Living and Working in *America*

A Survival Handbook

by
David Hampshire

SURVIVAL BOOKS • LONDON • ENGLAND

First published in 1992 (as Living and Working in the USA)
Second Edition 1995
Third Edition 1998
Fourth Edition 2002
Fifth Edition 2005

Survival Books Limited, 1st Floor,
60 St James's Street, London SW1A 1ZN, United Kingdom
☎ +44 (0)20-7493 4244, 🖷 +44 (0)20-7491 0605
✉ info@survivalbooks.net
🖳 www.survivalbooks.net
To order books, please refer to page 587.

British Library Cataloguing in Publication Data.
A CIP record for this book is available
from the British Library.
ISBN 1 901130 54 1

Printed and bound in Finland by WS Bookwell Ltd

Acknowledgements

M y sincere thanks to all those who contributed to the successful publication of this and previous editions of this book, in particular Beverly Laflamme (updating fifth edition), Catherine Wakelin (proofreading fifth edition), Kerry Laredo (desktop publishing fifth edition, and research, updating, proofreading and layout fourth edition), Joe Laredo (research and updating fourth edition), Tami Meehling (research fourth edition), Joanna Styles, Jo Allen, Hilda Fritze, Erik Gottschalk, Linda Hull, Adèle Kelham, Sheila and Paul Toffell, Linda and Philip Wenthe, Diana Sonderegger and Josephine Quintero. Finally a special thank-you to Jim Watson for the superb cover, illustrations, cartoons and map.

Titles by Survival Books

Alien's Guides
Britain; France

The Best Places To Buy A Home
France; Spain

Buying A Home
Abroad; Cyprus; Florida;
France; Greece; Ireland; Italy;
Portugal; South Africa; Spain;
Buying, Selling & Letting
Property (UK)

Foreigners Abroad: Triumphs & Disasters
France; Spain

Lifeline Regional Guides
Costa Blanca; Costa del Sol;
Dordogne/Lot; Normandy;
Poitou-Charentes

Living And Working
Abroad; America;
Australia; Britain; Canada;
The European Union;
The Far East; France; Germany;
The Gulf States & Saudi Arabia;
Holland, Belgium & Luxembourg;
Ireland; Italy; London;
New Zealand; Spain;
Switzerland

Making A Living
France; Spain

Other Titles
Renovating & Maintaining
Your French Home;
Retiring Abroad

Order forms are on page 587.

WHAT READERS & REVIEWERS

When you buy a model plane for your child, a video recorder, or some new computer gizmo, you get with it a leaflet or booklet pleading 'Read Me First', or bearing large friendly letters or bold type saying 'IMPORTANT – follow the instructions carefully'. This book should be similarly supplied to all those entering France with anything more durable than a 5-day return ticket. It is worth reading even if you are just visiting briefly, or if you have lived here for years and feel totally knowledgeable and secure. But if you need to find out how France works then it is indispensable. Native French people probably have a less thorough understanding of how their country functions. – Where it is most essential, the book is most up to the minute.

LIVING FRANCE

Rarely has a 'survival guide' contained such useful advice. This book dispels doubts for first-time travellers, yet is also useful for seasoned globetrotters – In a word, if you're planning to move to the USA or go there for a long-term stay, then buy this book both for general reading and as a ready-reference.

AMERICAN CITIZENS ABROAD

It is everything you always wanted to ask but didn't for fear of the contemptuous put down – The best English-language guide – Its pages are stuffed with practical information on everyday subjects and are designed to complement the traditional guidebook.

SWISS NEWS

A complete revelation to me – I found it both enlightening and interesting, not to mention amusing.

CAROLE CLARK

Let's say it at once. David Hampshire's *Living and Working in France* is the best handbook ever produced for visitors and foreign residents in this country; indeed, my discussion with locals showed that it has much to teach even those born and bred in l'Hexagone. – It is Hampshire's meticulous detail which lifts his work way beyond the range of other books with similar titles. Often you think of a supplementary question and search for the answer in vain. With Hampshire this is rarely the case. – He writes with great clarity (and gives French equivalents of all key terms), a touch of humour and a ready eye for the odd (and often illuminating) fact. – This book is absolutely indispensable.

THE RIVIERA REPORTER

A mine of information – I may have avoided some embarrassments and frights if I had read it prior to my first Swiss encounters – Deserves an honoured place on any newcomer's bookshelf.

ENGLISH TEACHERS ASSOCIATION, SWITZERLAND

HAVE SAID ABOUT SURVIVAL BOOKS

What a great work, wealth of useful information, well-balanced wording and accuracy in details. My compliments!

THOMAS MÜLLER

This handbook has all the practical information one needs to set up home in the UK – The sheer volume of information is almost daunting – Highly recommended for anyone moving to the UK.

AMERICAN CITIZENS ABROAD

A very good book which has answered so many questions and even some I hadn't thought of – I would certainly recommend it.

BRIAN FAIRMAN

We would like to congratulate you on this work: it is really super! We hand it out to our expatriates and they read it with great interest and pleasure.

ICI (SWITZERLAND) AG

Covers just about all the things you want to know on the subject – In answer to the desert island question about the one how-to book on France, this book would be it – Almost 500 pages of solid accurate reading – This book is about enjoyment as much as survival.

THE RECORDER

It's so funny – I love it and definitely need a copy of my own – Thanks very much for having written such a humorous and helpful book.

HEIDI GUILIANI

A must for all foreigners coming to Switzerland.

ANTOINETTE O'DONOGHUE

A comprehensive guide to all things French, written in a highly readable and amusing style, for anyone planning to live, work or retire in France.

THE TIMES

A concise, thorough account of the DOs and DON'Ts for a foreigner in Switzerland – Crammed with useful information and lightened with humorous quips which make the facts more readable.

AMERICAN CITIZENS ABROAD

Covers every conceivable question that may be asked concerning everyday life – I know of no other book that could take the place of this one.

FRANCE IN PRINT

Hats off to *Living and Working in Switzerland*!

RONNIE ALMEIDA

CONTENTS

12. HEALTH   299

13. INSURANCE   325

14. FINANCE 359

15. LEISURE 401

16. SPORTS 437

17. SHOPPING 471

IMPORTANT NOTE

The US is a vast country with many faces and numerous ethnic groups, religions and customs. Most importantly, each of the 50 states and the District of Columbia (the nation's capital) has different laws and regulations, encompassing a wide range of subjects (New York city is an exception to almost every rule!). **I cannot recommend too strongly that you check with an official and reliable source (not always the same) before making any major decisions or taking an irreversible course of action. However, don't believe everything you're told or read – even, dare I say it, herein!**

Useful addresses and references to other sources of information have been included in all chapters and in **Appendices A, B** and **C** to help you obtain further information and verify details with official sources. Important points have been emphasised, in **bold** print, some of which it would be expensive, or even dangerous, to disregard. **Ignore them at your peril or cost!** Unless specifically stated, the reference to any company, organisation or product in this book doesn't constitute an endorsement or recommendation.

AUTHOR'S NOTES

- The original (and geographically correct) title of this book was *Living and Working in the USA*. It was changed to **Living and Working in America** to distinguish it from other books with similar titles and because most people refer to the United States of America as simply 'America'. The United States of America is generally referred to in the text of this book as 'the US', and both 'US' and 'American' are used to mean 'pertaining to the United States of America'.

- All times are shown using am (ante meridiem) for before noon and pm (post meridiem) for after noon. Most Americans don't use the 24-hour clock. Some people refer to noon as 12am, while others call it 12pm; similarly midnight is either 12pm or 12am. To avoid confusion, the terms noon and midnight are used in this book. All times are local, so always check the time difference when making inter-state and international telephone calls (see **Time Difference** on page 531).

- The prices quoted in this book **don't** include state and city sales taxes (see page 474), which are almost never included in (quoted) prices in America. All prices are subject to change and should be taken as estimates only.

- His/he/him also means her/she/her (please forgive me ladies). This is done to make life easier for both the reader and (in particular) the author, and isn't intended to be sexist.

- Most spelling is (or should be) British English and not American English, except for the names of American organisations, e.g. the 'Bureau of Labor Statistics'. Where American English uses a different word from British English (e.g. 'faucet' for 'tap'), this is given in brackets.

- Warnings and important points are shown in **bold** type.

- The following symbols are used in this book: ☎ (telephone), ▤ (fax), ▱ (internet) and ✉ (email).

- Lists of **Useful Addresses**, **Further Reading** and **Useful Websites** are contained in **Appendices A, B** and **C** respectively.

- For those unfamiliar with the American system of weights and measures, conversion tables (to Imperial and metric measures) are included in **Appendix D**.

- A map of the US showing the 50 states is contained in **Appendix E**.

INTRODUCTION

Whether you're already living or working in America or just thinking about it – this is **THE BOOK** for you. Forget about all those glossy guide books – excellent though they are for tourists; this amazing book was written particularly with you in mind and is worth its weight in bagels. *Living and Working in America* is the most comprehensive (containing twice as much information as similar books) and up-to-date book about living and working in America, now in its fifth edition. It's designed to meet the needs of anyone wishing to know the essentials of American life, including immigrants, temporary workers, businessmen, students, retirees, long-stay tourists and holiday homeowners. However long your intended stay in America, you will find the information contained in this book invaluable.

General information isn't difficult to find in America and a multitude of books is published on every conceivable subject. However, reliable and up-to-date **practical** information specifically intended for foreigners isn't so easy to find, least of all in one volume. The aim of this book is to help fill this void and provide the comprehensive information necessary for a relatively trouble-free life. You may have visited America as a tourist, but living and working there is a different matter altogether. Adjusting to a different environment and culture and making a home in any foreign country can be a traumatic and stressful experience, and America is no exception. You will need to adapt to new customs and traditions and discover the American way of doing things.

With a copy of *Living and Working in America* to hand you will have a wealth of information at your fingertips – information derived from a variety of sources, both official and unofficial, not least the hard won personal experiences of the author, his family, friends, colleagues and acquaintances. *Living and Working in America* is a comprehensive handbook on a wide range of everyday subjects and represents the most up-to-date source of general information available to foreigners in America.

Adapting to life in a new country is a continuous process, and although this book will help reduce your 'rooky' (novice) phase and minimize the frustrations, it doesn't contain all the answers (most of us don't even know the right questions to ask!). It will, however, help you make informed decisions and calculated judgements, instead of uneducated guesses and costly mistakes. **Most importantly, it will help save you time, trouble and money, and repay your investment many times over.**

Although you may find some of the information a bit daunting, don't be discouraged. Most problems occur only once and fade into insignificance after a short time (as you face the next half a dozen!). The majority of foreigners in America would agree that, all things considered, they love living there. A period spent in America is a wonderful way to enrich your life, broaden your horizons, and with a bit of luck (or a job on Wall Street) make your fortune. I trust this book will help you avoid the pitfalls of life in America and smooth your way to a happy and rewarding future in your new home.

Good luck!

David Hampshire
January 2005

1.

FINDING A JOB

The main difficulty facing most people wishing to work in the US isn't usually finding a job, but obtaining a work visa. Contrary to the popular vision of the US as a land of opportunity for the world's oppressed workers, the **last** people the government welcomes are 'your tired, your poor, your huddled masses' (from the poem 'The New Colossus' by Emma Lazarus) – they have quite enough of their own! The US wants people who are rich, preferably with a university education, professional training and experience.

JOB MARKET

Until 1980, more Americans were employed in manufacturing than in any other sector of industry. However, manufacturing's share of the job market has been shrinking for decades (in the recession in the early '90s more than 1 million jobs were lost in manufacturing and construction), coupled with a boom in service industries. Today more than 65 per cent of the workforce is employed in service industries, 14 per cent in industry (compared with almost 30 per cent 20 years ago), almost 16 per cent in public service and a mere 1.5 per cent in agriculture. Fewer people are employed in manufacturing than at any time in the past 35 years. On the other hand, in certain sectors, such as healthcare, there's a high demand for experienced professional staff.

Recession & Recovery

The US made a full recovery from the recession of the early '90s, although the economy has recently suffered a number of setbacks, not least that occasioned by the disastrous events of 11th September 2001. The expansion which began in 1991 was the longest in recorded US history, with average growth in GDP of 4 per cent per annum. In 1998, inflation was around 1.5 per cent, the lowest for almost 25 years, although since then inflation has risen to around 2.7 per cent and it's expected to increase further after the presidential elections in 2004. Analysts credit the US's recovery to its flexible labour policy with its deregulated labour market, low-profile welfare state and weakened labour unions. Union membership has halved since the '60s and this has reduced the unions' stranglehold on major industries. The US has an extremely flexible and mobile workforce (the average American changes jobs around seven times in his working life) and most unemployed people will take almost any job to make ends meet, irrespective of their former position or salary.

The US labour market has been transformed in the last decade, during which the era of secure full-time employment with comprehensive employee benefits and lifetime guarantees has virtually ended. Nowadays an increasing number of full-time jobs are being replaced by part-time, freelance and contract work, with lower wages and no benefits (one in four jobs now comes into this category). Many people are also 'telecommuting' (working from home via telephone, fax and computer), through choice or because their employers have closed offices to reduce costs.

Unemployment

More than 15 million jobs were created between 1993 and 1998 (the most ever in such a short period) and by mid-2000 unemployment had fallen to below 4 per cent, its lowest in 30 years. Nevertheless, large companies continued to shed jobs during 2002 and 2003, using buzzwords (euphemisms) such as downsizing, restructuring and streamlining, an inevitable consequence of increasing competition made possible by computerisation and other new technologies. In the first four months of 2001 a record 572,000 people were made redundant, as unemployment climbed to 4.5 per cent, the hardest hit sectors being telecommunications and the automotive industry. Although the rate of large-scale redundancies (lay-offs) has declined, unemployment reached 5.4 per cent by mid-2004. It's estimated that a further 2 million long-term unemployed have simply given up looking for jobs at this point, causing them to drop out of the unemployment statistics altogether.

The US has a brutal and ruthless labour market and big employers increasingly treat their employees as a disposable commodity (company loyalty is almost non-existent in many companies). Whereas redundancies in the past were often temporary, with workers hired back by the same company after a few months, it's now believed that many jobs, particularly in the manufacturing sector, are gone for good. Employees don't have the protection and benefits that workers enjoy in many other developed countries, and employers have traditionally been free (and more than willing) to 'hire and fire'. Nevertheless, employers are having to offer better conditions and higher salaries to hire and retain skilled workers in a more competitive labour market.

Immigration

The US is a nation of immigrants and, although today less than 12 per cent of the population is foreign-born (compared with around 80 per cent 100 years ago), most Americans can trace their ancestors back to foreign settlers within five or six generations. Successive waves of immigration in the first half of the 20th century brought large numbers of Europeans and Chinese, who have been joined by an influx of immigrants from Asia, Mexico, Central and South America, and the Caribbean in the last few decades.

Annual immigration is around 1 million, added to which hundreds of thousands of illegal immigrants enter the country each year, over half from Mexico. Immigration isn't generally a contentious issue, although some Americans claim that immigrants lower the quality of life, take away Americans' jobs (although most new immigrants take jobs that Americans don't want), and import their own countries' social and economic ills. Since the terrorist attacks of September 2001, there has been considerable concern over the security issues related to immigration, including the overall tightening of entry requirements for visitors and immigrants alike. In the 2004 presidential campaign, the issue of employers moving jobs overseas to take advantage of cheaper labour rates was debated in areas hard hit by unemployment, where the issue of hiring foreigners can be a sensitive one. Those in favour of continued widespread immigration emphasise the cultural wealth and diversity of talents that immigrants have brought to the US since its foundation. Immigration also boosts the economy by billions of dollars per year.

An increasing number of cities with declining populations are mounting campaigns to attract immigrants to fill available jobs, including Pittsburgh, which has lost almost 10 per cent of its population in the past decade, Philadelphia, Louisville and Albuquerque.

Work Ethic

The US's recovery from recession was achieved by sheer hard work. A recent report by the International Labour Organisation indicated that the average American worker added almost a week to his working year during the '90s, reaching a total of almost 1,980 hours per year – more than his counterpart in any other western country (over 250 hours more than the average British worker and 500 hours more than the average German!). In companies that have fired workers to cut costs, it often seems that those surviving employees are simply picking up the workload of their departed colleagues. The higher you go up the ladder of success, the harder you're expected to work, and burn-out is common among managers and executives. Key employees routinely give up breaks and take work home with them, and it isn't unusual for them to be called at home or even when on vacation. Don't be misled by the informality and casual atmosphere or dress in many companies: Americans work long and hard.

Job Prospects

Job prospects are something of a mixed bag at the moment. It can be difficult to find employment of any sort if you don't have the right academic background or specialised qualifications, or if you're over the age of around 45. Recent changes to the visa application and approval processes may make some employers wary of hiring foreigners, particularly in industries where there have been recent redundancies. But for someone with the right qualifications and experience, there should be adequate opportunities available in the next few years. However, contrary to popular belief, the streets of the US aren't paved with gold and many immigrants find that it's easier to fail than to succeed. Although the US is the richest country in the world, it has a high poverty level and some 10 million people receive federal housing assistance. You don't have to be unemployed to live below the poverty line; some 20 per cent of families in this position have a head of household working full time. Nevertheless, the lure of the American Dream of rags to riches continues to attract millions of immigrants. The US remains the supreme land of opportunity and nowhere else on earth is it possible for a penniless immigrant to become rich in such a short time.

Further Information

The US Department of Labor publishes an abundance of information on employment trends and job prospects in the US, including the *Occupational Outlook Handbook*,

Occupational Projections and Training Data, Employment Outlook and the *Career Guide to Industries*, all of which are available from the Bureau of Labor Statistics, Publications Sales Center, Room 960, 230 S. Dearborn Street, Chicago, IL 60604 (☎ 312-353-1880) and online at the Bureau of Labor Statistics website (🖳 www.bls.gov). State and local job market and career information is available from state employment security agencies and State Occupational Information Coordinating Committees (SOICCs).

EMPLOYMENT & JOB SERVICES

The US Employment Service operates in partnership with state employment services to provide free counselling, testing and job placement in major cities across the country. State operated employment services operate a network of over 2,000 local offices, called Employment Service Centers, which help job-seekers find employment and employers locate qualified employees. Employment Service Centers are listed in telephone directories under 'Employment Services' or 'Job Service' in the 'State Government' listings section.

Employment Service Centers operate Job Banks containing computerised lists of vacancies in the local area and across the nation, so job-seekers can match their skills and experience to specific vacancies. You select the jobs that are of interest to you and obtain more information from staff, who can describe jobs in detail and arrange interviews. Service Centers employ counsellors who can test your occupational aptitudes and interests, help you to make career decisions, and channel you into appropriate training programmes through screening and referral services.

Many communities have career counselling, training, placement and support services for the employed and unemployed, although programmes are generally targeted at 'disadvantaged' groups such as women, youths, minorities, ex-offenders and older workers. Programmes are sponsored by a range of organisations, including churches, social service agencies, non-profit organisations, local businesses, the state employment service, and vocational rehabilitation agencies. Many libraries also have job search resources, including internet access.

EMPLOYMENT AGENCIES

Employment agencies are big business in the US and there are many in major cities and towns. Most large companies engage agencies to recruit staff, particularly executives (head hunters account for some 70 per cent of top level executive appointments), managers, professional employees and temporary office staff (temps). Most agencies specialise in particular trades or fields, e.g. computing, accounting, publishing, advertising, banking, insurance, sales, catering, teaching, health, engineering and technical, industrial and construction, or recruit particular types of staff, e.g. secretarial and office staff, bi-lingual people and domestic staff, while others deal with a range of industries and positions. Agencies may handle permanent or temporary, e.g. less than 90 day, jobs or both.

Many agencies, often calling themselves 'executive counsellors' or 'executive search consultants' (head hunters), cater for the lucrative executive market. US corporations go to extreme lengths to hire the right executives, and executive search firms are often employed to find the right person or make contact with someone who has been targeted as fitting the bill. Head hunters are extremely influential and, although many companies and managers consider it unethical to lure away a competitor's talented staff, most are happy to use their services. Critics claim that it encourages job-changing, forces up salaries and diminishes corporate loyalty (so does getting fired!). Be wary of agencies calling themselves 'career counsellors' or 'executive management services', as they often aren't employment agencies at all, but rather offer you suggestions regarding your lifestyle, dress or where and how you should look for a job. Most of these same 'services' are available for free or are things you can easily do for yourself. Before paying an executive counselling company a fee, make sure you know exactly what you will receive for your money, as many of their claims are completely bogus or even fraudulent. You should never have to pay an agency or recruiter to submit your résumé or job application to a potential employer. In the US, it's the employer who pays the recruiter for search services.

Employment agencies often must be licensed by state or local governments. Agency fees for permanent positions are usually equal to three months' gross salary or 25 per cent of gross annual salary and are nearly always paid by the employers looking for staff. Many agencies state in their advertisements that their services are 'fee paid', meaning that the employer pays for the agency's services, not the applicant. Some agencies act as employers, hiring workers and contracting them out to companies for an hourly rate. Employees of these sorts of agencies are paid an hourly rate (with weekly or bi-weekly wages) or receive a monthly salary. Benefits may include paid federal holidays and annual vacation after a qualifying period (like a regular job), but usually not medical insurance.

Temporary employment agencies usually take a percentage of employees' wages, e.g. 10 or 20 per cent, or may charge as much as your first two or three weeks' salary. Many also insist on a fee in advance with no guarantee of work. (Avoid these agencies unless you're truly desperate.) Wages are usually negotiable, so drive a hard bargain and ask for more than you're willing to accept. In some cities, good temps are hard to find, so you may have considerable bargaining power. Shop around different agencies to get an idea of the usual rates of pay and fees.

Temporary agencies usually deal with workers such as office staff, baby-sitters, home care workers, nannies and mothers' helps, housekeepers, cooks, gardeners, chauffeurs, hairdressers, security guards, cleaners, labourers and industrial workers. Nursing and care agencies are also fairly common and may cover a wide range of nursing services, including physiotherapy, occupational and speech therapy, and dentistry. Some agencies specialise in professional baby-sitters and domestic staff. Many agencies also employ people on a contract basis, e.g. computer professionals, nurses, technical authors, technicians and engineers. The internationally known agency Manpower is the country's largest temporary (and permanent) staff agency and fills around 100,000 jobs nationwide in summer.

Employment agencies make a great deal of money from finding people jobs, so if you've something to offer they will be keen to help you. If they cannot help you, they will usually tell you immediately and won't waste your time. To find your local agencies, look in the yellow pages under 'Employment Agencies'. If you have any doubts about the reputation of an agency, check with the local Better Business Bureau whether it has received any complaints.

CONTRACT JOBS

It's possible to find contract work in many occupations, particularly in computers, aerospace, defence, engineering and electronics, although there's also a strong market in providing cleaning, catering, maintenance and manual workers. Contractors are usually employed on the same general terms as permanent employees (see **Chapter 2**), but with no benefits or withholding of taxes provided by the 'employer'. Working as a contractor generally results in a higher salary, but don't forget to figure in the taxes, benefits and expenses you will be paying for yourself. There's considerable abuse in the area of contracting, mostly by companies hoping to cut corners on payroll costs, and the tax authorities generally question any contract arrangements that seem to skirt the edges of the law. Contracts are usually for a minimum of six months to one year (although open-ended contracts are also common) and may be extended for a number of years. If you wish to withdraw from a contract, penalties can be severe and may include repayment of relocation expenses, visa charges and air fares (if hired from abroad). Teacher exchange positions are available (usually for an academic year from August to August) through organisations such as The Central Bureau for Educational Visits & Exchanges in the UK (see page 30).

Contract jobs are available through employment agencies, some of which specialise in supplying contract staff to major companies, many of whom are increasingly contracting out non-core support work, from cleaning to computing, rather than hiring full-time, permanent employees. Professional contractors (or freelancers) often work from home. The potential for home-based work is huge, particularly within the computer industry, which is keen to capitalise on the number of people (particularly women) wishing to work part-time from home. There are a variety of websites offering free or low cost listings of work from home opportunities, but the area is also filled with scam artists. One free source of job listings, including information about finding and applying for work-from-home jobs is Workaholics4Hire (☎ 613- 841-4969, 🖳 www.workaholics4hire.com).

PART-TIME JOBS

Part-time jobs are available in most industries and professions and are common in offices, bars, stores, factories, hotels, cafés and restaurants. Often part-time workers are poorly paid and rates are usually around (or even below) the minimum wage of $5.15 per hour for unskilled workers, depending on the local unemployment rate and labour market. Part-time employees often have no protection from exploitation by employers, although some large employers allow them the same rights as full-time workers. Some companies operate a job share scheme, where two or more part-time workers do a full-time job between them. Many jobs listed under **Temporary & Casual Work** below are also available on a permanent part-time basis. Part-time jobs are also available through Employment Service Centers (see page 23) and employment agencies (see page 23).

TEMPORARY & CASUAL WORK

Temporary and casual work, legal and illegal, is available throughout the US. However, visitors (or anyone without a work visa) should be wary of working illegally (see page 42). One of the big attractions is that casual workers are often paid in cash at the end of each day's work. There are temporary employment agencies in most towns and cities. If you're looking for full-time work, a temporary job can often be a stepping-stone to a permanent position, as many employers use them as trial periods. Temporary and casual work includes the following:

- Work in restaurants and fast food establishments as a waiter, delivery person, dish washer, salad-preparer, short-order cook, etc. Experience is useful and you should apply in person, as telephone enquiries are usually ignored. Bar jobs can also be found in most cities and offer the opportunity to earn good tips.

- Agency work (see **Employment Agencies** on page 23) includes a variety of skilled and unskilled work, e.g. building and construction work, engineering, catering, office jobs, cleaning, baby-sitting and labouring. Temporary office jobs, e.g. clerks and receptionists, are available in all cities.

- Numerous jobs are available in resorts (winter and summer) during the high season. Try to arrive before the start of the season for the best jobs.

- Jobs as nannies, baby-sitters, house-cleaners and dog-walkers are available in most areas. People often advertise vacancies in supermarkets, drugstores, health food stores, bus shelters, and on college and university notice boards. You could also try placing an advertisement in such places or in a local newspaper.

- Painting and decorating jobs pay well and can be found through agencies, local companies, friends and acquaintances.

- Giving English and foreign language lessons can pay well (you can advertise in local newspapers and on notice boards).

- Jobs at exhibitions and shows, particularly setting up stands, catering (waiting and bar staff), and loading and unloading jobs.

- Work as an artist's model (male and female) can be found in major cities, working directly for artists or for art schools.

- Work in amusement and theme parks, travelling circuses and carnivals, erecting and dismantling tents and rides.

- A job as a nightclub doorman or bouncer.

- Gardening jobs are available in private gardens and public parks, and vacancies are advertised in local newspapers and magazines and on bulletin boards. Local landscape gardeners and garden centres are often on the look-out for extra staff, particularly in spring and summer.

- There are many farming jobs, particularly during the harvest season, for wheat, fruit (oranges, grapes, apples, etc.), vegetables and tobacco. Farming is a traditional form of work for casual labour (migrant workers), with jobs usually available somewhere in the US all year round. However, it's the poorest paid work and often involves severe health risks from pesticide exposure and other dangers. It's estimated that there are between 1 and 4 million migrant farm workers in the US, around 60 per cent of whom are Mexicans.

- Jobs on fishing boats, in fish processing plants and on game fishing boats during the tourist season.

- A variety of jobs on cruise ships are available through recruitment agencies, particularly in Florida and California.

- Market research, entailing asking people personal questions, in the street, house to house, or by telephone (telemarketing). Some companies aren't too particular about who they employ and often accept people with poor English. Market research companies also pay targeted consumers to complete questionnaires – anything from $50 to hundreds of dollars, depending on the number of hours' work involved.

- Selling, usually on a commission basis, particularly fast food or ice-cream in summer, and telephone selling. Many jobs are advertised in the classified advertisements of city newspapers, but don't believe a word of the claimed earnings potential. Jobs are also available selling door-to-door, e.g. Avon cosmetics, or through parties, e.g. Tupperware.

- Nursing in hospitals, clinics and nursing homes. Jobs are often available through nursing agencies, which provide temporary staff at short notice.

- Newspaper and magazine distribution.

- Courier jobs, where you usually provide your own transport, e.g. motorcycle, car or pickup. Other driving jobs include coach and truck drivers and delivering cars for manufacturers and rental companies. Jobs are often advertised in local papers for drivers with their own pickup (P/U) or mini-van.

- As a last resort (when you're really desperate), you can sell your blood to a hospital for around $10 a pint (but keep a few pints in reserve).

HOLIDAY & SHORT-TERM JOBS

Holiday (vacation) and short-term jobs in the US, lasting from a few weeks to six months, are arranged by a number of organisations. Youth programmes also provide summer jobs in state, city and county government agencies for low-income youths between 16 and 21, e.g. students, school dropouts and graduates entering the labour market.

Before coming to the US for a working holiday or a short-term job, check whether you qualify for a visa under existing immigration regulations. Bona fide vacation and short-term job applicants qualify for a J-1 cultural exchange visitor's visa, provided the employer or organiser is an official sponsor and can issue the necessary

DS-2019 form (see page 87). Most J-1 visas are issued to students, although many summer camp jobs are open to non-students. Generally, physically disabled people aren't eligible to receive non-immigrant visas, but it's often worthwhile making an application outlining the extent of your disability in a covering letter. Some of the largest programmes are outlined below:

The Student Exchange Employment Program (SEEP) is a reciprocal scheme allowing foreign students to work in the US for four months during the summer and American students to work in other countries for up to six months at any time of the year. To qualify for the Work America Program, you must be a full-time tertiary or advanced level student over 18, attend orientation courses in your home country and the US, and preferably know someone in the US who can sponsor you or arrange a job for you before departure. You can take any job anywhere in the US (except as an au pair, camp counsellor or medical intern) for any period between mid-June and early October. To qualify you need at least $950 of your own funds **or** a firm job offer from an American employer plus a minimum of $475.

Contact the US sponsors (Council on International Educational Exchange/CIEE, 3 Copley Place, 2nd Floor, Boston, MA 02116, ☎ 1-888-COUNCIL, 🖳 www.ciee.org) for information about whether the SEEP programme is available in your country. The CIEE also arranges seasonal jobs and provides tips on finding work and working in the US.

Camp America is the largest (over 7,000 participants annually) and most respected summer camp (see page 215) programme in the US. You must be at least 18 (by 1st June of the summer for which you're applying), be available to travel to the US no later than the end of June and be available to work for a nine or ten-week period. Applications are accepted from September for summer camps the following year, and you should apply as soon as possible, as all positions are usually filled by April or May. Family companions, who are similar to au pairs (see page 32), must be 18 to 24. Other general conditions are an ability to speak conversational English, physical fitness and no criminal record (you should also be calm, patient and caring). Positions in the kitchen, maintenance and office programmes (Campower) are open to bona fide students only. Counsellors are employed as general counsellors, who are responsible for overall activities and supervisory care of a small group of children, or special counsellors, responsible for instructing specific skills such as swimming, tennis or horse-riding.

Successful applicants are placed in a camp (or with a family if you choose the 'family companion' programme) with full board and lodging for nine or ten weeks. Free round-trip air transport is provided from the UK (London) to the US (you must pay the European airport taxes and fees, around $65). Applicants from Australia, India and New Zealand must make their own flight arrangements, for which $500 is paid as partial reimbursement. Pocket money from $600 to $1,100 is paid on completion of your nine or ten-week employment period, depending on your age and your assignment. All applicants are required to pay an initial 'good faith' deposit of between $40 and $120 (depending on the date of booking), which is forfeited if you withdraw after passing the interview. When a position is found, an additional deposit of $180 is payable plus the medical insurance fee (see below) and regional flight surcharge if applicable (see above).

At the end of your camp period, your deposit is returned and you may spend an additional ten weeks travelling independently in the US. Return flights are normally from New York City, although for an additional fee you can fly from California or Florida. Compulsory medical insurance of $250,000 is provided for $260, covering your period at camp and independent travel (baggage insurance of $2,000 can be provided for $96). Contact Camp America at 102 Greenwich Avenue, Greenwich, CT 06830-5504 (☎ 1-800-727-8233 or 203-399-5000, ☐ www.campamerica.aifs.com) or the American Institute For Foreign Study, 37 Queens Gate, London SW7 5HR, UK (☎ 020-7581 7373, ☐ www.campamerica.co.uk).

Another major employer of camp counsellors is Camp Counselors USA (CCUSA, Green Dragon House, 64–70 High Street, Unit 4CC, Croydon, CR0 9XN, UK, ☎ 020-8688 9051, ☐ www.ccusa.com), which places more than 8,000 camp counsellors (aged 18 to 30) per year in camps throughout the US. Other programmes include the YMCA's International Camp Counselor Program (ICCP, 5 West 63rd Street, 2nd Floor, New York, NY 10023-8800, ☎ 888-477-9622, ☐ www.ymcaiccp.org), which places counsellors (aged over 20) from more than 70 countries in some 500 camps throughout the US, and the British Universities North America Club (BUNAC, 16 Bowling Green Lane, London EC1R 0QH, ☎ 020-7251 3472, ☐ www.bunac.org). For further information about working as a camp counsellor, write to the US embassy or consulate in your home country.

Publications of interest to those seeking vacation or short-term jobs in the US include *Summer Jobs in the U.S.A.* (Peterson's Guides), containing details of thousands of summer jobs for students in the US and Canada, including ranches, summer camps, national parks, theatres, resorts and restaurants. For general information about work opportunities for international students contact any US embassy or consulate. You should also check the Student Jobs website of the US government (☐ www.studentjobs.gov) for information about programs open to non-citizens.

VOLUNTARY WORK & WORKCAMPS

The minimum age for voluntary work in the US is between 16 and 18, depending on the organisation, and most organisations require good or fluent spoken English. Special qualifications aren't usually required, and the minimum length of service varies from around one month to one year (there's often no maximum). Disabled volunteers are also welcomed by many organisations. Voluntary work is unpaid, although meals and accommodation are usually provided and some organisations also pay a small amount of pocket money. However, this is usually insufficient for your living expenses (entertainment, drinks, etc.), so make sure you bring sufficient money with you.

It's essential, before travelling to the US for any kind of voluntary work, that you check whether you're eligible and are permitted to enter the country under the immigration and employment regulations. You may be required to obtain a visa (see **Chapter 3**), so check the documentation necessary with a US embassy or consulate well in advance of your planned visit. The usual visa regulations apply to voluntary workers and your passport must be valid for at least one year.

International workcamps provide the opportunity for people from many countries to live and work together on a range of projects, such as building, conservation, gardening and community projects. Camps are usually run for two to four weeks between April and October. Normally, workers are required to work an eight-hour, five-day week, which can be physically demanding. Accommodation is usually shared with fellow 'slaves' and is fairly basic. Most workcamps consist of 10 to 20 volunteers from several countries, English being the common language. Volunteers usually pay a registration fee and their own travelling costs to and from the workcamp and may also be expected to contribute towards the cost of their board and lodging. An application to join a workcamp should be made through the appropriate recruiting agency in your home country. The CIEE (see page 28) provides places at international workcamps in the US and publishes *The Comprehensive Guide to Voluntary Service in the US and Abroad*.

There are many organisations that can help you find voluntary work in America, including the following:

- American Friends Service Committee (1501 Cherry Street, Philadelphia, PA 19102, ☎ 215-241-7000, 💻 www.afsc.org) maintains lists of internships, fellowships and volunteer opportunities on its website.

- American Hiking Society (AHS, 1422 Fenwick Lane, Silver Spring, MD 20910, ☎ 1-800-972-8608 ext. 207, 💻 www.americanhiking.org) requires volunteers to build and maintain mountain trails in national parks and forests throughout the US. Camping accommodation is provided usually with meals and partial travel expenses. Volunteers must pay a registration fee of $100, which includes a year's membership to the AHS (you receive a bi-monthly magazine called *American Hiker*). The AHS also publishes *Get Outdoors!* a directory of volunteer opportunities (see below) in parks and forests, which is updated every December (price $10).

- The Archaeological Institute of America (AIA, 656 Beacon Street, Boston, MA 02215, ☎ 617-353-9361, 💻 www.archaeological.org) publishes the *Archaeological Fieldwork Opportunities Bulletin*, listing archaeological sites throughout the US and details of the staff required at each site. It costs $19.95 and order information is available on the AIA website.

- The Central Bureau for Educational Visits & Exchanges (10 Spring Gardens, London SW1A 2BN, UK, ☎ 020-7389 4004) publishes *A Year Between*, a guide to taking a 'gap' year (GB£10).

- Gap Activity Projects (GAP, 44 Queens Road, Reading, Berkshire RG1 4BB, UK, ☎ 0118-959 4914, 💻 www.gap.org.uk) offers volunteer projects to young people taking a 'gap' year before going to university.

- Service Civil International (SCI International Voluntary Service, 5474 Walnut Level Road, Crozet VA 22932, ☎ 206-350-6585, 💻 www.sci-ivs.org), arranges places for young people over 15 in summer camps and workcamps (workcamps require a registration fee which varies according to the country from which you apply), as well as arranging long-term volunteer work.

- Student Conservation Association (SCA, 689 River Road, PO Box 550, Charlestown, NH 03603-0550, ☎ 603-543-1700, 💻 sca-inc.org), which claims to be the US's largest and oldest provider of community conservation programmes, requires volunteers aged 18 or over with an interest in conservation or resource management for projects in over 200 national parks, forests, wildlife refuges and similar areas throughout the US.

- Volunteers for Peace (1034 Tiffany Road, Belmont, VT 05730, ☎ 802-259-2759, 🖳 www.vfp.org) publishes the *International Workcamp Directory* and a newsletter.
- Volunteers of America (1660 Duke Street, Alexandria, VA 22314-3421, ☎ 1-800-899-0089 or 703-341-5000, 🖳 www.voa.org) is a spiritual organisation operating some 400 different programmes in more than 200 communities across the US.

Useful publications about voluntary work in the US include *Volunteer! The Comprehensive Guide to Voluntary Service in the US and Abroad* (CIEE – see address below) and *Make a Difference: America's Guide to Volunteering and Community Service* by Arthur I. Blaustein (Jossey-Bass).

TRAINING & WORK EXPERIENCE

A number of countries organise career development programmes in the US through the Association for International Practical Training (AIPT, Suite 250, 10400 Little Patuxent Parkway, Columbia, MD 21044-3519, ☎ 410-997-2200, 🖳 www.aipt.org). The aim of the programmes is to enable participants to gain practical experience for up to 18 months in the US and other participating countries. There are two categories of programme: general career development and hotel/culinary exchange (which is intended to benefit young people starting a career in the hotel and food service industries). A job offered to a trainee under the general career development programme must contain professional, practical training of a kind that develops his capabilities in his chosen field. Participants must be between 18 and 35 with at least two years experience and/or training in their chosen field. Applicants aren't considered if they've been unemployed in the six months before to their application. Most participants must find their own placements, but some assistance is available for qualified technical students. Participants may not change jobs without good reason and prior consultation with the AIPT.

Application forms can be downloaded from the AIPT's website and the application procedure takes from four to six weeks. Successful applicants are issued with a J-1 visa valid for a maximum of 18 months. There's a processing fee of $1,000 for short-term programmes (i.e. up to six months) and $2,000 for long-term programmes (6 to 18 months), payable by the applicant or his employer. There's an additional charge of $1,000 for programme 'extensions', which include insurance while in the US, and a fee of $250 if you bring your dependants with you. Trainees are subject to federal and state tax, but are exempt from social security payments. Salaries must be comparable with those paid to US employees with similar qualifications and experience, and are normally not less than $250 per week. For information about the career development programme in the UK, contact the Central Bureau for Educational Visits & Exchanges (for address see page 30).

AIPT in co-operation with the International Association for the Exchange of Students for Technology Experience (IAESTE) also provides on-the-job training in the US to full-time foreign university/college students in technical fields, e.g. agriculture, architecture, computer science, engineering, mathematics, and natural and physical sciences. Applicants should be aged 19 to 30 and have completed at least two, but preferably three, years in a technical major. Applications must be made by 10th December in your home country in order to gain acceptance for the following summer. Training periods can be as long as 18 months, although the majority of positions are for 8 to 12 weeks during the summer months. The IAESTE programme is available to students in more than 60 countries. For further information, ask your college or university for the address of the national committee in your home country or go to the IAESTE website, 💻 www.iaeste.org.uk.

A number of organisations arrange work experience programmes (internships) for overseas students. The Council on International Educational Exchange (CIEE, 3 Copley Place, 2nd floor, Boston, MA 02116, ☎ 1-800-COUNCIL or 617-247-0350, 💻 www.ciee.org) operates 'Internship USA', an annual programme for around 5,000 students from various countries, including the UK, Canada, Costa Rica, France, Germany, Jamaica, Ireland and New Zealand, who wish to work in the US. For information in the UK contact CIEE, 52 Poland Street, London W1F 7AB (☎ 020-7478 2000, 💻 www.councilexchanges.org).

Those wanting agricultural work experience should contact the Ohio International Agricultural Intern Program, 700 Ackerman Road, Commerce Suite 360, Columbus, OH 43202 (☎ 614-292-7720) and the Minnesota Agricultural Student Trainee Program (MAST International), 1954 Buford Avenue, Room 395, St Paul, MN 55108 (☎ 612-624-3740, 💻 http://mast.coafes.umn.edu).

In most countries there are government agencies handling educational exchanges and training in the US, e.g. the Central Bureau in the UK (see page 30). Contact your local US embassy or consulate for information. Information about exchanges between the US and the UK can also be obtained from the US Educational Advisory Service of the Fulbright Commission, 62 Doughty Street, London WC1N 2JZ, UK (☎ 020-7404 6880, 💻 www.fulbright.co.uk).

A useful publication is *Internships* (Peterson's Guides), which lists work experience opportunities within established US companies.

AU PAIRS

People aged 18 to 25 (yes, men also, but don't let your macho buddies find out!) are eligible to work as au pairs (also called 'child care providers') for up to a year. The purpose of the au pair programme is to increase the understanding of the US by young foreigners and to improve their English language fluency. On completion of a one year au pair programme, you're free to travel for one month in the US before your visa expires.

There are a number of official au pair schemes, the best known of which, Au Pair in America, is sponsored by the American Institute for Foreign Study (AIFS). Successful applicants must obtain a J-1 exchange visa, which is the only legal way to work as an au pair in the US. Contact Au Pair in America, River Plaza, 9 West Broad Street, Stamford, CT 06902-3788 (☎ 203-399-5000, 💻 www.aifs.co.uk). In Europe you can contact them at 37 Queens Gate, London SW7 5HR, UK (☎ 020-7581 7322).

Recruitment for the Au Pair in America programme is made all year round, although most placements start between June and September. In many countries, nationwide recruitment fairs are held throughout the year, where you can have an informal chat and meet former au pairs.

To qualify as an au pair in the US, you must hold a western European passport, i.e. Austrian, Belgian, British, Dutch, French, German, Greek, Irish, Italian, Luxembourg, Portuguese, Scandinavian, Spanish, Swiss or Turkish. You must also be between 18 and 25, hold an international driving licence or obtain one before the interview, have practical experience in caring for children (baby-sitting may qualify), speak English to a good standard, agree to the programme's code of conduct and rules and a full year commitment, not have a criminal record, and pass an interview and medical examination.

Au pairs are required to work up to 45 hours per week (over a maximum of five and a half days) caring for children and doing light housekeeping. Duties usually include feeding, dressing, bathing, playing with, supervising and baby-sitting children. Household chores should consist of simple cooking for children, clothes washing (with a machine) and ironing (for children only), washing up and drying dishes (although many US families have dishwashers), making beds, dusting, vacuum cleaning, and other light jobs around the home. You may also be required to take the family dog for a walk, drive the children to school and do the grocery shopping. Above all, an au pair should be treated as a member of the family and not as a servant or lodger.

At least one weekend per month (Friday evening to Monday morning) is free and you're entitled to two separate weeks' paid holiday during the year (by mutual agreement, although family holidays may count as part of the two-week allowance). You're provided with a private room, all meals, free medical insurance and pocket money of around $140 per week. Au pairs are guaranteed a minimum of four hours' study per week and the host family pays tuition costs of up to $500.

As an au pair with Au Pair in America, you pay $100 for a basic insurance plan that covers medical expenses of $100,000 (low for the US) during your employment period, although there's a one-time annual excess (deductible) of $200 if you make a claim. You can choose an optional insurance upgrade costing $250, which increases medical insurance to $500,000 and gives $1,000 baggage insurance ($25 excess) plus medical cover during the 13th month travel period, which isn't included in the standard policy. As evidence of 'good faith' (or rather so that you don't disappear as soon as you arrive in the US), you must pay a deposit of $400 before the visa forms are issued. This is refunded after satisfactory completion of your one-year assignment and can be used to fund your travel plans before returning home.

You should ensure that you have the money to return home, in case you're unable to complete the programme. If you're unhappy with the family you've been assigned to, you should contact the AIFS, who attempt to solve the problem through one of its community counsellors or find you another family. If you return to your home country without the agreement of the AIFS, you must pay your own return fare and forfeit your $400 deposit. This also applies if you're sent home because of dereliction of duty.

As an alternative to a year's au pair programme, it's possible to work as a family companion under the Camp America Summer Program (see page 215). The positions offered are similar to the au pair programme, but placements can be for as little as ten weeks and the pocket money is a total of $400. There are other established au pair agencies specialising in the US, including Au Pair Program USA, 6965 Union Park Center, Suite 360, Salt Lake City, UT 84047 (☎ 801-255-7722), whose UK agent is Childcare International, Trafalgar House, Grenville Place, London NW7 3SA, UK (☎ 020-8959 3611, 🖳 www.childint.com), and InterExchange, 161 6th Avenue, New York, NY 10013 (☎ 212-924-0446, 🖳 www.interexchange.org).

The au pair system has been referred to, uncharitably, as a minefield of guilt-ridden mothers, lecherous fathers and spoilt brats (usually by ex-au pairs who have had a bad experience). Your experience as an au pair depends entirely on your family. If you're fortunate enough to work for a warm and friendly host family, you will have a wonderful experience, lots of free time, and possibly holidays in the US and abroad. Many au pairs grow to love 'their' children and families, and form lifelong friendships. On the other hand, abuses of the au pair system are common and you may be treated as a servant rather than a member of the family and be expected to work long hours and spend most evenings baby-sitting. Many families employ an au pair simply because it costs only a fraction of the salary of the lowest-paid nanny (most Americans refer to their au pairs as nannies and many don't know the difference). Au pairs are also often expected to look after toddlers and babies, usually without any formal child or health care training. **If anything goes wrong, as it so easily can, you could be blamed and could even be charged with murder if a child dies while in your care (as happened in the Louise Woodward case in 1997).** Make sure that you know exactly what's required of you before choosing a family and if after starting work you have any questions or complaints about your duties, you should refer them to the agency that found you your position.

WORKING WOMEN

For many years, discriminatory laws in the US prevented women from competing equally with men and from entering male-dominated professions. However, in the last few decades, women have succeeded in breaking down many of the barriers and now (officially) compete on equal terms with men for education, professional training, employment, leadership positions and political power (although most women are too honest to get involved in politics). However, despite the Equal Rights Act (1964), which prohibited job discrimination on the basis of gender, women still encounter considerable resistance, and many inequalities still exist, not least in salaries. The Equal Pay Act (1963) 'guaranteed' that men and women filling the same jobs would receive the same pay, but more than 40 years later the reality has yet to match the theory. Although women's salaries, as a percentage of men's, **have** increased steadily in the last decade, women generally earn only some 78 per cent of men's salaries for comparable work, and women's pay rarely exceeds that of their male colleagues.

Professional women are common in the US and have more equality than their counterparts in other countries, although many find it difficult (or impossible) to reach the top ranks of their professions, thanks to what is called 'the glass ceiling'. The main discrimination against professional women isn't salary but promotion prospects, as many companies and organisations are loath to elevate women to important positions. Generally the closer women get to the top, the more they're resented. Among the Fortune 500 companies, women account for only around 14 per cent of the corporate executives and a mere 12 per cent of the boards of directors (the other US measure of power in business). Although 'the best man for the job is often a woman', it's seldom acknowledged by employers. It's more or less a given that women generally must perform twice as well as men to be treated as equals.

Nevertheless, in the US you're likely to come across women in top positions in all walks of life and will soon fail to be surprised when a professional, executive or manager turns out to be a woman. Men in certain professions or occupations, particularly those from countries where it's rare to have female colleagues or a female boss, may at first have difficulties accepting this situation (but you will get used to it unless you enjoy looking for a new job). In fact women are the main (or sole) breadwinners in one out of every six couples, and husbands are increasingly giving up their jobs in favour of their wife's career.

In most cases, however, there are increasing pressures on women to seek employment to supplement their husband's wages. Women make up around 45 per cent of the US labour force, and some 60 per cent of all women work full or part-time (over 70 per cent of women with adult children work). As a means of circumventing prejudice and low wages, many women have turned to self-employment. The number of women-owned businesses has increased significantly in recent years (despite the fact that banks and other financial institutions are often reluctant to lend them money). Female-owned firms account for around 9 million businesses, employing more than 27.5 million people.

There are a number of US magazines for working women, including *Working Mother* (🖳 www.workingmother.com) and *Women in Business*, published by the American Business Women's Association (ABWA), 9100 Ward Parkway, PO Box 8728, Kansas City, MO 64114-0728 (☎ 1-800-228-0007 or 816-361-6621, 🖳 www. abwahq.org). Annual membership to the ABWA costs around $50 and includes a subscription to the magazine, or you can order the magazine separately.

JOB HUNTING

When looking for a job (or a new job) in the US, you shouldn't put all your eggs in one basket, as the more job applications you make the better your chances are of finding the right job. Contact as many prospective employers as possible, by writing, telephoning or calling in person (see **Direct Applications** on page 37). Whatever job you're looking for, it's important to market yourself properly and appropriately. For example, the recruitment of executives and senior managers is handled almost exclusively by consultants who advertise in quality newspapers, such as the *New York Times* or the *Wall Street Journal*, and interview all applicants before presenting clients with a shortlist. At the other end of the scale, jobs requiring little or no previous experience (such as shop assistants) are advertised in local newspapers or in shop windows and the first able-bodied applicant may be offered the job on the spot. However, 'no experience necessary' may be a euphemism for poor working conditions and low pay or straight commission work.

When writing for a job, address your letter to the personnel director or hiring manager and include your résumé (see page 38) along with a covering letter presenting yourself and the type of job you're seeking. Writing for jobs from abroad is usually the least successful method of securing employment in the US, unless an advertisement is targeted at overseas applicants. Your method of job hunting depends on your circumstances, qualifications and experience, the sort of job you're looking for, and not least, your immigration status or eligibility for a visa. Your job hunt may include the following actions:

- Visit a state Employment Service Center in the US (see page 23). These mainly handle non-professional skilled and unskilled jobs, particularly in industry, retailing and catering.

- Contact local private employment agencies or executive recruiters in the area where you're looking for work (see page 23).

- Obtain copies of local and major city newspapers, most of which have 'Job Opportunities' or 'Help Wanted' sections on certain days, particularly Sundays. Most local and national newspapers are available in the reading rooms of local libraries in the US, so you don't must buy them. Jobs are also advertised in professional journals and trade magazines. Outside the US, some newspapers are available from international news agencies, US embassies and consulates, US trade and commercial centres, and US social clubs (although they don't always contain job advertisements). The jobs sections of most US newspapers can also be perused via the internet (see also below), e.g. 💻 www.nytimes.com, 💻 www. washingtonpost.com.

- If you have access to a computer, there are a number of job-hunting websites which include not only searchable job postings, but résumé building and posting features, as well as articles and information about job hunting. The great granddaddy of the job-hunting sites is Monster (💻 www.monster.com), which has merged with a number of other specialised sites. Monstertrak (💻 www.monstertrak.com) specialises in job listings for college students and recent alumni. Other useful sites include 💻 www.careermosaic.com, 💻 www. careers.org, 💻 www.hotjobs.yahoo.com, 💻 www.job-hunt.org, 💻 www.job smart.org, 💻 www.overseasjobs.com, 💻 www.jobweb.com.

- A number of sites 'host' your résumé for review by prospective employers, including 💻 www.resumenet.com (see **Résumés & Interviews** below).

- Apply to international and national recruitment agencies who act for US companies. These companies chiefly recruit executives and key managerial and technical staff, and many have offices worldwide and throughout the US. Some US companies appoint consultants to handle overseas recruitment in certain countries.

- Apply to multinational companies with offices or subsidiaries in the US and make written applications directly to US companies (see page 37). If you have a professional qualification that's recognised in the US, you can write to American professional associations for information and advice (addresses can be obtained from American Chambers of Commerce). Most professionals, e.g. in the medical and legal professions, must be licensed by individual states.

- Subscribe to job newsletters and digests such as the bi-weekly *Federal Jobs Digest*, containing up to 20,000 unadvertised openings throughout the US, available from Federal Jobs Digest, 325 Pennsylvania Avenue SE, Washington, DC 20003 (☎ 1-800-824-5000 or 914-366-0333 Ext. 1116, 💻 www.jobsfed.com). Many states also publish civil service job opportunities lists.

- Insert an advertisement in the 'Jobs Wanted' section of a local newspaper in the area where you would like to work (Sunday is the best day). Some newspapers allow unemployed job hunters to place free advertisements. If you're a member of a recognised profession or trade, you can place an advertisement in a newspaper or magazine dedicated to your profession or industry.

- Attend a 'Jobs Fair' in the US or in your home country, where hiring companies and agencies conduct massive job hunting campaigns in the attempt to woo new employees. Jobs Fairs are often targeted at specific professions, e.g. nurses or computer professionals, and are advertised in the jobs sections of regional newspapers.

- Networking (i.e. using business and social contacts) is a good way of finding out about job opportunities that may not be advertised. Ask relatives, friends or acquaintances working in the US if they know of an employer looking for someone with your experience and qualifications. If you're already in the US, contact or join expatriate social clubs, churches, societies and professional organisations, particularly your country's chamber of commerce. Many good business contacts can be made among expatriate groups.

- Apply direct to US companies, in person or using the companies' websites (see below).

- Free jobs and career newspapers are published in major cities and are often available from street vending machines.

Direct Applications

Your best chance of obtaining some jobs in the US is to apply directly to a company that interests you, when success is often simply a matter of being in the right place at the right time. When looking for a job where no special qualifications or experience are required, it isn't necessarily **what** you know, but **who** you know. Many small companies don't advertise vacancies, but rely on attracting workers by word of mouth and their own 'wanted' boards and may pay 'finders fees' to employees who present a successful candidate for an opening. Leave your name, address and a résumé or brief letter summing up your qualifications and background with a prospective employer, and if possible a local telephone number where you can be contacted, particularly if a job is likely to become vacant at a moment's notice. Many large companies post job vacancies on their company websites in hopes of avoiding employment agency or executive recruiter fees. Advertise that you're looking for a job, not only with friends, relatives and acquaintances, but also with anyone you meet who may be able to help. You can give Lady Luck a helping hand by cold calling prospective employers, checking notice and bulletin boards in large companies, and asking other workers.

When leaving a job in the US, you should ask for a written reference, if you think your work experience will help you obtain work in another country. Employers in the US don't normally like giving out written references addressed 'to whom it may concern'. They're considered unreliable (as anything bad said about the candidate could lead to a lawsuit) and subject to manipulation.

RÉSUMÉS & INTERVIEWS

Résumés and curricula vitae (CV) are of vital importance when looking for a job, particularly when jobs are thin on the ground and applicants are a dime a dozen. Never forget that the purpose of your résumé is to obtain an interview, not a job, and it must be written with this in mind. This means that it must be individually tailored to every job application. If you aren't up to writing a good résumé, you can employ a professional résumé writer who turns your humdrum working life into an epic that Indiana Jones would be proud of. Check to see that any professional résumé writer you employ is a member of the National Résumé Writers' Association (NRWA, P.O. Box 184, Nesconset, NY 11767, ☎ 888-NRWA-444, 🖳 www.nrwaweb.com). That assures adherence to a strict code of ethics (i.e. so you won't lose the job later for over-embellishing your life story) and some guarantee that your résumé is in the proper form for the region and industry where you're looking.

Job interviews should never be taken lightly in the US, where interviewing and being interviewed for a job is a science and creating a good impression can make the difference between being on the ladder of success or in the unemployment (or soup kitchen) queue. Dress smartly, even if the job is shovelling muck. The secret is in preparation, so do your homework on prospective employers and try to anticipate every question you may be asked and rehearse your answers. Most employers expect you to know something about the company, its products or services and general reputation in the press, all information you can check on in your local library. Some employers require prospective employees to complete aptitude and other written tests. In addition to a good résumé, employers usually require the names of three personal or professional references, whom they will contact (usually by telephone, so there's no incriminating documentation of any candid remarks exchanged). You may be asked to show proof of your immigration status or your eligibility for the appropriate visa. It is becoming increasingly popular to have job candidates sign a release authorising the employer to do a credit check on the candidate, even for jobs not directly involved with money or finance. (See **Credit Rating** on page 364). Interviews should always be followed up immediately with a letter, confirming your interest in (and suitability for) the job and thanking the interviewer for his or her time and interest. (In the US it pays to be obsequious!)

There are numerous books dealing with everything from writing a compelling résumé to how to answer (or field) questions during an interview, including *The Perfect Résumé* by Tom Jackson (Broadway) *The Damn Good Résumé Guide* by Yana Parker (Ten Speed Press), *Résumés for Dummies, Job Interviews for Dummies,* and *Cover Letters for Dummies* by Joyce Lain Kennedy (For Dummies), and *Knock 'em Dead With Great Answers to Tough Interview Questions* by Martin Yate (Adams Media Corporation).

SALARY

It can be difficult to determine the level of salary you should receive in the US, particularly for professional and executive appointments, where salaries and benefits aren't usually quoted in job advertisements. (The fanciful salaries quoted for sales appointments can be ignored!) On the other hand, 'Help Wanted' small advertisements, e.g. in the *New York Times*, may state salaries. Usually salaries are negotiable and it's up to you to ensure that you receive the level of salary and benefits commensurate with your qualifications and experience (in other words, as much as you can get).

If you have friends or acquaintances working in the US, or who have worked there, ask them what an average or good salary is for your trade or profession. Minimum salaries exist in some jobs, but generally it's every man for himself. Salaries in some companies and professions (particularly in the public sector) are decided by national pay agreements between unions and employers. Salary reviews vary between bi-annual and every 18 months, according to the employer, but in recent years, more and more employers have implemented salary freezes or even proposed wage or benefits cuts in order to avoid redundancies or bankruptcy.

When negotiating your salary, bear in mind that benefits and employment protection provided by US employers are less than in many other western countries (see **Chapter 2**). US jobs come with fewer fringe benefits than those in most European countries and may not include adequate health insurance or a company pension. If you're required to pay for health insurance, it can make a big hole in your salary. You should also take into account the (generally) longer working hours (see page 57) and shorter holiday allowances (see page 63). Americans are increasingly working longer hours, not necessarily to increase their bank balances, but simply to maintain their standard of living or keep their job.

Salaries vary considerably for the same job in different regions. Generally salaries are higher in Boston, New York City and California than in, for example, Chicago or Texas, although lower salaries are usually compensated for by a lower cost of living, particularly regarding accommodation. The salaries and conditions provided by multinational companies are fairly standard; nevertheless, you should obtain expert advice before accepting a job offer.

If you can claw your way to the top of a big company, you can expect an annual salary (with stock options and bonuses) of around $2 million. However, you should be a little wary of pay deals that include performance-related bonuses and stock options, particularly in young high-risk companies, where you may be better off with a decent monthly salary. At the other end of the scale, unskilled workers are often paid at, or around, the minimum wage and many people need to hold down a full-time job plus a part-time job (or two) in order to pay their mortgages. The average wage in 2003 was just over $700 per week or around $17.75 per hour, although this figure is inflated by higher-paid employees. Blue-collar workers average around $15 per hour, or a little over $10 for those in service trades. Almost 2 million workers, or around 3 per cent of all hourly workers, earn the minimum wage ($5.15 per hour) or less, over a third of them being employed in the food service industry. However, many industries, including fast food, retail and hospitality, are forced to pay more than a dollar above the minimum wage in order to hire and retain staff. With the exception of executives, salary rises in recent years have barely matched inflation and wage growth is non-existent for many low-paid workers. Most salary increases for blue-collar workers come from working longer hours, and salaries for non-executive staff have fallen (relative to the cost of living) in the last few decades.

SELF-EMPLOYMENT & STARTING A BUSINESS

Many Americans and immigrants have an ambition to start their own business and Americans are among the most enterprising people on earth, with small businesses providing some 40 per cent of the US's GNP. Entrepreneurs are respected and encouraged, and no stigma is attached to business failure, which often spurs people to even greater efforts. Even during the bleakest years of the recession in the early '90s, more than a million new businesses opened their doors, more than half of which were sole proprietorships or businesses with no more than two employees. Although many self-employed people come from the ranks of the unemployed, the majority leave secure and well-paid jobs to go it alone. As employers have increasingly been replacing full-time employees with freelancers, consultants and contractors, self-employment has become a necessity for many people rather than an option. In recent years, more than half of new companies have been started by women.

Business Visas

One of the main attractions of buying a business in the US for foreigners is that it offers one of the easiest and quickest methods of obtaining a non-immigrant (E-2) visa. The minimum investment figure isn't fixed, but the investment must be 'substantial' and not 'marginal', i.e. it mustn't solely provide a living for the investor and his family. It isn't necessary to use an immigration lawyer to make an E-2 visa application, although in some cases it's recommended. Always obtain a quotation in writing and shop around a number of immigration lawyers (but check their credentials and references), as fees can run into thousands of dollars, depending on the amount of work involved. The purchase of a business should always be made contingent on obtaining an E-2 visa. For further information see **Category E: Treaty Traders & Investors** on page 80.

Type of Business

There are four types of business structure you can choose if you're self-employed, including a sole proprietorship, partnership (general and limited), joint-venture or corporation. Because of the ever-changing and complex tax laws, you should consult a tax expert before deciding on the best type for you. You must also decide whether to buy an established business, a franchise or start a new business from scratch. When buying an existing business, always employ a licensed business broker (buyer's broker) to advise you on the purchase. Franchises have a much higher success rate than other start-up businesses and can be a reliable route to an E-2 visa (see above). Details of franchise opportunities can be found in the *Franchise Opportunities Guide*, available from the International Franchise Association (IFA, ☎ 1-800-543-1038, 🖳 www.franchise.org) for $17.

Professional Advice

Before investing in a business it's essential to obtain appropriate professional and legal advice. **If you aren't prepared to do this you shouldn't even think of starting a business in the US (or anywhere else for that matter).** Engaging the services of a business and investment consultant is usually the wisest course, although the quality of advice and service varies. Few foreigners are capable of finding their way through the ever-increasing web of legal requirements and regulations without expert advice (not to mention federal, state and local laws and regulations). The purchase of a business **must** be conditional on obtaining visas, licences, permits and any loans or other funding required. If you require financing, it must meet regulations and is usually limited to 25 per cent of the value of the business. While it's much easier to buy an existing business than start a new one, you must thoroughly investigate the financial status, turnover and value of a business (always obtain an independent valuation). It's also important to engage an accountant at the earliest opportunity.

Miscellaneous

The key to buying or starting a successful business is exhaustive research, research and yet more research (plus innovation, competitiveness and quality of service). Choosing the location for a business is even more important than for a home. Many business consultants advertise in the US and foreign press (see page 485), offering everything from a sandwich bar to a motel, a laundrette to a restaurant. Always thoroughly investigate an existing or proposed business before investing a dime. **As any expert will tell you, the US isn't a country for amateur entrepreneurs, particularly amateurs who don't do their homework and are unfamiliar with Americans and the US way of doing business.**

Local Information

There are many local, state and federal government agencies and departments providing information and advice about starting and running a business. The best place to start is the US Small Business Administration (SBA, 409 3rd Street, SW, Washington, DC 20416, ☎ 1-800-U-ASK-SBA, 🖳 www.sbaonline.sba.gov) with offices in all states (many located in local Chambers of Commerce). The SBA provides a wide variety of business counselling on finance, accounting, record keeping, business start-up and management, taxes, marketing, sales promotion, advertising, retailing, manufacturing, and on sales and service businesses. If you're thinking of starting a business or becoming self-employed, you will also find it worthwhile to join the National Association of Self-Employed (NASE, PO Box

612067, DFW Airport, Dallas, TX 75261-2067, ☎ 1-800-232-6273, 💻 www.nase.org). NASE publishes a wealth of information for small businesses and can save you considerable time, trouble and money via a multitude of services and discounts.

General Information

Most international accountants have offices throughout America and are an invaluable source of information (in English and other languages) on subjects such as forming a company, company law, taxation and social security. Many publish free booklets concerning doing business in the US, and most have a small business group or division in their US offices. AT&T publishes the *AT&T Business Guide to the USA* available from the American Chambers of Commerce, 75 Brook Street, London W1Y 2EB, UK (☎ 020-7467 7400).

Bottom Line

Whatever people may tell you, starting your own business isn't easy (otherwise most of us would be doing it) and it requires a lot of hard work (self-employed people generally work much longer hours than employees), a large investment and operating funds (most businesses fail because of lack of capital), good organisation, e.g. book keeping and planning, excellent customer relations (in the US the customer is always right, even when he is wrong!), and a measure of luck (although generally the harder you work, the more 'luck' you have). Almost two out of three new businesses fail within three to five years and that the self-employed must provide their own health and pension plans and don't qualify for unemployment insurance and workers' compensation.

ILLEGAL WORKING

There are literally millions of people working illegally in the US, and illegal workers are intrinsic to the economy, particularly in California, Florida, Illinois, New Mexico, New York, Texas and Washington DC. Most illegal workers are employed in 'transient' occupations such as those of bar staff, waiter and waitress, nanny and servant, farm worker (particularly during fruit and vegetable harvests), the fishing industry and construction worker, where workers are often paid partly or wholly in cash. Much of the middle class US couldn't survive without illegal servants and workers, who usually do the dirty jobs technology hasn't yet eliminated, and many local authorities turn a blind eye to illegal workers.

Although some employers are forced to employ illegal immigrants because of a shortage of local labour, most happily exploit illegal labour in order to pay low wages for long hours and poor working conditions, and naturally don't declare their illegal employees' earnings to federal, state or local governments. Before 1986, US law forbade illegal immigrants from working, but didn't penalise employers for hiring them. In 1986, a new immigration law was introduced that declared that a US employer couldn't employ anyone who wasn't a US citizen, a permanent resident with a green card, or a temporary resident with a non-immigration visa permitting employment (employers are supposed to take photocopies of their employees' identification documents). Fines of up to $20,000 and even imprisonment can be imposed on offenders.

To get a job in the US, an employee should have a social security number, which is issued to every American and legal immigrant. This has spawned a lucrative trade in false documents, which are sold for anything from a few hundred to thousands of dollars. **It's illegal for foreigners to work in the US without a visa or official permission, and if you work illegally with false documents the consequences are even more serious if you're discovered.** If you're tempted to work illegally, you should be aware of the hazards. A foreigner caught working illegally is usually fined, deported and refused entry into the US for five years. Illegal immigrants have no entitlement to federal or company pensions, employer-funded health insurance, unemployment benefits, accident insurance or other benefits.

LANGUAGE

One of the most important qualifications for anyone planning to live or work in the US is usually a good command of the English language (although some people seem to get along fine without it). You usually need to speak, read and write English well enough to find your way around the US, e.g. dealing with government officials, motoring, using public transport, and shopping, and to understand and hold conversations with people you meet. English proficiency is particularly important if you have a job requiring a lot of contact with others or speaking on the telephone and dealing with other foreigners, many of whom speak their own 'dialect' of English.

It's also important for foreign students to have a good command of English (unless they're studying English!), as they must be able to follow lectures and take part in discussions in the course of their studies. This may also require a wider and more technical or specialised vocabulary. For this reason, most colleges and universities won't accept students who aren't fluent in English, and most require prospective students to take a Test of English as a Foreign Language (TOEFL), set in many countries (see page 223). If you wish to improve your English before starting work or commencing a course of study in the US, there are English-language schools throughout the country (see **Language Schools** on page 222).

American English has deposed British English as the international *lingua franca*, and New York City has supplanted London as the world centre of English-language literature and publishing (although not English-language drama). If you already speak English fluently, you probably won't have too much trouble understanding Americans (unless you wind up in Texas or certain rural areas of the south), although if you don't speak with a US or southern English accent, they may have trouble understanding you. Unlike the rest of the world, which is constantly exposed to US accents on TV and in films, most Americans aren't used to English (or foreign) accents. Those who speak British English, plus Europeans, Australians, New Zealanders and South Africans (and various other nationalities) will find Americans incapable of distinguishing between their accents. British English speakers beware – American **is** a foreign language!

Although there's some truth in the assertion that the US and the UK are two nations divided by a common language (attributed to George Bernard Shaw), most American English and British English speakers understand each other most of the time. Nevertheless, there will inevitably be occasions, particularly during your first few months, when small misunderstandings will cause bewilderment, amusement and even embarrassment. Most differences between British and American English are found in terminology. Americans have a much richer assortment of slang and colloquial English than the British, and most cities, regions and ethnic groups have their own idioms. American English is more flexible and dynamic than British English; most new English words, whether slang or high-tech, come from the US and are quickly adopted around the world. However, the two languages are moving together, a process that has been accelerated by TV, film and tourism. Although some British people think American English is an abomination and lament the corruption of their language, a number of historians believe American English (in some parts of the country) is closer to that spoken in Elizabethan times, e.g. gotten, than British English. Shakespeare would probably feel more at home in today's Stratford, Connecticut than in Stratford-upon-Avon, England (and he wouldn't have to endure so many tourists).

Unlike some British English speakers, Americans don't drop their Hs, but drop their Ts, as in winner (winter), innerested (interested) and innernational (international). Americans delight in inventing new verbs and adjectives from nouns (transiting, faxing, partying, etc.), and in combining existing words to form new ones. They commonly dispense with hyphens, particularly when using prefixes. Americans also love acronyms, which are widely used and taken for granted. American English also throws up some 'interesting' words and expressions, e.g. slumgullion, rinky-dink, pixilated, hornswoggle, discombobulate and winningest (the team with the most wins). Written American English is much closer to British English and, spelling apart, the differences are usually much less obvious in the written word.

It comes as a surprise to many foreigners to discover that English isn't the official language in all states and isn't the primary language for some 15 per cent of Americans. One in seven (more than 30 million) US residents have grown up speaking a language other than English. Spanish is the main foreign language and is spoken by some 17 million people (almost half as many as in Spain!). In some cities it's common to see bi-lingual signs and advertisements in Spanish, usually directed at low-income families (the US has an increasing problem with Cubans and other Hispanics, many of whom refuse to learn English). In some neighbourhoods of New York City, Miami and many Texan cities, the predominant language is Spanish and you may rarely hear English spoken. Miami (often referred to as the capital of Latin America) has a 60 per cent Spanish-speaking population and has become America's first bi-lingual city.

Ethnic communities, particularly Spanish, have their own TV and radio stations, newspapers and schools. In public schools in most states children are taught in a variety of languages (in addition to English), including Armenian, Cantonese, Japanese, Korean, Russian, Spanish and Tagalog (Filipino). In addition to foreign tongues and native American Indian languages, a number of regional dialects survive in America, including the Cajun *patois* of Louisiana, and Gulla (of West

African origin) spoken by some African Americans in South Carolina and Georgia. Where applicable, differences in American and British English are indicated throughout this book (with the American English equivalent shown in brackets).

2.

WORKING CONDITIONS

Working conditions in the US are largely dependent on individual employment contracts and an employer's general working conditions. Some aspects of working conditions are decreed by federal or state law, civil service rules or teacher tenure rights, although most are negotiated between employers and employees through collective bargaining agreements, e.g. with unions, or individually and are set out in contracts and company personnel handbooks.

Government employees usually have considerably better job protection and legal rights than employees of private companies. Employees in the private sector are usually employed 'at will', meaning that they can lose their jobs without notice and for any reason (other than discrimination) or no reason at all (employees all dread hearing the euphemism 'We're gonna have to let you go.'). On the other hand, employees may also quit a job without notice and for any reason.

Most US employees receive few benefits and have little or no job protection. Employee benefits in the US lag behind other industrialised countries and are often provided at the whim of an employer, who can reduce or withdraw them at any time. Fringe benefits are rare, except for executives and key employees and those engaged or transferred from overseas. Employees hired to work in the US by foreign companies often receive more comprehensive fringe benefits and allowances than those provided to Americans.

Almost half of US employees in the private sector have no paid sick leave, more than 25 million workers and their dependants have no health insurance (provided voluntarily by employers), and most employed women have no paid leave for pregnancy or childbirth. Unlike European employers, US companies aren't liable for redundancy payments and are more likely to lay workers off when business is bad. Employee benefits provided by medium and large firms are generally much better than those provided by small businesses (companies with fewer than 50 employees are exempt from many aspects of employer legislation). Generally, US corporations fight tooth and nail to avoid providing employee benefits.

Job security is a thing of the past and many corporations now look upon employees as disposable resources to be exploited and discarded at will (although many employees regard their employers in the same way). Companies aren't restricted from laying off mid-level executives when they reach their mid-fifties, when finding a new job may be difficult. Job security comes not through long-term employment with one company, but through continual skill improvement. In general, Americans are increasingly working longer hours, having shorter annual holidays, fewer federal holidays and longer commuting times, and are earning lower basic salaries than in previous years.

Job titles are important in the US, as they define an employee's status and the perks that go with it (such as the key to the executive washroom). In the US, you are what your job title says you are. All large American corporations and employers have a strict hierarchy, including the federal civil service, which has 18 general grades and five executive levels. In some companies, employees are expected to conform to their employer's image in relation to dress and life-style (which may even extend to how they conduct their private lives).

DISCRIMINATION

It's illegal to discriminate against employees because of sex, race, national origin, colour, pregnancy, age, religion or weight. Federal law also bans employers from discriminating against ex-servicemen (veterans) and protects the disabled from discrimination by federal agencies and organisations receiving federal funds. Some state and local governments ban discrimination based on sexual preference, marital status (although unmarried partners, whether heterosexual or homosexual, don't count) and disability. In states with closed shop or union shop laws, it's legal to discriminate against an employee who doesn't wish to join or take part in the activities of a trade union.

Job advertisements should avoid references to race, age or sex, e.g. 'salesperson' should be used rather than 'salesman' (saleswoman). Often employers state in advertisements that they're 'equal opportunity employers', meaning all job applicants are (theoretically) judged equally. Employers may specify the age, religion, national origin or sex of applicants only when it's an essential qualification for the job, called a 'bona fide occupational qualification', e.g. a female fashion model (most men would look odd modelling tights). There's also protection from discrimination against the elderly and companies are prohibited from forcing active workers aged 65 and over to retire.

A woman doing an identical, or almost the same job as a man, with equal skill, effort and responsibility and similar working conditions, is legally entitled to the same salary and other terms of employment as the man. Under the discrimination laws, employers may not offer better benefits to male than female employees (or vice versa). For example, they aren't permitted to provide dependent health cover to married male employees and not to married female employees, nor have different retirement and pension plans for each sex. (It is, however, perfectly legal to restrict dependent health coverage or pregnancy coverage to married employees only.)

Racial discrimination continues to be a contentious issue in the US, where blacks (African Americans) and Hispanics often remain at a disadvantage in the job market, despite the success of 'affirmative action' – giving minority racial groups preferences and quotas in jobs and education. Some employers operate a mandatory Affirmative Action Plan (AAP), which (legally) discriminates positively in favour of ethnic minorities, in order to avoid or correct previous discrimination. This has caused resentment among non-minorities, who see themselves as victims of 'reverse discrimination'. Employers may state in ads that they're affirmative action employers.

In certain strictly defined cases, employers can demand that job applicants (and sometimes employees) take a lie detector test, for example for jobs related to government work, and national or company security. An employer can ask a credit bureau (see **Credit Rating** on page 364) for a report on a employee, but must inform him of this. Private employers are permitted to have dress or grooming codes, although public employers have less freedom to limit their employees' freedom of expression. Employers are, within limits, entitled to ask about an employee's life-style; however, this must not conflict with federal and state laws regarding discrimination.

It's almost impossible to prove discrimination on the grounds of sex and extremely difficult on the grounds of race, although it's widely acknowledged that discrimination is rife. However, because of the possibility of legal action by employees and rejected job applicants, large employers are normally extremely careful not to discriminate against prospective employees. If you believe you've been the victim of employer discrimination, contact your local office of the Equal Employment Opportunity Commission (EEOC) or their national office (1801 L Street, NW, Washington, DC 20507 (☎ 202-663-4900). The EEOC website (🖳 www. eeoc.gov) has an information sheet on how to file a discrimination complaint and there's a free telephone number available (☎1-800-669-4000) to automatically connect you with your local office. As with most issues in the US, there are lawyers who specialise in discrimination and employee-employer disputes.

TERMS OF EMPLOYMENT

Negotiating an appropriate salary is only one aspect of your remuneration, which may consist of much more than what you receive in your pay cheque. When negotiating your terms of employment for a job, the checklists on the following pages will prove useful. The points listed under **General Positions** below apply to most jobs, while those listed under **Managerial & Executive Positions** on page 53 may apply to executive and top managerial appointments only. Many companies offer a range of fringe benefits for executives, managers and key personnel, and it isn't unusual for executives to dramatically increase their annual salaries through profit-sharing, stock options and bonuses.

General Positions

- Salary:
    - Is the total salary adequate, taking into account the cost of living (see page 398)? Is it linked to inflation?
    - Does it include an allowance for working (and living) in an expensive region or city (e.g. New York City) or a remote area (e.g. in Alaska where workers often receive a hardship allowance)?
    - How often is the salary reviewed?
    - Does the salary include commission or bonuses (see page 56)?
    - Is overtime paid or time off granted in lieu of extra hours worked?
    - Is the total salary (including expenses) paid in dollars or is the salary paid in another country (in a different currency) with expenses for living in the US?
- Relocation expenses:
    - Are relocation expenses or a relocation allowance paid?
    - Do relocation expenses include travelling expenses for all family members?
    - Is there an upper limit? If so, is it adequate?

- Are you required to repay your relocation expenses (or a percentage) if you resign before a certain period has elapsed?
- Are you required to pay for your relocation in advance (this may run into thousands of dollars)?
- If employment is for a fixed period, will your relocation expenses be paid when you leave the US?
- If you aren't shipping household goods and furniture, is an allowance paid to buy furniture locally?
- Do relocation expenses include the legal and estate agent's fees incurred when moving home?
- Does the employer engage the services of a relocation consultant (see page 126)?

● Accommodation:
- Will the employer pay for temporary accommodation (or pay a lodging allowance) until you find permanent accommodation (see page 128)?
- Is subsidised or free, temporary or permanent accommodation provided? If so, is it furnished or unfurnished?
- Must you pay for utilities such as electricity, gas and water?
- If accommodation isn't provided by the employer, is assistance in finding suitable accommodation given? What does it consist of?
- What does accommodation cost?
- While you're living in temporary accommodation, will your employer pay your travelling expenses? How far is it from your place of employment?
- Are your expenses paid while looking for local accommodation?

● Working hours:
- What are the weekly working hours?
- Does the employer operate a flexi-time system (see page 57)? If so, what are the fixed (core time) working hours? How early must you start? Can you carry forward extra hours worked and take time off at a later date (or carry forward a deficit and make it up later)?
- Are you required to clock in and out of work?
- Can you choose to be paid or take time off in lieu of overtime worked?

● Part-time or seasonal work:
- Is part-time or seasonal work, e.g. during school terms (semesters), possible?
- Are flexible working hours or part-time working from home permitted?
- Does the employer have a job-sharing scheme?
- Are extended career breaks permitted with no loss of seniority, grade or salary?

● Holiday entitlement:
- What is the annual holiday (vacation) entitlement? Does it increase with service?

- What are the paid federal and state holidays?
- Is free air travel to your home country or elsewhere provided for you and your family, and if so, how often? Are other holiday travel discounts provided?

● Insurance:
- Is health insurance provided for you **and** your family? What does it include (see page 341)? **It's of the utmost importance to ensure that you and all members of your family are fully insured BEFORE you set foot in the US.**
- Is free life insurance provided?
- Is accident or any special insurance provided by your employer?
- For how long is your salary paid if you're ill or have an accident (see **Disability Insurance** on page 340)?

● Company pension:
- Is there a company pension scheme, and if so, what is your contribution (see page 60)?
- Are you required or permitted to pay a lump sum into the pension plan in order to receive a full or higher pension?
- What are the rules regarding early retirement?
- Is the pension transferable (portable) and do you receive the company's contributions in addition to your own if you resign? If not, does the employer pay into a private pension plan?
- Is the pension linked to the inflation rate (index-linked)?
- Do the pension rules apply equally to full and part-time employees?

● Employer:
- What are the employer's prospects?
- Is his profitability and growth rate favourable?
- Does he have a good reputation as an employer?
- Does he have a high staff turnover and has he laid off a high percentage of workers in recent years?

● Women:
- What is the employer's policy regarding equal opportunities for women?
- How many women hold positions in middle and senior management or at board level?
- Is paid or unpaid maternity leave provided?
- Does the employer have a policy of reinstatement after childbirth?

● Training:
- What initial or career training does the employer provide?
- Is training provided in-house or externally and will the employer pay for training or education abroad, if necessary?

- – Does the employer have an on-going training programme for employees in your field, e.g. technical or management? Is the employer's training recognised for its excellence (or otherwise)?
- – Will the employer pay all or part of the cost of non-essential education, e.g. a computer or language course?
- – Will the employer pay for day release to attend a degree course or other study?
- What are the prospects for promotion?
- Does the employer provide a free crèche (nursery or day care) for children below school age or a day care centre for the elderly?
- Is a travelling allowance paid from your home to your place of work?
- Are free or subsidised English language lessons provided for you and your spouse (if necessary)?
- Is a free or subsidised employee restaurant provided? If not, is a lunch allowance paid? Is any provision made for shift workers, e.g. breakfast or evening meals?
- Is free or subsidised parking provided at your work place?
- Are free work clothes, overalls or a uniform provided? Does the employer pay for the cleaning of work clothes?
- Does the employer offer inexpensive home loans, interest-free loans or mortgage assistance? A below base rate home loan can be worth thousands of dollars per year.
- Is a company car provided? What sort of car? Can it be used privately, and if so, does the employer pay for the petrol (gas)?
- Does the employer provide fringe benefits or subsidised services such as in-house banking, credit union, car discount scheme, travel discounts, employees' discount store or product discounts, sports and social facilities, fitness centre, subsidised theatre tickets, shopping services, shoe repairs, cleaners, florist, pharmacy, car servicing, on-site kindergarten or elementary school, and adult education?
- Do you have a written list of your job responsibilities?
- Have your employment conditions been confirmed in writing? For a detailed description of the possible contents of your employment conditions, see page 55.
- If a dispute arises over your salary or working conditions, under the law of which country will your contract (if applicable) be interpreted?

Managerial & Executive Positions

- Is private schooling for your children paid for or subsidised? Will the employer pay for a boarding school in the US or another country?
- Is the salary indexed to inflation or protected against devaluation and cost of living increases? This is important if you're paid in a foreign currency that fluctuates wildly against the dollar or could be devalued.

- Are you paid an overseas allowance for working in the US?

- Is a rent-free house or apartment provided?

- Are paid holidays provided (perhaps in a company owned house or apartment) or 'business' conferences in exotic places?

- Are all costs incurred by a move to the US reimbursed? For example, the cost of selling your home, employing an agent to let it for you, or storing personal effects.

- Will the employer pay for domestic help, e.g. a servant or cook?

- Does the employer provide profit-sharing or stock options (which may be worth more than your annual salary)?

- Is a car provided, perhaps with a chauffeur?

- Are you entitled to any miscellaneous benefits such as club memberships, free credit cards, or tickets for sports events and shows?

- Is there an entertainment allowance?

- Is extra compensation, e.g. a 'golden handshake', paid if you're laid off, dismissed or the company is taken over? This is important in the US's volatile job market!

EMPLOYMENT CONTRACT

Under US law, a contract of employment exists as soon as an employee proves his acceptance of an employer's terms and conditions of employment, e.g. by starting work. After an offer is accepted, employer and employee are bound by the terms agreed. A US employer isn't usually required by law to provide benefits such as holiday or sick pay, but if benefits are offered or promised the employer must fulfil his obligations.

If you're offered a job in the US, you should have a comprehensive and legally watertight, written contract detailing your terms and conditions of employment. However, most foreigners are dismayed to find that most US employers don't provide employment contracts. Contracts are generally reserved for high-level executives, certain professionals (such as university professors), engineers who work on a project basis and sports stars (who must have contracts by law). A written contract of employment should contain all the terms and conditions that have been agreed between the employer and employee. For the mere mortals who don't receive an employment contract, your offer letter serves as written proof of the terms you've accepted in taking the job. (And your new employer may ask you to return a signed copy of the offer letter when you accept employment.) Before signing a contract or an offer letter, you should know exactly what it contains. If your knowledge of English is imperfect, you should ask someone to explain anything you don't understand or have it translated.

Your employment is usually subject to satisfactory references being received from your previous employer(s) and/or character references. In the case of a school leaver or student, a reference is usually required from one or more teachers from your last school, college or university. For certain jobs, a pre-employment medical examination is required and periodical examinations may be a condition of employment, e.g. when good health is vital to the safe performance of your duties (see page 59). If you require a visa to work in the US, your contract may contain a clause stating that 'the contract is subject to a visa being granted by the US authorities'. Employees with a contract must be notified in writing of any changes in their terms and conditions of employment. Those with an offer letter will also be subject to any terms and conditions published in the employee manual, and these can be changed at any time.

EMPLOYMENT CONDITIONS

As used here, the term 'employment conditions' refers to an employer's general employment terms (including benefits, rules and regulations) applying to all employees, unless otherwise stated in an employment contract. You may receive a copy of these conditions on starting employment (or in some cases beforehand). If you don't receive employment conditions, generally the federal and state minimum legal requirements apply.

Employment conditions may cover: validity and applicability; place of work; salary and benefits; commission and bonuses; working hours; flexi-time rules; overtime and compensation; travel and relocation expenses; social security; medical examination; company car; company pension plan; workers' compensation insurance; unemployment benefit; sick pay and disability benefit; health insurance; miscellaneous insurance; notification of sickness or accident; annual holiday (vacation); federal holidays; personal and special leave; paid expenses; probationary and notice periods; education and training; pregnancy; part-time job restrictions; confidentiality and changing jobs; acceptance of gifts; long service awards; retirement; discipline and dismissal; redundancy (severance) pay; references; and union membership.

The above points are explained below or a reference is given to the chapter or page number where the subject is covered in more detail.

Validity & Applicability

Employment conditions may contain a paragraph stating the date from which they take effect and to whom they apply.

Place of Work

Unless you have an employment contract stating otherwise, your employer may change your place of work with or without your agreement or ask you to occasionally work at other locations. If your employer moves to another town or region, he may offer some or all employees relocation benefits to move to the new work place, but this isn't required by law.

Salary & Benefits

Your salary is stated in your offer of employment; salary reviews, overtime rates, bonus rates, planned increases and cost of living rises may also be included. Salaries are usually paid by cheque – weekly for hourly paid workers and bi-monthly or monthly for salaried workers. Only 35 per cent of workers have their salary paid directly into their bank accounts, most preferring to deposit (or cash) their own pay cheques. You must receive an itemised pay statement (pay stub) detailing all deductions, with your pay cheque or separately when your salary is paid directly into a bank account.

Minimum wages are set by the Fair Labor Standards Act (FLSA), although it does not apply to farm workers, disabled workers, full-time students, and 'student-learners' (mainly apprentices and those in work-study programmes). The tips of employees who regularly receive above a certain amount per month may be considered part of their wages for minimum wage purposes. The national minimum wage was $5.15 an hour in 2004 (it can be changed only by an Act of Congress) or around $10,300 per year for a 40-hour week. Although most states have no wage laws, some 13 states (including the District of Columbia) set a higher minimum wage than the federal government. The highest state minimum wage is $7.15 in Alaska.

Salaries are usually reviewed once or twice a year, depending on your position and the industry. It isn't unheard of, however, for employers to implement a pay rise freeze if the business is doing poorly, and occasionally there have been across the board pay cuts. Annual increases may be negotiated individually by employees, by an independent pay review board or by a union (by collective bargaining). Generally you're better off when you're able to negotiate your own salary increases.

Commission & Bonuses

Your salary may include commission or bonus payments, based on your individual performance, e.g. meeting sales targets, or your employer's profits. Bonuses may be paid regularly, e.g. monthly or annually, or irregularly (usually as the conditions for the bonus or commissions are met). Some employers in pay employees an annual bonus (usually in December or shortly after the end of the employer's fiscal year), although this may be limited to upper level executives or those directly connected with sales. When a bonus is paid it may be stated in your offer of employment, in which case it is obligatory, although the terms of the bonus can be changed. In your first and last years of employment any annual bonus is usually paid pro rata if you don't work a full calendar year.

Some employers operate an annual voluntary bonus scheme, based on an employee's individual performance or the company's profits (a profit-sharing scheme). If you're employed on a contract or freelance basis for a fixed period, you may be paid an end-of-contract bonus. When discussing salary with a prospective employer, take into account the total salary package, including commission, bonuses and benefits (such as free health insurance). Be sure to consider how attainable the bonus conditions are, as some employers like to set 'stretch' qualifications for bonus plans in order to inspire their workers to greater efforts.

Working Hours

Working hours vary according to your employer, your position and the type of industry in which you're employed. Unlike many other western countries, where employees are working progressively fewer hours, most Americans are working longer hours. Over 30 per cent of US employees work more than the standard 40-hour week; those in professional and management positions work an average of 45 hours a week, and in manufacturing the average (with overtime) is around 50. According to a recent UN report, the average US employee works 250 hours more each year than his British counterpart and almost 500 hours more than the average German worker (the equivalent of 13 weeks – an extra ten years in a working lifetime!). Not surprisingly, the number of leisure hours per week enjoyed by the average American has fallen from 24.3 in 1975 to below 20 today.

Generally the higher the position a person holds, the longer the hours he works, and many managers regularly take work home and receive business calls in the evenings, at weekends and even when on holiday! American white-collar workers often start work earlier than their counterparts in other countries, particularly on the west coast, where office hours may be dictated by office hours on the east coast, e.g. those of Wall Street, which are three hours ahead. Typical office hours are 8am to 5pm with a lunch break of 30 to 60 minutes.

Under federal law, most employees must have a meal break of at least 30 minutes for every five hours worked and a rest period of at least ten minutes for each four hours worked. Most medium-size and large companies have formal rest periods, such as coffee breaks and clean-up time for blue-collar workers, although in many offices employees take drinks and often even lunch at their desks. On average, employees in medium and large companies receive rest periods (not including a lunch break) totalling around 30 minutes a day. US employers are often reluctant to permit time off during working hours and may not allow paid time off to visit a doctor or dentist, which may be deducted from your sick leave or annual holiday entitlement.

Flexi-time Rules

Only 10 per cent of US companies operate flexi-time working hours, mostly for white-collar office workers. A flexi-time system normally requires all employees to be present between certain hours, known as core hours, e.g. 10am to noon and 2pm to 4pm. Employees may make up their required working hours by starting earlier than the required core time, reducing their lunch break or working later. Smaller companies may allow employees to work as late as they like, provided they don't exceed the threshold for overtime pay (see below).

Overtime & Compensation

Hourly paid employees can usually work up to 40 hours a week without earning overtime pay. Any hours above 40 **must** be paid at not less than 1.5 times the regular hourly rate (time-and-a-half). This also applies to certain salaried employees who qualify as 'non-exempt' (i.e. because they aren't exempt from the Federal minimum wage and overtime laws). The distinction between non-exempt and exempt employees (exempt being those who aren't entitled to overtime pay for extra hours worked) used to be fairly straightforward. But at the end of August 2004, the overtime laws were updated for the first time in nearly 50 years and there are still some questions about who is and isn't entitled to overtime pay.

There are three tests that determine whether or not you must be paid extra (time and a half) for working over 40 hours a week: the salary-basis test, the salary-level test and a duties test. Those who are paid on a salary basis are considered exempt, as they've been for the last 50 years. But, to qualify as salaried rather than hourly, you must be paid more than $455 per week ($23,660 per year). The previous threshold was a mere $155 a week. On the other hand, anyone who's paid more than $100,000 per year is automatically considered exempt from the overtime pay regulations. The third test is the tough one. An exempt employee is defined as one whose job is administrative, professional or executive in nature, based on the day to day responsibilities and duties performed. It's the definition of these three categories of duties that has been broadened in the new regulations. Before, you had to have supervisory responsibility over at least one or more subordinates, including the power to hire and fire them before you were considered exempt. Now, however, if you're consulted about hiring and firing, even if you don't have the final say, you could well fall into the exempt category even if you were entitled to overtime pay before.

Some states require overtime to be paid when a non-exempt employee works more than eight hours a day, although federal law is concerned only with the number of hours worked in a 'work-week' (any period of seven days in a row). Federal law doesn't require premium pay for work at weekends and on federal holidays, although some employers pay time-and-a-half (or double-time) for Sundays and some federal holidays.

An employer can give employees compensatory time off ('comp time') instead of paying overtime by mutual agreement with employees; comp time must be given at the overtime rate, e.g. for three hours' overtime, you're entitled to 4.5 hours off.

Travel & Relocation Expenses

Your travel and relocation expenses to the US (or to a new job in another region of the US) depend on your agreement with your employer, and may be detailed in an employment contract, offer letter or employee policies manual. If you're hired from outside the US, your air ticket (or other travel expenses) to the US is usually booked and paid for by your employer or his agent. You can usually also claim any incidental travel costs, e.g. the cost of transport to and from airports. Most employers pay your relocation costs up to a specified amount, although if you leave the employer before a minimum period elapses, you may be required to repay a percentage of the cost (or the full cost if you break your contract).

An employer may pay a fixed relocation allowance, e.g. $5,000, based on your salary, position and size of family, or he may pay the total cost of moving house irrespective of the amount. The allowance should be sufficient to move the contents of an average house (castles usually aren't catered for). A company may ask you to obtain two or three estimates when they're liable for the total cost. Generally you're required to organise and pay for the move yourself. Your employer usually reimburses the equivalent amount in dollars **after** you've paid the bill, although it may be possible to get him to pay the bill directly or make an advance payment. **Ensure that the relocation package is adequate.**

If you change jobs within the US, your new employer may pay your relocation expenses when it's necessary for you to move house. Don't forget to ask, as they may not offer to pay (it may depend on how desperate they are to employ you). (See also **Relocation Consultants** on page 126.)

Social Security

State social security includes retirement benefits (pensions), survivor benefits, disability benefits and some limited health insurance benefits, to which you and your employer each contribute 7.65 per cent of your gross salary. Social security contributions are compulsory for most US residents and are usually deducted at source from your gross salary by your employer. For details see **Social Security** on page 328.

Medical Examination

Many employers require all prospective employees to have a pre-employment medical examination performed by a doctor nominated by them. An offer of employment is usually subject to your being given a clean bill of health. This may be required for employees over a certain age only, e.g. 40, or for employees in particular jobs, e.g. where good health is of paramount importance for reasons of safety. Thereafter, a medical examination may be necessary periodically, e.g. every one or two years, or may be requested at any time by your employer. Medical examinations may also be required as a condition of membership in a company health, pension or life insurance scheme. Some companies also insist on employees having regular health screening, particularly senior managers and executives.

Federal law allows employers to require applicants to take medical exams or drug tests (60 per cent of prospective graduate employees are tested), provided they keep the results secret, although many states regulate drug testing. Employers are usually required to pay for medical examinations. Prospective employees are also regularly screened for background and criminal record and given psychological and polygraph (honesty) tests. There's no testing (yet) for smoking, alcohol abuse or sexual orientation.

Company Car

It's unusual for employees to be provided with a company car and they're rarely offered as fringe benefits. Even when a car is essential for your job, for example for a sales representative, your employer may insist that you provide your own, for which you're paid a mileage allowance for business use. If you're provided with a company car, you usually receive full details about its use and your obligations on starting employment. If a company car is provided, check what sort of car it is, whether you're permitted to use it privately, and if so who pays for the petrol for private mileage. Using a company car for private use affects your tax position.

Company Pension Plan

Many American companies provide a 401(k) company pension plan for employees. This includes around 80 per cent of employees employed by medium-size and large companies. Your contributions are deducted from your gross salary and vary considerably according to your age and your employer's pension fund. (See **Pensions** on page 336.)

Workers' Compensation Insurance

Almost all employers are required to have workers' compensation insurance, providing benefits for employees who suffer an injury (physical or mental) or illness as a result of their job. Workers are entitled to compensation for all job-related injuries, irrespective of whether they were at fault. If a worker dies as a result of an accident, his dependants receive the benefits. If a worker doesn't qualify for disability benefit, he is usually entitled to workers' compensation for work-related injuries, diseases and death. Workers who don't qualify for social security disability benefit (see page 332) or workers' compensation may be covered by other federal and state programmes. All states have some form of workers' compensation, although the benefits vary and some workers, e.g. farm employees, are exempt in some states or cover is optional.

Depending on the extent of injuries, employees receive hospitalisation and other medical care costs, and they may be entitled to medical or vocational rehabilitation. They may also receive a weekly disability benefit, depending on whether their disability is temporary or permanent, partial or total. Workers or their dependants receive a fixed weekly benefit, depending on their regular salary before injury. Most states pay a maximum of two-thirds of regular wages and stipulate maximum weekly payments. Payments vary considerably from state to state. Employees may also receive fixed (scheduled) benefits for losing a limb, organ or other part of the body.

If your employer isn't covered by workers' compensation, you can sue him for damages, but must show that the employer's negligence caused the injury.

Unemployment Benefit

All employers are required to pay tax under the Federal Unemployment Tax Act (known as FUTA tax) in order to provide workers and their families with a weekly income for a limited period when they're unemployed through no fault of their own, e.g. because of layoffs, plant closures or natural disasters. Unemployment tax (also, confusingly, referred to as unemployment insurance or 'reemployment insurance') is managed jointly by individual states and the federal government. The maximum rate of FUTA tax is 6.2 per cent of the first $7,000 paid to each employee each year, although employers with records of less unemployment (i.e. with fewer unemployment benefits paid to former employees) pay lower rates, down to a minimum of 0.8 per cent.

The law regarding the payment of unemployment benefit varies from state to state. In general, a waiting period of one week is necessary after a claim is filed before unemployment benefit is paid. To qualify for unemployment benefit you must not have quit your previous job without good cause or have been discharged because of misconduct, must not be involved in a labour dispute, and must be ready, willing and able to work. Self-employed people aren't eligible for unemployment benefits, nor are casual or temporary workers, minors working for their parents, and student interns.

If you're unemployed, you must register for work at your local state unemployment office as soon as possible (listed in telephone directories under state government 'Unemployment Insurance – Claims Office'). Take your social security card and pay slips with you, and any other documents that prove you're out of work and eligible for benefit. After filing you must report to the unemployment office periodically, usually weekly or when notified of job openings. Failure to report without good reason may result in a loss of benefit. If the unemployment office has a suitable job for you, you must accept it or lose your unemployment benefit unless you have a good reason for the refusal. However, a job must be suitable in terms of your qualifications and experience, and the wages, hours and working conditions mustn't be substantially less favourable than those for similar jobs in the community.

If you move to a new state, you can continue to receive unemployment benefit at your new address, as your new state acts as an agent for your old state (under the Interstate Reciprocal Benefit Payment Plan), which continues to pay your benefit. However, you must qualify for unemployment benefit under the laws of the new state. Benefit is paid only if you can prove that you've had a certain amount of past employment or earnings in a job covered by state law. The amount of earnings and the period used to measure them varies according to the state. The amount you receive also depends on your past earnings, the general aim being to provide a weekly benefit equal to around a third of your usual wages, up to a maximum set by law. In most states the total benefit you may receive in a 12-month period is limited to a percentage of your total wages in a prior 12-month period, as well as to a maximum number of weeks. In 2003, the maximum unemployment benefit varied from $133 to $558 (excluding allowances for dependants) per week, with an average of $235 for all states. Unemployment benefit may be taxable if your gross adjusted income reaches a certain level, depending on state and federal income tax reporting requirements.

Benefit is paid for a maximum of 26 weeks in all states (plus the District of Columbia) with the exception of Massachusetts and Washington State, where it's 30 weeks. During periods of high unemployment in a particular state, extended benefit may be available to workers who have exhausted their regular benefit. An unemployed worker may receive benefit equal to that which he received under the state programme for half the number of weeks of his basic entitlement, up to a maximum of 39 weeks (includes the period of regular benefit).

Further information is contained on the U.S. Department of Labor website (🖳 www.workforcesecurity.dol.gov).

Sick Pay & Disability Benefit

Short and long-term disability benefits, in the event of an illness or accident, vary considerably according to your employer, your length of service and whether you're a salaried or hourly-paid employee. Most employees receive short-term disability protection through sick leave, and sickness and accident insurance, although employers aren't required to provide sick pay. Under sickness and accident insurance, 80 per cent of participants have their benefit paid in full by their employers. The remaining 20 per cent usually pay a fixed contribution, e.g. $2 or $3 per month, or a percentage of their monthly salary. Sick leave is usually paid in full, whereas sickness and accident insurance usually amounts to half to two-thirds of normal pay. Sick leave plans commonly have a service requirement, e.g. three months, before new employees become eligible for benefit.

Sick leave is usually paid for a fixed number of days a year (annual sick leave plans) and employees are often permitted to carry over and accumulate unused sick leave from year to year (usually there's a maximum number of days). The average employee takes around seven days sick leave a year. Sick leave is more commonly available to salary-based white-collar employees than blue-collar workers, although many blue-collar workers have similar protection through sickness and accident insurance plans. Short-term sickness and accident benefits usually continue for a maximum of 26 weeks (six months).

Long-term disability (LTD) insurance typically replaces 50 to 60 per cent of income and usually begins after six months of disability and continues for a specified number of months or until retirement age, depending on the worker's age at the time of the disability. LTD insurance is more commonly provided for white-collar workers (some 60 per cent) than blue-collar workers (around 25 per cent). Employees are usually required to contribute towards the cost of LTD insurance and there are normally service requirements of from one month to one year before they become eligible. Some employees are eligible for an immediate disability pension under their company pension plan. If you aren't provided with short or long-term disability insurance by your employer, you can take out private disability insurance (see **Disability Insurance** on page 340).

Health Insurance

Health insurance is a common and important employee benefit, although the cover provided by employers varies considerably and comprehensive cover is rare. In fact, only around a third of employers pay 100 per cent of their employees' health insurance premiums and fewer than 20 per cent pay their employees' dependants' premiums. 100 per cent cover (including families) is usually restricted to government employees and employees of large corporations. For most employees, 50 to 90 per cent of their health insurance premiums are paid by their employers. Some 40 per cent of companies allow employees to remain members of company health insurance plans after their retirement. Many companies offer 'wellness' programmes designed to improve the health and fitness of employees, and some pay bonuses to employees who follow a healthy lifestyle. Health insurance cover doesn't usually include unmarried partners (whether heterosexual or homosexual). For more information about health insurance see page 341.

Miscellaneous Insurance

Miscellaneous insurance provided by your employer may include free life assurance. Most companies provide free life assurance equal to one to two times annual salary as part of a group health insurance plan. If applicable, miscellaneous insurance may be detailed in your employment conditions. (See also **Life Assurance** on page 355.)

Notification of Sickness or Accident

You're usually required to notify your employer of sickness or an accident that prevents you from working as soon as possible, i.e. within a few hours of your normal starting time. Failure to do so may result in your not being paid for that day's absence (if applicable). You're required to keep your boss or manager informed about your illness and when you expect to return to work. For periods of less than seven days, you're usually required to provide a self-certificate of why you were absent on your return to work, although some employers may require a doctor's certificate. If you're away from work for more than a certain number of days, e.g. seven, you **must** obtain a doctor's certificate.

Annual Holiday Entitlement

The biggest shock for many foreigners working in the US comes when they discover the length of their annual holiday (vacation). Most new employees of companies receive just one or two weeks' paid holiday a year, exceeded in every other leading industrial nation except Japan. Some employees may receive no paid holiday at all in their first year of employment. This will come as a severe blow to Europeans and other foreigners who are used to receiving four to six weeks' paid annual leave (the average in the US is 12 days a year compared with 25 in France and 30 in Germany).

Each year of employment raises your annual holiday entitlement by no more than a day or two, so it can take you 10 to 20 years before you're entitled to four weeks' paid holiday a year. The average holiday entitlement is nine days a year after one year of service, 17 days after 10 years and 20 days after 20 years. Your annual holiday entitlement usually depends on your profession, position and employer. White-collar employees usually become eligible for longer holidays after a shorter term of service than blue-collar workers. Holiday pay and entitlements are decided by individual or collective bargaining, e.g. by unions, and aren't a legal entitlement. Teachers and others employed in educational establishments will be dismayed to discover that there's no paid Easter holiday. The long summer holiday period is also often unpaid, so that teachers must often work in summer school.

Top managerial positions may offer additional annual holiday (but no time to take it). Many companies provide anniversary-year bonus holiday days, such as an extra week after 10 or 20 years' service (yippee!). Holiday entitlement is calculated on a pro rata basis (per completed calendar month of service) when you don't work a full calendar year. Part-time staff may be entitled to paid holiday on a proportional basis. Usually all annual holiday must be taken in the year in which it's earned, although many companies allow employees to carry some unused holiday over to the next year or choose to be paid in lieu of holiday. However, holidays are usually lost if they're unused at the end of the year.

Before starting a new job, check that any planned holidays are approved by your new employer. This is particularly important if they fall within your first 6 or 12 months. Usually white-collar workers must work six months before being permitted to take a holiday and blue-collar workers one year. Holiday may usually be taken only with the prior permission of your manager or boss and in many companies must be booked up to one year in advance. Most companies allow unpaid leave in exceptional circumstances only, although smaller companies are generally more flexible. If you resign your position or are given notice, most employers pay you in lieu of outstanding holiday, although this isn't an entitlement and you may be obliged to take your holidays at your employer's convenience.

Federal Holidays

When Americans talk about a 'holiday', they mean a federal holiday and not annual or school holidays (vacations – see above). Congress and the federal government designate the following ten days as federal or statutory holidays (public holidays). Although technically these apply only to federal employees and residents of the District of Columbia and it's left to individual states to designate their own holidays, most federal holidays are widely observed and are often considered to be national holidays. Banks, post offices, public schools, offices and most businesses are usually closed on federal holidays.

Date/Day	Holiday
1st January	**New Year's Day**
Third Monday in January	**Martin Luther King Day**
Third Monday in February	**Presidents' Day** – celebrates George Washington's birthday (22nd February) and Abraham Lincoln's birthday (12th February). It's also called Washington's Birthday or Washington-Lincoln Day.
Last Monday in May	**Memorial Day** – also known as Decoration Day and honours soldiers fallen in battle.
4th July	**Independence Day** – the most important US holiday.
First Monday in September	**Labor** Day – usually marks the end of summer.

Second Monday in October	**Columbus Day** – also variously called Pioneers' Day, Farmers' Day, Fraternal Day and Discoverers' Day.
11th November	**Veterans' Day** – formerly Armistice Day.
Fourth Thursday in November	**Thanksgiving Day** – generally known simply as Thanksgiving.
25th December	**Christmas Day**

Most private sector employees receive seven to nine holidays a year and a few receive as many as 12 (the average is nine). Other holidays may include extended holiday plans, such as the period between Christmas and New Year's Day, 'floating' holidays and personal holidays, such as employee birthdays. In addition to federally observed legal holidays, many states have local holidays, e.g. state days. Floating holidays may be decided by the employer or individual employees. Many companies give employees a full or half-day paid holiday on Christmas Eve and some also on New Year's Eve. Service and retail employees are required to work on most federal holidays, although overtime is paid, if applicable. Members of religious minorities (e.g. Jews or Muslims) are generally allowed to take their own major religious holidays off (e.g. Yom Kippur) sometimes in exchange for working Christmas Eve, Christmas Day, or other Christian holidays for co-workers who wish to observe those holidays.

When a holiday falls on a Saturday or Sunday, another day is usually granted to employees (or they receive an additional day's pay). When a public holiday falls on a Tuesday or Thursday, the day before or the day after, respectively, is sometimes declared a holiday, and most government offices are closed on the Friday following Thanksgiving. Foreign embassies and consulates in the US usually observe all US federal and local holidays **plus** their own national holidays.

Personal & Special Leave

Most companies provide paid personal or special leave on certain occasions, e.g. military leave, leave to attend the funeral of a family member (bereavement days), and leave for jury duty. An employer must allow an employee time off for jury duty, but isn't required to pay him (which may or may not be an acceptable excuse for refusing jury duty). A person selected for jury duty cannot be fired. Special leave for other occasions is usually limited to a number of days a year, e.g. three, and, in the case of funerals, may vary according to your relationship to the deceased. The grounds for compassionate leave may be listed in your employment conditions. An employer isn't required to allow employees time off work for religious observance, although he is required to accommodate religious beliefs to a certain extent.

Whether or not you're paid for time off work or time lost through unavoidable circumstances, e.g. public transport strikes, car breakdowns, inclement weather, depends on your employer, your status and position, and whether you're paid hourly or are a salaried employee. Executives and managers (i.e. white-collar workers), who admittedly often work much longer hours than officially required, usually have more leeway than blue-collar (hourly-paid) workers.

Some public sector employers allow employees to take sabbaticals and may even continue to pay them a percentage of their salary, although this is exceptional. Many employers don't allow employees to take unpaid leave, even in connection with a pregnancy (see page 67) or to care for a sick family member. However, around 35 states have some form of family or medical leave legislation, the majority limited to pregnancy leave; only ten states provide family and medical leave. In most states, companies aren't required to provide employees who are absent from work for an extended period, e.g. because of ill health or to attend a sick family member, with the same or a comparable job or to pay health or other employee benefits. In 1996, the federal government passed the Family and Medical Leave Act, under which an employee is eligible for up to 12 weeks' unpaid leave in a given year for the birth or adoption of a child, or personal or family health needs.

Paid Expenses

Expenses paid by your employer may be listed in your employment conditions. These may include travel costs from your home to a customer or client site, when travelling on company business or for training or education. Most companies pay a mileage allowance to staff who are authorised to use their own cars on company business (but make sure that business use is covered by your car insurance). Companies don't normally pay a lunch allowance, but may reimburse employees for certain working lunches or entertainment of customers or potential customers at lunch. Some companies pay a dinner allowance for employees working late into the evening, whether or not the employees are entitled to overtime.

Probationary & Notice Periods

For some jobs there's an official probationary period, varying from one or two weeks for hourly-paid employees to three months for salaried employees. During your probationary period, you can be let go (terminated) at any time with no notice at all for any reason or for no reason at all. It's not all that different after you've successfully completed your probationary period, although usually you receive a small pay rise or become eligible for certain benefits (e.g. sick leave or the company retirement plan) once you've completed your probationary period. Your notice period depends on whether you're employed 'at will' (see page 66) or whether you have a contract. If you're employed 'at will' and paid every two weeks, your notice period is two weeks, irrespective of how long you've been employed. Your notice period may also depend on your method of payment, your employer, your profession and your length of service, and may be indicated in your offer of employment or employment conditions. Notice periods are normally more a matter of common practice, though, and not legally enforceable. If you quit your job, and decide to leave right away rather than working out your notice period, you're still entitled to be paid for any outstanding holiday pay (and sometimes sick leave) you may have coming to you. But you risk receiving a less than favourable reference from your former employer. Most employers who terminate employees insist that they leave right away and in some cases may escort them from the premises to assure that they don't talk to colleagues or sabotage company equipment or projects.

Education & Training

The education and training provided by your employer may be stated in your employment conditions. In some professions (e.g. medicine, accountancy, teaching), you're required to complete a certain amount of continuing education in order to keep or renew your license to practice. It's in your own interest to investigate courses of study, seminars and lectures that you believe are of benefit to you and your employer. Some employers give reasonable consideration to a request to attend a part-time course during working hours, provided you don't make it a full-time occupation. For example, if you need to improve your English, language classes may be paid for by your employer. If it's necessary to learn a foreign language to do your job, the cost of language study should be paid by your employer. Many employers require you to pay for your own studies, including books and transportation to and from classes, and then reimburse you for your costs only after you have successfully completed the course.

In addition to relevant education and training, employers must also provide the essential tools and equipment for a job (although this is open to interpretation). It's also compulsory for companies to provide relevant and adequate health and safety training for all employees.

Pregnancy

Time off work in connection with pregnancy is usually given without question, but isn't always be paid or is deducted from your annual sickness allowance. Up to twelve weeks of unpaid maternity or paternity leave after the birth or adoption of a child is available to some 60 per cent of all workers under the Family and Medical Leave Act. Paid leave is rare, although some employers allow you to combine available short-term disability, sick leave and vacation time benefits. Pregnant women are entitled by law to pregnancy leave in many states, e.g. four months in California, and the same or a comparable job on their return to work. In 2004, California became the first state to allow a new mother to extend her short-term disability by an additional six weeks, with partial pay, in order to stay at home with the baby a bit longer. Other states have introduced similar legislation and may have programmes soon. Unpaid maternity and paternity leave can generally be taken after annual holiday and sick leave have been exhausted, and can usually continue for a limited period, e.g. around 20 weeks.

An employer cannot fire or refuse to employ a woman because of pregnancy (or for any reason connected with pregnancy or childbirth), force her to take maternity leave or penalise her reinstatement rights after a pregnancy. A mother's rights include the right to her job back (or a similar job) after she has given birth with no loss of wages, fringe benefits or seniority. The law requires employers to treat pregnancy and childbirth like a temporary disability, and health insurance plans must cover these conditions if they include temporary disabilities. A pregnant woman or nursing mother cannot be required to work overtime.

Part-time Job Restrictions

Restrictions on part-time employment for anyone other than your regular full-time employer may be detailed in your employment conditions. Many US companies don't allow full-time employees to work part-time (i.e. moonlight) for another employer, particularly one in the same line of business. Normally you must notify your full-time employer when you take on a part-time job, especially if it limits the hours you can work at your full-time job in any way. You may, however, be permitted to take a part-time teaching job or similar part-time employment (or you can write a book!).

Confidentiality & Changing Jobs

If you disclose confidential company information, in the US or overseas (particularly to competitors), you're liable to instant dismissal and may also have legal action taken against you. You may not take any secrets or confidential information, e.g. customer mailing lists, from a previous employer, but you may usually use any skills, know-how, knowledge and contacts acquired during his employ. You may not compete against a former employer if there's a valid, binding restraint clause in an employment contract. An employment contract may contain a clause defining the sort of information that the employer considers to be confidential, such as customer and supplier relationships, and details of business plans.

If there's a confidentiality or restraint clause in an employment contract that's unfair, e.g. it inhibits you from changing jobs, it is probably invalid in law and will be thrown out by a court. If you're in doubt, consult a lawyer who specialises in company law about your rights. If you're a key employee, you may have a legal binding contract preventing you from joining a competitor or starting a company in the same line of business as your employer (and in particular from enticing former colleagues to join your company) for a limited period.

Acceptance of Gifts

With the exception of those employed in the public sector, employees are normally permitted to accept gifts of a limited value from customers or suppliers, e.g. bottles of whisky or small gifts at Christmas. Generally any small gifts given and received openly aren't considered a bribe or unlawful (although if you give your business to someone else the following year, don't expect a gift next Christmas). Most US companies forbid the acceptance of any gifts of substance, and cash payments are totally out of the question (if you accept a real bribe, make sure it's a big one and that you have a secret bank account). You should declare any gifts received to your immediate superior, who decides what should be done with them. Some bosses pool all gifts and share them among their employees.

Long Service Awards

Most large companies present their employees with long service awards after a number of years, e.g. 15, 20 or 25. These are usually in the form of gifts, e.g. a watch or clock, so you can count the hours to your retirement, presented to employees by senior management. Periods of absence, e.g. maternity leave, usually count as continuous employment when calculating your length of service.

Retirement

The Age Discrimination in Employment Act (ADEA) prohibits employers who regularly employ 20 or more people from fixing a retirement age, and some state laws make compulsory retirement illegal (in which case you are simply fired!). Employees not covered by ADEA, e.g. police officers, prison guards and fire fighters employed by state and local governments, may be required to retire at 65 (anyone who wishes to continue working beyond 65 should seek psychiatric help). Many companies present retiring employees with a gift on reaching retirement age, the value of which usually depends on your number of years' service.

Discipline & Dismissal

Some large and medium size companies have comprehensive grievance and disciplinary procedures that must be followed before an employee can be suspended or dismissed. Some employers have disciplinary procedures whereby employees can be suspended with or without pay, e.g. for breaches of contract. Employees can also be suspended (usually with pay) pending investigation into an alleged offence or impropriety. Disciplinary procedures usually include verbal and official written warnings, and are to protect employees from unfair dismissal and to ensure that dismissed employees cannot (successfully) sue their employers. If you have a grievance or complaint against a colleague or your boss, there may be an official procedure to be followed to obtain redress. If an official grievance procedure exists, it may be detailed in your employment conditions.

Employees in the private sector are usually employed 'at will', meaning that they may lose their job without notice and for any reason or none at all; employees may also quit a job without notice and for any reason. Exceptions are employees covered by a collective bargaining agreement and those with contracts. Where formal discharge and disciplinary procedures exist, company policy may state that an employee be given notice before he can be fired, in which case he may have a legal right to notice.

Many states have exceptions to the 'at will' rule for private employees, e.g. employees fired because they refused to perform an act that violates public policy, or when the firing of an employee violated an oral assurance of job security. In these cases employees can sue for wrongful discharge. Employees of federal, state and local governments are covered by civil service laws and can be dismissed for 'just cause' only. In some states, you cannot be fired within a certain period of falling ill or before or after giving birth, provided you intend to return to work.

In general, employers can terminate an employee's employment at any time without justification and, unless the employee has a contract, he is entitled to little or no compensation. Unlike those in most European countries, US employers aren't liable to pay high redundancy payments and are likely to lay off workers when business is bad. Dismissal is common among executives and managers, particularly for older employees, and is generally accepted as a fact of life. The average executive has an unstable life and many live in a permanent state of 'red alert'. Companies often have a high turnover in senior executives and a shake-up at the top often works its way down the management ladder. US companies are ruthless in dismissing employees who don't measure up or fail to deliver the expected results.

Employers are fond of using euphemisms for firing someone, the most common of which are 'let go' or 'lay off' (Americans also have a number of terms for dismissal, including fired, canned, discharged, released, sacked and even terminated!). Dismissed employees are usually stripped of company keys, badges, passes and credit cards etc., and escorted from the premises by security guards, and may be given little or no time to say goodbye to colleagues or even to clear their desks (employers are fearful that they will sabotage the computer system or shoot their boss). If you're fired, you must be paid immediately and if you quit without notice you must be paid within 72 hours.

Redundancy Pay

Most employees have little or no right to redundancy (severance) pay, so US companies are more likely to lay off workers when business is bad than companies in some other countries. If you're employed in a volatile business, particularly in an executive or managerial position, it's important to have adequate financial compensation in the event of redundancy or severance written into your employment contract (one of the first jobs of any successful executive should be to make himself financially independent of his employer).

Executives may have a clause in their contracts, whereby they receive a generous 'golden handshake' if they're made redundant, e.g. after a take-over. Without a compensation clause in your contract, you are entitled to whatever your employer chooses to offer you. Some companies wishing to reduce their workforce may offer employees voluntary redundancy payments (pay-outs) or early retirement.

If you're entitled to redundancy pay, you may receive one to two weeks' pay for every year you've worked for a company, although you should try to obtain more if possible. You may also be entitled to be paid in lieu of any holiday, sick days and other days' leave owed to you, as well as a refund of your contributions to company pension plans. An employer must give redundancy pay if there are collective bargaining agreements or contracts that provide redundancy benefits. Although state laws may require redundancy pay under certain conditions, those employed 'at will' must usually rely on their employer's benevolence. If possible, you should ensure that you receive a cheque (or cheques) for the total redundancy package and all paperwork **before** you leave your work place for the last time. Redundancy pay doesn't affect your eligibility to claim unemployment benefit (see page 60).

References

An employer is under no legal obligation to provide employees with a written reference. If you leave an employer on good terms, he usually provides a written reference on request. Even if you're fired, you should ask whether your employer would be willing to serve as a reference (your boss may feel it's the least he can do under the circumstances). If your boss refuses to give you a reference or gives you a 'bad' reference, you should ask a sympathetic supervisor or even someone from another department to serve as a reference for you. It can be important to maintain contact with former colleagues so that you have current addresses and phone numbers for potential references.

Prospective employers usually contact your previous employer(s) directly for a reference, orally or written. This can be bad news, as you've no idea what has been said about you and whether it's true or false, although an employer shouldn't provide false information or hearsay that could be slander or libel (he shouldn't, but if he does it's almost impossible to successfully sue him). Some people advise having a friend call a former employer, posing as a potential employer to see what your former employer is saying about you, and there are services available that do this for a fee. Because of the dangers of being accused of slander, many employers refuse to give references and only reveal the dates of employment, the positions held and salary rates. However, in many states a former employer must provide certain facts to a prospective employer at a worker's request. In some states employees have access to their personnel files and must be given written notice of any referral given to others.

Union Membership

Some 16 per cent of the US workforce (around 16 million people) are union members (20 per cent in manufacturing, 35 per cent in the government sector and less than 10 per cent in the private sector), although the number has been falling steadily since the '50s, when more than a third of all employees were union members. The umbrella organisation covering trade unions is the American Federation of Labor and the Congress of Industrial Organizations (AFL-CIO, 815 16th Street, NW, Washington, DC 20006, ☎ 202-637-5000, 💻 www.aflcio.org), with a combined membership of around 13 million; a further 3 million workers belong to non-affiliated organisations. There are around 280 labour organisations in the US, the three largest unions (each with over a million members) being the United Automobile Workers (UAW), the American Federation of State, County, and Municipal Employees (AFSCME), and the Food and Commercial Workers (FCW).

Under the National Labor Relations Act (NRLA), employees have the right to form, join, or assist labour unions, and to bargain collectively through representatives of their own choosing on wages, hours and other terms of employment. They can also engage in concerted activities for the purpose of collective bargaining or other mutual aid or protection, such as striking to secure better working conditions (although employers have the right to hire permanent replacements for striking workers). The NRLA covers all private companies doing business in more than one state, shipping or receiving out-of-state goods, or whose actions affect interstate commerce.

Unions remain strong in traditional industries such as manufacturing and transport, but have little influence in industries such as services, finance, and retailing, and certain employees, such as farm workers, domestic employees of a family and managers, have no rights to collective bargaining. In the northern industrial states where unions are strong, e.g. Michigan, New York and Pennsylvania, the law gives unions protection. However, in the south and west, e.g. Florida, Mississippi and Texas, where state law is hostile to organised labour, unions are generally weak.

Employees aren't required to join or participate in a union, except where there's a 'union shop' (closed shop) agreement requiring all new workers to join the union within 30 days of being hired (employees must pay union dues, but aren't required to participate in union activities). With a closed shop agreement, only one union is recognised and given the right to negotiate contracts in each place of work. Closed shops are outlawed in around 20 southern and western states by 'right-to-work' laws, enacted to weaken unions and attract new industry. However, strong opposition from labour leaders has ensured that no major industrial state has introduced such laws.

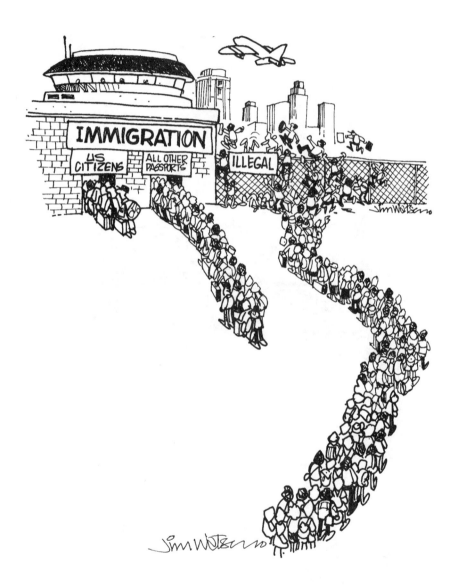

3.

PERMITS & VISAS

The notion that the US is a nation of immigrants is something of an illusion, as only 11 per cent of US residents are foreign-born, roughly the same as the UK and France, but less than Canada (around 16 per cent), Switzerland (17 per cent) and Australia (20 per cent). However, in terms of numbers, the US is way ahead of the field, with official immigration running at up to a million a year. In the wake of the terrorist attacks of 11th September 2001, there have been several changes to visa and immigration policies, and in some categories, visa applications have decreased as requirements have been tightened. Still, in recent years, it's estimated that over 7 million visas each year are issued for entry into the United States.

With the exception of certain visitors, all non-resident foreigners wishing to enter the US require a visa, even those just in transit on their way to another country. The US issues a bewildering range of visas which are broadly divided into immigrant (permanent resident) and non-immigrant (temporary resident) visas. An immigrant visa gives you the right to travel to the US to live and work there (and change jobs freely) on a permanent basis, with the possibility of qualifying for US citizenship after five years' residence. A non-immigrant visa allows you to travel to the US on a temporary basis, e.g. from six months to five years, and in certain cases to accept employment. Work permits aren't issued, as the appropriate visa serves the same purpose. A visa does not give you the right to enter the US, only to travel there for a specified purpose. This is because visas are issued by the Consular section of the Department of State, which only has the authority to pre-approve foreigners for travel. The Consular services issue 4 million visas annually.

For many years, the US immigration and naturalisation laws were enforced by the Immigration and Naturalization Service (INS) of the United States Department of Justice. After the terrorist attacks, the Department of Homeland Security (DHS) was created to co-ordinate the various services connected with national security. On 1st March 2003, the old INS became three new departments under the DHS: the US Citizenship and Immigration Service (USCIS), which handles the various immigration statuses and permits once an immigrant has been admitted to the country, Immigrations and Customs Enforcement (ICE), responsible for immigration-related investigations, detentions, deportation and the new registration system for students and exchange visitors (SEVIS), and Customs and Border Protection (CBP), which patrols the borders and entry points (and decides whether or not to admit arriving foreigners with a visa). Like the old INS, the USCIS maintains four regional service centres and more than 60 local offices throughout the US. Once admitted into the country by the CBP, it's now the job of the USCIS and the ICE to register and track all the various foreigners, make sure they're complying with the terms of their visas, and (especially) to make sure they go back home or at least leave the US when they're supposed to!

Possession of a visa isn't a guarantee of entry into the US. Entry into the country is strictly controlled and anyone who doesn't comply with immigration requirements (including being able to prove that they're indeed in compliance with the terms of their visa), can be fined, jailed or deported. In general, the US attempts to restrict entry of undesirables, i.e. anyone who's a threat to the health, welfare or security of the US (of which it clearly already has more than its fair share). Only holders of visas permitting employment may work in the US. Holders of other categories of visas may not accept employment, even informal work in a household as a nanny, au pair or mother's helper. Your passport must usually be valid for a minimum of six months after the termination of your planned stay. If your passport is close to its expiry date, you should renew it before travelling to the US.

There are many books that describe immigration procedures in detail including *Immigrating To The USA* by Dan P. Danilov (Staff Counsel Press), *Immigration Questions and Answers* by Carl R. Baldwin (Watson-Guptill) and *The Immigration Handbook* by Henry G. Liebman (First Books, Inc.). Further information is available on State Department websites (🖳 www.state.gov and 🖳 www.unitedstates visa.gov) and on the USCIS website (🖳 www.uscis.gov). (See also **American Citizenship** on page 504.)

Immigration is a complex subject and that the information contained in this chapter is intended as a general guide only. You shouldn't base any decisions or actions on the information contained herein without first confirming it with an official and reliable source, such as an American Embassy.

IMMIGRANT VISAS

An immigrant visa bestows upon the holder the status of a permanent resident. It comprises a stamp placed in your passport by an American embassy or consulate outside the US (as with non-immigrant visas), which allows you to enter the US to take up permanent residence. Holders of immigrant visas are issued with an Alien Registration Receipt Card, popularly referred to as a green card (although it's now pinkish-blue), consisting of a plastic identification card with your photo, thumb print and signature on the front. A green card serves as a US entry document for permanent residents returning to the US after a period abroad.

There are two ways most people can obtain a green card, through blood ties (or marriage) as an immediate or close relative of a US citizen or permanent resident, or through employment. Green cards are issued on a preferential basis and this can involve waiting many years, as only a limited number are issued each year. Immigrant visas give holders the right to live and work in the US (and change jobs freely) on a permanent basis and confers eligibility for US citizenship after three years for spouses of US citizens and five years for all others. The main difference between the rights of a permanent resident and those of a US citizen is that a permanent resident, although having all the responsibilities of a US citizen, is ineligible for certain welfare benefits, including some Medicaid and Social Security insurance benefits. Green cards are valid for ten years and cannot be withdrawn, provided the holder doesn't abandon his US residence or commit certain crimes.

Before applying for an immigrant visa you must establish that you fulfil the criteria for whatever category of visa you're applying for. Provided you qualify, you may apply for an immigrant visa under more than one category. When applying for an immigrant visa (and some non-immigrant visas) it may be advisable to employ the services of a qualified and experienced immigration lawyer, although it isn't always necessary. It depends on each case, although the procedure can be complicated and the rules and regulations change frequently. Many visa applications are rejected each year because the paperwork is incorrect, e.g. the wrong information has been provided, a form hasn't been completed correctly, the wrong visa application has been made, or a lawyer hasn't made the correct approach to the authorities. If someone makes an application on your behalf, you should, at the very least, check that the information provided is correct in every detail. If your application is rejected (for any reason) you're less likely to be granted a visa by appealing or re-applying, **so it's vital to get it right first time.**

There are literally thousands of immigration lawyers in the US and abroad, many of whom specialise in certain categories of immigrants only, e.g. those with lots of money to pay their fees. Lawyers' fees depend on the complexity of the case and range from $250 for a simple consultation to between $5,000 and $10,000 for a complex application involving a lot of work. You should engage a lawyer who's been highly recommended or who has a good reputation, as incompetent and dishonest lawyers aren't unknown. The most reliable source of information on US lawyers is said to be the Martindale-Hubbell list, which includes a rating of each lawyer. The ratings can be viewed on 💻 www.lawyers.com. **No lawyer, however much you pay him, can guarantee that your application will be approved.** Ensure that you know exactly how much you must pay and the exact services you will receive in return for your money. If you wish to appeal successfully against a refusal to grant you a visa or green card, you must probably engage the services of an immigration lawyer.

A cheaper alternative to immigration lawyers are the 400 or so immigration agencies operating throughout the country, some of which, such as the recently accredited Irish Immigration Center in Boston, charge no fees at all.

Categories

People immigrating to the US are divided by immigration law into categories, such as immediate relatives, family-sponsored and employment-based immigrants, diversity immigrants, special immigrants and investors, as described below:

Immediate Relatives

Immediate relatives are entitled to permanent residence **without** numerical limitation. They include the spouse (or a recent widow or widower), and unmarried children under 21 of a US citizen, and the parents of a US citizen who's over 21. Immediate relatives include step-parents and step-children, provided the marriage that created the relationship took place before the child's 18th birthday, and foreign children adopted before their 16th birthdays.

Preference Categories

Preference categories are those with annual numerical limitations (quotas) on the number of people who may enter as permanent residents. The total quota for all preference categories is 675,000 per year (the US immigration 'year' runs from 1st October to 30th September). Preference categories are further divided into family-sponsored immigrants and employment-based immigrants, as described below:

Family-Sponsored Immigrants

Relatives of US citizens and of permanent resident aliens (referred to as preference relatives) are limited to 480,000 a year. Immediate relatives (see above) are included in this number. However, there's no limit on the number of visas which may be issued to immediate relatives. Preference relatives receive all visas that aren't used by immediate relatives or a minimum of 226,000 per year. An additional 55,000 per year are allocated to relatives of amnesty recipients. Preference relatives are divided into the following four categories (minimum annual quotas for each are shown in brackets):

- **F-1 (First Preference)** – Unmarried children of US citizens and their children (23,400);

- **F-2 (Second Preference)** – Spouses, children, and the unmarried children of green card holders. At least 75 per cent of all visas in this category go to spouses and children, the remainder being allocated to older unmarried sons and daughters (114,200).

- **F-3 (Third Preference)** – Married children (of any age) of US citizens and their spouses and children (23,400);

- **F-4 (Fourth Preference)** – Brothers and sisters of US citizens and their spouses and children, provided the US citizen is over 21 years of age (65,000);

Employment-Based Immigrants

A total of 140,000 visas a year are available in the Employment-based Immigrant category, of which a maximum of 7 per cent can be allocated to people born in any one country. Employment-based immigrants are divided into the following five groups (annual quotas for each are shown in brackets):

- **E-1 (Priority Workers)** – People of extraordinary ability in the sciences, arts, education, business, or athletics; outstanding professors and researchers; and certain multinational executives and managers (40,000);

- **E-2 (Members of the Professions)** – Professionals holding advanced degrees or baccalaureate degrees plus at least five years of progressive experience in their field, and people of exceptional ability in the sciences, arts and business, e.g. professors and researchers (40,000);

- **E-3 (Professionals, Skilled and Unskilled Workers)** – Professionals holding baccalaureate degrees, skilled workers with at least two years' experience, and other workers whose skills are in short supply. Unskilled workers are subject to a quota of 10,000, which is included in the 40,000 total (40,000).

- **E-4 (Special Immigrants)** – Special immigrants include religious workers and ministers of religion, employees of certain international organisations and their immediate family members, specially qualified and recommended current and former employees of the US government and returning residents (10,000);

● **E-5 (Investors)** – People who create employment for at least ten full-time American workers (not family members) by investing capital in a new commercial enterprise in the US. The minimum amount of capital required is usually $500,000 (10,000).

In addition to the above quotas there are limits on certain sub-preferences, some of which are based on formulas which change each year. Please refer to a US Embassy for current details.

Diversity Immigrants

The Immigration Act 1990 created a new category, Diversity Immigrants, with the aim of providing immigration opportunities to people born in countries that have had the lowest numbers of immigrants in recent years (selection is based on country of birth rather than present residence or citizenship). Around 50,000 DV-1 visas are available each year through this scheme and are allocated by lottery (hence the scheme is commonly referred to as the 'Visa Lottery'). A maximum of 3,850 visas are issued to natives of each eligible country (to be eligible, a country must have had fewer than 50,000 visas, excluding diversity visas, issued to it during the previous five years). The UK has not qualified in the last five years, although Northern Ireland is eligible, as it is treated as a separate country for this programme only.

Applicants require a high school diploma (or equivalent) or a proven job skill requiring at least two years' training and two years' experience in that job within the last five years. No initial fee is payable on application, but successful applicants must pay a processing fee of $100 plus a $335 visa fee. The application period for DV-1 visas varies each year and usually lasts for two or three months only, e.g. the registration period for the 2006 programme ran from 5th November 2004 to 7th January 2005. Applications must be submitted online at the Diversity Lottery website (🖳 www.dvlottery.state.gov), including the submission of all photos and any supporting documents required. Only one application is permitted per person, although a husband and wife can each submit an application even when only one spouse qualifies. If more than one application is submitted, the applicant is disqualified for that year.

The lottery 'winners' are selected by computer and must apply for their visas as soon as possible after they receive written notification of selection. **Selection does not guarantee that a visa will be issued, as far more than 50,000 winners are selected each year.** Spouses and minor children can emigrate with the DV-1 winner.

Information about DV-1 visas and the application procedure can be obtained from US embassies and consulates or on the State Department visa website (🖳 www.travel.state.gov). No assistance is necessary from a lawyer or immigration expert, although many offer their services (often for a high fee that may claim to include a 'free' airline ticket or other prizes). **Avoid companies offering information or assistance in connection with the visa lottery, as they're simply a scam; no outside service can improve an applicant's chance of being selected!**

Petitions

In all cases when an applicant's qualification for an immigrant visa is based on his relationship to a US citizen or a permanent resident or on an offer of employment, a petition must be filed with the USCIS. Only after this petition has been accepted can you apply for a visa. The person who files the petition is known as the petitioner (or sponsor) and must usually be the US citizen or green card holder relative or a US employer. Some applicants, such as priority workers, investors, certain special immigrants and diversity immigrants, can petition on their own behalf.

Family-sponsored immigrants, who believe they're entitled to immigrant status based on their relationship to a US citizen or resident alien, must ask their relative to file a *Petition for Alien Relative* (form I-130) with their nearest USCIS service centre in the US. There's a $185 filing fee for the I-130 form. In certain cases where the sponsor is resident abroad, petitions can be filed at a US embassy or consulate, but in those cases, the sponsor must be in the process of moving back to the US themselves with the alien being sponsored. Sponsors must execute an *Affidavit of Support* (I-864) in which the sponsor agrees to support the intended immigrant and any dependants and to reimburse any government agency or private entity that provides the sponsored immigrant with federal, state or local public benefits. The sponsor must submit copies of their last three years' federal income tax returns, so make sure the relative sponsoring you has been filing! The obligation to support the alien relative continues until the immigrant becomes a US citizen, leaves the US permanently or dies.

Employment-based immigrants, who believe that they're entitled to immigrant status based on proposed employment in the US, require an approved *Immigrant Petition for Alien Worker* (form I-140) from the USCIS. The filing fee for this petition is $190. Some people who qualify as priority workers may petition on their own behalf with the USCIS, while most must have their prospective employer file the petition. Before filing, sponsors of applicants for classification as members of the professions, professionals, skilled and unskilled workers (second and third preference employment-based immigrants), must obtain 'labour certification' from the US Department of Labor, a protracted process requiring the employer to prove that there are no qualified American workers available to take the job, e.g. by advertising the job vacancy in newspapers and at his offices for a certain period.

Special immigrants, who qualify for immigration under a special category, must file a petition consisting of various documents, depending on the category. A US embassy or consulate or USCIS service centre will advise you what documents are required.

Investors must file an *Immigrant Petition by Alien Entrepreneur* (form I-526) with the USCIS, with a filing fee of $465.

If possible, you or your sponsor should file a petition in person, to be sure that your filing is recorded correctly. When you file in person, any obvious errors or omissions are pointed out on the spot, so you have the opportunity to correct them immediately or resubmit at a later date. When you file by post and errors or omissions are discovered, all forms, papers and documents are returned with a form explaining why, and the application is delayed.

Once a petition has been approved, the applicant is given a 'priority date' (or visa number). When this date is reached, the prospective immigrant is invited to submit his application for a visa to enter the US. In certain heavily oversubscribed categories, there's a waiting period of up to ten years before a priority date is reached.

The filing fee for a petition must be paid with a dollar cashier's cheque, dollar money order, international bank draft or in cash when filing a petition in person. Be wary of any prospective employer who asks you to reimburse him for the sponsor filing fees, especially before your arrival in the US. If the petition filed on your behalf is approved, the USCIS forwards it to the consular section of your local US embassy or consulate (if you filed abroad), who informs you of the subsequent steps to be taken to apply for the appropriate visa. If your petition is denied, the USCIS notifies you directly.

Applications

The application procedure and documentation for immigrant visas varies according to the immigrant category and the procedures of the local US embassy or consulate. Once your petition has been accepted (and you've received notification of this) you should receive a package of information from your local US consulate, *Instruction Package for Immigrant Visa Applicants*. Follow the instructions in this packet carefully, especially those related to how and where to pay the visa application fee (around $335)! Most consular offices outside the US can no longer accept visa applications by mail, unless the applicant is under 13 or over 80. All visa applicants are now required to have a face to face interview with a consular official, and these interviews can take anywhere from five minutes to two hours or more. The waiting period for scheduling visa immigrant interviews varies by consulate, anywhere from a few weeks to several months. Applicants are required to swear or affirm to the truth and accuracy of the visa application (form DS-230), and to submit certain documentary evidence to establish their eligibility for the visa. Documents required include your passport, birth certificate, marriage certificate, photographs, evidence of financial support, the form you received from the USCIS notifying you that your petition was approved (form I-797), police certificates, military records and a letter from your prospective employer (as applicable). Supporting documents not in English must often be translated, but this is part of the instruction package. You're also expected to have had a medical examination and bring all your immunisation records with you to the interview, as well as receipts showing that the various fees have been correctly paid.

If you have convictions for any criminal offences, including some driving offences, you may be required to provide official court records or a letter from the court giving details of the offence and the penalty imposed. You may also be required to prove that you won't become a 'public charge', i.e. that you have sufficient funds to support yourself in the US. You require documentary evidence, in duplicate, that you have sufficient funds to provide for yourself and your family or that you will have employment which will provide an adequate income. The proof required varies, but includes bank statements and a letter from your bank, ownership of property or investments, and income from investments or royalties.

Your sponsor (see above) must have executed an *Affidavit of Support* and you should have a copy of the receipt showing that this has been filed.

The cost of the medical examination must be borne by the visa applicant and varies according to the country, e.g. GB£85. If you successfully pass the interview (which may consist of a few innocuous questions only or a third degree, particularly if you were born in one of the countries considered by the US government to be a 'state sponsor of terrorism') and the medical examination and are over 14, you're finger-printed (those under 14 are finger-printed within 30 days of their 14th birthday). There's an $85 fee for the fingerprinting, which includes a search of FBI records to make sure aren't wanted already in the US! If all goes well, and your application is approved, you receive your ticket to paradise – the coveted green card – usually at the end of the same day as the interview. From the date your sponsor submits the petition on your behalf, you should expect to wait between six and nine months to obtain a green card, although it can take longer if the application is a 'difficult' one.

If you apply for a green card (to 'adjust status') while in the US, it's possible to obtain permission to travel abroad while waiting for a reply by applying for 'advance parole'. However, unless it's a matter of life and death, it isn't recommended and should never be undertaken without taking legal advice. If your application for an immigrant visa is denied and you believe that it hasn't been treated fairly, you can sometimes make an appeal. If this fails, you may have the option of a final appeal to the Board of Immigration Appeals in Washington. If all else fails, you can take your case to the federal court. **However, an appeal should usually be made only with the assistance of an immigration lawyer** (see page 77).

Once you've been issued with an immigrant visa, you must enter the US within six months; otherwise it expires. When you have a green card you shouldn't remain outside the US for longer than a year without obtaining prior authorisation from the USCIS. If you remain abroad for more than a year or make your permanent home in another country, your green card is cancelled (unless you've obtained a re-entry permit, allowing an absence of up to two years). In this case, you must apply at a US embassy or consulate for a special immigrant visa as a returning resident and prove that you didn't intend to abandon your residence when you left the US.

NON-IMMIGRANT VISAS

A non-immigrant visa gives a person the right to come to the US temporarily, e.g. from a few days to five years, and in certain cases to work, study or carry out some other activity. There's no limit to the number of non-immigrant visas issued each year. Many non-immigrant visas are valid for a set period (or a maximum period), often at the discretion of the immigration officer at the port of entry. It isn't always necessary to have a non-immigrant visa stamped in your passport, and a visa can be provided on a separate sheet and presented with your passport when entering the US. For example, this may be necessary in cases where the presence of a US visa in a passport will cause problems when returning home or travelling to other countries.

Many non-immigrant visas are of the multiple-entry type, allowing you to enter and leave the US as often as you wish during the visa's validity period. However, the period for which you're allowed to remain in the US may be affected by the validity of your passport. For example, for certain nationalities, if you have a non-immigrant visa that's valid for three years, but your passport is valid for three months only, you're admitted for just three months. This entry period is stamped on your *Arrival-Departure Record* (I-94) card (see page 104). If you have a valid non-immigrant visa and obtain a new passport, retain your old passport and take it with you when travelling to the US, as the visa remains valid. You must **never** remove the visa from the old passport, as this invalidates it.

Documentation

All applicants for non-immigrant visas filing at a US embassy or consulate (i.e. outside the US) must complete a *Nonimmigrant Visa Application* (form DS-156), which is a surprisingly small and innocuous looking piece of paper. All questions are fairly straightforward, although you should be careful to answer questions honestly, as US embassies and consulates maintain meticulous records and can easily check whether you've previously had a visa refused or cancelled. Nearly all visa applicants are now required to have an interview with the consular visa official, although the interview may last only five minutes if everything is in order. Males between the ages of 16 and 45, born in or citizens of certain 'high risk' countries must also submit a supplemental application (form DS-157) and there are supplemental forms for certain students, exchange programme participants and potential investors. Keep a copy of the forms for your own records and, if you're concerned about not being admitted, bring your copies with you when entering the US. A separate form must be completed for each visa applicant, including your spouse and children. There's a fee for a non-immigrant visa, currently $100, usually payable in local currency.

Foreigners already in the US applying for a change of non-immigrant status must complete an *Application to Extend/Change Nonimmigrant Status* (form I-539), and file their application at an USCIS service centre or online. The filing fee is $195 for a change of status. In order to make an American filing, you must qualify under the prevailing conditions for the non-immigrant status for which you're applying. Recent changes in policy have made US processing of status changes considerably more difficult. In some cases it may only be possible (or may be far easier) to file at a US embassy or consulate abroad. **A change of status is usually automatically cancelled when you leave the US.**

The documentation required to support an application for a non-immigrant visa varies according to the category. For certain categories, e.g. tourist, student and exchange visitor, you should be prepared to support your application with proof that you intend to return to your country of residence after your period in the US has ended. Certain non-immigrant visas, for example for a job, study or marriage, require a document to be provided or submitted, usually by someone in the US. In theory, whatever needs to be done in the US to obtain the initial permission should be carried out by the petitioner or sponsor, i.e. the person, institution or organisation 'requiring' your entry into the US. You're notified of the documents and other formalities when making your visa application. If you're accompanied by your spouse and children, you may need to provide a marriage certificate and a birth certificate for each child, as well as colour, passport-size photographs and passports for your spouse and each child. The US requirements for 'passport photographs' are somewhat different from the requirements in other countries. Usually, you cannot use photographs taken in do-it-yourself booths, but must go to a photographer familiar with the US passport photo requirements.

Visa Processing

The time required to process non-immigrant visa applications varies considerably according to the category of visa. Most non-immigrant visas are issued by US embassies and consulates directly. However, certain visas, e.g. employment visas, require a petition (see page 81) which must be approved by the USCIS before the visa application can be processed. In August 2001, the INS introduced a pilot programme, called the Premium Processing Service, whereby the employers of certain categories of 'special worker', e.g. scientists, athletes and corporate executives, may pay an extra $1,000 to have their petitions processed within 15 days instead of the usual two months or more. This programme has been continued under the new DHS departments dealing with immigration. When your petition has been approved, the Approval Notice must be presented with the application form and passport to the US embassy or consulate serving your place of residence. When applying for certain non-immigrant visas, it's recommended that you use an immigration lawyer (see page 77).

Many non-immigrant visas can be extended, provided your status remains unchanged and the period of admission originally granted hasn't expired, as stated on your form I-94 (see page 104). Applications for extensions must usually be made not more than 60 days before the expiry date and you must show that you acted 'in good faith', i.e. that you didn't plan to stay longer than originally permitted. An application for an extension for non-employed categories is made with an *Application to Extend/Change Nonimmigrant Status* (form I-539), which must be accompanied by a copy of your I-94 card and supporting evidence, if applicable, e.g. form I-129 for employment categories. If you file your application on time, you may remain in the US until you receive a decision, even if your authorised stay has expired. If your application is denied, there's no formal appeal and you must leave the country.

It's also possible to switch from one non-immigrant visa to another after arrival in the US, or even to 'adjust status' and obtain a green card. If you plan to do this, don't apply for a change of visa immediately after arrival, as the authorities may think that you had a 'preconceived intent' and deny your request.

Interview

It used to be the case that, if you were called in to the US embassy or consulate for an interview, it meant there was something wrong or suspicious about your application for a visa. With all the increased security concerns, nearly everyone requiring a visa must now appear in person at the local embassy or consulate before the visa is issued, although in most cases, the interview itself may last only a few minutes. You're much more likely to be subjected to a lengthy interview in countries where there's a lot of visa fraud or where governments are believed to be supporting known terrorist groups than, for example, in a western European country. The interviewers are well aware that many people travel to the US on a visitor's or student visa, while planning to work illegally or remain beyond the permitted period. Depending on the category of visa that you've applied for, the interviewer may ask questions about your employment or occupation, education and qualifications, finances, living circumstances, and personal background.

If you're prohibited from working in the US and you imply that you may look for work, your visa application may be rejected. If you're unemployed or have recently left school or university, your application will be closely scrutinised, as the consular official may suspect that you're planning to look for work in the US (unless you have a specific reason for your visit and can prove it). If you're going to the US as a bona fide visitor, you should have a return ticket, firm plans regarding your travels and what you intend to do after your holiday and, not least, sufficient funds to cover your expenses for the period you plan to remain there. You must contact the embassy or consulate to arrange an interview appointment, and if you're unable to attend for any reason, you should phone in advance to reschedule. If you're refused a visa, appeals are allowed in certain circumstances, although for certain non-immigrant visas, e.g. tourists, they're usually a waste of time. However, you're usually free to re-apply as often as you wish.

If you commit visa fraud, e.g. by completing form DS-156 dishonestly, providing false information, or untruthfully answering questions put to you at an interview, you can be permanently barred from entering the US.

Visa Waiver

Nationals of certain countries can visit the US under the Visa Waiver Program (VWP), including the citizens of Andorra, Argentina, Australia, Austria, Belgium, Brunei, Denmark, Finland, France, Germany, Iceland, Ireland, Italy, Japan, Liechtenstein, Luxembourg, Monaco, the Netherlands, New Zealand, Norway, Portugal, San Marino, Singapore, Slovenia, Spain, Sweden, Switzerland, Uruguay and the United Kingdom. If you're a citizen of one of these countries, you don't usually require a visa to visit the US, provided:

● You have a valid passport issued by a participating country and are a citizen of that country (not just a resident). In most cases, your passport should be valid for at least six months from the date of your arrival. Beginning in October 2004, your passport must be machine readable, i.e. have a standardised strip of machine readable characters on the main page. British passport holders should note that if their passport indicates that they're a British Subject, British Dependent Territories Citizen or British Overseas Citizen they don't qualify for travel without a visa.

● Your trip is for pleasure or business;

● Your stay is for a maximum of 90 days;

● You have a return or onward non-transferable ticket for a destination outside North America, issued by a participating carrier (i.e. most major airlines and shipping lines), and non-refundable except in the country of issuance or your home country. If you enter the US by land from Canada or Mexico, the return ticket requirement isn't applicable.

- There are no 'grounds of exclusion' or reasons why you shouldn't be admitted to the US (see page 100).

A *Nonimmigrant Visa Waiver Arrival-Departure Record* (form I-94W) must be completed, available from participating carriers (airlines and shipping companies), travel agents, US tourist offices, US embassies and consulates, and 'ports of entry' from Canada and Mexico. If you enter by land from Canada or Mexico, you must also pay a fee of $6. If you enter the US under the Visa Waiver Program, you cannot obtain an extension on the 90 day limit and you waive your rights to a hearing in the case of exclusion or deportation, except if applying for asylum. Thanks again to tightened security regulations, journalists entering the US to do any form of work-related activity must have the appropriate I visa (see page 95), even if they're from a Visa Waiver country and otherwise meet all the Visa Waiver Program requirements.

VWP travellers wishing to enter the US with passports issued on or after 26th October 2005 must have a passport that's machine readable and contains biometric information embedded in a chip that's part of the passport. This requirement has caused a certain level of panic in frequent traveller circles, but the deadline (which applies to the governments issuing the passports, not to individual travellers) has already been postponed at least once due, in part, to the need to develop an international consensus regarding what constitutes a 'biometric passport'. For additional information, check the website of the US embassy or consulate in your home country.

Students & Exchange Visitors

In 2003, the Homeland Security Department set up its Student and Exchange Visitor Information System (SEVIS), a centralised database designed to track visa holders engaged in academic and vocational studies, as well as participants in exchange programmes and fellowships. All schools, universities and exchange programmes that are approved to admit foreigners must participate in the SEVIS network. When a student or participant is admitted to a study or exchange programme that qualifies them for a visa (categories F, J and M below), they're registered in the SEVIS system and the appropriate form confirming this is sent to the participant (I-20, I-20M or DS-2019, depending on the type of programme involved). The confirmation form and proof of payment of the SEVIS fee (currently $100) are required as part of the documentation you must provide at your visa interview.

Those entering the US under any of the SEVIS visa categories aren't admitted into the country more than 30 days before the official start of their classes, course or programme, and in fact, ICE recommends that you don't arrive more than ten days in advance unless you can document the reason for your early arrival.

SEVIS has been a high priority issue for the HSD, due to the discovery that most of the terrorists who carried out the 11th September attacks had gained entry to the country using student visas for flight training schools. The manual system in place for tracking students was notorious for losing track of those who had never shown up for classes, dropped out of their programmes or simply failed to go home after completing them. The system is designed to track all activity of students and exchange participants, from the time they're first accepted into a school or programme through their arrival in the US, their enrolment in school, class attendance, grades received, eventual completion of the programme (or dropping or flunking out) and their return to their home country. More information is available on the SEVIS website (⊟ http://www.ice.gov/graphics/sevis/index.htm).

Categories

There are 18 categories of non-immigrant visa, each of which is designated by a letter, as shown in the table below. Rather surprisingly, there's no visa category for retirees (although it's always possible that one may be introduced in the future). Retirees may remain in the US for up to six months per year with a B-2 visa (see below), or longer with a green card. It isn't currently possible to qualify for immigration on the basis of retirement.

Category	Qualification
A	Ambassadors, diplomats, accredited officials and employees of foreign governments, and their immediate families, plus their personal attendants, servants and employees
B	Business visitors and tourists
C	Foreign travellers in transit through the US
D	Crew members of aircraft and ships who must land temporarily in the US
E	Treaty traders and investors and their immediate families
F	Academic or language students and their immediate families
G	Representatives of foreign governments coming to the US to work for international organisations, NATO employees, and their immediate families
H	Registered nurses, people working in specialised occupations, temporary agricultural and other temporary workers, trainees, and their immediate families
I	Foreign media representatives and their immediate families
J	Exchange visitors and their immediate families
K	Fiancé(e)s of US citizens coming to the US to get married and their unmarried children
L	Intra-company transferees and their immediate families
M	Vocational or other non-academic students and their immediate families

N	Children of certain special immigrants
O	People of extraordinary ability in the sciences, arts, education, business or athletics, essential support staff, and their immediate families
P	Internationally recognised athletes, entertainers (including those in culturally unique groups) and artists, and their immediate families
Q	Exchange visitors in international cultural exchange programmes and their immediate families
R	Ministers of recognised religions and their immediate families
V	Family members of second preference immigration visa applicants

Category A: Diplomats & Foreign Government Employees

Career diplomats, certain other accredited and accepted officials, and employees of recognised foreign governments and their immediate families are issued with a category A visa if their visit to the US is on behalf of their national government and to engage solely in official activities for that government. A-1 and A-2 visas are issued on the basis of reciprocity and are valid for the duration of the holder's assignment. A-3 visas for attendants, servants and personal employees are valid for one year and can be renewed annually. Certain holders of category A visas have diplomatic immunity.

Category B: Visitors

Anyone who wishes to visit the US on holiday or business and doesn't qualify for visa-free travel (see **Visa Waiver** on page 86) or who wishes to remain longer than 90 days must apply for a category B visa. Visitors' visas aren't required by Canadian citizens and most foreign residents of Canada (landed immigrants) who enter the US as visitors, or by Mexican nationals with a US border crossing card. Visitors' visas are the most commonly issued visas and are valid for visits for business or pleasure. B-1 visas are granted to visitors on business and B-2 visas to tourists, although combined B-1/B-2 visas are also issued.

B-1 and B-2 visas are valid for a maximum of ten years and may permit a single entry only or multiple entries. Since 1st January 1995, indefinite visas have been replaced by ten-year visas, and indefinite visas issued more than ten years ago are no longer valid. A ten-year visa allows the holder to enter and leave the US as often as he wishes during its ten-year validity period. However, B-2 visas normally allow an entry period of no more than six months at any one time (the actual period is decided by an immigration officer), although extensions may be granted. Factors which affect the entry period and the likelihood of admission with a B-2 visa include the expiry date of the visa, the number of entries made, the expiration date of your passport, and your history of travel to the US.

B visas normally **don't** give visitors the right to work in US companies, even if payment is made outside the country. This doesn't, however, apply to business conducted as a visiting businessman, e.g. as a representative of an overseas company, when no payment is received from a US source. The holder of a B-1 visa may consult with business associates, lawyers or accountants, take part in business or professional conventions, and negotiate contracts and look for investment opportunities. A category B-1 visitor must have a permanent overseas residence.

In addition to completing form DS-156 (see page 84) and DS-157 where required (see page 84), supporting documentation may be required in the form of an invitation from the person you're visiting or staying with in the US, if applicable. For a B-1 visa, you may require a letter from your employer verifying your continued employment, the reason for your trip, and your itinerary in the US. You may be required to 'submit evidence substantiating the purpose of your trip and your intention to depart from America after a temporary visit'. Examples of the evidence required are given on form DS-156. In the case of pleasure trips, this includes documents outlining your plans in the US and stating the reasons why you would return abroad after a short stay such as family ties, employment (a self-employed person may require a letter from his accountant or solicitor confirming that he is known to them and stating how long he has been in business), home ownership or similar binding obligations in your home country.

Applications for B visas must be made through a US embassy or consulate and require an in-person interview. At some consulates, you may receive the approved visa at the end of your interview, or you're asked to supply a stamped self-addressed envelope so that the visa can be sent to you as soon as it is available. If you make an application for a visitor's visa in a country other than your home country or country of residence (called an 'out-of-district' application), your application is subject to increased scrutiny, as it may be suspected that you're 'shopping around' for an easier port of entry.

It's possible to extend a B-2 visa for a maximum of six months at a time (see **Visa Processing** on page 85). An application to extend a B-1 business visa must be accompanied by a letter from your employer explaining why you need an extension. There's no entitlement to an appeal if the extension isn't granted. Technically you can leave the US after six months, return the following day and stay for a further six months, but you're unlikely to get away with this many times. Although many people use a B visa to remain in the US for a year or two, most eventually get caught and are refused admission. As a result of previous abuse by holders of B visas, immigration officials may regard you as 'suspect' and make checks to ensure that you aren't cheating the system.

Category C: Travellers in Transit

A C-1 visa is issued to foreign travellers in transit through the US and a C-2 visa is valid for transit from your own country to the United Nations Headquarters District in New York City only. There's also a C-3 visa for foreign government officials and their families and staff members in transit through the US. People who are issued with category C visas cannot change their status to another non-immigrant visa or become permanent residents. In August 2003, the US government suspended a 50-

year old programme of allowing transit without visa for foreigners making air connections at US airports. Unless you're from a Visa Waiver Program country (see page 86), you must now have a transit visa even if you're only changing planes in the US en route to another country. The application process for the necessary visa is the same as for any other category, and includes the need for an interview at a US embassy or consulate.

Category D: Aircraft & Ship Crew

The foreign crew of ships and aircraft who plan to leave with their ship or aircraft after a temporary stay in the US are issued with category D visas. People issued with D-1 visas cannot change their status to any other non-immigrant visa or become permanent residents. There's a C-1/D visa available for those crew members who transit through the US regularly and is valid for a period up to 29 days at a time.

Category E: Treaty Traders & Investors

Category E visas are termed Treaty Trader (E-1) and Treaty Investor (E-2) visas, and are issued to people wishing to invest in or trade with a company in the US. They're issued subject to certain conditions, but there's no restriction on the number issued each year. As the name suggests, category E visas are available only to citizens of countries with which the US has a commerce treaty. There are two types of treaty, one covering trade and the other covering investment. Currently, 70 countries have trade (E-1) and investment (E-2) treaties with the US, around 30 an investment treaty only and five a trade treaty only.

At least 50 per cent of the owners of a treaty business must be citizens of a single trade or investor country. An E visa holder must be a principal owner who controls at least 50 per cent of the company, or a key employee (with the same nationality as the principal owner) who's a manager, executive or a person with skills essential to the business.

Neither E-1 nor E-2 visas have a time limit, but continue to be valid as long as the holder maintains his status with the enterprise or business. **An E-1 or E-2 visa is valid only as long as the business continues to be viably operated.** The spouse and children under 21 of an E visa holder also receive E visas, although each family member must apply for their own visa. Spouses of E visa holders can work in the US, provided they apply for work authorisation with USCIS after arrival in the country. Children can attend college or university in the US until the age of 21, when they must qualify for a visa in their own right. No educational standards, job offer or experience are required, and an E-2 visa permits multiple entries and a potentially indefinite stay in the US. For further information contact Business Visa Specialists (🖥 www.immigrationvisas.com). (See also **Investors** on page 80.)

E-1 Visa: An E-1 visa is granted to those carrying out substantial trade with the US and the treaty country. The trade can be in goods or services. Substantial trade must be frequent, continuous and involve numerous transactions which provide sufficient income to support the trader and his family. The trading company must already be in existence when the application is made. To qualify for an E-1 visa, a company or individual must plan to establish an office in the US which will be principally engaged (i.e. generate over 50 per cent of its revenue) in trade between the US and the foreign country. The applicant must be employed in a supervisory or executive capacity, or possess highly specialised skills essential to the efficient operation of the firm.

E-2 Visa: An E-2 visa is granted to the principal owner or a key employee of a company that has invested a 'substantial amount of money' in a business enterprise in the US. The actual amount depends on the kind of business. There's no minimum, but most investments are over $100,000 and it's difficult to obtain an E-2 visa for an investment of under $80,000. Also, there are limitations on the percentage of financing permitted, which depends on the value of the business. A business can be jointly owned with a spouse or partner (who can be a US citizen).

More important than the amount of money invested is whether the business is likely to be profitable and whether it will employ Americans. The business must generate significantly more income than just to provide a living to the investor and his family. If you're establishing a new business, you must make appropriate expenditure before your visa application is considered, so it's generally easier to obtain an E-2 visa for an existing business than a new business. Anyone planning to buy a business should enquire about the likelihood of obtaining an E-2 visa **before** signing a purchase contract and should make the contract contingent on obtaining a visa.

Category F: Academic or Language Students

There are two main categories of visa for foreign students in the US, category F for full-time academic and language students, and category M-1 for vocational and non-academic students (see page 98). Students coming to the US on exchange visits are issued with J-1 visas (see page 95). Student visas (F-1 and M-1) are issued to those planning to pursue a full-time course of study leading to a degree, diploma or certificate at a government-approved institution or other recognised establishment. Virtually all public and accredited private colleges, universities and vocational schools have been approved by the USCIS. However, not all educational establishments are approved, so check in advance. All approved schools must be participants in the SEVIS tracking system (see page 87). A change of school or academic programme is permitted, but prior consent must be obtained from the USCIS. You must be proficient in the English language or must be taking a course in English to reach the necessary standard (unless all courses are taught in your native language). You must be accepted as a student by an approved school before you can apply for an F-1 visa, but you may visit the US as a tourist to inspect prospective schools. When you've been accepted as a student at a school, the school authorities register you in the SEVIS database and send you the appropriate form (I-20, I-20M or DS-2019) which you must then take with you to your visa interview along with your other forms and documents, and proof of payment of the SEVIS fee.

A student must be accepted for a full-time course of study and must continue in full-time education for the visa to remain valid. Your progress towards the degree or certificate for which you're enrolled is tracked in the SEVIS system so that the ICE can intervene if it appears you've dropped out or may be working illegally or doing anything else contrary to the terms of your visa. The criteria used to determine whether a course qualifies as full-time are the number of hours or credits scheduled during each term (semester) for post-secondary studies, and the period required to complete a course of study. F-1 visas are issued for the length of time it's estimated it will take you to complete your proposed studies up to a maximum of five years, although citizens of certain countries are issued visas for shorter periods, e.g. two months to four years.

To obtain a student visa, you must show that you can pay for your studies and support yourself financially in line with your circumstances for the period of your proposed stay. You must also show proof of a residence abroad to which you will return at the end of your studies. Students with F-1 visas are permitted to work up to 20 hours a week under certain circumstances. A student's spouse and children under 21, who are also granted visas, aren't permitted to work, although they may study.

As a result of a change in the law in 1997, F-1 visas are no longer issued for attendance at public (state) elementary schools (from grades K to 8) or publicly funded adult education programmes such as foreign language classes. Students may obtain an F-1 visa for public high school for a maximum of 12 months and must show proof that payment has been made for the full, unsubsidised cost of the education **before** the visa processing. This rule **doesn't** apply to dependants of individuals in other visa categories, who wish to study at public schools. Visitors who take a few classes for recreational purposes and students who have a spouse or parent in the US with A, E, G, H, J, L or NATO visa status, don't require a student visa. Holders of visitor (B-2) visas and those who entered visa-free under the Visa Waiver Program are prohibited from entering full-time study.

Category G: Foreign Government Representatives

Employees of international organisations, e.g. the United Nations, and their immediate families are granted category G visas if their visit to the US is in pursuit of official duties. G-1 visas are for representatives of a foreign government who are living and working in the US, and their staff. G-2 visas are for representatives of a recognised government travelling to the US temporarily to attend meetings of a designated international organisation. G-3 visas are for the representatives of non-recognised or non-member governments and G-4 visas are for individual personnel who are travelling to the US to take up an appointment at a designated international organisation. G-1 to G-4 visas are granted for the duration of the assignment. G-5 visas are for the attendants, servants and personal employees of G-1 to G-4 visa holders and are valid for one year and can be renewed annually. All category G visas include the spouse and children under 21 of visa holders. NATO visas also fall under this category.

Category H: Workers

If you wish to work in the US for a few years, you may qualify for a category H visa, some of which are valid (with extensions) for up to six years. In general these visas are based on a specific offer of employment from an employer in the US. The employment must be approved in advance by the USCIS on the basis of a petition (form I-129), filed by the American employer. There are six sub-categories of H visa; H-1B (workers in specialised occupations), H-1C (registered nurses), H-2A (seasonal agricultural workers), H-2B (workers filling jobs that cannot be filled by US citizens or residents), H-3 (trainees), and H-4 (immediate families of H-1, H-2 and H-3 visa holders). An employer should use an experienced immigration lawyer when applying for a category H visa, as the procedure is complicated and constantly changing.

H-1B visas are issued to workers in specialised occupations and the professions, e.g. lawyers, accountants, doctors of medicine, nurses, teachers and scientists, with a degree or equivalent experience, who are going to the US to perform services in a prearranged professional job. Applications made by those without a degree are subject to greater scrutiny and are more difficult to obtain. The position applied for must require a university graduate (it isn't possible for an employer to employ a professional person to fill a non-professional/non-graduate position) and the applicant must have the appropriate background for the position.

Most professions in the US are licensed and controlled by individual states, resulting in 50 different licensing procedures for each profession. One way to be granted an H-1B visa is to meet the requirements necessary to take the licensing examination and be licensed by the state where you plan to practise. An employer must file a Labor Condition Attestation (LCA) with the Department of Labor before he can sponsor someone for an H-1B visa. To prepare the LCA, the prevailing wage for that position in the locality must be obtained from the Department of Labor or another source. Form 129W must be included and there's a $1,000 petitioner fee.

As a result of increasing demand for H1-B visas among IT workers, e.g. in California's Silicon Valley, the government increased the annual quota from 115,000 to 195,000 in 2000, effective until 2003. But with the increase in unemployment among technical workers, particularly in the electronics and computer industries, the quota was slashed to a mere 65,000 new visas for 2004 and subsequent years.

H-1B visas are issued for up to three years, although citizens of certain countries are issued visas for shorter periods – from one month to two years. Extensions of up to three years may be granted, making a maximum of six years. It's possible for an H-1B visa holder to change his status ('adjust status') to that of a permanent resident while in the US.

H-1C visas were a new category introduced in September 2000 for registered nurses coming to the US to work in positions in 'health professional shortage areas' determined by the Department of Health and Human Services (DHHS). Only 500 visas were available annually up to and including 2003, but there are strict requirements and only a handful of hospitals are qualified to petition for nurses under this programme. They're valid for three years with no extensions. The programme was extended at the end of 2003. To qualify for an H-1C visa nurses must be fully trained and qualified.

H-2A visas are for temporary or seasonal agricultural workers coming to the US, usually to pick crops or do other short-term jobs on farms or ranches.

H-2B visas are for workers coming to the US to fill positions for which a temporary shortage of American workers has been recognised by the US Department of Labor. There are no educational requirements, and experience and qualifications depend on the job. Jobs offered to H-2B applicants must be strictly temporary, as far as the employer and employee are concerned. A typical H-2B applicant is a skilled technician employed by a foreign company and coming to the US to install machinery or train American staff. H-2B visas are also issued to entertainers who don't meet the criteria for category O and P visas. There's an annual quota of 66,000 H-2B visas, which are issued for an initial period of one year and may be extended for an additional two years (one year at a time), although citizens of certain countries are issued visas for up to six months only. A petition for an H-2B visa must be made by the prospective employer in the US, who must also obtain labour certification (see page 81). It takes considerably longer to obtain an H-2B visa than an H-1B visa – usually several months, depending on the state where you will be employed. After spending three years in the US with an H-2B visa, you must wait at least 12 months before you can apply for another one.

H-3 visas are for trainees coming to the US for on-the-job training or work experience in a field (such as agriculture, commerce, communications, finance, government, transportation or the professions) in order to further their careers in their home countries. The American employer must provide the USCIS with a statement describing the kind of training offered and the position for which the trainee is being trained, and explain why the training cannot be obtained in the trainee's own country. The training cannot be used to provide productive employment. An H-3 visa is issued for a maximum of 18 months and extensions are difficult to obtain, as training periods are generally assumed to be short-term.

H-4 visas are issued to the spouse and unmarried children under 21 of H-1B, H-1C, H-2 and H-3 visa holders, but they aren't permitted to work.

Category I: Foreign Media Representatives

Category I visas are issued to representatives of foreign information media, representatives of a foreign tourist bureau or film crew members holding professional journalism credentials and intending to work on news or non-commercial documentaries. Visas are only issued to those people involved in the newsgathering process. Therefore people involved in associated activities such as research, aren't eligible. All journalists must have an I visa when entering the US to work, even if they're from a Visa Waiver Program country and staying for less than 90 days. Visas are issued on the basis of reciprocity and include spouses and unmarried children under 21. They're issued for up to five years at a time and are renewable. It isn't possible for a foreign journalist to change employers in the US without prior permission from the USCIS.

Category J: Exchange Visitors

Category J-1 visas are issued to foreign exchange visitors including students, scholars, trainees, teachers, professors, medical graduates, research assistants, specialists or leaders in a field of specialised knowledge or skill, who seek to enter the US temporarily as a participant in an approved programme. The exchange programme also allows young people between 18 and 25 to work as au pairs for up to a year (see page 32). The kind of work that may be performed includes teaching, instructing or lecturing, studying, observing, conducting research, consulting, demonstrating special skills or receiving training. Foreign students may also be eligible for an F-1 or M-1 visa.

The period for which J-1 visas are issued varies according to the programme, e.g. from one to five years, although citizens of certain countries are issued visas for shorter maximum periods of between three months and four years, irrespective of the programme. A period of practical training may be permitted after the exchange programme has been completed. You must have an adequate knowledge of English in order to participate effectively in the exchange programme and must establish that you have adequate financial resources to cover all your expenses including tuition while in the US. Finance may consist of your own or your family's private resources, scholarships or a salary that's part of the programme. As most programmes include scholarships or employment, this requirement isn't usually difficult to meet. You're also required to prove that you have a residence abroad to which you intend to return at the end of your stay. Medical graduates must pass parts I and II of the US National Board of Medical Examiners Examination or the Foreign Medical Graduates Examination.

An exchange visitor must partake in a programme which is a participant in the SEVIS system (see page 87) and the programme must provide the SEVIS registration form (DS-2019) to the applicant, who completes it and presents it with his visa application.

One of the conditions of the J-1 visa for certain participants is that following the completion of your period as an exchange visitor, you aren't usually eligible for a green card or a temporary worker, trainee or intra-company transferee visa until you've spent at least two years outside the US, in the country of your nationality or last residence. You're ineligible if your exchange programme was financed in whole or in part, directly or indirectly, by a US government agency or by a foreign government, if you came to the US on a programme to learn skills that are in short supply in your home country, or if you're a medical graduate who entered the US to receive medical education or training. It's possible to obtain a waiver that allows you to work in the US before the two year qualification period has expired, but this may be difficult. The spouse and unmarried children under 21 of a J-1 visa holder are issued with J-2 visas and are permitted to study or, subject to approval from the USCIS, to work.

Category K: Fiancé(e)s

A category K-1 visa is granted to a fiancée or fiancé who's planning to marry a US citizen within 90 days of entering the US, together with his or her unmarried children under 21 (who receive K-2 visas). After the marriage takes place, the foreign spouse can apply for a green card. A K-1 visa holder can apply to work immediately after arriving in the US subject to permission granted by the USCIS, although if the intended marriage doesn't take place within 90 days, he or she must leave the country. There's no provision for extending the visa period or obtaining another category of visa. A couple must have met and seen each other within the past two years, unless their religion forbids them to meet before marriage.

It can take at least three months to obtain a K-1 visa to enter the US for marriage and most couples simply get married, in the US or abroad, and apply directly for a green card. However, it's illegal to enter the US as a visitor with the intention of getting married. It's also illegal to enter into marriage purely for the purpose of remaining in (or entering) the US and there are stringent checks for 'marriages of convenience' (satirised in the film *Green Card*). If you're legally in the US and meet and marry a US citizen, you can apply to adjust status and become a permanent resident. You mustn't, however, leave the US before receiving your green card without permission from the USCIS, as you must then apply for a visa to re-enter the country, which could take many months.

There's also a K-3 visa that can be granted to the spouse of a US citizen, allowing him or her to enter the US to wait while completing the immigration process. A K-4 visa is granted to unmarried children under 21 accompanying a K-3 visa holder. The American spouse must have already started the immigration process by filing the necessary petitions in the US, and the K-3 visa application must be made in the country where the wedding took place. The K-3 visa then allows the foreign spouse to join the husband or wife in the US while waiting for the green card application to be processed. On arrival, the foreign spouse can also apply to USCIS for permission to work.

You aren't eligible for a K visa to marry a non-US citizen who's a permanent resident (green card holder). If you marry a green card holder, you're subject to the quotas for family-sponsored immigrants and must usually wait a number of years for a green card. However, if the green card holder becomes a US citizen you immediately become eligible for a green card.

Category L: Intra-company Transferees

Category L-1 visas are granted to intra-company transferees. These are people employed abroad who are transferred to a branch, subsidiary, affiliate or joint venture partner of the same company in the US, which must be at least 50 per cent owned by the foreign company. To qualify you must have served in a managerial or executive capacity or possess specialised knowledge necessary to the US business and be transferred to a position within the US company at either of these levels, although not necessarily the same position. You must also demonstrate that the company has secured premises to house the new office.

The US employer or international company must file a petition at the USCIS service centre with jurisdiction over the place of employment in the US. Labour certification (see page 81) isn't required for an L visa. Large multinational corporations (for whom the L visa was created) can benefit from a 'blanket' L-1 rule, whereby they don't need to file an individual petition with the INS each time they need to transfer an employee to the US. They can provide the approval notice and form I-129S petition and submit an application to their local US embassy or consulate. To benefit, a company must have had at least ten intra-company transferees approved in the last year or have combined annual sales of a minimum of $25 million or a US workforce of at least 1,000 employees.

The L visa is initially issued for up to three years and may be extended for two years for a person with specialised knowledge and four years (two years at a time) for an executive or manager. One advantage of an L visa is that executives and managers can normally qualify for a green card as a Multi-National Manager.

However, the conversion of an L visa to a green card isn't automatic. An L-2 visa is granted to an L-1 visa holder's spouse and unmarried children under 21, although they aren't normally permitted to work unless they qualify for their own work visas.

Category M: Non-academic Students

There are three categories of visa for foreign students: category M-1 for vocational and non-academic students; category F for full-time academic and language students (see page 92); category J-1 for students coming to the US on exchange visits (see page 95). M-1 visas are issued for the estimated length of time it will take you to complete your proposed studies up to a maximum of five years, although visas aren't usually approved for programmes longer than 18 months. Students with an M-1 visa are permitted to attend only the specific school for which their visa has been approved and aren't permitted to change their course of study. All M-1 visa holders must be entered into the SEVIS system (see page 87) and must submit their copy of the registration form (I-20M) and payment of the SEVIS fee as part of their visa application. The spouse and unmarried children under 21 of an M-1 visa holder are granted M-2 visas. M-1 visa holders are only allowed to work if it's a required part of their training and the employment has been approved in advance by the USCIS. A student's spouse and children aren't permitted to work, although they may study.

Category O: People of Extraordinary Ability

Category O-1 visas are for people of extraordinary ability in the fields of science, art, education, business and athletics, and workers in film and television whose work has earned them 'sustained national or international acclaim'. This means that O-1 visas are granted to prominent people in their fields only. O-2 visas are issued to the support staff and crew of O-1 visa holders, e.g. a film or television production crew, but only if they possess skills and experience not available in the US. The immediate families of O-1 and O-2 visa holders receive O-3 visas. There's no annual quota for O visas. An O-1 visa can be issued for up to three years with an indefinite number of one-year renewals permissible.

Category P: Athletes & Entertainers

Category P visas are issued to internationally recognised athletes, entertainers and artists, and to essential support personnel. Individual athletes and teams are eligible for P-1 visas, which may be valid for five years in the case of individual athletes or six months for a team. P-2 visas are issued for individuals or groups involved in a reciprocal exchange programme between the US and one or more foreign countries, and a P-3 visa is issued for performers (individuals or groups) in a culturally unique programme. P-4 visas are granted to the spouse and unmarried children under 21 of people granted P-1, P-2 and P-3 visas. Dependants aren't allowed to work with these visas, although they're permitted to study. The qualifications necessary for P visas aren't as stringent as for O visas (see above), although there's a significant overlap between the uses and qualifications for O and P visas.

Category Q: Cultural Exchange Visitors

Category Q visas are for people involved in international cultural exchange programmes. Programmes must be designed to provide practical training, employment, and opportunities for sharing with US citizens the history, culture and traditions of your home country. The Q visa is an alternative to the J-1 visa, but unlike the J-1 visa prior approval from the USCIS and a two-year home residence aren't necessary. There's no registration with the SEVIS programme, either. However, Q visas are issued for 15 months at a time only (unlike J visas, which may be valid for up to five years). There's no provision for the issue of visas to the spouse and unmarried children under 21 of Q visa holders; dependants must qualify for a visa in their own right.

Category R: Religious Workers

Category R-1 visas are for workers who have been members of recognised religious groups for at least two years and are coming to the US to work for an affiliated religious organisation in any capacity. The term 'worker' includes counsellors, social workers, health-care workers for religious hospitals, missionaries, translators and religious broadcasters, but not janitors or fund-raisers. A petition isn't required for an R-1 visa, which is granted for an initial maximum of three years. The spouse and unmarried children under 21 of R-1 visa holders are granted R-2 visas and aren't permitted to work. Religious workers may also apply for a green card under the special immigrant category (see page 79).

Category V: Family Members

Category V visas were recently created to reunite families separated while waiting for their second preference immigrant visa applications to be processed. The V non-immigrant visa allows the holder to reside in and travel to and from the US until he becomes eligible to apply for an immigrant visa. People eligible for V visas are spouses and children under 21 of lawful permanent residents who have been waiting at least three years for their immigrant visa applications to be processed.

REFUGEES

The number of refugees permitted to enter the US each year is determined by an agreement between Congress and the President, and the rules concerning refugee status are complex. Refugees have no automatic right of entry and, although theoretically there's no quota, numerical limits may be imposed. A refugee is granted permission to come to the US before his arrival, while political asylum seekers apply for their status after arriving in the US as non-immigrants or illegal aliens. A refugee becomes eligible for a green card after a year; those who are granted political asylum are eligible for a green card two years after asylum is granted (which can take a long time). People from countries experiencing conditions of war or natural disasters may be given a safe haven in the US and granted Temporary Protected Status (TPS). This allows them to live and work in the US for a specific period, but doesn't make them eligible for a green card.

EXCLUSION & DEPORTATION

Exclusion is the term used for refusal of entry to the US, on arrival at a port or airport or when applying for a visa. There are many grounds for exclusion, some of which are listed on page 100. If you're excluded, it may be possible to obtain a waiver allowing you to enter the US.

There's a big difference between exclusion (being refused entry to the US) and deportation, which is the term used for expelling a foreigner from the US. If you're excluded, you may be able to reapply successfully later; if you're deported, you won't be allowed to return for at least five years. It's far easier to exclude someone from the US than it is to deport a legal resident (John Lennon didn't leave the US for many years, as he feared exclusion because of a minor drug offence). Grounds for deportation include violating the terms of a visa, e.g. by working illegally, and committing a crime.

Sometimes the CBP gives foreigners who have violated immigration laws the option of voluntary departure, rather than being deported. This means that you agree to leave the country without a deportation hearing and can apply for another visa after you've left. With the exception of those who enter the US under the Visa Waiver Program (see page 86), nobody can be deported without first being given the legal right to a deportation hearing in a US court. You should take legal advice before deciding whether to waive your right to a deportation hearing. The holder of a green card can be deported if he is convicted of a serious crime or participates in politically subversive activities.

If you exceed your permitted stay by six months or less, you can be barred on your next attempt to enter the country and may be banned from returning to the US for three to five years. If you overstay by a year or more, you can be excluded for ten years. (See also **Illegal Working** on page 42.)

4.

ARRIVAL

On arrival in the US your first task is to battle your way through immigration and customs. Fortunately, this presents few problems for most people. You should obtain some dollars before arriving, as this saves you having to change money on arrival. You may find it more convenient to arrive on a weekday rather than during the weekend, when offices, banks and stores may be closed. In addition to information about immigration and customs, this chapter also contains a list of tasks that must be completed before or soon after arrival, and includes suggestions for finding local help and information.

With the exception of certain visitors (see **Visa Waiver** on page 86), everyone wishing to enter the US requires a visa (see **Chapter 3**). If you stop in the US in transit to another country, you may be required to go through US immigration and customs at your first port of entry. Even if you're just going to sit in a transit lounge for a few hours, you probably require a US visa (see **Category C: Travellers in Transit** on page 90).

ARRIVAL/DEPARTURE RECORD

Before you arrive in the US by air or sea, you're given an USCIS *Arrival-Departure Record* card (I-94) to complete by the airline or shipping company. If you enter the US by road from Canada or Mexico, you're asked to complete it at the frontier and pay a fee of $6. If you're a visa-free visitor (see **Visa Waiver** on page 86), you're given an I-94W card *Nonimmigrant Visa Waiver Arrival-Departure Record*. The I-94/I-94W card is divided into two parts, an 'Arrival Record' (items 1–11) and a 'Departure Record' (items 14–17). You must complete it in pen in block capitals and in English. If you make a mistake, you may be asked to complete a new card. If you don't have an 'address while in the United States' (item 10), it's often wise to enter the name of a hotel in an area or city where you're heading or write 'touring', rather than leave it blank. If you're entering the US by land, enter 'LAND' under 'Airline and Flight Number' (item 7). If you're entering the US by ship, enter 'SEA' here. Complete the 'Arrival' and 'Departure' parts before arrival.

You're authorised to remain in the US until the date stamped on your I-94 card (departure record), entered by the immigration officer when you arrive. The I-94 card departure record is stapled into your passport and must be carried at all times. **It's this date, and not the expiry date of your visa, that determines how long you may remain in the US.** When you leave the US, the card is removed from your passport by an official of the transportation, e.g. airline or shipping, company. If you leave the US via Canada or Mexico or intend to remain out of the country for more than 30 days, you should surrender your I-94 card to a Canadian official at the Canadian border or a US official at the Mexican border.

Make sure that it's collected by the airline each time you depart the US; otherwise you could have problems on your next visit. If you fail to surrender your I-94 card (departure record) when you leave the US a future entry may be delayed. All I-94 cards are recorded in a computer, which makes it easy for immigration officials to check whether you returned your card or overstayed your last visit. If you overstay your visit (i.e. the date stamped on your I-94 card), it's a violation of the law. If you lose your I-94 card, you should replace it at the nearest US Citizenship and

Immigration Services (USCIS) field office. A list can be obtained by calling the USCIS National Service Center (☎ 1-800-375-5283) or online from the USCIS website (🖳 www.uscis.gov). Occasionally, a Customs and Border Protection (CBP) officer stamps your I-94 card with a date that precedes the expiry of your non-immigration visa. Although this is technically incorrect, it's best not to argue with a CBP admitting officer. If this happens to you, you can apply for an extension up to 60 days and not less than 15 days before the date on your I-94 card becomes due.

Many non-immigrant visas are of the multiple-entry type, which allow you to enter and leave the US as often as you wish during the visa validation period, e.g. ten years for a B-1/B-2 visa. However, the period that you're allowed to remain also depends on the expiration date of your passport. For example, if you have a non-immigrant visa valid for three years and your passport is valid for three months only, you're admitted for just three months, as stamped on your I-94 card. If you have a valid multiple-entry, non-immigrant visa and obtain a new passport, retain your old passport and take it with you when travelling to the US, as the visa remains valid. You must **never** remove a visa from your old passport, as this invalidates it.

IMMIGRATION

When you arrive in the US, the first thing you must do is pass through US Public Health Immigration & Naturalization. This is divided into two sections, 'US Citizens' and 'All Other Passports'; make sure you join the correct queue. Once in the US, you're under the jurisdiction of the USCIS, part of the Department of Homeland Security (DHS), who have dictatorial powers over you and have been variously described as aggressive, brusque, bullying, stern and intimidating (on a good day), despite the fact that they claim to 'treat you in a courteous manner'! Beginning in late 2004, all arriving foreigners will be fingerprinted and photographed, even those who are part of the Visa Waiver Program. This isn't as onerous as it sounds. They fingerprint only your two index fingers, using a digital scanning device (no ink to wash off afterwards!), and the photo is a quick full face picture taken by a digital camera. The CBP estimates it should take no more than 15 to 20 seconds if you follow the instructions, posted prominently in the queuing area. You should answer any questions put to you in a direct and courteous manner, however personal or irrelevant you may think they are. It never pays to antagonise immigration officials, for example, by questioning the relevance of certain questions.

US immigration officials are trained to suspect that **everyone** who doesn't have the right to live and work in the US is a potential illegal immigrant (most Americans believe that, given a choice, any sane person couldn't possibly wish to live anywhere other than in the US). Nationals of some countries may be singled out for 'special treatment', e.g. people from a country that's hostile towards the US, is considered to be harbouring terrorists or which has a reputation for illegal immigrants. It's an unfortunate fact of life that many immigration officials (like most people) are prejudiced against certain groups. If you're white, English-speaking, smartly dressed, sober and polite, you will have a much easier time than a black bohemian who doesn't speak English.

Immigration officers have the task of deciding whether you're permitted to enter the US and have the necessary documentation, including a visa if necessary. Even with a visa, you don't have the **right** to enter the US; only the immigration officer can make that decision. The length of time you're permitted to remain also depends on the immigration officer, irrespective of how long your visa is valid. If the officer believes that you may participate in activities, e.g. employment, prohibited by the terms of your visa, he can refuse to admit you. Present the following to the immigration officer, as applicable:

- Your passport (plus an old passport if it contains an unexpired visa);
- Your completed arrival/departure record card (I-94/I-94W);
- Your green card, if you're a permanent resident.

You should also have any documents or letters to hand that support your reason for visiting the US.

After entering the US with an immigrant visa, your passport is stamped to show that you're a permanent resident. You're permitted to travel abroad and re-enter the US by showing this passport stamp until you receive your green card, which you receive by post a few months later.

Some visitors may find themselves under close scrutiny, as people intending to live or work illegally in the US commonly enter the country as tourists, although most people are admitted with few formalities. However, if the immigration officer suspects you of not telling the truth he can search your luggage; read and/or photocopy any written or printed material, including personal letters; conduct a search of your person, including a strip search; arrest or detain you; prohibit you entering the US (although if you have a visa, you have the right to a hearing); parole you into the US, but require you to appear for a future hearing.

If a search of your person or baggage turns up evidence that contradicts the stated purpose of your visit or your visa status, e.g. work references and a résumé; letters from US companies or employment agencies offering you employment; letters from friends working illegally in the US; tools of your trade; or anything else which suggests you may look for work illegally you may be excluded. If you plan to visit the US before applying for a job or an immigrant or non-immigrant visa, you should mail any documents you may require, e.g. to a friend or to yourself c/o a post office, rather than bring them with you. A detailed search of your baggage and person is extremely rare (particularly a strip search).

The degree of questioning you're subject to may depend on many things, not least your nationality; the documentation you can provide supporting the reason for your visit or why you must return abroad (see below); the amount of money you have; whether you have friends or relatives in the US who can support you; whether you have a return ticket to your 'home' country; and your age and appearance.

Be extremely careful how you answer seemingly innocent questions from the immigration authorities, as you could find yourself being refused entry if you give incriminating answers (immigration officials **never** ask innocent questions). Whatever the question, don't imply that you may remain in the US longer than the period permitted or for a purpose other than that for which you've been granted permission. If you're singled out for closer examination, your passport and other documents may be placed in a red folder and you're asked to go to a separate waiting room for an interview.

If you enter the US from certain countries, you may be required to have immunisation certificates. Check the requirements in advance at a US embassy or consulate before travelling. An immigration officer can decide to send you for a routine (and random) health check, before allowing you to enter the US. Clearing immigration during a busy period can take a number of hours, so you should be prepared and take a thick book or half a dozen newspapers. Among the most notorious entry points for delays are New York's JFK and Miami airports. Immigration lines are shorter at smaller airports, although you may have little choice of entry point. The CBP website has charts of average waiting times for the major border crossings and airports of entry into the US (🖥 www.cbp.gov then use the 'quicklinks' or enter 'airport wait times' in the search function).

ENTRY REFUSAL

If you arrive in the US with a visa and an immigration official refuses you entry, you can insist on a review of your case before a judge. However, if you travel to the US as a visitor under the visa waiver program (see **Visa Waiver** on page 86), you 'waive any rights to a review or appeal of an immigration officer's determination as to your admissibility, or to contest any action in deportation' (other than on the basis of an application for asylum). If you have a visa you're entitled to:

● An exclusion hearing before a judge to determine your admissibility;

● An administrative appeal to the Board of Immigration Appeals;

● A judicial review or appeal of any, or all, of the above decisions.

If the immigration officer won't allow you into the country and says you will be sent back on the next flight, you must insist on appearing before a judge for an exclusion hearing. This is your right under US law, although the official may tell you it's impossible until the following day, which means you must spend the night in a hotel. The officer may try to put you in detention for the night, although this is illegal and you should insist on staying in a hotel.

If you're scheduled for an exclusion hearing, you should engage an immigration lawyer to represent you (see page 77). If you have a poor case, your lawyer may suggest that you agree to leave voluntarily, because if you're excluded from the US after a hearing it is entered on your permanent record. This makes it extremely difficult, if not impossible, to obtain a visa to enter the US in the future, as the exclusion must be recorded on all applications. If you voluntarily withdraw your application to enter the US, you're neither deported nor excluded, and the judge may allow you to remain for a few days to inform anyone necessary and make travel arrangements. However, your visa is cancelled and this must be declared when applying for a visa at a later date.

Alternatively, you may be admitted into the US on parole. This means that you must attend a deferred inspection interview on a specific date at the USCIS office nearest to your destination. This is preferable to an exclusion hearing before a judge, as you have a better chance of convincing a USCIS official that you should be allowed to remain in the US. You're entitled to a lawyer, which although not required, is recommended.

There are many grounds for exclusion from the US, listed in section 212 of the Immigration and Nationality Act, the purpose of which is to protect the welfare, health, safety and security of the US. Some of the most important grounds for exclusion relate to anyone who:

- Is afflicted with a contagious disease, e.g. tuberculosis, or mental illness or who's mentally disabled;
- Has been arrested and convicted for certain offences or crimes;
- Is believed to be a narcotics addict or trafficker;
- Has entered the US on the Visa Waiver Program (see page 86) and stayed longer than the permitted 90 days;
- Has been excluded or deported from the US within the last five years, removed from the US, or seeks or has sought or has procured a visa (or other documentation) or entry into the US by fraud or misrepresentation;
- Is or has been a member of a subversive or communist organisation;
- Was connected with the persecution of others in association with the Nazi government;
- Has detained, retained, or withheld custody of a child from a US citizen granted custody of the child;
- Seeks to perform skilled or unskilled labour (unlawfully);
- Seeks to engage in criminal or immoral activities.

CUSTOMS

If you travel to the US by air or sea, you're given a *Customs Declaration* form (6059B) to complete by the airline or shipping line. If you cross into the US via road from Canada or Mexico you're asked to complete it at the frontier. You must complete it in block capitals in blue or black ink (if you make a mistake you may be asked to fill in a new card). The form is available in several languages and should be completed in the language of the form (i.e. in French if the form is in French, English if the form is in English). Hand your completed form to the customs officer at your port or frontier of entry. The head of a family may make a joint declaration for all members residing in the same household and travelling together to the US. There are no restrictions on the amount of money you may take into the US, although if you take in more than $10,000 in currency or 'monetary instruments' you're required to state this on your customs declaration form (large sums of cash are often carried by criminals, particularly drug traffickers).

Some US ports and international airports operate a system of red and green 'channels', as is common in Europe. Red means you have something to declare and green means that you have nothing to declare, i.e. no more than the customs allowances, no goods to sell, and no prohibited or restricted goods. **If you're certain**

you have nothing to declare, go through the 'green channel'; otherwise go through the red channel. US customs checks are usually much stricter than in Europe and many other countries, and even when you go through the green channel you may be stopped, your customs declaration form inspected and you may be asked to open your bags. At ports without red and green channels, your baggage may be given a thorough inspection or you may be questioned by a customs officer while you're waiting to claim your bags. There are stiff penalties for smuggling.

A list of all items you're bringing in is useful, although the customs officer may still want to examine your bags. If you're required to pay duty or Internal Revenue Service (IRS) tax, it must be paid at the time goods are brought into the country. Import duty and tax may be paid in cash in dollars; by government cheque, money order or dollar travellers' cheques (provided cheques don't exceed the amount of the duty payable by more than $50); by personal cheque (made payable to the 'US Customs Service') for the exact amount of duty, drawn on a national or state bank or a trust company in the US; and with major credit cards, e.g. Mastercard and Visa. If you're unable to pay on the spot, customs keep your belongings until you pay the sum due. This must be paid within a certain period, noted on the back of your receipt. Postage or freight charges must be paid if you want your belongings sent on to you.

If you're discovered trying to smuggle goods into the US, customs may confiscate them, and if you hide them in a vehicle, boat or plane, they can confiscate that also! If you attempt to import prohibited items, you may also be liable to criminal charges or deportation.

If you have any questions regarding the importation of anything into the US, contact the customs representative at your local US embassy or consulate or check the 'Know Before You Go' document on the CBP website (🖳 www.cbp.gov). For information about personal exemptions, see **Duty-Free Allowances** on page 495.

Permanent & Temporary Residents

When you enter the US to take up permanent or temporary residence, you can usually import your personal belongings duty and tax free. Any duty or tax payable depends on where you arrived from, where you purchased the goods, how long you've owned them, and whether duty and tax has already been paid in another country. Personal effects owned and used for at least one year before importation are usually exempt from import duty. The duties levied on non-exempt items vary according to the classification of goods and their original value. All alcoholic beverages are subject to assessment of federal duty and internal revenue taxes (an additional tax is also payable in some states). If alcohol is included with unaccompanied shipments, customs may require the entire shipment to be thoroughly examined, which will incur delays and extra expense.

If you're coming to live in the US and are sending your household goods unaccompanied, you must provide US customs with a detailed list of everything brought into the country and its value. The detail officially required is often absurd and you're even expected to list such things as the titles of books, although in practice less detail is acceptable. A person immigrating to the US may bring professional equipment and tools of his trade with him. US embassies and consulates provide a free information package and sample inventory list.

You're required to complete customs form 3299 *Declaration for Free Entry of Unaccompanied Articles,* for presentation to the examining customs officer when your belongings are cleared through customs. It's not necessary to employ a broker or agent to clear your belongings, as you can do this yourself after you arrive in the US or you can authorise someone to represent you. If you're using a removals company, they usually handle customs clearance for you. Your belongings must be cleared within five working days after their arrival; otherwise they're sent to a warehouse for storage at your risk and expense until customs clearance can be made.

Your belongings may be imported up to six months before your arrival, but no more than one year after your arrival, after transferring your residence. They must not be sold, lent, rented or otherwise disposed of in the US within one year of their importation or of your arrival (whichever is later) without obtaining customs authorisation.

Visitors

If you're a visitor, you can bring your personal belongings to the US free of duty and tax without declaring them to customs provided that:

● They're brought in with you and are for your personal use only;

● They're kept in the US for no longer than six months in a 12-month period;

● You don't sell, lend, rent or otherwise dispose of them in the US;

● They're exported when you leave the US or before they've been in the US for more than six months, whichever occurs first.

For information about personal exemptions for non-residents, see page 495.

Returning Residents

If you're a US resident returning from abroad, you must declare all articles acquired abroad and in your possession at the time of your return, including:

● Articles you've purchased or inherited abroad;

● Gifts given to you while abroad, including wedding or birthday presents;

● Articles purchased in duty-free stores;

● Repairs or alterations made to any articles taken abroad and returned;

● Items you're bringing into the US for another person;

● Goods you intend to sell or use in your business.

You must also declare any articles acquired in American Samoa, Guam or the US Virgin Islands that aren't accompanying you at the time of your return. The price paid for each article must be stated on your declaration form in dollars or the equivalent in the country where it was purchased (if not purchased, an estimate of its fair retail price must be provided).

Returning residents may bring into the US personal belongings of US origin free of duty without proof, provided they're clearly marked as made in the US. Foreign-made personal articles taken abroad are dutiable when they're brought into the US, unless you've proof of prior possession, such as a receipt of purchase. Items such as watches, cameras, tape recorders, computers and other articles that can be readily identified by a serial number or permanent markings, can be registered with US customs before leaving the US. Customs will register anything with a serial number, identifying marks, or documented by a sales receipt or insurance document. You can also register in advance by filling out Customs Form 4457 after which you receive a carnet, an official Customs document listing the serial numbers of your equipment, which you can show as proof of your ownership.

Household effects and tools of your trade or occupation taken out of the US are allowed in duty-free when you return, provided they're properly declared and registered. All furniture, carpets, paintings, tableware, linens and similar household furnishings acquired abroad may be imported free of duty, provided they've been used abroad by you for not less than one year, or were available for use in a household where you were resident for one year. The year of use needn't be continuous nor must it be the year immediately preceding the date of importation. Items such as clothes, jewellery, photographic equipment, tape recorders, stereo components and vehicles are considered to be personal articles, and cannot be imported free of duty as household effects. The exemption doesn't include articles placed in storage outside the home or articles imported for another person or for sale.

If you took a car, motorcycle, boat, aeroplane or other vehicle abroad for non-commercial use, it may be returned duty-free provided you can prove that you took it out of the US, e.g. with a customs certificate or a US registration obtained before departure. A vehicle purchased abroad can be imported into the US on payment of duty of 2.5 per cent, but must meet US emission and safety standards (see **Vehicle Import** on page 254).

For residents who travel abroad more than three times a year, USCIS have introduced INPASS, a quick pass that works at ten major airports (it will eventually be used at 23 airports). You must have your palm scanned and then, whenever you pass through customs, you simply press your palm against a screen for identification. More information is available from USCIS field offices or on ☎ 1-800-755-0777.

General Information

General information about customs regulations for returning residents is contained in a leaflet, *Know Before You Go*, which is available via the internet (💻 www.cpb.gov). The following leaflets are also available from customs offices or from the US Customs and Border Protection, Office of Public Information (1301 Constitution Avenue, NW, PO Box 7407, Washington, DC 20229, ☎ 202-566-8195, 💻 www.cbp.gov): *United States Customs Hints For Visitors*, *Importing a Car*, *Pleasure Boats*, *Customs Guide for Private Flyers*, *Pets & Wildlife*, and *Trademark Information for Travelers*. The US Customs Service also provides detailed information regarding the importation of special items, and the US Department of Agriculture publishes

Travelers' Tips, available online at ⌨ www.aphis.usda.gov/travel. For information about importing: duty-free alcohol and tobacco (etc.) see page 495; cars, page 254; electrical apparatus, page 138; pets and animals, page 522.

REGISTRATION

The US doesn't require the registration of foreign nationals (aliens) at a local police station, although a change of address must be registered with the USCIS within ten days and you must report your address annually irrespective of whether it has changed. All permanently resident foreigners over the age of 14 are finger-printed before they're issued with their green card and those who attain the age of 14 while in the US should be finger-printed within 30 days of their 14th birthday. Non-immigrants intending to remain in the US longer than one year who are citizens of countries that require US citizens to be finger-printed, are also finger-printed. Permanent residents over 18 are required to carry their green cards (or a copy) at all times.

FINDING HELP

One of the biggest difficulties facing new arrivals in any country is how and where to obtain help with day-to-day problems. For example, finding a home, schools, insurance requirements and so on. This book was written in response to this need (and because the author needs to earn a living!). However, in addition to the comprehensive information provided in this book, you will also require detailed **local** information. How successful you are in finding local help depends on your employer, the town or area where you live (those who live and work in small communities are usually better served than those who inhabit cities), your nationality, English proficiency and sex.

Obtaining information isn't a problem, as there's a wealth of information available on every conceivable subject. However, finding up-to-date information, sorting the truth from the half truths, comparing the options available, and making the correct decisions is more difficult, particularly as most information isn't intended for foreigners and their needs. You may find that your friends, colleagues and acquaintances can help, as they're often able to proffer advice based on their own experiences and mistakes. But take care! Although they mean well, you may receive as much false and conflicting information as accurate (not always wrong, but possibly invalid for your region, community or situation). Americans are renowned for their friendliness and you should have no trouble getting to know your neighbours and colleagues, who will usually be pleased to help you settle in.

All communities have a wide range of clubs and organisations, for men and women. For new arrivals the most important is the newcomers club. Most US communities and towns pride themselves on the warm welcome they extend to new residents, and someone may contact you within a few weeks of your arrival in a new community. Some communities have a senior centre where help is provided for senior citizens, usually on a casual walk-in basis (these are also excellent places to meet people). In most communities there are local volunteer services designed to meet a range of needs. Services may be listed in telephone directories under a variety of names, including helpline, crisis centre, hotline, people's switchboard, community switchboard or 'we care'. Volunteer services can usually also direct you to a range of free or inexpensive local services.

Libraries (see page 432) are a mine of local information. Besides keeping reference books, telephone directories, local guidebooks, maps, magazines and community newspapers, they distribute useful leaflets and brochures about local clubs and organisations of every description. Library staff are helpful in providing information and answering queries and may even make telephone calls for you. Town halls, police headquarters (the police are usually helpful), visitors bureaux, tourist offices and chambers of commerce, some of which have multi-lingual staff, are also good sources of free maps and local information. Some large companies have a department or staff dedicated to assisting new arrivals or use a relocation company (see page 126) to perform this task. Relocation magazines are published in many areas (contact local chambers of commerce or estate agents for information).

There are expatriate and ethnic clubs and organisations in most areas. These may provide members with detailed local information regarding all aspects of living in the US, including housing costs, schools, names of doctors and dentists, shopping information and much more. Many clubs produce data sheets, booklets, newsletters and run libraries, and most also organise a variety of social events, including day and evening classes ranging from cooking to English-language classes. There are also numerous social clubs in most towns, whose members can help you find your way around (see page 416). Many countries have a number of consulates in the US, most of which maintain a wealth of local information about everything from doctors to social organisations. Many businesses, e.g. banks and savings and loan associations, produce books and leaflets containing valuable information for newcomers, and local libraries and bookstores usually have books about the local area (see also **Appendix B**). Other ways to meet people are to enrol in a day or evening class, join a local church or temple, and, if you have school age children, take part in the activities of the local Parent Teacher Association (PTA) or Home and School Association (HSA).

CHECKLISTS

Before Arrival

The following checklist contains a summary of the tasks that should (if possible) be completed before your family's arrival in the US:

- Obtain a visa, if necessary, for yourself and all your family members (see **Chapter 3**). Obviously this must be done before arrival.

- Visit the US before your move to compare communities and schools, and arrange schooling for your children (see **Chapter 9**).

- Find temporary or permanent accommodation and buy a car. If you purchase a car, arrange insurance (see page 267) and register it in the state where you will be resident (see page 255).

- Arrange for shipment of your personal and household effects.
- Apply for a social security card from your local US embassy or consulate.
- Arrange health insurance for your family (see page 341). This is essential if you won't be covered by your employer.
- Open a bank account in the US and transfer funds (you can open an account with many US banks from abroad). Have cheques printed with your US address as soon as possible.
- Obtain an international driver's licence (if your current licence isn't in English).
- Obtain an international credit card (which is invaluable in the US).
- Obtain as many credit references as possible, for example from banks, mortgage companies, credit card companies, credit agencies, companies with which you've had accounts, and references from professionals such as lawyers and accountants. In fact, anything which will help you establish a credit rating in the US (see **Credit Rating** on page 364).
- Collect and bring with you all your family's official documents, including birth certificates, driver's licences, marriage certificate, divorce papers, death certificate (if a widow or widower), educational diplomas, professional certificates, school records, student identification cards, employment references, curriculum vitae, medical and dental records, bank account and credit card details, insurance policies (plus records of no-claims' allowances), and receipts for any valuables.

After Arrival

The following checklist contains a summary of the tasks to be completed after arrival in the US (if not done before):

- On arrival at a US airport or port, give your passport, *Arrival-Departure Record* card (I-94/I-94W) and other documents to the immigration official (see page 106).
- Give your *Customs Declaration* form (6059B) to the customs officer and if you're importing more than your personal exemption (see page 495), provide a list.
- If you haven't purchased a car in advance you may wish to rent one (see page 257) for a week or two, as it's almost impossible to get around the US without a car (renting a car at an airport is the most expensive option).
- Do the following within the next few weeks:
    - Apply for a social security card from your local social security office.
    - Apply for a state driving licence (see page 265).
    - Open a current (checking) account at a local bank and give the details to your employer (see page 368).
    - Arrange schooling for your children (see **Chapter 9**).
    - Find a local doctor and dentist (see **Chapter 12**).
    - Arrange whatever insurance is necessary such as health, car, household and liability (see **Chapter 13**).

5.

ACCOMMODATION

In most areas of the US, accommodation (or accommodations – the plural is always used in American English) isn't difficult to find, depending of course on what you're looking for and whether you wish to rent or buy. There are, however, a few exceptions such as large cities, e.g. New York, and their suburbs, where rental accommodation is in high demand and short supply and rents can be astronomical. Rents and the cost of property in different regions and cities vary enormously, property in the most expensive areas costing up to ten times as much as in the cheapest. Accommodation usually accounts for 20 to 30 per cent of the average American family's budget, but can easily rise to 40 or even 50 per cent in high cost areas. Half of all renters spend more than a quarter of their income on housing and almost 15 per cent spend half their income.

Most Americans live in a house, flat (apartment) or a 'condominium' (abbreviated to condo), which is essentially an owner-occupied apartment. Some 65 per cent of American families (around 60 million) own their own homes, compared with around 70 per cent in the UK, 55 per cent in France, and 50 per cent in Germany and Spain. It's estimated that some 11 million Americans live in mobile homes (excluding those who live in vans, campers and trailers), which are popular with first-time buyers. Many Americans own a second (vacation) home, which may be a detached house, condo, town-house, cabin, mobile home or time-share.

Americans are extremely mobile, one in five moving home every year and the average home changing ownership every 12 years. Not surprisingly, many Americans are keen to ensure that buying a home won't restrict their mobility and that they will be able to sell for a profit when they move. However, for many people their worst fears were realised in the early '90s, when housing values, particularly in the Northeast and California, dropped by 10 to 20 per cent. Those who bought at the top of the market between 1988 and 1990 found that they were unable to sell without making a huge loss, although values have since recovered in most areas.

Although Americans are generally better housed than people in other western countries, poor Americans are likely to have worse housing than their foreign counterparts. Officially around 5 per cent of Americans live in overcrowded homes, defined as more than one person per room, although many believe the percentage is far higher. Among the poor it's common for a number of families, e.g. 15 to 20 people, to share a one or two-bedroom apartment (for many this is the only alternative to homelessness). It's estimated that up to 12 million Americans have experienced homelessness at some time and that there are between 600,000 and 800,000 people living in shelters and on the streets on any given night, a situation that has deteriorated in recent years. However, the number of shelters for the homeless has more than doubled in the last decade, and a range of free services are provided for the homeless in most areas. Public housing authorities also provide inexpensive housing for the poor in many cities and towns.

TEMPORARY ACCOMMODATION

On arrival in the US you may find it necessary to stay in temporary accommodation for a period before moving into permanent accommodation or while waiting for your furniture to arrive. Some companies provide rooms, self-contained apartments or hostels for employees and their families, although usually for a limited period. If you're hired from abroad or your company is transferring you to the US, you're usually provided with temporary accommodation until you find a permanent home.

In many cities and suburbs there are 'corporate' hotels. These are hotels which have been renovated and converted to serviced apartments and are rented on a weekly basis. In most major cities there are long-stay hotels such as Hyatt Residence Inns, which usually provide leisure facilities and sports for guests. You will also find more and more 'studio suites' hotels, where a hotel room also includes kitchen facilities, including a full sized American refrigerator, cooker, microwave oven and dishes, pots and pans to do your own cooking. In most large cities, particularly New York, self-contained, furnished apartments are available with their own bathrooms and kitchens (often termed 'corporate rentals'). Although expensive, they're more convenient and usually cheaper than hotel or motel rooms, particularly for families (considerable savings can be made by preparing your own meals). An advantage over ordinary apartments is that corporate rentals can usually be made on a daily, weekly or monthly basis.

Single people and married couples without children may be able to find temporary accommodation in hostels, such as those provided by the Young Men's Christian Association (YMCA) and Young Women's Christian Association (YWCA), both of which have hostels throughout the US. Alternatively, in most areas it's possible to rent a furnished room or bed and breakfast accommodation for a short period. Detailed information about hotels, motels, bed and breakfast, self-catering accommodation and hostels is provided on the following pages.

Hotels

The quality and standard of US hotels vary considerably, from luxury establishments (some with thousands of rooms) to seedy and rundown backstreet hovels (called flophouses), where you're unlikely to find a bedtime mint on your pillow. Nevertheless, the general standard of US hotel accommodation is among the highest in the world and most people should be able to find something to suit their budget and taste among the many thousands of hotels in the US. The US doesn't have many private family hotels, as are common and popular throughout Europe, although attractive 18th and 19th century inns, lodges and historic hotels can be found, particularly in New England.

All top class hotels provide air-conditioned rooms, tea and coffee making facilities, room service, radio and colour television (with cable television and pay-per-view satellite movies), bath or shower (or Jacuzzi), telephone (often dual-line or up to three handsets), mini-bar (wet bar), hair drier and trouser press. Additional facilities may include CD player, VCR/film rental, in-room fax machine and refrigerator, although these may only be provided on request and for an extra charge. Hotel services may include baby-sitting, laundry, parking, video and book libraries, theatre booking agencies, hairdressing and beauty salons, cinemas and shops. Many top class hotels also have a choice of restaurants, coffee shops, bars, health and leisure centres (with swimming pools, gymnasiums, steam rooms, solariums, saunas, whirlpools/spas and Jacuzzis), and a range of other sports facilities. Most quality hotels have rooms or even an entire floor reserved for non-smokers.

Large 'business' hotels also have 'executive' or 'club' floors, usually providing higher quality accommodation and a comprehensive business centre, including fax, secretarial/typing and translation services, computers (with internet access), audiovisual equipment, tele-conferencing, a business reference library, and links with an electronic business/stock market information service. However, if you require a non-standard business service, check that it's provided in advance.

A typical hotel room contains one or two double (usually queen or king sized) beds, two armchairs, a writing desk, walk-in wardrobe, colour television, WC, and bathroom with a shower or bath. WCs often have a paper seal which indicates that they've been 'sanitised', which is just the American way of saying cleaned (Americans are obsessed with toilet hygiene). You can normally fetch ice by the buckets full from a machine down the hall, and cold drinks and snacks from vending machines. Mini-bars are found only in the most upscale hotels in the US. Most hotels have safes, where you should leave your excess money, travellers' cheques and other valuables. Many chain hotels now offer high-speed internet access. A single room may have a single bed (in older hotels), but usually has at least a double bed, usually king or queen sized. Double rooms may have one or two double beds, or (rarely these days) two single beds (called a twin). Top class hotels usually provide suites (or Jacuzzi-suites), costing up to $2,000 per night, apartment-suites and rooms with kitchenettes. Rooms that are on a higher floor may be more expensive in some city hotels, where it pays to be as far away as possible from traffic noise.

Hotel accommodation can be expensive in the US, particularly in major cities where it's difficult to find budget hotels or the inexpensive and pleasant bed and breakfast or *pension* accommodation common in Europe. Cheaper hotel chains include Comfort Inn, Days Inn, Econolodge, Howard Johnson, Quality Inn, Ramada and Travelodge (see **Motels** on page 122); more upmarket chains include Hilton, Hyatt, ITT Sheraton and the trendy W hotels and Marriott. For a median level, particularly suitable for temporary accommodation on moving to a new area, there are the suites hotels, which include Summerfield Suites, Mainstay Suites, Homestead Suites, Amerisuites and Sierra Suites, where prices are similar to those of the cheaper chains, with the convenience of kitchen facilities. If money is no object, the top-rated chains are Four Seasons and Ritz-Carlton.

The table below provides a rough guide to rates for a double room in the largest and most expensive cities, e.g. New York. In smaller towns and cities, rooms are usually available for as little as half the rates shown below and you can find a decent room for as little as $60 per night. Hotel rates are always quoted per room and not per person and advertised rates don't include state or city taxes (or a 'bed or occupancy' tax), which may add another 5 to 15 per cent to the bill. Always ask for the rate inclusive of all taxes.

Class	Price Range ($)
Super deluxe	250 +
Deluxe	200 – 250
Expensive	150 – 200
Moderate	100 – 150
Inexpensive	Under 100

Hotel rates vary enormously according to the city and time of year (a room in New Orleans over Mardi Gras might cost three times what it would on a quiet weekday). Many hotels have reduced rates at weekends (during the week they're full of business people) or lower Sunday to Thursday rates if they're in popular weekend resorts; some have reduced rates in winter during the off season. Many hotels in summer resorts, particularly in New England states, are closed during the winter, i.e. from October to May, and those that remain open usually have greatly reduced rates. Conversely, in Florida the high season is the winter, when prices are 33 to 50 per cent higher than in summer. During off-peak periods, or at any time when room-occupancy is low, you're usually able to haggle over room rates. Always ask about discounts and special rates.

Among the many discount categories available are family, group, foreign visitor, students, senior citizens, youth hostel members, YMCA/YWCA members, plane/train/bus pass holders, rental car users, AAA or other automobile club members, Sierra Club or other environmental club members, government or airline employees, and military personnel. Corporate rates may be granted to anyone with a company identification or business card. Many hotel chains have periodic special offers, such as a four-for-one programme, where up to four people can stay in a double room for the price of a single. Another way to obtain a good deal is to book via the internet, as hotel chains sell to internet 'agencies' at rock-bottom prices. Sites worth visiting include 🖳 www.quikbook.com, 🖳 www.180096hotel.com, 🖳 www. 1800usahotels.com, 🖳 www.americaasyoulikeit.com and 🖳 www.usholidays.com.

If you're after a low-cost bed, look for accommodation described as student, budget, economy, no frills, rustic or European-style, all of which are euphemisms for basic. In major cities such as New York, there are long-stay hotels, some of which cater for women only. Rates vary and may be under $20 per night or even lower for weekly rates, depending on the facilities available and the length of your stay.

Most hotel chains have toll-free (800) booking (reservation) numbers, listed in the yellow pages, and any hotel in a chain can make bookings for you at other hotels in the chain. Some hotel chains provide free telephones at airports and main railway stations. Nearly all hotels, and certainly all hotel chains now have websites where you can book reservations, and many are now promising their best (i.e. cheapest) rates to those who book online. It pays to have a hotel booking confirmed in writing, by post, fax, or email depending on the time available. A deposit may be required when booking if you don't use a credit card. A booking guaranteed by a major credit card is kept all night; otherwise a room is usually held until 6pm only. If you plan to arrive later than this, inform the hotel in advance. If you wish to cancel a booking held with a credit card or an advance deposit, you must usually do so at least 48 hours in advance. However, it's often unnecessary to make a booking unless you're planning to stay in a resort area or a big city at peak times, when the best accommodation is full by 4 or 5pm. You can usually check in as late as you wish (provided there's a room available) and check-out is usually by 11am or noon. You aren't required to produce your passport or any identification when registering at a hotel in the US.

Resort hotels are common and provide a range of private facilities, including golf courses, tennis courts, horseback riding trails, bike and hiking paths, swimming pools, and ocean or lake beaches. Check whether the use of sports facilities and other activities is included in room rates; if not, they can add $30 or more per day to the cost. If you plan to stay at a resort hotel for a number of days, you may be quoted 'American Plan' (AP), which includes all meals (full board), 'Modified American Plan' (MAP), which includes breakfast and lunch or dinner (half board) or 'European Plan' (no meals).

Motels

Motels (motor-hotels, also called 'motel lodges' and 'motor inns') were invented in the US and are to be found throughout the country. They offer guests a clean and comfortable no-frills room at a reasonable price, and chains generally offer the same facilities throughout the country. Room rates range from $30 to $70 per night for a single room, depending on the location. Double rooms (i.e. with two beds) range from $50 to $100 per night. Many motels offer discounts for senior citizens. Motels generally provide better, cleaner and safer accommodation than inexpensive 'downtown' hotels.

The motel business is highly competitive and rates vary according to local competition. Most motels have neon signs outside stating 'vacancy' or 'no vacancy' and often quote their rates on huge billboards, although those **without** neon signs or on roads bypassed by new motorways are often cheaper, particularly during midweek. In some areas, there are few motels on major highways in any case. Motels don't usually have restaurants or provide room service or breakfast. However, family restaurants, fast food outlets, cafes and bars are usually located nearby (and may offer discounts to motel guests). Sometimes breakfast is available through room service, although it's generally expensive, or some motels offer a complimentary breakfast in the lobby, usually a 'continental breakfast' of rolls and coffee. If a motel has a restaurant, it's usual to pay for each meal separately, rather than charge them to your bill (as is usual in hotels). It's normal to pay in advance when you check in at a motel and you may be asked to pay a returnable key deposit.

Many motels furnish all their rooms with two double beds (queen or king size) or a double bed and two singles (twin beds). Additional folding beds (Z beds or cots) are usually available. Some motels have suites with more than one bedroom sharing the same facilities (intended for families or groups) and 'efficiencies', which are self-catering rooms with a small kitchen. If you're travelling as a family or group, ask how many people a room accommodates and whether there's a surcharge for extra people. Most motels (and hotels) don't charge for children under 18 sharing their parents' room or provide a camp bed in the parents' room for a small extra charge.

Motel rooms are usually similar with little individuality or character, although most are well appointed. All rooms have television (often with cable television and pay-per-view films), a private bathroom (with towels and flannel/washcloths), telephone, air-conditioning and heating, and possibly a fridge. Motels often provide washing machines and dryers, and vending machines for drinks and confectionery (candy). Ice is usually provided free, as most Americans are unable to drink anything without ice (including water and tea!). Ask to see a room before paying. Many large motels have swimming pools.

The largest and cheapest nationwide chains of motels include Days Inn with more than 800 locations, Motel 6 and Econolodge, both with over 500 locations.

There are also regional chains. If you're staying at a chain motel, the receptionist can book you a room at other motels in the chain. Most motel chains also have a toll-free (800) booking number and website. To find the toll-free booking number, call the toll-free information directory (☎ 1-800-555-1212). The American Automobile Association (AAA, see page 295) publishes booklets containing a list of approved motels and their rates. All motel chains publish directories containing directions, maps, facilities, addresses and telephone numbers.

Bed & Breakfast

Bed and breakfast (B&B) accommodation (often called bed and breakfast inns) is becoming increasingly popular in the US, particularly in small towns and holiday centres in New England, Virginia, California's wine regions and the deep south. American B&Bs are different from their British counterparts and tend to be in beautiful old houses full of antiques. Accommodation is generally geared towards couples, although single rooms are also available. Standards and prices vary considerably from around $35 per night for a single to $300 (on a par with a luxury hotel) for a double, depending on the location and the season (rates can vary by over 300 per cent between low and high season). The average is from $35 to $75 for a single and $50 to $100 for a double. Rates are higher in cities, e.g. in New York singles start at around $50 per night and advance booking is usually necessary. A private bath isn't always included, so check when booking. In New York and other major cities, B&B is a reasonably affordable way of staying 'downtown'.

B&Bs in the US aren't often individually advertised and are usually rented via official agencies or booking organisations. Unlike most other countries, not all B&Bs are hosted (where the owner or landlord lives on the premises and serves you breakfast). At an unhosted B&B, you're required to prepare your own breakfast from the provisions provided and prices start at around $100 per night. Guest houses and tourist homes are independent B&Bs which may not provide breakfast at all. The breakfast part of B&B varies from a roll and coffee or tea (i.e. continental breakfast) to a full cooked meal with many courses – the latter is more typical. Most B&Bs don't provide lunch or dinner, although some offer picnic baskets, as well as transport, tours and free services ranging from bike loans to the use of libraries, saunas, Jacuzzis/hot tubs, tennis courts and swimming pools.

The standards of B&Bs in the US are extremely variable, although there are a few organisations such as the American Bed & Breakfast Association (ABBA) that establish minimum national standards for their members. ABBA members are listed and evaluated in *Inspected, Rated & Approved* east and west membership consumer directories. In many regions B&Bs can be booked through booking agencies and lists may also be available from state and regional tourist organisations. In the last few years a wealth of US B&B guides have been published, including *Bed and Breakfast USA* by Peggy Ackerman (Plume), *The Complete Guide to Bed and Breakfasts, Inns and Guesthouses in the US and Canada* by Pamela Lanier (Lanier Publications), and the *Pelican's Select Guide to American Bed and Breakfasts* by Judi Russell (Pelican).

Another type of accommodation is offered by agencies such as America As You Like It (🖳 www.americaasyoulikeit.com), Affordable New York City (☎ 212-533-4001, 🖳 www.affordablenewyorkcity.com) and The B&B Agency of Boston

(⌨ www.boston-bnbagency.com), where you stay as a guest in a private home, a double room costing between $100 and $150 per night.

Self-catering

Self-catering apartments, houses and cottages are common throughout the US, particularly in cities, and mountain and beach resorts. Many resorts offer self-catering apartment hotels (housekeeping units) and condominium apartments (condos), both of which provide excellent accommodation for families. However, they don't always accept children, so check in advance. Accommodation usually consists of a studio or a one or two-bedroom apartment with a fully-equipped kitchen or kitchenette and a private bathroom with shower. Apartment hotels are usually owned by a company and designed for short-term rentals, whereas condos usually have individual owners, who let their apartments through management companies. Apartments and condos are particularly popular in Florida, where most are privately owned and purchased as investments (often by foreigners) and let to holidaymakers for most of the year.

Some condo complexes provide the same facilities as hotels, e.g. an entrance hall, lounge, coffee shop and restaurant, while others provide no services. Condos usually have double beds, fully equipped kitchens with a dishwasher, all linen, a washer and dryer (or shared facilities), televisions, and often air-conditioning and room telephones. Most resorts have a daily maid service and many provide a baby-sitting service. Other amenities may include swimming pools, tennis courts, golf courses, saunas, barbecue grills, and shops. When choosing self-catering accommodation, check the minimum and maximum rental periods, furnishings and equipment level (air-conditioning, phone, television, etc.), whether pets are allowed, sports and social facilities, local beaches, public transport, nearby shops, maid and baby-sitting services, and anything else of importance to you. Apart from serviced condos and hotel apartments, most self-catering accommodation doesn't provide a maid or cleaning service, although local services can usually be arranged.

A one-bedroom condo in a first class complex starts at around $100 per night for two adults and may be no more than $125 per night for four adults. Children under 12 may be accommodated free of charge when sharing an apartment with their parents. A quality two-bedroom apartment costs between $150 and $200 per night and accommodates up to six people. Weekly and monthly rates considerably reduce the cost per night: a two-bedroom condo in Florida can be had for as little as $295 per week, although luxury villas in Florida can cost $1,000 or more per week. At some resorts, rates vary according to the season (in Florida, summer rentals are around half those in winter) and in cities they may be much higher than average. It's usually cheaper to stay in a motel and eat out than stay in self-catering accommodation, although inexpensive motels are difficult to find in cities and are cramped in comparison with apartments. An apartment is often a good choice for a family; it's cheaper than a hotel room (particularly in major cities), provides more privacy and freedom, and you're able to prepare your own meals when you please.

Condo apartments can be rented through travel agents and are often offered as part of fly-drive packages. Bookings should be made as early as possible, particularly during holiday periods. Most guide books list agencies and organisations providing self-catering accommodation, and many establishments advertise in the travel and property sections of newspapers.

Hostels

For those travelling on a tight budget, one way to stretch your limited financial resources is to stay in hostels, which may be located in anything from a historic city building to an old lighthouse or adobe hacienda. Hostels are open to people of all ages and offer the cheapest accommodation available, from a few dollars up to $25 per night (average around $15), although there are far fewer hostels in the US (relative to its size) than, for example, in Europe. Most hostels recognise International Youth Hostel Federation (IYHF) membership, and it's usually cheaper if you join a national youth hostel federation outside the US in one of more than 60 countries affiliated to the IYHF.

To stay in the majority of hostels you must be a member of Hostelling International – American Youth Hostels (HI-AYH), 8401 Colesville Road, Suite 600, Silver Spring, MD 20910 (☎ 301-495-1240, 🖳 www.hiayh.org), although members of an overseas Youth Hostel Association can use HI-AYH facilities. Annual membership of HI-AYH costs $28 if you're 18 to 54 and $18 if you're over 54. There's no family membership, but children under 18 may join free. There are around 100 HI-AYH hostels, most of which are located in the Northeast, the Great Lakes area, Colorado and the Pacific Northwest. HI-AYH provide a members' directory ($3 or free if you join in the US) which lists and describes all hostels. Membership of HI-AYH provides discounts such as bicycle rentals at YMCA hostels.

Some hostels limit you to a maximum stay, e.g. three nights, and you should book in advance, particularly during holiday periods and in large cities. Some allow non-members to stay for a small extra charge, so that they can experience hostel life before becoming members. Hostels provide separate dormitories, e.g. 8 to 16 beds, for males and females. All hostels require guests to buy or rent (for around 50 cents a night) a sheet sleeping bag (sleep sack), which consists of two sheets sewn together, or to provide their own. Some allow you to use your own sleeping bag, although this is officially prohibited. Most hostels are open inconvenient hours and require guests to share light domestic duties. They don't provide meals, but usually have cooking facilities. There's a curfew after 10pm and alcohol, smoking and drugs are prohibited. However, US hostels are generally more relaxed than their European counterparts.

A variation on youth hostels is the home hostel, which is a private residence for the same price as a hostel. Some independent hostels in New York and other major cities provide dormitory accommodation for $15 to $25 a night. The cheapest city accommodation is often to be found at Young Men's Christian Association (YMCA) and Young Women's Christian Association (YWCA) hostels (known as Ys). Two-thirds of Y lodgings are 'coed' (mixed) and accept women and families, while the rest are for men only. Many Ys are located in run-down parts of big cities and are less of a bargain than they used to be, particularly for couples or groups. The room rates for Ys range from under $25 for a single in a small city, to $80 for a double in New York, where you may need to share a bathroom. It's usually necessary to book and pay in advance, for which you're charged a booking fee. Most Ys offer cheaper weekly rates and some offer packages which include room, half board (breakfast and evening meal) and excursions. Many Ys have swimming pools, gyms and other sports facilities. For further information contact Y's US Headquarters, 101 North Wacker Drive, Chicago, IL 60606 (☎ 312-977-0031) or consult the Rooms for Travellers section of their website (🖳 www.ymca.net).

The *Handbook of USA Youth Hostels* contains addresses, phone numbers, maps and practical information about youth hostels throughout the US and is available from YHA organisations worldwide. The US Servas Committee (11 John Street, Room 505, New York, NY 10038, ☎ 212-267-0252, 🖳 www.usservas.org) is a non-profit international co-operative which matches travellers with hosts who provide free accommodation for two to three days. Participation costs $50 per year. Student travel offices in North America and abroad usually sell a useful booklet, entitled *Sleep Cheap: North America*.

RELOCATION SERVICES

If you're fortunate enough to have your move to (or within) the US paid by your employer, he may arrange for a relocation service to handle the details. Services provided by relocation companies usually include house hunting (rent or buy), shipment of furniture and personal effects, school surveys, area information dossiers, orientation tours, financial counselling, home marketing, spouse counselling, and assistance after arrival. Relocation consultants' services are expensive and can run to thousands of dollars per day, although most people consider it money well spent (particularly if their employer is footing the bill!). You can find relocation companies in the yellow pages under 'Relocation Service'. Fees can vary considerably, so obtain a number of quotations and compare exactly what services are included. Most large property companies have relocation divisions and many offer a free relocation service to individuals.

If you just wish to look at properties for rent or sale in a particular area, you can make appointments with estate agents in the area where you plan to live, and arrange your own trip to the US. However, make **absolutely certain** that agents know exactly what you're looking for and obtain property lists in advance. Relocation guides are published in many areas and cities and contain house prices, guides to neighbourhoods, employment prospects, school examination scores, maps, entertainment and public services. Information is also available from local chambers of commerce.

AMERICAN HOMES

American homes are generally bigger, more luxurious and better equipped than homes in other western countries, particularly in rural areas. Homes are built in a huge variety of architectural styles, including villa, ranch, colonial, contemporary, Victorian, French manor, Spanish hacienda and English Tudor, all of which may be single, two-storey, split or multi-level. In addition to single-family detached homes and apartments, you can choose from a wide range of town houses. The average size of an older detached single-family house is around 1,800ft² (167m²) for owner-occupiers, and the average size of new single-family homes is up to 2,300ft² (207m²). Whereas land values constitute a large part of the cost of a home in many other countries, building plots in the US are relatively inexpensive and extensive prefabrication helps reduce building costs.

Kitchens in modern homes are usually large and include a dining area, plenty of worktop space, built-in cupboards (cabinets), dishwashers, waste disposal units, and possibly laundry facilities and/or a pantry. Kitchens in older homes are generally smaller and may have fewer facilities, unless they've been modernised. Most American families have a profusion of labour-saving devices, although many Americans don't use electric kettles to heat water for tea or coffee. Cookers (ranges or stoves) don't usually have grills, but broilers, which are larger than European grills and are located in or below the oven. Broilers have no temperature controls, so you cannot bake or roast and grill at the same time, unless you have a double-oven range. Many Americans use a portable grill or toaster oven in addition to their conventional oven. There's usually no facility for warming plates on ranges. American refrigerators are frost-free, huge (big enough to withstand a supermarket strike for at least a year) and modern models usually have ice-cube and chilled water dispensers on the **outside**.

Most bathrooms contain baths (tubs) and separate showers; many homes also have a separate shower room, or a shower or bathroom attached to the master bedroom (en suite). Modern two or three-bedroom family homes usually have two bathrooms. US baths may be small and uncomfortable and not very deep (but then most Americans prefer to shower). Bathrooms seldom contain a bidet. Americans also have what are called half-bathrooms (or a half-bath), which isn't a bath for babies, but a room **without** a bath. It usually contains a toilet and wash basin, and possibly a shower. Modern homes usually have a downstairs toilet. Showers supply water in torrents, rather than the trickle common in many countries, although in general, American plumbing leaves a lot to be desired (see **Water** on page 140).

In many parts of the US, particularly the affluent middle class suburbs of the Sunbelt states, many homes have outdoor or indoor heated swimming pools. If you have a pool, it will need a lot of attention such as filling, emptying, cleaning, filtering and chlorinating, although there are companies that will look after it for you (you can pay someone to do anything in the US). Many homes also have hot tubs or Jacuzzis (costing around $5,000), usually located outside the house where the climate is favourable. A hot tub consists of a large, usually circular, wooden tub containing hot water, the temperature of which is thermostatically controlled. Hot tubs usually accommodate a number of people and are intended as a relaxation rather than a bath.

Most modern houses have ultra-efficient heating, and air-conditioning (see page 141) is usually installed in homes in Sunbelt states. New houses usually include thermal insulation and extensive ventilation. New houses and apartments have an airing cupboard (linen closet), which may contain the hot water boiler (in older houses it's in the basement). Most homes in areas where it's cold in winter have double glazing, which may consist of two sets of windows, the outer of which are called 'storm' windows (these are often left open or removed altogether in summer).

Windows and doors in all areas usually have screens to keep out insects during summer, although storm windows may need to be removed to fit them. Because of the climate and abundant insect life in the US, infestations of cockroaches, ants, termites and other insects are common in many areas, even in new buildings. It's usual for residents in affected areas to use do-it-yourself deterrents and to periodically have pest-control agencies ('exterminators') fumigate their homes.

Modern homes usually have separate living, dining and 'family' rooms (the last often used as children's play rooms), a study (den), bar, cellar or basement, and maybe a utility or laundry room. Most houses have a paved or covered outdoor area such as a terrace, patio, loggia, deck or porch. Standard fixtures and fittings in modern houses are usually much more comprehensive and of better quality than those found in old houses. Common features are smoke and security alarms, humidifiers, copper wiring, electric door chimes, aluminium windows, skylights, and built-in cabinets and closets. Houses and apartments usually have light fittings in all rooms, although there may be no ceiling light fittings in living rooms and bedrooms. In many homes, curtains (drapes) are operated by drawstrings at the side of the window and windows are fitted with shades or blinds to keep out the sun. Most houses, furnished and unfurnished, are fully or partly carpeted and wooden floors are fairly common, particularly in older homes.

BUYING PROPERTY

Buying a house or an apartment in the US is usually a good investment and preferable to renting, depending on how long you're planning to stay. If you're staying for less than two years, you're usually better off renting. For those staying longer than two years, buying should be the better option, particularly as buying a house or apartment is generally no more expensive than renting, and you could make a large profit (or a loss!). The recession in the early '90s caused a serious slump in property prices, although the market has now fully recovered (yet once again there are rumblings of a 'housing bubble' that could burst).

As a long-term investment property remains difficult to beat, particularly detached single-family homes, and housing enjoys strong tax advantages over all other forms of investment. The interest charges on a mortgage can generally be deducted from your taxable income, and this should be taken into account when comparing buying with renting (for which there's no tax deduction). You can also sell a house and avoid paying capital gains tax (see **Capital Gains Tax** on page 394) on the profits, provided it's your principal residence and you've lived there a certain period of time.

Property values vary considerably from region to region. A house of 2,000ft^2 (185m^2) costs around $195,000 in Houston, Miami and New Orleans, $350,000 in Los Angeles, $385,000 in Chicago, $450,000 in Washington, DC, $600,000 in Boston and San Francisco, and a whopping $900,000 plus in New York. However, in rural areas and small towns (including many areas popular for holiday and retirement homes such as Florida) the same size home can be purchased for as little as $80,000. Most new homes are sold directly by developers, who are often also the builders. New town houses and apartments that are part of large complexes are often ready to move into, while single-family detached houses may be built to order. Whether you're buying a new or used property (two out of three buyers choose a used home), always haggle over the price.

In many states, hiring a lawyer for a property transaction is standard practice, although it isn't always necessary, as all states now have mandatory title insurance to protect against a future claim on the title by a third party. Before hiring a lawyer, compare the fees charged by a number of practices and check their experience of property transactions. Most people buy and sell their homes through estate agents (real estate agents), who must be licensed by local real estate boards. In the US, estate agents work from a database of all properties offered for sale through agencies in the area (crosslisting), so the usual practice is for a customer to engage a single agent. The estate agent's fee is paid by the seller, and where the buyer and seller have different agents, they split the fee between themselves. You should do business with a professional full-time agent or broker who's a member of a professional organisation. An agent with the title 'realtor' is a member of a local real estate board that has an affiliation with the National Association of Realtors (NAR), the largest and most respected organisation for brokers. Realtors subscribe to the NAR's code of ethics and must have completed a course of study. A 'realtist' is a member of the National Association of Real Estate Brokers (NAREB), which sets professional standards and has a code of ethics for members. The NAR and the NAREB have websites where you can find a local member estate agent, plus review homes for sale and information about mortgages and financing (💻 www.realtor.com for the NAR and 💻 www.nareb.com for NAREB). To get a 'rating' of agents by experience, success rate and commission rate, go to the website 💻 www.HomeGain.com.

Usually you pay an initial 'good faith' deposit of a few thousand dollars and sign a contract which is binding on both parties. **If you don't want to go through with the purchase, you will lose your deposit and can even be forced to go through with the purchase, so don't sign without taking legal advice.** The contract usually contains a number of conditions (riders or contingencies) that must be met before the contract becomes valid and binding, e.g. house and termite inspections and your ability to obtain a mortgage (if necessary) by a certain date. Conditions may vary from region to region and state to state. Some may be required by law, while others may be insisted upon by your estate agent or lender. The contract must list anything included in the price, e.g. furniture, fittings and extras such as a fireplace (for a new home), and should specify who pays the fees associated with the purchase. Standard contracts can usually be tailored to your requirements.

A number of US homes are sold by auction, whereby you pay a deposit of around 10 per cent and settlement is made between 30 and 90 days after the auction.

Most experts believe that you should always have a survey (house inspection) on a used house and a termite inspection is almost mandatory on an older home, as the US has countless varieties of wood-boring insects. Always use a certified and licensed professional inspector who's a member of the American Society of Home Inspectors, 933 Lee Street, Suite 101, Des Plaines, IL 60016 (☎ 1-800-743-ASHI, 💻 www.ashi.org) or another professional organisation. The average survey costs $250 to $500. In some states an owner must disclose any significant defects when selling a property and if he fails to do so you have a good chance of recovering damages if you sue. Note, however, that a claim must be made within a certain period, usually six months to a year after conclusion of the sale.

In California and some other states, your deposit and all other funds must be placed with a neutral third party, the 'escrow agent', who's usually selected by the buyer's estate agent (but is subject to approval by all parties). He is responsible for compiling and checking the documents and ensuring the transaction can 'close' within the period specified in the purchase contract. Once the deal is closed, the escrow agent records the deed and disburses the funds to the appropriate parties.

When calculating the cost of buying a home, allow around 5 per cent of the purchase price for closing (or settlement) costs. These may include a lender's valuation (appraisal) fee, legal fees, title search, title insurance, recording fees, survey/home inspection, household insurance, and mortgage tax. Make sure that all local taxes and water/sewerage bills have been paid by the previous owner, as these charges usually come with the property (and are passed on to subsequent owners!).

There are numerous books about buying a home in the US, including *Buying a Home in Florida* by yours truly (Survival Books). Although its title relates to Florida, much of the information contained in this book also applies to other states. Free booklets and magazines listing properties for sale are published in all regions, many of which (such as *Harmon Homes*, *The Real Estate Book*, *Real Estate News* and *Homes & Land*) are published in local editions throughout the country. They're available in local estate agents', shops, restaurants, supermarkets and libraries. *United Country* is a quarterly catalogue of country properties for sale throughout the US published by United Country Real Estate, 1600 N. Corrington Avenue, Kansas City, MO 64120 (☎ 1-800-999-1020, 🖳 www.unitedcountry.com). For information about mortgages, see page 378.

RENTED ACCOMMODATION

Rented accommodation is readily available in most areas, although choice and cost vary considerably. Renting is generally the best solution for anyone planning to remain in the US for less than two or three years. Long-term residents may want to rent for a year or two until they learn their way around their new area and develop an idea of the best places to purchase a house. Rented property can be found within a few weeks in some areas, while in others it takes much longer and you may need to compromise on what you're looking for. Large apartments and houses with four or more bedrooms are particularly difficult to find in most major cities, with the possible exception of luxury homes with astronomical rents.

The type of rented accommodation available depends on where you want to live. In cities most rental properties are apartments or town houses, while in rural and suburban areas, detached houses are most common. Rented accommodation in cities is often exorbitantly expensive and difficult to find. In major metropolitan areas, finding an apartment or house which suits your needs **and** your budget may take many weeks. The choice may often lie between a tiny apartment in the city close to your office or workplace, or a larger apartment or house out of town, with long commuting times. The area where you live is of paramount importance in determining your quality of life and has important implications for your family. The most desirable areas (often with the best public schools) are usually reflected in high rents and intense competition for rental properties.

Most property in the US is rented unfurnished and you may have difficulty finding a furnished apartment or house. Furnished apartments are usually equipped with the 'essentials' only, which include a cooker (range), refrigerator or fridge/freezer, beds, chairs, sofa, tables, lamps, china and glass, cutlery (flatware), curtains (drapes) and basic kitchen supplies. Some linen, e.g. bed, bath and table, may also be supplied. Unfurnished apartments usually have a cooker, refrigerator or fridge/freezer, air-conditioners and perhaps a dishwasher. Apartments are more likely to have a fridge than houses. Most property is centrally heated and homes in the south usually have air-conditioning. Most modern or post-1945 apartment blocks have a communal laundry room with commercial coin-operated washing and drying machines. Apartments and houses in modern urban developments usually have their own washer (washing machine) and dryer. Luxury apartment developments often have their own swimming pools, Jacuzzis, saunas, heated spas, racquetball and tennis courts, and a fully-equipped health club or fitness centre, all of which are 'free' to tenants.

Single people, particularly the young and students, may find it difficult to find accommodation that doesn't break the bank. The least expensive, single accommodation goes by a variety of names, the most common of which are studio, bachelor or efficiency. All of these are euphemisms for a one-room apartment in which you live, sleep and eat, with a separate kitchen and small bathroom. A walk-up is similar to a studio and is located in an apartment block without a lift (elevator). Cold-water apartments have no central hot-water system and you must install your own water heater (although most city apartment blocks have continuous hot water). One way single people can save money is to share accommodation. This is common in all areas and costs from $300 to $500 per month in a metropolitan area. Advertisements for sharers (roommates) can be found in most newspapers and in free 'singles' newspapers and magazines. It's possible to rent furniture, and student packages start at around $50 per month.

If you want rented accommodation for a short period only, for example while looking for a suitable property to buy, you may be better off taking short-term holiday accommodation. Short-term rentals, also called temporary housing, are available in many areas.

Finding a Rented Property

Your success in finding a suitable rented property depends on many factors, including the type of property you're looking for (a studio apartment is usually easier to find than a four-bedroom detached house), how much you want to pay and the area where you wish to live. When looking for accommodation in some cities, you must make up your mind quickly, because the next day the property will be taken. There are many ways of finding a rented property, including asking friends, relatives and acquaintances to spread the word, particularly if you're looking in the area where you already live (this is often the best way to find a place in New York and some other cities). Many local newspapers and magazines (including company 'house' magazines) have an 'Apartments for Rent' section and free monthly rental guides are published for many areas, including *For Rent* magazine (⌨ www.forrent.com), the *Apartment Guide* (⌨ www.apartmentguide. com) and the *Rental Guide Magazine* (PO Box 5018, Tallahassee, FL 32314-9959). Published rental guides can also be found in major supermarkets, estate agents' and relocation consultants' offices, chambers of commerce, banks, and street vending machines (in major cities).

Other ways to find a home include accommodation and renting agencies, estate agents, rental offices in large rental complexes, the managing agents of large rental corporations (who manage their own buildings), advertisements on notice boards in shopping malls, stores, supermarkets, colleges and company offices, and internet sites. To find accommodation through advertisements in local newspapers, you must be quick off the mark. Buy the newspaper as soon as it's published and start phoning immediately or scan the rental advertisements daily on the newspaper's website. You must be available to inspect the property immediately or at any time. The best days for advertisements are usually Saturdays and Sundays. In many cities the property section of Sunday newspapers, e.g. the *New York Sunday Times*, can be bought on a Saturday afternoon. You can insert a 'rental wanted' advertisement in many newspapers and on bulletin boards, but don't count on success using this method.

The numerous internet sites offering an apartment-finding facility include the websites mentioned above for the rental magazines, plus ⌨ www.homes.com, and the websites of most real estate chains, such as Century 21.

Many ploys are used to make apartments appear larger than they actually are. Always ask for room sizes (given in square feet) and when a number of rooms is listed, ask exactly what they are (sometimes kitchens and bathrooms are counted as rooms). Normally the total number of rooms includes bedrooms, lounge and dining room, so a three or three and a half room apartment usually has one bedroom. Generally the higher an apartment is in a block, the more expensive it is (you pay extra for the clean air, increased light, isolation from street noise and the view).

It's best not to deal with referral services or apartment finders, as you're likely to waste your time and money. Estate agents who list rental properties are normally paid by the landlord, not by the renter. Agents might try to charge you a 'registration' fee or get you to pay money in advance under some other pretence, e.g. a deposit, a waiting list fee, or a fee for a list of properties to view. This is usually illegal and you shouldn't pay any money until you've found a home and agreed to rent it. The agency fee or commission varies according to the agency and the length of your lease, e.g. half a month's commission for a one to two month lease; one month's commission for a three to six month lease; and 10 to 15 per cent of a year's rent (equivalent to 1.2 to 1.8 months' rent) for a lease of six months or longer (you may be able to negotiate). Some employers pay their employees' agent's fees. Find out how many weeks' rent you must pay in advance, whether there's a 'security' deposit against damages (usually one to two months' rent) and try to obtain a copy of a sample contract. **Don't hand over any money or sign ANYTHING before you know exactly what the conditions are.**

Rental Costs

Rental costs vary considerably according to the size (number of bedrooms) and quality of a property, its age and the facilities provided. Most importantly, rents depend on the neighbourhood and the region of the US. The rent for similar properties in different parts of the country can vary by as much as 1,000 per cent! As a general rule, the further a property is from a large city or town, public transport or other facilities, the less expensive it is. Average rental costs for unfurnished apartments and houses are shown in the table below:

Size	Monthly Rent ($)
Studio	400 – 600
1-bedroom	500 – 800
2-bedroom	600 – 900
3-bedroom	700 – 1,200
4-bedroom	1,200 – 1,500 +

The rents shown above are fair market rents for good quality modern or renovated properties in an average metropolitan area. They don't include properties in rural areas or in areas where there's a glut of new property, which can be much cheaper, and the downtown areas of major cities and exclusive residential areas, where the sky's the limit. In New York City, e.g. Manhattan, rents are often double (or more) the maximum shown above, while in some areas rents are less than the minimum shown. It's possible to find less expensive, older apartments and houses for rent, but they're rarer, generally small and don't offer the amenities of a new property. If you like a property, but think the rent is too high, try to negotiate a reduction or ask the agent to put your offer to the owner (which he may be obliged to do). Check the cost of extras such as maintenance, which may include grass-cutting, window-washing, and leaf and snow removal (you're normally responsible for clearing snow from the pavement in front of your house during a specified period). Sometimes rents include heating, air-conditioning, gas cooking and hot water, but don't usually include electricity.

In many US cities and towns there are laws protecting tenants' rights, the most common of which are 'rent control' laws. These laws place a limit on the maximum rent that can be charged for a particular apartment, which in many cases is well below the 'market' rent, i.e. what the landlord could get simply by renting to the highest bidder. If you wish to renew a lease, your landlord usually has the right to increase the rent, although the amount by which it can be raised may be controlled through a rent-control or rent-stabilisation law. There may, however, be an 'escalator' clause in the lease, under which the landlord can increase your rent if his expenses increase. Your landlord cannot increase your rent during the period of the lease (unless stipulated in the lease) and the percentage (reviewed annually) by which it can be increased may depend on the length of the lease. Note, however, that rents for furnished apartments, condominiums and co-operatives aren't controlled or stabilised, and owners can decide their own rent increases.

GARAGES & PARKING

A garage or parking space may not be provided when you rent an apartment, particularly in towns and cities. Houses in the suburbs usually have garages, often with space for two cars plus additional storage space. Smaller or older homes may have a one-car garage only, while large houses may have garaging for up to four cars (over 75 per cent of new homes have a two-car or larger garage). Garages are often an integral part of a house, with direct access to ground (first) floor rooms. Detached garages aren't popular, particularly in cold regions. In southern 'Sunbelt' states, apartments and town houses may have a car port or a parking space only. New houses and apartment buildings usually have adequate parking for residents and visitors.

If you live in a city, it may be difficult to find an apartment or town house with a garage or parking space, although new apartment blocks have underground parking which may be included in the rent. If parking isn't included, it usually costs between $100 and $200 per month, and can run to $500 per month in some cities, e.g. New York. It may be cheaper to use taxis locally and rent a car for longer trips. A lock-up garage is useful, particularly in areas with a high incidence of car theft, e.g. most cities. Free on-street parking is difficult or impossible to find in cities and large towns, and in any case isn't recommended for anything, but a wreck.

MOVING HOUSE

If you're moving to the US from abroad, it usually takes four to eight weeks to have your personal effects shipped, depending on the distance and route. Obtain at least three written quotations before committing yourself. Moving companies or movers (in the US movers are never called removal men, who are undertakers!) usually send a representative to carry out a detailed estimate. Most US companies charge by the weight of the goods to be shipped, not by the volume, as is common elsewhere, and you're entitled to go with the movers to the public scales where your load is weighed. Movers will pack your belongings and provide packing cases and containers, although this is naturally more expensive than packing them yourself. Ask how they pack fragile and valuable items, and whether the cost of packing cases, materials and insurance (see below) is included in the quotation.

If you're doing your own packing, most shipping companies provide packing crates and boxes. If you're moving within the mainland US, you should use a member of the American Moving and Storage Association, 1611 Duke Street, Alexandria, VA 22314 (☎ 703-683-7410), who publish a number of free leaflets. For international moves, it's best to use a shipping company that's a member of the International Federation of Furniture Removers (FIDI), the Overseas Moving Network International (OMNI) or the Association of International Removers. Members usually subscribe to an advance payment scheme, which provides a guarantee: when a member company fails to fulfil its commitments to a customer, the contract is completed at the agreed cost by another company or your money is refunded. Members of the British Association of Removers (BAR) who are 'overseas bonded' also offer a free finance guarantee protecting all pre-payments.

Make a complete list of everything to be shipped and give a copy to the shipping company. Don't include anything illegal, e.g. guns, bombs, drugs, pornographic material, etc. with your belongings, as customs checks can be rigorous and penalties severe. It's also pointless shipping items such as 220V electrical apparatus (the US has a 110V system), televisions (see page 183) and wardrobes (most US homes have built-in wardrobes). Give your shipping company the phone number and address in the US through which you can be contacted.

Fully insure your belongings with a well established insurance company during shipment or while in storage (warehouses have been known to burn down!). Around 50 per cent of moves result in some damage to possessions. Don't use the moving company's insurance policy, as this usually limits their liability to a paltry sum. You should make a photographic or video record of any valuables shipped for insurance purposes. If your stay in the US will be short, it may be wise to leave valued possessions at home, e.g. with relatives or friends, particularly if their insured value wouldn't provide adequate compensation for their loss or damage. Unless you're trying to save money, use a major shipping company with a good reputation and use a specialist company for international removals. If there are any breakages or damaged items, these must be noted and listed before you sign the delivery bill. If you need to make a claim, be sure to read the small print. Claims must usually be made within a limited period, sometimes within a few days. Send claims by registered post.

For house moves within the US you can rent a van or truck by the hour, half-day or day, and many people moving only personal effects rent a 'U-Haul' trailer (whose worrying advertising slogan is 'Make moving an adventure'). Many transport companies sell packing boxes in various sizes and rent or sell removal equipment (trolleys, straps, etc.), for those who feel up to doing their own move. See also the checklists in **Chapter 20** and **Customs** on page 108.

MOVING IN

Whether you're moving into a rented property or a purchased home, one of the most important initial tasks is to carry out an inventory of the fixtures, fittings and, if applicable, furniture and furnishings. If you've bought a property, you should check that the previous owners haven't made off with any fixtures and fittings that were included in the contract or anything which you specifically paid for, e.g. carpets, light fittings, curtains, cabinets or cupboards, kitchen appliances, garden ornaments or plants. It's common to do a final check or inventory, called a 'walk-thru', when buying a property (usually carried out one or two days before the closing).

If you're renting, you should complete an inventory of contents and a report on the property's condition. This includes the condition of fixtures and fittings, the state of furniture and furnishings, the cleanliness and state of the decoration, and anything damaged, missing or in need of repair (experienced renters advise taking photographs of any damaged fittings to add to the inventory). An inventory may be provided by your landlord or agent and may include every single item in a furnished property (down to the number of teaspoons). The inventory check should be carried out in your presence, when taking over and when terminating a rental agreement. If not provided by your landlord, you should make your own inventory and ask a witness and your landlord to sign it. Note the reading on your utility meters, e.g. electricity, gas, water and check that you aren't overcharged on your first bill. The meters should be read by utility companies before you move in, which you may need to organise yourself.

A rental property should be clean when you move in, as this is what your landlord will expect when you move out. You may be required to pay for a property to be painted when you leave, depending on the state of the decoration and the length of your tenancy. An allowance is made for 'normal wear and tear', including dirty paintwork, although it's open to individual interpretation. You should receive your security deposit within a specified period (14 to 60 days) of moving out of a rented property, and any deductions should be detailed in an itemised statement. Some landlords do almost anything to avoid repaying a security deposit and may make deductions for bogus repairs or cleaning, even when you leave a property spotless. If you disagree with deductions and are unable to come to an amicable agreement, you can file a suit in a small claims court to have your deposit returned.

You should also obtain written instructions from the landlord or previous owners about the operation of appliances and heating and cooling systems, maintenance of grounds, yard and lawns, care of special surfaces such as wooden floors, and the names of reliable local handymen who know the property and its quirks. Check with your local town hall regarding regulations and laws about such things as recycling, parking, and the upkeep of your yard, drive and front lawns. Many communities have local regulations requiring owners to keep buildings painted and in good condition. The storage of vehicles, trailers and boats, and the erection of fences and sheds may also be strictly regulated.

KEYS & SECURITY

When moving into a new home, it's often wise to replace the locks (or lock barrels) as soon as possible and fit high security (double cylinder or dead bolt) locks, as you've no idea how many keys are in circulation for the existing locks. If you're renting, you must obtain permission from the owner or landlord. If you own your home, you may wish to have an alarm system fitted, as this is usually the best way to scare away robbers and may also reduce your household insurance premium (see **Household Insurance** on page 349). Many door locks in the US don't lock automatically and you need a key to lock as well as open them. Most outside doors, particularly apartment doors in major cities, are fitted with a spy-hole and chains so that you can check the identity of a visitor before opening (or completely opening) the door. Inside doors often have locks that are operated by pressing and/or twisting a button on the centre of the door knob or by pushing or twisting the knob itself (these locks should be replaced if found on outside doors, as they're insecure).

No matter how secure your door and window locks, a thief can usually obtain entry if he is determined enough, often by simply smashing a window (although you can fit external steel security blinds). You can deter thieves by ensuring that your house is well lit, even (or particularly) when no one is at home, when it's often wise to leave a television or radio on (a timer switch can be used to randomly switch on and off a radio, television and lights). Most security companies provide home security systems connected to a central monitoring station. When a sensor, e.g. smoke or forced entry, is activated or a panic button is pushed, a signal is sent to a 24-hour monitoring station. Many local police offer free security assessments of your home and can suggest specific improvements to help foil thieves or vandals. **Remember, prevention is better than cure, as people who are burgled rarely recover their property.**

If you lock yourself out of your apartment (or car), there's usually a local locksmith on call day and night to help you. However, if you live in a small community, you should call the local police, who may be able to help you free of charge. A locksmith's services are expensive and it may be more economical to break a window to gain entry to your apartment (but difficult if you live on the 39th floor). If you vacate a rented house or apartment for an extended period, it may be obligatory to notify your building superintendent, agent or insurance company, and to leave a key with the superintendent or agent in case of emergencies. Fire prevention is also an important aspect of home security. If they aren't already fitted, it's wise to install smoke detectors in all rooms (required by law in some states) and keep a fire extinguisher handy. The US has one of the highest rates of house-fire deaths in the world.

UTILITIES

Electricity, gas and water companies in the US are called utility companies and are owned by private companies, local municipalities or the federal government (there are also co-operatives in some rural areas). The US produces some 20 per cent of its energy from nuclear power. (France is the world's highest nuclear producer with over three-quarters of its electricity coming from nuclear plants.) 70 per cent of the electricity in the US is produced using fossil fuels, including coal. Because utility companies were monopolies, state governments have established public utility or public service commissions (PUCs or PSCs) to set rates and monitor their operation in accordance with state law. The electric power industry in the US is in the process of being privatised (deregulated or restructured). Around 25 states are actively involved in the process, meaning that there are options for consumers when it comes to buying electricity. In some cities and regions you may be billed for electricity and gas (and/or water) by the same utility company or by your municipality. In others, there's no longer a monopoly on utility services, and you're free to choose your supplier from any of those serving your area. Electricity and gas bills are itemised separately.

If you're renting a property, your water is normally included in your rent. It's usually possible to apply by telephone to utility companies to have your electricity, gas or water service switched on, although you may have to fax them identity documents or your lease agreement. You may be required to pay a security deposit, depending on your credit history. When payable, a deposit may vary according to the size of the property, e.g. from $50 to $300. Deposits are usually held in an interest-earning escrow account and may be returned when you've been billed for a number of consecutive billing cycles, e.g. eight, or have paid most bills before the penalty due date in the past year or so. When moving into a property, you must sometimes pay a 'start-up' fee, e.g. $20, to connect the service and read the meter, which is included in your first bill. You must contact your electricity, gas and water companies (usually at least 48 hours in advance) to get a final meter reading and bill when vacating a property.

Electricity and gas meters are read and customers billed each month in most areas, although you're billed bi-monthly or even quarterly in some areas; the number of billing days is shown on the bill. Bills include a service or customer charge, e.g. $3 to $5 per month. If the meter reader is unable to read your meter, you receive an estimated bill, which is usually marked 'EST', 'Avg' or 'A'. A utility company may send a revised bill based on a meter reading provided by you. In some states regulations require at least one actual reading a year. You're usually given 14 days in which to pay a bill before it becomes overdue. If your payment arrives after the due date, it is added to your next bill and you may be charged a late payment penalty, e.g. 5 per cent of the outstanding amount. If you don't pay a utility bill, you eventually receive a 'notice of discontinuation of service', when you should pay the bill within the period stated, e.g. 15 days, even if you dispute the amount. In most states, utility companies are required by law to give adequate notice and a hearing before they can terminate a service.

Your utility company may offer a 'level billing' or 'budget' plan, where your annual energy costs are spread evenly throughout the year. You can also have a copy of your bill sent to a relative, friend or organisation. This is intended to assist people who are ill, elderly or away from their homes for long periods. In some states, utility companies have what are called 'lifeline rates' (or a 'baseline allowance'). These are electricity and gas rates designed to cover the service necessary to meet the energy requirements of the average household. Energy used above the lifeline rate is billed at a higher rate. Sales tax is charged on utility bills in some areas.

Most utility companies publish useful booklets explaining how to conserve energy, e.g. through improved insulation, and thus reduce your bills. However, this has little impact on most Americans, who are the most profligate consumers of energy in the world and habitually light and heat (or cool) their homes when they're empty. Most utility companies will perform a free home energy conservation survey and private companies will conduct a more in-depth examination for around $200. Always check the identity of anyone claiming to be a utility employee (or any kind of 'serviceman') by asking to see an identity card with a photograph.

More than 40 states have 'utility consumer advocates', who are public officials dealing solely with consumer problems concerning utilities. To find out whether your state has one, contact the National Association of State Utility Consumer Advocates, 8380 Colesville Road, Suite 101, Silver Spring, MD 20910 (☎ 301-589-6313, 🖥 www.nasuca.org).

Electricity

The electricity supply in the US is 110/120 volts AC, with a frequency of 60 Hertz (Hz) or cycles. Every resident, whether in an apartment or a house, has his own electric meter. This is usually located in the basement of an apartment block or outside a house, where it can be read when the occupants aren't at home. In many areas, electricity is charged at peak and off-peak (slack) period rates at different times of day and in different seasons (usually summer and winter). Electricity costs vary according to the area, e.g. from 8 cents to 14 cents per kilowatt-hour (KWH or KWHR).

It's possible to operate electrical equipment rated at 240 volts AC with a converter or a transformer, although generally it isn't worth bringing any electrical appliances to the US that aren't rated at 110 volts AC. Some electrical appliances, e.g. electric razors and hair dryers, are dual-voltage, and are fitted with a 110/240 volt switch. Check for the switch, which may be inside the casing, and make sure it's switched to 110 volts **before** connecting it to the power supply. Most people buy new electrical appliances in the US, which are of good quality and reasonably priced. Shop around before buying electrical appliances, as prices vary considerably, and check comparison tests in consumer magazines.

An additional problem with some electrical equipment that isn't made for the North American market is that the frequency rating is designed to run at 50Hz and not the US's 60Hz. Electrical equipment without a motor is generally unaffected by the increase in frequency to 60 Hz (except televisions). Some equipment with a synchronous motor may run with a 20 percent increase in speed; however, washing machines, cookers, electric clocks, record players and reel-to-reel tape recorders are unusable in the US unless designed for 60 cycle operation. To find out, look at the label on the back of the equipment; if it says 50/60Hz, it should run properly. If it says 50Hz, you might try it anyway, **but first ensure that the voltage is correct, as outlined above.** If the equipment runs too slowly, seek advice from the manufacturer or the retailer. For example, you may be able to obtain a pulley for a reel-to-reel tape deck or record turntable to compensate for the increase in speed.

The standard North American mains plug has two flat pins (live and neutral) plus an optional third pin (earth). It's possible to buy adapters for many foreign plugs, in the US and abroad, although it's more economical to change plugs. Most appliances sold in the US are fitted with a moulded two-pin plug, which will run off any outlet in the country. Some electrical appliances are earthed, which means they have a three-core wire and are fitted with a three-pin plug. If you need to fit a plug, the colour coding is usually white (neutral), black (live) and green (earth). **Always ensure that a plug is correctly and securely wired, as bad wiring can prove fatal. Never fit a two-pin plug to a three-core flex.**

In American homes, there are no switches on wall sockets, so electrical appliances should be fitted with their own on/off switches. On most switches, the UP position is ON and the DOWN position is OFF; some switches operate from left to right. The ON position may be indicated by a red spot on the switch. Standard and other lamps often have two or three-way bulbs which provide two or three levels of brightness. Often lamp switches (or knobs) must be turned in a clockwise direction or pushed and pulled. Electric light bulbs have a standard size screw fitting, which may be different from those in other countries. Bulbs for older appliances or foreign appliances, e.g. sewing machines, may not be available in the US, so bring a few spares with you.

Most American apartments and all houses have their own fuse boxes. If a fuse blows, **first turn off the mains switch.** This may be on the consumer unit or on a separate switch box nearby. Fuses in modern homes and homes with modern wiring are usually of the circuit breaker type; when a circuit is overloaded it trips to the OFF position. Switch off the mains switch and open the circuit breaker box. After locating and remedying the cause of the failure (if possible), switch the circuit breaker to the ON position. Close the circuit breaker box and switch on the mains switch. In many states, only a qualified electrician is permitted to install electrical wiring and fittings, particularly in connection with fuse boxes. Most electricity companies will service your major electrical appliances, e.g. a heating or air-conditioning system, and some provide service contracts.

Gas

Gas (usually natural) is available in most US cities. The same company may supply you with gas and electricity, when you will receive one bill for both, with gas and electricity costs itemised separately. Gas is available in all but the remotest areas of the US, although most modern houses are all-electric and aren't connected to the gas supply. Outside cities and in remote areas, gas may be supplied in bottles. Gas is charged by the cubic foot or the therm (a measure of heating 'value' roughly equivalent to 100 cubic feet). Costs have risen sharply in recent months, from around $0.70 per therm in 2001 to a little over $1 in the 2004-5 heating season. If you rent an apartment, your gas consumption may be included in your rent. Gas leaks are extremely rare and explosions caused by leaks even rarer (although spectacular and, therefore, widely reported). Natural gas is treated with a chemical to give it a 'rotten egg' smell that's easily detectible should you have a leak. You can also buy an electrically-operated gas detector that activates an alarm when a gas leak is detected.

Water

In many areas, you don't receive a water bill, as the cost is included in local property taxes. In other areas there's a charge and each building or apartment may have its own water meter, where you're billed each month or quarter for the water you use. Bills may include a meter charge, e.g. $10 per month. In most areas you're billed for water by your local municipality, possibly with your sewerage and rubbish collection. Water is charged by the unit, one unit being 100 cubic feet or 748 gallons. Rates are generally low, the first 36 units typically charged at around $1.40 per unit, the next 24 units at around $1.60 and additional units at around $1.90. Based on an average daily consumption of 100 gallons per person (less than one gallon of which is used for cooking and drinking), this equates to around $70 per person per year.

There's no interstate water system in the US; while half the country is bone dry, the other half is subject to flooding. In the west and south there are often restrictions on the use of water during the summer months, e.g. for private swimming pools, car-washing and watering gardens, particularly after a snow-free or dry winter. Water authorities produce conservation leaflets detailing how to conserve water and residents are asked to periodically check their homes for leaks to avoid waste and high water bills.

Despite billions of dollars spent in improving water quality, water pollution is common in many areas and water in rivers and streams is often unsafe to drink. Most Americans drink water straight from their house supply, although some people find the taste of the water or the purifying, e.g. chlorinating, chemicals unpleasant and prefer to drink bottled spring or mineral water (or American beer, which tastes like water). In many areas people install cold-water taps with filters, which are used when water is for drinking or cooking. You shouldn't drink water from rivers, wells, and streams, as it may be polluted (although in rural areas homes may have well water, which is usually excellent).

US taps (faucets) can be complicated for the uninitiated and may be fitted with a variety of strange controls, e.g. one common design is operated by a handle that works on a universal joint arrangement, where an up-and-down movement controls the flow and a left-to-right movement the temperature (left is hot); in the US the left tap is almost always the hot tap. When there are separate hot and cold taps in a shower, sometimes both taps turn in the same direction and sometimes in opposite directions; check them out before scalding or freezing yourself. Where a shower and bath are combined, a lever or knob is commonly used to convert the flow from bath to shower and vice versa. Most US baths and washbasins have a single mixer spout. Sometimes taps must be pulled or pushed rather than turned and a lever may also control the plug.

Before moving into a new home you should enquire where the main stop-valve or stopcock is, so that you can turn off the water supply in an emergency. If the water stops flowing for any reason, you should ensure that all taps are closed to prevent flooding from an open tap when the supply starts again.

HEATING & AIR-CONDITIONING

In many regions of the US the weather fluctuates between boiling and freezing, and many Americans consider air-conditioning (air or AC) and central heating as essential. Americans don't believe in doing anything by half, and heated and air-conditioned buildings are boiling or freezing (or the exact opposite of outdoor temperatures). All modern office buildings and many private homes have air-conditioning and many Americans would find it impossible to live without it (some homes even have **outdoor** air-conditioning). In the Sunbelt states, most Americans live in air-conditioned homes, drive air-conditioned cars to air-conditioned offices and stores, and never spend more than a few seconds in the heat (in case they melt). Elsewhere, most American homes have central heating, which may be a gas or oil-fired hot air or radiator system or an electric under-floor system. Modern homes often have a combined heating and cooling (air-conditioning) system which is thermostatically controlled. Many homes are also fitted with ceiling fans.

In older apartment buildings and single-family homes there's usually no central air-conditioning system and window air-conditioning units may be installed. These can be purchased in most electrical shops or department stores. You can install them yourself or most suppliers will install them for you for a small fee. If you do it yourself, make sure that the size and power of the unit is correct. Most window air-conditioning units have a choice of fan speeds and the fan can usually be switched on separately from the cooling system. The cooling system can be adjusted for temperature, and units often have a vent that can be opened to allow air into the room when they aren't in use. When using air-conditioning, all windows and outside doors should obviously be closed. You may find that some air-conditioners are extremely noisy and you may need to switch them off at night to get to sleep. Free-standing air-conditioners can be rented on a monthly basis in summer.

If you live in an apartment block, heating is usually centrally controlled and is turned on in the autumn (fall) and off in the spring. Apartment buildings in some cities must, by law, be heated to specified minimum temperatures during the coldest months, e.g. in New York from October 1st to May 31st the temperature must be 68°F between 6am and 10pm and 55°F between 10pm and 6am. If you live in an apartment in a building with a centrally-controlled heating system, you may have no control over room temperatures, apart from turning individual radiators on or off (although most radiators have a gauge with low, medium and high settings). In some apartment buildings the cost of heating and air-conditioning is included in your rent. If you're required to pay for heating/cooling separately, check the average monthly cost.

Central heating dries the air and may cause your family to develop coughs and other ailments. Those who find the dry air unpleasant can increase the indoor relative humidity by adding moisture to the air with a humidifier, vaporiser, steam generator or even a water container made of porous ceramic. Humidifiers that don't generate steam should be disinfected occasionally. In climates where high humidity is a problem, you can buy a dehumidifier to circulate room air and reduce the humidity. Most utility companies publish useful booklets detailing how you can save money on cooling and heating costs, and will perform a free energy survey of your home.

REFUSE COLLECTION & DISPOSAL

Americans are the ultimate consumers and produce considerably more household refuse (garbage or trash) per head than any other nation (people in Third World countries could live quite well on what Americans throw away!). Kitchens in modern homes are usually fitted with waste-disposal units, which usually dispose of anything up to and including chicken bones. Some apartments have rubbish compactors. US homes have their own individual dustbins (trash cans) and apartment blocks have large communal bins. Refuse collection (pickup) is organised by local communities or city authorities and may be contracted to a private company; there are usually one or two collections a week. The cost is included in local property taxes or you're billed around $10 monthly or bi-monthly (perhaps with your water and sewerage bill). You may be billed separately for the months prior to a charge appearing on your tax bill. All rubbish must be put into plastic bags and tied, and dustbins may need to be placed in a certain place, e.g. by the road, at a particular time (if you put your rubbish out too early you can get a ticket!).

Although recycling in the US is limited compared with many European countries, it has become a prominent issue in recent years and many states have introduced recycling laws (although there's no restriction on the amount of rubbish you can generate in the first place!). Among the most environmentally-conscious states are New Jersey, California, Oregon, Connecticut and Minnesota. Generally all paper, e.g. newspapers and magazines, aluminium cans and glass **must** be recycled, and many communities also recycle corrugated cardboard, plastic bottles, steel cans, motor oil, batteries and vegetative material such as leaves, grass and other garden debris.

Waste for recycling is usually stored in containers, e.g. barrels, provided by communities and is collected on specific days by local authorities. Waste collection information and schedules are published and delivered to all residents. Household rubbish and items such as furniture are picked up on certain days, although hazardous waste may need to be taken to collection facilities. In some communities residents maintain their own recycling centres, where some waste is taken to sites staffed by community volunteers. This saves communities hundreds of thousands of dollars in landfill tipping fees, as well as generating revenue from the sale of recyclable materials.

6.

POSTAL SERVICES

In the US, letters and parcels are called mail, which is mailed in a mailbox (which also refers to the box outside a home where letters are deposited), and delivered by a mail carrier. The United States Postal Service (USPS) is a government monopoly and operates over 38,000 post offices, denoted by a blue sign bearing an eagle and the words US MAIL. There are no 'sub' post offices operated by private individuals in the US. Unlike the post office in many other countries, the USPS handles mail and sells money orders only; no other services are provided.

The USPS delivers over 540 million pieces of mail per day and around 202 billion a year, comprising an amazing 40 per cent of the world's mail. The delivery standards for first-class mail are next day delivery in the same metro area, two-day delivery within 600mi (965km) and three-day delivery over 600 miles. However, around 25 per cent of all mail is delivered late, including 5 to 10 per cent of first-class mail, although delivery times vary from region to region (and some 10 per cent of mail is delivered **earlier** than set by the standards). Delivery between major cities is generally quicker than to small towns, and a letter travelling between two major cities, e.g. New York and Los Angeles, may be delivered quicker than a letter mailed to a small town in a neighbouring state. Although some people would like to see an end to the USPS monopoly on mail deliveries, most acknowledge that considering the huge volume of mail it handles it doesn't do a bad job.

If you have a complaint about the USPS you can complete a *US Postal Service Consumer Service Card*, available from mail carriers and post offices, or you can phone a complaint in to your local post office. If your complaint cannot be resolved there, you can contact the Consumer Advocate, US Postal Service, 475 L'Enfant Plaza, Room 5821, SW, Washington, DC 20260-2200 (☎ 202-268-2284). The USPS publishes information on the internet (🖥 www.usps.gov) and there are a variety of helpful pamphlets available in most local post offices. For information about telegrams and fax, see page 176.

Except for the delivery of letters, most mail services are also provided by private mail, business and communications service companies such as Mail Boxes Etc. (the 'post office alternative') who have offices nationwide. Their services include mailboxes, mail-holding, mail forwarding, call-in service (24-hour access), stamps, envelopes, postcards, packing supplies, air shipping/receiving, postal metering, American Express money orders, Western Union money transfers, telegrams, mailgrams, cablegrams, computer letters, email, voicemail, fax (minute mail), telex, copy service, telephone message service, and numerous other business services. Mail Box Etc. (6060 Cornerstone Court West, San Diego, CA 92121, ☎ 858-455-8800, 🖥 www.mbe.com) offices are usually open from 9am until 6pm Monday to Friday and 9am to 3pm on Saturdays. The USPS operates a domestic guaranteed overnight express mail service, as do private companies such as DHL, Emery Worldwide, Federal Express and UPS (who also provide express international parcel services). Companies guarantee next day delivery for domestic express items mailed before a certain time of day and offer a money-back guarantee if the stated delivery times aren't met. Pick-up services are provided by the post office and private companies.

BUSINESS HOURS

Post office business hours in the US are usually from 9am to 5pm, Monday to Friday, and some offices are open on Saturdays, e.g. from 8am to noon. Main post offices in major towns don't close at lunch times. Some main post offices are open 24-hours Monday to Saturday for important services, with a self-service section for weighing packages and buying stamps. In rural areas and small towns, post offices may have restricted and varied business hours and may open any time between 8am and 9.30am until between 2pm and 5pm Monday to Friday, or may open for a few hours each morning only and perhaps a few hours on Saturdays.

Central post offices in large cities provide 24-hour self-service machines in the lobby, where you can find stamp and change machines, scales, tables of postage rates, and mailboxes large enough to accept parcels. All post offices are closed on Sundays and federal holidays. Try to avoid post offices at lunch times and after 4pm when offices send their mail.

LETTERS & PARCELS

Domestic post in the US can be sent by express mail, priority mail, first-class mail or parcel post.

Express Mail

If you want a letter or parcel (up to 70lb/32kg) to arrive the next day, you must use express mail. The minimum rate is $13.65 for a letter weighing up to 8oz (225g); a parcel weighing 5lbs (2.2kg) costs twice that amount. Mail sent before 5pm between major business markets is guaranteed delivery by noon next day or by 3pm to other areas, as listed in the *Express Mail Next Day Service Network Directory*. The express mail service has a full money-back postage guarantee and merchandise is automatically insured for up to $500 against loss or damage. Other express mail services include merchandise and document reconstruction insurance (up to $50,000), shipping containers, shipment receipt, special collection boxes, return receipt service, collect-on-delivery (COD) service, and waiver of signature. There are over 27,000 express mail boxes throughout the US.

The post office also provides an express mail international service, called Global Express, to over 200 countries. It's possible to send letters or printed papers (up to 2kg), small packets (1kg) and books and pamphlets (5kg) by express mail to most countries, although this service isn't available from all post offices.

Priority Mail

Priority mail is delivered within two days (excluding Sundays) to most destinations and costs a minimum of $3.85 for items up to 1lb (450g). The 1lb rate applies for items of any weight, provided they fit inside the envelope provided. Post offices provide priority mail stickers, labels, envelopes and boxes, at no extra charge.

First-class Mail

Most correspondence is sent first-class, which is an air mail service costing 37 cents for the first ounce (25g) and an extra 23 cents for each additional ounce or fraction of an ounce, up to 13oz (330g) and the maximum charge of $3.13. Domestic mail weighing over 13oz and up to 70lb (32kg – the maximum permitted weight) is categorised as priority mail (see above). There are minimum and maximum sizes for letters.

Standard Mail

Standard mail (A) is a business service for newspapers, magazines and other periodicals (it cannot be used by the general public). Standard mail (B) is for parcels weighing 1lb or more.

Parcel Post

Circulars, books, catalogues and other printed matter (up to 70lbs/32kg) can be sent by parcel post. Rates are based on the weight, distance and shape of the package, and start at around $4.00 for items up to 1lb (450 g). Each item should be marked 'Parcel Post'.

Private parcel delivery services are operated by companies such as DHL, Emery, United Parcel Service (UPS) and Federal Express. These companies provide a next day air parcel service within the US and Puerto Rico, second day domestic air services, and international document and parcel services to over 180 countries and territories world-wide. Parcels can also be sent through postal, business and communication services, such as Mail Boxes Etc., who have offices nationwide.

Special mail rates apply to books, CDs, video tapes and 'recordings', called Media Mail and there are other rates for library books, publications or records for the blind, and certain controlled-circulation publications.

Postcards can be sent within the US for 23 cents and stamped cards can be bought for 25 cents. Rate tables are available from post offices and there's a postage calculator on the USPS internet site (🖳 www.usps.gov), as well as rate tables and information booklets for downloading.

International Post

There are four main categories of international mail: Global Express Guaranteed (which is an 'expedited' service), Global Express Mail (a 'high-speed' service), Global Priority Mail (an 'accelerated' service), and Letter-post (which presumably travels at normal speed).

Global Express Guaranteed

Global Express Guaranteed (GXG) can be used for sending documents and merchandise ('non-documents') to over 200 countries and costs from $24 for items up to 8oz (225g), including insurance up to $100 (for each additional $100 insurance, you pay an extra 70 cents up to a maximum 'document reconstruction' value of $2,500). There's a weight limit of 70lb (32kg).

Global Express Mail

Global Express Mail (known as EMS **not** GEM) is limited to around 175 countries, but includes insurance up to $500 (which can be extended to $5,000). The service costs from $15.50 for items up to 8oz (225g). Weight limits vary according to the destination, but are normally 44lbs (20kg).

Global Priority Mail

Global Priority Mail (GPM) can be used for certain countries in the Americas, Western Europe, the Middle East and Africa. Charges start at $6 for items up to 8oz (225g) and there's a weight limit of 4lbs (1.8kg). Flat-rate envelopes are available costing between $4 and $9 depending on the size and destination.

Letter-post

The standard service for items up to 4lbs (1.8kg) is Letter-post. All items up to 2lbs (900g) are automatically sent by airmail; items between 2lbs and 4lbs (1.8kg) may be sent airmail or surface mail (known as Economy). There are five price bands for various destinations, e.g. one for Canada, one for Mexico and one for Australia, Japan and New Zealand. The charge for sending a letter up to 1oz (28g) is between 60 cents and 80 cents; a 2lb (900g) parcel costs from $6.35 airmail or $5.60 economy. International postcards cost 50 cents to Canada and Mexico and 70 cents to all other countries. Aerogrammes (pre-paid airmail letters) cost 70 cents to all countries and are available from post offices and stationery shops.

Ask at your local post office for further information or use the USPS online rate calculator (💻 www.usps.gov).

General Information

Note the following when mailing letters and parcels in the US:

● If a post office considers that a parcel doesn't meet postal regulations they won't accept it until it's re-wrapped (not that any amount of protection will guarantee it won't be crushed in the mail). Generally, parcels should be secured with brown tape or 'strapping tape' which can be purchased from stationers, supermarkets and pharmacies. If you use any other method, e.g. string, adhesive tape, boxes and brown paper, post office staff may ask you to rewrap it, no matter how securely it's wrapped. If you're in any doubt, enquire in advance. Post offices sell a wide variety of packaging products, including tape, envelopes, padded bags, corrugated boxes, mailing tubes and cushioning material.

Parcels sent to addresses outside the US must be accompanied by a customs declaration form. Requirements in certain countries are met by using an adhesive form PP69, which is a combined customs and dispatch note. If the item being sent is of 'no commercial value' (NCV), you should write this on the customs form under 'value'. All forms are available from post offices. When sending such things as drawings, large photographs or paintings through the mail, **sandwich them between cardboard to prevent them being bent (writing 'Do Not Bend' is an open invitation to do just that!).** All parcels must be securely wrapped.

- You can rent a post office box with a lock for a small fee (varies considerably) at many post offices and collect your mail any time the post office lobby is open. A caller (pickup) service is also available during post office hours for customers who receive a large volume of mail or who need a box number address when no boxes are available.

- Affix airmail labels (available free from post offices) to all international airmail. Alternatively you can write or stamp 'PAR AVION – BY AIR MAIL' to the left and slightly above the mailing address. If first class mail isn't letter-sized, mark it 'first-class' or use a green diamond-bordered envelope.

- You can receive mail free of charge via any post office in the US through 'general delivery' (called *poste restante* in most other countries). Mail should be addressed as follows: Name, c/o General Delivery, Town, State and Zip Code (if known). General delivery mail is kept at a town's main post office (if there's more than one) and is returned to the sender if it's unclaimed after 30 days. Therefore when sending mail via general delivery, always put a return address on the envelope. You can also write 'hold for 30 days' on the envelope, although mail should automatically be kept for 30 days. Identification is necessary for collection and some post offices ask for two forms of identification, e.g. passport, green card, driver's licence or credit card.

  If you have an American Express card or use American Express travellers' cheques, you can have mail sent to an American Express office. Standard letters are held free of charge (registered letters and packages aren't accepted). Mail addressed to an Amex office should be marked 'client mail service' and is kept for 30 days before being returned to the sender. Mail can be forwarded to another office or address, but there's a charge. American Automobile Association (AAA) members can have their mail held free of charge at any AAA office, if marked 'hold for arrival'. Other organisations also provide mail holding services for members.

- If you have mail sent to you at a temporary private address in the US, have it addressed c/o the regular occupants. Otherwise the mail carrier may return it to the sender (he knows you don't live there). If a letter cannot be delivered it is returned stamped 'return to sender, 'not deliverable as addressed' or 'moved not forwardable' (or something similar). All mail should have a return address in case it cannot be delivered (you can have a name and address stamp made).

- Mailboxes are dark blue with a red and white stripe, bear the US Mail eagle logo in white lettering, and look like dustbins on legs (perhaps they're designed as junk mail repositories!). They're often located on street corners in cities, where many are positioned so that motorists can post letters without getting out of their cars (everything in the US is designed to ensure that motorists don't need to get out of their cars). Most mailboxes have a flap with a handle (which may be invisible from the top of the box) that you pull back to open the slot where mail is deposited. For security reasons, you may not mail any item weighing more than 1lb (450g) from a public mailbox. (Anything larger than this must be taken to a post office for mailing.) There are also mailboxes at railway stations, airports and in hotel lobbies. These are often simply a slot in a wall marked 'US MAIL'. Mail is also collected from private homes, post offices and businesses.

● In the suburbs and rural areas there may be no mailboxes, as mail is collected by the mail carrier when he does his rounds. In some areas, particularly where there are large houses with long driveways, houses have delivery/collection boxes located at the end of the drive. These have a small flag (a metal arm) which is raised to indicate to the mail carrier that there's mail to be collected. In apartment blocks there are usually rows of mailboxes in the foyer or entrance hall for residents' mail and a mailbox where residents can mail letters. In the suburbs there's one delivery/collection a day only. In city centres there may be a number of collections a day with the last collection at around 6pm or earlier on weekends. In most areas there's one delivery a day, in the morning or mid-afternoon, excluding Sundays and holidays. In some remote rural areas there's no mail delivery service and all mail must be collected from the local post office.

● When you receive mail from overseas on which duty is payable, the duty may be collected by the postal service, along with customs clearance and delivery fees on dutiable items. On packages containing dutiable articles, the customs officer attaches a customs form CF 3419 showing the tariff item number, rate of duty and the amount of duty to be paid. A customs processing fee of $5 is levied on all dutiable mail shipments. Packages that are passed by customs free of duty are endorsed 'Passed Free – US Customs'. Mail shipments unclaimed within 30 days are returned to the sender unless a duty assessment is being protested. For further information, obtain a copy of *US Customs International Mail Imports* from any customs office.

● Most mail in the US is sorted by machine, which is expedited by the use of full and correct postal addresses. The USPS divides the US into ten geographical zones, each consisting of three or more states and/or territories. Each area is identified by a digit (0 to 9) which is the first digit of a five-digit zip (zone improvement plan) code (numbered from 00001 to 99999, going from east to west) identifying a region, city or part of a city. In 1983, an extra four digits were added to zip codes (ZIP+4 code) to further identify addresses (of particular benefit to business mailers), although many people still don't bother to use them (in many cases, they don't even know what their full code is!). The zip code follows the state name or initials, as shown in the example below:

Elmer Whitmore Rand Jr
9753 Gold Rush Avenue
Suite 9423
Noname City
AZ 98765-1234
USA

The United States of America is usually written as USA (or U.S.A.). If you don't know your zip code or want to find someone else's, you can consult the official

US Zip Code & Post Office Directory, available at all main post offices or online. Other zip code directories include the *United States Zip Code Atlas* (American Map Corporation) and the *Rand McNally Zip Code Finder*. A list of local state zip codes is usually included at the back of local telephone directories. It doesn't, however, list all codes for cities with more than one code. Local zip codes may be shown on a map in telephone directories. Mail without a zip code may take longer to be delivered or may be lost entirely. When a PO Box number and street address are used, mail is delivered to the place indicated on the line immediately above the city, state and zip code line. The USPS has introduced a bar code system to speed up the reading of zip codes.

● When zip codes were established in 1963, two-letter state and territory abbreviations were also introduced. The following table lists the main codes:

Alabama	AL	Kentucky	KY	Ohio	OH
Alaska	AK	Louisiana	LA	Oklahoma	OK
Arizona	AZ	Maine	ME	Oregon	OR
Arkansas	AR	Maryland	MD	Pennsylvania	PA
American Samoa	AS	Massachusetts	MA	Puerto Rico	PR
California	CA	Michigan	MI	Rhode Island	RI
Colorado	CO	Minnesota	MN	South Carolina	SC
Connecticut	CT	Mississippi	MS	South Dakota	SD
Delaware	DE	Missouri	MO	Tennessee	TN
Dist of Columbia	DC	Montana	MT	Texas	TX
Florida	FL	Nebraska	NE	Utah	UT
Georgia	GA	Nevada	NV	Vermont	VT
Guam	GU	New Hampshire	NH	Virginia	VA
Hawaii	HI	New Jersey	NJ	Virgin Islands	VI
Idaho	ID	New Mexico	NM	Washington	WA
Illinois	IL	New York	NY	West Virginia	WV
Indiana	IN	North Carolina	NC	Wisconsin	WI
Iowa	IA	North Dakota	ND	Wyoming	WY
Kansas	KS	N. Mariana Is.	MP		

● Stamps can be purchased from vending machines (when not out of order) located in or outside post offices, airports, bus and rail stations, drugstores, banks and hotels. Many post offices have self-service machines (some of which may accept up to $20 bills) where stamps, stamp booklets, express mail stamps, postcards, and stamped envelopes are available. Some stamp machines also accept bank cards. In the US spirit of free enterprise, a (sometimes hefty) surcharge is usually levied when stamps are purchased anywhere other than at a post office. Prices vary, but they may cost 50 cents for a 37 cent stamp, or $1 for 4 x 20 cent stamps or 2 x 37 cent stamps, e.g. in hotels. Stamps can also be bought at shops such as stationers or drugstores selling postcards, usually for a 25 per cent surcharge (although some sell them at face value). Shops selling stamps exhibit a Stamps To Go logo. Whenever possible, buy stamps from a post office in booklets of 10 x 37 cent ($3.70), 20 x 37 cent ($7.40) and 20 x 20 cent ($4).

Under the 'easy stamp' service, many businesses offer stamps at face value. Other easy stamp services include the purchase of stamps, postcards and stamped envelopes by mail using a *Stamps by Mail Order Form*, available from post offices or from your mail carrier. Stamps can also be ordered by phone using a Discover, MasterCard or Visa credit card (☎ 1-800-STAMP24 or 1-800-782-6724) or online at the USPS store site (🖳 http://shop.usps.com). Small businesses (or even individuals) can subscribe to a program to print their own stamps on their computer printer. See the PC Postage programme on the USPS website.

Post offices also sell pre-stamped envelopes ($2.10 for a pack of 5) and single (20 cents) and double (reply) postcards (40 cents or 20 cents for each half). The reply half of a double postcard doesn't need to bear postage when originally mailed.

- Domestic money orders can be purchased from post offices for any value from 1 cent to $1000, for a fee of 90 cents for money orders up to $500, and $1.25 for $500.01 to $1000. International money orders up to a maximum value of $700 can also be purchased for certain countries (around 30 at present), for a $3.25 fee.

- Like many countries, the US provides services for philatelists. Post offices sell philatelic products such as first-day covers, stamp collecting kits, the Postal Service Guide to US Stamps, and mint sets of commemorative and special stamps. A free mail order catalogue of philatelic services is available from Stamp Fulfillment Service, US Postal Service, PO Box 419424, Kansas City, MO 64179-0997.

- It's a federal offence to tamper with anyone's mail, which may explain the proliferation of apparently unprotected mailboxes outside American homes. The USPS also claims a monopoly on the use of your mailbox, and it's illegal for anyone other than a mail carrier to place anything in your mailbox that hasn't travelled through the US postal system. This includes neighbours dropping off keys or personal notes, and if the mail carrier finds unauthorised items in your mail box, he can remove them without your permission or knowledge.

- Finally, carefully check all your mail and don't throw anything away unless you're certain it's junk mail (unsolicited direct mail, circulars, free newspapers, etc.). It isn't unknown for foreigners to throw away important correspondence during their first few weeks in the US (with luck some bills will be included!). Look for real letters mixed with your junk mail. Americans receive vast amounts of junk mail and if you would like to receive less (unfortunately there's no way of receiving none at all!) you can register with the Mail Preference Service (MPS). After registration you continue to receive mail from companies with which you do business and from charities and organisations that aren't subscribers to MPS. However, the amount of 'rubbish' you receive in your mailbox should be less. Send a letter or postcard, including your name, home address and signature to

Mail Preference Service, Direct Marketing Association, PO Box 643, Carmel, NY 15012-0643 or follow the instructions for MPS enrolment on the DMA website (💻 www.the-dma.org).

VALUABLES & IMPORTANT DOCUMENTS

The US post office provides a number of services for the delivery of valuables and important documents and letters:

Registered Mail

The safest way to send valuables is by registered mail. The cost depends on the value of your mailing, which must be declared when mailed, and whether you decide to insure it (recommended). For an additional fee, a receipt can be obtained stating when, where and to whom your mailing was delivered. The fee for registered mail is $8.00 (including insurance) for items valued up to $100, $8.85 for values from $100 to $500, and $9.70 for values from $500 to $1,000. Rates for values up to $25,000 can be obtained from post offices. Registered mail to Canada is subject to a limit of $1,000 and to all other countries the limit is $40.45 only. First-class or priority mail postage is necessary for domestic registered mail.

Insurance

Domestic mail can be insured for the following fees (payable in addition to postage): liability up to $50 (fee $1.30), $50.01 to $100 ($2.20), $100.01 upwards at $3.20 plus $1 for each additional $100 or fraction thereof (up to a maximum of $5,000). Insurance is available for **merchandise** sent as first-class mail only. You can insure mail for up to $200 online, but for values greater than that, you must go to a post office and fill out the appropriate insurance forms.

Collect on Delivery

Priority domestic letters and parcels can be sent collect on delivery (COD), where the combined price of the article and the cost of postage is collected from the addressee, up to the maximum value of $1,000. Ask at a post office for fees ($4.50 to $14.50, including insurance, depending on the amount) and mailing conditions.

Certified Mail

Certified mail provides the sender with a postage receipt and an identifying number for the item. The delivery must be signed for and a record of delivery is maintained at the receiving post office (no record is kept at the post office where mailed). It costs $2.30 in addition to postage and is available for first-class and priority mail. A certificate of mailing proves that an item was mailed and is available for a fee of 90 cents, but no record is maintained at the post office. You can limit delivery to the addressee or an authorised agent ('restricted delivery') for a fee of $3.50 plus postage. Certified mail isn't available for international mail, nor does it provide insurance protection.

Return Receipt

You can obtain a return receipt (proof of delivery) for COD, express, certified, insured (for over $50) and registered mail. A receipt showing the date, to whom delivered, signature, and the addressee's address (if different) costs $1.75, provided it's requested at the time of mailing. A delivery record (showing the date and to whom delivered) requested after mailing costs $3.25. A return receipt for merchandise showing the date and to whom delivered costs $1.50 and $3.00 for a delivery record.

Recorded Delivery

A recorded delivery service is available for international mail and is intended for letters, documents and items of little or no commercial value. It's for those who wish to know that a record of delivery exists, should it be necessary. For an additional fee you can purchase a return receipt at the time of mailing.

Special Handling

A special handling fee ensures that first-class mail, priority mail and parcel post are given 'preferential handling' (but not necessarily preferential delivery!). The fee in addition to postage is $5.95 up to 10lb and $8.25 over 10lb. Special handling doesn't mean special handling for fragile items, which should be packed with adequate cushioning and marked FRAGILE in **BIG** letters!

Should you need to make a claim for lost or damaged mail, obtain a copy of the *Customer Guide to Filing Indemnity Claims on Domestic Mail* from any post office.

CHANGE OF ADDRESS

Before you move home you should complete a *Change of Address* card (PS form 3575) at your local post office. You will receive a free change of address kit, including postcards to notify correspondents of your new address or you can use the online service (💻 www.usps.com/moversguide). Whenever possible, notify your local post office at least one month before you move and make sure that the effective date is entered on notification forms. First-class mail is forwarded free of charge for one year and second-class mail (including magazines and newspapers) is forwarded free of charge for 60 days from the date of the change of address order. When the forwarding time expires, mail is returned to the sender (including international mail). So don't forget to notify all correspondents of your new address well in advance. Publishers of periodicals usually need at least six weeks' notice to effect a change of address.

If you're going to be away from your home for a period of up to 30 days, you can have the post office hold your mail free of charge until you return. You can then pick up your mail or have it delivered. You must complete an *Authorization to Hold Mail* card at your local post office. If you receive mail for the previous occupants of a dwelling or office, or mail that isn't addressed to you, you have two choices regarding what to do with it (the third is to throw it away, which is illegal!). You can send it on to the addressee by crossing out your address, writing the new or correct address and dropping it in a mailbox, without a stamp. Or, if you don't know the addressee's new address, you can cross out the address and write 'Address Unknown' and drop it in a mailbox.

If you complete a change of address form, all your junk mail (which earns the post office $8 billion annually) automatically follows you, as the USPS sells its mailing list (including every change of address form) to companies.

UNSOLICITED MAIL & MAIL FRAUD

If you receive any unsolicited goods, don't use them unless you intend to keep and pay for them, and don't pay for any unsolicited goods sent cash on delivery (COD). Unsolicited goods may be returned without paying postage or can be kept until reclaimed. One of the most common practices in the US is for charities and organisations to mail unsolicited greetings cards and address stickers in return for a 'donation'. You may receive these several times a year from numerous charities. You aren't required to pay for them and can return them without a stamp, throw them away or use them **without** making a donation.

Beware of confidence tricksters who use unsolicited mail or adverts (such as work-at-home scams) to attract unsuspecting customers. Fraudulent mail promotions include sweepstakes and notices of prizes that require you to call a 900 number or buy a product; mailings that are made to look like they're from official government agencies; classified 'employment' or 'business opportunity' advertisements promising easy money for little work; and prize awards that ask for your credit card or bank account number. **Never forget that any mail offer that sounds too good to be true almost certainly is.** US postal inspectors warn you to be wary of scams requiring you to pay money before you know exactly what's involved. One of the sickest forms of mail fraud is a chain letter, which plays on superstitions and threatens people with dire consequences if they 'break the chain'. Chain letters are illegal and if you receive one you should hand it in at your local post office.

The sale of mailing lists is big business in the US and many companies sell or rent their mailing lists to non-competitor companies. If you receive unsolicited mail you don't want, you can demand that a company remove your name from their mailing list. For the rules regarding mail order, see **Mail-order & Internet Shopping** on page 492. The postal inspection service acts to protect you from mail fraud and publishes a brochure, *Postal Inspectors Protect Consumers*, to alert you to some of the most common mail fraud schemes. If you believe you've been the victim of mail fraud, send the details and all relevant documentation to the Postal Inspection Service, Consumer Protection Program, c/o Local Postmaster.

7.

TELEPHONE

A mericans are the most habitual telephone users in the world (some Americans have telephones permanently attached to their ears) and they make twice as many calls as people in most other countries. Some 98 per cent of Americans own a telephone (around 60 percent of homes have three or more) and around one third have an answering machine. The US telephone system is the most modern and cheapest in the world. Lines are generally clear, calls almost always go through first time, and you can get a telephone installed within a few days in most towns and cities. Thanks to new technology, customers can now use one line for voice, faxing and the internet, simultaneously!

American Telephone & Telegraph (AT&T) lost its 70-year monopoly in 1984. The increased competition in the long-distance telephone market (where more than 1200 companies compete) has resulted in call rates being driven down by 50 per cent, although local call rates have increased. In many, if not most, states the Baby Bells (the companies that took over most of AT&T's assets) no longer hold a strict monopoly on local services now that they're required to lease lines to competing providers. In recent years, the Baby Bells have been merging and can now offer long-distance calls. AT&T remains the leading long-distance telephone company, although their market share has been sliding in the past few years, followed by Worldcom (formerly MCI) and now Verizon has overtaken Sprint for third place. Verizon itself was created in 2000 when Bell Atlantic merged with General Telephone and Electric (GTE). Other telephone service providers include Capsule Communications (formerly US Wats), Planet Earth Communications (PEC) and SBC. Rates for domestic long-distance and international calls vary according to the telephone company, and one company may be cheaper for long-distance calls, but more expensive for international calls. Telephone companies are branching out into other areas and have already won approval to send news and advertising over telephone lines, and are starting to be allowed to send television signals over their lines.

In addition to traditional telephone services (so-called 'landline' or 'wireline' services), there are mobile phone (cell phone or wireless) providers and a variety of broadband internet service providers. Many telephone companies are now providing bundled services, which include local and long-distance with mobile phones and broadband internet services (including VoIP, telephone via the internet).

There have been telephone number changes in many states in recent years, as a result of telephone companies running out of numbers to allocate to new subscribers. If you have a problem contacting a subscriber, contact directory enquiries (assistance) (see **Operator Services** on page 168). **Emergency numbers are listed at the front of most telephone directories** (see page 177).

INSTALLATION & REGISTRATION

Homes in the US (new and old) are invariably wired for telephone services, although a telephone won't usually be provided when you move into a new home. Many US homes have telephone points in almost every room, although you should check the number and type of telephone points in advance. If you need additional wiring or points you can have it done by a local telephone company, a contractor or you can do it yourself. When not doing it yourself, obtain quotations from a number of companies. Installation of one jack plus wiring for a touch-tone telephone usually costs between $50 and $100.

If the latest modular jacks are already installed, you can simply plug your telephone in directly. The older type of jacks can easily be converted to a modular system by buying a four-prong-to-modular adapter or a modular jack (available from most telephone retailers). Books and leaflets explaining how to install modular jacks are available. However, you should check to see that your telephone company has installed a 'network interface jack', which allows you to disconnect your telephone wiring while you're working on the wires. If after changing the jacks your telephone doesn't work, check that they've been properly installed, because if you report a fault to your telephone company and there's nothing wrong with the line, you may need to pay for the serviceman's visit. If you suspect the telephone is at fault, check it by connecting it to another jack or attaching it to a neighbour's line. The local telephone company is responsible for the wiring only as far as the network interface jack, usually mounted on the outside of the house or building. Once the wires enter your home, they're your responsibility, although problems with interior telephone wiring are rare.

To have a telephone connected, contact the local telephone company (their number is listed in telephone directories under 'Customer or Consumer Guide'). You usually need to provide the following information:

- Your name;
- Your full address, including street and number (apartment number if applicable), town or city;
- The name of the former occupant or the previous telephone number (if available);
- Information about your previous telephone service, such as the telephone number and location;
- The type of monthly service you require;
- The social security number of the person to be billed;
- Credit information (if applicable), including employment details;
- A description of the types of telephone outlets (if any) at your new address;
- Your choice of long-distance company or the type of service bundle you would like from the local telephone company;
- How you would like your directory listing to appear, or whether you would like an ex-directory (unlisted) number (see page 175).

If you aren't a previous customer and are unable to establish credit, a deposit is required, usually equal to two months' estimated charges (you may be able to have an existing customer guarantee your bill payments). If your actual monthly usage is three times the estimated usage, you may also be asked for an additional deposit. The deposit earns interest and is returned within six months or one year, provided your telephone bills are paid on time.

You usually need to give only a few days notice for connection, for which there's a charge (depending on the telephone company) that's included on your first monthly bill, usually around $50 to $70. You're given a number when you apply. Many telephone companies don't rent or sell telephones and in any case it's usually cheaper to buy one from a retailer (see **Choosing a Telephone** below). All telephone company personnel carry identification cards, so if you're ever in doubt about a workman's identity, ask to see his identification.

CHOOSING A TELEPHONE

You aren't required to rent or purchase a telephone from your local telephone company and can buy one from any retailer. All telephones must be approved by the Federal Communications Commission (FCC). This is indicated by two numbers usually printed on a label on the bottom or back of the telephone; the 'FCC registration number', which certifies that the telephone won't damage the network, and the 'ringer equivalence number', which indicates how much ringing current the telephone requires. The ringer equivalence number allows you (or your telephone company) to calculate the maximum number of telephones that can be installed on a single telephone line. You may need these numbers when reporting a line fault to the telephone company. If a telephone doesn't have these numbers, contact your telephone company **before** connecting it to your telephone line.

There are two types of telephones; those that operate on the tone or Touch-Tone (trademark of AT&T) system where each key emits a different musical tone when pressed, and pulse telephones. Most homes now have tone telephones and many banks, credit-card companies and other organisations employ automatic systems which require them. However, before buying a tone telephone, make sure that your local telephone company provides tone lines, otherwise a tone telephone won't work (although a tone telephone may be switchable to pulse). You can also buy a tone adapter which converts a pulse tone telephone to tone operation. Pulse telephones are universal and work on pulse or tone lines. Old rotary-dial telephones usually work on the pulse system.

Renting a telephone is expensive, so it's better to purchase one which you can take with you if you move home. The price of a telephone usually depends on the quality of its construction (the most important attribute), country of origin, and not least, its features. A standard one-piece electronic telephone (with the keys on the handset) costs from $10, a basic cordless telephone with caller identification can be had for as little as $30, and a cordless with a built-in answering machine and speakerphone facility costs from $90. If you want an all-singing, all-dancing, wake-me-up-and-shave-me model, expect to pay around $200. Before buying a telephone, check prices and features as they vary considerably. Compare telephones from a number of retailers, and if possible, test them before buying (or buy from a retailer who provides a money-back guarantee). Also check the warranty period, e.g. 90 days to five years, and its terms before making a purchase and ask about local service facilities and parts availability. Buy a telephone with a modular (replaceable) cord rather than one that's permanently wired (in which case if the cord breaks the telephone is out of service).

Typical features of multi-function, electronic telephones include a mute (privacy) button (which allows you to talk to someone in the room without being heard by the caller); hold button or melody-on-hold, which 'entertains' the caller with 'muzak'; ringer selector, which lets you select or adjust the volume of the ring or even turn it off (when a light indicates ringing); a built-in loudspeaker (speaker-phone), so you can talk and listen without using the handset (hands-free); on-hook dialling; memory (speed dialling); automatic redial or last number dialled (LND); an LCD readout so that you can check the number dialled, the elapsed time of a call or the time of day; and an intercom system.

Telephone accessories include answering machines; headsets that allow hands-free operation; auto-diallers that can store hundreds of numbers and other information; amplifiers (for group discussions); locks to prevent unauthorised use; ringer cut-off switches (silencers); home controllers (to control lights and appliances by telephone) and security systems (which monitor fire, loss of electricity, floods, burglar intrusion, etc.); modems to connect to a home computer; and modular cords and 'T' adapters to connect accessories. You can also buy a two-line telephone which can be switched back and forth between business and personal numbers. Cordless telephones are popular. The handset can be operated from 100 feet (short range) up to 1,000 feet (long range) from the base station, depending on where they're used. If you're planning to buy a cordless telephone, make sure that it has a battery backup so it still works when there's a power failure. You should buy a cordless telephone with a lockout security feature. This ensures that when you place the handset in the base station, another cordless user cannot dial into your base station. If you're planning on having a Wi-Fi wireless computer network in your home, you will want to get one of the latest 5.8Ghz models, to avoid potential interference that affects 2.4 Ghz phones. (See also **Mobile Phones & Pagers** on page 175.)

USING THE TELEPHONE

Using a telephone in the US is much the same as in any other country, with the exception of a few American idiosyncrasies. Telephone numbers consist of a three-digit area code (123), a three-digit exchange code (456) and a four-digit subscriber number (7890), written variously as (123) 456-7890 (standard), 123/456-7890 or most commonly 123-456-7890 (as in this book). An area code may cover a part of a large city (212 covers parts of Manhattan, New York), a Metropolitan area (213 is the city of Los Angeles) or an entire state (207 is Maine). Canada uses the same code system as the US and area codes for the US and Canada are shown on maps in telephone directories. Many Caribbean islands and most of Central America also use the same code system and you could wind up with large international calling charges if you mistakenly assume that all numbers with the US format are national calls.

If you're making a call to a number within your local calling or service area, you may be able to dial the last seven digits only. More and more areas are now changing to 10-digit dialling, where you must dial the area code for all local calls, even if you're calling your next door neighbour. When making a call with the same area code but outside your local service area, you dial 1 + the ten-digit telephone number. If in doubt, dial the '1' anyway; if it isn't required, it is ignored (if you forget to dial it and it is required, a recorded message reminds you). When making a call to another area code, you dial 1 + area code + the seven-digit telephone number. Local calling and service areas are shown in telephone directories and may comprise towns in several different area codes.

Calls outside your local service area are called toll calls and are handled by a long-distance telephone company. In the US, states or regions are served by various local telephone companies, such as Verizon or SBC, regulated by state and federal agencies. For long-distance, e.g. interstate and international calls, there are independent long-distance telephone companies, such as AT&T, Worldcom and Sprint, although the local telephone companies generally offer their own range of intrastate and long-distance services to complement the local service. Most areas are served by a number of long-distance companies, although some have only one. You must designate (or pre-subscribe) a primary long-distance company when you apply to be connected and all calls made by dialling 1 (or 0) plus an area code are routed through that company. If you wish to place a call via an alternate long-distance company, you must make arrangements with that company. Be careful of a practice known as 'slamming' which involves the changing of your phone service to a different (usually more expensive) provider without your permission. Scam artists hide service change authorisations in the fine print of contest entry forms or conceal change requests in the rapid patter of a high pressure telemarketing call. The Federal Communications Commission offers information and advice on slamming and other forms of telephone fraud on its website (🖳 www.fcc.gov/cpb) under 'consumer alerts and factsheets'.

When you call a company or business number, you're likely to be connected to a recorded message stating that 'all lines are busy at the moment' and asking you to hold. Then you're connected to soothing muzak intended to keep you entertained until someone comes on the line. It's perhaps marginally preferable to getting an engaged signal or an answering machine, provided you have lots of time and money or it's a toll-free 800 number (see below). Many companies now make use of an automated call handling system, which transfers your call according to your responses to a menu of topics. ('Press one for customer service, press two for human resources, or stay on the line to be connected to an operator.') It's often difficult to get through to companies during peak business hours and you can wait a long time to be put through to the person or department required. Answering machines or voicemail systems are widely used in the US.

All telephone companies provide services for those with disabilities, including hearing and speech impaired customers, who are exempt from certain charges. There are also programmes available to low-income individuals and families to assure minimum telephone services. Handsets are available for the blind (with a nodule on the figure 5) and extra large key pads for the partially sighted. Telephones fitted with a flashing light, loud ring, a built-in amplifier or an inductive coupler (for those with behind-the-ear hearing aids) are available for the hard of hearing. A number of companies and organisations provide a Telecommunications Device for the Deaf (TDD) or teletype (TTY) line. These are typewriter-like devices that permit people with hearing or speaking difficulties to communicate via telephone lines and now there are systems for 'translating' between TTY systems and voice telephones. Ask your telephone company about TDD or other special services or check the FCC website (above) for their consumer factsheets on making telephone services accessible to everyone.

If you receive malicious or obscene telephone calls, you should hang up immediately. Never give your name or address to unknown callers and advise your children not to give personal information to strangers. You may be able to arrange for the operator to intercept calls for a limited period and your telephone company may also be able to stop all incoming calls to your number, while allowing outgoing calls only. Other measures include getting an ex-directory number. 'Caller ID' and 'call trace' services (see page 167) can help you identify or trace a caller. You can also buy an answering machine, allowing you to decide whether you wish to answer the telephone or not.

Most telephone companies offer an answering service or 'message centre'. This may be less expensive and more efficient than having your own answering machine. Features usually include timed messages, the ability to receive messages when you're on another call and the facility to erase messages selectively. Every member of a household can have a separate extension mailbox with a security code (so your messages are private and you don't have to listen to other people's messages). The cost is usually around $5 per month plus a start-up fee of around $10. In most cities you can employ a telephone answering service to answer your calls. They can have your telephone company connect your line to their service, for which they charge a one-time fee, or can assign you a new number. Answering services offer a choice of options and services, usually costing a minimum of $50 a month. If you just want to receive messages when you're away from your home or office, it may be cheaper to buy an answering machine or use a telephone company's answering service.

A major problem in recent years has been the increase in unwanted telemarketing calls, which usually seem to come in just as the family is sitting down to dinner, or at some equally inconvenient time. In 2003, the FTC and the FCC set up the National Do Not Call Registry, where you can register your home phone number as being unavailable to telemarketers and certain other sorts of unsolicited phone calls. (Business numbers aren't eligible to be placed on the Do Not Call register.) You can register by calling the FTC toll-free number (☎ 1-888-382-1222) or registering online at the Do Not Call List website (🖳 www.donotcall.gov). The law establishing the Do Not Call List exempted certain types of calls, most notably those from businesses with which you have a current relationship (i.e. where you have purchased something from them within the last few months), most charitable and religious organisations and political campaigns. (Laws do have to be passed by politicians, after all.) Registration is valid for five years.

When dictating numbers over the telephone, dictate one digit at a time, including repeated numbers, e.g. 11-222, **isn't** given as double one, treble two, but as one-one-two-two-two. Zero is usually read as the letter 'O' (oh).

TOLL-FREE NUMBERS

Toll-free numbers are indicated by one of four prefixes (800, 866, 877 or 888) and are provided by businesses, organisations and government agencies. For many years, 800 was the only toll-free prefix, so that the term '800 number' is now applied to all toll-free numbers, irrespective of the prefix used. Many organisations and businesses list their toll-free numbers in all correspondence, advertisements and on all documentation, and they're usually listed in directories alongside ordinary numbers. Most toll-free numbers are for interstate callers only and must be prefixed with a '1' (a local number is usually provided for in-state callers). Many 800 numbers can also be accessed from outside the US, although calls aren't usually free.

You can also obtain an 800 or 1-800 number for a residential line so that family members can call free from anywhere in the US and save money. This service is provided by a number of operators, e.g. AT&T, and by Call Home America (part of Global Crossing Communications, 1120 Pittsford-Victor Road, Pittsford, NY 14534, 🖳 www.callhomeamerica.com). Sometimes toll-free numbers are given as letters to make them easier to remember, e.g. ☎ 1-800-USA-RAIL for Amtrak. All telephones are marked with letters and numbers, so you just dial the number or press the key corresponding to a letter. For information about toll-free numbers, call the national toll-free directory assistance number (☎ 1-800-555-1212). **Some 800 series numbers are area codes and may indicate that you're calling a Caribbean island or Central America rather than a toll-free number!**

PREMIUM RATE NUMBERS

Don't confuse toll-free 800 numbers with 700 or 900 information or entertainment numbers, which are expensive. Information numbers provide information on a wide range of subjects, including health, weather, road conditions and sports, while entertainment numbers include music, chat, competition, horoscope and dial-a-prayer (or joke, meditation, etc.) lines. Some information provided by information and entertainment numbers is also provided free by public service numbers (see page 178).

Charges range from $1 to $5 for the first minute, usually with a lower rate for additional minutes. These numbers are often used by crooks, who make offers which seem too good to be true (they are!), e.g. 'guaranteed' credit or cash loans at low rates. **Companies with these numbers often make their living entirely from the income generated by calls.** The longer they can keep you on the line and the more times they can induce you to call, the more money they make. Be wary of any advertisements that fail to clearly disclose the cost of calls or make it difficult for you to determine the total cost. Information and entertainment numbers include those with an 'area code' of 550 (group conversation lines), 700, 900, 940 (adult programs) and 976.

The use of information and entertainment numbers is a huge growth industry, as there's no ceiling on charges which range from 50 cents to over $200 a minute. This has encouraged fraud whereby some line owners employ people to access private telephones (by deception, supposedly to call a local number) and make calls at $200 a minute. Most telephone companies offer a blocking option which allows you to block calls to 550, 700, 900, and 976 numbers from your home or office number. There's a one-time charge, e.g. $6, and there may also be an order processing charge, e.g. $20. All 940 lines are usually blocked, and if you want access to these numbers you must write to your telephone company for authorisation to remove the blocking. If you have a complaint about these numbers, contact the Federal Communications

Commission, 445 12th Street, SW, Washington, DC 20554 (☎ 1-888-225-5322, 💻 www.fcc.gov/cgb/complaints.htm).

CUSTOM & OPTIONAL SERVICES

All telephone companies provide a range of extra services, usually called custom calling or optional services, most of which require a tone telephone which provides faster dialling plus access to a range of computerised services. Some of these services are being built into electronic telephones to work with or instead of the telephone providers' services. Custom and optional services usually include the following:

- **Call Waiting** – This lets you know when another caller is trying to get through to you and allows you to speak to him without breaking off your current call (some companies allow you to suspend call waiting).

- **Call Forwarding or Diversion** – You can divert calls to another telephone number automatically, e.g. from home to office (or vice versa) or to a mobile telephone or pager. Some telephone services allow subscribers to set up a sequence of numbers to which the calls are transferred until one is answered.

- **Three-Way Calling** – This allows you to hold a three-way conversation.

- **Speed or Code Calling** – You can store frequently dialled numbers and simply press a one or two-digit code to dial them.

- **Repeat Call** – Your telephone redials a busy number for up to 30 minutes.

- **Home Intercom** – This allows you to call extension telephones in the same building.

- **Caller ID** – You can screen calls before you answer (a display unit is required). Some caller ID systems display the name of the person calling if their number is programmed into the telephone for speed dialling.

- **Repeat Call or Call Cue** – Also known as 'last call return', this function automatically redials the last telephone number you dialled.

- **Call Block** – You can block telephone numbers from which you don't want to receive calls, including callers who don't identify themselves for caller ID.

- **Priority Call** – You're alerted by a special ring when you receive calls from specified numbers.

- **Select Forward** – This allows you to transfer calls from specified telephone numbers to another phone.

- **Call Trace** – This lets you trace the number of your last caller.

- **Return Call or Call Return** – Allows you to dial the number of the last caller even when you cannot trace the number and is useful when you've just missed taking a call.

Custom calling or optional services can usually be ordered individually or as part of a package deal. Charges vary according to the service or package of services and range from a few dollars a month for a single service (average around $3.50) to $10 a month for a package.

OPERATOR SERVICES

The operator provides a number of services and can also help you in an emergency. If you're trying to make an urgent call and the number is continuously engaged, you can ask the operator to interrupt the conversation (there's a fee, e.g. $1). When the operator is making a connection, you should ask whether you're connected rather than 'through' to your number, as 'through' means finished in the US (also a line is said to be 'busy' and not 'engaged'). Operators are polite, if mechanically so, and long-distance operators often give their names and thank you for using their service, even when you had no choice.

If possible you should dial direct unless you're unable to obtain a number because of a fault, as operator assisted calls are expensive. If you dial correctly and obtain the wrong number, report the fault (see your telephone book for the number). The faulty call should be credited to your bill or, if you're using a payphone, you should be allowed a free call. Certain types of calls can be made through the operator only, including the following:

- **Person-to-person Call** – A person-to-person call is useful when you're making a long-distance or international call and wish to speak to a particular person only. The operator tries to obtain the required person for you and you pay for the call only when you reach him. However, you must pay for the service, which is the most expensive type of operator assisted call.

- **Collect Call** – A collect (reverse charge) call is where the person being called agrees to pay for the call. It's useful when you've no change, a payphone won't accept your coins or when you're calling your mother-in-law. To make a collect call, dial '0' followed by the area code and the number you wish to call. When the operator answers, tell him you wish to make a collect call and give your name and the number you're calling from. (If you're calling from a payphone, the call is automatically routed through the company that owns the telephone, and minimum charges for collect calls can run as high as $5 or more.) The operator may want an assurance that the number you're calling isn't a payphone. There are also cheaper automated (no operator) collect call services (dial 1-800-COLLECT) which charge 10 cents a minute plus a $1.50 service fee.

- **Third-number or Billed-to-third-number Call** – You can bill a call to a number other than the one you're calling from – your own or someone else's (provided he agrees to pay!).

- **Time and Charge or Real-time-rated Call** – When making a long-distance call, you can ask the operator to tell you the duration and cost when you've finished.

- **Conference Call** – You can talk with several people in different locations simultaneously via a conference call (set up by the operator). Desktop video-conferencing (DVC) is also possible via personal computers, where the person talking can be seen by other parties (as with a videophone).

- **Mobile & Marine Calls** – Calls to vehicles travelling outside their city of registration (roamers) and to vessels with telephones must be made via the operator, who connects you with the mobile or marine operator (as applicable).

There's a surcharge for the above services, e.g. $2 per call except for person-to-person calls, which cost around $5.

CHARGES

Depending upon the local telephone service provider, there may be several types of calls within the US. Local calls are generally billed based on distance, with the local service area divided into a free calling zone (normally within a radius of 3 to 5 miles, or 5 to 8 km) and one or more local call zones. Long-distance or toll calls usually are divided into in-state and national calls. In all states, telephone companies offer a variety of 'monthly calling plans' or measured services to residential customers. Plans are based on direct-dial calls made to exchanges within the area covered by your local telephone company, and rates vary according to the area, the number of free minutes permitted and the cost of calls. A typical service allows you to make as many local calls as you wish, at a low rate for a fixed monthly charge, e.g. $10 per month, or for a lower fee, e.g. $5, allow you to make calls at a slightly higher rate or give you a limited number of free minutes per month, e.g. 1,000, after which you're charged at an even higher rate. In some areas, you can choose 'selective calling', where for a flat fee you can talk to selected exchanges/communities for a number of hours a month, e.g. 20, and/or at a discount, e.g. 30 per cent. Local telephone companies may bundle local and long-distance services with a set monthly fee for unlimited local service plus some set number of long-distance minutes. And lately, many telephone companies are offering packages that include local and long-distance services plus mobile phone and internet services.

All residential and single-line business customers must pay an FCC approved subscriber line charge of no more than $6.50 per line, per month. Other charges include a change of name or a change in the type of service, including a change of your long-distance company. There's usually a connection charge that can range from $20 to $50, which appears on your first bill. Cable television (TV) operators are starting to offer telephone services on their cables, and you may have a choice of local telephone company in some areas. This should result in lower local toll rates, but increased basic service rates.

Call charges levied by US telephone companies are usually much lower than in other countries, particularly if you take full advantage of off-peak periods, calling plans and toll-free numbers. If you're going to be away from your home for at least one month, you can usually save on line rental by asking your phone company to temporarily suspend your service. There are low rates for those on low incomes and the elderly in some states. Residential customers are usually allowed a number of free directory assistance calls per line, per month, e.g. 3 to 10. After you've used your free call allocation, you're charged a flat rate for each call, e.g. 20 cents to 40 cents (or $1 via the operator). There's no charge for directory assistance calls from payphones. You may usually request two numbers each time you call directory assistance.

Calling plans covering the local service area and a designated toll call area (i.e. less than a long-distance call, but outside the free calling zone) cost from around $15 to $50 per month, depending on the area covered, the proximity of a large city such as Boston, New York or Atlanta, and whether you opt for unlimited calling or a set number of minutes or hours per month. Some call plans also include a selection of features (see **Custom & Optional Services** on page 167). Once you've exhausted your calling limit, calls are charged by the minute, at rates that can range from 1 cent a minute to 7 or 8 cents a minute. Telephone companies used to offer discounts of up to 60 per cent for calls placed during off peak hours (usually nights, weekends and public holidays) but over the last couple of years most providers now advertise their best rates as available 24 hours a day, seven days a week.

Long-distance Calls

Long-distance rates also vary according to your service provider. As well as the 'big three', these include, Capsule Communications, Excel Telecommunications, Long Distance Telecom, MTX Communications, Opex, ProDial, Qwest, SM Communications, TTI National and Unitel. Contact companies directly for information about their services, rates, billing, dialling arrangements and special services before choosing one. Many local telephone companies offer long-distance packages available only to those who agree to purchase bundles of services, combining local, long-distance and other services (such as internet or international calling). Most firms pay for you to switch from your present company (or pay any transfer charges levied by the company you're leaving) and may even pay for you to switch back if you aren't satisfied. Competition is intense, all companies offering discounts and rewards for switching carriers, e.g. frequent-flier miles, products and free calls valued at $50 to $75. Some 40,000 people a day switch carriers and many switch several times a year.

Long-distance charges are moving more and more to the flat-rate for a set number of minutes plans, although the per minute charges for calls over your allotted time can vary. All offer various calling plans, many of which offer discounts depending on the amount spent each month (or who you call). It has become increasingly difficult to determine which of the many available services and plans is the best, as it depends on your calling habits as well as the specific bundle of services you want and what other services you may use (e.g. mobile phones, calling cards or high speed internet connections).

There are a number of online sites that compare offers and rates for telephone services (e.g. 🖥 www.telecombeacon.com or 🖥 www.bettertelephonerates.com) and consumer magazines (see **Consumers' Organisations** on page 499) run frequent articles evaluating the latest offers for telephone services. On arrival in the US, you may want to opt for the most basic telephone service bundle from the local provider until you determine what your calling patterns are. Increasingly, long-distance companies are offering calls anywhere in the continental US (i.e. anywhere but Alaska and Hawaii) for a set rate, usually between 5 cents and 10 cents per minute.

BILLING & PAYMENT

Telephone bills are sent out monthly. Bills are divided into a number of pages and usually include a page to return with your payment. Local and long-distance calls are usually itemised with full details of each call. Bills are sent by your local telephone company and include charges from long-distance call companies, so you only need to make one payment. If you have any questions regarding your bill, the appropriate telephone number to call is shown on each section of the bill.

In addition to call charges, bills may contain an FCC (Federal Communications Commission) approved subscriber line charge, federal, state and local taxes, lease charges, wire maintenance plan charges, directory assistance call charges, 911 service fee, telecommunications relay service charge (to help pay for services for disabled people), universal service fund or connectivity fee (to support basic telephone services for low income people) and monthly service charges (local and long-distance). Service charges are billed a month in advance. Payment can usually be made in person at a telephone company office, at authorised payment agencies (usually retail outlets such as chemists and food shops), where you usually pay an additional fee, by post (a prepaid return envelope is included with your bill) or via the internet, using the telephone company's website or your bank's online bill payment service. Companies prefer you to pay them by post or internet. In some areas, bills can also be paid via the phone through local banks and financial institutions.

Your bill is usually dated and is overdue when payment isn't received by the 'due by' date printed on the bill, usually 10 to 20 days after the billing date. Payments received after the due date are shown as the balance on the next bill. If payment isn't received by the due date, you may be sent another bill warning you that your service will be suspended if it isn't paid within a certain period, e.g. seven days. You may also be charged a 'late payment' charge, e.g. 1.5 per cent of the amount due. If your service is suspended, a charge is made to restore the service and a deposit is usually required against future bills. If your line is out of order for 24 hours or longer, you're usually entitled to an adjustment on your local service bill.

INTERNATIONAL CALLS

Most private telephones allow calls to be dialled to more than 190 countries, and reverse charge (collect) calls to be made to around 140 countries. To make an international call, you dial the international access code (011), the country code, e.g. 44 for the UK, the area code **without** the first zero, and finally the subscriber's number. For example, to call the number 7123-4567 in central London, England (area code 020) you would dial 011-44-20-7123-4567. (The reason you don't get the operator after dialling the first 0 of 011, is that there's an automatic delay after you dial 0, during which time you can dial additional numbers.)

When making a direct-dial international call, you may need to wait up to a minute for the call to go through, although the connection may be quicker if you press the '#' (hash or pound) key after entering the last digit. When making a person-to-person, collect (not accepted by all countries), calling card or billing-to-a-third-number call, dial 0 instead of 011, followed by the country code, city code and number. The operator comes on the line and asks for details, such as the name of the person you're calling or your calling card number. If you cannot dial an international call directly, you must dial 00 and go through the international operator, when the cost is the same as dialling yourself. However, if you ask the operator to connect you when it's possible to dial yourself, the call is much more expensive. When using the operator, it saves time if you tell him the country code, the area code without the leading zero and the subscriber's number.

International calls are increasingly being billed at a flat rate with no off peak call discount. Check with your long-distance carrier for information about international calling packages, even if you only call overseas occasionally. The basic rate for international calls can be over $2.00 a minute if you don't have some sort of plan in place. For as little as $1 a month, that rate is cut to less than $1 per minute, and with other calling plans you should be able to reduce the charges further, particularly to the one or two countries you call most often. You can usually change your long-distance and international service options with a call to your long-distance provider or online on the carrier's website. The codes for major international cities are listed in telephone directories.

US long-distance telephone companies compete vigorously for overseas customers and all offer US citizens and residents calling cards, and cards which allow foreign customers to bill their international calls to a credit card. The benefits of international calling cards are that they're fee-free; calls can be made to and from most countries, usually from any telephone, including hotel telephones, and are made via an English-speaking operator in America (foreign-language operators are also available). **Most importantly of all, calls are charged at US rates (based on the cost between the US and the country you're calling from or to) and are usually much cheaper than calls made via local phone companies.** Those with high speed internet access (i.e. DSL) can now use VoIP to make long-distance and international phone calls via the internet for only 3 to 6 cents per minute, using a regular telephone. (See **Telegrams, Fax & Internet** on page 176.)

You should be aware that telephone calling card fraud is a huge and growing international problem. If someone gets hold of your calling card and code number, they can make calls at your expense. If you have a complaint about any telephone service provider, contact the Federal Communications Commission (see **Premium Rate Numbers** on page 166).

PUBLIC TELEPHONES

Public telephones (payphones) are plentiful on street corners in cities and towns, in airports, rail and bus stations, hotel and office building lobbies, bars and restaurants (many provide cordless telephones), libraries and other public buildings, many post offices, shops, department stores and drug stores, launderettes (laundromats), shopping malls, petrol stations, and at rest stops on main highways. Most are usually in working order. There are no public telephone offices and all long-distance and international calls must be made from payphones, many of which provide little shelter from street noise and the elements. In some residential areas payphones are rare.

Before using a payphone, read the operating instructions, which may vary with the area. AT&T provides public telephones in airports with a screen on which instructions can be displayed in English, French, German or Spanish (called a 'Public Phone Plus'). Some payphones are 'dial tone first', which means you get a dial tone before you insert any coins. Coins are inserted only after you've dialled and are connected to your number. These telephones allow you to dial an emergency number (or the operator, directory assistance, or a toll-free number) when you have no coins. With other payphones, you must insert the minimum call fee before you get a dial tone (even when calling an emergency service), although the fee is returned automatically if it's a free call. If you've inserted coins and there's no reply, you simply replace the receiver to get your money back. Some public telephones have a 'LOUD' button to increase the volume.

Payphones are privately owned and operated, and the FCC has no control over the charges for local or long-distance calls. The cost of a local call from a payphone varies across the country (and indeed may vary from one phone to the next in the same area), but is generally around 50 cents for unlimited time (although some payphones in large cities charge more after the first three minutes). Payphones usually accept nickels (5 cents), dimes (10 cents) and quarters (25 cents) only and don't give change, so insert the correct amount.

Charges for local and long-distance calls from payphones are set by the company that services the telephone. When you make a call from a payphone, check the dialling instruction card on the telephone to see which long-distance company services the telephone. If you wish to use a long-distance company other than the one assigned by the payphone, you must first dial that company's access code or use a calling card. Call the operator and ask for your preferred long-distance company's operator. Some payphones provide quick access to long-distance carriers by pushing a single button.

If you're paying with coins, you need a minimum of 60 cents for a three-minute long-distance call. As with local calls, your coins are returned if there's no answer. After three minutes a voice may interrupt you and tell you the cost for additional minutes. Sometimes if you continue speaking without inserting more coins, the operator waits until you've finished your call and calls you back immediately to ask for more money (sometimes by ringing the telephone). If you don't pay, the call is charged to the number you were calling (if a domestic number).

Payphones don't usually have directories (there's nowhere to put them), although you can obtain free directory assistance by dialling 1-555-1212 for numbers within your area code, 1 + area code + 555-1212 for other areas, or a local number, e.g. 411, in some cities. For directory assistance for toll-free numbers dial 1-800-555-1212.

You should be wary of using some private payphones, e.g. those located in bars, stores and restaurants, as owners can set their own high rates (they must, however, be indicated on the telephone). If you feel the calling rates are unreasonable, you must contact the payphone service provider (PSP) to file a complaint. The cost of long-distance calls from hotel rooms, direct-dialled or via the hotel switchboard, is usually high. To save money use a calling card. Local calls are, however, free in some hotels and you may be provided with a list of the local area codes and exchanges on check-in.

Payphones onboard aeroplanes on domestic routes ('airfones') accept all major credit cards and allow international calls. Telephones are built into the armrests of seats and located on cabin walls and you insert your credit card to release the handset (which you may take to your seat, if necessary). When you replace the receiver at the end of your call, the charge is automatically debited to your card and your credit card is released. A similar 'railfone' service is provided on certain Amtrak trains. Airfone and railfone calling is normally frighteningly expensive ($4 connection fee plus $4 per minute for calls within the US), but with some mobile phone carriers (see **Mobile Phones & Pagers** below) you can receive a discounted rate on incoming calls transferred to the airfone on your flight.

With most long-distance companies and calling cards you first dial a toll-free number to gain access to their system, then enter your account number and PIN, as directed. Check with your long-distance carrier for details about how to make calls from payphones or, when away from home, how to have them billed to your home number. It should be possible to call a toll-free number from most payphones without inserting a coin, but this isn't required by law. You're billed for all calling card calls on your regular monthly telephone bill or the amount is simply subtracted from your balance automatically (i.e. if you have a prepaid calling card). Cards can also be used to make international calls to the US from overseas.

Emergency call boxes are located on freeways and highways in most states, and are direct lines to request assistance with car problems or to report an accident or hazard only (they cannot be used to call your mum!).

DIRECTORIES

Telephone directories (commonly referred to as phone books) contain a wealth of information about telephone services, using telephones, US area codes and time zones, international codes, call rates, emergency numbers, service numbers, toll-free numbers, repair service, establishing or changing services, local service options, customer calling services, customer rights, telephone safety, billing and payment, directory assistance, area and long-distance calling, dialling instructions and operator assistance. There's often also information on local events and amenities, public transport, leisure and sports, parks, shopping, community services and zip codes, as well as maps of the local area. Emergency numbers are usually listed inside the front cover, and some directories include civil defence emergency information and a first aid and survival guide.

Directories are split into sections, e.g. general information, white pages (subscribers' numbers), blue pages (local, county, state and federal government offices) and yellow pages (business listings). Subscribers in white page directories are listed in a single alphabetical listing, no matter how many towns are included in the directory area. Yellow pages are indispensable and are often combined with white pages, except in major cities, where they're separate and may be divided into sections such as 'Consumer & Household' and 'Business & Industrial'. Subscribers in yellow pages are listed under a business or service heading (in alphabetical order) for the area covered. Small local 'Yellow Page' directories are published in most areas. In some cities, free local or ethnic directories are published, e.g. bi-lingual

(Spanish and English) yellow pages for consumers and tourists. You can usually order a free copy (or additional free copies) of any white or yellow pages published by your local telephone company by completing a pre-paid postcard in your local directory or calling their customer service number. Other directories can also be ordered (usually for a fee).

Telephone directories, including yellow pages, are available in bars, restaurants, hotel foyers and main post offices. Directories are also available in public reference libraries, some of which also keep foreign directories. National directories listing businesses, colleges and universities, associations and organisations, international organisations, and travel resources (resorts, car rental, hotels and motels, etc.) are also available.

With your basic telephone service you receive a listing in the white pages of your local telephone book, and business customers also receive a free listing in the yellow pages. Two people with the same family name can have both their first names listed and you can purchase additional listings for around 50 cents per month. It is possible to have only your name and phone number listed (i.e. with no street address) if you're concerned about people turning up on your doorstep. Anyone can get an ex-directory (unlisted) number for around $1 a month. This means that your number isn't included in the directory, but is available through directory assistance. For an additional fee, e.g. $2 per month, you can have a non-published number, which means your number is also unavailable through directory assistance. In most areas, white pages are published annually, one for each calling area, which may extend across more than one area code.

In most areas you dial a local number, e.g. 411, for local enquiries (directory assistance or information). Information for an area other than your local area code is available by dialling 1 + area code + 555-1212. Often numbers are given by recorded messages, so be ready to write them down. The operator will help you in an emergency (the emergency number is 911). Residential customers are allowed a number of free directory assistance calls per month (see page 169) and calls to directory assistance are usually free from payphones. There are a number of free directory assistance websites, white pages (residential) and yellow pages (business), but information on the sites is often out of date or just plain wrong, as telephone companies are loathe to share their subscriber lists with outsiders (other than for a fee).

MOBILE PHONES & PAGERS

There are over 165 million mobile phone (cell phone) subscribers in the US and costs have tumbled in recent years. In fact, many companies provide 'free' phones with a one or two-year service contract. Alternatively, you can buy 'pay as you talk' phones. Analogue phones are cheap, but digital phones are expensive (e.g. $300 or more), although the latest and greatest digital phones combine the features and functions of a handheld computer, including the ability to receive and send email as well as browsing the internet. However, you pay for incoming, as well as outgoing, calls (called 'paying for air time')! Mobile phone service is often referred to as 'wireless' service and it's normally possible to arrange for cell phone service as part of a package from your local telephone company.

Mobile phones are assigned telephone numbers within the local area code so that it isn't possible to tell from the phone number whether you're dialling a land line or a cell phone. Callers to your cell phone are billed for a local or long-distance call, according to the area code and exchange for your cell phone number. It's possible to have your cell phone number listed in the local directory if you wish, but there's usually an additional monthly charge for this. Also make sure your mobile number is registered with the Do Not Call Registry (see **Using the Telephone** on page 163) so that you won't have to pay for incoming telemarketing calls. When changing cell phone companies, you usually can keep the same phone number, thanks to recently enacted portability rules now in effect.

Some mobile phone companies provide access to an information service offering traffic reports, roadside assistance, vehicle services, and a wide range of other information and features. As a result of the proliferation of mobile phones, many restaurants, sporting venues, clubs, and hotels have banned or electronically block their use during performances or in quiet areas (see **Pagers** below). The GSM standard used in the US isn't the same as that used in Europe and other parts of the world. Foreign GSM phones must be tri-band or quad-band (often called world phones or world GSM phones) so that you can switch to the 1900 band used for GSM phones in the US.

Theft of mobile phone codes is a big business in the US, where crooks use scanners to 'grab' a caller's telephone number and identification number. You should lock your telephone when it isn't in use, keep your telephone and documents in a safe place, and report any bogus calls immediately (you should also disable international calling if you don't need it).

Pagers

A number of companies offer pagers, which are a less expensive alternative to mobile phones and can be used in places where mobile phones are banned. They allow you to send a brief message (up to 50 characters) and have a wider range than cellphones, as they operate via satellites. Pagers cost from around $50 but, as with mobile phones, they often come 'free' with a service contract, which costs around $40 per month for nationwide coverage and a number of 'calls' included.

TELEGRAMS, FAX & INTERNET

In addition to being home to the world's most frequent telephone users, the US also has the largest number of fax (facsimile) machines in the world. Faxes can be sent from a payphone-type machine and credit card operated machines, available in public places throughout the US, e.g. airports and railway stations, as well as in many shops. There are public fax bureaux in most cities (often located in copy shops such as Kinko's), and most hotels provide fax services, e.g. fax machines in foyers and sometimes in rooms.

You can also obtain a fax pager, where you ring a number to obtain information about your fax messages, e.g. the SkyTel Skyfax service uses a standard SkyTel pager to notify travellers of an incoming fax. The pager display tells you the name of the sender and his telephone number, and you can have the fax sent to a laptop computer or a nearby fax machine.

Not surprisingly, the US has the highest number of internet users in the world and enjoys the world's lowest internet access charges, thanks to intense competition between the many internet service providers (ISPs). More than half of all Americans are located in areas where high-speed internet (broadband) access is available, DSL or cable, and high speed access is rapidly replacing dial-up as the standard form of access. DSL is available from your local telephone company or from a number of independent ISP's, e.g. NetZero, AOL or Verizon. Cable internet access is available through many local TV cable companies. Some broadband providers are now, including VoIP services which allow you to make low cost long-distance and international telephone calls via the internet using a normal telephone plugged into the broadband modem or router.

For those living in areas not serviced by broadband providers, there are still many dial-up ISPs available, national and regional. Some even offer free access, although users must put up with a permanent 'ad bar' displaying advertising material. National dial-up services include AOL, Compuserve, MSN and AT&T Worldnet. Regional providers are listed in the yellow pages under 'Internet Service Providers'.

Many hotels in the US are now offering broadband Wi-Fi (wireless) internet access in guest rooms, often with free access. When travelling, there are also Wi-Fi hot spots located in airport lounges, book shops and coffee shops which you can use for an hourly fee or if you're a subscriber to certain Wi-Fi service provider networks.

If fax and email are too hi-tech and impersonal for you, you can always send a telegram via Western Union, from the Western Union website 🖥 www.western union.com or through a local Western Union agent. It takes a day to get there and costs $15, but what price nostalgia?

EMERGENCY NUMBERS

The national emergency number in the US is 911, for police, fire and ambulance emergencies, plus coast guard and cave and mountain rescue services. Emergency telephone numbers for local fire, police and ambulance services are listed inside the front cover of white and yellow pages and it's often advisable to use the local numbers rather than 911 in non life-threatening situations. Numbers for poison control, suicide prevention, state and metro police, county sheriff, FBI, US marshals service, US secret service (so secret they're in the directory!), drug enforcement agency, toxic chemical and oil spills, and the alcohol, tobacco and firearms departments are also listed.

Local police, fire and ambulance services often have the same telephone number. You can also call for a private ambulance (see 'Ambulance Service' in your yellow pages). **Make a note of your local emergency numbers and keep them in a prominent place near your telephone(s).** Local emergency services can often help with household crises, for example the local fire service may pump out a flooded basement free of charge and your local police force may help you gain access to your home or car when you've lost your keys.

If you're calling from a public payphone, the local emergency number is usually shown on the telephone dial or a notice. Emergency 911 calls are free from all telephones, including all payphones. **When making an emergency call, don't hang up, but let the emergency person end the conversation, as they may have important questions or instructions about what you should do until help arrives.** If you're unable to remain on the line, tell the operator the nature of the emergency, the exact location (address, town, etc.) where help is needed, and your telephone number. If you have a shared line that's required for an emergency call you're informed by the operator and **must hang up immediately**. If you call 911 from a mobile phone, you should give the exact location of the emergency first and then give the operator your phone number so that he or she can call you back if you get disconnected. Don't programme your mobile phone to automatically dial 911 when a single button is pressed, as 'accidental' calls tie up the emergency call centre lines and have caused delays in responding to genuine emergency situations. Be aware, too, that many states have short-dial numbers (e.g. #77 in Virginia) to use when reporting non life-threatening motorway accidents or breakdowns using a mobile phone. These numbers are indicated on signs on major motorways and in the front of your local phone book.

In addition to the above emergency services, in most areas there are local crisis hotlines for help and advice concerning missing children, youth crises and runaways, child abuse, battered women, deaf contact (or an emergency teletypewriter for the deaf), eye traumas, alcoholics anonymous, animal bites, crime victims, gays and lesbians, health, rape, suicide prevention, traveller's aid, STD clinics, AIDS, and drug abuse. These numbers are usually listed in local telephone books. (See also **Emergencies** on page 302 and **Psychiatry & Counselling** on page 315.)

PUBLIC SERVICE NUMBERS

There are no national service numbers, e.g. for road conditions and weather, although some private companies offer these services via 900 (premium-rate) numbers. Public service numbers are listed in telephone directories, for example in a 'Self Help Guide'. They may include arts, leisure and recreation, consumer problems, children's services, disabled services, discrimination, education, elderly services, employment, financial services, health, heat, information/referral services, landlord/tenant services, legal services, pollution, social security, social services, taxes, transport, veterans' services, voting information, weather and welfare. In most areas there are consumer information services (often free), e.g. Tel-Tips, which may be provided by your local Better Business Bureau. Ask them for a directory. All states provide a range of toll-free hotlines offering a wide range of information, including education, health, consumer and welfare information. Bi-lingual staff are often available to answer your questions. Some communities have a local 'special event telephone line' where residents can make community announcements.

8.

TELEVISION & RADIO

In the US, where television (TV) is a catchall for the banality and senselessness of much American culture, many believe Armageddon is already here and blame TV for destroying the fabric of American society. In many homes TV rivals family and religion as the dispenser of values, and is often referred to as the 'boob tube', the 'plug-in drug' or the 'idiot box'. Some 98 per cent of US households have at least one TV and around 70 per cent have two or more (almost all colour). The average American watches more than three hours of TV a day and a good 20 per cent of the public admit to more than four hours a day. Some 'couch potatoes' (people who spend all their time passively watching TV) leave their TVs on all day and even overnight, though in recent years, computer use, particularly surfing the internet, has cut into television time. (Whether or not this should be seen as a good thing is still undecided.) Prime time viewing is from around 7pm to 11pm and attracts an average 85 million viewers. A TV is an essential part of American life and even the most modest motel or hotel boasts a colour TV in every room. Airports now offer TV at each boarding gate showing travellers' channels and bus stations have coin-operated TVs built into the arms of chairs. Bars, clubs, dance halls and even launderettes have banks of TVs (often showing live ball games).

Most foreigners have little idea just how bad US TV can be. The US programmes sold around the world are the **best** they produce and many of the home market programmes are frighteningly bad (daytime talk shows and soap operas are referred to as 'trash TV', although lately even some of the trashiest of these are being sold to foreign markets). Most programmes are targeted at viewers with an IQ of a vegetable and an attention span of around five milliseconds. If something electrifying doesn't happen during that time (such as a graphic and gruesome murder or someone winning a jackpot prize), they're off zapping through the remaining 50 to 100 or more available channels. US TV can be condescending, boring, total rubbish and an insult to the intelligence (nobody ever lost money in the US by **underestimating** public intelligence). The sole purpose of US TV is to make money, not to entertain, educate or inform. However, not **everything** is drivel and US TV occasionally throws up some comedy gems such as *M*A*S*H*, *All In The Family* and *Cheers*, despite the Americans' occasionally bizarre sense of humour. US TV has its own annual awards for the 'least worst' TV programmes called Emmy's (TV's equivalent of the Oscar).

The main purpose of US TV is as a medium for advertisers, some of whom spend over $500 million a year on TV advertising (cigarette and hard liquor advertising is banned). TV programmes are advertised incessantly in much the same way as soap powder (although soap powder advertisements are usually more interesting) and programmes are even advertised during other programmes, as well as every few minutes in commercial breaks (you cannot say you weren't warned!). Often it's difficult to tell where a programme breaks and the advertisements start, as there's usually (deliberately) no warning that advertisements are about to start or have started (advertisements are also designed to look like programme trailers). Advertising on US TV is blatant, loud, amazingly frequent (as much as 30 minutes an hour), annoyingly repetitive and usually not funny (with certain hilarious exceptions). It has been estimated that the average 18-year-old American has watched 350,000 TV advertisements.

Even sports are interrupted every few minutes for a 'message from our sponsors' and, if there aren't enough natural breaks, the rules are changed to create more.

Advertising during sports programmes is unbelievable and makes some sports unwatchable. The major networks have nightmares about 'minor' teams (i.e. those not from a major, audience-rich metropolis) reaching the finals of major sports events, which would constitute ratings death (with a consequential loss of advertising revenue). The cost of a prime time 30-second advertisement spot leaps from around a mere few hundred thousand dollars to well over a million during the Super Bowl, which attracts viewers from 40 per cent of US households (if two unpopular teams got to the Super Bowl, there would be mass suicide among TV moguls). TV programmes (broadcast and cable) are listed in daily newspapers, many of which provide free weekly programmes with their Sunday editions. There are free TV guides in most areas (good for coupons) and many others are available on news stands, including the best-selling *TV Guide* (over 5 million copies sold weekly). For information about radio, see page 190.

STANDARDS

The standards for TV reception in the US **aren't the same as in most other countries.** The US transmission standard is NTSC (which stands for National Television Standards Committee – or 'never the same colour'), which is broadcast on 525 lines rather than the 625-line PAL standard used in most of Europe. TVs and video recorders that aren't manufactured for the NTSC standard won't function in the US (although dual-standard TVs are available). If you bring a TV to the US from abroad, you may get a picture or sound, but not both. Video recorders manufactured for non-US markets cannot be used to record or play back NTSC-standard videos (however, PAL-standard video recorders and TVs are useful for playing PAL-standard videos in the US and many PAL video recorders will play back NTSC videos on a PAL television set). The cost of a TV varies considerably according to the brand, screen size, features and, not least, the retailer (so shop around). High-definition TVs (HDTVs) with a 16:9 screen (proportioned to show feature films) are also widely available, although HDTV signals aren't available yet in all areas of the country. Flat screen televisions are also becoming more and more popular, in plasma and LCD versions.

Locating a particular station on a strange TV, e.g. in an hotel, is often a lottery, as there's often no relationship between the channel number selected and the channel number shown in the *TV Guide* or major newspapers. On the other hand, when you purchase a new set, the channels are fixed (channel 2 always comes in on channel 2), with no need to set or assign channel numbers to specific broadcast frequencies. There are no national broadcasters across the country and therefore ABC, CBS and NBC network stations may be found on any channel, depending on their local affiliate broadcaster. In most apartments there's no need to fit a private aerial (antenna), as all large buildings have a master antenna on the roof. If you have cable TV (see page 187), you receive all your stations via the cable link, which although provides better reception than a roof antenna, can be affected by power cuts and extreme weather conditions. Reception is poor in many remote areas, with snowy and fuzzy pictures the norm rather than the exception – and that's if you're lucky enough to be located close to a transmitter or have cable TV.

Broadcast TV in the US is carried on 82 channels, each assigned a specific broadcast frequency. Those numbered 2 to 13 are VHF (very high frequency) channels, while 14 to 83 are UHF (ultra high frequency) channels. Originally, there was a channel 1, but the frequency assigned to it was withdrawn for other (i.e. non-television broadcast) purposes. Most televisions purchased today have the capability to display at least 100 different channels when used with cable or satellite connections.

STATIONS & PROGRAMMES

US TV is the most competitive in the world, with national networks, local stations, cable and satellite TV stations all competing vigorously for your attention (not to mention telephone companies and others who plan to offer local TV services). There are five 'national' TV networks: the American Broadcasting Company (ABC), the Columbia Broadcasting Service (CBS), and the National Broadcasting Company (NBC), known as the big three, plus Fox TV and Warner (Brothers) TV. Other national networks include Pax, PBS and UPN.

Networks compete intensely for the 'best' (or rather most popular) programmes and sports events. New York City is the media capital of the US and the major networks all have their head offices there. In addition to the national networks, there are more than 800 licensed commercial TV stations and some 400 non-commercial public and educational stations. Major cities have up to 20 local broadcast stations and viewers in many areas can receive well over 100 stations when national and cable stations are included.

National TV networks are similar to a franchise, where local VHF stations (VHF signals reach more viewers and have a clearer signal than UHF) are affiliated to a network and take its programmes. The networks buy programmes from independent TV production companies (mostly located in Hollywood) and distribute them to local stations across the country. Local stations also show their own local news, sports and other broadcasts, which vary from incredibly amateurish affairs to reasonably competent programmes. Morning chat and news shows are often surprisingly unprofessional, even on the major networks, with two or more presenters often talking at the same time (when presenters must present live news without a script or prompter, chaos often ensues). There are also over 400 independent UHF stations (indies) which aren't affiliated to one of the national networks. Their output is often confined to showing old films and programmes or specialising in some way. Spanish language channels are becoming increasingly common throughout the country and there are several national Spanish language networks developing, such as Univison and Telemundo. Most TV stations are 24-hour, although some broadcast from 7am or 8am to 2am or 3am 'only'.

Programmes aimed at mass entertainment are preferred over educational and news programmes, and the major networks show virtually nothing targeted at minority interests. Most stations' output consists of a profusion of game shows, situation comedies (sit-coms), violent or old films and 'public access' programming (where amateurs do their utmost to make you switch off). 'Reality programmes' are a current favourite of network executives, given that they're far cheaper to produce than scripted series, and the genre has now expanded to include not only *Big Brother* and *Survivor* variants, but also big business reality (i.e. *The Apprentice*, featuring Donald Trump firing an ambitious would-be tycoon each week for not displaying sufficient ruthlessness), and a myriad of competitions daring contestants to eat live insects or dive into shark-infested tanks. An updated version of the old 'talent shows' is making a come-back, where aspiring performers compete to win recording contracts or studio time, with the TV audience voting for the winners via telephone or the internet. In some cases, even the losers become minor celebrities for daring to display their lack of talent on national TV. Another popular programme is the make-over, from home and landscaping make-overs to *Queer Eye for the Straight Guy* (where a team of gay, fashion and lifestyle consultants spiff up a straight geek) to *The Swan* (where a 'fashion' makeover includes radical plastic surgery to transform plain Janes into femme fatales). Public access channels include bulletin boards of local events and amateur video coverage of local high school sports and concerts. The only live programmes are local news and discussions and major sports events. There's little news, with the major networks presenting just two evening news programmes (usually at 6pm and 11pm), and the independents showing mainly local news.

News programmes last for around 30 minutes, at least ten of which are taken up with advertisements. They're often criticised for concerning themselves with entertainment (infotainment), rather than providing in-depth news, which is usually broken down into small easily-digestible pieces (caustically termed news McNuggets). CNN news is popular, although during peak viewing times it provides a confusion of sound-bites, miscellaneous statistics ('factoids'), celebrity and audience-participation interviews and advertisements. (CNN in the US is nothing at all like CNN International, shown outside the US, despite the common parent company and the occasional appearance of familiar 'international' presenters on the US programmes.) Local news generally consists of a catalogue of soaring crime (murders, robberies, arson and homicide body counts in the inner cities), flavoured with inane showbiz gossip. TV companies compete vigorously to bring instant pictures of disasters and on-the-spot reports from helicopter crews. Some local stations (channel 7 in Miami is one infamous example) specialise in gory crime news ('if it bleeds, it leads') and most Americans get their daily crime 'fix' from the TV. Crime stories dominate TV and justice has become a media circus, highlighted by the OJ Simpson farce in 1994/95 (aptly described as a 2,500 hour TV documentary).

Foreign news hardly exists in the US's insular news climate, except on PBS stations, and current affairs programmes are scarce (CBS's *60 Minutes* is a rare and notable exception). Sports coverage outside the popular US sports of baseball, American football, basketball, ice hockey, tennis, golf and motor racing is almost unheard of, and major international sports events are virtually ignored. US network TV is all about ratings, which are compiled daily; programmes which receive poor ratings are often axed at the drop of a hat. You never need to worry about missing a programme, particularly an episode of a popular soap opera, as they're usually shown at least five times a week. Indeed, many programmes are repeated hundreds of times on different channels.

The best programmes for discerning viewers are usually shown on the Public Broadcasting System (PBS) or public-service channels, although these aren't available everywhere. The PBS network of regional stations was developed as an antidote to the national networks, so that the 'few' discerning viewers (mostly foreigners) could watch some serious TV occasionally. PBS channels show some of the highest-quality programmes, many of which are foreign, e.g. British imports. PBS output includes comedy (British sitcoms are popular), children's programmes, e.g. *Sesame Street* and *Teletubbies*, drama, documentaries, discussion programmes, excellent science and nature features, live music and theatre, e.g. *American Playhouse* and *Masterpiece Theater*, and anything which is too highbrow (i.e. requiring a modicum of intellectual response) for national network viewers. However, as a result of its lack of funds, the PBS network is forced to broadcast many low-budget, narrow-interest programmes.

PBS TV used to be strictly non-commercial and survived on donations from government, foundations, business and individuals, which results in relentless, often wretched, fund-raising drives. Many viewers make annual donations, e.g. $50 or $100. Some PBS channels are heavily sponsored by oil companies, which has led to their being named the Petroleum Broadcasting System. PBS stations have started accepting some advertising; however advertisements are currently still limited to the breaks between programmes, and most advertisements aren't the same tacky ones seen on network TV. While you can watch a programme without being interrupted by advertisements every few seconds, programmes are interrupted to give details of future programmes and make requests for donations. Sponsors are acknowledged at the beginning and end of programmes. PBS stations often have fund-raising drives, e.g. a 'Britcom' (British comedy) night, where viewers may be invited to donate $100 in return for a 'gift' of British food (presumably there are people mad enough to pay!) or videos and DVDs of popular programmes. PBS channels publish monthly programmes for a nominal annual subscription.

Most TV programmes are taped and shown at different times in different time zones (see page 531), at whatever time best suits local stations. This results in stations switching back and forth between local and national programmes, and often leads to viewers joining programmes that are already in progress. Programmes are usually half an hour or multiples of half an hour in length, which is designed to make the co-ordination of stations and advertising easier. If a programme, such as a film, doesn't conform to this standard, it's ruthlessly cut (or padded out with ads) to ensure it's the right length. This has even led to cinema films being produced so they can be shown on TV without too much cutting.

US game shows (broadcast mostly during the day), which offer huge cash prizes for answering the most banal questions (usually about other TV programmes), must be seen to be believed. To qualify as a contestant you must be extrovert, exuberant and hyperactive, and capable of going bananas at the slightest provocation. This also applies to the live studio audience (ostentatious spectators are often invited back as contestants). Amazingly the number of game shows has been reduced in recent years because they were 'too intellectually demanding' on viewers and contestants, who have been described as 'having the brains of a golf divot'.

US network TV is among the most self-censored in the world and swear words, nudity (bare breasts are considered far more corrupting of the nation's virtue than any number of mutilated bodies), and anything which might offend is rigorously edited out (although allowed on cable stations). All swear words are 'bleeped out' and the major networks even bleep out the names of other networks (which are, in their eyes, the worst of all profanities). If you long for the sight of a bare breast or are desperate to hear some earthy language, there are plenty of cable stations where anything goes.

CABLE TELEVISION

Cable TV is available in around 60 per cent of US households (some 100 million). Most cable stations broadcast 24 hours a day and in the larger cities there are dozens of cable channels in addition to the national networks and PBS stations; many cable subscribers can receive more than 100 stations. Although there are some general entertainment cable TV channels, most channels are dedicated to a particular topic, including films, sports, religion, comics, game shows (yes, 24 hours a day!), pornography, local events, news, financial news, shopping (worth over $1 billion a year), children's programmes, weather, health, music (rock, country) and foreign-language programmes, e.g. Spanish. Most cable services also carry C-SPAN (Cable Satellite Public Affairs Network) which provides news about the federal government and covers what's happening in Congress (for those who have difficulty sleeping). Cable TV isn't subject to the same federal laws as broadcast TV and therefore channels may show programmes, such as pornographic films, which aren't permitted on network TV.

The cable channels available in a city or locality depend on the franchise agreement with the local municipality, although the most popular channels are usually available throughout the country. Until May 2001, over 40 per cent of the cable market was under the control of telecoms giant AT&T, but the Federal Communications Commission forced it to cut its share to no more than 30 per cent. AT&T's response was to merge its cable business with rival Comcast in a $72 billion deal that created the world's largest cable company!

There are generally three levels of cable service: basic, standard basic and premium. A basic service provides only local broadcast channels and costs around $10 to $15 per month; standard basic also includes the majority of cable channels (anything up to 100) for around $30 to $45 per month; premium services add a variety of film channels, e.g. Cinemax, Home Box Office, The Movie Channel, MovieMax and Showtime, for up to $50 to $75 per month. Other premium channels include Encore and Starz! Some premium channels offer Spanish as an audio programme to cater for Spanish-speaking viewers. Subscribers can buy or rent (for $3 to $5 per month) a special remote control. You can also subscribe to an FM stereo service (around $5 to $10 per month) in most areas, which improves FM reception on your stereo (radio) receiver.

Most cable stations also operate a pay-per-view system for TV games, current (first-run) films, exclusive specials and live sports events, such as wrestling and championship boxing (popular and expensive). Pay-per-view is increasingly being used by major networks to recoup broadcast rights to top sports events. Channels include In Demand, The Hot Network, Playboy TV and Spice 2 and charges vary between $4 and $30 per event or programme. Digital cable providers are now offering pay-per-view programming on demand, where you can choose to begin viewing (usually a film) anytime you like, in addition to using a digital video recorder (DVR) to pause, restart or replay portions of the film while you watch it.

One of the most contentious cable TV issues is companies deleting popular channels from the basic package and replacing them with pay-per-view channels. It isn't unusual for cable TV companies to change basic cable channels or increase premiums without informing subscribers. Cable companies have a monopoly in the areas where their franchise operates and although municipalities have consumer watchdog agencies to oversee services, companies do more or less what they like (and charge what they like). This also means the cable companies can censor what you watch and consumers often have little choice in the selection of channels. The total revenue of cable TV companies is around $20 billion a year.

Cable TV isn't available in remote rural areas. If it's available, but not installed in your house or apartment, you can usually have it hooked up for a one-time installation fee of around $50 (some cable companies offer free installation if you take premium channels). Cable companies also install multiple hook-ups (for an additional monthly fee) and may also hook up a VCR or a DVR for a nominal fee. Ask the superintendent of your building or your estate agent which company supplies your local cable TV service, and call and ask them about their rates and options. Modern TVs are 'cable ready' and no cable converter box is required. If necessary, cable companies provide subscribers with a converter box that fits between your house cable and your TV, and unscrambles the cable TV signals.

Cable TV is usually available in hotels, motels and even in some YMCAs and youth hostels (although some hotel pay-per-view films are expensive and the available cable channels may only be a limited selection from the normal household cable menu). Cable TV programmes are listed in TV magazines such as the *TV Guide* and in daily newspapers, where they may be divided into standard and premium channels.

SATELLITE TELEVISION

There are around 20 TV satellites in North America serving the US and Canada, each with a capacity to transmit up to 24 channels. Most satellite transmissions are broadcast exclusively for local cable TV companies, who pass the satellite signal through their cable network to subscribers. Every hotel, bar and club has a huge satellite dish (often 8 to 10 feet in diameter), which is mainly used to receive sports events. Many bars show a number of ball games simultaneously on different TVs.

However, many people are buying small satellite dishes, particularly those in remote rural areas where homes cannot be connected to a cable system, but also those who want to receive foreign TV stations. The two major service providers are DIRECTV (☎ 1-888-238-7177, 🖳 www.directv.com) and Dish Network (☎ 1-800-333-DISH, 🖳 www.dishnetwork.com). DIRECTV is the more popular of the two satellite systems, with over 10 million customers and a number of exclusive sports contracts. Packages vary from $40 to $91 a month and include up to 225 channels. Dish Network claims around 6 million customers and offers more international programmes, as well as two-way high speed internet by satellite. Dish Network packages are a bit cheaper, ranging from $25 to $78 a month. Subscribers to either satellite service receive a free satellite dish and receiver. Some cities are better served by DIRECTV than by Dish Network and vice versa. For a full comparison of the two, see the website 💻 www.dish-network-vs-direct-tv.com.

The contracts between the satellite owners, programmers and local cable TV companies are exclusive, so direct reception of individual channel or network satellite signals is illegal. There has been some controversy in recent years concerning a dish owner's right to freely receive satellite signals, although it's virtually impossible to enforce the law about the way you convert the satellite signal after it has entered your home. Satellite owners' attempts to scramble signals has had little effect and plans for pirate unscramblers are quickly on the market, sold through advertisements in magazines such as *Popular Mechanics*. It's estimated that some 70 per cent of satellite owners receive free programmes that cable viewers must pay for. If you have a large satellite dish, you may be interested in the *World Radio TV Handbook* edited by David G. Bobbett (Watson-Guptill Publications).

VIDEO & DVD

The US video market is the largest in the world and around 80 per cent of American homes have a VCR and almost 30 per cent have two or more; video cameras are also popular. However, DVD is fast superseding video tape, and rental shops stock approximately 50 per cent of each medium. In the last decade, there has been an explosion in the number of rental shops in the US (most towns have a few), although saturation point was reached some years ago in the major cities, where competition is intense. You can buy practically anything on video in the US, where there's a huge market in educational, training and sports videos. Videos sell for between $10 and $50, depending on the type of film, and DVDs can be bought for as little as $10.

Many video shops are open from around 9am until 8pm or 10pm, seven days a week. To rent a video you must be a member, for which shops require identification and proof of your address. If you're under 18, a parent is required to stand as a guarantor. Video rental charges are usually around $3 to $4 in the suburbs and $5 to $6 in major cities, depending on the film rating (new top ten films are the most expensive) and local competition. DVDs rent for around $1 more. Classic (i.e. old) films can be rented for just $1 or $2 from rental shops and public libraries. The standard rental period is three to five days from major video chains, or one to three days from independent shops. There's usually no extra charge for weekend rental, e.g. Friday to Monday. Most video shops also rent video games, for $3 to $6 for up to five days.

It's also possible to rent DVDs by mail, using the online rental service, Netflix (☎ 1-800-585-8131, 💻 www.netflix.com). For a set monthly fee of $18, you can rent all the films you want for as long as you want, although you're limited to having only three DVDs out at a time. Netflix pays the postage both ways, and as soon as you return one DVD, they send you the next one on your list.

Video shops sell second-hand videos and DVDs at reduced prices (e.g. $5 to $15) and also sell new videos at competitive prices (as do many other shops). However, the best place to buy videos is from a mail-order video club, most of which offer new members amazing introductory offers, e.g. six films for 39 cents each (plus shipping and handling), in return for an agreement to buy six more over a period of three years at regular prices (around $30 each). Many video shops sell food such as ice-cream, yoghurt, candy, popcorn, etc., to sustain you while you're watching a film.

RADIO

Radio flourishes in the US and has a growing audience, despite the competition from TV, cinema and videos. Radio reception is good in most parts of the country, including stereo reception, which is excellent in all but the most mountainous areas (where you're lucky to receive anything). The US has more than 10,000 local radio stations and in major cities you generally have a choice of 50 to 100 local stations, in stark contrast to some remote areas where you may be able to receive a few stations only. Like TV stations, many radio stations are affiliated to national networks such as ABC, CBS, and NBC. There are also over 100 regional radio networks. Although most stations are commercial, advertising on radio is a lot less obtrusive than on TV. There are also many 'special audience' radio stations, including a variety of foreign language stations and non-commercial stations operated by colleges, universities and public authorities.

US mainstream commercial radio (like commercial TV) is of little interest if you're looking for serious discussion or education, but excellent if you're into music, news or religion. Stations are classified as news, talk or music or a combination. As a general rule, news and talk stations broadcast on AM and music stations on FM (in stereo). There are lots of zany talk or chat shows where hosts are employed for their amazing ability to ramble on and on (and on) about nothing in particular for hours and hours. Music stations are highly specialised, the most common of which are categorised as adult contemporary, country, contemporary hits, easy listening, or middle of the road (MOR). In addition to these, there are stations specialising in top 40 hits, golden oldies or classic rock, urban contemporary (black music), adult oriented rock (AOR), light rock, jazz, blues, bluegrass, R&B, progressive, gospel, reggae and classical.

If you're looking for serious radio, then you must tune into National Public Radio (NPR), which like TV's Public Broadcasting Service (PBS), is non-commercial and specialises in news and public affairs. American Public Radio (APR) is also non-commercial and specialises in entertainment. NPR and APR survive on grants and sponsorship from large corporations and donations from individuals. Like PBS TV, NPR is considered highbrow, and it's usually the only choice if you want to listen to drama, serious talks, current affairs or world news (taken from the British Broadcasting Corporation). NPR and APR stations also broadcast live and recorded major classical concerts, sponsored by large corporations. NPR and APR transmit via satellite to around 5 million listeners through more than 300 affiliated stations across the US. People with cable TV can also subscribe to an FM stereo service in most areas, which improves FM reception on your stereo receiver.

Radio stations range from high-tech automated studios, where everything is recorded and the 'engineer' monitors the output in a local bar, to one-man shoestring set-ups with a pile of old LPs. Most stations are strictly local and when you're driving across the US you may need to find a new station every 50mi (80km) or so. Apart from news broadcasts, all programmes are generally local, and are a good way to find out about an area you're visiting or passing through. Stations are classified as AM (or medium wave) or FM (VHF, often stereo), and a few broadcast simultaneously on both wavebands; frequencies are quoted in KHz (AM) or MHz (FM). Radio stations are identified by a three or four letter call sign, e.g. WBZ, WCBS and KLOS; stations east of the Mississippi are prefixed with the letter 'W' and those in the west with a 'K'. A station's call sign is usually followed by AM or FM, e.g. WCBS FM.

BBC

The BBC World Service is broadcast on short wave on several frequencies simultaneously and you can usually receive a good signal on one of them. The signal strength varies according to where you live, the time of day and year, the power and positioning of your receiver, and atmospheric conditions. The BBC publishes a monthly magazine, *BBC On Air*, containing comprehensive information about BBC world service radio and TV programmes, which is available on subscription for around $35 a year. Contact BBC on Air, Room 310NW, Bush House, Strand, London WC2B 4PH, UK (☎ 020-7557 2803/2875, ⌨ www.bbconair.com).

9.

EDUCATION

The US has the most diversified education system in the world, with public and private schools ('school' usually refers to everything from kindergarten to university) at all levels flourishing alongside each other. Americans of all ages have an insatiable appetite for education and self-improvement, and no society in history has educated its young more persistently or at greater expense than the US. For the 2005 fiscal year, the federal Department of Education has a budget of nearly $63 billion, which is all the more impressive when you consider that most school financing is done at the state and local levels. Among the world's major industrialised nations, only Canada spends a higher percentage of its GNP on education. Around 85 per cent of students complete high school and the US also has a higher percentage of college graduates (some 55 per cent) than any other country. Many American universities and other higher education institutions are internationally renowned (the US arguably has the best undergraduate education system in the world) and their student bodies include thousands of foreign students from all corners of the globe.

Full-time education is compulsory in all states and includes the children of foreign nationals permanently or temporarily resident in the US for a minimum of one year. However, admission to a public school for foreign children is dependent on the type and duration of the visa granted to their parents, and attendance may not be possible. Compulsory schooling lasts from 8 to 13 years (depending on the state) and usually commences at the age of six or seven and continues until between 16 and 18. The typical American receives 12 years of education, although the average is lower in rural areas and small towns (apart from university towns), and higher in metropolitan areas.

There's no federal education system in the US, where education is the responsibility of individual states and districts. Consequently, education standards and requirements vary considerably from state to state and district to district. No fees are payable in public (state) primary and secondary schools, which are attended by around 90 per cent of children (schoolchildren of all ages are usually referred to as students). The other 10 per cent attend private fee-paying schools, most of which are church-sponsored (often Roman Catholic) parochial schools. Most public schools (pre-school, elementary and high) are co-educational (mixed) day schools. Private schools include day and boarding schools and are mostly co-educational (often abbreviated to 'coed', which confusingly also refers to female college students), although some are single sex. There's also a growing trend (an increase of 15 per cent per year) for children to be educated at home and it's estimated that some 2 to 3 million Americans (3 per cent of the school-age population) are taught by parents at home or in communal classes.

Formal education comprises three levels: elementary, secondary and higher. Vocational training, adult education, and special schools or classes also form part of the education programme in most states. Many states and communities provide schools or special classes for children with special educational needs, including those with emotional and behavioural problems, moderate and severe learning difficulties, communication problems, partial hearing or physical disabilities. There are also private schools catering for gifted and talented children, and most public schools have gifted and talented programmes (see **Special & Remedial Education** on page 209).

The US constitution requires the separation of state and religion and forbids religious observance in public schools (although there are plans to restore school prayers in some areas), but children are still expected to participate in the ritual morning pledge of allegiance to the American flag in many schools (although the words 'under God' are optional!). With the exception of a few private and some parochial schools, school uniforms are rare, although they're becoming more popular at public schools, particularly in large cities.

A unique aspect of the US education system is the high degree of parental involvement. 'Parent power' isn't only accepted, but is welcomed and encouraged through local Parent Teacher Associations (PTAs) and Home and School Associations (HSAs) attached to every school. PTAs and HSAs meet regularly and concern themselves with many aspects of a school's affairs including the curriculum, facilities, school hours and after-school activities and programmes. Parents are encouraged to attend meetings and show an interest in the school and their children's education (it's also a good way for newcomers to make friends). Schools organise parent days, 'back to school' nights and parent-teacher conferences, where parents can meet teachers and examine their child's school timetable.

In the last decade or so, there has been extensive debate over the declining standards and low achievements of American students, particularly when compared with students in other leading industrialised countries such as Germany and Japan (and even countries such as Korea and Taiwan). In tests given to American and foreign students, the US has had a poor showing. American high school students and graduates (from public and private schools) score particularly badly in mathematics (math) and science, many can barely read or write, and most know virtually nothing of the wider world or even their own history. Even colleges and universities haven't escaped censure and have been criticised for being too expensive, extravagant, having poor teaching standards, and inadequate planning.

In recent years, many parents concerned about the decline in public education have turned to private schools. Although the cost of private education is high, many American parents consider it an acceptable price to pay, particularly if the outcome is a bachelor's or master's degree from a prestigious university, with its resulting monetary value in the job market. Education for its own sake or the love of learning is rare in the US, where education and qualifications are judged primarily on their earning power (particularly MBAs). Foreign families resident in the US for a short period may prefer to send their children to a private international school, where they will be less indoctrinated in American ways. The organisation and curricula of most private schools and colleges are similar to those of public schools, although the administration differs.

Around one child in 20 enrolled in public schools cannot speak English or speaks it so poorly as to require language assistance. If your children don't speak English fluently, enquire whether English as a Second Language (ESL) classes are available or whether study is available in other languages. In some states children are taught in many foreign languages. For example in California public high schools commonly teach in Arabic, Armenian, Cantonese, Japanese, Korean, Russian, Spanish, and Tagalog (Philippines). In some other states students are taught in no foreign languages at all. Most public schools don't offer ESL courses unless they're located in areas where many new immigrants have settled. Private schools may also make no provision for students who don't speak English fluently.

In addition to a detailed look at public and private primary and secondary education, this chapter also contains information about summer camps, higher education, adult and further education, and language schools.

PUBLIC OR PRIVATE SCHOOL?

Before making any major decisions about your children's education, it's important to consider their individual ability, character and requirements. This is of particular importance if you're able to choose between public and private education, when the following points should be considered:

- How long are you planning to stay in the US? If you're uncertain, it's probably better to assume a long stay. Because of language and other integration problems, enrolling a child in an American school (public or private) with an American syllabus isn't recommended for less than a year, particularly for teenage children.

- The area where you choose to live affects your choice of public schools. Although it isn't always necessary to send your children to a local public school, it's unusual not to and you may have difficulty getting them accepted at another public school.

- Do you know where you're going after the US? This may be an important consideration regarding your children's schooling in the US. How old are your children and what age will they be when you plan to leave? What plans do you have for their education and in which country?

- What educational level are your children at now and how will they fit into the American public school system or a private school? The younger they are, the easier it is to place them in a suitable school.

- If your children aren't English-speaking or of English mother tongue, how do they view the thought of studying in English? Is schooling available in their mother tongue?

- Will your children require your help with their studies? Will you be able to help them, particularly with the English language?

- What are the school hours and the school holiday periods? How will they affect your family's work and leisure activities?

- Is religion an important consideration in your choice of school? In public schools, religious instruction isn't part of the curriculum. However, many private schools are maintained by religious organisations and they may make stipulations as to religious observance.

- Do you want your children to attend a co-educational or a single-sex school? All public schools and the majority of private schools are co-educational.

- Should you send your children to a boarding school? If so, should it be in the US or another country?

- What are the secondary and higher education prospects for your children in the US or another country? Are American examinations or qualifications recognised in your home country or the country where you plan to live after leaving the US?

- Do the schools under consideration have a good academic record? What percentage of high school pupils go on to two-year public colleges and four-year public and private colleges? What percentage of students take the ACT and SAT exams (see page 208) and what are the average combined scores? Other important indicators are the school dropout rate, the average daily attendance rate, expenditure per pupil (including textbooks), and the average teacher salary.

- What are the qualifications of teachers? How do teacher salaries compare with those in other schools?

- How large are the classes? What is the teacher-student ratio?

Obtain the opinions and advice of others who have been faced with the same decisions and problems as you, and collect as much information from as many different sources as possible before making a decision. Speak to the principals and teachers of schools on your short list. Finally, most parents find it's beneficial to discuss the alternatives with their children before coming to a decision. See also **Choosing a Public School** on page 199 and **Choosing a Private School** on page 212.

PUBLIC SCHOOLS

There isn't a federal government controlled or funded school system in the US. Publicly-funded state schools (public schools) are the responsibility of individual state departments of education and are funded largely from local and state taxes with some federal funds. Practices and policies regarding education (public and private) vary from state to state, where education is by far the largest area of expenditure, averaging around a third of total spending. State boards of education determine education policy in accordance with state laws. Each state's department of education is controlled by an elected board, headed by the superintendent of public instruction or the state commissioner of education. Board members are elected by local residents or appointed by the state governor and usually serve from two to six years. The board is responsible for setting policy relating to educational affairs such as the allocation of state and federal funds, certification of teachers, provision of textbooks and library services, records and educational statistics, and setting and enforcing the term of compulsory education.

The American public school system has an unusually high degree of decentralisation; i.e. schools are run largely by local authorities. Each state is divided into school districts (a total of over 16,000), many of which are the size of a city or county. Each district is governed by a superintendent and a locally elected school board (or board of education), usually with five to nine members. Working within the policies established at state level, school districts collect taxes, construct buildings, decide instructional policies, hire teachers, purchase equipment, arrange school terms (semesters) and holiday periods, and generally oversee the day-to-day running of schools.

The superintendent of a school is responsible for executing the policies established by the local board of education. Together with the board, the superintendent prepares the school budget, determines the level of taxes (usually property taxes) needed to finance the school programme, employs teachers and other school personnel, provides and maintains school buildings, purchases equipment and supplies, and provides transport for students who live beyond walking distance from school (many school districts provide school buses).

Teacher qualifications and standards vary from state to state. All states require teachers to have a licence or certificate to teach in public elementary and secondary schools, although the actual requirements for teacher certificates are set by state education departments. All states require a bachelor's degree for teaching elementary grades. Most states demand a bachelor's degree as the minimum qualification for teaching in secondary schools and a few require five years' study or a master's degree. Teachers unfortunately don't enjoy a high status in American society and even college and university professors don't receive the respect accorded them in many other countries. Low salaries and lack of status have led to an increasing shortage of teachers in many areas and the hiring of foreign teachers.

Until the '60s, public education in many (mostly southern) states was officially segregated, with blacks (African Americans) and whites attending separate schools. Desegregation heralded the controversial (particularly to whites) policy of 'bussing', which entailed transporting children by bus from one neighbourhood to another in order to balance racial groups (or achieve integration). This resulted in the bussing of both black and white children away from local schools and went against the long-established tradition of neighbourhood schooling. Although public schools are now integrated and officially blacks have equal educational opportunities, much education is in fact still segregated.

When bussing was introduced, many middle class whites simply abandoned the inner city schools ('white-flight') to blacks and moved to affluent suburbs where blacks were rare, or alternatively sent their children to 'white-only' private schools. However, although desegregation can hardly be hailed as an unqualified success, it has succeeded in narrowing the education gap between blacks and whites, and has reduced the high school dropout rate among blacks. Whereas in 1971, 23 per cent fewer non-whites than whites completed high school, the difference is now just 5 per cent. Blacks (and other minorities) are also attending colleges and graduate schools in greater numbers, although the percentage remains far lower than for whites. However, education opportunities for blacks (and other socially disadvantaged groups, such as Hispanics, native Americans, Asian-Americans and poor whites) remain woefully inadequate, and even when they've a superior education, it isn't necessarily reflected in increased employment opportunities.

Many school districts question whether bussing is necessary and would like to end it. Many people believe it would be better for children to attend local schools, rather than spend up to two hours a day on a bus. Despite bussing, 'segregated' schools are the norm in the US (particularly in cities) and the number of white pupils attending schools with black students is falling rapidly throughout the country.

Public education in the US has been in turmoil in the last few decades, partly as a result of years of experimentation and a neglect of the basics, such as reading, writing and maths (math). During the last ten years, one of the most important issues in American education has been curriculum reform and a return to the proven traditional methods of learning. The emphasis on the basics was reinforced in the '80s by a realisation of the need for training or orientation in technology-related fields such as computer science and communications. Traditional courses in science and the humanities have also been re-emphasised. In recent years, an increasing number of states and cities have radically altered the way they manage, finance and measure their schools. They've also redefined what children should know and how they should be tested, and have given new powers to principals, teachers, parents and students.

One of the most controversial issues in the last few years has been the 'privatisation' (or privatisation of management) of public schools, where outside contractors have been hired to manage schools. Initial results are encouraging, with better maintained and equipped schools, more motivated teachers, higher morale, and pride among pupils and teachers, all of which have helped raise academic standards. In some states, public schools are supported financially by local communities. There's nevertheless a general lack of funding in American schooling, highlighted by decaying school buildings for which the repair bill has been estimated at over $80 billion.

Choosing a Public School

For most American parents, one of the most important (if not **the** most important) criteria when choosing a new home is the reputation of the neighbourhood's public schools. This is often measured by the number of students schools send to famous American colleges (statistics are provided by all schools). If you intend to send your child to a public school, you should make enquiries about the quality of local schools before deciding where to live.

Generally, the more expensive the properties in a neighbourhood, the better the local public schools. Often you can estimate the quality of a neighbourhood's school simply by driving around town or checking the cost of property in the local papers. Because public education is largely locally funded (from property taxes), schools in wealthy areas are much better funded than schools in poor areas, such as inner-city and rural farming communities. Similarly, spending on education per student in the poorer states is less than half that in the wealthier states. The equipment available in affluent schools often includes educational television (TV), electronic and portable language laboratories, slides and viewers, and expensive computer systems. On the other hand, poorer schools often have a lack of basic supplies and equipment such as desks, lockers, books, general supplies, cafeteria facilities or gym equipment. Under the local funding system, the democratic ideal of providing equal education for all citizens is simply impossible to satisfy (equal opportunity is available to all Americans, provided they can afford to pay for it!). In many states, courts have ruled that over-reliance on local property taxes short changes poor districts and have compelled states to spend more on education and to spread the money evenly.

Some poor neighbourhoods in large cities have so-called 'magnet' elementary and high schools, whose superior curriculum (or special-emphasis programmes) and high academic standards attract students from a wide area. Other areas may have a select high school admitting students on the basis of high grades and test scores. Some public high schools specialise in a particular field of study such as science, maths, dance, music, drama, technology or vocational skills, where the teachers are trained specialists and student admissions are based on test results and achievements. On the other hand, most public schools lack extra programmes and have only a limited number of special teachers and tutors.

Foreign parents are often shocked at the apparent lack of discipline in many American public schools, although this may be largely due to the more relaxed atmosphere (of the country as a whole). Absenteeism is a huge problem in some (usually poor inner-city) schools, as is lateness for class (tardiness). This has led some authorities to make parents responsible for their children attending school and parents have been fined, had their welfare payments cut, been ordered to do community service, and even been jailed in some states for their children's truancy. Most schools periodically review attendance records and notify parents when students miss classes.

In the worst inner-city schools, drugs and violence are commonplace and arguments and fights are likely to be decided by knives or even guns. Violence by students against teachers is also common. At tough schools, students are routinely frisked for weapons, and metal detectors are used to dissuade students from bringing weapons to school. Some inner city schools resemble prisons with pupil identity cards, resident armed guards and police, high fences and locked exits during school hours. Under a new law, students who bring guns to school face a mandatory one-year suspension and are charged with possession of a firearm on school property. A number of schools throughout the country have had considerable success with a new programme whereby they offer rewards to students who (anonymously) report fellow students who bring guns or drugs to school.

The quality of public schools varies considerably from state to state and community to community; although some are dreadful, many are excellent. Many communities take pride in the quality of their local public school system (which is crucial in maintaining property values); where schools are well run, well supported and well funded by the local community, the quality of public education rivals any in the world and can offer opportunities seldom available in other countries. Even at schools where average standards are low, students who take full advantage of the opportunities afforded receive an excellent education. Many immigrant children do especially well academically in the US's public school system, particularly Asian students, who are gaining entry to the nation's best colleges and universities in increasing numbers.

Relocation guides are published in many cities and regions. These usually include profiles of local schools and comparative scores for different grades. It's also possible to compare high school ACT and SAT scores (see page 208).

Organisation

Most children start school before the age of six, when compulsory schooling usually begins, in a nursery school or a kindergarten (see page 204). The maximum 13 years of formal elementary and secondary education covers education from 5 to 18, divided into increments called grades (kindergarten to grade 12). Children usually start in kindergarten or grade one at the age of five or six and go up one grade each year until reaching grade 12 at the age of 17. Occasionally a student must repeat a grade because of prolonged absence or low marks, although this is rare. The 12 years following the kindergarten year are usually organised under what is known as the '6-3-3 plan' where grades 1 to 6 are in elementary (primary) school, grades 7 to 9 in junior high or middle school and grades 10 to 12 in a (senior) high school, as shown in the table below:

Age	Grade	School
2 – 5	-	Pre-School
5 – 11	K – 6	Elementary or Primary
12 – 14	7 – 9	Junior High or Middle
15 – 18	10 – 12	Senior High or High

Variations on the 6-3-3 plan include 5-3-4 and 6-2-4 schemes as well as the older 8-4 and 6-6 plans. Under the 8-4 plan students spend eight years (grades 1 to 8) in elementary school and four years (grades 9 to 12) in high school. Under the 6-6 plan students spend six years (grades 1 to 6) in elementary school and six years (grades 7 to 12) in a combined junior and senior high school. Irrespective of which plan is followed in a given school district, the basic state-decreed curriculum for each grade remains the same. Usually a student has one teacher for all major subjects during his first six years of schooling (elementary) and a different teacher for each subject during the last six grades in middle and high schools.

Although a child can legally leave (quit) school at 16 (known as drop-outs), this is generally discouraged (the job prospects for anyone in the US without a high school diploma are worse than dismal!) and the vast majority of students stay at high school until 18.

Registration

At elementary and secondary levels, students usually attend a public school close to their home. If you have a preference for a particular public school or school district, it's usually necessary to buy or rent a property in that area. It's quite normal for Americans to ask an estate agent to find them a home in a particular school district. All schools prefer children to start at the beginning of a new term (semester), although this isn't necessary.

Parents should enquire at the school district's central office or Board of Education to find out to which school(s) their children will be assigned and the documents required for registration. Usually you must produce proof of residence, a birth certificate (or a certified copy), and details of your child's medical history, including immunisations (see **Health** on page 202). It may be necessary to provide proof of a complete medical examination during the year prior to registration. It's also necessary to provide past scholastic records, including a school report from your child's last school. This is used to assign students to a class or grade and should be as detailed as possible, with samples of essays, projects and examinations.

Many towns provide transport to school (buses), although it may be provided for certain schools or ages only, and may depend on the travelling distance to school, e.g. there may be bussing only when the distance from home to school is over 2 or 2.5 mi (3 to 5.5km). Some towns provide buses for children in special education only.

Terms & School Hours

The school year usually runs from early September until May or June (nine months) and is divided into 'quarters' or terms (semesters). Some schools use the quarter system, which comprises three sessions: fall (September to December), winter (January to March) and spring (March to May or June). Others use a semester system made up of two sessions: fall (September to December) and spring (January to May). School vacation dates are published by schools well in advance, thus allowing parents plenty of time to schedule family holidays during official school holiday periods. Normally parents aren't permitted to withdraw children from classes, except for visits to a doctor or dentist, when the teacher should be informed in advance whenever possible. If you wish to take a child out of school during classes, you must obtain permission from the principal. This is rarely given. It's particularly unwise to take a child out of school when he should be taking examinations or during important course work assignments.

The school day in elementary schools is usually from 8.30am to 3pm or 3.30pm, with an hour for lunch. In high schools, hours are usually from 7.30am to 2pm or 2.30pm. This is divided into six one-hour classes or four 90-minute classes (with a five-minute break between classes) and a 30-minute lunch break. Extra-curricular activities and sports are scheduled after school hours. Lessons in public schools are held from Monday to Friday and there are no lessons on Saturdays or Sundays.

Over the past ten years a new system has evolved (starting on the west coast), designed to overcome the serious overcrowding in some schools, particularly in major cities. Class sessions are held for 45, 60 or 90 days, followed by a break of 15 to 42 days, all year round. This means that at any one time a third of the school's students and teachers are on holiday, thus allowing a school with a capacity for 1,200 students to accommodate 1,800. Around 6,000 schools now operate on this basis, although many parents don't like it, as it plays havoc with family holiday plans.

Some high schools also provide summer sessions, which offer students the opportunity to make up for work they've missed or subjects they've failed. It also allows them to take additional subjects for which they receive college-level credits. Summer classes are usually held in the mornings, with afternoons devoted to sports, trips or leisure activities. Some parents enrol their children in summer classes to familiarise them with a new school, make friends or to improve their English when it isn't their mother tongue (or just to get them out from under their feet).

Health

In most states, school children must be immunised against a range of diseases before starting school. These may include polio, DTP (diphtheria, tetanus and pertussis or whooping cough) and MMR (measles, mumps and rubella or German measles). Tuberculin screening may also be necessary. (If your children have been vaccinated against tuberculosis, be sure the school knows this, as they will test positive when screening is performed.) Evidence (in English) of the appropriate inoculations, including exact dates, is required when you apply to a school. Most schools have full or part-time nurses (who may cover a number of schools) or at the very least staff trained in administering first-aid. Most states require students to have periodic medical examinations (physicals), by their family doctor (physician) or by a school appointed doctor. School nurses conduct routine checks for such things as sight, hearing, curvature of the spine, lice, height and weight. Special examinations are necessary to take part in some sports activities. Dental checks aren't carried out at schools, but many schools promote a dental health week.

Health education is provided in elementary and secondary schools, including sex education (e.g. the dangers of AIDS) and the perils of drugs and smoking (which are combined with community programmes). In some cities, e.g. New York, high schools issue free condoms to children as young as 12 (usually without their parents' knowledge or agreement, which is a contentious subject). This isn't only to combat AIDS, but to reduce unwanted pregnancies (in some inner-city schools over half the girls in the senior class are pregnant at the end of the school year). Although AIDS is primarily a male disease among those over 25, there's little difference in the incidence between teenage boys and girls. In many communities, volunteer ambulance corps members teach children about safety and accident prevention.

Provisions

It's common for children at elementary level to take a packed lunch to school, although many children also go home for lunch when they live close to school. Milk is usually sold at elementary schools at snack and lunch times. Most elementary and secondary schools provide a self-service cafeteria where children may purchase lunch, and some children receive free lunches under local welfare programmes. The 'equipment' required by students varies considerably and may include the following (at elementary school, teachers may send parents a list of the items required):

- School bag or backpack (buy a good quality bag or pack, as inexpensive ones don't last) and/or a lunch box and thermos for a packed lunch;

- Pencils (with eraser tops), pens, glue or paste, scissors, paper, notebooks, folders, binders, etc.;

- Gym or physical education (phys ed) clothes, including shoes, sports shorts/ skirt, shirt/blouse and a towel;

- Sports bag for the above (if the school bag is too small).

High school students are provided with lockers where they can store their books and other possessions. Schools provide cycle racks for students who cycle to school and high schools provide car parks (parking lots). Elementary school children must usually reach a certain grade and pass a cycling proficiency test before being permitted to cycle to school. Bicycle safety helmets are encouraged and are mandatory in some states and towns.

There's often a charge for participation in sporting activities and extra-curricular activities such as driver education or marching band.

Pre-school Education

As used here, pre-school education embraces all formal and informal education before the age of six (when compulsory schooling starts). It includes tots and toddler programmes, play school, nursery school (collectively known as pre-kindergarten) and kindergarten. Attendance at school for children under six isn't compulsory, and the provision of schools for children under six varies according to the finances and circumstances of local communities. Most public elementary schools provide a pre-school kindergarten (K) year for five-year-olds, which is usually the first year of elementary school (see page 205).

There are various types of pre-schools, including non-profit co-operative schools, church-affiliated schools, local community schools, private schools and Montessori schools. A co-operative school is usually the least expensive, as parents work voluntarily as teachers' aides alongside professional teachers. Church-affiliated schools are usually attached to religious centres and may include religious education (it isn't always necessary for children to follow the same religion as the school). Private schools are the most expensive and vary considerably from small home-run set-ups to large custom-built schools. A number of private nursery schools use the Montessori method of teaching, developed by Dr Maria Montessori in the early 1900s. Montessori is more a philosophy of life than a teaching method and is based on the belief that each child is an individual with unique needs, interests and patterns of growth. Some Montessori schools have 'pre-school' (for children aged two-and-a-half to six) and elementary levels (ages 6 to 12).

In many areas, private classes are offered for children aged from six months to three years. These combine the theory and practice of play groups and day care centres. Many areas also have what are termed 'toddler' or 'tot' programmes, which usually accept children from two to four years of age. Activities generally include arts and crafts, music, educational games, perceptual motor activities and listening skills. Most communities also have informal community schools or learning centres, playgroups, morning programmes at local YWCAs, and other inexpensive alternatives to private schools. Community colleges also offer a variety of courses for small children, e.g. painting, dancing and cooking, once or twice a week, e.g. on Saturday mornings.

Many children attend private nursery schools for two to six-year-olds and some private elementary schools have a pre-nursery or nursery programme. Fees for private nursery schools range from $5,000 to $15,000 per year for full-time schooling, depending on the school and area. School hours vary, but children usually attend for a few hours in the morning, e.g. from 9am to 11.30am, or afternoon, e.g. 12.45pm to 3.15pm, or both. Some schools allow you to choose a number of morning or afternoon sessions only, thereby reducing the fees. Many day care centres are designed for working parents and combine nursery school and (extended) day care, with centres open from 6.30am to 6pm.

Pre-school education programmes maintain a close relationship with the home and parents and are intended to introduce children to the social environment of school and concentrate on the basic skills of co-ordination. Activities are often expanded to include alphabetic and numerical orientation, so children entering kindergarten or grade one at the age of five or six who haven't attended pre-school are usually at a disadvantage. Research in a number of countries (including the US) has shown that children who attend pre-school usually progress at a faster rate than those who don't. A much lower proportion of children (around 60 per cent) attend pre-school in the US than in Japan and many European countries (e.g. Belgium and France, where it's 95 per cent). In some areas (e.g. New York City), nursery schools are in short supply and it's necessary to put your child's name on a waiting list as soon as possible (before conception!). Some of the more 'prestigious' (and expensive) nursery schools require pre-admission testing and interviews (of the potential students and their families), as some people believe the choice of the 'right' nursery school is essential for eventual university admittance. Ensure that a pre-school or day care centre is licensed and meets local and state standards.

Nursery school is highly recommended for all children, particularly those whose parents' mother tongue isn't English. After even a few months in nursery school, a child is integrated into the local community and is well prepared for elementary school (particularly when English isn't spoken at home). Parents can also make friends in the community through pre-school contacts.

Elementary School

The first years of compulsory schooling are called elementary or primary school (just to confuse the issue, elementary schools are also called grade or grammar schools, although these terms are considered rather old-fashioned). Elementary education starts at the age of five or six, depending on the particular state and whether a kindergarten (K) year is provided. Even when provided, attendance at kindergarten isn't always compulsory. To qualify for kindergarten a child must be five years old on or before a 'cut-off' date, e.g. 1st September or October, to attend that year. Usually a child must be enrolled in kindergarten or first grade in the calendar year in which he turns six. Elementary school, which is almost always co-educational (mixed boys and girls), is usually attended from the age of 5 or 6 until 11 (grades K to 6), when students go on to a middle or junior high school. In some districts, students attend elementary school until 13 (up to grade 8) before attending a senior high school.

The elementary school curriculum varies with the organisation and educational aims of individual schools and local communities. Promotion from one grade to the next is based on a student's achievement of specified skills, although a child is required to repeat a year in exceptional circumstances only. (Some school districts are returning to testing as a means of determining when a child is ready to move to the next grade, in an effort to reduce reliance on 'social promotion,' and this is becoming yet another contentious issue.) Elementary schools provide instruction in the fundamental skills of reading, writing and maths, as well as history and geography (taught together as social studies), crafts, music, science, art and physical education (phys ed) or gym. Foreign languages, which used to be taught at high schools only, are now being introduced during the last few years of elementary school in some areas (although in some cities, state schools don't offer any foreign language teaching). Elementary students are usually given regular homework, although in many schools few children complete it.

Secondary School

Secondary education is for children aged 12 to 18 (grades 7 to 12). It generally takes place in a high school, which is often divided into junior and senior high (housed in separate buildings or even separate locations). Junior high is for those aged 12 to 14 (grades 7 to 9) and senior high for students aged 15 to 17 (grades 10 to 12). During the four years in senior high school, students are usually referred to by the following terms:

Term	Age	Grade
Freshman	14 – 15	9th
Sophomore	15 – 16	10th
Junior	16 – 17	11th
Senior	17 – 18	12th

In some districts, students attend a combined junior/senior high school or attend a middle school until 13 (grade 8) before transferring to a four-year senior high school. Like elementary education, secondary education is co-educational. American high schools are often much larger than secondary schools in other countries, and regional high schools with over 2,000 students are common in some rural areas and city suburbs.

Secondary school students must take certain 'core' curriculum courses for a prescribed number of years or terms, as determined by each state. These generally include English, maths, general science, health, physical education and social studies or social sciences (which may include American history and government, geography, world history and social problems). Students are streamed (tracked) in some high schools for academic subjects, where the brightest students are put on a 'fast track'. In addition to mandatory subjects, students choose 'electives' (optional subjects), which supplement their future education and career plans. Electives usually comprise around half of a student's work in grades 9 to 12. Students concentrate on four subjects each quarter and are seldom 'pushed' beyond their capability or capacity for learning.

High schools offer a wide range of subjects from which students can choose a programme leading to college/university entrance or a career in business or industry. The courses offered vary from school to school and are listed in school curriculum guides. Around the ninth grade, students receive counselling as they begin to plan their careers and select subjects that are useful in their chosen fields. Counselling continues throughout the senior high school years and into college, particularly in junior college or the first two years of a four-year college programme. Larger schools may offer a selection of elective courses aimed at three or more tracks:

academic, vocational and general. Students planning to go on to college or university elect courses with an emphasis on academic sciences (biology, chemistry, physics), higher mathematics (algebra, geometry, trigonometry and calculus), advanced English literature, composition, social sciences and foreign languages.

The vocational programme may provide training in four fields: agricultural education, which prepares students for farm management and operation; business education, which trains students for the commercial field; home economics, which prepares students for home management, child care and care of the sick; and trade and industrial education, which provides training for jobs in mechanical, manufacturing, building and other trades. Students interested in entering business from high school may take typing, shorthand, book-keeping or 'business' English.

The third programme is a general or comprehensive programme providing features of the academic and vocational programmes. Its introductory courses provide an appreciation of the various trades and industrial arts, rather than training students for specific jobs. Those who don't want to go to college or enter a particular trade immediately but want the benefits of schooling and a high school diploma often follow the general programme.

Upon satisfactory completion of 12th grade, a student graduates and receives a high school diploma. (In the US, students graduate from high school, junior high school, elementary school and even nursery school.) At high schools (as at colleges and universities) there are ceremonies to celebrate graduation complete with caps, gowns, diplomas, and speeches by staff and students. Graduation ceremonies are often called 'commencement', because it marks the start of a new stage in a student's life. Americans are enthusiastic about 'life cycle events' (milestones) and graduations are a time of great celebration and feting of students. It's a particular honour for a student (usually the top student) to be chosen as the 'valedictorian', who gives the valedictorian oration or farewell speech at the graduation ceremony.

With the exception of physical education (phys ed) classes, school sport is usually extra-curricular, i.e. takes place outside school hours. Team sports have a high profile at many high schools and being 'on the school team' is more important to many students than being top of the class. (Actually, in terms of securing scholarships for university, they may be right!) Students who excel at sports are often referred to disparagingly as 'jocks', implying that they're too stupid or lazy to succeed at their academic work. Although the jock stereotype doesn't always ring true, sports stars do tend to neglect their school work. This has led some schools to introduce 'no pass/no play' rules, where only students who pass their courses may participate in after-school sports. High school sport is central to school activities and the ceremony that goes with college sport is also found at high school level.

In addition to sports, many other school-sponsored activities take place outside school hours, including science and nature clubs, musical organisations (e.g. band and choir), art and drama groups, and language clubs. Nearly every school has a student-run newspaper and a photographic darkroom is also usually available. Colleges and universities place considerable value in the achievements of students in high school extra-curricular activities, as do employers. High schools are also important social centres, and participation in school-organised social events such as homecoming parades (with homecoming queens) and school dances is widespread.

Examinations & Grades

When a student enrols in a public school, a 'cumulative file' or 'folder' is opened for him (which follows him throughout his school years) and there's a continuous evaluation system throughout all grades. Students are marked on each essay (paper), exam (test) and course taken in each subject studied throughout their 13 years of education (grades K to 12) and the Grade Point Average (GPA) is calculated during high school. In many elementary schools, students' work may be classified as E (excellent), S (satisfactory) or U (unsatisfactory). The following grading system is used in high schools throughout the US:

Grade	Classification	Points
A	Excellent	4
B	Good	3
C	Average/fair	2
D	Poor	1
E/F	Fail	0

All grades are internal and are related to the general standard achieved at a particular school, which usually makes it difficult to compare standards in different schools and states. Marks depend on a range of criteria, including a student's performance in tests given at intervals during the year, participation in class discussions, completion of homework assignments, and independent projects. Students receive a report card at least twice a year (in some school districts it may be up to six times), which shows their grades in each subject they're studying. Commercially prepared tests are also given in many areas at all levels to assess students' and schools' achievements, and locally developed end-of-year examinations are given in many schools. Some states, e.g. New York, have state-wide exams prepared by the state department of education. The federal programme, No Child Left Behind, introduced by the Bush administration in 2002, has also encouraged school districts to implement regular testing of children in order to prove the schools are achieving various goals and thus are eligible for federal funding.

High schools maintain a school 'transcript' for each student, summarising the courses taken, the grades attained and other relevant data. If a student wishes to go on to college or university, his high school submits copies of his transcript to the college. College or university acceptance is also based upon personal recommendations from teachers, achievements outside school (e.g. extra-curricular and sports achievements), and college aptitude tests. Students in their junior year may take the Preliminary Scholastic Aptitude Test (PSAT), which is a good guide to their chances of acceptance by the college of their choice. They may also take the National Merit Scholarship Qualifying Test (NMSQT), which is used to screen the top academic students in the nation for scholarship consideration.

Students planning to go to college take national college aptitude tests during their last two years in high school, set by various independent institutions. Some colleges also require students to take Achievement (Ach.) Tests. Tests are of the multiple-choice type and aren't based directly on school work, but are designed to measure aptitude and verbal and mathematical skills rather than knowledge (tests are often accused of testing nothing but a student's ability to take the test itself). The best known and widely used tests are the American College Testing (ACT) programme and the Scholastic Aptitude Test (SAT), both of which are recognised by accredited universities to evaluate potential students.

The maximum SAT score is 1,600 (800 mathematical and 800 verbal skills), with the average score usually between 900 and 1,000. To gain entry to an Ivy League university (see page 216), students must usually score over 650 in each section or a combined total of over 1,300. Each college or university sets its own admission requirements, the subjects necessary (for a given course), and the minimum GPA acceptable. In some states, state-wide examinations are used to determine admission to public colleges and universities. High school students can attend 'cramming' colleges where they're coached in passing these exams or improving their ACT or SAT scores. Numerous books on how to improve ACT and SAT scores are available from libraries and book shops. Students who score highest in ACT and SAT tests are offered scholarships to top universities.

Students in many high schools can follow an Advanced Placement (AP) programme. This is an advanced curriculum sponsored by the College Board and adopted by high schools in addition to their state-determined curriculum. Students who elect to enrol in an AP course for a given subject complete one academic year of course work paralleling an introductory college-level course, i.e. the first (freshman) year. On completion of the course, students take the AP exam, and if they pass are granted college placement or credits (or both). The AP programme isn't an automatic option, as it's generally expensive for schools to adopt and is therefore offered to outstanding students only. If you're interested in following the AP programme, you should make enquiries well in advance.

SPECIAL OR REMEDIAL EDUCATION

Special education (special ed) is provided for children with moderate or severe learning difficulties (the 'learning impaired'). These are usually due to a physical disability or an emotional problem, which prevents or hinders them from attending a mainstream school or class for their age group. School districts may provide special classes or schools for children with special educational needs, including those with emotional and behavioural difficulties, moderate and severe learning difficulties, communication problems, hearing or sight impairment or other physical disabilities. If you have a child who requires special education, check that the town where you intend to live provides appropriate tuition **before buying or renting a home**.

Since the early '70s, American public schools have been required by law to provide an education for all students, and consequently all states now provide special and remedial schools or classes for disabled children. Special education may take place in certain schools only or in all public schools within a particular school district. The No Child Left Behind legislation requires all school districts to demonstrate improvements in the education of disabled and special ed students.

Over 4 million disabled children benefit from three federal grant programmes: Handicapped State Grants, Pre-school Incentive Grants and Title-1 State Administered Programs. These have been expanded to include educational options for emotionally disturbed children and vocational education for mildly 'impaired' students. In some areas, there are special schools for children who lead 'stressful' lives in broken homes and dangerous neighbourhoods, and special schools for delinquent young criminals (similar to boot camp for military conscripts).

Most public schools also have a gifted and talented programme or special 'fast-track' classes for exceptionally bright children (those with very high IQs or special talents, such as designing spaceships or practising brain surgery at the age of three). There are also special 'magnet' programmes or schools in major cities catering for gifted and talented children (see **Choosing a Public School** on page 199).

PRIVATE SCHOOLS

There are numerous private fee-paying schools in the US, serving a multitude of educational needs and educating around 10 per cent of children, a total of almost 5 million students in elementary schools and 1.2 million in secondary schools. Private schools include single-sex schools, schools sponsored by religious groups, schools for students with learning or physical disabilities, and schools for gifted children. Some private schools place the emphasis on sport or cater for students with talent in art, drama, dance or music. There are also schools emphasising activities such as outdoor living or adhering to a particular educational philosophy such as Montessori (see page 204) and Rudolf Steiner schools.

Although most private schools prepare students for entry to an American college or university, some international schools prepare students for the International Baccalaureate (IB) examination (see **International & Foreign-language Schools** on page 214). Many international schools teach classes in a number of languages, e.g. English, French, German and Spanish. Some private schools teach exclusively in a foreign language, e.g. Japanese, follow foreign curricula and prepare students for examinations set by examining boards in their home country.

Religious instruction isn't permitted in public (state) schools, so many private schools are based on religious principles, ranging from Catholic convent schools to fundamentalist academies. Church-run schools are usually referred to collectively as 'parochial' schools, although the term is commonly used to refer to schools run by the Catholic Church. In some areas, particularly the south, parochial schools are seen merely as an attempt to create all-white schools, while in some northern cities, the Catholic schools are considered the best way for minority students to escape problems in city public schools.

Private schools are organised like public schools (see page 197), although the curricula and approach differ considerably, and are usually aimed at securing admission to a top university. Private schools range from nursery schools to large day and boarding schools, from experimental and progressive schools to traditional institutions. They include progressive schools with a holistic approach to a child's development and schools with a strict traditional and conservative regime and a rigid and competitive approach to learning. School work in private schools is usually rigorous and demanding, and students often have a great deal of homework and pressure (in stark contrast to most public schools). Many parents favour this competitive 'work ethic' approach and expect their offspring to work hard to justify the cost. Some private schools are run on the lines of a military academy with uniforms (although these are rare), strict discipline and punishments (corporal punishment isn't illegal in the US).

Private 'prep' schools aren't the same as public preparatory or primary schools, but are single sex high schools that prepare students for prestigious 'Ivy League' universities. Prep schools have a social cachet and are roughly equivalent to British public schools (e.g. Eton and Harrow). They flourish in the eastern states, but are rare in the west, where they're seen as elitist and decadent. Although most private schools are day schools, they include a number of boarding schools, particularly in the New England states where it has long been a tradition among affluent American families to send their offspring to board. Note, however, that most American boarding schools cater for high school students only and there are few boarding schools for younger children.

Fees vary considerably according to a variety of factors, including the age of students, the reputation and quality of the school, and its location (schools in major cities are usually the most expensive). Annual fees start at around $1,000 for elementary schools and around $2,000 for secondary schools, but can be as high as $15,000 in some regions. Boarding school fees can run to $30,000 per year, although this may include books and school trips. In some states, school districts subsidise private schools through a voucher system, and around a third of private school pupils receive some sort of financial assistance. Most private schools provide scholarships for gifted and talented students, which may be reserved for children from poorer families or ethnic minorities. Some schools have large endowments, enabling them to accept any students they wish, irrespective of the parents' ability to pay.

Fees aren't all-inclusive and additional obligatory fees are payable plus fees for optional services. Private school fees tend to increase by an average of 5 to 10 per cent annually (unless you're rich or someone else is paying, start saving **before** you have any children). In addition to tuition fees, most private schools solicit parents for contributions (some schools are quite aggressive in their 'requests').

Most private schools provide a broad-based education and generally offer a varied approach to sport, music, drama, art and a wide choice of academic subjects. Their aim is more the development of the child as an individual and the encouragement of his unique talents, rather than teaching on a production-line system. This is made possible by small classes, which allow teachers to provide students with individually tailored tuition. Private schools employ specialist staff, e.g. reading specialists, tutors to help those with difficulties, and specialists to assist those who wish to accelerate their learning or work independently. Most private schools also offer after-school classes, sports teams, clubs and 'enrichment' programmes.

When making applications, do so as far in advance as possible. It's usually easier to gain entry to the first grade than to get a child into a later grade, where entry is strictly limited. Entry is often facilitated for some foreign children, as many schools consider it an advantage to have students from several countries. Gaining entrance to a prominent private school is difficult, particularly in major cities, and you can never guarantee that a particular school will accept your child (unless you're the President of the US). Although many nursery and elementary schools accept children on a first-come, first-served basis, the best and most exclusive schools have a demanding selection procedure, including tests and personal interviews with the potential student and family members, and many have waiting lists. Don't count on enrolling your child in a particular school and neglect other alternatives.

Before enrolling your child in a private school, make sure that you understand the withdrawal conditions in the school contract, particularly if you expect to be in the US for a short time only. Before sending a child to a particular private school you should consider carefully his needs, capabilities and maturity. For example, it's important to ensure that a school's curriculum and regime is neither too strict nor too liberal for your child.

There are a number of guides to private schools, including Peterson's *Private Secondary Schools*, which provides a detailed analysis of private day and boarding schools, in the US and abroad. Directories of private schools are available in most reference libraries. Over 1,000 private schools are members of the National Association of Independent Schools (NAIS, 1620 L Street, NW, Washington, DC 20036-5695 ☎ 202-973-9700, 🖳 www. nais.org), whose website has a search facility for finding a private school in your area. See also **International & Foreign-language Schools** on page 214 and **Pre-school Education** on page 204.

Choosing a Private School

The following checklist provides a guide to some of the things you must consider before selecting a private school:

- Does the school have a good reputation? Does it belong to a recognised body for private schools such as the Incorporated Association of Preparatory Schools? How long has it been established? Is it financially stable?

- Does the school have a good academic record? For example, what percentage of students obtain high marks in the ACT and SAT examinations and go on to top universities? What subjects do students do best in? All schools should provide exam pass rate statistics. Parents of children who aren't exceptionally bright may prefer to send them to a school with less academic pressure.

- What does the curriculum include? A broad and well-balanced curriculum is best. Ask to see a typical student timetable to check the ratio of academic to non-academic subjects. Check the number of free study periods and whether they're supervised.

- Do you wish to send your children to a single-sex or a co-educational school? Some parents believe that children make better progress without the distractions of the opposite sex (although their 'social' education may suffer as a result).

- Day or boarding school? If you're considering a day school, what are the school hours? If you've decided on a boarding school, what standard and type of accommodation is provided?

- Do you intend to send your children to an elementary or secondary private school only, or both?

- How many children attend the school and what is the average class size? What is the teacher-student ratio? Are student numbers increasing or decreasing? Check that class sizes are in fact what they're claimed to be. Has the number of students increased dramatically in the last few years (this could be a good or a bad sign)?

- What are the qualification requirements for teachers? What are the teachers' nationalities?

- Are you required to pay for extras? For example, optional lessons (music, dancing, sports, etc.), lunches, art supplies, sports equipment, school trips, telephone calls, clothing, insurance, textbooks, stationery and parking.

- Which countries do most students come from?

- Is religion an important consideration in your choice of school? What is the religious preference of the school, if any?

- Are special English classes provided for children whose English doesn't meet the required standard? Usually if a child is under nine, it doesn't matter if his English is weak. However, children over this age may not be accepted unless they can read English fluently (as printed in text books for their age). Some schools provide intensive English tuition for foreign students.

- What languages does the school teach as obligatory or optional subjects? What facilities are provided (such as a language laboratory)? If you wish your children to learn foreign languages, you may need to send them to a private school or pay for a private tutor.

- What is the student and staff turnover?

- What are the school terms and holiday periods? Private school holidays are usually much longer than those for public schools, e.g. four weeks at Easter and Christmas and ten weeks in the summer, and often don't coincide with public school holiday periods.

- What sort of discipline and punishments are imposed, and are restrictions relaxed as children get older?

- What are the withdrawal conditions should you need or wish to remove your child? A term's (semester's) notice is usual.

- What examinations are set and in which subjects? How do they fit in with your child's education plans?

- What sports instruction and facilities are provided?

- What are the facilities for art and science subjects, e.g. arts and crafts, music, computer studies (how many computers?), science, hobbies, drama, cookery and photography?

- What sort of excursions and holidays does the school organise?

- What medical facilities does the school provide (e.g. infirmary, resident doctor or nurse)? Is health and accident insurance included in the fees?

- What reports are provided for parents and how often? How much contact does the school have with parents?
- Last but not least, unless someone else is paying, what are the fees?

Draw up a list of possible schools and obtain a bulletin or prospectus from each (some schools provide a video prospectus). If applicable, obtain a copy of the school newspaper or magazine. Before making a choice, visit the schools on your list and talk to the head, staff, students, and if possible, parents and former students. Most parents find it helps to discuss the alternatives with their children and, if possible, allow them to make the final decision. See also **Public or Private School?** on page 196.

INTERNATIONAL SCHOOLS

In addition to the many private schools that follow the American curriculum, there are a number of international and foreign-language schools. International schools accept students of all nationalities and religious backgrounds, who are taught in English. Where necessary, students whose mother tongue isn't English receive intensive English tuition. International and foreign-language school fees may be higher than those at many American private schools, particularly fees for boarders.

Most international schools prepare students for the two-year International Baccalaureate (IB) pre-university examination, although some offer an American curriculum in addition to the IB curriculum. The IB diploma is recognised as an entry qualification by universities worldwide and is particularly important if you're planning to continue your child's college or university education outside North America. It should be noted that an American high school education is academically up to two years behind those in most other industrialised countries, and a high school diploma isn't accepted as a university entrance qualification in many countries (e.g. most European countries).

The IB curriculum is introduced during a student's last two years of secondary school, and study is undertaken in a wide range of subjects, selected under the guidance of a school-appointed IB co-ordinator. The subjects that comprise the core of the IB curriculum are divided into six groups (from each of which candidates must select one subject): language A (literature); language B (modern foreign languages); individuals and societies (social studies); experimental sciences; mathematics; and a sixth elective (optional) subject. Three subjects are studied at Higher level and three at Subsidiary level. In addition, students are required to complete a course unique to the IB curriculum, called Theory of Knowledge. This reflects the philosophy of the IB, which is that students should be taught 'how to learn'; a deliberate compromise between the preference for specialisation in some countries and the emphasis on general knowledge preferred by others.

Further information about the IB, including a list of participating American schools, can be obtained from International Baccalaureate North America (IBNA), 475 Riverside Drive, 16th Floor, New York, NY 10115 (☎ 212-696-4464), from the international headquarters (Organisation du Baccalauréat International, Route des Morillons 15, 1218 Grand-Saconnex, Geneva, Switzerland, ☎ +41 22 791 7740) or on the IBO website (🖳 www.ibo.org).

Foreign-language schools cater for nationals of a particular country or those speaking a particular language, and students usually study for entry to higher educational institutions abroad. Among the many foreign-language schools in the US (usually located in major cities such as Los Angeles, New York and Washington DC) are Canadian, Chinese, Dutch, French, German, Greek, Japanese, Norwegian, Spanish and Swedish schools. Information about international and foreign schools is available from embassies and consulates in the US (see **Appendix A**). See also **Private Schools** on page 210 and **Choosing a Private School** on page 212.

SUMMER CAMP

Going to summer camp ('day camp' or 'sleep-away camp') is a long tradition in the US. Some 8 million children aged between 6 and 18 attend over 10,000 camps each year. Summer camp is considered to be an adventure and an important part of a child's development, where he learns independence, self-sufficiency, responsibility and friendship (and self-defence!). Many children attend camp for two weeks only, although some go to camp for almost the entire ten weeks of the summer holiday.

An American summer camp is usually a permanent structure, with separate areas for activities, administration and sleeping (in cabins called 'bunks'). Camps are located in rural surroundings in areas of great natural beauty, usually close to a lake where there's ample space and equipment for water sports, including canoeing, sailing, swimming and water-skiing. Other sports facilities may include tennis and basketball courts, riding stables, archery and rifle ranges, a golf course, plus open areas for field sports such as baseball and football. Non-sporting activities may include arts and crafts (perhaps with a wood shop, craft shop, pottery studio and photographic darkroom), exploratory trips, campfires, science and the performing arts. Many camps have a dining hall and an amphitheatre, where the entire camp community can socialise. Although some camps specialise in the arts, most camps put the emphasis on physical outdoor activities; sing-songs, camp plays and concerts usually make up the indoor activities.

Many camps are lavishly equipped (even extending to electricity in the cabins), while others are more primitive and emphasise the back-to-nature element of camping. Some camps have no windows or bug screens in cabins and provide makeshift sports facilities only. Camps run by Boy or Girl Scout organisations usually have platform tents rather than cabins for sleeping, and concentrate on activities such as camp craft, hiking and canoeing. Camp staff (e.g. counsellors, office, cleaning and kitchen staff) often include university students, many of whom are recruited abroad by organisations such as Camp America (see page 215). Depending on your child's personality, you may wish to choose a specialised or a single-sex camp rather than a more traditional camp. It's possible to visit most camps and speak to the camp director or owners or attend a camp presentation in your area. Many of the best camps are accredited by the American Camping Association (ACA) or other associations such as the Western Association of Independent Camps.

There are various types of camps, including private or independent camps, organisational or agency camps (sponsored by organisations such as the Boy or Girl Scouts, YMCA/YWCA, Jewish Youth Centers, or a church or charitable institution), special needs or institutional camps, camps for the underprivileged, and day camps (where children attend during the day and return home in the evening).

Camp guides include *Peterson's Summer Fun: Traditional and Specialty Camps*, listing over 3,000 summer opportunities in the US and worldwide, and the online guide of the American Camping Association (5000 State Road 67 North, Martinsville, IN 46151 (☎ 765-342-8456, 🖳 www.acacamps.org), listing over 2,000 residential and day camps throughout the US. Summer camps are advertised in Sunday newspapers such as the *New York Sunday Times* and in free family-oriented newspapers throughout the spring.

HIGHER EDUCATION

Higher education refers to study beyond secondary school level and usually assumes that a student has undertaken 13 years of study and has a high school diploma. There are three main levels of higher education: undergraduate studies (bachelor's degree), graduate studies (master's degree) and postgraduate studies (doctor's degree). The minimum age for enrolment at university is usually 18, and some 40 per cent of college students are 25 or over, many of them taking advanced degrees.

Degree level courses are offered by around 3,500 accredited colleges and universities, with a wide variety of admission requirements and programs. Of the total college population of 15 million students (12 million in public colleges and 3 million in private), around 500,000 are overseas students, roughly half of which are working on graduate level degrees. Hundreds of American colleges recruit students in countries such as the UK, Hong Kong, Japan and Malaysia. Although the terms 'college' and 'university' are often used interchangeably, a college may be independent or part of a university (both colleges and universities are also referred to simply as schools). An American college typically offers a blend of natural and social sciences and humanistic studies. Students are usually 18 to 22 and attend college for around four years to earn a bachelor's degree in arts or science. On the other hand, a university is usually composed of an undergraduate college of arts and sciences, plus graduate and professional schools and facilities. The four years of undergraduate study for a bachelor's degree are referred to as freshman, sophomore, junior and senior (also used in high schools).

One of the most surprising and unique aspects of the US education system is that many of the most prestigious universities are private foundations and receive no federal or state funds (their main source of income in addition to fees is endowments). The most famous universities include the Ivy League universities (so called because they've been sufficiently long established for ivy to have grown on the walls): Brown, Columbia, Cornell, Dartmouth, Harvard, Pennsylvania, Princeton and Yale. The Ivy League, together with the 'heavenly seven' or 'seven sisters' (Barnard, Bryn Mawr, Mount Holyoke, Radcliffe, Smith, Vassar and Wellesley) of once all-female colleges, are the most prestigious American universities. Although some people claim their fame rests more upon their social standing than their academic excellence, attending one of these colleges usually pays off in the job market, particularly at executive level. Other world-renowned American higher education institutions include the Massachusetts Institute of Technology (MIT) in

Cambridge (Massachusetts), the California Institute of Technology (Caltech) and Stanford University in California, all of which have earned distinguished international reputations for their research and academic excellence.

The academic standards of American colleges and universities vary greatly, and some institutions are better known for the quality of their social life or sports teams than for their academic achievements. Establishments range from vast educational 'plants' (with as many as 50,000 students) offering the most advanced training available, to small private academies emphasising personal instruction and a preference for the humanities or experimentation. Major universities are like small cities with their own shops, banks, police and fire departments, and are usually renowned for the excellence of their teaching, research facilities, libraries and sports facilities.

The main difference between higher education in the US and that in many other countries is that in the US, the system is designed to keep people in education rather than screen them out. Some 55 per cent of American high school graduates (55 per cent of whom are male and 45 per cent female) go on to some sort of higher education (a total of over 14 million). Many Americans look upon a bachelor's or master's degree, rather than high school graduation, as the natural completion of school life. With the exception of the top dozen or so, American colleges and universities are geared to the average rather than the brighter student. The academic standards required to earn a bachelor's degree in the US are lower than in many other countries. Some colleges accept almost any high school graduate and are disparagingly referred to as 'diploma mills' (which has diminished the value of degrees). It's at the graduate schools (where students study for a master's degree) that American universities are seen at their best, where serious students receive an education rivalling that of any country.

Most universities have excellent professors, due in large part to paying vast salaries which enable them to attract the best brains (many from abroad). Professors have a much higher social standing than school teachers and are permitted a high degree of autonomy in their teaching methods (associate and assistant professors are fancy names for readers or lecturers).

Community & Liberal Arts Colleges

The US has two unique higher education institutions: the two-year community or junior college and the four-year liberal arts college. Two-year community colleges are largely locally controlled and publicly funded. They offer studies leading to technical and semi-professional occupations, and studies which prepare students for entrance to a four-year degree institution. A two-year college awards an associate degree after two years' study, e.g. Associate of Arts (AA) and Associate of Science (AS) degrees. The four-year liberal arts college may be one of the constituent parts of a university complex or an independent establishment. It provides pre-professional training of four years or less for students who proceed to advanced professional schools, such as law or medicine, and offers a liberal education for students who don't enter professional or graduate school. A university college of liberal arts often serves students in parallel undergraduate professional colleges, such as engineering and business administration, by providing them with courses in basic disciplines. In many states, the top 10 to 15 per cent of graduating high school students are admitted to four-year universities, the next 20 per cent or so go to state colleges, and the remainder attend two-year community colleges.

Terms & Grades

Most colleges and universities have two terms (semesters) or sessions a year of around 14 weeks each: fall, from September to late December, and spring, which extends from late January to late May (some divide the academic year into three sessions: fall, spring and summer). Those who miss or fail a course can catch up by attending summer school, an intensive eight-week course offered between terms. Most students complete ten courses per academic year and usually take four years (although it can be much longer) to complete a bachelor's degree requirement of around 40 three-hour courses or 120 credits. Those who achieve the highest grade point averages (GPAs) graduate (or 'are graduated') as Summa cum Laude (excellent), Magna cum Laude (very good) and Cum Laude (good). All other successful students are awarded ungraded degrees. As bachelor's degrees have become commonplace, more students are pursuing postgraduate studies (almost always called 'graduate school'), particularly professional degrees in law (JD) and business (MBA), and PhDs.

Fees, Grants & Scholarships

Tuition fees vary widely among colleges and universities and no two institutions charge the same fees. Public state colleges and universities charge significantly lower fees for in-state residents (also applies to resident foreign students) and higher 'out-of-state' fees to non-residents. One year's residence in a state is usually necessary to qualify for the resident tuition rate. Higher fees may also apply to out-of-county students at a two-year community college.

Average tuition fees for public (state) four-year colleges and universities are around $3,500 per year and for private institutions around $15,000 per year, although you can pay twice as much for tuition at an Ivy League college. Fees for private universities have increased alarmingly in recent years and many colleges have reduced their entrance standards (called 'dumb-downscaling') to attract students who can afford the fees. In addition to tuition fees, there are also fees for registration, health centre, sports centre and parking (all of which must be paid at the start of each semester). Room and board, books and supplies, transportation, and other expenses cost (on average) an additional $8,000 to $15,000 per year, depending on the area, whether you attend a public or private institution.

A car is often essential, as public transport is usually poor. Health insurance is compulsory, although students may be automatically enrolled in the university health insurance plan. All in all, paying for a child's college education is a major investment for parents, most of whom can expect to spend between $50,000 and $100,000 to put a child through college. Most families participate in savings and investment schemes to finance their children's college education, and an increasing number expect their offspring to take an active role in paying for their own education through loans and evening and summer jobs. Many students obtain part-time employment to finance their studies, during term-time and summer breaks (foreign students should check in advance whether their visa allows such employment), while others receive grants, scholarships and loans to help meet their living expenses.

Scholarships are awarded directly by universities as well as by fraternal, civic, labour and management organisations (around a third of students at Harvard receive a scholarship). Although public universities don't usually give financial aid to foreign students at the undergraduate level, it's possible for foreign students to obtain a scholarship or partial scholarship for their tuition fees from a private university. Full scholarships covering all tuition expenses are rare, so unless you're able to contribute at least 50 per cent from your own resources, it generally isn't worth applying.

A foreign student can apply directly to an American university for aid, a scholarship or work-study option, and can also apply to educational programmes in his home country. American embassies can provide information about the range of scholarships and grants available. A request for financial aid from a college or university doesn't affect an entrance application in any way, as each is considered independently. Around half of all college students (some 5 million) receive some form of financial assistance, and having wealthy parents doesn't ban a student from receiving aid (although 25 per cent of American students and parents don't ask for help).

Qualifications

Entry qualifications for American colleges and universities vary considerably; generally the better the university (or the better the reputation), the higher the entrance qualifications. Some specialist schools, such as law schools, have a standard entrance examination. Usually overseas qualifications which would qualify students to enter a university in their own country are taken into consideration. It's important for mature students returning to full or part-time college education to provide any diplomas or certificates showing the education level they've attained (otherwise they must take basic tests). Whatever your qualifications, each application is considered on its merits. All foreign students require a thorough knowledge of English and those whose mother tongue isn't English must take a TOEFL test (see page 223). Some colleges and universities also require all foreign students to take the SAT (see page 208). Contact individual universities for details of their entrance requirements.

Applications

Applications must be made to the Director of Undergraduate Admissions at colleges and universities. If you plan to apply to highly popular colleges and universities, such as those in California, you must apply in the summer or autumn (fall) for admission in the **following** fall term (August/September), although you should start the process 18 months in advance. State universities in California are closed to foreign students by December for admission the following autumn. For less popular universities, the latest a foreign student can apply for September admission is March of the same year, as overseas applications usually take at least six months to process. With changes to the student visa requirements (see **Immigrant Visas** on page 77), you should plan on extra time for your visa application, which cannot be started until after you've been accepted by a school. The number of applicants each university receives per available place varies considerably and you would be wise not to make all your applications to universities where competition for places is fierce (unless you're a genius). It's best to apply to three universities of varying standards, e.g. speculative, attainable and safe.

Accommodation

Following acceptance by a college or university, students are advised to apply for a place in a university dormitory (dorm) or in other college accommodation. Campus accommodation is limited, although many universities give priority to foreign students. The cost of college accommodation and board (meals) ranges from around $2,000 to $8,000 per year. Many students rent rooms in shared apartments or houses. However, in many areas this kind of accommodation is difficult to find and expensive.

Clubs & Facilities

All colleges and universities have a wide variety of societies and clubs, many organised by the students' union or council, which is the centre of campus social activities. Some universities ban alcohol on campus and there are no students' bars. Students found drinking alcohol on campus may face suspension or even expulsion.

American colleges and universities usually have excellent sports facilities and go to great lengths to recruit the best high school athletes. Most colleges provide full academic scholarships to athletes, often risking their academic reputation in the process. There's an unwritten agreement between college Directors of Admission and potential sports stars that they enrol in college purely to play sports (with luck they will use intercollegiate competition as a springboard to a professional career). Sports teams generate huge incomes for colleges and are a commercial necessity (inter-college competitions are big business), although the situation often embarrasses college administrators and angers other students, who resent the preferential treatment given to athletes. Faced with criticism, some universities have initiated support programmes to improve the academic performance and graduation rates of athletes.

All colleges and universities devote a lot of time to wooing their former students ('alumni/alumnae'), who are persuaded to keep in touch with their old college (alma mater), and most importantly, send lots of money. Many colleges have annual events called 'homecomings' (also held by high schools), when alumni are encouraged to return to college and take part in various activities. Colleges also hold other strange events such as a 'fathers' day' or 'siblings' weekend', which are often linked with sports events.

Information

American college catalogues are available in high school guidance offices, libraries and book shops. There are also numerous guides to choosing a college, including *Barron's Profiles of American Colleges*, US News & World Report magazine's *Ultimate College Guide* and Money Guide magazine's *Best College Buys*. Many state Departments of Higher Education have a toll-free 'education hotline' where you can obtain information about all aspects of higher and further (adult) education. The Fulbright Commission provides an Educational Advisory Service in many countries (e.g. 62 Doughty Street, London WC1N 2JZ, UK, ☎ 020-7404 6994, ▭ www.fulbright.co.uk) for students planning to study at an American college or university. The United States International Information Programs section of the State Department also provides information (▭ http://educationusa.state.gov). The Institute of International Exchange (IIE) publishes *Academic Year Abroad*, *Short-Term Study Abroad* and *Intensive English USA*, which provide useful advice and study options (available from IIE Books, P.O. Box 1020, Sewickley, PA 15143-1020, ☎ 412-741-0930, ▭ www.iiebooks.org).

FURTHER EDUCATION

Further education generally refers to education undertaken by adults of all ages after leaving full-time study, often after years or even decades of intervening occupation. It doesn't include degree courses taken at college or university directly after leaving high school, which come under higher education (see page 216). It also excludes short day and evening classes, e.g. those held at community colleges and usually termed 'continuing education' (although there's often a fine distinction between further and continuing education). Further education includes everything from basic reading and writing skills for the illiterate to full-time professional and doctorate degrees at university. On many university campuses, more students are enrolled in further education courses than in regular degree programmes.

Often adult education students don't need to be high school or college graduates or take any tests or interviews, and they're generally admitted on a first-come, first-served basis. A high school diploma is required for some courses, although General Educational Development (GED) tests allow students to earn a high school equivalency diploma (also called the Graduation Equivalency Diploma). This is important to those wishing to continue their education in college or in career-oriented programmes. There are a number of books detailing how to pass the GED, many of which include a mock test that can be taken before the exam. To make courses available to the widest possible number of people, course and tuition fees are kept to a minimum, and retirement age students and the unemployed may receive a discount. Recent innovations, including Learning Anytime Anywhere partnerships between colleges and businesses, in order to promote distance learning, and Community Technology Centers, which are being established in rural and 'economically distressed' areas, are helping to increase access to further education.

Adult education courses may be full or part-time and are provided by two and four-year colleges, universities, community colleges, technical schools, trade schools, business and technical schools, and elementary and high schools. Courses are also provided by private community organisations, government agencies, job training centres, labour and professional organisations, private tutors and instructors, business and industry, industrial training programmes, museums, clubs, private organisations and institutes, correspondence course schools, and educational TV programmes. More and more adult education programmes are becoming available on the internet, including courses which offer university or continuing education credits for completion.

Over 4,000 trade schools provide training for 130 occupations from aviation mechanic to X-ray technician. However, you should avoid schools that aren't state-licensed and nationally or regionally accredited by an agency approved by the US Department of Education. Many colleges, such as community colleges, offer a comprehensive range of continuing and professional education classes. Many further education courses are of the open learning variety, where students study mostly at home. Correspondence colleges, most of which are private commercial organisations, offer literally hundreds of academic, professional and vocational courses, and enrol many thousands of students annually.

Each year millions of students attend further education courses at universities alone, many of which are of short duration and job-related, and scheduled in the evenings, at weekends and during the summer break. Lecturers may be full or part-time faculty members or professionals practising in the fields in which they lecture. Students generally aren't required to take a minimum number of courses per term or to take courses in succeeding terms. You can register in a formal vocational programme or simply take a course for pleasure.

The most popular fields in further education are business administration and management, education, engineering, health professions, fine and applied arts, physical education, language, literature, religion and psychology. The federal government underwrites the cost of basic further education, so that older students (particularly members of minority groups) can go back to school for the rudiments of an education they failed to get as children, including reading, writing, maths, history and geography. Further education also gives students the opportunity to complete their high school studies, which in some cities can be undertaken in Spanish and other languages. Many cities and states offer career, vocational and continuing education programmes in public schools, including English as a Second Language (ESL) classes.

LANGUAGE SCHOOLS

This section is mainly concerned with English-language schools, although much of the information also applies to all language schools. If you don't speak English fluently (or you wish to learn another language) you can enrol in a language course at numerous language schools. There are English-language schools in all cities and large towns; however, the majority of schools, particularly those offering intensive courses, are found in the major cities. Many adult and further education institutions provide English courses, and many American universities hold summer and holiday English-language courses. Colleges and universities often run an American

Language Program, which is a pre-academic English-as-a-Second-Language (ESL) course for students whose native language isn't English.

Obtaining a working knowledge or becoming fluent in English while living in the US is relatively easy, as you're constantly immersed in the English language and have the maximum opportunity to practise (provided you don't spend all your time speaking in your native tongue). However, if you wish to speak English fluently, you probably need to take lessons. It's usually necessary to have a recognised qualification in English or pass a Test of English as a Foreign Language (TOEFL) in order to be accepted at a college or university. You can find out information about taking a TOEFL test by contacting the Educational Testing Service (ETS, Rosedale Road, Princeton, NJ 08541, ☎ 609-921-9000, 💻 www.ets.org/toefl). Foreigners who wish to study English full-time can enrol at one of the many English language centres at American universities where, provided you study for a minimum of 20 hours a week, you're eligible for an F-1 student visa (see page 92).

Most language schools offer a choice of classes according to your current language ability, how many hours you wish to study a week, how much money you plan to spend and how quickly you wish to learn. Courses vary in length from a week to six months and cater for all ages. Full-time, part-time and evening courses are offered by most schools, and many also provide residential courses (often with half board, consisting of breakfast and an evening meal), which are usually excellent value. If you must find your own accommodation, particularly in a major city, it can be difficult and expensive. Language classes generally fall into the following categories:

Category	Hours per Week
Standard	10 – 20
Intensive	20 – 30
Total immersion	30 – 40 +

Course fees are usually calculated on a weekly basis. Fees vary considerably and depend on the number of hours tuition per week, the type of course, and the location and reputation of the school. Expect to pay $175 to $225 per week for a standard course and between $250 and $300 per week for an intensive course. Half board accommodation usually costs between $200 and $300 extra, depending on the location, and various self-catering options are generally available costing between $150 and $350 per week, depending on whether you want a shared or single room. It's possible to enrol at a good school for an all-inclusive (tuition plus half board accommodation), four-week, intensive course for as little as $400 per week. Total immersion or executive courses are offered by many schools and usually cost $2,500 or more per week. Not everyone is suited to learning at such a fast rate, even if they can afford it!

Whatever language you're learning, don't expect to become fluent in a short time unless you have a particular flair for languages or already have a good command of a language. Unless you desperately need to learn a language quickly, it's probably better to spread your lessons over a long period. Don't commit yourself to a long course of study (particularly an expensive one) before ensuring that it's the correct course for you. Most schools offer a free introductory lesson and free tests to help you find your appropriate level. Many language schools offer private and small group lessons. It's important to choose the right course, particularly if you're studying English in order to continue with full-time education in the US and need to reach a minimum standard or gain a particular qualification.

You may prefer to have private lessons, which are a quicker but more expensive way of learning a language. The main advantage of private lessons is that you learn at your own speed and aren't held back by slow learners or left floundering in the wake of the class genius. You can advertise for a private teacher in local newspapers and magazines, on shopping mall notice boards, at town halls, libraries, universities or schools, and through your (or your spouse's) employer. Your friends, colleagues or neighbours may also be able to help you find a suitable teacher.

For further information about languages in the US, see **Language** on page 43.

10.

PUBLIC TRANSPORT

With the notable exception of air travel and rush-hour urban rail and bus services in some cities, public transport in the US is generally slow and infrequent (or even non-existent). Except for a few cities such as New York and San Francisco, public transport is nowhere near the standards enjoyed and taken for granted in Europe and would be considered hopelessly inadequate in any country less reliant on the car. In fact many areas outside major cities and holiday destinations aren't served by public transport at all! Nevertheless, despite its manifest inadequacies, public transport in the form of a subway or urban rail system is faster than travelling by car in most major cities.

The one area of public transport where the US excels is in air travel, where Americans enjoy the most comprehensive and cheapest services in the world. For most Americans, air travel and taxis are the only means of public transport worth considering. Airlines account for some 10 per cent of total passenger miles, compared with 0.5 per cent for inter-city buses and just 0.2 per cent for rail travel. The success of the airline industry has been at the expense of the railways, where an infrequent and relatively expensive national passenger service survives thanks only to federal subsidies. The US has a comprehensive long-distance bus service (Greyhound), although it's slow and provides little competition to airlines. It isn't **always** essential to own a car in the US, particularly if you live in a city with adequate public transport (and where parking is expensive or impossible). However, if you live in the suburbs or a rural area or do a lot of out of town travelling, a car is essential. When travelling long-distance, the choice is usually between flying and driving.

As people move out of the cities into the surrounding suburbs and countryside, more are commuting to work, creating (one would think) a huge demand for fast and frequent public transport; however, even where trains and busses are available, most commuters steadfastly prefer to rely on their own cars. The US has no long-term unified national transport policy, balancing the needs of the public transport user against those of the motorist. The present system is heavily weighted in favour of private cars and the level of public transport subsidies are among the lowest in the world. The lack of comprehensive public transport services contributes hugely to the incessant traffic jams, particularly in major cities such as Los Angeles and New York, where a short road journey during rush hours can take hours.

Reduced fares for senior citizens and the disabled are provided in most areas, and many transport authorities and companies publish information leaflets for disabled travellers. There are also reduced public transport fares for children, youths and students in most regions. Many cities and towns offer park and ride services, where inexpensive or free parking is combined with low cost public transport into town centres. Most public transport operates reduced services on weekends and on federal holidays.

The single busiest travel period for all forms of public transport is the Thanksgiving holiday period. If you plan to travel any time during the week of the Thanksgiving holiday you should book your train, bus or airline tickets well in advance or you may not be able to travel at all. When booking a holiday you should be wary of travel and holiday deals which seem too good to be true, as they most likely are! Don't give your credit card details or send any money in response to an advertisement until you know more about the company and have received written details of an offer. Better still, book through a travel agent who's a member of the American Society of Travel Agents (ASTA), who can usually organise and book all your travel arrangements and save you time and money.

TRAINS

The railway (railroad) was responsible for opening up the west in the 19th century and played a major role in the development and exploitation of the whole North American continent. However, it fell into rapid decline in the latter half of the 20th century, losing much of its former business to the car, air travel and long-distance buses. The American national railway network, known as Amtrak, is operated by the National Railroad Passenger Corporation, a federally administered semi-nationalised corporation. Amtrak was created in 1971 with the merging of the passenger routes of 13 privately-owned railway companies, which after years of neglect were bankrupt and facing collapse. In recent years Amtrak has suffered badly from lack of investment.

The US rail network covers more than 186,000mi (300,000km) of tracks and is the largest in the world. However, in terms of passenger miles per head of population, it rates well behind other industrialised nations. The fastest and best trains carry freight, which has priority over (and subsidises) the passenger service. The passenger rail system covers only 22,000mi (35,750km) of track and excludes two mainland states (South Dakota and Wyoming), as well as Alaska and Hawaii. There are no direct transcontinental train services and connections must be made through Chicago, in the north, and New Orleans, in the south. The rail network links over 500 cities and towns, but many cities aren't connected. (Amtrak provides Thruway buses to link train services and to serve areas where there are no rail services.) Local trains are operated by state and regional rail companies in many states.

In general, services are slow and infrequent (Amtrak is God's way of telling Americans to slow down!). American trains are on average twice as slow as those in most European countries and four times as slow as French and Japanese high-speed trains. Late trains are common, particularly on long-distance routes, and some routes have one train a day only. In an effort to win back customers, Amtrak introduced 'on-time' guarantees on certain services, where passengers on late trains (even one minute late) receive a free ticket on the same route. Nevertheless, more people travel by rail today than 30 years ago – around 24 million each year. The busiest stations are New York, Washington DC, Philadelphia, Chicago and Newark – each handling over a million passengers per year (over 4 million in the case of New York).

Amtrak's rolling stock, track and auxiliary services vary from excellent to poor. The tracks (apart from those in the Northeast) are still owned by the old freight companies (such as Topeka & Santa Fe and Chesapeake & Ohio) and are mostly ancient and badly maintained, with the exception of those commercially maintained by the busy freight network. On some routes the ride is uncomfortable and derailments aren't unknown. Stations are occasionally grand buildings (e.g. New York's Grand Central and Washington's and Los Angeles' Union stations), but most are run-down and neglected, and in the major cities are home to tramps and derelicts.

The rail system is at its best in the Northeast 'corridor' (the Boston-New York-Philadelphia-Baltimore-Washington route), served by 120mph Metroliners and a new service called Acela, which whisks you from Boston to New York in three and a half hours and from New York to Washington DC in two and a half. The southern Californian system is also good, where distances are short and getting to and from airports would otherwise be inconvenient and expensive. In these regions, rail travel from city centre to city centre is as fast as air travel and compares favourably with European rail services. Rail is generally the quickest way to travel between city centres less than 300mi (483km) apart; beyond this distance it's quicker to fly (even allowing for the time spent travelling to and from airports). Outside the Northeast and southern Californian regions, almost the only people who use trains are train buffs, tourists with lots of time, and those who are afraid of flying. Crossing the US by train takes around three and a half days at an average speed of around 40mph and is reminiscent (speed-wise) of rail travel in China or India. Long-distance train travel is usually little cheaper than flying and often more expensive, although Amtrak offers regional passes for 15 and 30 days' travel for around $210 and $270 off-peak, and $325 and $405 during peak periods. Peak periods are during the summer months and over the Christmas holidays. Nationwide passes are available for $295 and $385 off peak, or $440 and $550 during peak periods.

The advantages of rail travel are the spaciousness of the carriages (particularly on medium and long-distance journeys) and the chance to relax, read and enjoy the changing landscape (or the industrial wasteland). Many trains have observation lounges with wrap-around windows. Service is the equal of that on any railway in the world and you can usually eat and drink well at what are reasonable rates by international standards. As a means of travel for tourists with plenty of time and a wish to see some of the world's most spectacular scenery, trains are ideal. The evocative names and routes of many of Amtrak's long-distance trains recall the golden age of American rail travel and include the Champion, Empire Builder, Silver Meteor, Silver Palm and Silver Star, South Wind, Sunset, and Vacationer.

Amtrak provides accommodation for wheelchair-bound passengers (indicated by a wheelchair symbol on the outside of cars) on all trains, including specially designed sleeping accommodation and bathrooms on overnight trains. New Amtrak carriages, such as Amfleet trains and Metroliners, can be boarded without steps at most stations (although steps are necessary at some stations). Wheelchairs are available on request at most stations, although disabled, elderly and other passengers who need assistance (such as those in wheelchairs) should notify Amtrak (☎ 1-800-USA-RAIL) 72 hours before departure. Guide dogs may ride in passenger cars free of charge, although **no other animals are permitted on Amtrak trains**. Amtrak publishes a free brochure, *Access Amtrak*, for disabled passengers.

For information about Amtrak services, write to Amtrak Distribution Center, PO Box 7717, 1549 Glen Lake Ave, Itasca, IL 60143 or check the Amtrak website (🖳 www.amtrak.com). Amtrak publishes a bi-monthly magazine, *Express*, available free from stations and agents, as well as a comprehensive free travel planner, *Amtrak's America*, containing information about all Amtrak's long-distance routes, sleeping accommodation and travel advice. Amtrak stations, offices and approved travel agents provide information about tours, connections with other train services and buses, rail trips in Canada, hotel bookings, and car rental. In addition to its regular services, Amtrak offers around 75 package tours, many of which include hotels, meals, sightseeing and theatre shows (☎ 1-800-321-8684).

In addition to the Amtrak system and local rail services, there are a number of scenic narrow gauge railways operating restored steam locomotives on lines negotiating some of the most spectacular terrain in the US (particularly in the Rockies, where the romance of the railways survives). Deserving special mention are the Grand Canyon Railway (💻 www.thetrain.com), which uses vintage steam trains and runs along the southern rim of the Grand Canyon, and the Durango and Silverton Line (💻 www.durangotrain.com) offering trips aboard a refurbished 19th century steam train. Another popular journey is the Napa Valley Wine Train (💻 www.winetrain.com), employing Pullman cars built in 1917 and offering the added bonus of the opportunity to sample some of the region's best wines.

If you're interested in chartering a private train, the American Association of Private Railroad Car Owners publishes a directory available from AAPRCO, 421 New Jersey Avenue, SE, Washington, DC 20003 (💻 www.aaprco.com). Two excellent books for rail lovers are *Rail Ventures: Complete Guide to Train Travel in North America*, by Jack Swansen (Roberts Rinehard Publishers) and *USA by Rail* by John Pitt (Bradt Publications).

Tickets

Single tickets in are called 'one-way' tickets and return tickets 'round-trip' tickets. (Round-trip tickets normally cost exactly twice the one-way fare.) Circle trips are round-trips within a region, where the return journey is via a different route from the outward journey. Excursion fares are for round-trips during off-peak times and cost little more than regular one-way tickets. With the exception of round-trip excursion fares, all tickets entitle you to break your journey (stop over) as often as you wish. It's cheaper to buy a through ticket to your final destination, rather than buy tickets between stopover points.

Rail tickets for Amtrak services should be purchased from a ticket office, online or by telephone **before** commencing your journey. There's a $15 surcharge for tickets purchased on Amtrak trains when the ticket office was open at the time of departure (except for senior citizens and the disabled) and you won't be able to claim any promotional discounts or travel offers. With few exceptions, discounted, excursion or round-trip tickets cannot be purchased on trains, although sleeping car, club service and custom class accommodation can be, subject to availability. If you wish to upgrade your accommodation, you should consult the conductor or 'on board services' (conductors aren't required to change notes larger than $20). When you present your ticket to the conductor (or buy a ticket from him on a train), he puts a receipt in front of your seat or beneath the overhead baggage rack. If you change seats or leave your seat temporarily, take the receipt with you and replace it when you return.

Fares

Standard Amtrak accommodation is called 'coach', and on selected trains in the Northeast corridor and Metroliner trains a superior Club Service is provided (with wider seats). Regional train services, the Acela Express and Metroliner have fares that vary with the time you're travelling (off-peak, shoulder and peak hours). Children under two travel free and those aged 2 to 15 pay half-fare (based on off-season adult fares). Children under eight aren't permitted to travel alone and children aged 8 to 11 may travel unaccompanied under certain conditions only and with written permission from the person in charge at the boarding station. Full adult fares are charged for children under 11 travelling alone. A sleeper berth costs between 125 and 200 per cent of the standard fare. Senior citizens over 62 receive a discount of 15 per cent on most tickets and disabled travellers receive a 15 per cent discount on full fare tickets, although proof of disability is required. Students with a Student Advantage card also receive a 15 per cent discount. Discounts don't apply to sleeping accommodation and cannot be combined with other discounts.

Payment

All Amtrak ticket offices and the Amtrak website accept American Express, Carte Blanche, Diners Club, Discover, Mastercard, and Visa provided the fare is more than $25. Credit cards are also accepted at some ticket offices and aboard trains for tickets and dining car meals. Personal cheques are accepted for fares over $25 in all states except California, where cheques are accepted from customers aged 62 or over only. Passengers paying by cheque must produce photo identification and a credit card. At major stations, tickets can be purchased from automatic ticket machines called Quik-Trak kiosks, which may accept bills up to $20 and credit cards (e.g. American Express, Diners Club, Discover, Mastercard and Visa).

Bookings

Amtrak advises passengers to arrive at a station 30 minutes before departure time. This is, however, generally necessary only when you need to buy a ticket or have baggage to check in. Bookings are required for Club Service and Custom Class travel, seats on long-distance trains, sleeping car accommodation, Metroliner trains and some Empire Corridor trains. If you're in doubt about whether you need to book, check in advance. If you're planning to take a long-distance train during the summer or on a federal holiday, you should book well in advance to be sure of a seat. Bookings are required for all club and sleeping accommodation and on long-distance trains indicated on Amtrak timetables as 'all reserved trains'.

You can make bookings at city railway stations, Amtrak ticket offices and most travel agents. When you book a seat or sleeper you're given a booking number and a time limit to pay for your ticket. If you arrive at a station without a booking and seats are still available, you are assigned a seat and sold a ticket on the spot. Amtrak has a computerised booking system which you can call free on 1-800-USA-RAIL. The best time to call is early morning or late at night (see also **Timetables & Maps** on page 240).

Cancellations & Refunds

Tickets for sleeping accommodation are refunded if bookings are cancelled at least 24 hours before departure. If cancelled less than 24 hours prior to departure (but before departure), the accommodation charge isn't refundable, but can be credited to a future booking. If not cancelled before departure ('no show'), the accommodation charge is neither refundable nor may it be carried forward. Club Service seating cancelled less than an hour before departure is not refunded, but may be applied to other Club Service travel on the same date only. Refunds of the unused value of most tickets are available at Amtrak ticket offices upon presentation of the original tickets (refunds aren't given for lost, stolen or destroyed tickets).

Local Trains

Local (state or regional) rail companies offer a wide range of tickets usually including: one-way; round-trip; weekly (typically saving 15 per cent) and monthly (saving 30 per cent) commuter tickets; round-trip excursion (RTX, off-peak only); children's fares (e.g. aged 5 to 11, 50 per cent reduction); 10 or 20-trip; senior citizens and disabled; student monthly; and groups (e.g. 15 or more people). On local trains, senior citizens (aged over 62 or 65) and disabled people with a valid Reduced Fare Card or Medicare Card may be eligible for reduced fares for off-peak travel, i.e. any time **except** on trains scheduled to depart between 6am and 9.30am and between 4pm and 7pm, Mondays to Fridays. In some areas, a Weekend and Holiday Family Supersaver Fare allows two children under 12 to travel free with a full-fare paying adult. In most areas, children under five travel free when accompanied by a full-fare paying adult, although this is often restricted to one free child per adult. Local one-way and round-trip tickets may be valid up to 180 days.

Tickets for suburban services can normally be purchased on trains, although there may be a surcharge (e.g. $2 during peak hours and $1 during off-peak hours) when tickets are available at a local outlet. At some suburban stations there are ticket outlets during peak hours only, outside which tickets must be purchased on trains. In some areas, where tickets are not available at the local station, they can be purchased at nearby shops. **If in doubt, check in advance.** Ticket machines may be provided which accept all coins (except pennies) plus $1, $5, $10 and $20 bills. Monthly tickets can usually also be purchased by post. Information about local commuter train services can usually be found in the front of your local telephone directory.

Accommodation

The cheapest rail accommodation (called accommodations in the US) is called 'coach', where reclining aircraft-type seats are provided, with ample leg room. Seats are comfortable and have trays, reading lamps, and sometimes a fold out leg and foot rest. Pillows are provided free on overnight trains, although you should bring a blanket (souvenir blankets are sold in lounge cars) to counter the freezing, night-time air-conditioning. Most people find they sleep well in the reclining seats.

Superliners, operating in the west, are Amtrak's premier long-distance trains and offer restaurants, bars, a cinema, video entertainment, taped music programmes and social centres. Superliner accommodation varies, but usually consists of coaches, observation or dome cars, full-service dining cars, and sleeping cars. At least one toilet is provided in each car. Sleeping accommodation includes economy single and double bedrooms, deluxe bedrooms with shower, washbasin and toilet, family bedrooms sleeping two adults and two children, and bedrooms for passengers with mobility problems. In the east, Amtrak's older Heritage long-distance trains are in service, although these are being replaced by new Viewliner carriages. Heritage trains are equipped with a range of sleeping accommodation including:

- Slumbercoaches: private single and double rooms equipped with a toilet and washbasin, and lounge seats converting into a single bed or upper berths at night;

- Roomettes: private single rooms converting from a sitting room to a sleeping room, with a full-length bed and private toilet facilities;

- Bedrooms: private rooms designed for two adults or one adult and two children, with a private bathroom. Bedrooms can be combined into suites.

General Information

- Smoking is prohibited on all Amtrak trains except for the Auto Train, where passengers may smoke in a designated area of the lounge car only. Passengers may smoke on station platforms when the train stops, provided that there are no local laws forbidding smoking at the train station, but must remain ready to re-board immediately when notified that the train is about to depart.

- Many trains in the Northeast Corridor and on the West Coast now offer quiet cars. Seating is available on a first-come first served basis, and those sitting in the quiet car are requested not to use mobile phones, pagers, handheld video games or computers that make noise. Passengers are asked to speak softly and the lights on board may be dimmed to allow travellers to relax.

- All trains have toilets or bathrooms. These are often quite spacious on older trains, with the toilet separate from the washing facilities and seats for those required to wait. Trains often have separate bathrooms for men and women.

- Long-distance Amtrak trains often have baggage check-in facilities. On trains where you can check in your baggage, you must have photo identification (to reclaim your bags) and you're restricted to three checked-in bags, none of which can weigh more than 50lbs (25kg). Excess baggage can be checked in for a fee of $10 per additional bag. You're limited to two pieces of carry-on luggage. Checked in and carry-on bags must be labelled with the passenger's name and address.

- Announcements are usually made when trains are approaching stations, although you shouldn't rely on (usually unintelligible) announcements for information about when to disembark or change trains. Often stations are poorly signed and many have one or two small signs only. Platforms (tracks) in some areas are marked inbound (into city) and outbound (out of city).

- Most long-distance trains have dining or restaurant cars and tavern lounges, where you can have a quiet drink. Meals are reasonably priced by international standards (around $15) and above average for rail fare. However, Amtrak snack bars are poor and for the starving only. Food and drink must be provided by law on any train journey of over two hours. All long-distance trains with a dining car service provide children's dishes and a special food service, e.g. low fat and kosher meals (although these must be ordered in advance). Passengers may bring their own food on board, although Amtrak employees are not allowed to heat it up or serve it to you.

- Most trains also have a bar-car, where in addition to alcohol, you can often buy drinks and snacks all day long. The bar may open and close at strange times, as the sale of alcohol is subject to the licensing laws of whatever state the train is passing through. Passengers are permitted to consume privately purchased alcohol in private sleeping car accommodation only. Alcohol may not be permitted on local trains unless there's a bar-car.

- Railfone public telephones are provided on all Metroliner Service trains and most long-distance and express trains, calls being paid for by credit card.

- Earphones must be used when listening to radios, cassettes and compact disc (CD) players on trains.

- Inexpensive daily parking is available at or near most suburban stations.

- All main stations offer a choice of restaurants and snack bars, although the food may leave much to be desired. Food and drink machines are also provided at many stations.

- Travel insurance for rail passengers is available from major stations.

UNDERGROUND & URBAN RAILWAYS

A number of US cities have underground railways (subways), including Atlanta, Boston, Los Angeles, New York, Philadelphia, San Francisco and Washington DC. Many cities also have an efficient urban railway system, including Chicago, New York, San Francisco and Washington DC. The Atlanta MARTA and the Washington Metrorail systems are the most modern in the US and among the best in the world. Unlike the New York City underground, they're efficient, clean, comfortable, quiet and generally free of smoke, graffiti and crime. A few cities, such as San Francisco, New Orleans and Philadelphia, still have trams (streetcars) and some smaller cities are building new tram lines (called light-rail service). There are cities with elevated railways or monorail systems, such as Chicago's elevated railway (called simply the 'el') and the Miami elevated railway known as the Metrorail (also referred to as the Downtown People Mover).

Tickets or tokens are usually available from automatic machines (which may not provide change) and may also be available from ticket offices. A range of tickets is available, which may include one-way, round-trip, daily, weekly, two-weekly and monthly tickets. The standard fare is usually around $1.50 to $2.00 for any journey, but New York and other large cities have introduced commuter passes that resemble plastic credit-cards and can hold up to $100 of discounted fares. Senior citizens (e.g. 65 and older) and the disabled usually qualify for half fares (known as 'reduced fares'). Reduced fare tickets may not be available from stations, but from special outlets only.

Smoking, eating, drinking, and playing radios and cassette/CD players aren't usually permitted in stations or on trains, and only guide dogs are allowed on trains. There are car parks at most suburban stations and some have bicycle racks and lockers. Bicycles can be taken on some trains, although usually outside commuting hours only. Most undergrounds and urban railways operate from around 6am to 2am, Mondays to Fridays, with reduced operating hours at weekends and on public holidays.

There are a few rules that should be observed when travelling on undergrounds, particularly in New York City:

- Avoid using undergrounds between 11pm and 7am. If you use them at night, try to use a carriage with a guard (motorman or conductor), the centre cars or those that are most crowded. During the day most trains are safe, but you should avoid empty or near-empty carriages if possible.

- While waiting on a platform, stand in a brightly lit area or close to a manned ticket booth (more crime occurs on station platforms than on trains). In New York City there's an 'off hours waiting area' marked in yellow, which indicates where trains stop during off-peak hours.

- Don't stand too close to the edge of the platform, as people are occasionally pushed under trains.

- Keep a firm grip on your bags and wallet, particularly if you're sitting or standing near the doors (a favourite snatching spot). Undergrounds are a favourite hunting ground for pickpockets, particularly during rush hours.

BUSES

There are two main kinds of bus service in the US: urban (town/city) bus services and long-distance buses (which aren't called coaches in the US). Buses are the most widespread form of local public transport in the US, where more than 1,000 inter-city and suburban bus companies operate services to around 15,000 cities and towns, the vast majority of which have no other public transport services. The bus network covers around 280,000mi (450,000km) of routes, on which some 350 million passengers are carried annually. Each region has its own bus companies providing local town and country services.

Long-distance Buses

Long-distance buses are the cheapest and most popular form of public transport in the US, particularly among the poor, the car-less, eccentrics and the downright weird (you meet some 'interesting' people when travelling on long-distance buses). Although there have been cutbacks in services in recent years caused by increased competition from domestic airlines, long-distance buses continue to survive and even to prosper. You can travel almost anywhere in the US by bus on an extensive network of scheduled routes with good connections.

A number of companies provide long-distance services, by far the largest of which is Greyhound Lines (Greyhound), formed when Greyhound acquired Trailways Lines. Greyhound operates some 250 million miles of regularly scheduled services with 18,000 daily departures to more than 2,600 destinations and carries over 25 million passengers each year. It has depots in most cities and large towns throughout the US and Canada. Greyhound offers the cheapest option for independent travellers seeking door-to-door transport to small towns, and areas that aren't served by Greyhound are usually covered by regional and local bus companies (many of which accept Greyhound bus passes). It also claims an excellent safety record – around 20 per cent of the average commercial vehicle accident rate.

Bus terminals offer a host of services and usually have a restaurant, travel information office, ticket office, toilets, left baggage lockers, and baggage and parcel services. Terminals also usually have a baggage depot, where charges are around $1.50 per item, per day. Bus passes often entitle you to discounts at bus terminal restaurants (although it's usually cheaper to eat away from terminals), nearby hotels and on sightseeing tours. Although bus terminals are usually safe places, they're often located in run-down, inner-city areas and aren't the best places in which to spend a lot of time (many are meeting places for drug addicts, few of whom plan to catch a bus!). Try to plan your arrival so that you arrive in time to find a place to stay in a more appealing area.

You must usually buy your ticket at a bus terminal or a central office before boarding a bus; however you can also now purchase tickets online for mail delivery or pick-up at the terminal. Allow plenty of time, as there are often long queues. Tickets aren't generally sold on buses, except in some rural areas and on-city (urban) routes. Obtain information about timetables, connections and fares, and confirm them by checking the posted timetables. **Always ask for the cheapest available fare, which may not be advertised.** You can buy open-dated tickets from bus terminals or travel agents in advance, although usually it's unnecessary or even impossible to make a reservation. Point-to-point tickets are usually considerably cheaper if purchased at least seven days in advance. Normally when a bus becomes full, another is simply put into service (which means you can arrive ten minutes before departure and be assured of a seat).

You can make as many stopovers as you wish, provided the entire journey is completed before your ticket expires (although there may be restrictions on special fares and sightseeing tours). Bus pass coupons must be validated each time they're used, so you should arrive early at bus terminals to have your ticket stamped. In addition to boarding a bus at a bus terminal, buses also stop at designated 'flag stops'. When you see your bus approaching you must flag it down by waving at the driver to get his attention (if a bus doesn't stop, it's probably full).

Fares depend on a number of considerations, including whether you're making a one-way or round-trip, the time of travel and when you are returning. Children under two travel free (limit of one child per adult paying customer) and those aged 5 to 11 travel for half fare when accompanied by an adult (limit of three children per adult paying customer). Military personnel receive a 10 per cent discount and in addition can travel anywhere (on Greyhound) for a maximum fare of $198 round-trip. People over 62 years of age receive a 5 per cent discount and students up to 15 per cent off. A companion may ride free to assist a passenger with a disability, but must be able to provide needed assistance during the trip and must accompany the disabled passenger for the entire trip (a guide dog may also accompany a passenger with a disability). There's a variety of discount and promotional fares available, although these don't usually apply during holiday periods. Regional and national passes offering unlimited travel within a set period can cost less than $10 a day (for a 60-day pass valid throughout the US).

Passengers are allowed two pieces of free baggage with a total weight of up to 100lb (45kg); children travelling for half fare are allowed 50lb (22kg). Baggage liability is limited to just $250. As with planes and trains, baggage is checked in before boarding a bus, for which you should allow around 45 minutes in cities and 15 minutes in small towns. You should identify your baggage with a name tag and keep your claim ticket in a safe place. When two buses are running on the same service, make sure your baggage is put on the correct bus, as it isn't unusual for bags to end up on the wrong one. You can take a small bag on to a bus provided it fits into the overhead baggage compartment. Always keep any valuables with you on the bus.

Most long-distance interstate buses have air-conditioning, heating, toilets (essential when travelling with children), and reclining seats with headrests and reading lamps. The seats are comfortable, with the smoothest ride being in the middle of the bus away from the wheels (the best view, however, is at the front, where you also have the most leg room). Window seats are often cooler than aisle seats, particularly at night when drivers usually turn up the air-conditioning to keep themselves awake. Take a warm sweater, jacket or blanket on to the bus with you, as the powerful air-conditioning is freezing at anytime. If you plan to sleep on a bus, an inflatable pillow or sleeping bag (to use as a pillow, not to bed down in the aisle) is useful. Ear plugs are also recommended if you're a light sleeper.

If you use a radio or cassette player on a bus, you must wear earphones. Smoking and alcohol are prohibited on all buses, although people often sneak off to the rest room for a puff (however, if you break the rules, drivers are more than willing to throw you off a bus). If you're travelling across the US, bear in mind that distances are often vast and a coast-to-coast trip takes three days, with only brief stops at fast food joints or bus terminals every few hours and no overnight sleep stops or stops for showers (the main consolation is that you don't need to pay to sleep on the bus). At rest stops, you may have only a few minutes to stretch your legs or grab a hamburger and the driver may drive off without warning if aren't on the bus on time! Many people provide their own food and drink, so that they can eat at their leisure. On long journeys you may need to get off the bus occasionally for it to be cleaned. For further information contact Greyhound Lines (☎ 1-800-229-9424, 🖥 www.greyhound.com). Greyhound publishes a huge and excellent *United States of Greyhound* map showing all Greyhound routes plus major parks, monuments and attractions. (See also **Timetables & Maps** on page 240.)

City & Rural Buses

Each region of the US is served by a number of local bus companies, providing local city, suburban and rural services. Many cities also have trolley buses or coaches, operated electrically from overhead wires. Cities and states often have their own local transport authority which controls and sometimes subsidises local public transport (as does the federal government). In a few cities (e.g. Seattle) buses are even free within certain downtown areas. Amtrak provide Thruway buses to link train services and service areas where there are no rail services.

However, compared with Europe, urban bus services in the US are often poor. City buses are slow and crawl during rush hours, when it's often quicker to walk (although bus and commuter lanes speed up traffic in some cities). Services usually operate from around 6am or 7am to 11pm, seven days a week, and in major cities there's a 24-hour service on the most popular routes. However, services during the evening (e.g. after 6pm), at weekends and on federal holidays are often severely curtailed, when you may need to wait up to an hour for a bus (some services run infrequently at all times).

Bus drivers may not provide change, particularly when the fare is deposited in a box. In many cities there's a flat fare (e.g. $1 to $1.50) for a one-way journey, irrespective of the distance. In New York City you must buy a token to travel on a city bus (tokens are also valid on the subway). You can often transfer to another bus free of charge or for a small additional fare (e.g. 25 cents) within a short period, usually one hour; ask when boarding, as you may need a transfer ticket. Transfers cannot be used for a round-trip or circular journey. In some areas you must buy a ticket from a ticket office before boarding a bus and give it to the driver when boarding.

In most cities you can buy daily, weekly and monthly bus passes offering large savings. You can also save money by buying a book of 10 or 20 tickets. In all cities there's free travel or reduced fares (typically 50 per cent reduction) for senior citizens (those aged over 60 or 65) and disabled people, although these may be applicable only during off-peak hours. Children under five usually travel free and those aged 5 to 12 usually travel for half fare. There are reduced fares (25 to 50 per cent reduction) for students or those under 18 in some cities.

Bicycles aren't permitted on buses. Collapsible pushchairs (strollers) must be folded before boarding a bus (don't forget to remove your child first!). With the exception of guide dogs and small pets in cages, animals aren't permitted on buses. Many city buses are equipped with wheelchair lifts at the rear door and most are air-conditioned in summer. Smoking and alcohol are banned on rural and city buses throughout the US. In major cities there are 'regular' or local buses operating at frequent intervals (e.g. ten minutes) and stopping every one or two blocks. Limited stop buses often travel the same routes as regular buses, stopping at around a quarter of the regular stops. Express buses make few stops and mainly provide shuttle services to the suburbs.

Bus stops may be indicated by yellow kerbstones, bus shelters and signs showing bus routes, timetables and intersections. Destinations and route numbers are shown on the front of buses, but are often difficult to read. You usually enter buses at the front and exit from the middle. In many cities all stops are request stops, which means that if nobody is waiting to board and no-one has signalled to get off, a driver won't stop. Most buses have a bell cord or a pressure-sensitive strip to signal the driver when you want to get off. Drivers may announce the names of stops, although understanding them can be difficult. A 'STOP REQUEST' sign may be illuminated at the front of the bus when a stop has been requested.

In many cities there are tourist or 'culture' bus routes, where buses follow a loop and stop at places of interest. For a flat daily fare you can get on and off buses at any stop. In some cities visitors can buy a pass allowing unlimited travel on all local public transport for a period of one to seven days. Some communities provide a local commuter bus service to and from local rail stations. Bus companies provide route maps and timetables, although you shouldn't pay too much attention to bus times.

TIMETABLES & MAPS

All US public transport companies produce free comprehensive national and local timetables, route maps and guides. Amtrak publishes bi-annual national and regional (e.g. Northeast) timetables for spring/summer (May to October) and autumn/winter (November to April), available free from Amtrak stations and sales offices. They contain details of all Amtrak services plus information about interline services to locations that aren't served by Amtrak. Many state Amtrak timetables (sometimes in English and Spanish) and individual route timetables are also published. Nearly all public transport companies in the US now have websites where you can download route maps and timetables as well as make use of their route planning guides that give you the most direct route from one address to another.

Most US transport companies don't accept any responsibility for inconvenience, expense or damage resulting from errors in timetables. Amtrak timetables and services shown in timetables aren't guaranteed, are subject to change without notice and form no part of the contract between Amtrak and a passenger. Amtrak disclaims liability for inconvenience, expense or damage resulting from errors in their timetables, shortage of equipment or delayed trains (they don't plan on getting sued!). However, when a delay causes a passenger to miss a guaranteed connection, Amtrak provides alternative transportation on Amtrak or another carrier, or overnight hotel accommodation at their discretion. If you have a complaint or any comments about Amtrak's services, write to the Office of Customer Relations, Amtrak, Washington Union Station, 60 Massachusetts Avenue, NE, Washington, DC 20002.

Sunday timetables apply on federal holidays, e.g. New Year's Day, Memorial Day, Independence Day, Labor Day, Thanksgiving and Christmas Day. On certain other holidays such as Presidents' Day, a Saturday timetable may be operated. Americans don't use the 24-hour clock, even on transport timetables, where pm (afternoon) times are often shown in **bold** print, which can be confusing. Bus timetables aren't usually displayed at stops, although free timetables can be obtained from bus companies, local libraries and other public offices.

TAXIS

Taxis (cabs) are inexpensive in the US compared with many other countries and are plentiful in most cities (except when it's raining, you have lots of bags, or you're late for an appointment). Taxis are usually easily distinguishable, and most often are painted bright yellow. Many taxi drivers in US cities are recent immigrants who speak little English (a knowledge of Spanish often comes in handy), take circuitous routes (because they're lost or because they're crooks) and often charge whatever they can get away with (so make sure the meter is working). You should take a street map so that you have some idea of whether you're taking a direct route or are being given the grand tour. Don't hesitate to tell the driver if he is going the wrong way or point out on a map where you want to go (New York City cabbies have been known to give passengers a blank look when asked for the Empire State Building or Grand Central Station).

Most taxi drivers are supposed to take English and city-knowledge tests, although you would never guess (English is the **second** language of more than half of New York City's cabbies). New York cabbies have a reputation for being among the rudest and most aggressive drivers in the world. Many Americans' vision of hell is hurtling from pothole to pothole in a New York cab during the height of summer (naturally without air-conditioning), with the lunatic driver attempting to run down pedestrians and push other vehicles off the road while roundly cursing everyone and everything in sight in a foreign tongue. However, spare a thought for the much maligned taxi driver, who's in constant danger of being mugged or even murdered.

At US airports and major railway stations there's often a taxi 'dispatcher'. His job is to get you a taxi, advise you on fares and help prevent you being swindled by cab drivers (or bogus cab drivers). At some airports and rail stations, fares to popular destinations are posted on notice boards. At smaller railway stations there are often taxi telephones. At many airports you can arrange to be picked up by a limousine (limo), a monster stretched car with three or four rows of seats. Make sure you get the price in writing, unless you've just won the lottery, although in a few areas, most notably around Chicago, limos can be an economical alternative to taxis to and from the airport. Minibus shuttle services are also available at most airports; like taxis, they take you exactly where you want to go, but the fare is lower as it's shared with your fellow passengers.

In some cities, e.g. New York, taxis have their tariff posted on their doors. In New York there's a charge (flagdrop) of $2 for the first 1/5 mile, 30 cents per additional 1/5 mile or 20 cents per minute. When the cab is moving at more than 9.6mph the meter clocks distance and when it's stopped or moving at less than 9.6mph, the meter clocks time. This method of calculating fares is standard throughout the US and conforms to federal standards for taximeters. At night (between 8pm and 6am) and all day Sundays there's a surcharge of 50 per cent (or a 100 per cent surcharge if you take a cab outside city limits, plus toll fees). Baggage that can be carried by one passenger is usually free, although some companies make a charge, e.g. $5 for the use of trunk space or a charge per piece (around $1) above a certain size, e.g. over 24in (60cm) long.

In addition to what's shown on the taxi meter, you can be charged tolls (trunk, bridge and ferry) and specified surcharges, such as a night or Sunday surcharge. Special rates may apply to some destinations, usually posted in cabs. Cabbies expect a tip of 15 per cent and aren't happy when it isn't forthcoming (and usually tell you so!). Most don't like changing anything larger than a $10 or $20 note, but don't mind keeping the change.

To hail a cab, just raise your arm (there's no need to yell 'Taxi!'). Taxis are obliged to stop if they're on call, usually indicated by a light on the roof, e.g. 'ON CALL' (signs vary from city to city). A licensed cab must take you anywhere within the city limits or their official area, and a driver may not ask your destination before you get in and then refuse to take you (so don't tell him where you want to go until after you get in). Most cab drivers won't take you to dangerous areas at any time. Get the driver to repeat the destination so that you're sure he knows where you want to go (although this doesn't guarantee that he won't get lost or take you somewhere else). In some areas a driver may be forbidden by law to get out of his taxi (e.g. to help you with baggage) as a security measure. Passengers **always** ride in the rear of a taxi (this is to protect the cabbie rather than the passenger).

There are unregulated radio cabs or 'livery cars' in all towns and cities (New York has some 32,000) that can be hired by pre-arrangement only. Some companies may not respond to your telephone call unless you're already known to them. Some radio cabs are limousine standard and although fares are usually higher than regulated cabs, they're generally clean, comfortable and air-conditioned. Limousines can be rented by the hour, day, week or month and are the best way to travel, provided someone else is paying or you're a millionaire. Rates range from around $50 to $75 per hour (usually for a minimum number of hours, e.g. three or four) plus tolls and tips (around 15 per cent is expected). You should avoid 'gypsy' or 'pirate' taxis, particularly at airports, as they're meter-less, unregistered, unlicensed and uninsured, and often crooks (even worse than licensed cabbies). If you're desperate and all you can find is a pirate taxi, always agree the fare in advance.

If you have a complaint about a taxi, note the cab number which is displayed on the roof, the outside of the passenger door, on the dashboard, or on the rear of the front seat (or all four). Also note the driver's licence number (usually posted inside the cab, e.g. in the rear or on the dashboard next to the driver) and the name of the taxi company. This information should be listed on a receipt, which must be provided on request.

AIRLINE SERVICES

The American airline business (international and domestic) is extremely competitive, and consequently Americans enjoy the cheapest air travel in the world and are the world's most frequent fliers (The US has around ten times as many flights a day as Europe). Major American airlines (most of which are excellent), such as American Airlines and United, can feed passengers to some 250 domestic destinations. Each day more than a million Americans make a domestic flight as routinely as people in other countries hop on a train or bus. Between New York City and Washington DC alone, there are more than 100 shuttle flights in each direction every day. When travellers are able to choose between plane, bus or train, over 90 per cent choose to go by air (which is cheaper per mile than car travel).

The huge volume of air traffic does, however, have its drawbacks. Flights from many airports suffer long delays and weather disturbances (thunderstorms, tornados, hurricanes, blizzards and other frequently occurring phenomena) can play havoc with flight timetables across the country. During peak periods this often means that departures can be delayed for up to an hour and arrivals have to 'stack' while waiting for a landing slot. The majority of domestic flights out of major airports are delayed. When travelling between US cities you may spend more time on the ground getting to and from airports than in flying time. You should check in at least an hour before a domestic flight and two hours before an international flight, as airlines often over-book. It's also becoming increasingly common to encounter delays at security check-in points. If you arrive late (i.e. within ten minutes of departure on a domestic flight or within 30 minutes on an international flight), you may get bumped (put on a later flight), even if you're holding a boarding pass. When flying to the US, there are notoriously long immigration queues at some airports (e.g. New York's JFK and Miami), where you may be delayed for up to two hours.

The deregulation of domestic air routes in 1978 opened up the airways to scores of competing airlines (many of which had been restricted to regional routes) and was supposed to stimulate competition and reduce fares. However, as with most things conceived in Washington, things didn't go exactly according to plan. While fares on the most competitive routes have decreased, fares on less popular routes have soared and many smaller communities have lost their scheduled air services entirely. The shake-up also caused a dozen airlines to go bankrupt (or file for protection from their creditors), including America West, Continental, Pan American Airways and TWA. (Although the idea was to weed out inefficient airlines, this was only supposed to happen to the opposition!) The surviving US air carriers were also dealt a heavy blow when air travel fell off following the September 11th attacks. Increased security precautions at all airports since that time have helped reassure the flying public (though tales of abuses by security personnel have put some Americans off flying altogether!). Increases in costs for the major airlines, particularly fuel costs, have caused even the largest companies to teeter on the brink of bankruptcy lately.

Since 1990, smoking has been banned on all flights scheduled for six hours or less within the US and its territories (including direct flights with a stopover, but no change of plane). This includes flights (under six hours) between the continental US and Alaska, Hawaii, Puerto Rico and the US Virgin Islands. The smoking ban applies to domestic and foreign carriers. Smoking is still permitted on international flights into or out of the US, although many airlines have banned smoking on selected routes (most transatlantic flights are smoke-free) and the US is moving towards a complete ban on flights that originate in or leave the country. Pipes and cigars have long been prohibited on all US airlines, even in smoking sections. Smoking may also be banned in airport terminal buildings or permitted in designated areas only.

Airports

The US has some of the busiest airports in the world, of which the main international airports (termed 'gateway' airports) include Boston, Chicago, Denver, Los Angeles, Miami, New Orleans, New York (JFK and La Guardia), Newark, Orlando, Philadelphia, San Francisco, Seattle, Washington (Dulles and National). Each gateway airport acts as a hub for US carriers and regional/commuter airlines (which operate services to scores of smaller airports).

In terms of passenger numbers, around 30 of the world's 50 busiest airports are located in the US. Hartsfield-Jackson International Airport in Atlanta was the world's busiest in 2002, with Chicago's O'Hare in second place and Los Angeles' LAX in fifth place. New York's JFK ranks 21st busiest and Newark 23rd. US and international airlines offer scheduled services to more than 1,000 airports in the continental US. Airports are often vast places with many terminals (Los Angeles international has seven and JFK ten), some of which are miles apart. When catching a plane, check which terminal you require in advance. (This information is normally printed on your ticket or itinerary, but it can be difficult to find or decode.) Allow plenty of time when travelling by road to an airport, as some have restricted access which causes delays, especially during rush hours or periods of bad weather. Most airports, however, have adequate short and long-term parking (although it can cost as much as your flight!). Private off-airport car parks are often a much more economical choice, although you may need to locate and book space in advance.

Most US international airports have separate international and domestic terminals. Unlike most foreign airports, domestic terminals in the US are far bigger and more numerous than international terminals. Domestic terminals usually also cater for flights to Canada and Mexico, and many regional airports operate a small number of international flights. Major airports are organised by airline, where each carrier has separate check-in desks, gates, lounges and even exclusive terminals at some airports. Signs at international airports are sometimes in English and Spanish, and most airports have information desks and centres with multilingual staff. If you have any problems, go to the ticket booth of the airline with whom you're travelling. Flight departures aren't always announced, but are displayed on information screens and departure boards.

Since the attacks of September 11th, security has been increased at all US airports, sometimes to what seems like absurd levels. It's increasingly important to arrive at the airport early enough to be able to negotiate the security procedures. All checked-in bags are now subject to being x-rayed and searched if necessary. If you lock your checked-in bags, you may find the locks have been broken or cut off to do a search, and many travel experts advise you not to lock your luggage at all. (Also not to pack anything valuable in your checked-in luggage!) Queues for the security checkpoint can be long at peak times. As in most other airports in the world, they x-ray and possibly search all carry-on bags. In most US airports, you are asked to remove your shoes so they can be passed through the x-ray machine, and you must remove any computers from carry-on bags (including small hand held computers, like a Palm). Computers are x-rayed separately and often are swabbed for traces of explosive residue. The Transportation Security Administration (TSA) has a section of its website devoted to air travel (🖳 www.tsa.gov, then follow the link for 'Travelers and Consumers'), where you can find the latest lists of prohibited carry-on items and general tips for what to pack and how in order to avoid problems.

It's sometimes wise to avoid major airports, such as New York's JFK, as this usually saves you time and trouble, particularly when you're travelling on domestic flights. You may have a long walk to the luggage reclaim area, although there are moving walkways (speedwalkers) in most airports. Luggage trolleys must be rented at many airports for around $3 using coins, bills or a major credit card. Trolleys are usually available free of charge only in the international arrivals area, so if you're a foreigner arriving in the US, you should be prepared to pay for a luggage trolley, particularly if you have a connecting flight.. Most international airports have full service banks, currency exchanges, automatic teller machines (ATMs), and stamp and travel insurance machines. All international airports have executive and VIP passenger lounges, and publish free passenger information booklets. Major airports have emergency clinics (and sometimes a dental service), restaurants, bars, gift shops, luggage storage, lost property offices, fax machines, photocopiers, computer rentals and other business services. Duty-free has a low priority in the US and duty-free shops are small or even non-existent at the smaller international airports (you must usually pay for duty-free goods at a shop and collect them at the departure gate). US airports don't have comprehensive shopping malls.

Public transport to and from major airports includes buses, taxis, mini-buses, limousines and sometimes rail or subway services. Often there's a dispatcher whose job is to find you a taxi and advise you about fares. Many hotels and motels provide courtesy bus services at major airports, although smaller airports may have no bus services at all. A shuttle minibus or mini-van door-to-door 'taxi' service is often provided and can be booked to pick you up. Air taxis, both helicopters and light aircraft, are available at all major airports and many smaller regional airports. In some cities, e.g. New York, a helicopter service is available between international airports and a central downtown terminal (usually provided free for first-class passengers). Helicopter and light aircraft sightseeing tours are often available. An *Airport Transit Guide* containing details of fares, public transport and timetables for travel between 55 US and Canadian airports and local city centres is published by Salk International Travel Premiums (💻 www.airporttransitguide.com). For current arrival/departure, gate and luggage information you should call the relevant airline.

International Fares

International air fares to and from the US are among the lowest in the world for long-haul flights. When travelling to the US, particularly from Europe, it's cheaper to travel from a major city where a wide choice of low-cost fares is usually available. London is the main European gateway to the US and attracts the bulk of transatlantic traffic, although it's expensive for business flights. If you're travelling from London, shop around travel agents and airlines for the lowest fares, and check the travel pages of *Time Out* magazine and British Sunday newspapers such as *The Sunday Times* and the *Observer*. Fares from London to New York vary from over $7,000 for a first class one way fare to less than $300 for a discounted Apex return. There has been a number of US casualties in the airline business in recent years, during which fare 'wars' have pushed many US airlines to the edge of extinction. You can insure against an airline going bust and leaving you stranded or buy your ticket with a charge or credit card offering protection against bankruptcy.

With the exception of full-fare open tickets, fares depend on the number of restrictions and limitations you're willing (or able) to tolerate. These include minimum advance purchase periods; limitations on when you can fly; a minimum and maximum period between outward and return flights; and advance booking of outward and return flights with no changes permitted and no refunds (or high cancellation penalties). Apex (advanced purchase excursion) fares are generally the cheapest, particularly for midweek flights. Apex seats must usually be booked between 7 and 21 days in advance and there are restrictions on the length of your stay, e.g. a minimum of seven and no more than 21 days. The main disadvantage with all discounted tickets is that they're non-refundable and cannot be used on other flights or airlines. Before buying a ticket, carefully check the restrictions. Many Apex tickets carry 15 to 100 per cent penalties for reservation changes or cancellations. It pays to shop around before buying a ticket, as it's easy to pay a lot more than is necessary. The cheapest round-trip ticket to/from the US is usually cheaper than any one-way flight. **Book well in advance when travelling to popular destinations (such as Florida, New York and California) during peak periods.**

The cheapest international flights can usually be purchased from 'bucket shops' and 'consolidators' (in the US and abroad), which are companies selling surplus seats at large discounts. They deal mainly in international and transatlantic flights, and rarely offer domestic flights (on which discounts are insignificant). Fares change frequently (a deal that's available one day may not be the next), so if you're looking for the lowest fares check the travel and business sections of major newspapers (e.g. the Sunday editions of the *New York Times*, *Los Angeles Times* and the *Chicago Tribune*), where promotional flights are widely advertised, or contact a travel agent who specialises in low cost fares. Although it's easier to ask a travel agent than call individual airlines or consult their websites, some travel agents won't always tell you about the cheapest fares because it reduces their commission.

If you're flying to the US and plan to make a number of domestic flights, it's usually much cheaper to buy your tickets abroad, where you qualify for an air pass under the Visit US Airpass (VUSA) scheme. Under the VUSA scheme, you can buy coupons for domestic flights. Most airlines no longer offer standby air passes, as they proved too popular! With air passes you may need to pre-arrange your schedule, although exact dates and flights can usually be left open. You must buy your VUSA before you arrive in the US and at least a week before you wish to use it; the validity period (e.g. 30 days) starts from the date of the first flight. To qualify for VUSA discounts, tickets must be purchased in conjunction with a transatlantic or intercontinental ticket and you must provide proof of foreign residence. For details, check with a travel agent, or go to the airline website (e.g. Delta, American, American West, etc.).

Domestic Fares

Flying is the quickest and most convenient way of travelling in the US, which has the lowest domestic air fares in the world (some even lower than Greyhound buses). Fares have been reduced by up to 70 per cent in the last few years, as airlines have fought desperately to maintain their market share (or merely to survive) in the face of increasing competition from low-fare, no-frills 'peanut' airlines. These offer no luxuries (e.g. snacks rather than meals or no food service at all) and the cabin may be more cramped than with a major carrier, but the fares are unbeatable. Like international fares, domestic fares vary according to ticket restrictions (see above) and are heavily influenced by the time of day, the day of the week, how far in advance you book, and the season. The largest domestic carriers are Delta, American, United, USAir, Southwest, Northwest, Continental, and America West. Airports which are most used by low-fare airlines include Atlantic City, Tampa, Islip Long Island, and Reno; those used infrequently or not at all include Charlotte, Cincinnati, Richmond, and Pittsburgh. A 300-mile (480km) flight from Atlantic City airport can cost as little as $85 with a low-fare airline, whereas a flight of a similar distance from Cincinnati can cost almost $300.

There are generally three fare seasons; high or peak (summer and holiday periods), 'shoulder' (e.g. October or November with the exception of the Thanksgiving travel peak) and low or off-peak, which is all other times (particularly during school terms). The summer peak season runs from Memorial Day (the last Monday in May) to Labor Day (the first Monday in September). Thanksgiving, Christmas and New Year are peak periods for domestic flights, but not usually for international flights. Shoulder periods often include the days immediately preceding a federal holiday. When planning a flight during a holiday period, book **well** in advance.

American Airlines recently introduced a 'simplified' ticket structure with just four classes: first-class, full-coach (also called economy or tourist class) and two discount fares, and many other airlines followed suit. One-class economy seating is popular on short domestic flights and many airlines are replacing first class with a better business class. The most expensive fares are open return tickets, for which there are no advance booking requirements and flights can be booked or cancelled at any time. Open tickets are usually valid for a year, during which a full refund can be obtained at any time. Excursion and discount fares usually apply to round-trip flights only and tickets must normally be purchased in advance, e.g. 7 or 14 days.

Other common conditions are minimum and maximum stay requirements, such as 6 to 14 days or one to six days, including a Saturday night. Discount fares are generally non-refundable, although you can usually change your flight for an additional fee (e.g. $50). It's much cheaper to buy a discounted ticket and pay to change the return flight (if necessary) than to buy a full-fare ticket. On long domestic flights (usually over an hour), services are much the same as on international flights, with meals, drinks and films (although you must usually pay for alcoholic drinks and films on domestic flights). Short flights (less than an hour) are often coach class only, while long flights usually have first/business and coach class compartments.

Infants under two travel free on most domestic flights, provided they don't occupy a seat, although some airlines charge 10 per cent of the full adult fare. The fare for children aged 2 to 11 is generally 75 per cent of the adult fare. This is also charged for a second infant (under two) when two infants are travelling with one adult. There are usually no child rates for Apex tickets. Note, however, that a discounted adult fare is often cheaper than a full child fare. Many airlines also offer discounts for youths, students and senior citizens (over 60 or 65).

As a result of deregulation, promotional fares can be offered at almost any time and there's usually at least one airline offering a promotional flight to most major destinations. Promotional fares or special offers on major routes can make a journey of 1,000 miles cheaper than a hop of a 100 miles or so. The most heavily discounted routes are along the eastern and western coasts. You can usually save around 30 per cent by travelling by 'night coach' (or 'red-eye' flights) or in the evening or early morning, any time on Saturdays, and on Sundays before the evening rush period. Some airlines offer discounts if you travel on a flight making a number of stops.

Other deals include two-for-one (twofer) promotions where two people travel for the price of one. Many smaller airlines are able to offer inexpensive domestic flights by using little-used airports. Some smaller regional airlines offer all seats at the same low fare, which may be lower than the lowest fare offered by larger national airlines.

Sometimes it's cheaper to buy a round-trip than a one-way ticket and leave the return trip unused. Charter flights are often the cheapest, but they don't provide the same security as a discounted seat on a scheduled flight. Other inexpensive flights are available through travel clubs, although members may be given little advance notice of flights or tour packages. As with international fares, domestic rates change frequently, and a deal that's available one day may not be the next.

With the exception of walk-on shuttle flights, often referred to as 'flying buses', you should reserve a seat on a domestic flight. When you book your flight, you're usually allocated a seat number and can check in at the gate if you have hand luggage only. If you need to travel on a particular flight, book as early as possible. There's no penalty for missing a domestic flight after you've booked a seat and on average around 15 per cent of passengers fail to turn up ('no-shows'). If you don't have a booking, arrive early and ask to be put on the waiting list.

Most airlines routinely over-book flights (when not half-empty) as an insurance against 'no-shows'. This sometimes results in passengers with bookings being 'bumped' (denied a seat) and forced to travel on a later flight, for which they may be entitled to 'denied boarding compensation' (DBC). Airlines always ask for volunteers before denying a passenger a seat. If you're bumped involuntarily, the amount of DBC depends on how late (after your original scheduled arrival time) you arrive on a substitute flight. If the delay is less than an hour, no compensation is paid. If you're delayed between one and two hours after your original arrival time, you're entitled to compensation equal to the value of the flight up to a maximum of $200; over two hours' delay and your compensation is doubled (up to a maximum of $400). In some cases you're offered an upgrade on the next flight, or even a free return ticket to any destination on the airline's domestic network (generally the more over-booked a flight, the higher the compensation). Most airlines offer you the choice of a free flight voucher or its dollar value. Compensation applies to flights originating in the US only and excludes charter flights and cancellations due to an aircraft malfunction or bad weather.

To avoid being bumped, try to check in at least an hour before the scheduled departure time for a domestic flight and always check in by the time specified. If you check in late and are bumped, you won't be entitled to claim DBC. One way to increase your chance of having a seat is to visit an airline office (or some travel agents) and obtain a boarding pass and seat number in advance. When the weather is bad in the local area or the area where your flight terminates, you should confirm your flight before arriving at the airport (recommended **any** time, even for domestic flights). Some airlines require you to 're-confirm' your flight 48 to 72 hours in advance. Although the 'OK' under status on your ticket means that a booking has been made, a confirmation may still be necessary.

Most US airlines operate a 'frequent flyer' or 'mileage club' scheme for regular passengers, who receive free tickets, bonus miles, free upgrades and discounts after travelling a number of miles, e.g. 10,000 (16,000km). Benefits may also include car hire and hotel discounts. Membership of these schemes is free, although you must join at the check-in counter before flying and must have an American address. Bonus miles can also be earned by using car hire companies, hotel chains and credit cards affiliated to frequent flyer schemes. An 'air miles' scheme introduced in 1992 allows buyers of certain products and services to earn flight discounts. Contact airlines for information or take out a subscription to *InsideFlyer* magazine (1930 Frequent Flyer Point, Colorado Springs, CO 80915, 🖥 www.webflyer.com), which costs from $36 for 12 issues. Most US airlines also operate airline clubs for travellers who, by law, must pay for membership. Membership privileges include the use of private airport lounges, computers and fax facilities, ATMs, showers, cheque-cashing facilities, and other services.

Flights can also be booked via the internet, through sites such as Expedia, Onetravel, Orbitz and Travelocity, or direct with over 30 airlines. Some of the discount airlines only accept bookings from their website. The latest innovation is ticket-less travel (employed by most new budget airlines) which may also mean you receive no boarding pass or seat number (you sit wherever there's a spare seat). Tickets are booked with a credit card and you receive a reference number, which is quoted (you must show identification) on arrival at the airport. It's estimated that doing away with tickets will save airlines billions of dollars a year.

11.

MOTORING

The US has a passionate and enduring love affair with the car. Most Americans simply won't walk anywhere (it's virtually unconstitutional), hence the proliferation of drive-in services, including banks, dry cleaners, fast food outlets, espresso bars, grocery shops, religious services, clinics and marriages. In the US, the car is God and it's every American's birthright to own one as soon as he reaches puberty (the legal age is usually between 16 and 18). Many high schools teach driving as part of their curriculum and any teenager who cannot drive is regarded as something of a freak. Americans wear their cars as people in other countries wear the latest fashions and lately it seems the bigger, the better. Giant sports utility vehicles (SUVs), sort of a small lorry (truck), now account for over half the personal passenger vehicles on the roads!

The US has over 230 million vehicles, while the total population, including those too young to drive, is little more than 288 million – the highest ratio of vehicles to population in the world (by comparison, 60 million Britons own a mere 28 million vehicles). The number of registered vehicles exceeds the number of licensed drivers (191 million) and in some areas, e.g. greater Los Angeles (Autogeddon!), half the metropolitan area is occupied by roads and car parks. The US has the most extensive motorway (freeway) network in the world, covering some 46,500mi (74,500km) of a total of over 3.9 million miles (6.25 million km) of roads. Because of the total dominance of cars over public transport, it's almost mandatory to own at least one car in the US.

Not surprisingly, with so many vehicles rushing around, there are many accidents, including a motor vehicle injury on average every 15 seconds and a death every 12 minutes. The US has a worse road death rate relative to its population than most other 'civilised' countries (including many notorious for their mad drivers, such as Belgium, France, Italy and Spain). There are more than 41,000 motor-vehicle related deaths (more than 6,000 of which are teenagers and almost 5,000 pedestrians) and some three million injuries (many serious) a year, costing over $100 billion. In an effort to reduce teenage deaths, restrictions have been imposed on teenage drivers in many states in recent years, including prohibiting them from carrying teenage passengers (many 'accidents' are a result of teenagers showing off to their friends, often when drunk).

The first thing you notice when driving any distance in the US is that it's a BIG country. In some regions, you can drive for miles without seeing another vehicle, and people living in remote rural areas think nothing of spending four or five hours behind the wheel to visit friends or do the weekly shopping. Highways and city streets are generally kept as straight as possible (American cars aren't noted for their cornering ability), and streets in most cities are laid out on a grid pattern. In the north of the country severe frosts and lack of maintenance leave many roads (particularly in the cities) in poor condition with huge potholes. Federal, state and local communities fight a constant battle to keep roads and bridges in an acceptable condition and many interstate highways are in urgent need of repair.

If possible, you should avoid rush hours, which can be a nightmare. Times vary according to the city, but are usually between 7am and 9.30am, and from 4pm to 6.30pm. In some cities, rush hours start earlier and/or end later. In Los Angeles, for example, rush hours last from 7am to 11am and from 3pm to 8pm, particularly on the motorways. In fact, Los Angeles has a more or less permanent traffic jam. Small towns usually have shorter rush hours, e.g. 7.30am to 8.30am and 4.30pm to 5.30pm. Around 10 million residents of major cities spend at least 90 minutes each day driving to and from work, and in southern California three-hour 'commutes' are common (many people leave home at 5am or 6am to avoid morning rush hours and stay late to avoid the evening crush). In many cities there are special driving rules on major thoroughfares during rush hours, where parking is prohibited.

Many areas experience heavy traffic jams on Fridays, when the mad weekend rush starts, and on Sundays when the lemmings return. It's best not to drive at all in some cities unless absolutely necessary, as traffic congestion can be horrendous at most times and parking costly (illegal parking is even more expensive). Park-and-ride car parks are provided in the suburbs of many cities, although they aren't widely used, as public transport is poor and parking isn't usually difficult to find, except in major cities. Publicly funded car pooling (or ride sharing) schemes and car pool lanes have been introduced in most states during the last decade or so in an effort to ease traffic congestion, and high occupancy vehicle (HOV) lanes have been created on urban freeways in many areas. These are reserved during peak hours for buses, minibuses and cars with a minimum number of passengers (usually two or three). However, they've had little success, as commuting times in most areas haven't increased sufficiently to force people to seek alternatives to driving alone (a sharp rise in petrol prices coupled with better public transport might do the trick).

The US is slow to invest in fast, frequent and inexpensive public transport. In fact, it isn't happening at all in many cities. It's indicative that the metropolitan area with the worst traffic problems (Los Angeles) also has one of the worst urban public transport systems in the US (and the world). In 2001, President Bush scrapped his predecessor's $1.45 billion five-year programme to develop (conventional) fuel-efficient vehicles capable of 80mpg (3.5l per 100km) in favour of a (presumably equally costly) plan to encourage the development of hydrogen-powered vehicles, which emit nothing but water vapour, although it could be ten years before such vehicles can be mass-produced. Meanwhile, some states are independently taking steps to reduce pollution. California was the first state in the nation to introduce a separate car emissions testing (smog testing) programme, designed to force car manufacturers to produce cleaner vehicles. In 2004, the state further tightened its anti-pollution requirements, giving manufacturers until 2009 to reduce emissions by 25 per cent in cars and light trucks, and by 18 per cent in sports utility vehicles (SUVs) and heavier trucks.

The highway system is the responsibility of state, county and municipal authorities, and not the federal government. Therefore traffic laws often vary from state to state, although all Americans drive on the same side of the road (except perhaps when drunk!) and there's general uniformity with respect to road signs and traffic (stop) lights. Most road signs are uniquely American, although international signs are being introduced in many areas. **Never assume that the motoring laws in one state are the same as in another.** Detailed information about motoring laws in all states, US territories, and Canadian provinces is provided in the *Digest of Motor Laws*, published annually by the American Automobile Association (see page 295) and issued free to members.

VEHICLE IMPORT

If you plan to import a motor vehicle or motorcycle, temporarily or permanently, first make sure that you're aware of the latest regulations. Taking a new or relatively new car to the US is usually an expensive and pointless exercise, as apart from the import duty, bureaucratic hassles and different standards, cars can be purchased in the US far cheaper than in most other countries. All imported motor vehicles must meet certain standards under the Motor Vehicle Safety Act of 1966 (revised under the Imported Vehicle Safety Compliance Act of 1988). They must also conform to bumper standards under the Motor Vehicle Information and Cost Savings Act of 1972 (which became effective in 1978), and meet air pollution control standards under the Clean Air Act of 1968. Unless a vehicle manufactured abroad conforms to the required standards, it's unlikely to meet the regulations. The cost of modifying a car to meet emission regulations, for example, is between $1,000 and $2,000, depending on the make, model and year of manufacture. If a vehicle is unable to meet the emission standards, hasn't passed the US safety (crash-control) and bumper tests, or doesn't meet the US theft prevention standards, it is refused entry or is destroyed at the port of entry. Always check the latest regulations before attempting to import a vehicle.

The duty on foreign-made cars (new and used) imported into for personal use or resale is 2.5 per cent and on motorcycles 2.4 per cent. A non-resident can import a car without paying duty, although if it's sold duty must be paid. Savings can be made when importing some cars and motorcycles, although generally it isn't worth the time, trouble and expense involved.

For further information contact the Department of Transportation, National Highway Safety Administration, 400 7th Street, SW, Washington, DC 20590, ☎ 202-366-0123, 💻 www.nhtsa.dot.gov) or the Environmental Protection Agency (Ariel Rios Building, 1200 Pennsylvania Avenue, NW, Washington, DC 20460, ☎ 202-272-0167, 💻 www.epa.gov) who publish an *Automotive Import Facts Manual*, which can be downloaded from their website. US Customs publish a pamphlet, *Importing or Exporting a Car*, available from the 'Travel' section on the US Customs and Border Protection website (💻 www.cbp.gov).

VEHICLE EXPORT

Personally exporting a car from the US is a relatively simple process and usually yields huge savings, particularly exports to most European countries, where car prices are up to twice as high as those in the US. Cars purchased in the US have usually been manufactured to US specifications and are left-hand drive (apart from right-hand drive collectors' items) and cars exported to some countries may need expensive modifications to meet local 'type approval' regulations.

For a car to qualify as a 'personal export' (or personal import), many countries insist that it's driven (a short distance is usually enough) in the US, and that you personally arrange for the export of the car. Taxes for personal car imports vary considerably from country to country and may include car tax, import duty and value added tax (VAT). However, the bottom line is that after paying all expenses (shipping, taxes, duty, etc.) you often end up with a car costing around 25 to 30 per cent less than the local new price (even greater savings can be made when buying a used car). However, before exporting a car from the US, thoroughly investigate prices, registration requirements (type approval), taxes and import duty, shipping costs, and foreign regulations and residence requirements.

VEHICLE REGISTRATION

Every vehicle in the US must have a certificate of ownership (title) showing the name of the registered owner. The title contains the owner's name and address, the registration plate (licence plate or tag) number and other details about the vehicle. A new title must be issued each time there's a change in the details printed on it, e.g. a change in the address of the owner. A certificate of title must be applied for immediately after a new or used vehicle is purchased; without it you cannot obtain a registration plate. Applications must be made to a state office, e.g. the Department of Motor Vehicles (DMV), or the local county clerk's or treasurer's office. The fee for a certificate of title may range from $5 to $50 (more for a title with a lien, i.e. a vehicle which hasn't been paid for), depending on the state. Upon transfer of ownership, a seller must usually endorse the certificate of title and give it to the buyer, who surrenders it to the issuing office and is then issued with a new certificate. A seller may also be required to notify the issuing office of a sale, e.g. within ten days.

To register a car you usually require the following papers:

- Certificate of title (unless you're applying for a title and registration);
- Proof of ownership, e.g. bill or certificate of sale with purchase price and date;
- Proof of identity and date of birth;
- Proof of insurance or financial responsibility;
- Sales tax clearance (i.e. receipt for sales or use tax); if sales or use tax hasn't been paid before registration, it is collected when you register or title a vehicle;
- Current registration card, if applicable;
- Safety and emissions inspection certificates, if applicable (see below);
- Registration authorisation, if you aren't the owner of the vehicle;
- Completed vehicle registration application form;
- The registration fee.

Motor vehicle registration rules and fees vary from state to state. Fees for registration plates (often reflecting or 'reflectorised') range from around $10 to $50 per year and include state road taxes. The registration fee may be a flat fee or be based on a car's weight, age or value (or a combination). Upon registration, you're issued with one (affixed to the rear of a vehicle) or two licence plates, the expiry date (month/year) of which is shown on the rear plate. A variety of personalised plates are available in most states (for an extra cost) and all states provide special plates for the disabled (a medical certificate is required).

Registration fees are usually paid annually, on a fixed date for all owners, or more often staggered, often based on your birthday or the first letter of your family name. There are usually penalties for late renewal and you can be arrested for displaying an out of date (dead) plate, although some states allow a grace period. Registration is validated by a sticker affixed to the rear registration plate. Duplicate plates and registration papers are available for a small fee.

If you're moving from one state to another, you must re-register your vehicle. This can usually be done before entry, although you may require a local address. Otherwise, a vehicle must be re-registered immediately or within a designated period of taking up residence, e.g. 10 to 60 days. In some states, a non-resident must register his vehicle if his stay exceeds a certain period, e.g. 30 to 90 days; in a few states a visitor's permit is required after a period. A car's registration plates may remain with a car when it's sold or be retained by the seller, who may need to return them to the issuing office, e.g. when the new owner transfers a vehicle out of the state. Refunds are usually granted on unexpired plates when a car is permanently removed from a state or is scrapped.

Cars imported into the US by tourists can be driven on foreign registration plates for up to one year from the date of arrival, provided the country of registration is party to the UN Convention on Road Traffic (Geneva, 1949) and the Convention on the Regulation of Inter-American Automotive Traffic (Washington, 1943). If your home country isn't a signatory to these conventions, you must obtain registration plates from the authorities in the state where the vehicle is landed. A foreign registered car must display the appropriate international sign at the rear (excluding Canadian and Mexican registered vehicles). If you own a car with foreign plates and intend to work or study in the US, you must obtain US plates in accordance with the regulations in the state where you're residing. The regulations applicable to registration plates for tourists and residents also apply to foreign driving licences (see page 265).

Detailed information about vehicle importation and registration is provided by state Departments of Motor Vehicles (DMVs) and is contained in the US Customs Service's leaflet, *Importing or Exporting a Car* (see above), and the *Digest of Motor Laws* published annually by the AAA (see **Motoring Organisations** on page 295).

ROAD TAX

There's no federal road tax, although all states levy an annual registration fee, which varies considerably from state to state, e.g. $10 to $50 per year. For more information, see above.

SAFETY & EMISSIONS TESTS

An annual safety inspection is necessary in around 25 states, including Alaska, Arkansas, Delaware, Hawaii, Louisiana, Maine, Massachusetts, Mississippi, Missouri, New Hampshire, New Jersey, New York, North Carolina, Oklahoma, Pennsylvania, Rhode Island, South Carolina, Texas, Utah, Vermont, Virginia, West

Virginia, and the District of Columbia. In some states, all vehicles must be inspected upon resale or transfer, sometimes within seven days of registration. The annual test fee is usually around $10 to $20.

Most inspections include a car's lights, brakes, windscreen (windshield) wipers and horn, and some include the tyres (tires), windows, body, and seat belts. All states authorise private repair shops and car dealers to make inspections, and a few have government operated inspection stations. In many states, a used car sale isn't final until the car passes the inspection and in other states failing the inspection cancels the sale at the buyer's option. If your car fails the inspection, you usually have a grace period to get it repaired or take it off the road. In most states, police are authorised to inspect a vehicle at their discretion or on reasonable grounds, e.g. when bits are falling off it.

Some states and counties also have emissions (smog) tests, which cost around $25 (in some states they're free). In California, most vehicles must be tested when they're first registered and, with certain exceptions, upon change of ownership. (Californians are also encouraged to report 'smoking' vehicles to the air pollution control service.) In most other states that have emissions tests, they're required periodically, e.g. every two years. When your vehicle passes a safety and/or emissions test, you're given a sticker for your windscreen or rear number plate.

CAR RENTAL

Car rental (Americans don't use the term 'hire') is common, as public transport is generally poor. When travelling long distances, most Americans go by air and rent a car on arrival (air travellers represent 80 per cent of business). Airlines, charter companies, car rental companies and tour operators all offer fly-drive packages (which often include accommodation). It's often wise to book a car in advance, particularly during holiday or peak periods when rented cars are in high demand. Many fly-drive holiday packages (particularly when booked in Europe) include a 'free' rented car, although fly-drive deals may not be as good as they appear at first glance, as many contain restrictions or apply to expensive cars only. Some companies charge a daily airport access fee (plus tax) and it may be cheaper to throw away a fly-drive car voucher and arrange a local deal yourself by calling local rental companies listed in the yellow pages.

The biggest national car rental companies include Alamo, Avis, Budget, Dollar, Hertz, National and Thrifty. National rental companies have offices in all major cities and at international airports that are open from around 8am to 10pm, and provide national toll-free telephone numbers. Of the major companies, Dollar and Thrifty are generally the cheapest, although all companies offer special rates, e.g. corporate, 24-hour, weekend, weekly, off-peak, holiday, and extended period on certain categories of cars, as well as bonus coupons for airline tickets. You should shop around by telephone or on the internet to compare rates, which may vary considerably. However, 'all inclusive' doesn't necessarily mean that and you may have to pay extra for an extra driver or local fees and taxes (plus petrol). Airports are generally the most expensive places to rent a car, followed by city centre (downtown) offices.

There are also cheaper rental companies in all major cities, ranging from companies with a few run-down heaps to medium-sized, state-wide agencies. Some nationwide chains (e.g. Rent-a-Heap, Rent-a-Junk, Rent-a-Wreck and Ugly Duckling) also rent older cars, usually three to five years old. Although cars are well worn, they're usually mechanically sound and rental rates are around half those of new models. However, some local agencies have high mileage charges and other hidden costs. Wherever you rent a car, if you suspect that it has a fault you should return it immediately and insist on a replacement.

You must usually be 21 to rent a car and must have held a licence for a minimum of a year. A few companies, e.g. Avis, rent to 18-year-olds in most cities, although Hertz have a minimum age requirement of 25. Many rental companies levy a 'young driver' surcharge of between $20 and $25 (depending on the state) per day on all drivers under 25, although women under 25 may be charged a lower premium than men, as they're less accident prone. If you have a foreign licence without a photograph, e.g. an old British licence, you may be asked to show your passport. You should also have an International Driver's Permit (IDP), which must be used in conjunction with your foreign licence (it won't be accepted on its own). All drivers planning to drive a vehicle must provide these documents (there's often a surcharge of $5 to $10 per day for extra drivers).

When renting a car it's imperative to ensure you have sufficient liability insurance (see page 352). Many states no longer oblige car rental companies to provide third party cover, so check what insurance is provided. When included in the basic cost, third party cover may be restricted to in-state only and there may be a high surcharge for interstate travel. Check the cost of out-of-state insurance, personal accident insurance (PAI), collision (or loss) damage waiver (CDW/LDW), personal effects protection (PEP), which may be included in your travel insurance, and supplementary liability insurance (also known as top-up liability insurance) or extended protection (SLI/EP), which increases third-party liability to $1 million (from the standard $300,000 per accident and $100,000 per person plus $25,000 property damage). US residents can usually extend their personal motor vehicle insurance to include rented vehicles, although your policy must usually include collision insurance (unless you pay for CDW/LDW).

If you pay for a car with a credit card (e.g. American Express or a Gold Mastercard/Visa card), your card company may provide free CDW, but check the extent of cover provided, as most pay the excess (deductible) only after your insurance company pays on a claim. In some states CDW has been banned in favour of a mandatory excess ($100 to $200) when a rental car is damaged; elsewhere you may be asked to pay between $15 and $20 per day. If you're a visitor, it's usually cheaper to extend rental insurance before travelling to the US. If you decline CDW, you may be held responsible for all damage to a car (however caused), even minor scratches. SLI or EP can add $15 per day to your rental costs and PEP, a further $7 per day. See also **Car Insurance** on page 267.

Rented cars are graded into classes or sizes by body size, not engine capacity, e.g. economy or sub-compact (the smallest), compact, mid-size or intermediate, and standard or full size. Groups are usually identified by a letter, e.g. A to H. Many companies also rent coupes, premium and luxury models, convertibles (or roadsters) and sports cars, four-wheel drive or sports utility vehicles (SUVs), and mini-vans. A sub-compact costs from around $30 per day and a compact around $40 per day, both with unlimited mileage. With limited mileage, rates may be around $10 per day cheaper plus 10 cents to 20 cents per mile (above 100 or 150 free miles per day), although this option is seldom available. Standard or full-size models cost upwards of $40 per day with unlimited mileage. Weekly rates are generally more economical, although you're charged the full daily rate for each day over a full week you have the car.

Rates vary considerably from state to state: Chicago and New York are among the most expensive (around twice the national average), while Florida and California are the cheapest. Rental of a sub-compact car from Avis or Hertz varies from around $30 a day in Florida up to an astronomical $150 or more per day in New York. Many factors affect the rate, including the day of the week and the season, the size of the town and the popularity of the local tourist attractions. When comparing rates, check any minimum periods, as some companies' lowest rates are for a minimum period of three days and always ensure that the rate you're quoted includes all insurance.

Local sales tax (see page 474) must be added to rental rates and is usually payable even when a rented car was provided free. Extras such as insurance, taxes and surcharges can easily double or treble the basic daily rental rate. Almost all rental cars have automatic transmission, radios and air-conditioning. Many larger models have power steering, cruise control and other 'luxury' features. Child car seats, which are compulsory for children under four, cost between $4 and $5 per day. Manual transmission cars won't start unless you have your foot on the clutch and automatic transmission cars won't start if they're in neutral (sometimes they get stuck there and you must step on the brake to release the transmission).

Many rental companies insist on payment with a major credit card and won't accept cash unless you make prior arrangements, including a hefty deposit. This is so that they can trace you if you steal or damage the car and also because they can deduct extra charges from credit cards. The estimated cost of the rental is deducted or 'blocked off' your card's credit limit as soon as you drive off, so make sure that this doesn't leave you short of credit during your trip. When paying by credit card, check that you aren't charged for unauthorised extras or for something that you've already paid for, such as petrol. Most rental companies expect you to fill up the tank before returning the car; otherwise you are charged double or more the going price for petrol for 'topping the tank'.

Vans and pick-ups are available from major rental companies (and U-Haul van rental) by the hour, half-day or day, and sometimes from smaller local companies (usually cheaper). You can also rent a camper (recreational vehicle or RV), motor home, caravan (trailer) or mini-bus from a number of companies (prices vary with the season).

Some rental companies provide inexpensive one-way rental deals, called 'returns', for those who are willing to deliver a car to another city, although there's sometimes a drop-off charge. This can vary greatly between rental companies, e.g. from $50 for short distances to $500 for a coast-to-coast route, depending on the distance of the drop-off from the rental location.

One of the cheapest ways to get from A to B (provided B is where you want to go!) is with a 'driveaway' car. A driveaway is a unique American concept, where you receive the free use of a car or truck in return for delivering it to a specified destination. There are driveaway companies in most major cities. Look in the yellow pages under 'Driveaway Cars', 'Auto Delivery', 'Automobile and Truck Transporting' or 'Automobile Transporters and Driveaway Companies'.

BUYING A CAR

Most cars are cheaper in the US than in other countries and hardly anyone pays the list price. Car dealers are usually willing to negotiate and prices may vary considerably from dealer to dealer. Generally, there aren't long waiting lists for new cars, although in recent years some new sports and luxury models have been in short supply, in which case instead of obtaining a discount you're likely to be charged a premium. Dealerships are usually grouped in one part of a town, which makes comparing cars and prices relatively easy.

There are taxes on new and used cars; these vary from state to state and include a sales or use tax. Sales tax is levied on the proceeds of retail sales of tangible personal property, including cars. All but five states have a sales tax (see **Sales Tax** on page 474) which applies to new and second-hand cars (states without sales tax may levy a special car tax). Some states levy a lower or higher sales tax on cars than on other goods. In most states, sales tax is payable on the balance of a sale after the value of any trade-in has been deducted. A city or county sales tax may be payable **in addition** to state sales tax. Sales tax on a used car may be levied only if it wasn't previously registered in the state. Any vehicle sold by a person other than a licensed dealer, manufacturer or dismantler may be subject to a 'use tax', which is comparable to the sales tax collected by licensed dealers. Any sales or use tax due must be paid at the time of registration.

All states have 'lemon' laws covering new and used cars, which protect buyers from buying a clunker, i.e. a vehicle with major defects.

New Cars

Although comparisons between new car prices in different countries are often difficult to make because of fluctuating exchange rates and the different levels of standard equipment, most new cars are much cheaper in the US than in most other countries. American consumers have a huge choice of cars and, in addition to a wide range of US models, most European and Japanese cars are available. Ever since the introduction of the sports utility vehicle (SUV), the average size of American cars has been increasing, which isn't surprising, given that SUVs are a sort of small truck (often with comparable handling and road-holding abilities). SUVs now make up a good half of the personal passenger cars on the road. They've completely replaced estate cars (station wagons) as the family vehicle of choice, and some Americans are now lusting after a Hummer, derived from the military armoured vehicle, the Humvee. 'Compact' (or 'economy' or 'mid-size') models are around the same size as larger European cars, such as a Jaguar or Mercedes. 'Sub-compact' is the name given to small family cars such as the European Ford Focus or VW Golf, open sports cars are called roadsters or convertibles. Traditionally, American cars have had prodigious thirsts, and the current fad for SUVs has certainly brought the US back to those cherished traditions. In the view of many (and not just foreigners), American cars still handle poorly, are too big for many people and consume too much petrol, which is why over 30 per cent of Americans buy imported cars. Petrol consumption is measured as miles per gallon rather than by consumption per a set distance (i.e. litres per 100km).

Many American cars (or cars made for the US market) are liberally adorned with 'idiot' gadgets and buzzers, for example those informing you that your seat belt isn't fastened, your lights are on or your keys are in the ignition. Some American cars have combination locks on the doors that can be used to lock or open them when you've locked your keys inside the car (provided you haven't forgotten the combination). Cruise control is fairly common and highly desirable when you're driving hundreds of miles on a dead-straight road at 55mph or 65mph; it decreases your fuel consumption, helps prevent speeding and is less tiring. Air-conditioning is standard on most cars and certainly isn't a luxury in the hotter states (or during the height of summer in New York City), although it decreases power and increases petrol consumption. Some 90 per cent of American cars are fitted with automatic transmission and most have power steering, both of which increase petrol consumption. Air bags have become standard on all cars and trucks because of federal safety requirements, but may be disabled by an authorised dealer.

The basic price of a car without options, but including warranty and freight, is usually called the base sticker price; this is shown on a label in the car window. In addition to the base price, the sticker shows the manufacturer's installed options with the manufacturer's transportation charge and the fuel economy (miles per gallon). The sticker may only be removed by the purchaser. The dealer sticker price, usually shown on the same sticker, is the base price plus the suggested retail price of dealer-installed options, and additional dealer mark-up (ADM) or additional dealer profit (ADP), dealer preparation and undercoating.

The dealer mark-up on new cars is much lower than in most other countries and most of a dealer's profit is made on options and on finance and insurance packages. Many 'options' may be already fitted to a showroom model and you must pay for them whether you want them or not (or look elsewhere). These may include electric windows and mirrors, central locking, sun roof, alloy wheels, stereo radio/cassette/compact disc (CD), power steering, anti-lock brakes (ABS), air bags, automatic transmission, leather or power seats, cruise control, headlamp cleaning, trip computer, split/fold rear seats and air-conditioning. Some manufacturers (particularly Japanese) include many of these items as standard equipment (termed 'fully loaded'), while others (particularly German) make you pay heavily for them and usually have a list of options as long as your arm. Sticker prices don't include local taxes, licence plates and registration. Many car dealers also include a high charge, e.g. around $150, for the paperwork associated with buying a car (haggling may get it reduced or cancelled).

Before you enter a showroom to buy a car, decide on the make and model you want and check its price, and repair and safety records, with a reliable guide. You should know in advance how much you're willing to spend. Don't fall for come-on advertisements such as '$100 over dealer's cost', called 'low-balling' in the trade. Once you're in the showroom they start adding options that drive up the cost. ('High-balling' is offering an unrealistically high trade-in price, which later drops dramatically if you don't have it in writing.) You can drive a hard bargain when a dealer's expecting a shipment of new cars and wants to get rid of his 'old' models. When the price isn't right, show that you're prepared to walk away from the deal and the price is usually reduced.

The US car industry has been stuck in a period of flat or falling sales for the last couple of years, and most car dealers are offering rebates, low or even zero-rate financing for terms up to five years (most banks only lend you a maximum of 80 per cent of the cost of a new car over 36 to 60 months) and other incentives to try and boost lagging sales. Dealers may also offer incentives such as free AAA membership, service discounts, options or special equipment, and a free loan car for up to five days when a repair or service is required. Many manufacturers offer optional extended warranties, which are good value if you do high mileage or intend to keep a car for a long time.

Most dealers offer personal contract purchase (PCP) or lease deals, usually with a 30 per cent down payment, a contract term of 25 or 36 months and an annual mileage allowance of 12,000, 24,000 or 36,000, above which you must pay up to 35 cents for every mile covered. All leasing offers stipulate 'qualified buyers only', which means that unless you have an excellent credit rating you won't be eligible for a lease. Leased vehicles have a guaranteed buy-back value, known as the 'minimum guaranteed future value' (MGFV), and at the end of the contract you can buy the car outright by paying the MGFV, return it to the dealer, or trade the car's MGFV against a replacement vehicle. If you return a car, it is inspected for damage and you can be faced with a large repair bill. Shop around and compare a number of leasing deals, as some deals are deliberately confusing and offer poor value. Although leasing gets you behind the wheel of a car you otherwise couldn't afford, there's a hefty price to pay to satisfy your ego.

There are numerous consumer magazines and guide books for car buyers, with which you can make comparisons until your head spins. These include the *Standard Guide to Cars & Prices* (Krause Publications) and *Consumer Reports* (see page 264) magazine's annual *Car Buying Guide*. The AAA (see page 295) and *Money* magazine (☎ 1-800-633-9970 or 407-444-7000) also provide car price guides. Car magazines regularly show 'list' and 'best' (offer) prices, and also list dealer margins, so you know exactly how much profit a dealer is making. One of the best guides is *The Car Book*, a free guide to new cars, safety, fuel economy, maintenance, warranties, insurance, tyres, used cars and consumer complaints, published by the Center for Auto Safety, 1825 Connecticut Avenue NW, #330, Washington, DC 20009-5725 (☎ 202-328-7700, 🖳 www.autosafety.org), which also publishes other information for motorists.

Used Cars

Used (also called second-hand, previously owned or 'pre-owned') cars are excellent value, particularly low mileage cars less than a year old, where the savings on the new price can be as much as 25 per cent. The minute a new car leaves the showroom it's usually worth at least 10 per cent less than the purchase price. Some models depreciate much faster than others and represent excellent second-hand buys.

Inexpensive used cars can be purchased for as little as $500, although obviously you should be more circumspect when buying a 'junker'. If you want a car for a short period only, an older car reduces your losses if you sell it within a short period. Old V-8 gas-guzzlers can be an excellent buy, as the low-stressed motors last for ever (although the body and other parts rust and fail, as on any car). However, the often eccentric handling may frighten you to death. Fuel consumption is horrendously high and may vary from around 8mpg (35.3l per 100 km) in town to 15mpg (18.8l per 100 km) on a run (compared with 20 to 30mpg – 14 to 9.4l per 100 km - with a compact or sub-compact). The use of air-conditioning in under-powered older cars increases petrol consumption, reduces engine power, and increases the possibility of overheating when in traffic jams or climbing long mountain passes.

If you don't want a gas-guzzler, Japanese cars are generally among the cheapest and are usually reliable and economical. Old Volkswagens are also good value and it's easy to get them repaired and find spare parts. Obtaining spares for some imported cars is difficult or even impossible. The number and location of dealers in imported cars varies considerably from state to state. In some states, you may find that the nearest dealer is hundreds of miles away. Older classic European sports models can be bought in the US for much less than in Europe, although their condition is often poor and finding spares and expert mechanics can be difficult.

When you're buying a second-hand car in an area which has a lot of snow, you should check it carefully for rust, as a vast amount of corrosive salt is used on roads. The Sunbelt states are the best place to buy, as there's usually no snow in winter. However, prices are generally higher on the west coast than the east (because of stricter emission regulations).

A car with high mileage can be a good buy, particularly cars sold by rental companies, although you should be careful when buying a car with average (e.g. 10,000mi per year) or high mileage that's over four years old, as this is the time when it may need expensive repairs. Most Americans are reluctant to have their cars serviced and generally follow the old adage 'If it ain't broke, don't fix it'. This means that even simple preventive maintenance such as a change of oil, oil filter, plugs and belts may be done rarely, if at all, and a 'tune-up' may be done only when a car is running badly. Around one in five cars tested by the AAA fails maintenance tests and many people drive cars that are in a dangerous condition. Cars under four years old, therefore, usually represent the best value.

Buying a car privately may be cheaper than buying from a dealer, although you won't get a warranty and must usually know what you're doing. It's important to have a car checked mechanically before buying it. Unless you're an expert, take someone knowledgeable with you. Alternatively, most service stations and repair shops will check out a car on the spot and it's usually inexpensive (although getting a dealer or private buyer to allow you to do this may be difficult). The price of a used car depends on its make and size, its age and condition, the time of year, and the area where it's for sale.

You may get a better deal from a new car dealer who also sells used cars of the same make than from a used car dealer selling used cars only (usually of any make). However, if you're looking for an inexpensive car, a used car dealer may be the better bet. Whenever possible, use a dealer who has been recommended. It's often better to buy a car from a small town dealer than a dealer in a major city. In small towns, a dealer relies more on local business and is likely to be careful to maintain his good reputation. You can usually check whether there have been a large number of complaints against a dealer through a local consumer protection agency or Better Business Bureau.

A 'buyer's guide' sticker must be displayed in the windscreen of all used cars sold by dealers. This includes information about who must pay for repairs after purchase, whether there's a warranty (e.g. 6 months/6,000mi) and what it covers, whether a service contract is available, and general points to note when buying a used car. Dealers sell cars with no warranty (as seen or 'as is', although in some states your rights to redress in the case of serious problems are protected by law) or with a full or limited warranty.

When purchasing a car privately, obtain a bill of sale, the proper title and registration, and copies of all financial transactions. Be sure to obtain a title or (e.g. in New York State) a notarised bill of sale. Check the registration month and year on the rear registration plate, because if a vehicle is unregistered you could be held responsible for the past year's registration fee. If you're stopped by the police, you must show proof of ownership and in some states it's illegal to drive without it.

One of the best places to buy second-hand cars (and to compare prices) is through local newspapers, e.g. the Sunday edition of the *New York Times*. Free car shopper magazines and newspapers are also published in all areas. You can get an idea of the value of second-hand cars from guides such as the National Automobile Dealers Association's (NADA) *Used Car Price Guide*, Edmund's *Used Car Prices* (🖳 www.edmunds.com) and the Kelley *Blue Book Auto Market Guide* (available through several websites, including 🖳 www.cars.com). *Consumer Reports* magazine provides a telephone used car price service (☎ 1-800-422-1079 – calls are free, but the information costs $10).

Do your own research in your local area by comparing prices at dealers, in local papers and in the national press. Many private sellers are willing to take a considerable drop and dealers also negotiate over prices. The average mileage for a car in the US is around 10,000 per year. Cars with high mileage, e.g. 20,000 per year, can usually be purchased for substantially less than the average price and may offer excellent value, provided they've been regularly serviced. Used cars are usually paid for in cash or with a certified cheque or a money order.

SELLING A CAR

The main points when selling a car are:

- Whenever possible, sell a car in the state where it's registered. To sell a car legally in a state other than that where it's registered, you must re-register it in that state and fit new licence plates. It's possible to sell an out-of-state car, although you may need to drop the price considerably to compensate for the legal hassle involved on the buyer's part. A car with an automatic gearbox is much easier to sell than one with a manual box (stick shift).

- A potential buyer cannot test drive your car unless he is covered by your or his insurance. You're responsible if someone drives your car without valid insurance, even with your permission.

- Inform your insurance company. Cancel your policy or transfer it to a new car. When you sell a car, you may be required to notify your state's Department of Motor Vehicles (DMV) by completing part of the registration or title paper. The new owner of the car must also register his ownership.

- If you're selling your car privately, you should insist on payment in cash or by certified cheque or money order. There are crooks who, given half a chance, happily give you a dud cheque and drive off with your car. If someone insists on paying with a personal cheque, you shouldn't allow him to take your car until the cheque has cleared.

- Include in the receipt that you're selling the car in its present condition (as is) without a guarantee, the price paid and the car's odometer (mileage) reading, which must be stated by law.

- You can advertise a car for sale in local newspapers, on free local notice boards, in the weekend editions of major newspapers, and in motoring newspapers and magazines. The best place to advertise a car depends on its make and value. Inexpensive cars are best sold in local newspapers, while expensive and collectors' cars are often advertised in the motoring press and in newspapers such as the *New York Sunday Times*. Buyers usually travel a long way to view a car that appears good value. (If nobody calls, you will know why!)

- Last, but certainly not least, obtain the best possible price for your car, which may mean taking time to sell it. If you must sell a car in a hurry, you may need to sell it to a used car dealer, who will usually offer you a derisory sum.

DRIVING LICENCE

The minimum age you can obtain a 'regular' (car) driving licence (called a driver's license or sometimes an operator's license) varies from 14 in 'rural' states such as South Dakota to 17 in Minnesota and New Jersey. However, in the majority of states it's 16. For commercial vehicles up to 7.5 tons laden weight, the age limit is 18 and for heavy goods vehicles (HGVs) it's 21. Most states allow people to obtain a restricted (learner's) permit at a younger age than a full driving licence (usually 14 to 16), subject to certain qualifications, e.g. written parental or guardian's consent, enrolment on an approved driver education training course, and the driver must be accompanied at all times by a licensed adult driver. In some states, junior licences for those under 18 or 21, allow teenagers to drive to and from high school only and are subject to a curfew. Other restrictions have been introduced in recent years in an attempt to reduce the high accident rate among teenage drivers.

An application for a driving licence is usually made to a state office, e.g. the State Motor Vehicle Division or Department of Motor Vehicles (DMV), although in some states licences are issued by county clerk's offices or local driver licensing examination stations. Your local DMV is listed in the phone book; and most now have websites where you may be able to make appointments. DMVs are normally open between 8am and 5pm Mondays to Fridays with one late evening opening. Applications must often be made in person, although renewals can usually be made by post or even over the internet. Fees for licences vary considerably, e.g. from around $10 to $40. Licences are usually valid for four to six years, although in some states licences for those under 18 and over 70 are valid for a shorter period, e.g. one or two years. Licences usually expire on the holder's birthday.

In most states, you must pass a 'knowledge test', which can be done before you reach licensing age. To prepare for the test, you can usually obtain a 'driver's handbook' free or for a nominal sum (Florida has a good one, which is free). The test itself, a series of multiple-choice questions, is taken at a DMV office on a touch-screen computer and takes around half an hour. In some states, you must make an appointment to take the test. Once you've passed the written test, you can apply to take the road test – in some states a few days later, in others a few weeks. The test costs around $20 and you usually must provide your own car (which is inspected before the test to make sure you aren't putting the examiner at risk!). Drivers over a certain age, e.g. 75, must usually take a driving and/or eye test every time they renew their licenses. (Elderly drivers are a controversial subject in the US, where drivers over 75 are twice as likely to have an accident as the average motorist.)

To obtain a licence you must take proof of your identity and 'true full name', date of birth and your social security number (or evidence that you've applied for one) to your local DMV. The 'true full name' requirement is one of the new security enhancements, whereby any changes from the name listed on your birth certificate must be properly documented and the name you use for your license must agree with how your name appears on your social security card. If possible, you should always make an appointment with the local DMV (unless you like standing in long queues for hours on end). Most licences require a photograph (some must be in colour), but these are nearly always done at the license office as part of the procedure. If your licence expires and is allowed to lapse for more than a year, a driving test may also be necessary. Licence renewals usually include an eye test and may include a simple written test, depending on your driving record. When taking up residence in a new state, you must obtain a new licence within a certain period, e.g. 10 to 30 days. You must usually pass vision and written tests and surrender your old licence. If you don't want to surrender your old licence, you may need to take a driving test. Holders of out-of-state licences aren't usually required to take a driving test. Holders of foreign licenses may be able to simply exchange their home country license for a state license, if their home country offers licensing reciprocity for Americans from that state. (Check with your home country embassy or consulate for details.)

Tourists may drive in the US for up to a year with a foreign driving licence, provided the issuing country is party to the UN Convention on Road Traffic (Geneva, 1949) and the Convention on the Regulation of Inter-American Automotive Traffic (Washington, 1943); most countries are signatories. If your licence wasn't issued by a country which is a signatory to these conventions or you intend to work or study in the US, you must obtain a driving licence (usually within 30 to 90 days) in the state where you land or where you're a resident. This may result in the confiscation of your foreign or existing licence (or your American licence may be stamped 'valid in state only'). You may need an American licence in order to obtain car insurance (see page 267).

If your foreign licence doesn't contain a photograph or is written in a language other than English, it's wise (but not mandatory) to obtain an International Driver's

Permit (IDP). Always carry your foreign licence as well as your IDP. Without an IDP it may be necessary to obtain a certified English translation of your foreign driving licence, usually obtainable from your country's embassy in the US. You must always carry your driving licence when driving in the US, where a licence is also the most common form of identification (in some states you can have your car impounded if you're stopped by the police without your licence). If you don't drive, you can obtain an official identification card (usually annotated 'This is not a driver's permit') from DMVs in most states and from agents in most cities for around $5 to $15. This is useful to prove your date of birth or name and address, for example when cashing personal cheques or buying alcohol.

Most states operate a points system, whereby drivers are given penalty points for traffic offences. In some states, you can take a six-hour driving course organised by the AAA and community schools, which reduces your licence point count by two, or opt to attend a driver improvement class (traffic school) at your expense in lieu of a violation being placed on your record. When you accumulate a number of points within a 12-month period, e.g. 12 in New Jersey, your licence is automatically suspended, e.g. for 30 days. When renewing your licence, you must take a written test if you accumulate more than a certain number of points, e.g. eight in Colorado. A driving licence can be suspended or revoked. Suspension involves the temporary withdrawal of your right to drive (most states emphasise that driving is a privilege and not a right). The state may reinstate that right after a designated period on payment of a fee. (However, thousands of Americans continue to drive after they've had their licences suspended.) If your licence is revoked, it's usually permanent.

CAR INSURANCE

One of the most surprising things about car insurance is that it isn't mandatory in all states, e.g. Alabama, Iowa, Mississippi, New Hampshire, Pennsylvania, Rhode Island, Tennessee, Utah, Virginia, Wisconsin and the District of Columbia. These states have 'financial responsibility' laws, requiring you to post a bond, cash deposit or approved self-insurance with the state to cover damages if you're involved in an accident. Evidence of financial responsibility includes car insurance in some states. Motorists in states where car insurance is compulsory must provide proof of insurance at the time of vehicle registration and may be required to carry it in their vehicles at all times. Buying car insurance is more complicated in the US than in most other countries and may include the following types of cover:

Liability Insurance

Liability insurance includes bodily injury liability, i.e. injuries you cause to someone else, and property damage liability, which is damage caused to someone else's property, including other vehicles. In most states, liability motor insurance is compulsory, although it doesn't necessarily include unlimited liability. Most states have laws setting minimum levels for liability insurance, but these are usually woefully inadequate. 'Responsibility' limits are set by each state for death or injury to one person, death or injury to more than one person, and property damage in excess of a certain amount, e.g. $250 or $500. These amounts are usually expressed as three figures and they may be as low as $10,000 in respect of personal injury or the death of an individual and $5,000 in respect of property damage. (Some insurance companies express liability limits as a single figure, which is a better system, as it provides more flexibility in resolving claims against you and is a lot simpler to understand!) If your liability after an accident exceeds your amount of insurance and you have personal assets, these are used to pay damages, if necessary, until you're bankrupt.

Lawsuits often run into millions of dollars and litigation lawyers are among the richest legal vultures. Experts recommend that you have total cover of at least $250,000 and preferably $500,000, depending on your personal assets. Liability limits can usually be raised significantly (e.g. to $1 million) for a modest extra premium. To protect yourself against astronomical damages, you can also take out a personal liability umbrella policy (see page 353) which increases your liability limits to a level that covers almost any event.

No-fault Insurance

Around 25 states and the District of Columbia have some form of Personal Injury Protection (PIP) or no-fault insurance law. This means that if you're involved in an accident, you can claim (up to certain limits) from your own insurance company for personal injury sustained in an accident (see below), rather than go to court and try to prove that the other party was at fault. In states without a no-fault law, the victim files a claim against the other driver, irrespective of whether or not the driver is insured, and is paid only if it can be proved that the other driver was responsible for the accident. If you weren't to blame and can prove it through witnesses or a police prosecution of the other driver, make sure your insurance company is informed, or you may lose your good driver (no-claims) discount.

Where applicable, PIP insurance is usually compulsory and covers bodily injury only and not vehicle damage. Those insured under PIP insurance receive prompt payment from their own insurance company, but their right to sue for general damages is usually restricted. Motorists insured in states with liability laws should ensure that their insurance covers them when travelling in states with no-fault laws. Most insurance companies automatically extend their policies to cover states with no-fault laws. **PIP cover may duplicate insurance provided by health or disability insurance policies.** PIP insurance provides benefits for medical and hospital costs (the level depends on your policy), plus lost wages or income continuation (e.g. $2,000 per month or 75 per cent of the actual loss), replacement/essential services (e.g. $25 per day), survivors' loss/death benefit (e.g. $10,000), and funeral expenses (e.g. $5,000). Lost wages and replacement services are payable up to a maximum amount for maximum periods, e.g. one to three years.

PIP Medical Expenses Insurance

It's possible to buy Personal Injury Protection cover for medical expenses only. PIP medical expenses pays the medical expenses of anyone injured when travelling in your car, irrespective of fault. Depending on your policy, it may also pay your medical bills when you or your family members are travelling in someone else's car, or if you're hit by a car while walking. Unlike other health policies, the medical payments part of a vehicle policy pays for all medical expenses incurred, without excesses (deductibles) or co-payments (called 'first dollar coverage'). If you have comprehensive health insurance, you may not require this protection, although it also covers anyone travelling in your car. In some states, you can choose your PIP health insurance provider, who can be someone other than your car insurance company, e.g. your employer's health insurance company.

Catastrophic Medical Expenses Insurance

Some insurance companies offer catastrophic medical expenses cover, protecting you against abnormally high medical bills. Whether or not you have this type of insurance depends on the level of your health insurance. If it has limitations, you're advised to have catastrophic medical expenses cover.

Uninsured Motorist Insurance

To protect yourself against accidents with uninsured motorists and hit-and-run accidents (whether driving or walking), you should have uninsured motorist insurance. Uninsured motorist laws have been enacted in many states, requiring insurance companies to include in their basic policy cover against damage caused by motorists who aren't insured. Uninsured motorist cover is usually equal to the minimum financial responsibility limits set by a state (see above under **Liability Insurance**) and is compulsory in some states. If you have collision insurance (see below), you usually don't need uninsured motorist insurance. In many states (where liability insurance is compulsory), the penalties for driving without insurance are derisory, e.g. a fine of $100 to $200 and possible licence suspension (e.g. a year in California), and there may be no penalty at all unless you have an accident. However, when the paltry financial penalties are compared with the often high insurance premiums, it's hardly surprising that there are so many uninsured motorists. If you have an accident involving another vehicle, the chances of the driver being uninsured are extremely high in some cities, so it's important to calculate the financial consequences of an accident involving an uninsured motorist.

Under-insured Motorist Insurance

This is similar to uninsured motorist cover and covers you when another motorist is responsible, but has insufficient insurance to cover the injuries or damage to property (although, if he has sufficient assets, you can still sue him).

Collision Insurance

Collision cover is for damage caused by you to your own vehicle, irrespective of who was responsible for the damage. Collision cover usually has an excess (deductible);

the higher the excess, the lower your premium. Whether it's necessary (or wise) to have collision cover (or comprehensive cover described below) usually depends on the value of your car. Collision and comprehensive cover are usually required by a car loan or a leasing company. With collision insurance, you usually don't need uninsured motorist insurance (see above).

Comprehensive Insurance

Comprehensive cover is for loss of the vehicle resulting from fire, theft, vandalism, collisions with animals, storms, floods, riots, explosions, earthquakes, falling objects, plus accidental glass breakage, e.g. from a stone thrown up by another vehicle. It doesn't cover you against accidents involving other vehicles or objects, for which you require collision cover (see above). Comprehensive cover usually has a lower excess than collision cover.

Miscellaneous Extra Insurance

This insures you against a wide range of costs, including a rental car when your car is being repaired, and towing and labour in the event of an accident or breakdown (also provided by automobile clubs). If you frequently use rented cars, you may be interested in a policy that includes collision damage waiver (CDW) for rented cars, which may also be provided free by a credit card (see page 373).

Premiums

Insurance premiums are high, particularly for men under 27 and those who live in inner cities, where driving conditions are more hazardous and where car theft is endemic. If you have no driving record in the US, you can expect to pay between $1,000 and $2,000 per year for full coverage. Many factors influence the cost of car insurance, including:

- The make and type of car (and how expensive it is to repair);
- The type of insurance cover required;
- The age and value of the car;
- Your age, sex (some companies offer a discount to women drivers) and occupation;
- What you use your car for (e.g. business or pleasure);
- Your driving experience and driving record;
- Your accident record and no-claims bonus (good-driver discount);
- Who will drive the car;
- Your health (you may be required to pay an excess if you suffer from epilepsy or diabetes);
- Where you live and whether your car is stored in a locked garage overnight;

- The number of miles you do each year (some policies offer reduced rates for those who do low mileage, e.g. 7,500mi per year);

- Any extras required, such as a rented car when your car's being repaired after an accident.

Shop around a number of insurance companies, as rates can vary by up to 400 per cent. Among the largest US car insurers are State Farm, Allstate, Farmers and Nationwide. State Farm is a mutual insurance company and customers sometimes receive a refund from excess profits. You should ask your family, friends and colleagues for their advice regarding car insurance, although you should also make your own comparisons.

Some ways to reduce your insurance are to:

- **Make comparisons - shop 'til you drop!**

- Insure your car with your household insurance company (see page 349), which may yield a discount of 5 to 10 per cent.

- Consider an excess (deductible) of $500 to $2,000 on collision and comprehensive insurance. An excess may be compulsory for young drivers.

- Drop collision and/or comprehensive cover on older cars worth less than around $2,000.

- Take advantage of insurer's discounts, usually 5 or 10 per cent of the premium. Most insurance companies offer discounts for cars fitted with air bags, automatic seat belts, anti-theft devices or anti-lock brakes. Many also provide low-mileage discounts and discounts for more than one car, no claims (good-driver discounts, e.g. if you make no insurance claims in three years), drivers aged over 50 or 55, driver training courses (e.g. defensive-driving), and even good student grades (are diligent students safer drivers?). Drivers aged over 65 can complete a 'mature driving course' in some states, guaranteeing them a three-year discount on their insurance premiums.

- Don't get uninsured motorist cover unless required by state law. If you're hit or injured by an uninsured motorist, repair and medical bills are covered by your collision insurance (provided you have it!), PIP cover and other medical insurance.

- Drop your reimbursement for a rented car. If you're a two-car (or more) family, you may be able to do without a rented car while one car is being serviced or repaired. Insurance companies have limits on what they pay for a rented car.

- If you have an employee hospitalisation plan, you could drop your car insurance medical payments, which duplicates medical insurance you already have.

- Drop the emergency towing service, which you probably don't need unless you have an old car susceptible to breakdowns. Insurers often limit what they provide for a tow, e.g. $25, which is too little anyway. Join the AAA or another automobile club providing an emergency towing service (see page 295).

- If your car isn't a status symbol, consider buying a 'low profile' car with a low insurance rating and, if you're considering a house move, choose a low insurance area.

- **One thing not to do in order to save money on car insurance is reduce your liability limits!**

There's no correlation between the premium you pay and the quality of service you receive, so paying a high premium doesn't guarantee the best service. Some 25 states publish information comparing the insurance rates of different companies. For information contact your state insurance regulator (see page 326). Premiums can be increased at renewal time only (every 6 or 12 months), which is likely if you've made any claims in that period. Many insurance companies allow premiums to be paid in instalments, e.g. quarterly or monthly.

When completing your insurance proposal form, make sure that you state any previous accidents or driving offences; otherwise your insurer can refuse to pay out in the event of a claim. Drivers who have been banned for drunk or dangerous driving must usually pay at least double the standard premium for three years (even penalty points on your licence increases your premium). Your insurance company may cancel your policy if you're found guilty of drunk driving, speeding or recklessness resulting in injury or death. For general information on car insurance contact the Insurance Information Institute, 110 William Street, Floor 24, New York, NY 10038 (☎ 212-346-5500, 💻 www.iii.org). (See also **Insurance Companies & Brokers** on page 326 and **Insurance Contracts** on page 327.)

AMERICAN ROADS

The standard of American roads varies enormously from eight-lane freeways in urban areas to gravel or dirt tracks in remote rural areas (usually in the western states). Generally, American roads have fewer road markings (e.g. studs or 'cat's eyes') than European roads. Streets in most cities are laid out in a grid pattern (hence the word gridlock for traffic jam), with all roads running north-south or east-west. In the central (downtown) areas of main cities, every other street is usually a one-way street. Streets are usually marked as north, south, east or west of a dividing line and every corner is given a letter (N, S, E or W). It's often important to know whether you want uptown or downtown when asking for directions.

In some cities (e.g. Los Angeles), you're confronted with multiple layers of interconnecting roads 12 lanes wide and a mile high, with direction signs two blocks wide and four storeys tall (which can unnerve even the most hardened motorist). Finding the right entrance or exit road can be a nightmare; needless to say, it's best to avoid rush hours. Direction signs in the east are sparse (particularly on freeways), inconsistent and poorly placed. They're usually unlit at night in urban areas and therefore difficult to read. In many suburbs, counties may be signposted, but not major towns. **If you get lost and end up in a 'rough' area, don't stop a stranger to ask the way, but find a policeman or police station (or ask at a well-lit restaurant or petrol station).**

Suburban roads and freeways are generally well surfaced and maintained, although roads in some cities are poor, e.g. in New York City, where many roads are full of potholes. Most roads have wide 'shoulders', although in rural areas there may be a steep drop in the level between the road surface and the dirt shoulder. Cars with low ground clearance can be a liability, as holes, bumps, dips and humps (e.g. for railway lines) in roads can damage exhaust pipes and body panels. Freeways are badly maintained in some areas, where the surface is rough and full of holes (the reason American cars have such soft suspension). The hard shoulder (or 'berm') of freeways is often littered with stripped tyres from trucks and other debris.

As you may already have discovered, the US is a large country and vast distances look small on maps (unless you have a very small scale map). When estimating journey times, carefully calculate distances and take into account road quality and terrain. Although it's possible to travel 500mi/800km in a day on freeways (e.g. at an average 50mph/80kph), your range is greatly reduced on secondary roads, particularly in mountainous areas, where speeds may average just 20mph or 30mph (32kph to 48kph). Most people reckon on covering between 300mi and 400mi per day (six to seven hours' driving) or 200mi to 250mi (four to five hours) when travelling with children (unless you tranquillise them).

If you have the time, you will find travelling on state and country roads much more enjoyable than on interstate highways. Driving long distances on dead-straight highways at a constant speed of 55mph or 65mph is deadly boring and can induce 'highway hypnosis', which manifests itself in drowsiness and lack of concentration. You can avoid this by taking regular breaks for food and drink and to stretch your legs. Never drive when you're tired; get someone else to take the wheel for a spell or pull well off the road and take a nap (drowsiness is estimated to contribute to around 10,000 road deaths a year in the US). Never park on the hard shoulder of a freeway, but get off it and go to a rest stop.

Multi-lane highways are generally referred to as freeways (except in Los Angeles, where freeways are known locally as parking lots). Other names for multi-lane highways include beltways (ring roads), expressways, interstates, parkways, speedways, superhighways, throughways (or thruways) and turnpikes.

Many freeways have just two lanes in each direction, although in urban areas and major cities there may be up to eight. Most freeways have huge central reservations (dividers). The rules for motoring on freeways are much the same as on fast roads in other countries and include no stopping (except in emergencies). The maximum speed on freeways varies from 55mph to 65mph according to the state, so look for speed limit signs (see page 275); there's usually also a minimum speed, e.g. 40mph or 50mph, although this is rarely enforced (especially in LA, where you're lucky if you can reach 40mph).

Many freeways have 'pool lanes', reserved for high occupancy vehicles (HOV) during peak hours (in the peak direction), including buses, minibuses and cars with a minimum number of passengers (usually two or three). Pool lanes are usually indicated by diamond road markings and signs indicating the period of operation (which may be all day). Information about pool schemes can often be obtained by dialling telephone numbers shown on signs on freeways. Shared cars aren't required to pay a toll on some roads. In some cities, e.g. New York, there are bus lanes and suburban areas throughout the US have cycle lanes.

Many freeways have 'exit only' lanes, where all traffic on the inside lane must leave the freeway. Freeway exits are often unmarked and you may find yourself leaving a freeway without realising it. This makes driving in the inside lane less relaxing than it is in most other countries. One of the most unusual and frightening aspects of American freeways is that exits are sometimes from the outside lane, particularly in urban areas and at junctions. These often aren't indicated very far ahead, and if you're in the inside lane you must quickly cross several lanes of traffic to exit. When driving on unfamiliar freeways with more than two lanes, it's best to avoid the inside and outside lanes. Most interstate highways have considerable distances between exits. Another bizarre and dangerous feature of American freeways is that the sliproad (ramp) onto a freeway is often situated just before the sliproad off the freeway rather than after it.

Most drivers join a freeway without indicating and with little regard for other traffic, which they expect to pull over or slow down. In some states (e.g. California) you drive up a sliproad where there's a small traffic light with the sign 'one car per green'. After getting a green light you continue onto the freeway itself, where there's another sign saying 'merge'. Somehow you're supposed to find a gap in the wall-to-wall traffic. (If it isn't stationary, it is travelling at 65mph to 75mph). Beware of merging lanes, e.g. where two four-lane highways merge into one, as these are often poorly signposted and may come as a complete surprise.

Turnpikes (usually shown in green on maps) are privately constructed freeways on which tolls are levied; thruways, parkways and expressways (plus others) may also be toll roads. The name turnpike comes from the first toll highways, the entrance to which was barred by revolving poles called 'turn pikes'. Turnpikes are mostly located in the Northeast, although they're also found in other areas such as Florida, Kansas and Oklahoma. They're usually known by names, e.g. the 'Atlantic City Expressway' and the 'Massachusetts Turnpike'. Tolls are usually payable on entry to, or exit from, a turnpike, and sometimes during a journey. On shorter journeys, tolls may be paid by dropping the fee, e.g. 50 cents in quarters, in a funnel in an 'exact change' lane. If you don't have the exact change, you must queue in a lane with a cashier. (Don't be tempted to drive through a toll without paying, as there are concealed barriers and heavy fines to deter non-payers, and booth attendants radio offenders' registration numbers to waiting highway patrol cars.) On longer turnpikes you're given a card when you join it and pay at a tollbooth when you exit. Turnpikes are often better quality roads than non-toll freeways and have service areas with restaurants and petrol stations. There are also toll bridges and tunnels in many cities (e.g. New York).

The following are the official categories of main road in the US:

Interstate Highways

The Interstate and Defense Highway System (originally funded by the Defense Department), as it's officially called, includes a comprehensive network of freeway-standard roads with at least two lanes and a hard shoulder in each direction. Interstate highways are prefixed with the letter 'I' and numbered using even numbers for east-west roads and odd numbers for north-south roads. The lowest numbers are in the south and west and the highest numbers in the north and east, e.g. the I-10 runs across the southern US border from Jacksonville (Florida) to Los Angeles (California), the I-90/I-94 crosses the northern edge, the I-5 runs down the west coast, and the I-95 down the east coast. When you come to a junction, the direction of an interstate may be indicated, e.g. I-10 East or I-95 North/South.

Most interstate roads have one or two digits. Three-digit numbers usually indicate short urban spur freeways, where the first digit denotes whether the spur goes around or into a city. Even-numbered prefixes indicate spurs that go around a city, e.g. the I-435, which is a circular spur from the I-35 around Kansas City. Odd-numbered prefixes signify a spur that goes into a city, e.g. the I-710, which is a spur into Los Angeles from the I-10.

Some interstates bear names as well as numbers, e.g. the 'Golden State Freeway', although these can generally be ignored, as they usually change or disappear after a few miles. However, names are often part of the local language and are unavoidable (when giving directions, a local person may use names rather than numbers).

Interstates are provided with rest areas, picnic sites and viewpoints, which have toilets (restrooms or bathrooms) and drinking fountains, but don't usually have other facilities, e.g. petrol stations and restaurants, unless they're turnpikes (see above). However, petrol stations and restaurants (usually referred to as 'truck stops') are usually located close to interstates and are well signposted, usually in neon. If you cross a state border (line), the first rest area after the border usually has information leaflets on things to see and do in the state you've just entered and sometimes a person you can ask for details. If you're touring, you may be interested in the National Geographic Society's publication *The Interstates Crossing America*.

Federal Highways

Federal highways bear the prefix US and are the most important roads after interstate highways, which they duplicate on some routes and with which they provide links. They vary from large dual carriageways (divided highways), virtually indistinguishable from interstates, to ordinary suburban streets. Federal highways are numbered in the same way as interstate highways; north-south odd and east-west even.

State Highways

State highways vary in quality more than any other major road. Some are of freeway standard, while others are little more than dirt or gravel tracks. There's no conformity in the numbering system, which is decided by state authorities, and the numbers of through routes often change at state borders. All states provide road condition and road construction telephone hotlines.

SPEED LIMITS

Speed limits vary from state to state and are usually signposted (shown in miles per hour). The federal recommended maximum speed limit on freeways is 55mph (89kph), often referred to as the 'double nickel'. This has been increased to 65mph (105kph) on rural interstate highways in some 40 states. Check local speed limits and look out for speed restrictions. The following speed limits are guidelines only and apply to cars and motorcycles:

Type of Road	Speed Limit
Interstate freeway	55mph (89kph) or 65mph (105kph)
Other freeways and dual carriageways	40 – 55mph (64 – 89kph)
Rural road	45 – 55mph (72 – 89kph)
Urban road	25 – 35mph (40 – 56kph)
Business districts	25 – 30mph (40 – 48kph)
Residential districts and school zones	15 – 25mph (24 – 40kph)

On freeways there's often a **minimum** speed limit of 40mph or 45mph (64kph or 72kph), unless otherwise indicated, although this is rarely enforced. Some areas are designated as 'speed zones', where speed limits are restricted and there are often 30mph to 35mph (48kph to 56kph) zones immediately after leaving a freeway, which are strictly enforced. Speeding in a school zone is a serious offence. Many small towns control their own roads and often have speed limits as low as 25mph (and signs such as 'This is God's country. Please don't drive through it like hell!'). Some speed limits are advisory, e.g. at sharp bends on open roads, and are shown on a yellow background rather than white. (In the New England states, speed limits at bends are compulsory.) Speed restrictions are often signposted at level (grade) crossings, alleys and uncontrolled junctions, where visibility is limited.

The 55mph or 65mph speed limits are widely ignored, although most motorists drive 5mph or 10mph above the limit only (except in Los Angeles, where there's a two-speed system: dangerously fast and stopped). Most truckers and many motorists have Citizens Band (CB) radios, distinguishable by their huge antennas. Among other things, these are used to broadcast the location of police patrol cars (Smokey the Bear) and speed traps. Speeding (called a 'moving violation') is usually less risky when you're in a group, as it's unlikely that the police will book a whole convoy of vehicles. Following a speeding trucker (72mph is considered to be the 'trucker's speed' in 65mph zones) may help you avoid a ticket, but don't count on it. Speeding is the main factor in over 25 per cent of accidents, particularly in mountain areas, where it's more likely to result in the loss of your life than the loss of your licence.

The enforcement of speed limits depends on the particular state, although speeding is generally taken much more seriously in the US than in many other countries. In most states, non-freeway speed limits are more rigorously enforced than freeway limits and are, therefore, more widely observed. Speed limits are enforced by state, county and city police using radar guns, fixed radar traps, marked and unmarked cars, helicopters, and light aircraft (e.g. on interstate highways). Radar warning signs are usually erected at state borders and along highways, although there are no warnings in some states. All states except Connecticut, Michigan, Virginia and the District of Columbia permit the use of radar detector devices (in wide use), but radar jamming devices are illegal in all states. Drivers often warn oncoming drivers of radar traps by flashing their headlights, but this is often illegal and can result in a fine. An increasing number of authorities now use photographic speed traps that snap a speeder's registration number (used successfully for many years in Europe).

Speeding fines vary from harsh to a paltry $10, particularly on interstate highways, where the degree of enthusiasm for the maximum speed limit of 55mph or 65mph varies from state to state. Some western states reluctantly enforce federal speed limits, under the threat of the loss of federal highway grants. (If over 50 per cent of vehicles checked by underground traffic monitors fail to observe the 55mph speed limit, federal grants are cut.) The average fine for speeding is around $50 for up to ten miles over the limit, plus a further $5 or $10 for each additional mile per hour.

GENERAL ROAD RULES

The following list includes some of the most common road rules and some tips designed to help you adjust to driving conditions and avoid accidents. However, like most things in the US, road rules vary from state to state. For detailed information on road rules in individual states, contact your state Department of Motor Vehicles (DMV) or see the *Digest of Motor Laws* published annually by the AAA (see page 295).

- Traffic drives on the right-hand side of the road (in all states!). You may find this a bit strange if you come from a country driving on the left; however, it saves a lot of confusion if you do likewise. Take extra care when pulling out of junctions and one-way streets and at roundabouts (traffic circles or rotaries); remember to look first to the left when crossing the road. If you aren't familiar with driving on the right, you should be prepared for some apprehension and disorientation (some people have problems adjusting to it).

- When you want to turn left at a junction, you must pass in front of a car turning left coming from the opposite direction, and not behind it. At major junctions in some cities there are green-arrow signals for left-hand turn lanes. Certain lanes are signposted 'RIGHT LANE MUST TURN RIGHT' or 'EXIT ONLY' and mean what they say. If you find yourself in these lanes by mistake and leave it too late to change lanes, you must turn in the direction indicated. You should signal when changing lanes, although few Americans do, particularly on freeways.

- Rear indicator (turn) lights on many American-made cars aren't always coloured orange or yellow, but are often red and an integral part of the rear light cluster. This makes them difficult to see or distinguish from brake or rear lights. Hand signals are usually necessary only when your indicators fail. The hand signals used in all states are: left turn, arm horizontal; right turn, arm upward; stop or slow, hand and arm downward.

- Use of a horn is prohibited in some cities; they should in any case should be used sparingly, e.g. to prevent an accident.

- Each state has rules and regulations regarding the towing of trailers or another vehicle.

- There's no automatic priority to the right (or left) on any road, although generally, a turning vehicle must give way to one going straight ahead. 'STOP' signs are red and octagonal; 'YIELD' (give way) signs are an inverted triangle, usually yellow. You must stop completely at a stop sign before pulling out from a junction (motorists who practise the 'rolling stop' are a favourite target of traffic cops). When approaching a main highway from a secondary road, you must usually stop, even where there's no stop sign. At a 'YIELD' sign you aren't required to stop, but must give way to other traffic. Not all junctions have signs.

- Yellow centre lines mark the separation of traffic lanes moving in opposite directions, and white broken lines separate lanes moving in the same direction. A solid yellow line to the right of the centre yellow line (i.e. on your side of the road) means that passing is prohibited; two solid yellow lines prohibit passing in both directions. Solid yellow lines are usually accompanied by 'DO NOT PASS' or 'NO PASSING ZONE' (pennant-shaped, black on yellow) signs. Yellow lines are also used on the left edge of one-way roads and dual carriageways. White road edge lines are intended to guide drivers in poor visibility.

- At roundabouts (traffic circles or rotaries), vehicles on the roundabout (coming from the left) have priority and not those entering it, who are faced with a 'YIELD' sign. This shouldn't be a problem, as most roundabouts are found only in a handful of states, such as Massachusetts (which is why you should always beware of American registered vehicles at roundabouts in your home country). In place of roundabouts, Americans have what is called a four-way stop. This is a cross-roads indicated by a 'STOP' sign with '4 WAY' underneath, at which all motorists must stop (it was obviously invented by bureaucrats!). Priority goes to the vehicle stopping first. When two vehicles stop at the same time, a driver is supposed to give way to the vehicle on his right. When you approach at the same time as a car coming from the opposite direction, the vehicle that's turning should yield to the one going straight on through the intersection. (Roundabouts are a much better idea!)

- Occasionally, you will come across a three-way stop, where traffic from one direction has priority and vehicles from the other three directions must stop. Needless to say, these junctions cause a lot of confusion and it isn't always easy to establish who has priority. Priority isn't always clearly indicated by signs (which may be obscured) and there may be no line indicating where to stop. If in doubt, stop and proceed only when it's clear to do so or when other motorists clearly cede priority. Failure to obey (or understand) right of way signs is a factor in over 10 per cent of fatal accidents and nearly 20 per cent of all accidents.

- You must use dipped headlights (low beams) after dark (usually half an hour after sunset and half an hour before sunrise) in all states. You're usually prohibited to drive on side (parking) lights. Headlights must generally be used when visibility is reduced to less than 500 or 1,000ft. Many people drive with headlights on during the daytime (which is legal), particularly in the southern states, where heat haze often makes unlit cars difficult to see. Full beam (high beams) must usually be dipped when a car approaches within 500ft (150m) or when you're following within 200ft or 300ft (60m to 90m) of another vehicle.

Headlight flashing has a different meaning in different countries. In some countries it means "after you", while in others it means "get out of my way". It can even mean "I thought that was the windscreen washer". **In the US, headlight flashing usually means "me first!".** Drivers often warn oncoming traffic of potential hazards (including police radar traps) by flashing their headlights (which may be illegal). Hazard warning lights (both indicators operating simultaneously) may usually be used to warn other drivers of an obstruction, e.g. an accident or traffic jam on a freeway, although in some states it's illegal to use them while a vehicle is moving.

- The sequence of traffic (stop) lights is usually red, green, yellow and back to red, although some are simply red-green-red. Yellow means stop at the stop line; you may proceed only if the yellow light appears when stopping might cause an accident. A green filter light may be shown in addition to the main signal, which indicates you may drive in the direction shown by the arrow, irrespective of other lights showing. Traffic lights are frequently set on the far side of a junction, sometimes making it difficult to judge where to stop, and are also strung across the road rather than fixed to posts by the roadside. A 'Delayed Green' sign at some stop lights indicates that the green light opposite changes first, usually to allow motorists to make a turn across your lane. In some suburban areas, there are flashing red lights to indicate traffic lights ahead. Jumping (running) red lights is a major cause of accidents in cities.

  Traffic lights in cities are usually set for traffic travelling at a certain speed, e.g. 25mph. These may vary according to the area, traffic density and the time of day. If you maintain the set speed, you're able to 'make' most lights when they're green. At night or in the early hours of the morning, some junctions and crossroads have flashing traffic lights. A flashing red light indicates 'STOP' (as at a four-way stop) and a flashing yellow light means 'YIELD', i.e. you can proceed without stopping if it's safe to do so.

- One of the most surprising rules is that in all states you may make a right turn at a red stop light, unless otherwise indicated. The only exception is New York City, where there's no right turn on red (although the rule does apply in other parts of New York State). **You must, however, treat a red light as a stop sign and stop before making a right turn.** You must also give way to pedestrians crossing at the lights. Busy junctions often have signs indicating that turning on a red light isn't allowed (e.g. 'NO TURN ON RED') or is allowed at certain times only. If you're stopped and the motorist behind you is sounding his horn, it probably means you can turn right (though it sometimes means that the motorist behind you cannot see the 'NO TURN ON RED' sign). Although it appears to be a sensible rule, some people claim that it increases accidents. In some states you can also make a left turn on a red light from a one-way street into another one-way street, where indicated.

- Always approach pedestrian crossings (see page 296) with caution and don't park or overtake another vehicle on the approach to a crossing. Pedestrians have the legal right of way once they've stepped onto a crossing without traffic lights and you must stop; motorists who don't stop are liable to heavy penalties. When crossing a public footpath, e.g. when entering or emerging from property or a car park, motorists must give way to pedestrians.

● On-the-spot fines can be imposed for traffic offences in some states. However, never offer to pay a fine, as it may be interpreted as an attempted bribe (on the other hand, it may be accepted with pleasure). Convictions for many motoring offences result in licence penalty points being imposed (see page 267). Fines can also be exacted for all offences, although the maximum fine is rarely imposed. Serious offences such as dangerous or drunk driving involving injury or death to others may result in a prison sentence. Traffic fines can usually be paid by post and many communities have a local office, e.g. Violations Bureau, where fines (e.g. parking) can be paid. Using a mobile phone while driving is now illegal in some states (e.g. New York, where you can be fined around $100) or you may be required to use a hands-free system.

● A black 'X' in a yellow circle with RR indicates a level (railroad grade) crossing, with or without an automatic barrier. Many railway crossings don't have barriers, although some are provided with flashing lights and/or a bell to warn motorists of an approaching train, while others rely on motorists to check that the line is clear before crossing. Trains usually whistle when approaching a level crossing. Only public railway crossings are required to have warning signs, which leaves some 120,000 crossings (out of 300,000) where no signs are required. It's mandatory to stop at railway crossings in some states (usually indicated by a sign), although this may apply to buses and trucks only. **Approach railway crossings with extreme caution and, if you have any doubts about whether it's safe to cross, STOP and check for trains.** Some 500 people are killed and thousands more injured annually in collisions at railway crossings.

● Be wary of cyclists, moped riders and motorcyclists. It isn't always easy to see them, particularly when they're hidden by the blind spots of a car or are riding at night without lights. **When overtaking, ALWAYS give cyclists a wide . . . WIDE berth.** If you knock them off their bikes, you may have a difficult time convincing the police that it wasn't your fault; far better to avoid them (and the police).

● Children getting on or off school (or church) buses, usually painted 'school bus' yellow, have priority over all traffic. In many states, buses are equipped with flashing yellow lights to warn motorists that a bus is about to stop, followed by flashing red lights when it actually stops. Take care when approaching a stopped school bus without flashing lights, as they could have failed. All motorists **must** usually stop not less than 20ft or 25ft behind or facing a school bus with flashing lights or 'stop arms', even when it has halted on the opposite side of the road (children are instructed to cross the road in front of the bus while traffic is stopped). However, vehicles travelling in the opposite direction on a dual carriageway aren't required to stop. Motorists must remain stopped until the bus moves off or the driver signals motorists to proceed. **Never pass a school bus with flashing red lights!** The law regarding school buses is taken very seriously and motorists convicted of passing a stopped school bus may fined up to $1,000, imprisoned or required to do community service, and may receive up to five penalty points on their driving licence. School zones and school crossings are indicated by a sign showing children on a yellow background, in the shape of an arrow facing upwards.

● Drivers of foreign-registered cars must have the appropriate international sign affixed to the rear (except for cars registered in Canada or Mexico). American registered cars don't need a 'USA' international sign when used in Canada or Mexico.

● Hitchhiking or picking up hitchhikers is prohibited in some states and motorists can nullify their insurance by doing it. It's also a risky business, as a hitchhiker can be anyone from a mugger to a rapist or serial killer. You should also be wary of taking children (other than your own) over a state border, which is a federal offence on a par with kidnapping.

● All states publish local rules of the road, obtainable free from state Departments of Motor Vehicles (DMVs). The American Automobile Association (see page 295) publishes a *Digest of Motor Laws* containing all state traffic regulations, including motor vehicle registration, taxes, driving licence, traffic rules, towing and trailer information, motorcycle and moped rules, and other information. It's available from any AAA office and is free to AAA members. The AAA Traffic Safety Department also publishes a wide range of brochures and leaflets to help improve driving and increase safety.

MOTORCYCLES

Motorists with a full car driving licence (US or foreign) may ride a motorcycle (up to 125cc) without passing a test or obtaining a special licence. (Although often 'underpowered' motorcycles are not legal on the roads, or they're treated like bicycles and mopeds and must stay to the far right of the roadway, out of the way of the vehicular traffic.) US motorcycle tests are mostly superficial and in most states there's no restriction on the size of bike a rider can ride after passing his test. No test is necessary for moped riders.

In general, motoring laws applying to cars also apply to motorcycles; however, there are a few points which apply to motorcyclists only. Proof of ownership (title) and registration of motorcycles is required in all states (see **Vehicle Registration** on page 255). No title is required for mopeds, which must be registered in most (around 35) states plus the District of Columbia. A motorcycle licence is required in all states, although this may be an authorisation on a car licence; a moped licence is required in most states. The minimum age for riding a moped (up to 50cc) is 10 in Arkansas, 13 in New Mexico, and between 14 and 16 in all other states. For motorcycles over 50cc, the minimum age is 14 in Alabama, Alaska and Kansas, 15 in Florida, Hawaii, Louisiana and Mississippi, and between 16 and 18 in all other states. In some states riders under a certain age, e.g. 18, must complete an approved motorcycle rider education programme.

A crash helmet of an approved design is obligatory for all motorcycle riders and passengers in some 20 states. In most other states, helmets must be worn by riders under 18 or 19. Three states currently have no helmet laws in place (Colorado, Illinois and Iowa), although this is subject to change. In Delaware, all riders must carry helmets, but only those under 19 are required to wear them (Americans' heads get harder as they age!). Rhode Island requires only passengers to wear a helmet. Failure to wear a helmet incurs a fine of around $100, with higher fines (e.g. $250) and prison sentences for persistent offenders. Moped riders must wear helmets in around 20 states, half of which require only those of a certain age to wear them, e.g. 16 to 19 (even though more middle-aged riders are involved in accidents than teenagers). Many bikers are vehemently opposed to wearing helmets and argue that they have a right to kill themselves, although when they're injured it's often the state that has to pick up the bill (estimated at $100 million per year in California alone). In many states, you're also required to wear goggles if a windscreen (windshield) isn't fitted to your bike. Note also the following:

- In general, motorcycles registered for use on public highways must meet the equipment requirements in the state in which they're registered, in addition to federal safety standards.

- Only bikes over 50cc are permitted to use interstate or limited access highways.

- In many states, motorcyclists are required to use headlights at all times.

- Riding between lanes of traffic is prohibited in all states and riding two (or more) abreast is also prohibited in some states.

- A strong lock is recommended for all bikes.

Insurance for motorcycles is high and similar to that for cars. The cost of insurance depends on your age (riders under 25 pay **much** more), type and cubic capacity of your motorcycle, and the length of time you've held a licence. You should have liability insurance well above the legal minimum (see **Car Insurance** on page 267). In most states, you can be eligible for significant discounts on motorcycle insurance if you've completed the state motorcycle training classes.

Like cars, motorcycles are inexpensive. If you want a bike for a short period only, it's probably best to buy a used model, as you won't have to bear the initial depreciation. Most dealers sell new and used bikes (on which sales tax must be paid). The procedure and legal requirements when buying a bike are much the same as for buying a car (see page 260). It's also possible to rent a motorcycle or moped in most areas.

Some American motorists think all bikers are Hell's Angels and are often hostile towards them. They won't usually run you off the road, but you may need to put up with a certain amount of abuse.

SEAT BELTS

The wearing of seat belts is compulsory for drivers and front-seat passengers in the District of Columbia and all states except New Hampshire, where only those under 18 are required to belt up. Seat belt laws usually apply to children (e.g. up to age 16) in any seat and in some states, adult passengers in rear seats must also wear them. Fines of between $10 and $50 are levied for violations, depending on the state. However, in 38 states, you cannot be stopped for not wearing a seat belt; a police officer must find some other reason for stopping you and can then fine you for being 'unbuckled' (although you cannot incur licence penalty points).

Around two-thirds of Americans regularly wear seat belts, with around 10 per cent more women wearing them than men. The most conscientious belt wearers are Californians, 87 per cent of whom regularly buckle up. In some states, failure to wear a seat belt may reduce the amount of damages awarded by a court as the result of an accident. In some older American cars, shoulder seat belts operate automatically when you close the door (although you must fasten the lap belt yourself).

In all states and the District of Columbia, young children must ride in a federally-approved child safety seat or use seat belts. Age requirements vary from state to state. Generally, children under three or four must be secured in a safety seat, above which age a seat belt may be used. Some states stipulate any child under 40 pounds or 40 inches (do police officers carry scales and tape measures?) must be secured in a safety seat. Depending on the state, drivers can be fined between $20 and $500 for each child not properly secured and a court hearing may be necessary. In some states, child restraint laws don't apply to out-of-state drivers.

Whether or not you're required by law to wear a seat belt, it's always wise. It has been estimated that seat belts would prevent some 75 per cent of deaths and 90 per cent of injuries caused to people involved in accidents who weren't wearing seat belts (air bags would save most of the remainder). **However, rear seat lap belts (used on their own) can cause serious internal and back injuries, and should be avoided (by children as well as adults).** If you're exempt from wearing a seat belt for medical reasons, a seat belt certification is required from a physician. Taxis, emergency vehicles, buses and trucks weighing 18,000 pounds or more are exempt from seat belt and child restraint laws. **If you wish to be safer, at least as a driver or front passenger, buy a car fitted with air bags.** For more information about seat belts and other aspects of motoring safety, write to the National Highway Traffic Safety Administration, Information Department, 400 7th Street SW, Washington, DC 20590 or visit their website (🖳 www.nhtsa.dot.gov). The AAA (see page 295) publishes a free guide to child safety seats. It's even possible to buy seat belts for pets!

AMERICAN DRIVERS

Like motorists in all countries, Americans have their customs and idiosyncrasies, many of which are peculiar to a region, state or city. Chicago has the reputation of being one of the worst places to drive, and the traffic in New York City may frighten you to death (certainly New York cabbies will!). It's debatable where the worst drivers come from; some say Bostonians or New Yorkers are the worst, while others cite redneck southerners. Drivers on the east and west coasts tend to be more disciplined than those in the Midwest, west and south. The worst cities to drive in based on traffic density are New York, Los Angeles, Houston, San Francisco and Washington DC. Wherever you drive in the US, the traffic density and different road rules (or lack of them) can be intimidating. In cities, one of the main causes of accidents is drivers 'running' red lights.

Attitudes towards pedestrians vary from hostility to deference, according to the locality and driver. As in most countries, drivers are usually more polite and respectful of pedestrians in small towns than in major cities. In country or wilderness areas, you should keep an eye open for deer and other wildlife which may run into your path. (Also beware of drivers who stop suddenly to look at the wildlife.) Many Americans, particularly southern Californians, are fair-weather drivers and are totally lost in heavy rain (or any weather other than bright sunlight), when they're likely to slow to walking pace and are a hazard to other motorists.

In general, however, Americans have a reputation for being good and careful drivers. Drivers tend to be relaxed, courteous and considerate and, unlike many Europeans, are usually happy to give way to a driver waiting to enter the flow of traffic or change lanes, although road manners have deteriorated in recent years. A combination of straight, wide roads, big comfortable cars, low maximum speeds (compared with most other western countries) and vigilant police tends to result in a relaxed and civilised driving style. The extra comforts provided as standard in many American cars, such as automatic transmission, cruise control, power steering and power-assisted brakes, and air-conditioning, also help make driving more relaxing. That's not to say that there aren't crazy, incompetent and aggressive drivers in the US (as in other countries, 'road rage' is on the increase), but they're very much in the minority (contrary to the impression given by American films and television).

One of the main differences between motoring in the US and in other western countries is that on most roads with more than one lane, it's legal to 'pass' on the inside, i.e. on the right. This is strange at first and can be unsettling when you're being passed by giant lorries on both sides. Officially, it's illegal to overtake on an inside lane, i.e. to deliberately move to an inside lane in order to overtake a slower vehicle and then return to the outside line, and lane hopping can earn you a ticket (sometimes to the next life). Passing, however, is when you're already in an inside lane in which traffic is moving faster or you have a clear road. Needless to say, there's a thin dividing line between 'passing' and 'overtaking', and many Americans swap lanes (lane dodge) continuously without signalling (Americans rarely signal when changing lanes on freeways). You should, therefore, take care when changing lanes, as it's the major cause of freeway accidents. You should look over your shoulder first, as wing mirrors (particularly on monster American cars) usually have a blind spot as big as a house. Although freeways usually have a 'slow' (through) and a 'fast' (passing) lane, because of the passing either side rule, many motorists stick to 'lane driving', i.e. get into one lane and stay there. However, in some states the outside lane is exclusively for overtaking. Take care when passing lorries, as they're often large and long, and create considerable side winds.

American drivers often drive too close (tailgate) to the vehicle in front of them, particularly on freeways, and have no idea of safe stopping distances. This is particularly true of lorry drivers, who often try to intimidate you into driving faster or moving over by driving a few feet from your rear bumper (fender). (Lorries aren't allowed in the outside lane of freeways with three or more lanes.) After passing manoeuvres, driving too close to the vehicle in front is the biggest cause of accidents in the US. As a safety precaution, try to leave a large gap between your vehicle and the one in front. This isn't just to allow you more time to stop should the vehicles in front decide to get together, but also to give a tailgater more time to stop. **The closer the vehicle behind you, the further you should be from the vehicle in front.**

Wherever you drive in the US, drive defensively and always expect the unexpected (or the worst) from other drivers. However, provided you avoid rush hours, you will probably find driving in the US less stressful than in many countries. If you come from a country where traffic drives on the left, take it easy at first and bear in mind that there are other motorists around just as confused as you are.

DRINKING & DRIVING

Drunk driving is a serious problem in the US, where excessive alcohol is estimated to be a factor in some 40 per cent of all traffic fatalities (that's almost 15,000 deaths per year). More than 1.8 million people are arrested for drunk driving each year, a small fraction of the millions who drive while under the influence of alcohol. Random breath (or sobriety) tests are permitted in some states, while in others police need a reason to stop a vehicle before they can ask you to take a breath test. Often a police officer tries to detect alcohol by sniffing the air and he may try to goad you into giving him a reason to demand a sobriety test. A test may consist of reciting the alphabet or counting numbers, standing on one foot for a designated period, walking in a straight line, or touching the tip of your nose with an index finger with your eyes closed (this is serious!). Chemical tests can consist of a breath, blood, urine or saliva alcohol test, or a test for drugs (narcotics). If you have a choice, experts suggest that you request a urine test. A refusal to take a test usually results in your driving licence being automatically suspended or revoked, e.g. for six months or a year. In some states, there are periodic purges when road blocks are set up throughout a county or state and all drivers are given a breath test.

You're no longer considered fit to drive when your breath contains 35 micrograms (mg) of alcohol per 100ml, or your blood contains 80mg of alcohol per 100ml or your urine 107mg per 100ml. In most states, you're considered to be driving while intoxicated (DWI) or driving under the influence (DUI) when your blood-alcohol content (BAC) or level is 0.1 per cent (it's occasionally lower, e.g. 0.08 per cent or even 0.05 per cent for minors). In some states, if your BAC is above a certain level, e.g. between 0.05 and 0.09 per cent, you may be charged with 'driving while ability-impaired', although this is usually done only after an accident or in a case of reckless or dangerous driving. You're entitled to two chemical tests, which must measure within a certain percentage of each other, e.g. 0.02.

Penalties include fines, imprisonment, on-the-spot licence suspension or revocation, and community service. A first conviction for drunk driving results in a heavy fine (e.g. $250 to $500) and revocation of your licence for up to six months. In some 40 states, imprisonment from 1 to 60 days is mandatory after the first or second offence for driving while intoxicated (exceptions are Arkansas, Michigan, Minnesota, Mississippi, New York, Oklahoma, South Dakota, Wisconsin and the District of Columbia). In many states, offenders must participate in a programme of alcohol education or rehabilitation. If you have an accident while drunk, the penalties are usually more severe, particularly if you cause an injury or death. However, many people believe that the penalties are too lenient and that tougher action is needed to deter habitual drinkers from driving.

There's a strong lobby against drunk drivers, spearheaded by Mothers Against Drunk Driving (MADD), many of whose members have lost children in road accidents involving drunk drivers. In some areas people are encouraged to dial 911 (the emergency number) to report drunk drivers. Even carrying an open alcohol container in the passenger compartment of a vehicle is a serious offence in many states (where alcohol must be transported in sealed containers, e.g. unopened bottles or cans, and be locked in the boot). It's an offence to carry alcohol across some state borders. Riding a moped, bicycle or horse while drunk is also illegal (and may cost you points against your driving licence!), and driving under the influence of drugs carries the same penalties as those for drunk driving.

ACCIDENTS

If you're involved in an accident, the procedure is as follows:

1. Stop immediately. If possible, move your car off the road and keep your passengers and yourself off the road. If you have an accident (or a breakdown) on a freeway or other fast road, don't stay in your vehicle whatever the weather (even if parked on the shoulder), as there's a danger that another vehicle may run into you. Failing to stop after an accident, or failure to give particulars or report to the police is a serious offence. However, if you have an accident in a dangerous area, you should drive to the nearest police station to report it.

2. Warn other drivers of an obstruction by switching on your hazard warning lights (particularly on freeways). If necessary, for example when the road is partly or totally blocked, turn on your car's headlights and direct traffic around the hazard. In bad visibility, at night, or in a blind spot, try to warn oncoming traffic of the danger, e.g. with a torch (flashlight) at night.

3. If anyone is injured, immediately telephone for an ambulance, the fire department (if someone is trapped or oil or chemicals are spilled) or the police, or get someone else to do it. Motorist aid call boxes with a direct line to the local highway patrol are located on some freeways and highways. Use them to request assistance for breakdowns and report hazards and accidents. Give first-aid only if you're qualified to do so. Don't move an injured person unless absolutely necessary to save him from further injury and don't leave him alone except to telephone for an ambulance. Cover him with a blanket or coat to keep him warm.

4. There's no requirement to report an accident to the police if there are no injuries or damage to property (other than your own). Calling the police to the scene of an accident may result in someone being booked for a driving offence. In all cases you mustn't say anything that could be interpreted as an admission of guilt (even if you've ploughed into a stationary vehicle!). Don't agree to pay for damages or sign any papers except a traffic ticket (which you must sign), before checking with your insurance company or an attorney. Let the police and insurance companies decide who was at fault.

5. If you or the other driver(s) involved decide to call the police, don't move your vehicle or allow other vehicles to be moved. If it's necessary to move vehicles to unblock the road, take photographs of the accident scene if a camera is

available or make a drawing showing the positions of all vehicles involved before moving them.

6. Check immediately whether there are any witnesses to the accident and take their names and addresses, particularly noting those who support **your** version of events. If a motorist refuses to give his name, note his registration number. Write down the registration numbers of all vehicles involved and their drivers' and owners' names and addresses, vehicle registration certificate, driving licence and insurance details. You must by law also give these details to anyone having reasonable grounds for requiring them (e.g. anyone injured or the owner of damaged property). **Don't, however, reveal how much insurance cover you have.** Note also the names and badge numbers of any police present.

7. All accidents involving death or bodily injury must usually be reported immediately to the local police, sheriff or highway patrol. If death, injury or property damage above a minimum amount, e.g. $250, is involved, the safety-responsibility laws of most states require that you must also report the accident to the state Department of Motor Vehicles (DMV) and establish financial responsibility within a given period, e.g. 5 or 10 days. This is in addition to any report made to the police, highway patrol, or your insurance company. **If you fail to report an accident, your driving licence may be suspended for a year.** In general, you should report **all** accidents immediately to the local police, whether they're called to the scene or not, and inquire about other reporting requirements. Make sure your report is officially recorded by the officer on duty and obtain a copy. If you have an accident involving a domestic animal (except a cat) and are unable to find the owner, it must also be reported to the local police. This also applies to certain wild animals, e.g. deer, which are a danger on rural roads, including some freeways.

8. If you're arrested by the police, you aren't required to make a statement, even if they ask for one. The best policy is not to say or sign anything until you've spoken to a lawyer and obtained legal advice.

9. Finally, you should report all accidents to your insurance company in writing as soon as possible, even if you don't intend to make a claim (but reserve your right to make a claim later). Your insurance company asks you to complete an accident report form, which should be returned as soon as possible. The claim procedure depends on your insurance cover and that of anyone else involved in the accident (see **Car Insurance** on page 267).

In some areas you should be extremely wary of stopping at what looks like the scene of an accident, e.g. on a deserted highway, as accidents are sometimes staged to rob unsuspecting drivers (called highway hold-ups). You may, however, be obliged to note the location of the 'accident' and call for help from the first available telephone.

TRAFFIC POLICE

Despite the TV and film image of speeding reckless drivers, traffic laws in the US are taken seriously and strictly enforced. Each state has an agency responsible for enforcing highway traffic rules and regulations, e.g. state troopers or the highway patrol, employing patrol cars, motorcycles and aircraft. Traffic laws are also enforced by local police, such as county sheriff's officers or municipal police. If a policeman wants you to stop, he usually drives along behind you flashing his overhead lights (which may be red, blue or yellow or a combination) and possibly sounding his siren. You should pull over and stop, if possible on the hard shoulder. Once you've stopped, stay in your car and let the officer come to you. Keep your hands in view, e.g. on the steering wheel, and don't do anything that could be misconstrued, like reaching for your licence in the glove compartment (an officer may think that you're going for a gun). If you're stopped by an unmarked vehicle, ask to see the officer's identification.

Whatever you're stopped for, the officer will ask to see your licence and may want to see your car registration document and insurance card, so always carry them with you. Don't joke with or antagonise an officer, as this may lead to a ticket, whether you've done anything illegal or not. A foreign accent and an apology may help you get a warning rather than a ticket. **Although some people attempt to bribe patrolmen by inserting a $20 bill inside their licence, this practice isn't recommended!** If you're stopped for speeding or another 'minor' offence such as failing to stop at a 'STOP' sign or making an illegal turn, you may get away with a caution (called a 'friendly warning') in some states. If you receive a ticket for a motoring offence, you may have the choice of paying a statutory fine or going to court. If you're stopped for drunk driving (see page 285) or another serious offence, you may be arrested.

If you're arrested for a traffic violation, you may be taken directly to court, to the police department, or before some other agency or person authorised to set and accept bail. There you must decide whether to plead guilty, no contest or not guilty. A plea of guilty or no contest may result in a fine, which you must pay before you're released. If you plead not guilty, the court sets a hearing date and asks you to post an appearance bond, which is a sum of money to guarantee your appearance on that date.

Some 40 states and the District of Columbia accept AAA Bail and Guaranteed Arrest Bond Certificates in lieu of cash or surety bonds for traffic violations, although only 30 states are required by law to accept them. You must deposit your AAA membership card (see page 295) and bond with the court and may then leave the jurisdiction. If you appear for trial, your card and certificate are returned to you or your AAA club. If, however, you elect to forfeit your bond and don't appear for trial, the court notifies the AAA club of the forfeiture. The AAA then arranges for payment and recovers your membership card from the court. You must then reimburse the club for the amount spent on your behalf and your membership card is returned. Most states accept AAA bonds for amounts from $200 to $1,000. In states without mandatory acceptance of AAA bonds, acceptance is at the discretion of the magistrate who sets bail. In some states police may accept your driving licence in lieu of a bond.

If you break the law, you may be 'tagged' by the police, but not stopped and may receive a summons later. If you're driving a rented car, the rental company receives the summons and may debit the amount of any fine from your credit card.

CAR THEFT

Car theft is rampant in the US, where a car is stolen on average every 20 seconds (over 1.5 million per year) and thefts from motor vehicles run into tens of millions. If you're driving anything other than a worthless heap you should have comprehensive insurance, which includes cover for theft (see page 267). It's wise to have your car fitted with an alarm, immobiliser (system interrupter) or other anti-theft device, plus a visible deterrent, such as a steering or transmission shift lock (many new cars are fitted with door dead locks and sophisticated alarm systems as standard equipment). This is important if you own a car that's desirable to car thieves, which includes most new sports and luxury models, often stolen by professional crooks to order. A good security system won't prevent someone breaking into your car (which usually takes most crooks a matter of seconds) or even prevent your car being stolen, but it at least makes it more difficult and may persuade a thief to look for an easier target.

Radios, tape and CD players attract a lot of (the wrong) attention in most cities (e.g. New York), particularly in expensive foreign cars. Often drivers put a sign in their car windows proclaiming 'No Radio' (or 'No Valuables', 'Trunk is Empty' and 'Doors Open'), to deter thieves from breaking in to steal them. If you buy an expensive stereo system, get one with a removable unit or with a removable control panel (which you can pop in a pocket). However, never forget to remove it, even when stopping for a few minutes. Cover an empty slot with a dummy cover, so that it appears that no radio was installed; otherwise a crook may break in and look for the removed unit.

When leaving your car unattended, store any valuables (including clothes) out of sight or in the boot (trunk) if you're unable to take them with you. This shouldn't be done immediately after parking your car in some areas, where it isn't wise to be seen putting things in the boot. Boots aren't a safe place to hide belongings unless fitted with a protective steel plate or you have a steel safe installed **inside** the boot. Don't leave your car papers in your car, as this not only helps a thief to sell it quickly, but also hinders its recovery (particularly if you don't have a copy of the papers). If possible, avoid parking in long-term car parks, as these are favourite hunting grounds for car thieves. When parking overnight or when it's dark, park in a well-lit area, which may help deter car thieves.

If your car is stolen (or anything is stolen from it) report it to the police in the precinct where it was stolen (but don't expect them to find it). You can report it by telephone, but must go to the station to complete a report. Report a theft to your insurance company as soon as possible. It's now possible to subscribe to a service that combines global positioning satellite (GPS) technology with an integrated mobile phone to allow police to locate your car (and, one hopes, the thieves) within minutes of it being reported as stolen or missing. The same service can also provide custom directions when you're lost and send help to find you when your car breaks down, as well as unlocking your car for you remotely if you've lost your keys.

PARKING

Parking in most cities and towns isn't usually a problem (except in New York, which is an exception to **every** rule). However, parking is restricted or prohibited in many streets. Parking regulations may vary according to the area of a city, the time of day, the day of the week or even the season. Most cities are divided into parking zones, which may be indicated by colours. Usually suburban areas are unrestricted, except perhaps for the main thoroughfares and town centre (downtown) areas, where on-street parking is usually metered. In some towns there are parking regulations during rush-hours on major thoroughfares, where no parking is permitted on one or both sides of the street at certain times (this may also include streets with parking meters in town centres). In winter, some streets are designated 'snow streets', meaning you mustn't park there when snowfall exceeds a certain depth (shown on a sign), in order to leave the road free for snow ploughs.

In some streets, there are parking restrictions at certain times only, e.g. no parking between 9am and 11am Monday to Thursday. Some streets have signs prohibiting parking on certain days for street cleaning, e.g. 2am to 7am (offending vehicles are towed away), although times aren't always shown. Parking may be prohibited overnight, e.g. 1am or 2am to 6am or 7am, in some areas. If you have visitors who must park overnight on the street, inform your local police.

In some cities, parking restrictions are indicated by the kerb (Americans spell it curb) colour; for example, a red kerb indicates no parking at any time, a yellow kerb may signify a limited truck loading zone, a green kerb a limited parking period, a blue kerb disabled parking only, and a white kerb passenger loading and unloading. No parking areas, e.g. at street corners, may be indicated by yellow lines. Always read all parking signs carefully.

Apart from the obvious illegal parking spots, such as across entrances and at bus stops, be careful not to park within ten feet (3m) of a fire hydrant, often indicated by a large gap between parked cars, as you're liable to have your car towed away. Other restricted areas are in front of fire and ambulance stations and schools, often indicated by a red kerb, and on bus stops and taxi ranks, where you may stop briefly, but mustn't get out of your car.

Reserved parking spots for disabled motorists are provided in most towns and cities. In all states, disabled residents are issued with special registration plates, allowing parking privileges in designated spaces close to all public facilities. In some cities, you can be fined up to $500 for illegally parking in a space reserved for a disabled motorist. Most cities provide free parking permits for residents.

You must always park in the direction of the traffic flow on the near side of the road. Often, parking spaces are diagonally aligned and 'head-in', which means the front of your car must be facing the pavement (sidewalk). If you're used to driving small foreign cars (sub-compacts), parking an American monster, or worse, an SUV in a tight space can be decidedly tricky. When parking on a hill, always 'kerb your wheels', i.e. turn your wheels towards the street when facing uphill and towards the kerb when facing downhill. It's also wise to leave the car in gear or 'park' and apply the hand brake. The following parking restrictions are in widespread use:

- **No Stopping** – Means what it says: no stopping at the side of the road.

- **No Standing** – You may stop only to pick up or drop off passengers or goods if you do it quickly. You must not leave your car in a 'no standing' area.

- **No Parking** – You may stop only to pick up or drop off passengers or goods. If you're stopping for longer, the driver should stay in the driver's seat so that he can move the car if necessary.

Parking on highways in rural areas is forbidden and you must pull completely off the road if you wish to stop. Overnight off-road parking is prohibited or restricted in many states for caravans (trailers) and recreation vehicles (RV) and you must use an official trailer or RV park.

Meters

Parking meters are common in most towns and cities, and usually accept nickels, dimes and quarters. In a small town centre 50 cents buys up to 30 minutes' parking with a maximum permitted period of one or two hours (some allow three or four hours). In larger towns meter parking may cost $1.50 per hour (up to a maximum of $10). There are often 12 or 24-hour meters (also called posts) at main railway stations, where parking costs around 25 cents for 1.5 hours. Don't park if a meter isn't working or a parking bay is suspended, as you can get a ticket. Meter feeding (i.e. inserting more coins once your initial time allocation has expired) is usually permitted unless there's a maximum time indicated. Parking attendants often ride around on three-wheeled motorcycles and chalk the tyres of cars parked in limited-period parking areas without stopping (except to write tickets!). Parking meters are usually in operation from 8am or 9am to 6pm or 6.30pm Mondays to Saturdays (except holidays); check meter times, as they may vary from street to street.

Fines

Parking regulations are controlled by city police and private companies, who are zealous, as they're paid on a results basis and usually have quotas to meet. If you get a parking ticket, you may be given an envelope in which to post payment to the appropriate office. Payment must usually be made within 30 days to avoid incurring a penalty. Few states swap parking ticket information, particularly those without common borders, so if you receive an out-of-state ticket it's unlikely that you will receive a summons for non-payment.

Some streets and areas are designated 'tow away' zones (often graphically depicted by a sign showing a red axe embedded in a car or a car being towed away). There's usually a fine of at least $100 when your car is towed away (plus the associated time and hassle). To collect your car from the pound, you must show proof of ownership, insurance card identity, registration document and your driving licence. The towing fee must usually be paid in **cash** before you get your car back, as towers don't normally accept personal cheques or credit cards.

Wheel clamps (colloquially called the 'boot' or 'Denver shoe', as they were first used there) are in wide use. To free your car from this heinous (but effective) device you must go to the clamping station listed on your ticket, pay an unclamping fee and return to your car to await release (expect to wait at least an hour or longer during busy times). After a clamp has been on your car for a certain period, e.g. 72 hours, it may be towed away, when you will also be liable for towing and storage costs.

If in doubt about whether on-street parking is legal, don't take a chance, but park in a car park (parking lot) or garage.

Car Parks

Private and municipal car parks (parking lots) are provided in most cities, with parking costing from $10 to $25 per day; short-term parking usually costs from 75 cents to $3.50 per hour (but can be much higher, e.g. up to $10 for the first hour!), although in a few towns car parks are free. Outside central areas, parking costs around $5 to $10 per day or $4 for an evening. Many car parks offer 'early bird specials', i.e. all-day parking for $10 to $15 per day ($20 in New York) provided you arrive before a certain time. Often waste ground is used, although car parks on waste ground aren't as secure as purpose built parks (particularly after dark) and usually have rough surfaces. In most cities, garages provide daily parking for commuters, although monthly rates can be $300 or more, e.g. in central Manhattan. Cheaper garages can usually be found outside central areas a short bus or subway ride from city centres. Some cities have park-and-ride systems. These can cost over $6 per day (e.g. in New York City), but if you use them regularly, you can pay a monthly charge which works out as little as $1 per day. Car parks catering for commuters have restricted opening hours and are usually closed overnight. Indoor and outdoor car parks are provided close to major airports, from where free transport is provided to and from terminals.

Often there are humps and bumps at the entrance or exit to car parks and garages, so drive slowly. **When using a car park, be sure to use the correct entrance and exit. Sometimes spikes (guaranteed to rip your tyres to pieces) are laid to prevent customers leaving without paying.** In some (usually outdoor) private car parks, you park in a free stall (space) and pay by poking the fee (usually a fixed daily or evening fee) in folded dollar bills into a slot on a board corresponding to your stall number. A 'stuffer' is provided to push bills through the tiny slot (whatever happened to the high-tech US?). Shopping centres (malls), banks, supermarkets, large shops and other establishments often provide free parking areas for their customers. In cities, you may be required to make a purchase and have your receipt stamped, or free parking may be limited, e.g. to three hours. In suburban areas, large shops and shopping centres usually provide enormous and completely free car parks. If you remain too long or park after hours, you may be given a ticket or even be towed away. Different parking levels may be indicated by symbols, e.g. fruit or vegetables, to help you remember where you parked. Some car parks and garages provide valet parking (common at hotels and restaurants), with cars parked by attendants.

PETROL

Three grades of unleaded petrol, known as gasoline (or gas), are available: regular (87 octane), special or mid-grade (89 octane) and premium or super (93 octane) as well as diesel, which is used by most small trucks, but few cars. Leaded petrol has been banned in the US since 1996. Petrol is sold by the US gallon, which is equal to 3.8 litres and is smaller than the British 'imperial' gallon (4.5 litres).

Petrol is much cheaper in the US than in other western countries (petrol tax is just 10 cents to 20 cents per gallon in most states), although the cost fluctuates according to the world oil price. In 2004, the average cost of a gallon of regular unleaded was around $2.00; it was as much as $2.40 in some cities and remote areas and as little as $1.80 in other cities and towns. (Prices are usually higher during holiday periods.) Premium petrol is typically 30 to 40 per cent more expensive than regular. Prices are lowest in cities and suburban areas, where there's lots of competition, and highest on turnpikes, freeways and in rural areas (where the next petrol station may be 100 miles away). Unless you're desperate, it's best to avoid petrol stations that don't display their prices. On suburban highways, the first and last stations may be the most expensive. Independent petrol stations are usually cheaper than those run by large oil companies, although many oil companies provide stamps or tokens that can be exchanged for gifts.

When motoring in rural areas, you should keep your tank topped up (and check your oil and water), as petrol stations are often few and far between, and may be closed on Sundays and holidays (many petrol stations are also closed in the evenings and at weekends). In some states, e.g. California, it's an offence to run out of petrol, for which you can be fined, so it pays to pay attention to the fuel gauge. In many states, it is illegal to carry cans or other reserve supplies of petrol in the boot of your car due to the danger of explosion and fire if you're struck from behind (rear-ended). If you wish to purchase a reserve supply of petrol, you must have a regulation steel petrol can (gas can), made specifically for the storage of petrol. These can be purchased at most petrol stations and automotive supply shops.

Petrol (gas) stations have 'full-serve' or 'self-serve' ('U-serve') pumps, although it isn't always easy to tell whether a station has self-serve pumps (except in New Jersey and Oregon, where there are none!). At full-serve pumps, the attendant checks your oil and cleans your windscreen free of charge and also checks your tyres and radiator water level if asked (it's unnecessary to tip for these services). When buying petrol, make sure that the pump is reset to zero, particularly if an attendant is filling your car. It's best to check your own oil level, as a garage attendant may 'short stick' the dipper so that it doesn't register. These services aren't available at self-serve pumps, but the price of petrol may be slightly lower. At many petrol stations, you must pay before filling your car, particularly at 24-hour and late night stations (common in cities). You pay the clerk and collect any change after filling your car.

Some self-serve stations are simply old stations (with old equipment) where the owner has decided to dispense with full-serve. They aren't equipped with automatic pumps informing the cashier how much you owe, and the attendant must take your word for how much petrol you've used or check the pump himself (thus defeating the object of self-serve stations). When filling your own car, check the instructions. Usually, you insert the pump in your tank and push it down to lock it into position, then pull up the base of the pump holder to signal to the attendant that you're ready. Take care not to splash yourself with petrol. It may come out faster than you expect or the automatic cut-off device may not function properly (particularly with old pumps). US petrol stations (particularly those in rural areas) tend to be far more dilapidated than their counterparts in Europe.

Some petrol stations accept only cash, others only credit cards, and some stations may make a surcharge of a few cents per gallon for credit card payments ('discount for cash'). Most garages also accept dollar travellers' cheques. Major oil companies issue 'credit' cards to pay for petrol, servicing and spares at petrol and service stations (application forms are available from service stations). Although generally called credit cards, most oil companies' cards are charge cards, with the monthly balance due in full at the end of each month, although a few companies allow you to pay off the balance over a period.

Most petrol stations have toilets (restrooms), sometimes located outside the main building, when it may be necessary to ask an attendant for the key (cleanliness varies). Some petrol stations also sell confectionery (candy), hot and cold drinks (usually from vending machines), motoring accessories, newspapers, household goods and various other items. Oil is normally sold by the quart, equivalent to 0.9 litres or 1.6 'imperial' pints, and is less expensive from discount shops.

REPAIRS & SERVICING

You must be extremely careful who you choose to service or repair your car, as vehicle repairs generate more consumer complaints than any other service industry. Repairs and servicing at new car dealers and service stations are the most expensive (particularly in major cities), while the cheapest are small, specialised repair shops, department store chains and general repair shops. However, the quality of work can be extremely variable and it's always best to choose someone who has been personally recommended by family, friends or colleagues. Shop around and compare prices, but don't be taken in by low prices or gifts, as they may be worth little and may disguise hidden extras.

Repair shops are usually efficient and friendly, and most do servicing and repairs (however major) on-the-spot if you're from outside the state. Some garages, however, carry out unnecessary repairs, replacing parts such as brake pads and exhausts needlessly, or even puncturing tyres so that they can sell you a new one or do a repair. These sharp practices are reportedly more prevalent in some western states, particularly at garages close to freeways and on cars with out-of-state plates. If you need minor emergency help, you should remain with your car while it's being repaired, or the mechanic may replace the engine!

You generally have a better chance of redress with a new car dealer or a garage that's a member of a trade association or approved by an automobile club. More than 4,000 car repair shops are approved by the AAA (see page 295) and provide AAA members with a guarantee of all estimates and work. Should a dispute arise between an AAA member and an AAA approved garage, the AAA arbitration service resolves the problem. Garages and repair shops that are members of the Automotive Service Association (ASA, PO Box 929, Bedford, TX 76095-0929, ☎ 817-283-6205, ⌨ www.asashop.org) abide by a code of business ethics. Another safeguard is to check whether a mechanic has been tested and certified by the National Institute for Automotive Service Excellence, in which case he is entitled to display the ASE certificate in his shop.

In some states, it's difficult to find dealers or repair shops that can work on European cars, and obtaining spares is often difficult or impossible. The number and location of dealers in imported cars varies considerably from state to state and in some states, you may find that the nearest dealer is hundreds of miles away. It's wise to carry a selection of basic spare parts, as service stations in small towns are unlikely to stock them and you may need to wait several days for them to be sent from another state. If you need spares, it's cheaper to buy them from shops such as Sears or from major service stations such as Mobil and Shell than from small petrol stations or dealers.

When a car is under warranty, it must usually be regularly serviced by an approved dealer so as not to invalidate the warranty. Most dealers have a set price for regular services (e.g. at 10,000mi intervals) and certain repairs. Service stations don't usually provide a loan (loaner) car while yours is being serviced, although you can usually rent a car cheaply (see page 257). Some collect your car from your home or office and deliver it after a service, or drop you at a railway or bus station or in a local town and pick you up when your car is ready for collection.

ROAD MAPS

There are a huge number of road maps available, from town street plans to atlases covering the whole country. Unlike maps in most countries, American road maps are often organised by state (listed in alphabetical order and drawn to different scales), which makes planning an inter-state trip difficult. Route maps are, however, arranged in geographical order and good sheet maps can be obtained from petrol stations, information offices and in local book shops. City plans certainly come in handy, for example in Los Angeles, where there are 6,500mi of streets and 40,000 junctions.

Among the best American road maps is the large format *Rand McNally Road Atlas: US, Canada and Mexico*, available in paperback and hardback versions (Rand McNally have their own shops in major cities). Similar maps include the *Mobil US Road Atlas* and the *Hamlyn Motoring Atlas USA, Canada and Mexico*. Rand McNally also publish a *Standard Reference Map and Guide* for each state. Free state maps are available from main tourist, publicity or welcome centres and many local tourist bureaux. Some state tourist offices, including welcome centres located on main routes just inside state borders, provide free official state highway maps to personal callers.

The AAA (see page 295) publishes more than 1,000 regional, state and local maps, including the *AAA US Road Atlas* ($5 to members). The AAA and other automobile clubs offer members excellent free maps and regional touring guides, a holiday planning and routing service (including the quickest or most scenic routes, as required), plus detailed maps of towns en route. Town maps are often available from local book and stationery shops. **A good map could save your life, as people who get lost in dangerous neighbourhoods are occasionally murdered!**

MOTORING ORGANISATIONS

There are many national and regional motoring organisations (automobile clubs), providing emergency breakdown and repair services for motorists. Around a third of the US's 160 million motorists belong to an automobile or motor club, by far the largest of which is the American Automobile Association (AAA or 'triple A'), with around 36 million members in the US and Canada and more than 1,000 offices. The AAA is split into regional (usually state) clubs, called chapters, which are listed in telephone books.

Basic AAA membership includes 30 minutes' free mechanical help at the scene of a breakdown or towing to an AAA approved service station (totalling 26,000), additional labour, parts or towing fees (beyond three miles) must be paid by members. The AAA provides a wide range of services and a comprehensive information and advisory service for members, including a holiday planning and routing service with free maps. The AAA also operates the largest retail travel agency in the US and offers low-cost air fares and competitively priced cruises. Basic AAA Membership costs around $65 (fees vary by chapter). For an extra $10 to $30 the AAA Plus service provides all the advantages of basic membership plus up to 100 miles free towing, emergency road service anywhere up to 100 miles, free petrol to get you to the nearest open petrol station, up to $100 in parts and labour, plus locksmith and extra winching services if required. A special membership, known as Plus RV, applies to recreational vehicles (RVs), motor homes, caravans (trailers) and motorcycles and costs around $100.

The AAA provides reciprocal services for members of foreign motoring organisations affiliated to the AAA. The national AAA breakdown service 24-hour telephone number (☎ 1-800-AAA-HELP) can be used by members when travelling outside their local club area to obtain emergency road services. Other AAA services include: guaranteed repairs at AAA approved garages; travel and other insurance; fee-free AAA/Visa credit card; fee-free American Express travellers' cheques; hotel/motel discounts; up to $1,000 ($2,000 AAA Plus) legal fee reimbursement; discounts on new and used cars; emergency personal cheque cashing when travelling; AAA Bail and Guaranteed Arrest Bond Certificates (see page 288); and international driving permits.

For further information contact the AAA National Office, 1000 AAA Drive, Heathrow, FL 32746-5063 (☎ 1-888-859-5161 or 407-444-7000, 🖥 www.aaa.com) or your local AAA chapter (listed in the yellow pages). The AAA publishes *The Handicapped Driver's Mobility Guide* plus numerous safety leaflets and brochures available free to members from local offices or by post from AAA Foundation for Traffic Safety, 1440 New York Avenue NW, Suite 201, Washington, DC 20005 (🖥 www.aaafoundation.org). The AAA also offers services such as driver education and improvement programmes, and provides driver test and training equipment.

Those who are wedded to their RVs might like to join the Good Sam Club, reputedly the world's largest RV owners' organisation (🖥 www.goodsamclub.com).

PEDESTRIAN ROAD RULES

The US is a dangerous place for pedestrians, where they comprise some 13 per cent of all motor vehicle related deaths (almost 5,000 per year) plus tens of thousands of serious injuries. (This is no doubt only partly the reason for the American aversion to walking.) When crossing any road you should take extreme care and whenever possible cross at a pedestrian crossing or walkway, traffic lights, junction or other 'safe' place. If you're in doubt about where to cross, follow the example set by other pedestrians – but not too closely, as Americans are among the world's most ill-disciplined pedestrians.

It's possible to be fined (e.g. $20 or $25) for 'jaywalking', i.e. crossing a road at an unauthorised place or against a pedestrian light, although you would have to lie down in the road to get booked in most cities. In large cities (e.g. New York), almost everyone ignores pedestrian lights, and motorists (who also ignore lights) are surprisingly tolerant of pedestrians wandering across the road. A good indication of pedestrian anarchy is a sign stating 'LOOK FOR PEOPLE CROSSING' on freeways in California (they aren't official pedestrian crossings – even Americans don't put them on freeways!).

Busy pedestrian crossings usually have signs saying 'WALK' and 'DON'T WALK'. Some have a red hand to indicate don't walk and a white 'walking man' for walk. Some crossings have an audible signal for blind pedestrians. Pedestrian crossings are often badly marked and vary from state to state and even from city to city. Many consist of simply two white lines at junctions, perhaps joined by diagonal lines. At pedestrian crossings without pedestrian lights, you should take care when crossing, as motorists may be disinclined to stop (although they're generally better than motorists in most other countries). Signs and road markings for crossings are often abbreviated 'PED XING' for pedestrian crossings or 'BIKE XING' for bicycle crossings.

Parents should never allow young children out alone on roads and should walk between them and traffic, always keeping a tight hold on their hands. If you're unable to do this, then use reins or secure them firmly in a pushchair. Pedestrians **must** use footpaths (sidewalks) where provided and, if walking on a road without a footpath, should keep to the left-hand side, facing oncoming traffic. There are manned patrols at road crossings on busy roads outside or near schools.

12.

HEALTH

After wealth, the subject which most concentrates American minds is health. The US has the most expensive health care in the world, consuming some 14 per cent of GDP – around twice as much as in the UK, Germany and Japan. US hospitals are jam-packed with the latest high-tech equipment, and highly trained and motivated staff; a total of around 2.5 million surgeons, doctors (physicians), nurses and dentists (although, somewhat surprisingly, the US has a shortage of nurses); 6.2 million are employed as health care practitioners and technicians. The US leads the world in high-tech surgery such as transplants, and heart and brain surgery. The average life expectancy is 75 for men and 80 for women (which ranks the US 42nd in the world, behind the UK, Japan and Greece), although it's significantly lower for the poor and underprivileged groups. The infant mortality rate of around seven deaths per 1,000 live births is one of the highest among western countries, ranking the US a lowly 30th in the world, in terms of this statistic.

However, although health care for the wealthy and securely-employed is the best in the world, it can be sparse to non-existent for the poor and unemployed. Health care for all isn't a national priority in the US, where medicine is a huge growth industry and a profitable sector of the free-market system. Many Americans are terrified of falling ill with a long illness, which could bankrupt them. Americans universally agree that health care is far too expensive. The average American family spends around 15 per cent of its income on health care and the nation around $1 trillion (that's $1,000 billion). And despite all that money changing hands, the government coughs up another $2,168 per capita each year for health care – nearly 18 per cent of its annual expenditure. Not surprisingly, Americans are extremely health conscious and agonise over their diet and whether they're getting enough exercise, hence the proliferation of fitness and food fads (a dime of prevention can avert a million-dollar cure).

Around 42.5 million Americans (over 15 per cent of the population) don't have any health insurance at all and a further 65 million have inadequate insurance. Publicly-funded health schemes are provided for the over 65s and the disabled (Medicare), and the poor (Medicaid), although most people without private insurance must pay for their own medical treatment if they want treatment at all. Consequently, many patients arrive at public hospitals (which treat the poor on a near charity basis) chronically sick and in need of expensive care, and hospitals are finding it impossible to cope with the demand.

Every other industrial nation has found a way to provide their citizens with comprehensive health care at a fraction of the cost of the US and with far better health results. Americans question why health insurance costs them far more than it does in other western countries, where health care standards are comparable (although Americans don't think so) and doctors aren't exactly starving. In many countries in Europe, everyone has health insurance, nobody is denied coverage or charged extra because of a bad medical history, there are few or no waiting lists, patients can choose their own doctors, and hospitals are equipped with the latest technology and highly-trained staff, all of which is provided at a fraction of the cost in the US.

The Clinton administration came to power in 1992 vowing to provide health care for all, but initial proposals (described variously as too ambitious, too bureaucratic and too expensive) failed to gain approval by Congress. Under the Bush administration, a much touted Patients' Rights bill was defeated due to controversy over litigation limits. Medicare benefits have finally been extended to include prescription drug coverage for the over 65s, but this won't begin until 2006. There's still an enormous controversy raging over the real cost of this program, which was kept from Congress until after they had voted on the measure.

Meanwhile, the cost of medical insurance and treatment continues to soar. Apart from the cut-throat profit motivation of almost everyone associated with the medical profession (doctors, hospitals, clinics, nursing homes, drug manufacturers, and insurance companies), there are a few mitigating reasons for the high cost of medical treatment. Medical training is expensive and medical students and their families often incur large debts to pay for their degrees. Doctors are required to have expensive malpractice and accident insurance, and must take extreme and expensive measures to avoid law suits. The price of medical technology increases almost daily, with new and highly expensive treatments for cancer, AIDS and other ailments (the cost of sophisticated life support systems runs into millions of dollars). The US also has a rapidly growing elderly population, which consumes a disproportionate share of health resources and is expected to double by the year 2030. Other factors contributing to high costs include abuses of the Medicare and Medicaid programmes (see **Chapter 13**) and the high level of services necessary for victims of crime, drugs and accidents. On top of everything, there's the all-American aversion to death, which is seen as the ultimate failure. It's not uncommon for family members to insist on the latest and greatest high-tech wonder drug or procedure in the hope of saving their 102 year old granny. Some famous (and rich!) people even arrange to be frozen after death, in the hope that modern science will devise a way to extend their lives at some later date, when they can be thawed out and revived.

Before arriving in the US, even for a short stay, you should ensure you have adequate health insurance, generally considered to be a minimum of $250,000. Only emergency patients are treated without prior payment and treatment may be refused without evidence of insurance or a deposit. If you're planning long-term residence in the US, you should have a thorough medical examination, including a dental and optical check, before you arrive. If you've been putting off elective medical or dental treatment, e.g. a 'nose job' or having your teeth capped, it's likely to be less expensive to have it done outside the US. Before deciding where to live in the US, compare the availability of neighbourhood doctors, specialists and hospitals, as facilities vary greatly from community to community.

Generally, the US is a healthy place to live provided you have health insurance and avoid inner cities after dark! Apart from the dangers to your health posed by your fellow man, your main health problems will be those associated with the hustle and bustle of life in a modern-day society, including stress (expatriate stress is a recognised mental condition), poor diet, lack of exercise, obesity (some 64 per cent of Americans are officially overweight and 30 per cent are considered obese), drugs and alcohol. Influenza (flu or grippe) epidemics are common, causing schools to close in many states. The major health issues (apart from health insurance) include AIDS, drug addiction, alcoholism, abortion, euthanasia and care for the elderly. The leading causes of death are heart disease, cancer and strokes. Despite the fact that many Americans have never had it so good, they're popping ever-increasing quantities of 'lifestyle' pills, particularly those prescription medications that are now freely advertised on the television.

Many Americans have an irresistible desire to improve on nature and the US leads the world in cosmetic (plastic) surgery. In the US, if you haven't had some part of your anatomy 'improved', or at least your teeth straightened or capped, you're either an Adonis or impoverished. Modern day Frankensteins (easily recognisable by their million-dollar smiles and Rolls Royces) will 'lift' your face (chin, cheekbones, ears, eyelids, nose), provide instant weight loss (stomach, hips, thighs, bottom) or increase the size of your breasts or penis (small, medium, large, extra large), as quickly as you can say $5,000. More than 150,000 breast implants are performed each year (using implants made of water rather than silicone since the scare). The latest craze in California is for men to have chest, buttock and calf implants to match their wives' silicone-augmented breasts (some 700,000 American men a year have cosmetic surgery). Hair implants or 'weaving' are also fashionable among American men (a full head of hair is even more important than perfect teeth if you want to attract the opposite sex or keep your job in the face of younger competition).

The US has many health magazines and newsletters. If you require general information regarding any health matter, contact the National Health Information Center (Department of Health & Human Services, PO Box 1133, Washington, DC 20013-1133, ☎ 1-800-336-4797 or 301-565-4167, 💻 www.health.gov/nhic). General information about most medical problems is also available from health agencies providing pre-recorded telephone information, usually available in English and Spanish, sometimes in other languages. Most recordings last for three to five minutes and a wide range of topics are covered. For information about the largest network, Tel-Med, check your local telephone directory or contact Tel-Med Inc., 24769 Redlands Blvd #L, Loma Linda, CA 92354-4025 (☎ 909-478-0330 💻 www.tel-med.com).

You can safely drink tap water in the US – the water from Yucca Valley in California was voted the world's tastiest in 2000, but Californian wine is even nicer. (See also **Health** on page 202.)

EMERGENCIES

The action to be taken in an 'emergency' depends on the degree of urgency. In most cities, emergency medical services are among the best in the world. **Keep a record of the telephone numbers of your doctor, dentist, local hospitals and clinics, emergency ambulance service, poison control and other emergency services (fire, police) next to your telephone. In the US, 911 is the universal emergency access number for reaching the police, ambulance, and other emergency services.**

● In a life-threatening emergency, you should telephone 911 and request an ambulance. Most ambulances are staffed by paramedics and equipped with cardiac, oxygen and other emergency equipment. In some cities you may need to wait for a city (public) ambulance and you may be better off calling a private ambulance, which should come immediately (see 'Ambulance Service' in your yellow pages). Private ambulances are expensive and a trip to the local hospital costs $100 to $200 (which may or may not be paid by your health insurance, depending on the circumstances), although some accept Medicare and Medicaid (see **Chapter 13**). Many small towns provide a free ambulance service, funded by donations and local fund-raising, and operated by volunteer ambulance crews.

● If you're physically capable, you can go to the emergency room of the nearest hospital, many of which are open 24 hours a day (check the location of your nearest hospital and the quickest route from your home, in advance). You should check, in advance, which local hospital is best equipped to deal with emergencies such as heart attacks, car accident injuries, burns and children's injuries. If you have a minor injury or complaint, you can go to a 24-hour 'walk-in' clinic (see page 310).

● If you're sick and too ill to go to a doctor's office, you could call your doctor for advice, although over 90 per cent of doctors don't make house calls. In most larger cities, there are 'house-call' doctor services who send a doctor (or a nurse, paramedic, or physician assistant) to your home at any time of day or night (usually within a few hours) for a fee of from $100 to $150. House-call doctors perform routine diagnostic tests and call for an ambulance if necessary although their services are intended for use by the elderly or those who are housebound. You may be better off getting someone to drive you to a doctor or to a hospital emergency room.

● If you need urgent medical advice or drugs, you can check the yellow pages for the telephone number of a local doctor, hospital or pharmacy. Police stations keep a list of doctors' and pharmacists' private telephone numbers in case of emergencies.

● Each region has a Poison Control number, usually listed inside your telephone book cover or in the white or yellow pages. Alternatively, you can obtain your region's toll-free number by calling 1-800-555-1212. Obtain your local Poison Control number in advance and keep it by your telephone with other emergency numbers.

● If you have an emergency dental problem, telephone your own dentist. If he doesn't provide an emergency service outside normal surgery hours, telephone another dentist who does (often listed in yellow pages). Most dentists use an answering service outside normal surgery hours and return your call (or you're called by a 'stand-in' dentist). In an emergency, you may be able to obtain treatment at a university or dental hospital, where a dental surgeon is on duty. However, a dentist isn't obliged to treat anyone, even in an emergency.

Although you may have heard stories about emergency patients without insurance or the means to pay being turned away from a hospital, if your condition is critical (life-threatening) a private hospital **must** take care of you, whether you're able to pay or not. However, if you're unable to pay, once your condition has stabilised you're usually transferred from a private to a public hospital (see page 309).

DOCTORS

There are excellent doctors (physicians) in all areas of the US. The usual way to find a doctor is to ask your colleagues, friends, neighbours or acquaintances if they can recommend someone (but don't rely on their recommendations alone). The availability of medical services varies greatly according to the area and in some areas doctors (and other medical practitioners) are scarce. Most American doctors won't take jobs in remote areas (such as the Midwest) and inner cities (e.g. Brooklyn), where positions are increasingly filled by overseas doctors with J-1 visas (although the AMA is implacably opposed to hiring foreign doctors).

Your employer may advise you about medical matters and many large companies have a company doctor or an arrangement with a Health Maintenance Organisation/HMO (see page 306). These differ from conventional health care in that doctors, specialists and hospital treatment are all provided by an HMO for an inclusive monthly fee. Students may be required to register at a college student health centre. You can ask at your local hospital for a recommendation or contact your local city, county or state medical society, who will provide you with a list of local doctors. Family doctors are listed alphabetically by specialisation under 'Physicians and Surgeons' in the yellow pages. In small communities where there's insufficient business to support a profitable practice, there may be no local doctors.

If you need a doctor who speaks a particular language, your local embassy or consulate in the US should be able to help you (many keep lists of doctors). If you want to be attended by a doctor who practises at a particular hospital, e.g. a prestigious hospital or one close to your home, you can call the hospital administrator's office and ask for the names of doctors who practise (have privileges) there. Many hospitals have doctor referral services and you can often find background information on staff members on a hospital's website, searchable by speciality. A hospital won't recommend a doctor, but will give you several names. When a doctor has privileges at a prestigious (e.g. teaching) hospital, it's usually an excellent recommendation. Finally, you can check a doctor's credentials in the *American Medical Directory* or the *Directory of Medical Specialists*, usually available in local libraries. If you're covered by Medicare (see page 333), you must choose a Medicare-participating doctor who accepts Medicare assignment. If you're seeking a specialist, you may wish to consult one of the numerous guides to finding 'the best' or 'top' doctors in the US, but be advised that these guides aren't always objective, and some try to sell advertising services to the very doctors they're rating.

Most people have what's termed a 'primary-care physician' (similar to a family doctor), who's the doctor you depend on for routine medical treatment (e.g. prescription medicines), and who refers you to specialists or admits you to hospital, should it be necessary. Most doctors in large cities specialise in one or two areas, even in general practice, the most common being internal medicine, family practice, paediatrics, obstetrics and gynaecology, anaesthesiology, and emergency medicine. The best primary-care physician for your family depends on the ages of your family members and their medical history.

Most Americans go to an internist or a family practitioner (FP), who provides routine care for all family members. The term GP (general practitioner) is becoming rare in the US and only around 5 per cent of doctors use this title. GPs have generally been replaced by FPs, whose training is more intensive. An FP is usually the best choice of primary-care physician for a family with small children. However, most parents take their children to a paediatrician, who cares for them from infancy to adolescence. All schools need a health report and examination from a doctor before a child begins school (see **Health** on page 202). The most common family doctor is an internist, who's a specialist in internal medicine (heart, lungs, kidneys, etc.), and therefore suited for middle-aged or older patients. It's common for a woman during her child-bearing years to see an obstetrician-gynaecologist (OB/GYN or gyne).

It's wise to find a primary-care physician as soon as possible after your arrival, rather than wait until you're ill, when you may not have time to choose. You may wish to choose a doctor who's part of a group practice or a health maintenance organisation (HMO), where patients have access to a number of doctors (see page 303). However, some group practices don't permit patients to choose the doctor they see. Before registering with a doctor, you may wish to make some enquiries in advance, for example:

- What sex is the doctor?
- What is the doctor's age, training and medical background?
- At which local hospitals does he practise?
- Is it a group practice?
- What are the surgery hours?
- Does the doctor make house calls (most don't, but you can always ask)?
- Does the doctor practise preventive or complementary (alternative) medicine?
- Last, but not least, if you're a private patient and paying the bill yourself, what are the doctor's fees, e.g. for an office visit, a first medical and an annual medical (see below)? Can bills be settled directly by your insurance company?

It's often wise to meet a prospective doctor before deciding whether to become a patient. You should telephone and ask to meet and speak with the doctor. (Also to ask if he is accepting new patients, as some doctors limit their practices to a certain number.) Stress that you require only five minutes of the doctor's time (you may, however, still be charged the regular office fee). If a doctor refuses to meet you, you may want to cross him off your list.

Doctors' surgery hours vary, but are typically from 8.30am to 6pm or 7pm, Monday to Friday, with the surgery sometimes closing earlier one day a week, e.g. 5pm or 5.30pm on Fridays (evening surgery hours may also be held on a few evenings a week). Surgeries are also usually open on Saturday mornings, e.g. from 8.30am to 11.30am or noon, and some doctors have Sunday surgery hours for emergencies. Most doctors use an answering service outside surgery hours, who will give you the name of the doctor on call and his telephone number.

All doctors operate an appointment system. You cannot just turn up and expect to be seen. If you're an urgent case, your doctor usually sees you immediately, but you must still telephone in advance. If you miss an appointment without giving sufficient notice, your doctor may charge you a standard fee (although unlikely). Most doctors work with a full staff, including nurses and nurse practitioners, receptionists and even billing specialists (to keep track of all the insurance paperwork). Normally, when you go in to see your doctor, you talk first with a nurse, who may then take your temperature, blood pressure and do any other routine tests or measurements the doctor needs. Unfortunately, most doctors are scheduled in 15 minute increments so it's not at all uncommon for the doctor to be running late, often by as much as an hour or more. On the other hand, having to wait for your doctor is an indication that he is giving each patient the time they need rather than simply rushing through the day's schedule.

Your doctor may wish to be paid the day you see him in order to eliminate paperwork, although many send you a bill once you've established yourself as a regular patient. Doctors usually expect immediate payment in cash from foreign residents, but most accept payment by credit card. Fees are high, e.g. up to $150 for a consultation (although the average fee is around $65), $100 for a laboratory (lab) test, and $30 for antibiotics or vaccines given by injection. If you must see a specialist, he will charge up to $300 for a consultation and possibly another $175 for lab tests. The cost of malpractice suits means that doctors usually err on the side of over-treatment. Many prescribe medicines, tests and treatment that may be unnecessary and that probably wouldn't be prescribed in many (or any) other countries (although insurance companies are increasingly questioning diagnostic tests).

Your family doctor can give advice and provide information on any aspect of health or medical after-care, including preventive medicine, blood donations, home medical equipment and counselling. If you would like a second opinion on any health matter, your doctor should be happy to refer you to a colleague or a specialist (however, in many cases where a second opinion is sought, the second doctor **doesn't** confirm the first doctor's diagnosis). If your doctor treats a request for a second opinion as criticism of his competence, you should find another doctor. There are a number of occasions when a second opinion isn't only desirable, but essential (thousands of unnecessary operations are performed annually). Many insurance policies require patients to seek a second opinion before surgery and demand certification that hospitalisation is necessary.

If you plan to remain in the US for a number of years, you should bring your medical and dental records with you (including test results, X-rays, laboratory reports, hospital records, etc.) or ask your overseas doctor to send them to your doctor in the US. This is important if you have an unusual health history or suffer from a long-term condition, as it can save considerable time and expense on tests or background studies. If you change doctors in the US, ask your old doctor(s) to forward your medical records to your new doctor (your medical records are your property).

If you wish to complain about professional misconduct or unfair charges, call your state Department of Health's Professional Medical Conduct Division.

Health Maintenance Organisations

In addition to traditional fee-for-service or indemnity health plans, many employers (around 60 per cent) provide employees with medical care through health maintenance organisations (HMOs). HMOs place the emphasis upon preventive medicine and outpatient treatment, and their members are hospitalised less than half as frequently as people who make use of more traditional fee-for-service medical care. When you belong to an HMO, your medical bills are taken care of for a fixed monthly fee averaging around $200 per family (usually paid in full or in part by employers), and often supplemented by a small fee (called a co-payment) for each doctor visit. This is some 30 per cent less than conventional fee-for-service insurance plans, although you must use specified health care providers and appoint a primary care physician (PCP) to 'manage' your health care needs, i.e. refer you to relevant specialists. (Women may also appoint a woman's principal health care provider or WPHCP.) HMOs may be sponsored by the government, medical schools, hospitals, employers, labour unions, consumer groups, insurance companies or hospitals.

Fees generally cover medical services, hospitalisation and surgery, home health care, outpatient surgery and some nursing home services. Preventive care services such as regular (e.g. annual) examinations and immunisation are an important element of HMO programmes. A typical HMO is a group practice with its own clinical facilities and salaried doctors and staff. Practices usually include a number of different specialists, who provide for a wide range of family needs. Some HMOs are attached to hospitals, but most are independent with doctors being registered to practise at local hospitals.

HMOs have experienced huge growth in the last 20 years and now treat more than 30 million patients. The main drawback of an HMO is that you're restricted in your choice of doctors, although many think this is a small price to pay for the lower costs. Critics of HMOs (usually free-spending doctors and hospitals) claim that HMO doctors are forced to put economy before the patient's well-being and accuse HMOs of restricting the treatment available based on cost cutting concerns. However, studies have shown that HMO care can be as good if not better than that provided under fee-for-service schemes (most European countries employ a similar system where insurance companies and the medical profession work together to control costs, without compromising the quality of health care).

Preferred Provider Organisations

Even more popular than HMOs are preferred provider organisations (PPOs), which combine major medical insurance with the group practice concept. Members are encouraged to use participating doctors and hospitals, but can go outside the PPO network for an additional cost. An estimated 110 million Americans are enrolled in PPO programmes, which have multiplied dramatically in recent years. As with all medical insurance plans, carefully check the extent of clinical and hospital facilities or affiliates, and compare the overall costs and benefits of a PPO plan with those available through a conventional fee-for-service insurance plan. For further information about PPOs contact the American Association of Preferred Provider Organizations, PO Box 429, Jeffersonville, IL 47131-0429 (☎ 812-246-4376, 🖳 www.aappo.org).

MEDICINES

Americans take more pills and potions than people in most countries, and in the past few years pills have overtaken psychoanalysis (therapy) as the preferred treatment for that quintessentially American ailment, depression. (Almost 6.5 million people are being treated for depression at any time, three times as many as in 1987, the year Prozac was launched.)

Medicines (medication or drugs, which doesn't necessarily mean 'hard drugs') can be obtained from chemists (pharmacists or druggists), general stores (drugstores) and supermarkets, and are usually cheaper than in other western countries. Brand name prescription medication is, on the other hand, often much more expensive than in other countries, thanks to the fact that there's no pricing regulation on prescription medicines in the US. Shops are packed with medicines for every ailment under the sun (hypochondriacs will think they've died and gone to heaven), which may include medicines that are available in other countries on prescription only. There are medicines to make you feel happy, help you lose weight and increase your sexual potency (one day, happiness, youth and lifelong vitality will come in a single tablet). However, there are strict controls on the licensing and sale of most medicines (apart from illegal drugs such as cocaine and heroin, which you can buy on any street corner). Some medicines, sold freely in other countries, require a doctor's prescription in the US. Many chemists keep a comprehensive record of all customers and the medicines dispensed (required by law in some states), and you may be asked to complete a questionnaire if you're a new customer.

Some items common in other countries are difficult to find in the US, e.g. soluble aspirin. Americans take tablets containing acetaminophen rather than paracetamol for headaches; tablets containing codeine can be bought on prescription only. Brand names for the same medicines vary considerably from country to country and even in different areas of the US, so ask your doctor for the generic name of any medicines you take regularly. Any medicines you take with you to the US (you shouldn't take non-prescription medicines) should be accompanied by a doctor's letter explaining why you need them. You should keep imported medicines in their original packaging (US customs officials are extremely suspicious of anything other than aspirin).

If you're visiting the US for a short period, you should take sufficient medicines with you to cover your stay, as prescription medicines can be expensive and insurance policies don't usually cover existing medical conditions (you may also be unable to obtain your usual medicine). In some states, chemists fill prescriptions from state-registered doctors only. If you must refill a prescription from a doctor who's resident in another state (or abroad), you must get a local doctor to write a copy prescription (for a large fee). A hospital emergency room or walk-in clinic may refill a prescription from its own pharmacy or write a prescription that can be filled at a local chemist.

Brand name medicines can cost up to 30 times more than generics in the US. In 2003, President Bush signed into law the Medicare Prescription Drug Improvement and Modernization Act, which will pay for prescription drugs for Medicare members, starting 1st January 2006. Until that date, those over 65 can purchase a drug discount card entitling them to discounts of around 10 per cent to 20 per cent on the average prices of prescription drugs. The drugs covered varies by plan (many of the drug cards are being offered by pharmaceutical companies), and each Medicare participant can take part in only one discount card program. Further information about the scheme can be obtained from a Medicare hotline (☎ 1-800-MEDICARE).

An alternative method of obtaining cheap medicines, which can vary in price by up to 100 per cent within the US, is to import them from Canada, where medicine prices are limited by law, through an online chemist such as The Canadian Drugstore. Some insurance plans allow members to buy prescription medicines by post. Although this practice isn't illegal, it's the subject of considerable state and federal debate and may come under regulation at some future date.

Medicines prescribed by a doctor are available from chemists' and drugstores and are usually paid for by health insurance plans. At least one chemist is open in most towns during the evenings and on Sundays for the emergency dispensing of medicines. A list is displayed on the doors of chemists and published in local newspapers and guides. In most large cities, there are chemists open 24 hours, seven days a week, some of which provide a free delivery service in the local area, e.g. within five or ten streets (blocks). If you need medicines urgently when local chemists are closed, you should contact your doctor, a hospital or the local police station for help.

Most chemists provide free advice regarding minor ailments, suggest appropriate medicines, and sell non-prescription medicines, toiletries, cosmetics, health foods and cleaning supplies. Alternative therapies such as herbal and homeopathic medicines are popular and widely available. Health food shops sell health foods, diet foods and eternal-life/virility/youth pills and elixirs, all of which are extremely popular.

Always use, store and dispose of unwanted medicines safely, e.g. by returning them to a chemist or doctor, and never leave them where children can get their hands on them.

HOSPITALS & CLINICS

People are referred to hospitals and clinics in the US more often than in most other countries, although this may be for tests or treatment as an out-patient only. Many doctors refer patients to hospitals to take advantage of their specialist staff and superior facilities and equipment. You may also be admitted to hospital for observation as a precautionary measure. Preventive surgery is common in the US and if there's an indication that an operation **may** be necessary, the vast majority of doctors have little hesitation in operating (a doctor would rather send you to hospital to have your appendix removed than be sued by your relatives after you've died of peritonitis!).

If you're admitted to a hospital in the US, you will usually receive the best medical treatment available anywhere in the world. However, every test, doctor's visit, pill, meal and fluff of your pillows is added to your bill. The cost of a hospital room alone is likely to exceed the cost of the most expensive hotel room (a private room can cost over $1,000 a day) and even a stay of a few days is likely to result in a bill for thousands of dollars. This also applies if you're giving birth in hospital, which won't be covered by health insurance if you were pregnant before taking out a policy. If you have insufficient insurance, you may be discharged from hospital earlier than would otherwise be the case (but not if your condition is critical). You should ensure that you have adequate hospital insurance (see page 333) before an emergency arises, as without it hospitalisation can be a financial disaster.

The hospital care available to you depends on two factors: who your doctor is and where you live. In some rural areas, there may be only one local hospital with limited facilities. If you require treatment in a better equipped hospital and want to be treated by your regular doctor, he must be registered to practise there. In an emergency, you're admitted to the nearest hospital. Most towns have at least one clinic or hospital, although the choice varies considerably according to the city or town. Hospitals include university hospitals, city hospitals, veterans' administration hospitals, state and regional hospitals, community hospitals and assorted private hospitals. University hospitals are teaching hospitals affiliated to a medical school and are the best equipped and staffed, and able to perform all major surgery and diagnosis. Apart from a house doctor and nurses, there are no house staff at private hospitals (unlike university hospitals), where you're attended by your private doctor. City hospitals are public hospitals, operated and funded by the city or state, as are Veterans' Administration hospitals, which are exclusively for US military veterans (who are treated free of charge). In many cities, public neighbourhood medical clinics are affiliated to a major city hospital. Many private hospitals are funded by religious organisations.

A general community hospital is adequate for most medical problems and is likely to offer service in surgery, internal medicine, obstetrics and paediatrics. For a more serious illness or major surgery, you're usually better off at a university or teaching hospital, where specialised skills are available, or in a hospital or clinic that specialises in your complaint. Most hospitals provide different types of accommodation, e.g. private and semi-private rooms and wards.

In many areas, there are walk-in medical clinics or urgent care centres ('doc-in-a-box'), where you may be treated for such complaints as a sprained ankle, ear ache or even a broken arm. No appointment is necessary at a walk-in clinic, many of which are open 365 days a year. They're often located in large shops or shopping centres, so you can drop in for a quick X-ray while doing the shopping. Walk-in clinics usually have a minimum charge of $50 to $75, to which must be added the cost of treatment or tests. Most require immediate payment and accept personal cheques and major credit cards, although some will wait for payment from an insurance company. Most public hospitals also have walk-in clinics and medical centres.

If your condition is critical (i.e. life-threatening), you're usually taken to the nearest hospital, even if you have no medical insurance and are unable to pay. However, if you're admitted to a private hospital, you may be transferred to a public hospital once your condition has stabilised. If you're uninsured and need non-emergency hospital treatment, you can go to the out-patient department of a public hospital, where, although you may need to wait a long time, you're treated without advance payment. However, treatment isn't free and a public hospital must sue you for payment, even if you're penniless, in order to receive reimbursement from the local, state or federal government. If you're unable to pay a court judgement against you, the judgement remains in effect for a long time (20 years in some states).

An acute shortage of resources means that there are long waiting lists for non-emergency treatment in public hospitals, and hospital stays are kept to the absolute minimum. Public hospitals are unable to deliver adequate health care for the millions of people without insurance, which is exacerbated by increases in homelessness, AIDS infection, drug abuse and immigration. Some public hospitals, such as

Bellevue Hospital in New York City, have excellent facilities (particularly for emergencies), although few people choose to be treated in a public hospital if they can afford to use a private one.

The admission procedure for private hospitals varies, but is essentially the same everywhere. The first question you're likely to be asked on arrival is about your medical insurance or how you intend to pay for treatment. You must report to the admitting office, where you're asked to complete the following paperwork (if you're in pain or unable to handle the paperwork and answer the questions, take someone with you):

● An admission application form;

● A room and floor card;

● A telephone request;

● A consent for treatment form;

● A consent to release information to the state medical department;

● A financial agreement.

The financial agreement depends on whether you have medical insurance covering your hospitalisation. If you have insurance, take your insurance card or proof of coverage with you. Insurance usually covers a semi-private room only and if you want a private room you must usually pay a deposit of around $500 per week. If you don't have medical insurance, you must pay a large deposit, which could be as much as $3,000 to $4,000 for a week's stay or from $1,500 to $2,500 for a stay of three days. A deposit can usually be paid in cash, by cheque or by credit or charge card. You should check the admission procedure in advance and ask how the deposit (if applicable) should be paid.

Hospital bills must usually be paid in full before a patient leaves the hospital. If you have a company or private health insurance policy, your insurer usually pays the bill for you. If you're sent a bill for which your insurance company is liable, don't pay it, but refer all requests for payment to them. According to some audits, 95 per cent of hospital bills contain errors, including duplicate billings and services, inflated services (drugs and other items are often charged at extortionate rates, e.g. $10 for an aspirin), unrequested items and other 'phantom' charges, and clerical errors. When a bill is paid by an insurance company, many of these 'errors' go unnoticed, as the company usually has even less idea what treatment has been given than the patient (and doesn't care too much what the costs are anyway, as it can simply increase its premiums to cover the cost of claims). **If you're paying your own hospital bill, obtain an itemised statement, check it thoroughly and query anything you don't understand or disagree with.**

CHILDBIRTH & ABORTION

The traditional place to give birth in the US is in the maternity ward of a hospital, where a stay of just two days is normal (and costs around $4,000 **plus** an obstetrician's fees – see below!), although there has recently been an increase in home births using professional midwives. If you plan to have a child in the US, it's important to find a good obstetrician-gynaecologist (OB-GYN), who makes all the necessary hospital arrangements and deliver the baby (and charge you around $3,750!). If you wish to have your child at home, you must find a doctor and/or midwife (see below) who's willing to attend you. Many doctors are opposed to home births, particularly in cases where there could be complications, when specialists and hospital facilities may be required. You can hire a private midwife (a qualified nurse with special training) through an agency to attend you at home throughout and after your pregnancy. A 'compromise' between giving birth at home and in hospital is to use a maternity or birth centre staffed by experienced midwives, where mother and baby usually go home around 12 hours after the birth.

For hospital births, you can usually decide (with the help of your doctor or midwife) the hospital where you wish to have your baby. You aren't required to use the hospital suggested by your doctor, but you should book into a hospital as early as possible. Your doctor may refer you to an obstetrician or you can find your own. Find out as much as possible about local hospital methods and policies on childbirth, either directly or from friends or neighbours, before booking a bed. 'Natural' childbirth is common and many hospitals expect mothers to attend natural childbirth lessons requiring the participation of the father or other family member to act as 'coach' during delivery. Lessons are available at hospitals, clinics and in groups run by nurses.

The policy regarding a father's attendance at a birth may vary from hospital to hospital. A husband may not have the right to be present with his wife during labour or childbirth (which is usually at the consultant's discretion), although some doctors may expect fathers to attend. If the presence of your husband is important to you, you should check that it's permitted at the hospital where you plan to have your baby, plus any other rules that may be in force. Birth centres usually allow family members to be present during the birth.

In the US, midwives are increasingly responsible for educating and supporting women and their families during the childbearing period, usually working in conjunction with your OB-GYN rather than going solo. Certified Midwives (CM) and Certified Nurse Midwives (CNM) can be located through your doctor, the local birthing centre or by contacting the American College of Nurse-Midwives, 8403 Colesville Rd, Suite 1550, Silver Spring MD 20910 (☎ 240-485-1800, 🖳 www. midwife.org). Midwives can advise women before they become pregnant, in addition to providing moral, physical and emotional support throughout a pregnancy and after the birth. Your midwife may also advise on parent education and ante-natal (pre-natal) classes for mothers. Information about contraception, pregnancy and abortion is available from your family doctor.

Abortion is legal in the US (since 1973) and around 1.6 million abortions are performed each year (around one million unmarried teenagers become pregnant each year – almost 10 per cent of the female population between 15 and 19, the highest rate in the industrialised world). Abortion is a highly contentious subject, particularly given the tendency of some religious leaders to get involved in the issue. Anti-abortion groups are becoming ever more vociferous and violent in their opposition and some extremists have resorted to bombing clinics and murdering doctors. For information about abortion and counselling, contact the National

Abortion Federation, 1755 Massachusetts Ave NW, #600, Washington, DC 20036-2123 (☎ 1-800-772-9100 or 202-667-5881); for information about the alternatives to abortion, contact Right-to-Life (☎ 1-800-848-LOVE).

Health insurers in won't pay for any medical costs associated with childbirth or abortion if you were pregnant before you took out health insurance. If you have health insurance, don't forget to inform your insurance company about your new arrival. Some health insurance plans don't cover pregnancy and childbirth unless the mother is insured with her husband on the same policy. Many insurance plans don't cover abortion services unless the abortion is necessary to save the life of the mother or to save her from serious injury if she were to carry the child to term.

DENTISTS

American dentists use the most up-to-date techniques, including pain-free, laser technology, to provide possibly the best (and certainly the most expensive) dental treatment in the world. The best way to find a dentist is to ask your colleagues, friends or neighbours (particularly those with beautiful teeth) if they can recommend someone. Your local city, county or state dental society will give you the names of local dentists, although it won't recommend one. Dentists are listed alphabetically in the yellow pages with their areas of specialisation, e.g. general (or family) dentists, paediatric dentists, and those specialising in oral and maxillofacial surgery, endodontics, orthodontics and periodontics. There's no must register with a dentist, and in many areas there are walk-in dental clinics in health centres, department stores and shopping centres.

Check what arrangements a dentist provides for 24-hour emergency service, and for evening or Saturday surgery hours (many dentists have evening surgery hours on one day a week or on Saturday mornings). Most dentists work with one or more dental hygienists, who may handle much of the routine work of dental examinations and cleaning. If you miss a dental appointment without giving 24 hours' notice, your dentist may charge you a standard fee. Most dentists send you a postcard to remind you of a check-up every six months and call the day before to remind you about an appointment (so you really must work hard to forget!).

If you plan to live in the US for a number of years, you should take a copy of your dental records with you. This is important if you have an unusual dental history, when it may save you time and money. Have your teeth checked and (if necessary) fixed before arriving in the US, as dental treatment is expensive, particularly cosmetic treatment which can run to many thousands of dollars (it pays to keep your mouth shut during dental check-ups). A standard health insurance policy may cover emergency dental treatment only, although most insurance companies provide an optional dental plan (see page 348). Dental treatment is often included in the services provided by an HMO group insurance plan (see page 306). Dentists may expect payment on the spot (credit cards are usually accepted), although many provide payment plans when major (expensive) treatment is necessary.

Orthodontia (teeth straightening) is fairly common in the US, where it appears that half the teenage population wear braces on their teeth and adult orthodontia is becoming more and more common. It is believed that straight teeth can alleviate a variety of health complaints, especially stress related issues such as grinding teeth or clenching your jaw while you sleep. Americans who can afford it have their teeth capped at enormous expense (not that they need much persuading, as a dazzling smile is a prerequisite for success in the US). And many dentists offer tooth whitening treatments designed to brighten your smile and make you look 'years younger'. You should obtain a written detailed quotation before starting a course of treatment (a 'rough estimate' will be only a fraction of your final bill) and an itemised bill when work is complete. If you have regular check-ups and usually have little or no treatment, you should be suspicious if a new dentist suggests you need a lot of treatment. If this happens, obtain a second opinion before going ahead, but bear in mind that two dentists rarely agree on the treatment required. If you have a complaint that you're unable to resolve with your dentist, contact your local dental society or your state board of dentistry.

OPTICIANS

There are three kinds of professionals providing eye care in the US. The most highly qualified is an ophthalmologist, who's a specialist doctor trained in diagnosing and treating disorders of the eye. In addition to performing eye surgery and prescribing drugs, he may also perform sight tests and prescribe glasses and contact lenses. You may be referred to an ophthalmologist by an optometrist or your family doctor. An optometrist is licensed to examine eyes, prescribe corrective lenses, and dispense glasses and contact lenses. They're also trained to detect eye diseases and in many states may prescribe medicines and treatment. A US optician isn't the same as an optometrist and may not examine eyes or prescribe lenses. Opticians are licensed in many states to fill prescriptions written by optometrists and ophthalmologists, and to fit and adjust spectacles (glasses).

As with dentists, there's no must register with an ophthalmologist or optometrist. You simply make an appointment with anyone of your choice, although you should ask your colleagues, friends or neighbours if they can recommend someone. Opticians and optometrists are listed in the yellow pages, where they may advertise their services. Ophthalmologists are normally listed in the yellow pages under Physicians as specialists.

The optometrist business is highly competitive and unless someone comes highly recommended, you should shop around for the best deal. Prices for spectacles and contact lenses vary considerably, so it's wise to compare costs (although make sure you're comparing similar services and products). On average, an eye examination costs $50 to $65 and a good pair of spectacles around $250 to $300. Contact lenses can be had for $100. There are many opticians offering discounts and deals (e.g. 'buy one get one free'), many of which advertise via the internet, but these aren't necessarily good value. You should ask about extra charges for eye examinations, fittings, adjustments, a lens-care kit, follow-up visits and the cost of replacement lenses (if they're expensive, it may be worthwhile taking out insurance). Many opticians and retailers offer insurance against the accidental damage of spectacles for a nominal fee.

Around one in ten Americans wears contact lenses, two-thirds of whom are women. Disposable and extended-wear soft contact lenses are also widely available, although medical experts warn that extended-wear lenses should be treated with extreme caution, as they greatly increase the risk of potentially blinding eye infections. **Obtain advice from your doctor or ophthalmologist before buying them.**

You aren't required to buy your spectacles or contact lenses from the optometrist who tests your sight, and he must give you your prescription at no extra charge. However, this doesn't apply to a lens-fitting prescription for contact lenses. There are many optical retail chain stores where you can have a pair of spectacles made within an hour and in many states, you can find an optometrist office operating as part of the optical chain.

COUNSELLING & PSYCHIATRY

Counselling and assistance for health and social problems is available in the US from a variety of local community groups, volunteer organisations, national associations and self-help groups. If you must find help locally, you can contact your local community public health office for advice. Most states operate toll-free helplines for a wide range of problems, and counselling is also available by telephone. Many colleges and educational establishments provide a counselling service for students. Look in the yellow pages under 'Social Service Organizations' for local organisations.

Problems for which help is available are numerous and include: general health complaints; substance abuse; alcoholism (e.g. Alcoholics Anonymous) and alcohol-related problems; gambling; dieting (e.g. Overeaters Anonymous); smoking; teenage pregnancy; attempted suicide and psychiatric problems; rehabilitation; homosexuality-related problems; youth problems; parent-child problems; child abuse; family violence (e.g. battered wives); runaways; marriage and relationship problems; and rape. Many communities provide a range of free health services for the homeless. In times of need, there's nearly always someone to turn to and all services are strictly confidential. As with everything else in the US, it's always possible to consult with private counselling services for a (sometimes hefty) fee.

If you, or a member of your family, are the victims of a violent crime, the police will put you in touch with a local victims' support scheme. In major towns, counselling may be available in your own language if you don't speak English. If you need help desperately, someone who speaks your language can usually be found. One association providing community-based, family counselling and support services across the US is the Alliance for Children and Families (formerly Family Service America), 11700 West Lake Park Drive, Park Place, Milwaukee, WI 53224 (☎ 414-359-1040, 💻 www.alliance1.org). For counselling and help regarding drug abuse, see page 317. For help for those suffering from AIDS, see **Sexually Transmitted Diseases** on page 320.

Many Americans, particularly the rich and famous, regularly consult a psychiatrist or psychoanalyst (usually referred to as an analyst or 'shrink') and some even take their pets. Americans seek through psychoanalysis (therapy) to identify and overcome their faults rather than adjust to them. To most Americans, their analyst is someone who lends a sympathetic ear rather than 'fixes' their lives. Along with higher education and religion, psychotherapy is one of the few fields in which anything goes, and therapies range from the most conservative to the most radical and extreme approaches. However, because of rising costs, insurance companies and HMOs now limit the therapy for which they pay and since the late '80s the number of people receiving psychoanalysis has dropped from over 70 per cent to a 'mere' 60 per cent. There's an increasing tendency for psychiatrists to prescribe medications for conditions such as depression, behavioural disorders and even shyness (called 'social interaction disorder'), thanks to the frequent advertising of prescription drugs on television and in magazines.

LONG-TERM CARE

Long-term care is a general term usually used to describe a wide range of medical, nursing, social and community services for the disabled, those suffering debilitating illnesses, and those unable to look after themselves. The subject of long-term care has been thrust into the spotlight in recent years, as more and more people live into their eighties and nineties (the number of Americans aged over 80 increased by more than 30 per cent to over 9 million between 1990 and 2000), and families confront the problem of caring for mentally and physically ill relatives. By the age of 75, one in every three people needs long-term care and by 85 the figure is one in two. The number of Americans needing long-term care is expected to reach 14 million by the year 2020.

Some 80 per cent of long-term health care is provided in family homes by family members. However, more and more families are turning to long-term care services, including: home medical and nursing services; community services such as adult day care and home-delivered meals ('meals on wheels', costing around $5 to $10 each); patient and family counselling; nursing homes and assisted living arrangements; and many other services geared to helping those with disabilities. Many communities offer a variety of services in 'senior centres', including meals, recreational and social activities, health screening, and comprehensive information about programmes for senior citizens. If you must pay for professional home care from a home care agency, costs can be $100 to $150 per day or $20 to $35 an hour for a registered nurse or therapist (or $100 per visit).

There's an acute shortage of nursing homes (and nurses), although the biggest problem for many families is paying for, rather than finding, a nursing home. Americans spend well over $50 billion a year on nursing-home care. Fees are prohibitively expensive, averaging $40,000 - $50,000 per year. Medicare (see page 333) usually pays for a stay of up to 100 days in a nursing home, but under certain conditions only. Medicaid (see page 334), which is a federal programme for people on low incomes or those who have used most of their assets to pay medical bills, pays half of all nursing home care. Standard health insurance policies don't cover nursing homes, for which a specific long-term care insurance policy is required (see page 347).

The US Department of Health and Human Services runs an Eldercare locator service available by phone (☎ 800-677-1116) Monday to Friday 9.00am to 8.00pm (ET) or a 24 hour service on the internet (🖳 www.eldercare.gov). All states have a department handling long-term care services, such as a Division or Office of Aging. For the address of your local unit contact the National Association of State Units of

Aging, 1201 15th Street, NW, Suite 350, Washington, DC 20005 (☎ 202-898-2578, 🖳 www.nasua.org) or the National Association of Area Agencies on Aging, 1730 Rhode Island Ave., NW, Suite 1200, Washington, DC 20036 (☎ 202-872-0888, 🖳 www.n4a.org). (See also **Long-term Care Insurance** on page 347.)

DRUG & ALCOHOL ABUSE

The topic of 'drug abuse' covers three separate, but related, problems: the abuse of illegal (usually narcotic) drugs such as heroin, cocaine or the so-called 'club drugs' (e.g. ecstasy), the abuse of prescription medications (also called drugs in the US) and the abuse of legal drugs and other substances (including alcohol, tobacco and inhalants). The US is the world's largest market for legal and illegal drugs, despite decades of effort on the part of the government to win their 'war' on drugs.

Illegal drugs are still being imported into the US, despite drug education programmes for the young (e.g. 'Just Say No To Drugs' and 'Partnership For a Drug-Free America'), drug rehabilitation programmes and federal attempts to intercept drugs. Americans spend between $40 and $50 billion (over $1.5 billion by high school and college students) annually on illegal drugs (cocaine, heroin, marijuana and others). In many suburbs, areas around schools are designated 'Drug-Free School Zones' to warn off drug pushers. Some 60 per cent of high school children try drugs and seven out of ten teenagers who commit suicide are abusing drugs or alcohol. Around 13 million Americans (10 million of whom use marijuana) are estimated to be regular drug users, according to the National Institute on Drug Abuse (🖳 www. nida.nih.gov). Drug abuse is so widespread that an increasing number of employers, including the federal government, now screen employees for drug use. Another 9 million Americans are estimated to be using legal prescription drugs for non-medical purposes. Tranquillisers, pain killers and other legitimate medications can cause addiction problems or can be misused by others looking to get high. Misuse of prescription drugs is a becoming an increasing concern for substance abuse professionals, as it can be harder to detect.

The possession and use of hard drugs is a serious offence in all states, particularly for dealers, who face five or more years in prison and fines of up to $4 million for a first offence. Almost 60 per cent of federal prison inmates are drug offenders! The law regarding so-called 'soft' drugs, such as marijuana, varies from state to state. Smoking marijuana is legal in Alaska and has been 'decriminalised' in around ten other states, meaning that if you have less than one ounce, you receive a fine only. If you have more than an ounce, you may face a criminal charge for dealing and possibly a prison sentence. In most other states, possession of marijuana is a misdemeanour. The exceptions are Arizona and Nevada (the most liberal state with regard to gambling, liquor and prostitution), where possession is punishable by a lengthy prison sentence. Don't forget, too, that you can be denied an immigrant visa to enter the US if it's found that you're a drug abuser, or drug trafficker, or if your police record turns up any drug-related arrest in any country in which you've lived, even if the arrest is considered a misdemeanour in the country where it occurred. If this information is discovered after your move to the US, you can be deported for having concealed the information on entry to the country.

There are drug help organisations in most cities (e.g. in New York City there's Cocaine Anonymous, Drug Abuse Information Line, Drugs Anonymous and Narcotics Anonymous, to name but a few). Many have toll-free lines, which can be found by calling 1-800-555-1212. Look in the yellow pages under 'Drug Abuse & Addiction' or 'Social Service Organizations' or call information for the telephone numbers of local help organisations. For general information about drug abuse contact the American Council on Drug Education, 164 W. 74th St., New York, NY 10023 (☎ 1-800-488-DRUG, 🖳 www.acde.org). Parents should obtain a copy of the free government leaflets *Growing Up Drug Free* and *A Parent's Guide to Prevention* from the US Department of Education (☎ 1-800-624-0100).

The number one drug problem (excluding tobacco – see below) is alcohol, estimated to be directly responsible for 100,000 deaths a year. Apart from the tragic direct and indirect loss of life, alcohol abuse costs American industry billions of dollars each year in loss of production due to absenteeism. It's estimated that some 25 million people have alcohol-related problems, many of whom are 'blissfully' unaware of them. Drunken driving is widespread and an increasing problem (see page 285). Alcoholics Anonymous have groups in every city in the US, where recovering alcoholics meet to encourage each other to stay sober. If you can afford to pay for private treatment, a number of private clinics and hospitals specialise in providing treatment for alcohol (and other substance) dependency. For further information about alcohol abuse, contact the National Institution on Alcohol Abuse and Alcoholism (🖳 www.niaa.nih.gov).

SMOKING

Smokers are public health enemy number one in the US, where they're a persecuted minority threatened with extinction. Around 45 million smokers have quit in the last decade and of the 25 per cent of Americans who still smoke (among the lowest percentage of any country) around 90 per cent want to quit. The number of teenage smokers has been in continual decline since 1996. It has long been known that smoking causes lung and other types of cancer, heart disease, bronchial complaints and a variety of other life-threatening illnesses (costing the government an estimated $50 billion per year). Health warnings on cigarette packets warn of dire consequences for those who smoke, particularly pregnant women (who are warned that 'smoking during pregnancy can result in foetal injury, premature birth and low birth weight').

In recent years, the effects of passive or 'sidestream' smoking, i.e. inhaling the smoke from smokers' cigarettes, cigars and pipes, has become a heated issue. Many local governments and most states have some sort of non-smoking laws. Most states have passed laws banning smoking in restaurants, work areas and other public places. Smoking is banned on most public transport such as taxis, buses, subways, trains and flights. In most cities, smoking is also prohibited in public toilets, shops, banks, hotel foyers and lifts, sporting venues, shopping centres and public schools. Many hotels have no-smoking rooms, although the number is surprisingly low considering non-smokers outnumber smokers three to one. Smoking is usually banned in cinemas and theatres. New York City has banned cigarette vending machines in all public places except bars, and in California, Draconian laws introduced in 1998 made it illegal to smoke in all bars, restaurants and private clubs (even in cigar bars and private smokers' clubs!). At least three states, California, Delaware and New York, have banned smoking indoors in nearly all buildings open to the public, and some cities and towns have forbidden smoking outdoors in public parks or on beaches. Parents who smoke have even been denied custody of children in divorce cases!

Before you light up in a public place, check whether smoking is permitted. A 'Thank You For Not Smoking' sign is a polite way of saying "try smoking here and you're in trouble, buster!" Even in places where it's legal to smoke, people may even ask (or tell) you to put out your cigarette, or fall about in a paroxysm of coughing if you light up a cigar or pipe. In the US, anti-smoking hysteria knows no bounds, and many Americans won't allow guests to smoke in their homes. If you're an incurable addict and are invited to dinner, check whether you are allowed to smoke (or that there's a nice 'smoking' bar nearby). Many people believe that smoking will eventually become (like sex) an activity that can be conducted only in private among consenting adults.

Most businesses and government offices restrict or ban smoking in the workplace and many run programmes to encourage employees to quit. In fact smoking is fast becoming a career hazard, as some employers refuse to employ smokers on the grounds that their habit may lead to costlier health insurance and working days lost to sickness (smoking is directly responsible for millions of sick days each year), not to mention lawsuits for illnesses caused to other employees. Some companies impose a health insurance surcharge on smokers or offer discounts to non-smoking employees. US life assurance companies often offer discounts to non-smokers. However, most Americans are opposed to setting anti-smoking conditions of employment, as is the American Civil Liberties Union (ACLU). Many states prohibit employers from firing or refusing to hire people who smoke outside work (although thousands of companies don't employ smokers). It's not uncommon to see job advertisements posted noting 'smoke free environment' or that this is a 'no smoking office.'

There's a ban on advertising tobacco products on radio and television and in many publications (many people believe cigarette advertisements directly target children). American public schools run vigorous campaigns to discourage young people from smoking (it's a federal offence to sell cigarettes to anyone under 18).

Tobacco companies are under attack from all sides, particularly since 1992, when the US Supreme Court ruled that the Surgeon General's warning on cigarette packets **doesn't** protect tobacco companies from liability for illness and death caused by smoking. Companies have been accused of adding extra nicotine to cigarettes (to increase addiction), targeting children and minorities, and pushing their products on the developing world. In recent years, courts have awarded huge damages to smokers with lung-cancer, and states have been suing tobacco companies for smoking-related public health care expenses (tobacco companies have made a number of multi-billion dollar settlements).

For information about smoking regulations and the rights of non-smokers contact Action on Smoking and Health (ASH), 2013 H Street, NW, Washington, DC 20006 (☎ 202-659-4310, 🖳 www.ash.org).

SEXUALLY-TRANSMITTED DISEASES

The US has more than its fair share of sexually-transmitted diseases (STDs), including genital warts, herpes, chlamydia, gonorrhoea, syphilis and the fatal Acquired Immune Deficiency Syndrome (AIDS), which was first identified in the US in 1981. The number of AIDS cases officially recorded is over 886,000, of which more than 501,000 have died. It has been estimated that hundreds of thousands more Americans may be infected with HIV (human immunodeficiency virus), which leads to AIDS, although the epidemic forecast in the '80s hasn't materialised. Mothers infected by HIV can pass it on to their babies. Conservative estimates are that a quarter to a half of all those infected with HIV will eventually develop AIDS, although some experts believe the percentage will be much higher.

AIDS takes an average of ten years to develop and is always fatal, although recent developments in treatment have prolonged patients' life spans. (The drugs used in these treatments are hideously expensive and not always covered by health insurance.) AIDS is contracted by the exchange of bodily fluids, primarily through sexual contact and needle sharing. The spread of AIDS is accelerated by the sharing of syringes by drug addicts, among whom AIDS is rampant (many of America's heroin addicts are infected with HIV). In an effort to reduce syringe sharing among HIV positive drug addicts, syringe exchange centres have been set up throughout the country. Around half the men and two-thirds of the women who contract HIV do so as a result of heterosexual contact with partners who are intravenous drug-abusers.

The high level of publicity accorded AIDS and a number of high profile celebrities who have come down with the disease has led to greater awareness and some changes in behaviour that have helped to limit the spread of the disease. Virginity has been revalued, celibacy has become more common (even among couples in their twenties) and monogamy is sounding better every day. Health care workers and even police and fire fighters routinely use precautions, such as latex gloves or face masks when dealing with high risk people or situations.

The most common protection against AIDS, as well as other sexually transmitted diseases, is for men to wear a condom, although they aren't a guarantee (against AIDS or pregnancy) and the only real protection is celibacy. Condoms are on sale at chemists', drugstores, some supermarkets, men's hairdressers, and vending machines in bars and other public places. The AIDS epidemic spawned a flood of condom shops across the US, with snappy names such as Condomania, Condom Nation and Condomplation. Between 150 and 200 condom styles are offered, including flavoured and glow-in-the-dark condoms, and condoms sealed inside nutshells and fortune cookies.

All cases of AIDS and HIV-positive blood tests in the US, must be reported to local health authorities (patients' names remain anonymous). If you would like to talk to someone in confidence about AIDS or other sexually transmitted diseases, there are organisations and self-help groups in all cities providing information, advice and help, including local and state health departments. Check the local information section in the front of your yellow pages for hotlines and counselling centres. There's also a national STD telephone hotline (☎ 1-800-227-8922), a national AIDS hotline (☎ 1-800-342-2437) and information about STDs is available from the Centers for Disease Control and Prevention (🖳 www.cdc.gov).

BIRTHS & DEATHS

Births and deaths in the US must be reported to the local town hall in the town in which the birth or death took place. If the birth or death took place in a hospital, birthing centre, nursing home or other type of medical facility, the event is usually automatically reported to the local town hall for registration.

Either parent can register a birth by going to the town hall registrar within two to six weeks of the birth and giving the child's details . If the parents aren't married, they may both be required to report to the registrar if they want both their details to be included on the birth certificate. In some states, if an unmarried mother registers a birth, only her details are shown. (In some states, the birth certificates of children born out of wedlock used to be stamped with the word 'bastard' across the face of the form. Fortunately this practice died out around 30 or 40 years ago, but the certificates themselves are now conversation starters.) You should usually apply for a social security number (see page 328) for your child when you provide information for a birth certificate and many hospitals provide you with the forms to do so. Births and deaths of foreigners should be reported to an embassy or consulate to obtain a national birth certificate and a passport, or to register a death in the deceased's country of birth. (See also **Childbirth** on page 311.)

Like being born, dying is expensive in the US, where there's no such thing as a simple send-off. Undertakers (morticians) are exorbitantly expensive (unlike doctors and other health practitioners, they get only one bite of the cherry and must make the most of it). The average 'traditional' funeral costs around $6,000, plus the cost of the cemetery plot. US graveyards are among the most expensive property in the world and a burial plot usually costs around $1,500 (equivalent to around $1.5 million per acre!). In 1963, Jessica Mitford published her book, *The American Way of Death*, a scathing (but at the same time funny) critique of the funeral industry. She managed to update the book just before her death in 1996, and the revised edition is definitely worth a read if you expect to have to deal with death and a funeral while living in the US. Partly in response to the original edition of the book, the Federal Trade Commission passed a variety of laws requiring funeral directors to disclose the various costs and requirements for funerals, but enforcement of the laws has not been consistent. Grieving family members are often persuaded to opt for expensive embalming, elaborate caskets and funerals costing thousands of dollars. Although it's not normally the time for hard bargaining, you must be shown the cheapest available options if you ask for them and a funeral home must tell you what services are required, either by law or by the cemetery. It's customary for family and friends to attend a 'viewing' or 'visitation' of the deceased the day before the funeral and to inspect the body in the open casket (hence the 'need' for embalming), which often remains open during the funeral service. Cremation is a simpler and somewhat cheaper alternative, costing around $2,000. The ashes (called 'cremains' in the trade) can then be scattered, buried in a cemetery plot or retained by the family. A death notice is normally run in the local newspaper (for a fee, which can be $20 to $150), giving information about the funeral or memorial services, although this isn't always required.

In the event of the death of a US resident, all interested parties must be notified (see **Chapter 20**). You need around a dozen copies of the death certificate, e.g. for the will, pension claims, insurance companies and financial institutions. The funeral director can normally arrange for you to receive an initial supply of copies of the death certificate. If you must obtain a copy of a birth, marriage or death certificate, the cheapest way is to apply to the registrar for the town or county where the event was registered. There's a fee of anywhere from $5 to $15 per copy. You can also obtain copies of vital documents online through state and county websites or from online vital record services, such as VitalChek (🖥 www.vitalchek.com). (See also **Wills** on page 396.)

13.

INSURANCE

Americans spend around $2,500 per capita each year on insurance, most of which is spent on health, household, liability, disability and life insurance. This equates to around 12 per cent of GDP, one of the highest percentages in the world. However, the range and scope of mandatory insurance (including social security) provided by the state and employers in the US is less comprehensive than that provided in most other western countries. Federal social security provides for only the most basic needs and only those living below the poverty line rely exclusively on state benefits.

There are a few occasions where insurance is compulsory, which include liability insurance for vehicles (required by law in most states), and household (homeowner's), fire and in some cases mortgage life insurance (usually required by lenders) for homeowners. If you lease a car or buy one on credit, your lender will insist that you have collision and comprehensive car insurance (see page 267). Voluntary insurance includes private pensions, disability, health, legal, dental, travel, car breakdown, and life insurance. Free state health treatment isn't provided for residents or visitors in the US (except if you're poor, over 65 or disabled), so it's imperative to have health insurance (see **Health Insurance** on page 341).

It's unnecessary to spend half your income insuring yourself against every eventuality, from the common cold to being sued for your last nickel, but it's important to be covered against any event that could precipitate a major financial disaster (such as a long illness or unemployment). **The cost of being uninsured or under-insured in the US can be astronomical.** As with anything connected with finance, it's important to shop around when buying insurance. Simply picking up a few brochures from insurance agents or making a few telephone calls could save you a lot of money. Regrettably, you cannot insure yourself against being uninsured or sue your insurance agent for giving you bad advice. If you wish to make an insurance claim against a third party or someone is claiming against you, you should seek legal advice, as US law is likely to be different from that in your previous country of residence and you should never assume that it's the same.

Many excellent books about insurance are available, including *Insurance for Dummies* by Jack Hungelmann (For Dummies). Each state has its own laws and regulations governing insurance. If you require information about local state insurance laws or wish to make a complaint (almost 50 per cent of complaints to Better Business Bureaux concern insurance), contact your state insurance regulator listed in the blue pages (state government listings) of your local telephone directory. Many state insurance departments publish buyers' guides to insurance which are available from insurance companies and agents as well as from the state department. For general insurance information, contact the Insurance Information Institute, 110 William Street, New York, NY 10038 (☎ 212-346-5500, 💻 www.iii.org).

INSURANCE COMPANIES & BROKERS

Insurance is big business in the US, where the industry writes over 40 per cent of the world's insurance business. There are numerous insurance companies to choose from, many providing a wide range of insurance services, while others specialise in certain fields. The major insurance companies have offices or agents throughout the

US, including most large towns. Most agents provide a free analysis of your family's insurance needs. The largest insurance companies include State Farm, AIG, Metropolitan Life, Zurich/Farmers, Allstate, St. Paul Travelers and Liberty Mutual.

The majority of Americans buy their insurance through insurance brokers (agents). Before buying any insurance, shop around among brokers and companies, and ask your colleagues, friends, neighbours and acquaintances for their recommendations. Although most brokers are honest, many are incompetent and try to sell you more insurance than you need or the wrong policy, so seek out a reputable broker who has been recommended. You're usually better off dealing with an independent broker who deals with a number of insurance companies, rather than a broker who sells the policies of one insurance company only (a so-called 'captive'). Brokers or companies who charge a flat fee for their advice, rather than earn commissions for selling policies, are usually the most objective.

According to independent experts, most brokers offer terrible advice, particularly regarding life insurance, and are interested only in selling policies (**any** policy). Obtain recommendations from at least three brokers, but bear in mind that this will almost certainly result in wildly different recommendations. When you've found a reliable broker, it's often wise to buy all your insurance through him, but still obtain quotations for new insurance from other brokers or companies. Never allow yourself to be rushed into buying insurance (experts recommend that you 'shop 'til you drop' when buying insurance).

The least expensive policy isn't necessarily the best value, particularly regarding the prompt payment of claims. Ask a broker how long particular companies take to settle claims; although all insurance companies are pleased to take your money, many aren't nearly so happy to pay up. Some companies use any available loophole to avoid settling claims, particularly if they can prove negligence, and you may need to threaten them with litigation before they pay. If you must make a claim, don't send original bills or documents to your insurance company **unless absolutely necessary** (you can send a certified copy). Keep a copy of all bills, documents and correspondence, and send letters by registered post. **If you receive a cheque in settlement of a claim, don't bank it if you think it's insufficient to cover your claim, as you may be deemed to have accepted it as full and final settlement.**

Be extremely wary when choosing your insurance company, as there's no Federal Deposit Insurance Corporation for insurance companies as there is for banks, and thrifts (see page 367). If your insurance company fails, you're on your own, so pick one with an AAA credit rating.

INSURANCE CONTRACTS

Read all insurance contracts before signing them. If you don't understand everything, ask a friend or colleague to 'translate' it or take legal advice. If a policy has pages of legal jargon and 'gobbledegook' in small print, you have a right to be suspicious, particularly as it's common practice nowadays to be as brief as possible and write clearly and concisely in simple language. Some states have laws requiring all agreements and contracts between commercial institutions and consumers to be written in plain language. Be wary of policy exclusions, which may invalidate the very protection you think you're paying for. Be careful how you answer questions on an insurance proposal form; even if you unwittingly provide false information, an insurance company can refuse to pay out when you make a claim. A medical report may be required for certain insurance policies, e.g. health insurance, a pension plan or life assurance.

Most insurance policies run for a calendar year from the date you take out the policy. All premiums should be paid punctually, as late payment may affect your benefits or a claim (although if this is so, it should be noted in your policy). Before signing any insurance contract, you should shop around and take a few days to think it over. Never sign on the spot, as you may regret it later. With some insurance contracts you have a 'cooling off' period, e.g. 10 or 30 days, during which you can cancel a policy without penalty.

SOCIAL SECURITY

Social security, which costs around a third of the annual federal budget, is the name given to state benefits applicable to over 95 per cent (some 156 million) of US workers. Under the Social Security Act, everyone who works regularly in the US is covered by social security, including self-employed people, and domestic and farm workers. Social security contributions are called taxes and are usually referred to by the initials of their acts. There are three main pieces of legislation: the Federal Insurance Contributions Act (FICA tax) for employees, the Self-Employed Contributions Act (SECA tax) and the Federal Unemployment Tax Act (FUTA). Under FICA, employers and employees contribute 7.65 per cent (6.2 per cent for retirement, survivor and disability insurance, and 1.45 per cent for Medicare hospital insurance) of an employee's gross salary up to a maximum salary of $87,900 (the benefit or earnings base). Under SECA, self-employed people pay double an employee's contribution (15.3 per cent) – 12.4 per cent on income up to $87,900 and a Medicare levy at 2.9 per cent on all income. Contributions and salary limits increase each year in line with inflation (known as the Cost of Living Adjustment, or COLA, which was 2.1 per cent for 2004). Employees' social security contributions are deducted at source from their gross salary and are usually shown on salary slips as FICA tax. Self-employed people pay their contributions annually with their income tax.

Employees of state and local governments are covered under voluntary agreements between the states and the Commissioner of Social Security. Each state decides whether it will negotiate an agreement and, subject to conditions that apply to retirement system members, what groups of eligible employees are covered. At present over 75 per cent of state and local employees are covered.

Officially, Social Security (capitalised to refer to the federal programme) refers to retirement, disability and survivors' benefits, although people often use the term 'social security' (no capitals) to refer to Medicare, Medicaid, Supplemental Security Income (SSI) and welfare payments such as Aid to Families with Dependent Children (AFDC), food stamps and public housing. Social security benefits, particularly Supplemental Security Income (see page 334), vary considerably from state to state, and states that pay high welfare payments attract huge numbers of welfare recipients from lower-paying states.

It's now possible to apply for a social security card at the same time you apply for an immigrant visa, just by checking 'yes' to questions 33a and 33b on the Form DS-230. On admission to the US, the Social Security office sends your card directly to your US postal address. Social security cards issued to non-immigrants without the right to work in the US are marked 'not valid for employment'. The social security number is a nine-digit identification number issued to every US citizen and resident alien upon application. Social security numbers are used by banks, insurance companies, and many other businesses and government agencies as a means of identification. If you don't have a social security card when you arrive in the US, you should apply for one at your local Social Security Administration (SSA) office. There are around 1,300 of them, and you can find your nearest office by calling the SSA's toll-free information number (☎ 1-800-772-1213) or using the locator service on the website (🖳 www.ssa.gov and then click on 'Contact Us'). There's also a multilingual gateway with information in 15 different languages (🖳 www.ssa.gov/multilanguage). You can obtain an application form (SS-5) by calling the information number or downloading it from the SSA's website (🖳 www.ssa.gov), but you must take the completed form, plus your birth certificate, passport, I-95 customs form and original visa (if applicable) to the office, in person. It can be two or three weeks before you receive your social security card, but your number is normally available within a day or two (by telephoning ☎ 1-800-772-1213) and you can obtain a temporary letter confirming it, if you cannot wait to receive the card. A social security number may be required when applying for a driving licence or a job or opening a bank account and is the most widely recognised and most frequently used record-keeping number in the US. The social security card isn't, however, an identification card, and you shouldn't carry it with you in your wallet or purse. Due to the increase in identity thefts (see page 365), you should be careful about giving out your social security number or using it (or any part of it) as a password or PIN. If you lose your card, apply for a duplicate one (i.e. **not** a new card number) from your nearest social security office. When a woman marries and changes her family name, she should apply for a new card showing her married name (it will have the same social security number).

It's recommended that you periodically (e.g. every few years) check that your social security earnings have been credited and what your total estimated benefits are, by calling the social security hot-line (see below) and asking for form SSA-7004. This form is used to apply for a Personal Earnings and Benefit Estimate Statement (PEBES), which describes and estimates your benefits and provides a year-by-year record of your earnings subject to social security taxes, and the total taxes paid. This information can be requested online (🖳 www.ssa.gov/pebes), but the statement is sent to you.

To qualify for most social security benefits, you must have been employed for a minimum number of calendar quarters (three-month periods). In 2004, you gained one social security 'credit' for each $900 in earnings, up to a maximum of four credits a year; i.e. a minimum of $3,600 must have been earned to qualify for four credits. The earnings figure is increased each year to keep pace with increases in average wages. The number of quarters required depends on your age and the particular benefit, although most people need 40 credits (ten years' work) to qualify for benefits. Your local social security administration office will tell you how long you must work to qualify for particular benefits. Certain categories of person are exempt from FICA tax (and similarly are ineligible for benefits), e.g. exchange visitors under a J visa and foreign students with F, M or Q visas.

Through international 'totalisation' agreements, the US social security programme is co-ordinated with the programmes of other countries. These agreements benefit workers and employers. First, they eliminate dual coverage and taxation when people from one country work in another country and would otherwise be required to pay social security taxes to both countries for the same work. Second, they prevent the loss of benefit protection for workers who have divided their careers between two or more countries. The agreements allow the SSA to add US and foreign coverage credits if you have at least six quarters of US coverage. Similarly, you may need a minimum amount of coverage under a foreign system in order to have US coverage counted towards the foreign benefit eligibility requirements. The United States currently has totalisation agreements with 20 countries (Australia, Austria, Belgium, Canada, Chile, Finland, France, Germany, Greece, Ireland, Italy, Luxembourg, the Netherlands, Norway, Portugal, South Korea, Spain, Sweden, Switzerland, and the United Kingdom).

You can make a claim for social security in person, by post, or by telephone at any social security office or online on the Social Security website. Addresses are available at post offices and are listed in telephone directories under the federal government listing 'Health and Human Services Department – Social Security Administration'. You must provide proof of identification and other details according to the type of claim (the social security office will tell you what's required). You can appeal if a claim is rejected and can receive social security cheques outside the US, provided you remain eligible.

Once you reach your official retirement age (65 for those born before 1938), you can work all you want without losing any social security benefits. If you apply for retirement benefits before reaching your retirement age (early retirement), your benefits are reduced according to how much you're earning. The retirement age is gradually being raised from 65 to 67, depending on your year of birth. Those born in 1960, or later, will have to work until they're 67 to receive full retirement benefits.

If you have a complex query, e.g. the amount of your benefit cheque suddenly drops, you should call at a social security office in person. For straightforward enquiries call social security toll-free on ☎ 1-800-772-1213 from 7am to 7pm, Mondays to Fridays. The best time to call is before 9am and after 5pm (it's best to avoid the first week of the month when cheques are sent out, as this results in a torrent of calls).

The Social Security Administration produces a number of publications on specific benefits and on the social security system in general and many publications are available in a variety of languages and formats (e.g. large print or braille). Publications can be downloaded on the Social Security website (🖥 www.ssa.gov), picked up at local social security offices or ordered by telephone (☎ 410-965-2039) or by post (Social Security Administration, Office of Supply and Warehouse Management, Attn: Requisition and Quality Control Team, 239 Supply Building, 6301 Security Boulevard Baltimore, MD 21235). Other publications of interest include *Social Security Benefits Handbook* by Stanley Tomkiel III (Sphinx) and *Social Security, the Inside Story* by Andy Landis (Crisp Publications).

Retirement Benefits

The age at which you become eligible for the full federal retirement benefit is currently 65, although you may take early retirement at 62 and receive 80 per cent of the full benefit. Between the ages of 62 and 65, 80 to 100 per cent of the benefit is paid. The age at which beneficiaries are eligible for full retirement benefits will increase to 65.5 in 2005, 66 in 2016 and 67 in 2027. Reduced benefits will still be available from the age of 62.

Retirement benefit is based on your social security earnings (usually those after 1950). These are updated (indexed) to the year you reach the age of 60, or two years before you become disabled or die, and reflect the increase in average wages since the earnings were paid. If you were born in 1929 or later, you need 40 credits (i.e. ten years' contributions) to qualify for retirement benefits. If you delay your retirement past the age of 65 or don't receive the benefit for a number of months after the age of 65 because of high earnings, you receive a credit which may result in a larger benefit.

The social security benefit structure is progressive, in that it provides higher benefits for low paid workers in relation to their pre-retirement earnings than for higher paid workers. For workers retiring at 65, social security benefits provide approximately 60 per cent of earnings for low-income workers, 45 per cent for mid-income earners and 25 per cent for high-income earners. The law provides a minimum monthly retirement benefit for people who have received a low income. The average monthly benefit paid to those who have worked continuously since the age of 22 is $947. If you retired in 2004 at the age of 62 with a final salary of $40,000, you would receive a benefit of around $831 per month. The benefit would increase to $1139 per month if you wait until age 65 to retire, and would be $1571 if you wanted to wait until age 70 before drawing your Social Security benefit.

If your spouse is also 65, he or she can receive a spouse's benefit equal to half your benefit. If your spouse is aged between 62 and 65, he can draw a reduced benefit. The amount depends on the number of months he starts receiving the benefit before the age of 65. For example, if he draws his benefit at 62, he receives around 37.5 per cent of your basic benefit. This benefit remains the same for the rest of his life, unless you die first, in which case he is entitled to widow's benefits (see **Survivor Benefits** below). If your spouse is entitled to a retirement benefit based on his own earnings, he can draw whichever amount is the larger. If he is entitled to a benefit which is less than his spouse's benefit, he receives his own retirement benefit plus the difference between the spouse's retirement benefit and his benefit.

You can obtain a Personal Earnings and Benefits Estimate Statement from the SSA giving an estimated projection of the value of social security benefits you will receive at retirement (see above). Further information about retirement benefits is provided in a *Retirement* booklet (number 05-10035) available from SSA offices. (See also **Pensions** on page 336.)

Survivor Benefits

Survivor benefits provide life assurance protection for your family, possibly totalling as much as $100,000 over a number of years. The deceased must have been fully covered by social security at the time of his death and a marriage must usually have lasted for at least nine months. The amount of benefits is based on what a worker would have been entitled to had he been 65 when he died and the number and age of his survivors. The maximum family survivor benefit in 2004 was $3,282 per month for a spouse with two children, the average benefit being $1,882.

Benefits include: a one-time cash payment of $255; a benefit for each child under 18, or under 19 if a child is a full-time student at an elementary or secondary school, or at any age if a child is disabled before age 22; benefit for a widow at any age if she has children under 16 or disabled and in care. If there are no children under 16 or disabled, a widow's benefit is equal to 71.5 per cent of the basic amount at age 60 or a full benefit at 65 (benefits start at 50 if she is disabled). Parents can sometimes collect survivor benefits if they were dependent on you for at least half of their support. Further information is provided in a *Survivors* booklet (number 05-10084) available from SSA offices.

Disability Benefits

Under social security law, to be classified as disabled you must be blind or must be unable to engage in any substantial activity because of physical or mental impairments for a period of one year. Disability benefits are paid to various groups, including disabled workers and their families, and disabled widows and widowers. If you're a worker and become severely disabled, your eligibility for disability benefits depends on the number of years you've contributed to social security and when. If you're under 24, you need six social security credits (18 months' payments) during the three-year period before your disability. If you're aged 24 to 30, you need credits for half the period from the age of 21 to the time you became disabled. If you're 31 or over, you need up to 40 credits (ten years' payments), depending on your age at the time of your disability, 20 of which must have been earned in the ten years before your disability.

If you believe that you're entitled to disability benefits, contact your local social security office. You should submit a medical history plus a detailed statement from a doctor giving the reasons for your disability. The office will also require details of your work history, education and other personal data.

Benefits begin after a waiting period of five months, and no benefits are paid for the first five months' disability. Some disabled people under 65 are entitled to Medicare (see below), including disabled workers of any age, those who become disabled before the age of 22, and disabled widows and widowers aged 50 or over who have been entitled to disability payments for two years or more. Average monthly benefits in 2004 were $866 for a single worker and $1,344 for a worker with a family (spouse and child). Benefits increase automatically in line with a rise in the cost of living. While you're receiving benefits, payments can also be made to certain members of your family.

If you aren't covered by social security disability benefits, you're usually entitled to workers' compensation for work-related injuries, diseases and deaths (see page 321). Further information is provided in a *Disability* booklet (number 05-10029) available from SSA offices. (See also **Disability Insurance** on page 340.)

Medicare

Medicare, which costs the federal government some $200 billion a year, is a federal health insurance programme for people over 65, disabled people under 65 who have been receiving disability benefits for at least two years (or have worked long enough to qualify for Medicare), and insured people and their dependants of any age who require a kidney transplant or dialysis treatment because of permanent kidney failure. Around 15 per cent of Americans are covered by Medicare, or some 40 million people, around 1 million of whom pay more than $2,000 towards their treatment. Medicare is paid irrespective of income.

To qualify for Medicare you must have lived in the US for at least six months and be a permanent resident. (Those who have lived in the US for less than 5 years should contact the Social Security office to ask about their eligibility for Medicare.) If you're receiving social security (or railway retirement monthly benefits) you automatically receive information about Medicare around three months before you become eligible. All others must file an application form at their local social security office. To ensure your protection starts the month you reach 65, apply for Medicare around three months before your 65th birthday (even if you aren't planning to retire). If you're entitled to Medicare, you receive a Medicare card, which must be produced when registering for medical or hospital care under Medicare.

Medicare insurance consists of two parts: hospital insurance (Part A) and medical insurance (Part B). Part A helps pay for the cost of in-patient hospital care and certain kinds of follow-up care, such as nursing facilities and home health care. People aged 65 or older in 2005, who aren't eligible for benefits may purchase hospital insurance coverage for a monthly premium of $206, if they have 30 to 39 quarters of social security coverage. For those with fewer than 30 quarters of coverage, the monthly premium is $375. Part B is offered free to all beneficiaries who are entitled to part A insurance, and can be purchased by those not qualified for $78.20 per month. Part B helps pay for the cost of doctors' services, out-patient hospital services, durable medical equipment, and a number of other medical services and supplies that aren't covered by Medicare hospital insurance. The main difference between Medicare medical insurance and hospital insurance is that you don't need to qualify under the social security system to enrol in the medical plan.

If you're entitled to Medicare health insurance, you may choose your own doctor, but he must be a Medicare-participating doctor. While Medicare pays most of the costs of many illnesses, it doesn't offer protection for long-term or mental illness. Therefore you shouldn't cancel your private health insurance when you qualify for Medicare, although you may wish to consider a new policy covering only the portion of health care not covered by Medicare. Many private health insurance companies offer policies supplementing Medicare cover, called Medicare supplement or Medigap insurance (see page 344).

In 2005, Medicare hospital insurance pays for the first 60 days of hospital care in each benefit period, except for the first excess of $912. After the first 60 days, you must pay $228 per day for the next 30 days. If hospital care is necessary for between 90 and 150 days, you can use some of your 60 lifetime 'reserve days', when you pay $456 per day. After 150 days in hospital, Medicare ceases to make any contribution towards bills. There's an annual excess of $100 for Medicare medical insurance, after which Medicare generally pays 80 per cent of the approved amounts for any care received during the year.

Starting in 2006, Medicare will introduce a new prescription drug plan option, costing around $35 a month. The new drugs coverage pays 75 per cent of the first $2,250 prescription drug costs, after an annual excess of $250. After that, you're expected to pay the next $3,600 out of your own pocket and then Medicare pays around 95 per cent of the costs above that amount. In the interim, there's a system of drug discount cards, available for use during 2004 and 2005. The available drug discount cards offer discounts of 10 per cent to 25 per cent on a specific list of prescription medications. For certain low income individuals, the card offers a $600 credit towards drug costs. The system is fairly complicated and requires you to choose from a large offering of available discount cards. The Medicare website (see below) offers a number of publications about the prescription drugs programmes and has a questionnaire online to help you choose among the various discount cards available.

For further information about Medicare, obtain a copy of *Medicare and You* (10050) or *Your Medicare Benefits* (10116) from your local social security office or from Medicare Publications, Health Care Financing Administration, 7500 Security Boulevard MS N1-21-19, Baltimore, MD 21244 (☎ 1-800-MEDICARE or 1-800-633-4227, ⌨ www.medicare.gov). (See also **Health Insurance** on page 341 and **Long-term Care Insurance** on page 347.)

Medicaid

Medicaid is a joint federal/state means-tested programme that supplements Medicare by providing comprehensive health care benefits for people aged 65 and older, and disabled people with low incomes and few or no assets. It covers around 35 million poor Americans, although it doesn't include all the poor and excludes almost as many as it covers (eligibility for Medicaid varies from state to state). If you're receiving AFDC (see **Welfare** on page 335) you usually receive Medicaid, although this depends on the state where you live. Most Supplemental Security Income recipients (see below) also qualify. Contact your state or local welfare office for information about Medicaid.

Medicaid costs the government around $200 billion yet reimburses doctors and hospitals for only 60 per cent of what private plans pay. This means that those covered by Medicaid cannot always obtain care, as many practitioners refuse to accept Medicaid rates.

Supplemental Security Income

Supplemental Security Income (SSI) is a federally funded programme designed to ensure a minimum level of income for those with limited earnings and resources, or who are aged 65 or over, blind or disabled. Around 6.5 million Americans receive SSI, which costs the government some $25 billion annually. How much you can earn and still obtain SSI depends on whether you work and the state where you live. To qualify for SSI payments, your assets (in any state) must be valued at less than $2,000 for one person or less than $3,000 for a couple. Assets exclude the house you live in and the land it's built on, generally one car and other possessions. Social security offices will explain exactly what information and evidence are required in order to claim SSI and provide assistance if necessary.

In 2004, the basic federal SSI payment was $564 per month for an individual and $846 for a couple. However, in some states SSI payments (and earnings limits) are much higher, as the federal payments are supplemented by state payments. In most states, if you receive SSI you're also entitled to Medicaid (see above), as well as food stamps, free school meals and other types of welfare (see below). In many states, an application for SSI is also treated as an application for Medicaid. Further information is provided in an SSI booklet (number 05-11000) available from SSA offices or by telephoning ☎ 1-800-772-1213.

Welfare

Welfare refers to miscellaneous social services, such as subsidised school lunches, winter heating allowances and energy assistance programmes, food stamps (given to some 25 million people), special needs payments to pregnant women, veterans' benefits, rent subsidies, public housing for the homeless and programmes such as nutrition for Women, Infants and Children (WIC) and Temporary Assistance for Needy Families (TANF – see below). Many cities have senior centres offering meals as well as social, cultural, recreational and health-promotion programmes for the aged. Other local welfare services include reduced public transport fares, community-organised transport services, services to the house-bound (e.g. shopping, housekeeping, minor repairs, personal care, escort assistance, library service), home sharing, meals on wheels and senior services.

Under the TANF programme, nearly all recipients must work after two years of assistance and cannot receive assistance for more than five years in total (states can specify fewer years and exempt up to 20 per cent of recipients from the five-year time limit). After these time limits, states can elect to provide non-cash assistance and vouchers to families, using Social Services Block Grant or state funds. Parents must work a prescribed number of hours per week: single parents 30 hours the first year and couples 35 hours. Work can be unsubsidised or subsidised employment, on-the-job training, work experience, community service, 12 months of vocational training, or child care provided to individuals participating in community service. Exceptions are parents with a child under six who cannot find child care, and single parents with children under one, and six weeks' job-search time is excluded.

Reducing welfare payments is a topical theme in the US, particularly among politicians, for whom it's a certain vote winner (during his campaign in 1992, President Clinton pledged to "end welfare as we know it", but ten years later it's still recognisable). Most Americans would like to see welfare cut drastically or even eliminated altogether (at the very least they would like to make able-bodied people work for their welfare cheques). In the last few years many states have slashed welfare payments in a bid to balance their budgets.

Nevertheless, welfare payments are a way of life for many Americans and have been for generations. However, the popular image of the 'welfare queen' who fills her grocery trolley with caviar and steak and gets into her Cadillac couldn't be further from reality (but it's a convenient stereotype for those wishing to cut welfare). Families receiving TANF and food stamps live well below the poverty line in all states, except Alaska and Hawaii. It's also a myth that welfare is bankrupting the country, as only some 2.5 per cent of federal funds go towards TANF and food stamps. It is, however, true that many foreigners go to the US and live on welfare (including, unbelievably, thousands of illegal immigrants) and that many people abuse it, costing the country billions of dollars in fraud.

PENSIONS

The US has the same problems with a falling birth-rate and ageing population as other western countries, and the federal government is keen to reduce expenditure on state pensions. If nothing is done to reduce pension costs, the IMF calculates that by 2020 the US will need over 40 per cent of its GNP just to finance state pensions (other countries would be in an even worse position). Federal policy is to encourage workers to extend their working lives, and the age when they receive maximum federal retirement benefits will be increased to 65.5 in 2005, 66 in 2016 and 67 in 2027 (although reduced benefits are still available from age 62). However, although Americans are living longer, they're retiring earlier, not later. Early retirement (before age 65) is normal and by the age of 62 almost half of workers have retired. However, early retirement may cost you hundreds of thousands of dollars, so be cautious about accepting an early retirement offer from your employer.

For workers retiring at 65, federal retirement benefits (see page 331) currently provide approximately 60 per cent of earnings for minimum-wage workers, 40 per cent for mid-income earners and 25 per cent for those on high incomes (over $87,900 per year – the social security tax earnings limit). However, it's estimated that you need 70 to 80 per cent of your last working year's wages to maintain your living standard in retirement. Many people cannot afford to retire at all, particularly single women, and it isn't uncommon to find people working full or part-time well into their 70s. It's particularly important for women to plan for retirement or they can be forced to continue working. Nearly one in six women over 65 live in poverty and most get only half the social security benefits of men and around 40 per cent of the pension benefits.

Further information about the different kinds of pension plans can be found via the internet (⌨ www.retirement-plan-online.com).

Company Pension Plans

Some 86 million Americans (an increase of more than 30 per cent in the last 20 years) contribute to company pension plans (known as retirement plans), which are offered by the majority of large companies, but only around 40 per cent of those with fewer than 100 employees and a mere 10 per cent of those with fewer than 25. Company plans may be financed entirely by the employer or by employer and employee contributions. On average, companies put in 50 cents to every $1 an employee contributes up to 6 per cent of an employee's salary or a maximum of around $10,000 per year. The employer contribution (known as the 'company match') can be as high as $1 per $1 or it may be zero, or it may vary from year to year according to the company's performance.

Employer pension plans are defined benefit plans, where the amount of benefit is fixed, but not the amount of contributions, or defined contribution plans, where the amount of contribution is generally fixed, but the amount of benefit isn't. The best type of company pension plan for workers who change jobs or careers is a portable defined contribution plan, which you can roll over and take with you when you leave a company (or leave to your dependants when you roll over!). Defined contribution plans include profit sharing plans, employee stock ownership plans (ESOPs), 401(k) plans (see below) and money purchase plans.

Two new plans have been introduced in recent years to encourage small businesses to offer company plans: the Simplified Employee Pension and Simple pension plans, known as SEP-IRA and Simple-IRA. Under a SEP-IRA, an employer isn't required to contribute every year; under a Simple-IRA, employers contribute 2 or 3 per cent of income and you can contribute up to $6,000 per year.

Some 75 per cent of company pension plans permit employees to borrow half the total in their account up to a maximum of $50,000. However, you must get in before your employer, as many employers legally dip into employee pension funds when they need a bit of cash (particularly when they're in financial trouble and close to bankruptcy). Company pension funds can be raided at will by companies who consider them to be over-funded (however, when a fund is under-funded, they aren't required to bail it out or even repay funds removed!). When a company crashes with a pension fund covered by the Pension Bank Guarantee Corporation (PBGC), the taxpayer (as usual) must repay what owners have 'stolen'. Without PBGC cover, employees can lose their pensions.

Most company pensions are covered by the federal Employee Retirement Income Security Act (ERISA), which protects the rights of workers who participate in pension plans. Your employer provides you with a copy of the conditions regarding your company pension and further information can be obtained from the Pension Rights Center, 1350 Connecticut Ave NW, Suite 206, Washington, DC 20036 (🖥 www.pensionrights.org).

If you change jobs before retiring, you're entitled to all your accrued benefits from an employer pension plan. You may put these funds into an IRA or Keogh pension plan (see below) or transfer them to a new employer's pension plan to avoid taxation. If you're transferred to the US from abroad, permanently or temporarily, you may be able to transfer your existing company pension or keep up payments in a foreign pension fund while you're in the US or until you reach retirement age.

401(K) Plan

Those who have the opportunity contribute to a company tax-deferred pension plan, in which you can invest up to $13,000 of your annual income (the amount is adjusted annually for inflation). Employees over the age of 50 can invest up to $16,000 a year. The most common of these is known as a 401(k) plan (after an obscure section of the tax code). Since its introduction in the mid '80s, the 401(k) has become the US's most popular pension plan. An estimated 25 million Americans have around $1 trillion invested in 401(k) plans. However, not all companies are obliged to provide one and benefits vary enormously. The maximum an employee can contribute to a 401(k) plan varies, e.g. between 2 and 17 per cent, the typical maximum contribution being around 15 per cent. In a few companies, employees are obliged to contribute to a 401(k), while more than half of plans don't allow employees to start contributing immediately after joining the company. Some of the best 401(k) plans are offered by manufacturers and high-paying companies with stable workforces and strong unions, while some of the worst are offered by companies in the retail and service industries, the fastest growing sectors of the economy, although this isn't always the case.

In recent years, companies have been under pressure from the Department of Labor to pay more of the fees associated with 401(k) plans out of pension surpluses, which means that less is available to employees when they retire. Pension regulators have found that one in four companies deducts excessive fees from 401(k) plans and many have been forced to reimburse plan members. Some companies encourage 401(k) plan members to buy company stock through their 401(k) plans (and may, in fact, make matching payments in company stock rather than in cash). Many Enron employees discovered too late that betting your retirement on the stock performance of your employer can have disastrous results. Most 401(k) funds allow you to shift investments from company stock to a variety of funds, and most advisors urge employees to make sure their 401(k) investments are properly diversified.

Personal Pension Plans

Many people who are members of company pension plans also contribute to a personal pension plan, such as an Individual Retirement Account (IRA) or a Keogh Retirement Plan (for the self-employed), in order to supplement their state and company pensions. Most financial institutions offer IRAs and Keogh plans, including banks, savings and loan associations, stockbrokers, insurance companies and investment companies, all of which provide leaflets and further information.

Individual Retirement Account

One of the most common personal pension plans is an Individual Retirement Account (IRA). These are offered by most financial institutions, including banks, savings associations, stockbrokers, insurance companies and investment companies. Part, or all, of your contributions to an IRA may be tax deductible, depending on your salary level and whether your employer provides a pension plan. If your employer doesn't provide a pension, profit sharing or stock bonus plan, your contributions to an IRA are tax deductible, irrespective of your income. This tax deduction applies to federal income taxes only and you must check local state law for the impact (if any) of IRA contributions on state income taxes.

If you, or your spouse, are covered by a company pension plan, your eligibility to make a tax deductible IRA contribution depends on your total salary or self-employment earnings, reduced by certain other tax advantaged savings plan deductions. Those earning up to $40,000 (one person) or $60,000 (couple) can make the same maximum contribution each year as someone not covered by a company pension plan. The allowable deductible amount is reduced by around $1 for every $3 above the limit. If you're covered by an employer's pension plan and earn above $50,000 (one person) or $70,000 (couple), you cannot make a deductible IRA contribution, but you can contribute to a (non-tax deductible) Roth IRA, where the Adjusted Gross Income (AGI) limits are $110,000 (single person) or $160,000 (couple), contributions being graduated if your AGI is above $95,000 (single) or $150,000 (couple). In fact, even if you're eligible to contribute to a traditional IRA, a Roth IRA could earn you more money in retirement.

You may contribute to an IRA until the age of 70 years and six months, up to a maximum of $3,000 per year if you're single, $3,500 if you're married and file a joint return with your spouse (irrespective of whether your spouse has any earnings), or $6,000 if you're married, file a joint tax return, and you and your spouse have sufficient earned income. Unlike other investments, the interest on IRAs isn't subject to tax each year.

Keogh Retirement Plan

A Keogh Retirement Plan is a pension plan designed exclusively for the self-employed, e.g. sole proprietors, partners and professional people, as well as employees who have freelance or outside income. There are two types of Keogh plan: money purchase and profit sharing plans. With a money purchase plan, a set amount or set percentage of your earnings is paid into the plan each year, up to a maximum of $30,000 or 20 per cent of your total earned income, whichever is the smaller. With a profit sharing Keogh plan, a fixed percentage of business profits is set aside in the plan. This is limited to the lesser of $30,000 a year or, currently, 13.04 per cent of earned income (the percentage is liable to annual adjustment). If you're unsure of your income, a profit sharing plan is recommended, as contributions can be varied; with a money purchase plan they must remain the same each year. Depending on your AGI before your IRA deduction (see above), you may be able to contribute to an IRA in addition to a Keogh plan.

Withdrawals

Tax deductible contributions to an IRA, Keogh or 401(k) plan are tax-deferred until cash is withdrawn; non-deductible contributions (e.g. to a Roth IRA) aren't taxed upon withdrawal. You can start making withdrawals from your IRA, Keogh or 401(k) plan at the age of 59 and a half, provided you've retired, except if you wish to make a first-time (!) home purchase, pay for (eligible) higher education or become disabled. Withdrawals before this age are subject to a 10 per cent federal tax penalty (plus regular income tax). However, you **must** start withdrawing from your plan no later than 1st April of the year following that in which you reach the age of 70 years and six months. In general you can take your IRA, Keogh or 401(k) payment in the form of an annuity, in instalments or in one lump sum. A 15 per cent tax penalty (in addition to regular income tax) is levied on large annual withdrawals from all pension plans, including IRAs, Keogh and 401(k) plans, although this doesn't affect the vast majority of taxpayers, as withdrawals must exceed $112,500 before they're subject to the tax penalty. If you close an IRA, Keogh or 401(k) plan before the agreed term, the penalties are severe and you will lose most, if not all, of your tax benefits.

If you die before receiving any benefits from an IRA, Keogh or 401(k) plan, all funds in your plan are paid to your beneficiaries, in a lump sum or in periodic payments. Tax breaks help you to minimise taxes when you retire and take funds from your plan. You can transfer your IRA or Keogh funds between financial institutions. For example, with the drop in bank interest rates in recent years, many investors moved their funds from low-interest bank Certificates of Deposit (CDs) into stock and bond mutual funds. IRA and Keogh plans may be covered by the FDIC insurance scheme (see page 367), but not when you choose your own investments.

ACCIDENT INSURANCE

It's rare for Americans to have a specific insurance policy for accidents. Accidents are usually covered by health insurance (see page 341), car insurance (see page 267) and disability insurance (see below) policies. Employees are usually covered by workers' compensation insurance (see page 60), social security disability benefit (see page 332), and sickness and accident insurance (see page 340), although these usually cover short-term disabilities only.

DISABILITY INSURANCE

Disability or income protection insurance provides you with an income when you're unable to work. For the vast majority of Americans, social security or employer benefits paid in the event of illness, injury or invalidity, are insufficient to meet their financial commitments. Disability insurance guarantees you a fixed amount each week or month, or a percentage of your salary when you're ill for a long period or permanently disabled, without which you could lose your home and other assets or could even be bankrupted. On average, your chance of being disabled between the ages of 35 and 60 is four times greater than your chance of dying.

Like all forms of insurance, disability insurance must be reviewed and updated regularly to reflect your current requirements. Homeowners need disability insurance to ensure they can continue to pay their mortgages. Disability insurance may be linked to your mortgage (a mortgage disability policy) or your mortgage insurance policy (which pays off your mortgage on your death). There are two types of disability insurance: short-term and long-term. Short-term disability policies pay benefit for a few months or years only, e.g. up to two years, while long-term coverage may continue payments indefinitely until you return to work or reach retirement age (e.g. 65) or longer. In some states, e.g. New York, short-term disability insurance is required by law for most employers. Some employers also provide long-term disability insurance. Under an employer's short-term disability group plan, the period during which your salary is paid usually depends on your length of service, for example:

Period of Service	No. of Weeks' Salary
Less than 13 weeks	0
13 weeks – 2 years	8
2 years – 5 years	10
5 years – 10 years	15
More than 10 years	26

All disability policies specify a qualifying period before benefit payments begin, e.g. two to six months. The longer you can wait for your disability insurance to pay out, the lower your monthly premiums. Usually, you can choose when the payments start, e.g. 30, 60 or 90 days or even a year after the disablement. Your employer may, for example, continue to pay your salary for a period after an accident or the onset of an illness, in which case you can choose to defer payments from your disability insurance for this period.

Look for a policy with low cost that's renewable, non-cancellable and with benefits indexed to inflation. A typical policy pays between $250 and $1,000 per month. The maximum amount that can be insured is usually 60 to 75 per cent of your net monthly earnings, as benefit from a disability policy isn't taxed so you must replace your after-tax income only. The longer the period for which you require cover and the higher the monthly income required, the higher your monthly premiums. Therefore by reducing the amount of monthly income or terminating payments after you reach retirement age, you can lower your premiums. The younger you are, the lower your premiums, which can vary between $13 per month for a person under 30 to $65 per month for someone over 60 for a monthly benefit of $250 (from $50 to $260 per month for a monthly benefit of $1,000). Depending on your age and type of job, some insurance companies may require you to have a medical examination or will obtain a report from your family physician (non-smokers may pay lower premiums). Many professional organisations offer low-cost policies.

Many states have a compulsory State Disability Insurance (SDI) scheme, usually financed by workers through payroll deductions. Benefit normally begins after the eighth day of a disability or the first day of hospitalisation and is based on wages paid during a specific 12-month period. In California, for example, benefit ranges from $50 to $266 per week and is payable for up to a year. (See also **Sick Pay & Disability Benefit** on page 332.)

HEALTH INSURANCE

With the exception of the poor, those aged over 65 and the disabled, there's no national system of free health care or inexpensive health insurance. There's also no free treatment for visitors who fall ill in the US. It's therefore important to ensure that your family has full health insurance cover before you arrive in the US, which may be provided by a holiday or travel insurance policy. However, if possible it's usually better to extend your present health insurance policy (most policies can be extended to provide international cover) than to take out a new policy. This is important if you have existing health problems that won't be covered by a new policy (this also applies when changing jobs). The health insurance cover required when visiting most other countries is totally inadequate in the US, where the recommended minimum cover is $250,000 or $500,000. When travelling in the US, always carry proof of your health insurance with you. If you arrive in the US without health insurance, you can obtain temporary cover from a number of American companies.

Not surprisingly, most Americans are extremely health conscious and are terrified of an accident or long illness which could bankrupt them and leave them (or their survivors) paying off the debt for many years afterwards. Most employers provide their employees with health insurance (see below), although it's voluntary and few companies pay 100 per cent of premiums. Never assume that your employer will take care of your health insurance, but check to make sure; if you need to pay your own premiums, it will make a big hole in your salary. It's estimated that over 42 million Americans (25 per cent of them children) are without health insurance and a further 65 million have inadequate insurance.

Residents over 65 and the disabled are covered by the Medicare federal health insurance programme (see page 333), although cover is limited and there's no protection for long-term or mental illness. Residents with low incomes are covered free by Medicaid (see page 334), although cover is extremely basic.

If you're living or working in the US and aren't covered by a compulsory policy, it's extremely risky not to have private health insurance for your family. If you're under-insured, you could be faced with astronomical medical bills. When deciding on the type and extent of health insurance, make sure that it covers **all** your family's present and future health requirements in the US, before you receive a large bill.

When changing employers or leaving the US, you should ensure that you have continuous health insurance. If you and your family are covered by a company health plan, your insurance will probably cease after your last official day of employment. If you're planning to change your health insurance plan, ensure that no important benefits are lost, e.g. existing medical conditions usually aren't covered. When changing health insurance companies, you should inform your old company if you have any outstanding bills for which they're liable.

Company Insurance Plans

Most US companies provide their employees with some kind of health insurance, and some 60 per cent of Americans have health insurance paid partly or wholly by their employers. Most large and medium size companies have a group insurance plan in which all employees and their families are enrolled from their first day of employment (although there may be a qualification period for some benefits). Group cover is usually provided without an individual medical examination. Large multinationals and the US government provide employees and their families with free comprehensive health insurance, although most companies pay a percentage of premiums only, e.g. 50 to 90 per cent.

Only some 10 per cent of American employers pay the entire cost of traditional fee-for-service medical coverage. Employers have been battling for years to reduce health care costs and many small firms simply cannot afford to insure their employees or their families; over 80 per cent of the total number of uninsured people are workers or their dependants (see **Families** on page 346). Some company insurance plans aren't open to foreign employees until they've been resident in the US for six months. In this case you should be covered by an individual health policy. **If you're offered a job in the US, carefully check the health insurance cover provided.**

In recent years, group insurance rates have risen by up to 15 to 20 per cent a year and individual direct-pay rates at up to 30 per cent a year. Some insurance companies offer less expensive health care plans for small companies, which reduce premiums by up to 50 per cent. An increasing number of employers are replacing traditional fee-for-service or indemnity plans with less expensive group plans offered by health maintenance organisations (HMOs) and preferred provider organisations (PPOs), which combine fee-for-service insurance with the group practice concept (see pages 306 and 307). Under HMO plans, there are less likely to be restrictions on the number of days' hospital care, no dollar maximums on benefits, and no required payments by individuals. There's also a broader range of services available and less paperwork to be completed, although some HMOs impose an affiliation period of up to three months, during which you receive no benefits. HMO plans nearly always include cover for hearing treatment, physical examinations, infant care, and immunisation and inoculations (required under the HMO Act), which aren't usually covered by fee-for-service plans.

The average employee contribution is around $50 per month for individuals and over $100 per month for families, and the average employee excess is $500 per year per family member ($1,500 maximum per family). The trend is for employers to shift more of the cost of health insurance to employees. In order to reduce costs, many employers pay 50 per cent of their employees' health insurance only, where they previously paid 90 or 100 per cent. If you're an employee and are required to pay a percentage of your health insurance, it's automatically deducted from your salary in equal instalments throughout the year.

Some companies impose a health insurance surcharge on smokers and a few even refuse to employ smokers on the grounds that their habit may lead to costlier health insurance and more working days lost to sickness (see **Smoking** on page 318). Being overweight or a heavy drinker may also increase your health insurance costs. Some companies even prohibit employees from indulging in 'hazardous activities and pursuits', although many states have passed legislation prohibiting employers from curtailing their employees' (legal) leisure activities. Some employers offer health insurance discounts to non-smoking employees or those who take regular exercise. Some employers provide free or low-cost group insurance for retirees.

If you're a member of an employer funded group insurance plan, check whether it can be continued or converted to individual coverage (at group rates) when you or your spouse retire. Continuing free or low-cost company insurance after you retire isn't a right and if your employer wishes to he can cancel or increase the cost of your health insurance at any time.

Medical Savings Accounts

If you work for a small employer, defined as one with fewer than 50 employees, you may be eligible to set up an Archer Medical Savings Account (MSA). This is a tax deferred savings plan linked to a high deductible health plan (HDHP) provided by your employer. You can also have an MSA if you're a small business owner and meet the other requirements. To set up an MSA, your employer's HDHP must be your only form of medical insurance, other than long-term care, dental or vision coverage. The HDHP plan excess must fall within certain limits (i.e. between $1700 and $2500 for an individual, or $3350 to $5050 for a family) and there must be a cap on the maximum out of pocket costs for members of the plan (currently $3350 for individuals and $6150 for a family).

An MSA is set up with a trustee, usually a bank or investment company, and contributions are made to the MSA by the employee or employer, limited to 75 per cent of the plan deductible or the employee's earned income for the year. This pool of money is then available to the employee to pay for qualified medical costs that fall under the deductible amounts of the HDHP. When distributions are made from the MSA, the amounts must be added to taxable income, but most qualified distributions also qualify as deductible medical expenses on the employee's tax return. If distributions are made for anything other than qualified medical expenses, there's a 15 per cent additional tax on the amount distributed, unless the distribution is made after the account holder is disabled, reaches the age of 65 or dies. On the death of the account holder, the money can be transferred, tax free, to the MSA of the spouse or distributed to the beneficiary (in which case it is taxed as normal income to the recipients).

The government is trying to encourage use of MSAs and there's a programme available to those on Medicare, where the government contributes to the MSA. The programme, initially called Medicare + Choice, has been reworked to coordinate with the 2003 Medicare changes related to prescription drug coverage. The new programme is called Medicare Advantage.

Medigap Insurance

If you're covered by Medicare (see page 333), it's recommended that you take out Medicare supplement insurance, known as a Medigap policy, for the portion of health bills not paid by Medicare. Most private health insurance companies offer Medigap policies. A Medigap policy should be guaranteed renewable for life and you should avoid existing condition restrictions and time limits until cover begins. For the six months following enrolment in Medicare medical insurance (Part B), people aged 65 or older cannot be denied Medigap insurance because of existing health problems.

The cost of Medigap insurance varies dramatically, from $500 to $2,000 per year, depending on the insurer, the cover required and, in some cases, the area. Some companies charge higher premiums initially or conversely have increasing premiums, and some charge more if your health is poor, although in New York, premiums are subject to community rating. Premiums for a basic plan average around $100 per month and for maximum coverage around $225 per month. Some HMOs insure over 65s for between $75 and $150 per month. However, your spouse may not qualify for the same benefits as you. A disadvantage of Medigap insurance is that you may be restricted as to the doctors and hospitals you may use.

The major US health insurance companies include Blue Cross, Blue Shield, Major Medical, Prudential, Group Health Insurance and Aetna. Free Medigap insurance counselling is provided in many states. For further information obtain a copy of the *Guide to Health Insurance for People with Medicare* (publication number 02110) and *Medigap Policies and Protections* (10139) from any social security office.

Extent of Cover

The extent of health cover varies considerably from one policy to another. Some offer 'no-frills' insurance for basic medical expenses, while others are comprehensive plans (although few cover all medical expenses). Most insurance plans offer a range of medical 'packages', e.g. basic protection and major medical, plus optional or supplementary packages such as dental, optical, maternity and disability insurance.

Major Medical

The usual health insurance policy is called major medical and includes: physicians', surgeons' and anaesthetists' fees; out-of-hospital prescription drugs; consultations with specialists; hospital accommodation and meals; any operation or other treatment necessary (e.g. physiotherapy, radiotherapy, chemotherapy); X-rays and diagnostic tests; maternity care (after a 12-month qualification period); medicines, X-rays and dressings while in hospital; treatment for mental health problems; substance abuse treatment; and home nursing and extended care facilities.

Exclusions & Options

Basic health plans (particularly direct-pay plans) usually **don't** include: dental care; maternity and infant care; routine physical examinations; eye and ear examinations; hospice care for the terminally ill; intensive care; disability; and organ transplants, all of which are usually available as options or supplements. A basic plan also usually excludes extras for hospital in-patients such as a telephone, television or visitors' meals. Infant care, routine physical examinations, dental care, and eye and ear examinations are usually included in an HMO or PPO plan (see pages 306 and 307). Treatment of any medical condition for which you've already received medical attention, or which existed before the start of the policy (called 'pre-existing'), may not be covered. Health insurance doesn't cover childbirth if you were pregnant when you took out health insurance; however, comprehensive medical insurance usually covers complications associated with childbirth, such as a Caesarean section. If possible, verify before a pregnancy that regular maternity charges are covered as 'any illness'. Some health insurance policies don't cover childbirth in a hospital, but usually cover the cost of a birthing centre.

Families

Insurance provided by an employer often covers the employee only and **not** his family. Less than 20 per cent of employers provide health insurance for their employees' dependants and some 40 per cent of children aren't covered by employer-based insurance plans. Children over 18 may not be included in a family policy. In many areas, it isn't possible to include 'domestic partners' (i.e. anyone to whom you're not legally and officially married) under employer health policies, although this is changing. You should always check with the insurer before making any assumptions.

Students

Full-time students in US colleges or universities may be able to pay a college infirmary fee entitling them to receive infirmary treatment. Students' families aren't covered by a student's college infirmary fee and must be covered privately. Students can also buy additional, low cost accident insurance, which is recommended and may be compulsory. All US colleges and universities provide foreign students with information about compulsory and recommended health insurance before their arrival in the US.

Travellers

If you do a lot of overseas travelling, ensure that your health plan covers you outside the US (most do). All bills, particularly those received for treatment outside the US, must include precise details of all treatment and prescriptions received. Terms such as 'Dental Treatment' or 'Consultation' are insufficient. It's also helpful if bills are written in English.

Premiums & Payments

Health insurance in the US is **very** expensive; a typical policy for a family of four costs thousands of dollars a year ($500 to $1,000 per month is typical). Health insurance is particularly high for the self-employed, e.g. those with E-2 visas, who don't qualify for group rates. Immigrants without medical records tend to be put into a high risk category until they've built up a sufficient medical history. However, it may be possible to take out a cheaper foreign insurance policy that covers you in the US, e.g. some travel companies insure immigrants for a year after they arrive. Before buying health insurance, shop around among different agents and companies and ask your colleagues, friends and neighbours for recommendations.

Premiums can vary by up to 50 per cent from one insurance company to another. Premiums for men are usually lower than for women, although the highest premiums are usually for infants under two years old. Some policies levy an excess (deductible) on a variety of services, e.g. $10 for each routine visit to a doctor, 20 per cent of ambulance costs, and 20 per cent or $1,000 per hospital admission (as an in-patient). Under an HMO or PPO plan, members usually make a 'co-payment' of $5 to $20 for each service rendered. Most policies have an annual excess, typically $100 to $250 for an individual and $500 to $1,000 for a family. This is the amount you must pay towards your total medical bills in any year **before** your insurance company starts paying. Consider taking a higher excess, e.g. $1,000, if you're young and/or in good health rather than paying higher premiums, and avoid buying excess cover (i.e. more than you need or something you don't need). There may be a maximum limit on the amount an insurer will pay in any one year, e.g. $50,000, and a lifetime maximum such as $1 million. Many insurers require a second opinion or a pre-admission review on non-emergency surgery and may penalise you (e.g. up to $1,000) if you don't follow the rules. File all claims promptly, as some insurers reject claims not filed within six months of treatment.

If your employer doesn't provide a group insurance plan, you must purchase private health insurance or a direct-pay plan for you and your family. You may qualify for low-cost group insurance through a professional association or another organisation, and you may also be able to obtain inexpensive insurance through an HMO or PPO (see pages 306 and 307). If you don't qualify for a group rate, your premiums may be much higher (possibly even higher than your rent or mortgage). However, never assume that a group rate is lower than a direct-pay plan, as some organisations levy huge commissions. Retirees can obtain a low-cost policy from the AARP (formerly the American Association of Retired Persons), 601 East Street, NW, Washington, DC 20049 (🖳 www.aarp.org).

With some plans, the more claims you make, the more your insurance premiums increase. If you have a long-term illness or a poor medical history, you may be unable to obtain health insurance at any price (although some states operate a state insurance scheme for those who have been rejected for coverage by two or more insurance companies). If you or a member of your family contracts a serious, expensive or chronic disease, you may find that your health insurance is cancelled or that your premiums rocket (it isn't uncommon for an insurance company to cancel the policies of its sickest patients!). You may be required to pay your own medical bills and receive reimbursement from your insurance company later (less the percentage for which you're liable, if applicable). On the other hand, your insurance company may settle bills directly with doctors or hospitals and send you a bill for your contribution. Always obtain itemised medical bills, check them thoroughly and query anything that you don't understand (see also **Hospitals & Clinics** on page 309). For Medigap insurance premiums, see page 344.

LONG-TERM CARE INSURANCE

Very few health insurance policies cover the cost of long-term health care, which usually includes skilled nursing care, intermediate care, custodial care and home health care. Many Americans take out a long-term health care (or nursing home) insurance policy, provided by many US insurance companies, and some employers offer long-term care policies as an employee benefit. Make sure you know exactly what long-term care insurance covers and under what circumstances benefits apply. The vast majority of long-term care plans have severe restrictions covering hospital admissions, level of care, length of coverage, custodial care, cancellation provisions, and Alzheimer's disease exclusions. **Policies with these restrictions should be avoided.** One in five people makes a claim on a long-term care insurance policy.

Always buy a policy where you're evaluated first and complete a medical questionnaire before you become ill (called front-end underwriting). Many people discover that they aren't covered only when illness forces them into a nursing home. As with disability insurance, the longer the elimination period (i.e. the period before you start to receive benefit), the lower your premiums. You can set up a Medicaid Trust to protect some of your assets, under which Medicaid pays your nursing home bills after a 30-month waiting period, which means you require long-term care insurance for 30 months only. Always use an experienced lawyer to set up a Medicaid Trust. Following exhaustion of your personal assets, long-term care is paid by Medicaid, although this limits your choice of facilities and may result in a reduction in the quality of care. For information about long-term care insurance, obtain a copy of *A Shopper's Guide To Long-Term Care Insurance* from your state insurance department or the National Association of Insurance Commissioners, 2301 McGee, Suite 800, Kansas City, MO 64108-2604 (☎ 816-842-3600, ▭ www.naic.org). (See also **Long-term Care** on page 316.)

DENTAL INSURANCE

Dental insurance is often provided by employer health insurance plans. It can be part of a comprehensive medical and dental plan or a separate plan offered in addition to medical coverage. Often employers offer separate dental cover, which can be linked to a choice of medical plans. Some two-thirds of workers in medium and large companies participate in an employer dental plan, around half of whom are required to contribute towards their individual dental costs and two-thirds towards family dental cover. Dental benefits are also available through a dental HMO (see page 306) and under some foreign health insurance policies or international health schemes (although usually optional).

Dental plans usually cover preventive and restorative treatment and most also cover orthodontic expenses, particularly for children. Preventive care typically includes examinations, cleaning and X-rays, while restorative treatment includes fillings, periodontal and endodontic care, prosthetics and crowns. Preventive care is usually covered at 80 to 100 per cent; fillings, surgery, endodontics and periodontics are covered to 60 to 80 per cent; and expensive inlays, crowns, prosthetics and orthodontia to 50 per cent. Under some plans, members are offered a reimbursement based on a schedule of cash allowances for restorative services, such as fillings and crowns. The percentage of dental expenses paid by a plan may be increased each year, provided you're examined regularly by a dentist.

Some plans require members to pay a fixed co-payment, e.g. $10 for preventive care, after which benefits are paid in full. Often a member must pay an annual excess, e.g. $50 a year. Most plans have an annual maximum benefit, e.g. $1,000 a year, and orthodontic services usually have a lifetime maximum of around $1,000. 'Expensive' treatment, e.g. over $200, usually needs pre-authorisation from your plan. Premiums average between $12 and $20 per month for an individual.

HOUSEHOLD INSURANCE

The following types of household (homeowner's) insurance policies are offered, although some companies don't use the standard 'HO' categories:

- **HO-1 (Basic Policy)** – The basic household policy insures your home and possessions against losses caused by the 11 'common perils': fire or lightning; windstorm or hail; explosion; riot or civil commotion; aircraft; vehicles; smoke; vandalism or 'malicious mischief'; theft; breakage of glass (that constitutes part of the building); and volcanic eruption. The basic policy is inadequate for most homeowners.

- **HO-2 (Broad Policy)** – The broad household policy, which is more popular than the basic HO-1 policy, insures your home and possessions against losses caused by the 11 'common perils' (see above) and a further six perils: falling objects; weight of ice, snow or sleet; sudden or accidental tearing apart, cracking, burning, or bulging of a steam or hot water heating system, an air-conditioning or automatic fire protective sprinkler system, or an appliance for heating water; accidental discharge or overflow of water or steam from within a plumbing, heating or air-conditioning system, or automatic fire protective sprinkler system, or an appliance for heating water; freezing of plumbing, heating or air-conditioning systems, or sprinkler system, or of a household appliance; sudden and accidental damage from an 'artificially generated electrical current' created by appliances, devices, fixtures and wiring.

- **HO-3 (All-risk or Special Policy)** – An all-risk or special policy protects your home against all the perils included in an HO-2 policy, plus any other perils not specifically **excluded** in the policy. Your possessions, however, have the same cover as the HO-2 policy. This is the most popular form of household policy.

- **HO-4 (Renter's Policy)** – A renter's policy provides the same protection as an HO-2 policy for the personal possessions and home improvements made by someone who's renting a property. The building itself isn't insured.

- **HO-5 (Comprehensive Policy)** – A comprehensive policy covers everything, including your personal possessions, on an all-risk basis, with the exception of any exclusions listed in the policy. It's the 'Cadillac' of policies and the most expensive.

- **HO-6 (Condominium & Co-op Policy)** – In most condos, the master policy normally covers only those parts of a property that are co-owned. An HO-6 policy covers personal possessions and improvements, but excludes the dwelling itself (which is insured by the condominium or co-op association).

- **HO-8 (Older Homes Policy)** – An older homes policy is similar to a basic HO-1 policy and is specifically for older homes which would be prohibitively expensive to replace. It ensures that an older home is returned to serviceable condition, but not necessarily to the same state as previously.

- **General** – An HO-3 (all-risk) or HO-5 (comprehensive) policy provides the most extensive protection and includes everything except flood, earthquake, war, nuclear accident and certain other risks specified in your policy. An HO-3, and most other household policies, also provide protection against loss of use, i.e. when your home becomes uninhabitable and you're required to find alternative accommodation and incur additional living expenses.

All household insurance policies include your personal possessions, such as furniture, clothing, electrical and electronic equipment, and household appliances. If you don't own your home, you can take out a household renter's policy (HO-4), covering your personal possessions and, most importantly, damage caused by you to the property you're renting. When insuring your possessions, don't buy more insurance than you need. Unless you have valuable possessions, the insurance may cost more than replacing your possessions. You may be better off insuring a few valuable items only. Possessions aren't usually insured for their replacement value (new for old), but their 'actual cash value' (cost minus depreciation). You can, however, buy replacement-cost insurance, although policies often include limits and are more expensive.

To calculate the amount of insurance you require, make a complete list (inventory) of your possessions containing a description, purchase price and date, and their location in your home. Some insurance companies use a formula based on the insurance cover on your home, although this is no more than a 'guesstimate'. Keep the list and all receipts in a safe place (such as a safety deposit box). Add new purchases to your list and make adjustments to your insurance cover when necessary. There are maximum limits on cover for individual items in a standard household policy (listed in contracts).

A basic household policy may not include such items as credit cards (and their fraudulent use), cash, musical instruments, jewellery, valuables, sports equipment and bicycles, for which you may need to take out extra cover. A basic policy doesn't usually include accidental damage caused by you or members of your family to your own property (e.g. 'accidentally' putting your foot through the television during a presidential speech) or your home freezer contents (in the event of a breakdown or power failure). The highest level of cover usually includes damage to glass (windows, patio doors, etc.) and porcelain (baths, washbasins, etc.), although you may need to pay extra for accidental damage, e.g. when your son blasts a baseball through a window. Ask your insurer what isn't covered and what it costs to include it (if required).

High-value possessions (called 'scheduled property') such as works of art and jewellery, aren't fully covered by a standard policy and must be insured separately for their full value or through a basic policy 'rider' or 'floater', which may also insure your property if it's stolen from somewhere other than your home, e.g. a car or hotel room. The value of scheduled property must be certified by a bill of sale or a professional appraiser's report. The cost of floaters varies considerably according to the area and the local crime rate.

If you're buying your home with a mortgage, your lender usually insists that it's covered by a household insurance policy. When the mortgage is paid off, it's unnecessary to have household insurance, although it's recommended. Many people lose their homes each year as a result of natural disasters such as earthquakes, fires, floods, hurricanes and tornadoes. Around 5 per cent of owners don't carry any household insurance and it's estimated by the Insurance Information Institute that eight out of ten homeowners have insufficient insurance for their homes and possessions. The amount you should insure your home for isn't the current market value, but its replacement value, i.e. the cost of rebuilding the property should it be totally destroyed. Many insurers insist that you insure your home for at least 80 per cent of the replacement cost. If you insure for less than 80 per cent of the replacement cost, you receive a pro rata settlement of any claim, however small. For example, if you insure for 50 per cent of the replacement cost, you receive only 50 per cent of the value of a claim. If you own or rent a second home or other property, it must be covered by a separate household policy.

All agents and insurance companies provide information and free advice, and usually inspect your home to assess your insurance needs, if requested to do so (if not, go elsewhere). An assessment should be performed by a professional appraiser, e.g. a Member of the Appraisal Institute (MAI), and the cost varies considerably.

Some policies are index-linked and the amount of cover is automatically increased each year based on the federal Consumer Price Index (CPI) or a state CPI (this may be called an 'inflation guard' provision). Even with an index-linked policy, you should review your policy regularly, e.g. annually. Household insurance must usually be renewed each year and insurance companies are continually updating their policies, so you must ensure that a policy still provides the cover you require when you receive the renewal notice (although sometimes the cost is simply added to your monthly mortgage payments). It's your responsibility to ensure that your level of cover is adequate, particularly if you carry out expensive home improvements that substantially increase the value of your home.

A household insurance policy usually includes liability insurance of $100,000 or more in respect of bodily injury and property damage (see **Liability Insurance** below). Most companies offer optional extra cover, e.g. cover of $300,000 for an extra $10 a year.

Premiums

The cost of household insurance varies widely according to the value of your home and its location (i.e. the state and neighbourhood), and may also depend on other factors such as whether your home is constructed of bricks/concrete or wood (timber-frame homes are more expensive to insure) and how far it is from a fire hydrant. Most policies have an excess (deductible), which is the amount of the loss you must pay. You can reduce your premium by accepting a higher excess, e.g. $250 (or even $1,000) instead of $100. Excesses are limited by law in some states. If you have extra security, such as high security door and window locks, an alarm system, fire extinguishers, sprinklers, or smoke alarms, you usually receive a discount. You may also receive a discount if you're over 55 or if you buy your car insurance from the same company. Rates for the same level of cover from different companies can vary by as much as 100 per cent, so shop around and obtain at least three estimates. However, make sure that all quotes are for the same level of cover. 2001 saw increases of up to 15 per cent in property insurance premiums. As a **rough** guide, a $75,000 household policy with a $250 excess would cost between

$150 and $500 per year for a masonry home in Florida (10 to 20 per cent more for a timber-frame home).

Owners of houses vulnerable to subsidence (e.g. those built on clay) are likely to have to pay much higher premiums. In some areas, flood insurance is mandatory (under the National Flood Insurance Act of 1994), as it's specifically excluded from most household policies. (If you live in a flood plain you should have a sump pump and should call the fire department if you have a flood.) You can insure against flood risks through the National Flood Insurance Program, operating in more than 18,000 communities and backed by the federal government (☎ 1-888-379-9531, 🖳 www.floodsmart.gov). You can also insure against other natural disasters such as earthquakes and hurricanes, although in high risk areas cover is prohibitively expensive (e.g. in California only some 15 per cent of homeowners have earthquake insurance). Premiums have increased considerably in regions that have been hit by hurricanes and floods and other natural disasters in recent years, although lower premiums may be offered in return for a higher excess.

Claims

If you make a claim, you may need to wait months for it to be settled. Generally, the larger the claim, the longer you must wait for your money, although in an emergency a company may make an interim payment. If you're dissatisfied with the amount offered, don't accept it and try to negotiate a higher figure or take legal advice.

LIABILITY INSURANCE

Liability insurance is the second most important insurance to have in the US (after health insurance), where suing is a national sport (baseball is also popular, but not nearly so rewarding). People sue each other at the drop of a hat for the most trivial and ludicrous reasons, irrespective of who (or whether anyone) was at fault. Even more astounding, in many of the most bizarre cases (most of which would be laughed out of court in other countries) plaintiffs are awarded millions of dollars in damages, often out of all proportion to the incident. For example a burglar successfully sued for injuries sustained while breaking into a house and a couple sued a hospital for $4 million for distress and permanent emotional damage when their baby was harmlessly and temporarily dyed blue.

The practice of dragging your spouse, friends, neighbours, host, employer or doctor into court at the drop of a hat is (to many foreigners) one of the most appalling aspects of the American way of life. If someone slips in your drive or on your carpet, or trips over your vacuum cleaner lead, they may sue you for millions of dollars. The system is designed to keep litigation lawyers (of which there are zillions) and insurance companies in luxury. They're aided and abetted by the courts and judges, who seem to take it for granted that people have liability insurance with which to pay the farcical 'damages' awarded. If you don't have personal liability insurance, you could find yourself in serious financial trouble.

Liability insurance covers you against claims from third parties due to injury or property damage, medical bills, loss of earnings, and pain and suffering as a result of an accident on your property (or something occurring on your property, e.g. if a branch falls off your tree and injures someone or your child bites someone through your fence). Considering the low cost of liability insurance and the high cost of law suits, most experts recommend $300,000 to be the **minimum** cover necessary.

Work-related losses aren't covered by a standard household policy, e.g. injury and damages incurred by clients, customers, business associates or domestic employees working for you on your property. If you use your home as an office or work place, you must take out additional liability cover or a separate policy (including malpractice insurance). Damage or injuries caused by your children while working on someone else's property also aren't covered, but can be included for a small additional fee.

Liability insurance is usually offered as part of a household policy (see page 349), but it can be purchased separately. Many people also take out a personal liability 'umbrella' policy to extend the cover of their household and vehicle policies, and usually include protection against claims arising from business activities and other claims, such as slander. An umbrella policy provides liability cover over and above the amount in your basic policies and isn't a replacement for these policies. (See also **Legal Insurance** below and **Legal System** on page 516.)

LEGAL INSURANCE

Legal insurance pays part of your lawyers' fees when you're being sued or when you must take legal action against a third party. A legal claim could arise for a large number of reasons, including problems with a new house, a ruined holiday, a car accident, bad workmanship, personal injury, unfair dismissal or compensation in respect of faulty goods, to give but a few examples. With lawyers' fees at hundreds of dollars per hour, few people can afford to pursue their rights in law. In the US, even if you win your case you must still pay your own lawyer's fees. **One of the hidden benefits of legal insurance is that when your opponent knows (or thinks) that you have the financial 'muscle' to go the distance, he is often willing to settle out of court.**

However, full legal expenses insurance, which pays all your legal expenses, isn't available. Nevertheless, there are a variety of prepaid legal plans on the market, where you pay an annual or monthly fee, e.g. $10 or $20 per month. This entitles you to unlimited telephone calls to a lawyer to discuss personal legal problems and a number of office consultations. The service may also include contract reviews, a free will, and discounts for complex legal matters. Some prepaid legal plans pay up to $5,000 in lawyers' fees during the first year; if you don't use it, the amount may increase to $25,000 after five years. Other benefits also usually increase after a number of years. But be wary of prepaid legal services offers coming to you from unknown sources, especially those advertised over the internet. Many of these are set up as pyramid schemes or other forms of scams that benefit mainly the people selling the services. Legal expenses insurance is often included as an option in other policies, e.g. car insurance, and is usually worthwhile having. Personal liability insurance and a personal liability umbrella policy also provide a certain amount of legal insurance protection (see above).

HOLIDAY & TRAVEL INSURANCE

Holiday and travel insurance is recommended for anyone who doesn't wish to risk having his holiday or travel spoiled by financial problems or to arrive home broke. As you know, anything can and often does go wrong with a holiday, sometimes before you even get started, particularly when you **don't** have insurance. The following information applies to US residents travelling within the US and abroad, and to those visiting the US on holiday. **Nobody should visit North America without adequate travel and health insurance!**

Travel insurance is available from many sources, including travel agents, insurance brokers, banks, automobile clubs and transport companies (airline, rail and bus). Package holiday companies and tour operators also offer insurance policies, some of which are compulsory (although **most don't provide adequate cover**). You can also buy 24-hour accident and flight insurance at major airports, although it's expensive and doesn't usually offer the best cover. Before taking out travel insurance, carefully consider the range and level of cover you require and compare policies (cover, conditions and premiums vary considerably).

Short-term holiday and travel insurance policies may include insurance against: holiday cancellation or interruption; missing your flight; departure delay at the start **and** end of a holiday (a common occurrence); delayed, lost or damaged baggage; lost or stolen belongings and money; medical expenses and accidents (including evacuation home); personal liability and legal expenses; default or bankruptcy (e.g. the tour operator or airline going bust).

The cost of travel insurance varies considerably according to your destination. Many companies have different rates for different areas, e.g. North America, Europe and worldwide. Premiums may also be increased for those over 65 or 70. Generally, the longer the period covered, the cheaper the daily cost, although the maximum period is usually limited, e.g. six months. With some policies an excess (deductible) of around $50 or $100 must be paid for each claim. For people who travel abroad frequently, whether on business or pleasure, an annual travel policy provides better value, but carefully check exactly what it includes.

Travel insurance for visitors to the US should include personal liability (e.g. $1 or $2 million) and repatriation expenses. If your travel insurance expires while you're visiting the US, you can buy further insurance from an insurance agent, although this won't include repatriation expenses. Flight insurance and comprehensive travel insurance is available from insurance desks at most airports, including travel accident, personal accident, worldwide medical expenses and in-transit baggage.

If you must make a claim, you should provide as much documentary evidence as possible in support. Although travel insurance companies eagerly take your money, they aren't always so keen to settle claims, and you may need to persevere before they pay up. Be persistent and make a claim **irrespective** of any small print, as this may be unreasonable and therefore invalid in law.

CAR INSURANCE

Third party car insurance (or liability) is required in most states. All states set minimum financial responsibility limits, for which insurance is the easiest (and least expensive) way to meet the requirements. Additional third party and comprehensive insurance is available from numerous insurance companies. For more information see **Car Insurance** on page 267.

CAR BREAKDOWN INSURANCE

Breakdown insurance for cars and motorcycles is available from a number of US motoring organisations (see page 295).

LIFE ASSURANCE

Although there are worse things in life than death, such as spending an evening with a life assurance salesman, your dependants would probably rate your death without life assurance high on their list. There are more than 2,000 life assurance companies in the US and only the Japanese and Canadians buy more life assurance (relative to income) than Americans. There are some 400 million current life policies in the US providing total cover of over $7,500 billion. Although usually referred to as life insurance, US life policies are almost always for life assurance. Assurance is a policy covering an eventuality that's certain to occur (for example, like it or not, you will die one day). Thus a life assurance policy is valid until you die. An insurance policy covers a risk that **may** happen but isn't a certainty, e.g. that you will have a car accident. There are two basic types of life assurance policies: term and permanent (or full or whole life).

Term Assurance

Term assurance is, as the name suggests, for a limited period (term), e.g. 10 or 20 years or until the age of 65, and pays out only if you die within the term covered by the policy. It provides straight insurance protection, with the whole premium going towards purchasing insurance. Premiums typically increase periodically, e.g. at five or ten-year intervals, and become increasingly expensive as you get older and the risk of death increases.

Permanent Assurance

In contrast to term assurance, permanent (or whole life) assurance provides protection for your whole life. One important benefit of permanent assurance is that the premiums remain the same no matter how long you live; although they're higher than for term assurance in the early years, they're lower in later years. A permanent policy provides life assurance coupled with a savings or investment account. A big attraction of permanent assurance is that the investment part of the policy grows at a tax-deferred rate, so income tax on the profits doesn't need to be paid until the policy is cashed in (or withdrawals are made).

Other types of policy include single premium life, where you pay one (large) premium for a fully paid up life assurance policy, and annuities. With an annuity, you pay premiums in return for a guaranteed regular income for life. Annuities can be single premium or annual premium, and payments can begin immediately or can be deferred. The main disadvantage of an annuity policy is that payments cease on the death of the holder and the lump sum is lost, so you may be better off investing your lump sum and living off the income (if possible). You should be suspicious of anyone who tells you to sell your investment portfolio to buy an annuity. Over 90 per cent of full-time employees in medium size and large companies receive free life assurance as an employment benefit. This is usually equal to one to two times your annual salary and can often be increased at low cost.

One disadvantage of all life assurance policies is the large commissions paid to agents, plus expenses and maintenance costs. Commissions may be equivalent to a year's premiums, so it pays to shop around and ask agents about their commission rates. It's usually best to buy no-load life assurance, where you buy direct from an insurance company such as Ameritas Life or USAA Life, and don't pay a commission. When you buy through an agent, you may pay 100 per cent commission in the first year, 50 per cent in the second and 2 per cent every year thereafter. You can usually save money by paying your premiums annually. Commissions on cash-value permanent policies are five times higher than on term assurance.

When buying life assurance, you're usually better off buying from an independent agent, who deals with a number of insurance companies, than from one who sells the policies of a single life assurance company (a so-called 'captive'). Obtain recommendations from at least three agents, check out the financial stability of life assurance companies at your local library, and never substitute life assurance for investments.

Be wary of replacing an existing life assurance policy and carefully check your eligibility (e.g. medical and other qualifications) for a new policy. If you require additional life assurance, it's usually wise to retain your existing policy and take out an additional policy, rather than cancel an existing policy. **After taking out a life assurance policy, you have ten days in which you can cancel the policy without penalty.**

Many state insurance departments publish life assurance buyers' guides, and a *Consumer's Guide to Life Insurance* is published by the American Council of Life Insurance, 1001 Pennsylvania Ave. NW, Washington, DC 20004-2599 (☎ 202-624-2190). A good general guide to life assurance is *New Life Insurance Investment Advisor* by Ben Baldwin (McGraw-Hill).

Whether you must undergo a medical examination depends on the insurance company, your age, state of health, and the amount of insurance required (non-smokers often pay lower premiums). You must complete a medical questionnaire and, depending on your age and health record, your doctor may be required to provide a medical report. If you have no family doctor or previous medical history, you may need to have a medical examination. Most policies don't pay out when death is due to an AIDS-related illness. Finally, you should leave a copy of all insurance policies with your will (see page 396) and with your lawyer. If you don't have a lawyer, keep a copy in a safe place at home and make sure your family knows where it is. A life assurance policy usually needs to be sent to the insurance company upon the death of the insured, with a copy of the death certificate.

14.

FINANCE

The US is the richest country in the world, with a GDP of around $11 trillion ($11,000,000,000,000) in 2003 and a per capita GNP of around $35,000. However, contrary to popular belief, the streets of the US aren't paved with gold and it also has one of the world's highest poverty levels, nearly 36 million Americans (12.5 per cent of the population) living below the official poverty line.

Despite the widespread use of credit and charge cards (the average American has eight); people still use cash (particularly criminals). In fact, payments are made in cash some 70 per cent of the time (more often than in most European countries), compared with 10 per cent by cheque (check) and 20 per cent with credit and debit cards. However, some businesses virtually insist on payment by credit card (e.g. car hire companies). Americans are suspicious of personal cheques (particularly drawn on out-of-state banks), as payment cannot be guaranteed. Consequently many businesses require three separate pieces of identification, at least two major credit cards, birth certificate, passport, and security in the form of an arm or leg (or your first born) until the cheque has cleared!

More than half of all Americans have credit debts. Although the recession and resulting widespread job losses in the early '90s led many consumers to drastically reduce their buying on credit, credit is still a way of life and not to have any debts is considered un-American. (If everyone paid off their debts, the whole economy would collapse.) In some circles, your financial standing depends on the amount of credit and debt you carry, which comes as little surprise in the nation that gave the world junk bonds and where the government has run up a massive national debt. Your financial status may also be determined by the number of credit cards you carry, although newcomers find it difficult to obtain even one.

Most foreigners find the US financial services industry surprisingly unsophisticated. There is little use made of direct debit or standing orders to simplify consumer bill paying, although banks are making more and more services available to their customers over the internet. There's no integrated nationwide banking system and many foreigners initially find it difficult to establish a credit rating (see page 364), as banks and lending institutions have tightened their credit standards because of the number of personal bankruptcies and the increasing prevalence of identity theft. Although money can buy almost anything in the US, if you arrive with a suitcase full of dollars you may find it difficult to even open a bank account (they will think you're a drug dealer!). Banks are often difficult to deal with and are wary of extending credit, irrespective of your income. If you have an international credit card issued by a foreign bank, you should retain it until you've replaced it in the US.

When you arrive to take up residence or employment, make sure you have sufficient cash, travellers' cheques, luncheon vouchers, coffee machine tokens, silver dollars, gold bars and diamonds to last at least until your first pay day (which may be some time after your arrival). Don't, however, carry a lot of cash. During this period you will find a major credit card (e.g. American Express, Diners Club, MasterCard, Visa) invaluable, as without one you're expected to **prepay** many bills, including hotel rooms and car hire.

Personal finance is the US's favourite subject, although according to a survey conducted in 1996 (commissioned by The Investor Protection Trust) four out of five Americans are financially illiterate and their ignorance costs them a lot of money.

There are numerous books on personal finance, including the *Wall Street Journal Guide to Understanding Personal Finance* by Kenneth Morris (Fireside), *Making the most of Your Money* by Jane Bryant Quinn (Simon & Schuster) and *Consumers Report Money Book* (National Book Network), plus many personal finance magazines such as *Money*. The government even offers a free adult education program called Money Smart, which you can order on the FDIC website in English, Spanish, Chinese, Korean or Vietnamese. (🖳 www.fdic.gov/consumer/moneysmart) The Money Smart program is also available through some banks and employers. (See also **Social Security** on page 328, **Pensions** on page 336 and **Sales Tax** on page 474.)

US CURRENCY

Unless you've just arrived from another planet, you're no doubt aware that the American unit of currency is the US dollar (US$). The US$ is everyone's favourite currency (particularly counterfeiters) and it's the world's leading international currency (although it's expected to be challenged by the euro as the premier international reserve currency in the next decade). It's used for most international trading and practically all international lending and borrowing transactions. Consequently, American interest rates are of major concern to foreign debtor nations. In many countries, particularly in Central and South America, Asia and Eastern Europe, the US$ acts as an unofficial second currency and is often preferred to local currency (which may not be accepted at all by some people). The US$ has been highly volatile in the last decade, although it stabilised for a while. Budget pressures caused by the war in Iraq and large tax cuts pushed through by the Bush administration have caused the dollar to tumble at the end of 2004. The Federal Reserve's benchmark interest rate was cut repeatedly from early 2001 until hitting a 40 year low in mid 2004 of only 1 per cent. Rates since then have been inching upwards, approaching 2 per cent by the end of 2004. Rates charged by the banks, on the other hand, are as high as 5 to 8 per cent and rising.

The dollar is divided into 100 cents (¢) and US coins are minted in 1 cent (penny), 5 cent (nickel), 10 cent (dime), 25 cent (quarter) 50 cent (half-dollar) and $1 (formerly a 'silver dollar', but since 2000 a new 'golden' dollar coin has been introduced). 'Two bits' is slang for a quarter (25 cents), but the names given above are official names and are printed on the coins. US coins don't have their value in numbers anywhere, making them particularly difficult for foreigners to get used to. With the exception of the penny (copper), all coins are silver in colour (the nickel is made of nickel and the quarter of an amalgam of silver and copper). The nickel is slightly smaller than a quarter, but is larger than a dime. The quarter and the dime have serrated edges. The dime is the smallest of all coins. Half-dollar and dollar coins (although legal tender) are rare. There's been talk of phasing out the penny, as it's worth so little and is more valuable as scrap metal than currency. The quarter is the most useful coin and you should always carry some with you for parking meters, bus and underground fares, road tolls, payphones, luggage lockers, vending machines, tips, etc. The Treasury has been trying to introduce a smaller, lighter one dollar coin to the public for many years now to replace the old silver dollar. The first attempt, the Susan B. Anthony dollar, was issued in 1979, but was not terribly popular because it was easily confused with a quarter. In 2000, the 'golden dollar' coin was first issued, exactly the same size and weight as the Susan B. Anthony, but made of a metal alloy that has a 'golden' colour. The edges of the golden dollar are smooth, so that blind people can distinguish it from the quarter. Still, most Americans are unenthusiastic about giving up their dollar bills for dollar coins.

Just to confuse everybody (especially foreigners), all US banknotes (bills) are the same size and have similar designs, although a different president's face adorns the front. Notes are printed in denominations of $1 (Washington), $5 (Lincoln), $10 (Hamilton), $20 (Jackson), $50 (Grant), and $100 (Franklin). The $2 (Jefferson) and $500 bills are no longer printed (although still legal tender), and $1,000 and $10,000 bills aren't in general circulation (Americans rarely even carry $100 notes!). Since 1929, banknotes have been printed in a distinctive shade of green (hence the familiar name of 'greenbacks'); however, the Treasury has finally decided to add some colour to US money. The first 'subtly' coloured banknotes made their appearance in late 2003, adding blue, peach and metallic tones to the $20 bill. The $50 note with a coloured background appeared at the end of September 2004 and eventually all banknotes, except the $1 and $2 notes will be redesigned to incorporate various anti-counterfeiting features, including various shades of colour. The dollar has a number of slang names, the most common of which is buck; a fin is a $5 note and a sawbuck a $10 note. If you're unfamiliar with US notes, you should stick to low denominations (up to $20) and check them carefully to avoid errors, when receiving notes in change and when spending them. Notes above $20 are often treated suspiciously, as they're a favourite target of counterfeiters the world over. They may not be accepted by some shops, although this depends on what you're buying. US notes are the most counterfeited in the world.

You should obtain some US notes before arriving in the US and familiarise yourself and your family with them. You should have some US dollars in cash (e.g. a total of $50 to $100 in small notes) when you arrive, which saves you having to change money on arrival at a US airport (where you often receive a poor exchange rate). Rather than changing money at all, you may be better off using a bank machine to simply withdraw US cash from your account back home. However, avoid carrying a lot of cash.

OTHER CURRENCY & TRAVELLERS' CHEQUES

The US has no currency restrictions and there's no limit on the amount of money you may bring in or take out of the country. However, any amount over $10,000 in 'monetary instruments', including US or foreign currency, travellers' cheques (checks), money orders, bonds or securities, must be declared to customs on arrival in, or departure from, the US. The import of gold must be declared on arrival.

Most shops and businesses don't accept foreign currency or travellers' cheques in foreign currencies and it's best to avoid bringing them to the US. It is becoming more and more difficult to find a bank or other financial institution that exchanges foreign currency or travellers' cheques in foreign currencies, even in large cities such as New York. You usually receive an unfavourable exchange rate or pay a high commission when changing money at a hotel or bureau de change. You may be asked for identification (ID) when changing foreign notes at a bank and some banks only change foreign money for their own customers. US dollars can be used in Canada, although Canadian dollars aren't accepted in the US.

The most widely recognised and accepted travellers' cheques are issued by American Express, followed by Visa and Thomas Cook. The normal fee charged when buying travellers' cheques worldwide is 1 per cent of their value, although this may be waived when travel arrangements are made with the company issuing the cheques (e.g. American Express or Thomas Cook). The commission on American Express cheques may be higher when they aren't purchased directly from an American Express office. Some US organisations such as the AAA (see page 295) provide members with fee-free travellers' cheques. Travellers' cheques can be cashed at most banks, although some levy a fee (ask first).

Almost all businesses and retailers (exceptions include taxi drivers and some small businesses) in the US readily accept US$ travellers' cheques and give you change as if you had paid in cash. $10 or $20 cheques are accepted almost everywhere, while larger denominations may be accepted only for expensive purchases (so don't try to pay for a coffee with a $50 cheque). You may be asked for identification when cashing travellers' cheques at a bank, e.g. a driving licence or credit card, and may also be asked for identification in shops. The sign 'No Checks' applies to personal cheques only and not to travellers' cheques. Many hotels change travellers' cheques for residents, as will a few shops, although they usually give a poor exchange rate.

Keep a record of cheque numbers and note where and when they were cashed. American Express provides a free, three-hour replacement service for lost or stolen travellers' cheques at any of their offices worldwide, provided you know the serial numbers of the lost cheques. Without the serial numbers, replacement can take up to three days. Most companies provide toll-free numbers for reporting lost or stolen travellers' cheques, including American Express (☎ 1-800-221-7282), Citicorp (☎ 1-800-645-6556), MasterCard (☎ 1-800-223-9920), Thomas Cook (1-800-223-7373) and Visa (☎ 1-800-227-6811).

If you have money transferred to the US by banker's draft or a letter of credit, it may take up to two weeks to clear. You can also have money sent to you by international money order (via a post office or a bank), a cashier's cheque or a telegraphic transfer, e.g. via Western Union (☎ 1-800-325-4176 or 1-800-CALL-CASH), which is the quickest and safest, but also the most expensive method. A telegraphic or cable transfer to the US from overseas takes 24 to 48 hours and costs around $20. Within the US, a cash wire transfer via Western Union costs a minimum of $12 (depending on the amount) and takes as little as 15 minutes. You can send money by telephone, in person at any Western Union agent, or via the internet. To send $1,000 by Western Union's online service costs $75! It costs around $3 to collect transferred funds from any of Western Union's 9,000 US offices and, for an additional $3, they notify you by telephone when it arrives. Western Union has over 100,000 agents in almost 200 countries. Up to $2,000 can be sent from a MasterCard or Visa account via Western Union (☎ 1-800-325-4176).

American Express cardholders can transfer up to $10,000 (depending on the card holder's credit limit) by 'MoneyGram', within the US and internationally. A less expensive way to transfer funds to the US from some countries is by purchasing an international money order from a bank, for which there's a standard charge. The money order is made payable to you at a receiving US bank at face value. Transfers can also be made by airmail letter, which although takes longer, e.g. around eight days to Europe, is much cheaper. You can have money sent to you in the US in the form of a certified cheque (cashable at any bank) and send money within the US via a post office money order, which can be purchased or cashed at any US post office (American Express also provide money orders). You need your passport or other identification to collect money transferred from abroad or to cash a banker's draft (or other credit note). **If you plan to transfer a large amount of money to the US, for example to buy a business or property, shop around for the best deal.** One specialist company that claims to offer the best deal in the UK is Currencies Direct, 6th Floor, Hanover House, 73/74 High Holborn, London WC1V 6LR, UK (☎ 020-7813 0332).

If you're sending money abroad, it's best to send it in the local currency, so that the recipient doesn't need to pay conversion charges. You can send money direct from your bank to another bank via an inter-bank transfer. Most banks have a minimum service charge for international transfers, generally making it expensive, particularly for small sums. Overseas banks also take a cut, usually a percentage (e.g. 1 or 2 per cent) of the amount transferred.

CREDIT RATING

It has become more and more important in the US to establish and maintain a 'good' credit history or credit rating. Even if you don't believe in borrowing money to pay your bills, your credit history is often required when applying for a job, obtaining a credit or debit card, renting an apartment or applying for insurance or government benefits.

In the US, everyone's credit history is maintained by private companies called credit-reporting agencies or credit bureaux (e.g. Equifax, TransUnion and Experian, formerly TRW). They collect information from banks, mortgage companies, shops and other businesses. Your credit record contains information such as your current and prior addresses, bank accounts and major credit cards you hold, judgements or liens against you or your property, bankruptcies or foreclosures, as well as failure to pay your debts on time or at all, e.g. payments on revolving charge accounts. Credit bureaux can legally report negative credit information for seven years and bankruptcy information for ten years. The only information that can be changed in your credit report is incorrect items and items outside the seven or ten-year reporting periods. Credit bureaux are only supposed to release your credit history report to creditors or those with a legitimate business need for the information, but in practice this can include almost anyone interested in your business and willing to spend the money to obtain the report.

You're normally entitled to receive a free copy of your credit history report if you've been denied credit, employment or insurance within the past 60 days; and you can always request a copy of your own report for a nominal fee (around $10). Starting in 2005, all credit bureaux will be required by federal law to provide consumers with one free copy of their credit report each year.

It can be difficult for new arrivals in the US to establish an acceptable credit history, and for some things, having no credit history (or no available report from the credit reporting agencies) may be worse than having a less-than-perfect credit rating. The best way for a foreigner (or anyone else for that matter) to build up a good credit rating is to be employed by the same employer for a year or more (even better if you have your salary deposited directly), have a couple of bank accounts (checking and savings) and to always pay your monthly bills on time without your account going into overdraft. Due to the rise of identity thefts (see below), it is strongly advised that everyone check their credit history report at least once a year, to find any mistakes or suspicious items and also just to see who has been requesting your credit history. If you find a mistake or a transaction you don't recognise, you should ask to have the error corrected, although credit agencies can refuse to make any changes. You're entitled to add your own explanation of the item (up to 100 words) which must be added to your report. Be advised, though, that your addition to your report may take 45 days or more to appear.

Identity Theft

In the last few years, identity theft has become a serious concern for US consumers. Identity theft involves the fraudulent use of another person's identification to establish credit, bank accounts or other financial arrangements. In the US, many banks and lenders have routinely used a customer's social security number for identifying accounts. So, if a crook gets hold of your social security number, combined with your name or a bank or credit card number, it's possible for them to do considerable damage to your finances or to your credit history before you have any idea that there is something wrong. Identity thieves have drained victims' bank accounts and run up huge debts on credit cards working mainly over the internet. In some cases, they open new accounts in their victims' names, with the bills delivered to fake addresses, so that there is no indication of anything wrong until the victim is refused credit or turned down for a job based on a bad credit report.

Identity thieves get hold of social security and account numbers by a variety of means, including email messages requesting you to 'confirm' your account information, theft of purses and wallets containing cards, stealing post containing account statements or new credit cards or simply rifling through rubbish bins for discarded identity information. **Don't use your social security card or number for identification except when absolutely necessary!** You should never give out bank account numbers, your social security number, passwords or any other financial details to someone who telephones or otherwise contacts you. If they claim to be calling from your bank, offer to call them back at the telephone number listed on your statement. The US government offers several pamphlets on identity theft, including *ID Theft: What's it All About?* and *ID Theft: When Bad Things Happen to Your Good Name*, available online or from the Government Printing Office (see **Appendix C**). There is also a government website devoted to identity theft (💻 www.consumer.gov/idtheft), if you think you've been a victim or just want additional information.

If you have a bad credit rating, avoid so-called 'credit-repair' companies like the plague. These companies charge from $50 to over $1,000 to 'fix' your credit report. In most cases they do nothing at all or nothing you cannot do yourself for free or for a few dollars. Never give anyone advertising easy credit approval or low credit card interest rates your current account number, which may be used to fraudulently withdraw money from your account. Finally, if you're refused credit, look on the bright side; without credit you cannot run up any debts! For further information obtain a copy of the *Consumer Handbook to Credit Protection Laws* available free from the Federal Reserve System, 20th Street, 18 Constitution Avenue, NW, Washington, DC 20551 (☎ 202-452-3245, 🖳 www.federalreserve.gov/pubs).

BANKS

There are thousands of independent banks in the US, although the number has fallen dramatically in the last decade or so because of take-overs and bank failures (merger mania has been rife in recent years). There are also branches of many foreign banks (around 300) in the major cities. Consequently, there's a mind boggling choice of banks in most towns and cities and competition is fierce. Around 1,500 privately owned banks are required to maintain interest-free reserves with the Federal Reserve. The 'Fed' is composed of 12 Federal Reserve banks that act as the country's central bank, execute national monetary policy and set interest rates in co-operation with the Treasury.

There are two main types of bank: 'commercial' banks and 'savings' banks or savings and loan associations, known as S&Ls or thrifts. You may also be eligible for membership in a credit union, a non-profit co-operative financial institution that operates much like a savings bank. Commercial banks usually offer a wider choice of services, while savings banks may offer a better rate of interest. Savings banks and thrifts are granted government charters to collect deposits and make home loans, and they hold 50 per cent of US home mortgages. Since deregulation of the savings and loan industry in 1982 (intended to increase competition), the number of thrifts has fallen from over 4,000 to around 1,000. The US's commercial banks, on the other hand, have made record profits in the last few years, with higher fees accounting for some 25 per cent of income, and cash-rich banks are increasingly concerned about finding borrowers for their money. Credit unions, on the other hand, are non-profit organisations, owned and operated by members who generally share a common bond of some sort, a common employer, school, church or professional or social organisation.

When selecting a bank, you should choose one that's covered by the FDIC guarantee (see below). Among the largest US banks (by assets) are J.P. Morgan Chase & Co, Bank of America, Citibank, Wachovia, Banc One, Wells Fargo, Fleet Boston (recently acquired by the Bank of America), USBC, Suntrust Banks and HSBC North America. However, that you may be better served by a small bank or credit union, where you're more likely to be treated as an individual than an account number. You should also ask about such things as credit card fees and interest rates (see page 373), loans, overdrafts and other services. Banks advertise extensively on local television and in newspapers. Friends and colleagues are usually anxious to share their experiences with local banks. To find if you're eligible for credit union membership, check with your employer, neighbours (some credit unions serve a geographical area) or any clubs you belong to.

The US invented drive-in or drive-up banks, where Americans (who live in their cars) can obtain cash without leaving their vehicles. Some banks have auto-tellers placed at car window height while others have a complicated system of vacuum pipes, microphones and loudspeakers used to conduct business with an invisible teller. If you're unfamiliar with this method of doing business, take time to read the instructions before attempting it. You can also drive up to a window and conduct business face-to-face with a teller as you would in any bank. Drive-in banks can also be used by motorcyclists, cyclists and even pedestrians.

Nearly all banks and credit unions now offer online and telephone banking services, usually free of charge. After all, it saves them money if you do all the work yourself from your own computer! With online access, you can check your balances, preview your statements and issue stop payment orders. You can also transfer money among your accounts, pay your credit card and often pay some or all of your bills online.

In some respects, the US banking system is 'primitive' in comparison with other western nations and standards vary considerably. Many banks' business is restricted to a particular city, county or state (or a number of states). Some banks have just one branch (or even no branches at all, in the case of online banks) and many have just a few local branches. There are no nationwide banks with the vast branch networks and influence of, for example, major European banks. For many years, major banks were prohibited from interstate branching to protect smaller banks from unfair competition, although a bill passed in 1994 allowed banks to open branches anywhere in the US from 1st June 1997. Consequently, the US banking system is far less integrated than the European system.

FDIC Insurance

Because of a spate of bank failures in the 1930s, the federal government established the Federal Deposit Insurance Corporation (FDIC, 🖥 www.fdic.gov) to guarantee deposits in the event of bank failures (there's a similar insurance for savings and loan associations called the Federal Savings and Loan Insurance Corporation, the FSLIC, and the National Credit Union Administration for credit unions). The maximum amount insured in any one bank, credit union or savings association is $100,000 for a single person or $200,000 for a couple. Note, however, that deposits maintained in different rights, capacities or forms of ownership, are separately insured, so it's possible to have more than one insured account with the same insured bank, although retirement funds such as an IRA, Keogh or 401(k) plan aren't insured separately. Make sure that each separate deposit isn't more than $100,000 (or $200,000 for a joint account) and that all deposits in any financial institution are covered by the FDIC guarantee. Separate accounts in different branches of the same bank (e.g. cheque and savings accounts) are treated as **one** account for the purposes of the FDIC insurance. **Never deposit any money in a bank that isn't covered by the FDIC, FSLIC or NCUA (insured institutions must display an official sign).**

Banking Hours

Usual bank opening hours are from 9am to 5pm, Mondays to Fridays, although business hours often vary according to the bank, the branch, its location and the type of service. Most banks in urban areas provide a combination of full, teller (walk-up), drive-in (or drive-up) and lobby services, all of which may have different open hours. Full service includes a bank's total range of services and has the most restricted business hours, e.g. 9am to 3pm Mondays to Thursdays, 9am to 7pm on Fridays, and perhaps 9am to noon on Saturdays. Teller service is provided during full service hours and may also be provided for a few extra hours, e.g. 8am to 9am and 3pm to 4pm Mondays to Thursdays. Drive-in banking hours may be the longest, e.g. 8am to 6pm Mondays to Thursdays, 9am to 7pm on Fridays and 9am to 1pm on Saturdays. There's no shutdown over the lunch period in cities and large towns. All banks are closed on federal and local state holidays.

Drive-in and Saturday service is usually provided at certain branches only. In urban areas, most banks have extended business hours, until 7pm or later, on one day a week, usually a Thursday or Friday (the most common day). Saturday opening, e.g. from 9am to noon, is fairly common in large towns and cities. On the other hand, banks in small rural towns may close at 2pm or 2.30pm. Some banks are opening branches in large grocery shops ('superstores') and these branches may be open the same hours as the hosting shop, including Sundays and holidays.

There are full service banks at some airports (usually with 'standard' banking hours) and currency exchange facilities (e.g. from 7.30am to 11pm) at most international airports. Automated Teller Machines (ATMs) are provided in most terminals. Most banks have 24-hour ATMs (see page 372) at all branches or separate ATM centres for cash withdrawals and deposits, often located in shopping centres.

BANK ACCOUNTS

Most Americans are paid by cheque (hence their preoccupation with the size of their 'pay check'), bi-weekly or monthly, which they then cash or deposit in a bank account. If you want to cash a cheque, you must take it to the branch where it was drawn or a branch of the same bank (usually banks are inundated by employees cashing their pay cheques on Fridays). It's estimated that around 15 per cent of American families don't have a bank account (bankers have the same low public esteem as lawyers, politicians and used-car salesmen). If you're paid by cheque, one of your first acts should be to open an account with a bank, S&L or credit union. US employers are increasingly paying their employees' salaries directly into bank accounts (it's cheaper and easier for them than printing and distributing 'pay checks.'). Ask about 'direct deposit', even if it isn't standard practice at your place of work.

Before opening an account you should shop around among local banks and compare accounts, interest rates, services and fees. You should take note of a bank's fees (there may be 200 or more!), which have increased in the last few years and have caused considerable outrage among customers. To avoid fees, you should never overdraw your account or accept cheques from unreliable sources, and you should keep a minimum balance in the account, use your own bank's Automated Teller

Machines (ATMs) free, obtain overdraft protection (see below) and read your bank's fee-disclosure literature.

There are two main types of bank account: current accounts (known as checking accounts) and savings (deposit) accounts. Many Americans have at least two accounts, a current account for their pocket money and day-to-day transactions and a savings account. Many banks offer combined cheque and savings accounts or automatic transfers between accounts.

Current Accounts

The best type of account to open initially is a current (checking) account, which is the usual account for day-to-day financial transactions. To open an account, simply go to the bank of your choice and ask to open an account. You need a permanent address and a social security number (see page 328), although you may be asked to provide further identification such as a state identification card, driving licence or passport. You may also be asked for a reference or co-signer, although most banks waive this requirement in the never ending quest for new customers. All banks provide a range of personal and business current accounts, which usually include regular current accounts, special or basic current accounts, and NOW (and Super NOW) accounts:

Regular Account

A regular current account usually requires a minimum balance, e.g. $300 to $2,000. There's usually no charge for writing cheques and no monthly account fees and usually the account pays interest. If the balance falls below the required minimum, there's a monthly service fee, e.g. $5 to $10. This type of account may not be worthwhile unless you write at least 20 or 25 cheques per month, as you get a better rate of interest in a savings account.

Special or Basic Account

Special or basic current accounts don't require a minimum balance, but may have a monthly service fee, e.g. $5 to $10, and/or a per cheque charge of 20 cents to 35 cents. Some banks may levy a monthly service fee plus 75 cents for each transaction over a certain number (e.g. eight) in each statement period, irrespective of the account balance. A free basic account may also be available that pays no interest, but also has no monthly or transaction fees.

NOW Account

Negotiable order of withdrawal (NOW) accounts require a minimum deposit and are a combination of cheque and savings accounts, with no interest rate ceiling or floor. The interest rate is calculated on a sliding scale according to the account balance. A Super NOW account requires a higher minimum balance than a standard NOW account. Some NOW accounts require a high minimum deposit, e.g. $5,000 to $10,000, and include privileges such as no bank charges, a no-fee credit card, lower credit card interest rates, overdraft protection and a premium savings rate.

Many banks used to provide gifts (e.g. a toaster or blender), 'prizes' or goods at a discount when you opened an account (particularly for a savings account with a large minimum deposit), although gifts have largely been phased out and replaced by interest payments. Other inducements include free cheques for a number of months (or life), a free gold credit card for a year (or life), extended warranty and 90-day purchase protection, $20 off your local telephone bill and free cheques (often the first 50). Although incentives may be attractive, you shouldn't let them influence your choice of bank or the type of account you open (unless, of course, all other terms, fees and conditions are equal).

Most banks offer free cheques or accounts free of service charges (and a range of other inducements) for customers under 18 and over 55 or 65, particularly if their income is paid by direct deposit. Many banks also offer low cost current accounts, e.g. $3.50 per month and no per-cheque charges, and students may be offered accounts with no per-cheque fees or monthly service charges during the summer months. Some accounts are a combination of cheque, savings and credit card accounts and may combine the balances of cheque and savings accounts as well as other investments.

Cheques aren't provided free by banks and typically cost $10 to $20 for a box containing five pads of 20 to 25 cheques. It's cheaper to buy your cheques from a cheque printing company, such as Checks in The Mail, 2435 Goodwin Lane, New Braunfels, TX 78135 (☎ 1-866-639-2432, 🖳 http://secure.checksinthemail.com). If you use a computer program such as *Quicken* or *MS Managing Your Money*, you can also purchase cheques to print with your financial management software. Most banks return cancelled cheques (or a scanned image of the cheques) with your monthly statement. You should keep track of these cancelled cheques, as they're often needed for proof of payment or for challenging a fraudulent or erroneous cheque transaction. Some banks offer an itemised statement or cheques that produce a carbonless copy instead of returning the cancelled cheques to customers.

Cheque Usage

Although most Americans have current accounts, few banks issue cheque guarantee cards (so cheques cannot be guaranteed). Cheque theft is rife, so cheques are subject to far more scrutiny than in most other countries, and may be accepted only when drawn on a local or in-state bank, or by a business where you're known personally. Most retailers have strict rules regarding the acceptance of cheques and some businesses won't accept cheques at all, e.g. petrol stations and restaurants often have signs proclaiming loudly 'NO CHECKS'. On the other hand, in shops where you're well known you may be allowed to write a cheque for **more** than the amount of your bill and receive the difference in cash. When paying by cheque in some shops and supermarkets, you must go to a special desk and have your cheque approved before going to the checkout desk. Some shops insist that customers are issued with a store identification card (a check-cashing card) before they will accept personal cheques.

All cheques must be printed with your name and address. You also need identification, usually a state driving licence and a credit card, green card, passport, or employer or college identification card. In this age of identity theft (see page 365) you should **never** offer your social security number when writing a cheque. You may also be asked for your employer's name and telephone number, and to deposit two pints of blood until the cheque has cleared.

When writing cheques, Americans write cents as a fraction, e.g. $107.42 is written:

$$\text{One hundred and seven } \frac{42}{100}$$

When you deposit a cheque in a bank, most banks require you to endorse it with your signature or an endorsement stamp. This must be done on the back of the cheque, across the short side, just behind the left side of the front of the cheque. The entire endorsement and signature must fit in the 1.5 inch area usually indicated on the back of the cheque. Americans don't use crossed cheques; therefore it is possible for you to sign over a cheque written to you to another person (though it's not generally a good idea to do so, nor to accept cheques from others like this). To deposit a cheque in your bank account, you should precede your signature with the words 'for deposit only' and the account number in which you want the money deposited. The date is written month/day/year and not day/month/year, e.g. 12th September 2005 must be written 9/12/05 and not 12/9/05, which would be 9th December.

Foreigners should be aware that US banks are much stricter than foreign banks with regard to overdrawing current accounts, which is even illegal in some states. Many US businesses have signs stating 'All checks must have ID' and there may be others stating that a 'bounced' cheque will cost you (and the retailer) $15 to $25. If a cheque bounces, the payee will want to find you to recover the money plus administrative costs and the penalty payment charged by their bank. Most banks charge customers a fee, e.g. $5 to $25 (average $15) for each bounced cheque. Californian law makes the drawer of a bounced cheque liable to three times the face value of the cheque or $100, whichever is the greater, plus a re-presentation fee of around $20. Many banks close your account automatically after a certain number of 'bad' cheques have been written. It's even possible to go to jail for bouncing cheques (unless you're a member of Congress and use their banking facilities), e.g. in California bad cheques totalling $1,500 or a record of writing bad cheques can get you locked up. However, you can avoid a criminal record by making restitution on overdrawn cheques, paying $40 in administrative fees (plus $25 per cheque), and attending a four-hour 'bad-cheque diversion school' (similar to traffic school). The names of those whose accounts have been closed because of cheque bouncing are entered into a national database (containing details of 7.5 million accounts), and many banks refuse to open new accounts for listed cheque bouncers. Most important of all, if you bounce a cheque you may damage your credit rating (see above). Nevertheless, cheque bouncing (or 'writing rubber checks') is a national sport in the US, where some 400 million cheques are bounced annually.

All banks offer customers overdraft protection on particular accounts, thus protecting customers from 'inadvertently' bouncing cheques. Overdraft protection is sometimes linked to a credit card or savings account, where the additional funds are debited to the account holder's credit card or savings account.

After the foregoing catalogue of restrictions, suspicion and threats to your liberty, you may wonder whether it's wise to use cheques at all. They do, however, have their uses and are good for paying bills by post (such as rent and utilities) and shopping at local shops, and are accepted by most professionals.

Savings Accounts

All banks and S&Ls and various other financial institutions offer a wide range of savings accounts, most of which are intended for short or medium term savings, rather than long-term growth. Thrifts and credit unions generally offer a higher rate of interest than commercial banks, and brokerage houses may offer even higher rates of interest (but won't insure your money). When opening a savings account, the most important considerations are how much money you wish to save (which may be a lump sum or a monthly amount) and how quickly you need access to it in an emergency. It doesn't pay to keep long-term savings in a savings account if interest rates are low, when treasury securities and money market mutual funds pay higher interest.

It's often wise to have your cheque and savings accounts at the same bank, e.g. a bank may automatically transfer money from your savings account to cover an overdraft on your current account or provide a free current account if you maintain a savings account with a minimum balance, e.g. $300 to $1,000. You can also avoid fees (average around $5 per month) by keeping a minimum amount on deposit. Shop around for the best deal. All banks will transfer a fixed amount periodically or surplus cash from a current account to a savings account. Most banks also provide a range of combined cheque and savings accounts (e.g. NOW accounts – see above), where interest is paid on deposits, usually on a sliding scale according to the balance.

There are two main types of savings account: statement savings accounts and passbook savings accounts. With a statement savings account you have access to funds via ATMs (see below) and receive regular monthly or quarterly statements. With a passbook savings account, all transactions are recorded in a passbook, which must be presented to the teller each time you deposit or withdraw funds.

Tax must be declared and paid on the interest earned on most savings accounts, although there are some tax-free or tax-deferred savings accounts for special purpose savings, such as pension accounts, medical expenses and educational costs. For more information, see **Chapter 13**.

DEBIT CARDS

One of the most important innovations in banking in the last few decades has been the introduction of Automated Teller Machines (ATMs) and the ATM or debit (cash) card. A debit card allows bank account holders to withdraw money from their accounts 24 hours a day, seven days a week. The freedom from queuing, banking hours and bank tellers (who, let it be said, are usually very agreeable people) provided by debit cards is convenient, and you should think twice before opening an account with a bank that doesn't provide (lots of) local ATMs.

Usually you can withdraw a maximum of $300 daily (provided you have the money in your account) and make deposits, transfer funds between accounts, check balances and make payments at an ATM. There's no charge for using a debit card when you use an ATM at a branch of your own bank, but there's normally a charge of $1 to $3 or 2 per cent of the amount withdrawn when you use an ATM at another bank. ATMs are located in the lobbies of most banks and can also be found in shopping precincts, supermarkets, department stores, airports and railway stations.

Point of sale purchases using a debit card are often free, although some merchants add a small fee of 10 cents or 15 cents to debit card transactions. Many merchants who accept debit and credit cards now have point of sale card readers that you operate yourself rather than having the clerk or cashier handle paper forms revealing your card number. To pay for your purchases, you 'swipe' the card (draw the magnetic strip through a track that allows the machine to read it) and then indicate whether this is a debit or credit card. (Some cards can be used either way.) If you're using a debit card, you enter your personal identification number (PIN) to validate the sale. Credit or charge cards require your signature.

ATMs are linked into networks, allowing customers of different banks to draw cash from machines in major cities across the country. All banks have their own network of ATMs and most are linked with other domestic networks (e.g. Cirrus, Exchange, Honor, Mac, Nyce, Plus, Presto, Pulse and Star) and abroad (e.g. Cirrus). Cirrus (owned by MasterCard) is the largest North American network with over 500,000 ATMs worldwide. Your bank can provide you with a listing of ATM sites in any region of the country or abroad and this information is readily available on the internet on the network company and bank websites.

When using ATMs abroad, you receive the wholesale bank exchange rate, which is a better rate than you can get over the counter anywhere. If possible, you should use a debit card that allows you to tap into a cheque or savings account, rather than a credit card which incurs interest on cash advances and a hefty fee. However, never rely solely on ATMs to obtain cash, as they can be fickle things and may not accept your card or may even 'swallow' it. Sometimes your card may be rejected by a machine in one city and accepted by a machine of the same network in another city.

For security reasons, you should destroy your PIN as soon as you've memorised it and never write it down. Don't keep a lot of money in an account for which you have a debit card and **never** have a debit card for a savings account with a large balance. Don't use ATMs in 'high risk' areas at night, as muggings occasionally occur. If you lose your debit card, you must notify the issuing bank as soon as possible to avoid being held responsible for transactions made by others. Provided that you report the missing card promptly, your liability is normally limited to around $50.

CREDIT & CHARGE CARDS

Credit and charge cards are referred to collectively as credit cards, although only 'bank' cards such as MasterCard and Visa, and store cards such as Discover (created by Sears, Roebuck & Co.), are 'real' credit cards where the balance can be paid over a period of time. Cards such as American Express, Carte Blanche and Diners Club are charge or 'convenience' cards, where you must pay the full balance owed when you receive your monthly statement (usually within 30 days). However, most charge cards operate an extended payment plan for air travel and other prepaid travel arrangements. The other major difference is that credit card holders have a credit limit, while charge cards usually have no limit (or a much higher limit) on the amount that can be 'borrowed' in any month.

Credit and charge cards are widely used (Americans are born clutching a credit card and the average person has eight). Before issuing a credit or charge card, card companies require an assurance that you won't disappear owing them a fortune and they check your bank, your employer and credit bureaux to ensure that you're credit worthy (see **Credit Rating** on page 364). To qualify for a credit or charge card you must usually earn a minimum of $15,000 per year and must have been employed with the same company for two or three years. It's often difficult for newcomers to obtain credit or charge cards, even when they have excellent references or have previously held cards in another country. New arrivals should enquire at their bank or employer to see if there are any options for securing a major credit card. Some employers issue company credit cards, or the bank may be able to arrange for a credit card with a low credit limit or higher rate of interest for use during your first year.

You can apply for a MasterCard or Visa card from your bank or from any bank in the country, whether or not you have an account there, but American Express and Diners Club applications must be made direct to the card companies. If your application is approved, you usually receive your card within two to four weeks. You can obtain as many credit and charge cards as you wish, although you should bear in mind the annual fees, e.g. $40 to $65 for charge cards. The annual fees for MasterCards and Visa cards vary considerably, e.g. from zero to $50, with the average around $20. Cards with annual fees often charge lower interest rates than those without annual fees. Only two things matter when obtaining credit cards, the card's annual fee and its interest rate, **so shop around for the best deal you can find**. If you know that you're able to pay off the balance each month, you should choose a card with no annual fee and offering other benefits.

Some banks charge interest on credit cards from the purchase date, so even if you pay off the total owed each month you still incur interest charges. Interest is usually charged at a high annual rate, e.g. three or four times the current savings rate. As a response to the demand for lower interest rates, many banks have lowered their rates, although the average is still around 15 per cent higher than the rate banks pay to borrow money. Most cards have a grace period of 20 to 25 days for repayment, and charge fees (or increase interest rates) for late payment and overstepping your credit limit. RAM Research Cardtrak publishes reports and newsletters about credit cards and credit card offers. Their website includes a credit card search feature and you can even apply for some of the cards online from their website. (PO Box 1700, Frederick, MD 21702, ☎ 301-631-9100, 🖳 www.cardweb.com).

When using a credit card in the US, you may be subject to a more rigorous check than in other countries. For example, you may be asked for further identification (e.g. a driving licence or other photo ID) and some banks encourage you to have your photo put on your card. Many shop clerks are extremely lax about checking signatures or bothering to look at the photo, which makes it easy for crooks to use stolen cards. (If the crook decides to use your card on the internet, though, even a photo on the card won't help.) Keep all receipts (print off the transaction confirmation when buying online) and check them against your credit card statements, as dishonest businesses may add a digit or two to their copy of the sales receipt or use your card number for other transactions.

You can use MasterCard and Visa cards to obtain cash from ATMs and banks displaying the MasterCard or Visa symbol (Discover Card holders can obtain cash advances at over 500 locations nationwide). MasterCard and Visa customers can also obtain cash advances at over 65,000 ATMs and participating banks worldwide. Banks levy an additional fee (e.g. around $3) for cash advances and interest charges start from the moment the cash leaves the machine. It's normally much cheaper to use your debit card (see **Debit Cards** above) provided you have money in your bank account.

American Express and Diners Club cards allow you to cash personal cheques and buy travellers' cheques for limited sums, and provide free travel, car rental collision damage waiver (CDW) and luggage insurance. Many MasterCard and Visa cards also provide free travel accident insurance and some cards provide a free 90-day insurance against accidental damage to purchases, extended warranties, and price protection schemes. In addition to standard cards, most banks issue 'gold' and 'platinum' cards offering additional services and extra 'status', although there's usually a fee of $50 to $75 per year and cards are seldom worth the extra cost.

Many credit and charge cards participate in bonus or points schemes, such as 'frequent flyer' schemes, where cardholders earn air miles each time they use their cards (see page 248), and Visa's 'rewards' scheme, where customers receive points exchangeable for credits on travel, brand-name goods and discounts at department stores. Often 1,000 to 5,000 bonus miles are awarded just for signing up with a card company. However, before obtaining any credit or charge card, compare the annual fee, interest rates, interest-free credit period and benefits, as you may pay heavily for such incentive schemes. Card companies can cut back on card privileges at any time.

Credit and charge cards can be used to purchase goods by mail or over the telephone, in the US and abroad. However, when you use your card in this way, you're open to all sorts of problems, including non-delivery, faulty goods, problems regarding cancelled goods and fraud, to name but a few. See **Mail-order & Internet Shopping** on page 492 for details.

If you lose a credit or charge card or it's stolen and you report the loss before it's used, the card company cannot hold you responsible for any subsequent unauthorised charges. If a thief uses your card before you report it, your liability is limited to $50. You can register all your cards with a card security club for a few dollars a month. If your cards are stolen, a telephone call to the club ensures that all your cards are cancelled and that new cards are issued. You should keep a list of the numbers of all your credit and charge cards and keep it separately from the cards. If you lose a card, report it immediately to the police and the issuing office (e.g. bank or shop – the phone number is usually indicated on your monthly bill) or telephone the 24-hour, toll-free number provided by the card company, e.g. American Express (☎ 1-800-221-7282), Carte Blanche or Diners Club (☎ 1-800-234-6377), Citicorp (☎ 1-800-645-6556), Discover (☎ 1-800-347-2683), MasterCard

(☎ 1-800-622-7747) and Visa (☎ 1-800-336-8472). Obtain the name of the person to whom you reported the loss and note the date and time of the call. Confirm the loss as soon as possible in writing.

Even if you don't like plastic money and shun any form of credit, credit cards do have their uses and anyone in the US without a number of them is considered financially unreliable. They can be used to pay many people who don't usually accept credit cards in other countries, such as doctors, dentists or hospitals, post offices, taxis, cinemas, car parks, fast-food restaurants and telephone companies. Note, however, that not all businesses and professionals accept cards. Many inexpensive (budget) shops and businesses don't accept credit cards in order to keep their costs to a minimum. Some outlets, e.g. petrol stations and restaurants may accept one card only (always the one you don't have!). The credit cards most widely accepted in the US are Visa and MasterCard, although you should always check before making a purchase (particularly if you have no cash or travellers' cheques). Many restaurants and shops have a minimum spending level, below which they won't accept payment with a credit card. Car hire companies and hotels may 'block off' hundreds of dollars of credit on your credit card (thus reducing your available credit) as a safeguard against non-payment of bills and theft or damage to a vehicle or your room.

Other benefits of credit and charge cards include no deposits on hire cars, no pre-paying hotel bills (plus guaranteed bookings), obtaining cash abroad (at a cost), simple telephone, mail-order and internet payments, safety and security (compared to carrying large amounts of cash), and above all, convenience. They're also useful for separating company and private expenses for tax purposes. All major purchases can be paid with one cheque each month or can be paid directly from a bank account.

In the wrong hands, credit cards are a disaster and they should be avoided by anyone who's reckless with money (e.g. politicians). Non-profit credit counselling is available in most regions from the Consumer Credit Counseling Service, whose services may include paying your creditors each month, in the same way as a debt consolidation service (but without any charges). For information about non-profit credit counselling services, contact the National Foundation for Consumer Credit, 801 Roeder Road, Suite 900, Silver Springs, MD 20910-3713 (☎ 301-589-5600, 💻 www.nfcc.org). Compulsive spenders can obtain help from Debtors Anonymous, PO Box 920888, Needham, MA 02492-0009 (☎ 781-453-2743, 💻 www.debtorsanonymous.org).

LOANS

When you need a loan, it pays to shop around, as many borrowers pay too much interest. Interest rates vary considerably according to the bank, the amount borrowed, the period of the loan, and most importantly, whether the loan is secured or unsecured. A secured loan, where you must provide collateral (e.g. stocks, bonds or home equity – see below) as a guarantee against defaulting on the repayments, is cheaper than an unsecured loan. Your bank may offer you an overdraft facility or 'revolving credit line' (often linked to a cheque or savings account) that can be used when required and is free until you use it. Loans are also possible through life assurance policies and 401(k) pension plans. You can usually borrow against 75 to 90 per cent of the cash-value of an insurance policy and up to half of your vested account balance in a 401(k) plan, up to a maximum of $50,000. This is often the most economical way to borrow, as the interest rate is usually only 1 per cent above the prime rate. Besides banks, insurance companies and employee pension plans, there are a whole host of private lenders ready and willing to lend you money, offering various terms, conditions and collection methods.

The rate of interest charged on loans in the US is quoted as the Annual Percentage Rate (APR). This is an annual rate that relates the total finance charge to the amount of credit you receive and the length of time you have to repay it. All interest rates on goods must, according to federal law, quote an APR figure so that you're able to instantly compare rates. However, as the rules for calculating the APR aren't clearly defined, different lenders calculate them in different ways. Therefore, although it pays to shop around and compare APRs for loans (which vary considerably), you should also ask what each lender's fees are. It may be unnecessary to have an account with a bank or thrift to obtain a loan from them. If interest rates drop, you may be able to save money by refinancing a loan, resulting in considerable savings over the term of the loan.

One of the most popular forms of loan in recent years has been home equity or home-secured loans (or a second mortgage). With a home equity loan, you take out a loan based on the equity in your home, calculated by deducting any outstanding mortgage debt from your home's current value. Banks loan 75 or 80 per cent of the equity value of your home, although some banks have lowered their limits to 50 or 60 per cent in recent years. Many homeowners have a home equity 'line of credit', allowing them to borrow against the equity in their home at any time. One big advantage of home equity loans is that the interest is usually tax deductible. A disadvantage of home equity loans is that you can end up paying much more in interest over the longer term of the new loan. A home equity loan can be a good way to pay off all your other debts, **provided you stop all other borrowing!**

Homeowners can also take out a reverse mortgage loan, which, like an equity loan, is for a homeowner who wants to take money out of his property. Reverse mortgage loans are targeted at elderly homeowners who need income. Loans don't need to be repaid until a house is sold, e.g. after the owner has died or moved into a nursing home. Because of the high closing costs associated with equity and reverse mortgage loans (possibly thousands of dollars), a loan should be large enough to justify the fees. If you default on a loan where your home is the security, **you could lose your home!**

No matter where you take out a loan, make sure you understand the terms you're agreeing to and always read the fine print! Private lenders and finance companies aren't regulated like banks and insurance companies are, and often charge high rates of interest or outrageous 'loan initiation fees.' although many of these are legal and valid lenders, others are scam artists or loan sharks. Loan scams are often advertised under 'Money to Lend' or similar headings in newspaper and magazine advertisement columns, usually using (expensive) 900 numbers. If you're dubious about a loan broker or scheme, contact your local consumer-protection office or Better Business Bureau for advice or to check a 'lender's' credibility. In general, the more desperate your financial situation, the more suspicious you should be of anyone who's willing to lend you money (except your mum!).

MORTGAGES

Mortgages (home loans) in the US are available from a number of sources, including savings and loan associations (who provide over half of all mortgages), commercial banks, credit unions, mortgage bankers, insurance companies, builders and developers, and government agencies. Mortgages comprise almost 80 per cent of savings and loan business, compared with around 30 per cent of commercial banks' business. (Savings and loan associations are, by law, required to make mortgages at least 60 per cent of their business.)

Most US lenders won't lend more than 70 or 80 per cent of the market value of a property to non-residents (residents may be able to borrow up to 95 per cent), meaning that if you want to buy a $100,000 home, you must usually find a deposit (down payment) of at least $20,000. If you pay less than a 20 per cent deposit, most mortgage lenders insist that you have a mortgage life insurance or private mortgage insurance (PMI) policy. This pays off the outstanding balance on your mortgage if you die before the end of the term. PMI normally costs between $30 and $60 per month, but can usually be cancelled once a certain amount of a mortgage has been repaid. Overseas buyers must normally make a deposit equivalent to between three and six months' mortgage payments.

Lenders evaluate a property to confirm its value and check your credit rating (see page 364), employment history, income, assets, residence and liabilities. You should check your own credit rating before applying for a mortgage, to make sure there isn't anything that could adversely affect your application.

The maximum amount you can borrow depends on your income. Most lenders insist that a mortgage is no more than three times your annual salary or that monthly repayments are no more than around 30 per cent of your gross monthly income. When calculating how large a mortgage you can afford, take into account all closing costs, which average 3 to 6 per cent of the sale price of a property and depend on its location, cost and other factors. 'Non-income status' mortgages of 65 to 70 per cent with no proof of income or tax returns are also available, although borrowers usually require a significant amount of money in savings or investments. It's often difficult or more expensive to raise finance for an American property from abroad. It takes between 30 and 90 days to arrange an American mortgage, depending on its complexity.

The sort of mortgage deal you're able to negotiate depends on a number of factors, not least the state of the housing and money markets. Lenders usually charge a fee for granting a mortgage, expressed as a number of points, each of which is equal to 1 per cent of the loan amount. In a competitive market you may be offered a mortgage with no points. However, when there's a glut of buyers looking for loans, you're charged a fee of one to four points, which can increase the cost of your mortgage considerably. To attract new customers, lenders may offer inducements such as below-market interest rates (or interest-free for the first year), exceptional long-term loans, discounts, rebates and give-aways (gifts), most of which don't provide real savings or long-term advantages. Transferable (assumable) mortgages, which can be sold with a property, are often an attractive proposition, and it's possible to assume an existing fixed-rate mortgage, which is a good deal if the interest rate is lower than the current market rate.

If interest rates drop, you may be able to save money by refinancing a loan, resulting in considerable savings over the term of the loan. Refinancing is generally worthwhile only when the interest rate on your mortgage is at least 2 per cent higher than the prevailing market rate. It can take months to refinance a home loan and you must take into account all associated fees and other payments. Refinancing costs usually range from 4.5 to 5 per cent of your mortgage value, so it may not be worthwhile if you have only a small mortgage.

Interest rates fell dramatically in the US during the last couple of years, hitting 40 year lows in early 2004. A combination of factors has led to a turnaround, though, and rates began slowly climbing in the months before the 2004 elections. Rates vary slightly by region, but on a typical 30-year fixed-rate mortgage, the average rate in mid-2004 was 5.75 per cent and the average on a 15-year fixed-rate mortgage was 5.14 per cent. Average interest rates apply only to so-called 'conforming' mortgages, which can be resold through the government's mortgage repurchase agencies, a sort of 'insurance' for home mortgages. The maximum for a conforming mortgage was $333,700 as of September 2004. Mortgages for more than this limit are called jumbo mortgages, and generally incur an extra 0.25 to 0.5 per cent interest to compensate for the increased risk. **Shop around for the best deal you can find (including closing services and all costs).** The Real Estate section of most Sunday newspapers carries listings of current mortgage rates in the area and there are a number of websites that connect you with lenders according to your requirements such as HSH Associates, a financial publisher (🖥 www.hsh.com). Using the services of a mortgage search company or an independent mortgage broker is another way to find a good mortgage deal, or you can search the internet (e.g. 🖥 www.eloan.com).

You should take time to investigate all the options available, taking into account your present and probable future income. Note, however, that although salaries increase, your higher income may be swallowed up by a larger family, inflation and higher interest rates. Generally the more money you put down as a deposit, the more choice you have. Be sure to check if you can pay off a loan early (called accelerating payment) and reduce your interest.

Mortgage Period

The traditional American mortgage period is 30 years, although lenders also offer 10 or 15-year fixed-rate mortgages, requiring a higher deposit or higher monthly repayments than a 30-year mortgage (or sometimes both). If you can afford the repayments, a 10 or 15-year mortgage can save you a considerable amount in interest compared with a 30-year mortgage. For example, monthly repayments on a 15-year $100,000 mortgage at 10 per cent would be $1,075, compared with $878 over a 30-year period – a difference of $197 per month or $35,460 over the 15-year term. However, the 15-year mortgage would result in interest savings of $122,580 over the period of the loan at a flat 10 per cent. In fact, a 15-year mortgage is usually offered at a slightly lower interest rate (e.g. a 0.25 to 0.75 per cent reduction) than a 30-year mortgage, meaning you make even greater savings.

The most common types of mortgage in the US are fixed-rate mortgages and adjustable-rate mortgages (ARMs).

Fixed-Rate Mortgage

This is the traditional American mortgage where the interest rate is fixed, irrespective of whether interest rates go up or down, and can be repaid over 10, 15, 20 or 30 years (see **Mortgage Period** above). It's paid off in equal monthly payments comprising principal and interest (called amortisation), until the debt is paid in full. A fixed-rate mortgage offers stability and long-term tax advantages, although interest rates are initially higher than with an adjustable-rate mortgage. A fixed-rate mortgage may not be assumable, i.e. a buyer won't be able to take over the seller's original below-market rate mortgage. If your income is fixed or rises slowly, you're generally better off with a fixed-rate mortgage, although some people don't qualify because their income is too low. With a low interest rate, experts recommend taking a fixed-rate mortgage.

Adjustable-Rate Mortgage

With an Adjustable-Rate Mortgage (ARM), the interest rate is adjusted over the life of the mortgage, resulting in changes in monthly repayments, the loan term and/or the principal. Payments usually change periodically, normally once a year or once every six months, with changes in interest rates based on a specified index, such as US Treasury securities or state and national inflation indices. An ARM is initially available at a lower interest rate than a fixed-rate mortgage. You should choose an ARM with a ceiling or cap on the rate of interest that can be charged (irrespective of how high the index goes). Caps can be annual or over the full period of the mortgage. Generally, an ARM's rate cannot rise or fall more than 2 percentage points per year or six points over the loan's life. Note, however, that if interest rates rise considerably, a cap may cause negative amortisation, where the balance on the loan increases instead of reduces, despite the fact that you're making maximum monthly payments.

An ARM is a good choice for someone who expects his income to rise sufficiently to offset the likely higher repayments. When comparing the cost of an ARM with a fixed-rate mortgage, bear in mind that an increase of just 1 per cent in the interest rate, e.g. from 7 to 8 per cent, on a $100,000 mortgage, costs $75 per month or around $27,000 over 30 years. Most ARMs can be converted to fixed-rate mortgages.

There are also other types of mortgage available, including:

Two-Step Mortgage

A two-step mortgage is a 30-year mortgage whose rate adjusts once only, after five or seven years, the initial rate being around half a point lower than a fixed-rate loan.

Low Deposit Mortgage

For those who cannot afford the 20 per cent deposit required by most lenders, the federal government provides mortgages insured by the Federal Housing Authority (FHA) for deposits of as little as 3 per cent. The Federal National Mortgage Association (popularly known as Fannie Mae) is a government-created corporation whose purpose is to make home loans available to low and moderate-income families. It doesn't lend money to consumers, but buys mortgages from a national network of 4,000 approved lenders and specialises in 15-year mortgages. A 20 per cent deposit is normally required or private mortgage insurance covering up to 20 per cent of a property's value, although loans with a 3 per cent deposit are now available to low-income families. The FCIC (see **Appendix C**) has a booklet on the FHA program, *Guide to Single-Family Home Mortgage Insurance*, available for $1 by post or free on their website.

Bi-weekly Mortgage

The normal repayment frequency for mortgages is monthly. However, one of the most popular forms of mortgage in recent years has been the bi-weekly mortgage, where payments are made every two weeks (most Americans are paid bi-weekly). The big advantage of a bi-weekly mortgage is that a loan that usually takes 30 years to amortise is paid off in 19 to 21 years when paid on a bi-weekly basis. The reason is that bi-weekly payments (26 a year) are equivalent to 13 monthly payments, meaning the loan is paid off much faster and resulting in significant interest savings. The bi-weekly mortgage (for all its financial benefits) costs around one monthly payment (i.e. 8 per cent) more per year than a monthly fixed-rate mortgage, but the extra amount is evenly distributed throughout the year.

Interest rates for bi-weekly mortgages are usually similar to those for standard 30-year, fixed-rate mortgages. However, because repayments of a bi-weekly mortgage are slightly higher than for a 30-year, fixed-rate mortgage, income requirements are usually higher. Mortgage payments for a bi-weekly mortgage are made directly from your bank account, so if you're paid bi-weekly, your payments correspond to the deposit of your pay cheque.

Other Mortgages

There are many other types of mortgage, including a balloon, re-negotiable rate (roll-over), graduated-payment, purchase money, shared-appreciation, shared-equity, seller take-back, wraparound, growing-equity, land contract, buy-down, reverse-annuity, convertible and rent with option (where a renter has the option to buy at a specified time and price). These 'creative financing' mortgages are usually offered in times of high interest rates and tight money and may not be offered when mortgages are readily available.

A wealth of information is published about buying homes and obtaining mortgages in the US. Most banks can provide you with a variety of government booklets and publications, and the US Government web portal (see **Appendix C**) can guide you to information available online. Books available include *The Field Guide to Home Buying in the US* by Stephan M. Pollan and Mark Levine.

INCOME TAX

In the US, you may have to pay more than one form of income tax. Everyone is liable for federal income tax (see below); in some states you must also pay state income tax (see page 391), and in certain cities or counties, local income taxes as well. US federal income tax is levied on the worldwide income of US citizens and resident foreigners, and on certain types of US income of non-resident foreigners. If you earn income in the US, you may need to file a US income tax return even if you're only visiting the country. If you're a non-resident foreigner (alien) and you work or are engaged in a trade or business in the US, you must file a tax return (form 1040NR) irrespective of the amount of income or whether it's exempt from US tax. Some tax laws that apply to non-residents are different from those that apply to resident foreigners. Generally, non-residents are taxed only on income from sources in the US. You're classified as a non-resident foreigner if you aren't a US citizen and you don't meet the 'alien registration card (green card) test' or the 'substantial presence test'.

Under the 'green card' test, you're a lawful permanent resident of the US for tax purposes if you had a green card at any time during the previous tax year (January to December). Under the substantial presence test, you're liable for US federal income tax if you spend more than 31 days in the US during the current year **and** a total of 183 'qualifying' days (six months) during the current year and the two previous years. All days spent in the US in the current year qualify towards the 183-day total, but only a third of the number of days spent in the previous year and a sixth of the number of days in the year before qualify. For example, if you spent 90 days in the current year, e.g. 2004, these are counted in full. In the previous year, i.e. 2003, you spent 120 days in the country, a third of which is 40; in the preceding year of 2002, you spent 60 days, a sixth of which is 10. The sum for 2002 to 2004 would therefore be 10+40+90, a total of 140 days, or 43 days fewer than the necessary 183 days. In other words, a presence of 122 days in each of three consecutive years satisfies the substantial presence test.

During the year you arrive in or depart from the US, you may have dual status and be a non-resident and a resident foreigner, when special rules apply. This subject is described at length in IRS publication 519, *US Tax Guide for Aliens*, available free from any IRS office or via the IRS website (🖥 www.irs.gov).

If there's any doubt, the Internal Revenue Service (IRS) may use 'intention' as a yardstick for establishing your country of domicile and therefore who gets your taxes. The US has tax treaties with many countries to prevent people paying double taxes. Under tax treaties, certain categories of people are exempt from paying US tax or qualify for benefits, including short-stay visitors, teachers and professors, employees of foreign governments, trainees, students and apprentices. Treaties also cover the payment of capital gains tax (see page 394). If part of your income is taxed abroad in a country with a treaty with the US, you won't usually need to pay US tax on that income. Contact your nearest IRS district office for information about your

US tax obligations. Even if you aren't liable for US taxes, you may have to complete a tax return, e.g. a 'non-resident alien' return (form 1040NR).

Reducing your tax burden is a national sport and an obsession in the US, where a wealth of tax books, magazines and free advice in financial magazines and newspapers is published, particularly during the few months leading up to April 15th (tax filing day). The best selling tax guides include the *Ernst & Young Tax Guide*, and J.K. Lasser's *Your Income Tax* (John Wiley & Sons). Cheaper magazine-style guides include the World Almanac's *Cut Your Own Taxes and Save*. All tax guides (and computer programs) are updated annually and are tax deductible.

In addition to US taxes, you may also be liable to tax in your home country, although citizens of most countries are exempt from paying taxes in their home country when they spend a minimum period abroad, e.g. one year. If you're in doubt about your tax liability in your home country or country of domicile, check with your country's embassy in the US (see page 554).

Federal Income Tax

The US now has six rates of federal income tax, 10 15, 25, 28, 33, and 35 per cent, the top rate being one of the lowest in the industrial world (although state and local taxes must be added in most states). With the reduction in top tax rates during the '80s, the tax burden was shifted from corporations and the rich to the middle class. At the other end of the scale, more than 6 million people with incomes below the poverty level pay no tax at all. Despite the relatively low upper tax rates, the top-earning 5 per cent of taxpayers pay over 50 per cent of the federal income tax bill. The tax system was supposed to have been simplified and rationalised under any number of major tax reforms over the last twenty years, but each administration wants to add its own distinctive 'improvements' to the system. The latest changes have been three successive tax cuts passed in 2001, 2002 and 2003 by the Bush Administration, which were supposed to be designed to jump-start a sluggish economy and generate more jobs. Critics contend the cuts unfairly benefit the rich, and that the true cost of the tax cut plan was kept from Congress before the measures were voted upon. One new and complicating factor, introduced in the Bush tax cuts, is the notion of the 'Sunset Rule.' Rather than simply changing the tax law, as has been done in the past, many provisions of the tax cut were enacted into law for a limited period of time, like a trial period. If Congress doesn't act to renew these sections of the law, they're set to expire after 2, 5 or 10 years, with the law going back to what it was before. Everyone claims that Congress will certainly act in time to make the cuts permanent, but they've been known to miss these sorts of deadlines before.

One yardstick used to compare the average US citizen's tax burden with that of previous years is 'tax freedom day', the day of the year on which the average person has earned enough to pay his federal taxes. Tax freedom day had become progressively later each year since 1993 when it was 18th April. By 2001, it was 3rd May. Aided by the Bush tax cuts (although affected by many other factors), Tax Freedom Day has been brought back to 11th April in 2004, the earliest since 1967. (For further information go to the Tax Foundation's internet site, 🖥 www. taxfoundation.com).

The agency responsible for the administration of federal tax laws and the collection of taxes is the Internal Revenue Service (IRS), part of the US Treasury Department. In the US, your employer is responsible for deducting income tax from your salary (called withholding) and paying it to the IRS. The rate of withholding depends on your income and the information you give your employer on form W-4, *Employee's Withholding Allowance Certificate*. The amount withheld is credited against the tax owed when you file your US tax return (see page 388). The US tax system is based on self-assessment, which, although it requires a smaller bureaucracy than in many other countries, puts the onus on individual taxpayers. The withholding should equal 90 per cent of your tax liability for the year in question or 100 per cent of the amount paid in the previous year. If your tax withholding amounts to less than 90 per cent of your tax liability, you must usually compensate by making quarterly estimated tax payments. If you have self-employment income, you **must** make quarterly estimated tax payments (as no tax is withheld at source) by 15th April, 15th June, 15th September and 15th January.

Although the IRS are usually helpful, they have sweeping powers at their disposal and aren't slow to use them if they suspect somebody of fraud. Tax fraud is a major crime (felony) in the US and is estimated to cost as much as $150 billion annually. The IRS carries out random checks and can demand a full-scale inspection or audit of any taxpayer at any time. They can insist on receipts or other evidence to support all tax claims for the previous three years. Many people are fearful of the IRS and their imagined 'reign of terror', but as long as you aren't a crook, you have nothing to fear. Most 'little' people are extremely honest with their tax returns. It's the big fish who can afford expensive tax lawyers who 'legally' evade billions of dollars in taxes each year.

Each year the IRS selects around a million tax returns for audit or examination, and although the chance of being selected is less than 1 in a 100, if you earn over $50,000 per year or are self-employed, the odds increase significantly (so take extra care when preparing your tax return). Among the most common abuses relate to taxes on IRA deposits, Keogh plans, home offices, retirement payments and depreciation. If your return is selected for examination, it doesn't mean that the IRS suspects you of fraud, although you have a right to be alarmed, as 80 per cent of audits result in extra tax being assessed. (Only a small percentage result in a refund!) The IRS may notify you that an examination is to be conducted by interview or you can request an interview. You can have professional representation at an interview or have someone represent you in your absence. If you're found to owe additional tax, you must pay interest from the due date of your tax return, although when an IRS error caused a delay, you **may** be entitled to a reduction in the interest. Publication 566, *Examination of Returns, Appeal Rights, and Claims for Refund* explains the review process in detail.

The IRS attempts to solve tax disputes through an administrative appeals system. If you disagree with your tax bill after an audit of your tax return, you're entitled to an independent review of your case. The IRS recommends that you keep all tax documents for at least three years after filing your return. The IRS may disclose your tax information to state tax agencies (with which it has information exchange agreements), the Department of Justice and other federal agencies, and certain foreign governments under tax treaty provisions, although there are strict guidelines.

If you're a foreign US taxpayer, you must satisfy the IRS that all income tax has been paid and obtain a certificate of compliance (known as a sailing or departure permit) from the IRS before leaving the US to take up residence abroad. This is done by filing form 1040C, *US Departing Alien Income Tax Return*, or form 2063, *US Departing Alien Income Tax Statement*. For further information obtain a copy of *Tax Information for Visitors to the United States* (IRS Publication 513), the *US Tax Guide for Aliens* (519) and *US Tax Treaties* (901). Departure permits aren't required by representatives of foreign governments with diplomatic passports and employees of foreign governments or international organisations.

The IRS provides a number of toll-free hotlines, including one for tax help for individuals (☎ 1-800-829-1040) and a separate National Taxpayer Advocate service for help in resolving disputes (☎ 877-777-4778), and a postal Problem Resolution Program and walk-in tax assistance at IRS offices throughout the country. You can also call Tele-Tax (☎ 1-800-829-4477) which provides recorded information on around 140 topics of tax information. The IRS also has a variety of video and audio tapes that you can borrow for yourself or for professional or civic organisations, and publishes more than 100 free taxpayer information publications on a range of subjects, including a *Guide to Free Tax Services*, *Your Rights As A Taxpayer* and *Federal Income Tax* (covering most of what the average taxpayer needs to know). You can order IRS publications, tax forms and instructions by phoning 1-800-829-3676, writing to the IRS Forms Distribution Center (PO Box 25666, Richmond, VA 23260-5666) or downloading them from the IRS website (🖥 www.irs.gov).

Taxable Income & Rates

Your liability to file a tax return depends on your filing status, your adjusted gross income (AGI) and your age. If your AGI is **below** the income shown in the table overleaf, you don't need to file a tax return. There are certain exceptions to the standard filing status listed in the table. For example, 'married filing separate returns' cannot be used if either spouse is claimed as a dependant on another person's tax return, and anyone who receives earned income credit must file a tax return, irrespective of their gross income. For tax purposes it's your marital status on 31st December of the tax year in question that counts. If you're in the process of divorce, you may be liable for income tax even if your spouse earns all the income – unless you qualify for 'spousal relief'! A head of household is a US citizen or resident who's unmarried, but supports a child, parent or other relative. A qualifying widow(er) is one whose spouse died in either of the two years **before** the tax year in question. If your spouse died more than two years before the tax year, you may be able to use the head of household rates.

Filing Status	Gross Income ($)
Single:	
Under 65	7,950
65 or older	9,100

Married Filing Joint Return:	
Both spouses under 65	15,900
One spouse 65 or older	16,850
Both spouses 65 or older	17,800
Married Filing Separate Returns:	3,100
Head of Household:	
Under 65	10,250
65 or older	11,450
Qualifying Widow(er):	
Under 65	12,800
65 or older	14,000

A child may be claimed as dependent if he is under 19 or a full-time student under 24 irrespective of income; if he isn't a full-time student and is over 19, or if he is over 24, he can be claimed as a dependent only if he earns less than $3,100 per year. A dependent child must generally file a tax return if he has unearned income over $800 or earned income (or total income) over $4,850. A self-employed person must file a tax return if his net earnings from self-employment for the year are $400 or more.

Your tax rate depends on your salary and your marital status as shown in the table below. 'Married (Joint)' is a married couple filing jointly or a qualifying widow(er); 'Married (Separate)' is a married couple filing separately; 'Head' is a head of household.

		Income ($)		
Rate (%)	**Single**	**Married (Joint)**	**Married (Separate)**	**Head**
10	0–7,150	0–14,300	0–7,150	0–10,200
15	7,151–29,050	14,301–58,100	7,151–29,050	10,201–38,900
25	29,051–70,350	58,101–117,250	29,051–58,625	38,901–100,500
28	70,351–146,750	117,251–178,650	58,626–89,325	100,501–162,700
33	146,751–319,101	178,651–319,100	89,326–159,550	162,701–319,100
35	Over 319,100	Over 319,100	Over 159,550	Over 319,100

Not all income is taxable; some is fully taxable, some is tax exempt, and some is partially exempt. Taxable income includes: all wages; back and severance pay; interest and dividends; alimony; net income from a business or profession; property gains; annuities; social security benefits; prizes from contests, lottery and gambling winnings, rewards and royalties; income from estates, trusts and partnerships; director's and jury duty fees; rental income (e.g. from a holiday home); state unemployment compensation; sick pay; and, believe it or not, embezzled and other forms of illegal income. (Back in the roaring Twenties, the government found it was easier to catch gangsters such as Al Capone for evading taxes than for any of the crimes they had committed!!).

Income that **isn't** taxable includes: interest on tax-free securities (municipal bonds); inheritances, most life insurance proceeds and bequests; gifts (which may, however, be subject to gift tax – see page 395); scholarships and grants; workers' compensation; employer child-care allowances and child support payments; pay for voluntary work; employer health insurance (or 25 per cent of premiums paid by the self-employed) and pension plan contributions; Christmas and other employer gifts with a nominal value; and employer courtesy discounts.

Deductions & Exemptions

All taxpayers can claim a number of deductions, exemptions and allowances, commonly referred to as tax breaks, in order to reduce their tax bills. If you're married, you and your spouse may file separately or you may file a joint return. Usually, a couple saves money by filing a joint return, although in certain cases filing separately can save taxes. To find out the best method, calculate your taxes using separate and joint tax returns or consult a tax adviser. If you file separately there are a number of deductions and credits you may not take.

The most important decision all taxpayers must make is whether to itemise their deductions or choose the standard deductions. To decide the best method, make a rough calculation by totalling your itemised deductions and comparing them with the relevant standard deduction (see below). If your itemised deductions are greater than the standard deduction, you will pay less tax by itemising. If you decide to itemise, it's important to claim for **everything** that's legally deductible. If you're part of a married couple, filing separately, you cannot take the standard deduction unless your spouse does so too.

If you choose to itemise your deductions, you can make the following major deductions: state and local income and property taxes; medical and dental expenses exceeding 7.5 per cent of your AGI; interest payments and finance charges on your home mortgage and investments; contributions to qualified organisations (e.g. charities); damage and theft losses (a limited amount only); certain educational expenses for your children or yourself; and miscellaneous deductions (to the extent by which they cumulatively exceed 2 per cent of your AGI). Employees may also deduct a range of business expenses (to the extent that the total exceeds 2 per cent of AGI) such as meals and entertainment, business travel, car expenses, and the upkeep of a home office. You may also deduct moving expenses, depreciation, losses on loans and worthless securities.

Home ownership enjoys strong tax advantages over all other forms of investment, as the interest charges on a mortgage and property taxes can be deducted from your taxable income, and you can also avoid paying capital gains tax when you sell your home (see page 394). In the early years of a mortgage, most of the monthly payment is interest, so almost the entire payment is deductible when you itemise deductions on your income tax. Keep records of all home improvements, because when you sell your home the cost of improvements increases your tax cost (basis) in the property and decreases your capital gains tax liability. If you sell your home, you must complete a *Sale of Your Home* form (2119) when you complete your 1040 tax form.

Instead of itemising your deductions, you may choose to take a standard deduction (as shown in the table below). If you're blind or aged over 64, you're entitled to additional standard deductions: single people and heads of households receive an extra $1,200 ($2,400 if over 64 **and** blind), and married taxpayers filing jointly or separately and qualified widow(er)s, an extra $950 ($1,900 if over 64 **and** blind) each.

Filing Status	Standard Deduction ($)
Single or married filing separately	4,850
Married filing jointly	9,700
Head of household	7,150

If you're claimed as a dependant on another taxpayer's return, e.g. children who are claimed as dependants on their parents' return, your standard deduction is limited to the greater of $800 or your earned income plus $250, up to the normal standard deduction amount.

An exemption for each dependant is available to taxpayers with AGI under certain limits. For 2004, taxpayers were allowed to claim $3,100 for each dependant (including their spouse if filing jointly). You cannot take the exemption for yourself if you're claimed as a dependent on someone else's return. Each individual you claim as a dependent must have their own social security number or taxpayer identification number, even babies born on the 31st December. A tax credit of $1000 can also be claimed for each dependent child under 17 (plus an additional credit if you have more than three children under 17).

Tax Return

If you're an employee and receive wages subject to US income tax withholding, you must complete a tax return. If you're an employee, the amount of tax due is compared with the tax withheld by your employer and the difference is payable or refunded. If you want to receive a refund, don't forget to tell the IRS if you move home! Tax forms are available from libraries, government offices and IRS offices, or the IRS may send you a form. All forms are available for download from the IRS website (🖳 www.irs.gov). Public libraries provide a variety of information resources to assist taxpayers with preparing federal, state and city tax returns. People who have difficulty reading the print on IRS documents can obtain large-print versions of the most common tax forms (☎ 1-800-829-3676). These forms are only intended for reference use, not for filing.

There are a number of different tax forms, depending on your income and the complexity of your tax affairs. The blue 1040 'long' form is the standard tax form, comprising many separate forms, although few taxpayers need to complete them all. There are also two short forms, the pink 1040A and the green 1040EZ (EZ stands for 'easy'), which the IRS estimates can be used by one in three taxpayers. The 1040A form can be used by individuals and couples of any age whose taxable income after deductions and exemptions is below $50,000 and who take the standard deduction rather than itemise. It allows you a bit more flexibility than the 1040EZ form, e.g. divided income, estimated income tax payments, IRA contributions and claims for dependants. The 1040EZ is for single people and married couples filing jointly who are under 65 (and not blind), take the standard deduction, have no dependants and report less than $50,000 of taxable income. Income must be of the most straightforward type, e.g. wages, tips, and a maximum of $1500 in interest earnings.

Most people can complete the 1040A and 1040EZ forms without professional help, although this shouldn't influence your decision to use either of these forms, as using them may cost you money. When using a short form, make sure that it allows you to include all your deductions. Anyone who itemises deductions, reports income or losses from capital gains, deducts expenses for running a business, has sold a home, receives alimony, or who earns $50,000 or more, **must** file the 1040 long form.

Most people find completing the 1040 long form a complicated and irksome task, and over 55 per cent employ some kind of professional help, e.g. a tax preparation service, an enrolled agent (an expert certified by the Treasury Department), a certified public accountant (CPA) or a tax lawyer. The best way to find a qualified professional is through a recommendation from a friend, relative or business associate. Fees vary considerably, for example the fee charged by H&R Block, the leading chain of tax preparation services, is less than $100, while a lawyer's fees can run into thousands of dollars. Enrolled agents' and CPAs' fees average around $200 to $500 depending on the complexity of your situation. The advantage of using an enrolled agent or CPA is that he is professionally accountable for his actions and must pass rigorous examinations. As with all professional services, the size of the fee is determined by the complexity of your return and the number of forms prepared. The most appropriate professional isn't the least expensive, but the one who best meets your tax requirements. You should be wary of using anyone other than a reputable company or professional to complete your return, as anyone can set himself up as a tax 'expert'. Note, however, that whoever you choose, most tax preparers are unable to complete totally error-free returns!

The IRS has been encouraging online filing of taxes (e-filing) for several years now. (And why shouldn't they? It's less work for them in terms of data entering your information and having to check your calculations for errors!) Many professional tax preparers can e-file your taxes for you, which can result in a quicker refund if you have one due you and it's now possible to make your tax payment online using a credit card. If you have a home computer, you may prefer to complete your own 1040 tax return using a program (the cost of which is tax deductible) such as *Tax Cut*, *TurboTax* or *TaxAct*. Several tax software vendors make their tax return programs available for free over the internet as part of the effort to encourage e-filing (although they may make a charge for e-filing the resulting return, usually around $10 to $15). The IRS estimates that 60 per cent of individual taxpayers are eligible for the free online e-filing services. Be sure to check the IRS website if you're considering using any of the free online services to make sure you're dealing with an authorised e-filing vendor. There are reports of scam artists luring taxpayers to bogus IRS or tax filing websites, where they then harvest social security numbers, bank account information and other financial data for identity theft purposes.

Tax returns are sent to taxpayers at the beginning of the year and should be completed and returned to the appropriate office by April 15th for the previous tax year (January to December). If you're a non-resident foreigner, your tax return for the previous year is due by 15th June. In certain cases you can establish a tax year other than the calendar year. You can obtain an extension (until August 15th) by submitting form 4868, *Application for Automatic Extension of Time to File US Individual Income Tax Return*, sought by around 5 per cent of taxpayers or more than 6 million people. **However, this isn't an extension of time to pay your taxes, which must still be paid by midnight on April 15th.** If you apply for an extension, you should estimate your tax obligations and pay the amount owed. If you're unable to pay by April 15th, you must pay interest for the period from April 15th until the tax is paid and possibly a late payment penalty. If you underestimate the amount due, you must pay interest and must also pay a penalty if the unpaid amount is more than 10 per cent of your tax for the year. If you apply for an extension, you must use form 1040 or 1040A when you file your return (you cannot use form 1040EZ). You can also apply for a second extension, although this is granted in exceptional circumstances only.

If you don't have an extension, but cannot pay the full amount due by April 15th, pay as much as you can and file your tax form on time anyway. The penalty for filing late, as opposed to merely paying late, runs at 5 per cent per month and up to 25 per cent of your tax debt. It's usually better to borrow and pay your tax bill on time than delay paying it and pay interest and penalties. If you cannot meet the deadline for completing your tax form, file form 4868 and pay any tax due. If you're unable to pay your tax bill when you receive a balance-due notice from the IRS, you can ask to set up an instalment agreement. This is usually granted if you have a good tax payment record over the past three years and owe less than $10,000.

Before posting your tax return, check that you've signed it (you **and** your spouse must sign if filing jointly) and that your CPA or tax adviser has also signed (if applicable). Around a million people forget to sign each year! Check that your address and social security number are entered correctly, and write your social security number on each page of your return to identify them. Double check everything, including **your maths**. If you submit an unprocessable return, you can be fined $500. Attach all necessary schedules to your return and, if you owe tax, make sure you've enclosed a (signed!) cheque or money order (with your social security number written on the reverse). **Finally, photocopy all pages and attachments and retain them for at least three years.** If you've e-filed, make sure you make a copy for yourself (or receive one from your tax preparer) along with the confirmation of receipt from the IRS.

If you discover that you've made a mistake after filing your return (particularly one which will result in a refund!), you can file a form 1040X *Amended US Individual Income Tax Return*. You can file a corrected return for the previous three years only, e.g. a corrected return for 2001 must be filed before 15th April 2005 or you will lose any refund. Don't have nightmares about the IRS; the worst they can do is bankrupt you and seize your home. You cannot get the death penalty for tax evasion – yet.

State & Local Income Tax

State income tax rates vary considerably from state to state, although guidelines are set by the federal government. Several states (Alaska, Florida, Nevada, New Hampshire, South Dakota, Tennessee, Texas, Washington and Wyoming) have no state income tax, and in New Hampshire and Tennessee state income tax applies only to dividends and interest income. In Rhode Island, state income tax is levied at 25 per cent of the federal income tax rate. Some of the remaining 38 states levy a flat rate, which favours the wealthy, although many have been making their income tax more progressive in recent years, levying higher taxes on those with higher incomes. The following table shows the taxes charged by these states, as well as the personal exemptions applicable. These are individual tax rates and there are sometimes reductions for couples. Where the amount under personal exemption is marked with a letter 'c', it is a tax credit rather than an exemption.

| State | Rates (per cent) | | | Income Brackets | | Personal Exemption ($) | | |
	Low	High	No.	Low ($)	High ($)	Single	Married	Child
Alabama	2.0	5.0	3	500	3,000	1,500	3,000	300
Arizona	2.87	5.04	5	10,000	150,000	2,100	4,200	2,300
Arkansas	1.0	7.0	6	3,999	27,500	20c	40c	20c
California	1.0	9.3	6	5,962	39,133	80c	160c	251c
Colorado	4.63	4.63	1	Flat rate		0	0	0
Connecticut	3.0	5.0	2	10,000	10,000	12,500	24,000	0
Delaware	2.2	5.95	6	5,000	60,000	110c	220c	110c
Georgia	1.0	6.0	6	750	7,000	2,700	5,400	2,700
Hawaii	1.4	8.25	9	2,000	40,000	1,040	2,080	1,040
Idaho	1.6	7.8	8	1,104	22,074	3,100	6,200	3,100
Illinois	3.0	3.0	1	Flat rate		2,000	4,000	2,000
Indiana	3.4	3.4	1	Flat rate		1,000	2,000	1,000
Iowa	0.36	8.98	9	1,211	54,495	40c	80c	40c
Kansas	3.5	6.45	3	15,000	30,000	2,250	4,500	2,250
Kentucky	2.0	6.0	5	3,000	8,000	20c	40c	20c
Louisiana	2.0	6.0	3	12,500	25,000	4,500	9,000	1,000
Maine	2.0	8.5	4	4,250	16,950	4,700	7,850	1,000
Maryland	2.0	4.75	4	1,000	3,000	2,400	4,800	2,400
Massachusetts	5.3	5.3	1	Flat rate		3,300	6,600	1,000
Michigan	4.0	4.0	1	Flat rate		3,100	6,200	3,100
Minnesota	5.35	7.85	3	19,440	63,860	3,100	6,200	3,100
Mississippi	3.0	5.0	3	5,000	10,000	6,000	12,000	1,500

Missouri	1.5	6.0	10	1,000	9,000	2,100	4,200	2,100
Montana	2.0	11.0	10	2,199	76,199	1,740	3,480	1,740
Nebraska	2.56	6.84	4	2,400	26,500	94c	188c	94c
New Jersey	1.4	6.37	6	20,000	75,000	1,000	2,000	1,500
New Mexico	1.7	6.8	5	5,500	26,000	3,100	6,200	3,100
New York	4.0	7.7	7	8,000	500,000	0	0	1,000
N. Carolina	6.0	8.25	4	12,750	120,000	·3,100	6,200	3,100
N. Dakota	2.1	5.54	5	28,400	311,950	3,100	6,200	3,100
Ohio	0.743	7.5	9	5,000	200,000	1,200	2,400	1,200
Oklahoma	0.5	6.75	8	1,000	10,000	1,000	2,000	1,000
Oregon	5.0	9.0	3	2,600	6,500	151c	302c	151c
Pennsylvania	3.07	3.07	1	Flat rate		0	0	0
S. Carolina	2.5	7.0	6	2,400	12,300	3,100	6,200	3,100
Utah	2.30	7.0	6	863	4,313	2,325	4,650	2,325
Vermont	3.6	3.9	5	29,050	319,100	3,100	6,200	3,100
Virginia	2.0	5.75	4	3,000	17,000	800	1,600	800
W. Virginia	3.0	6.5	5	10,000	60,000	2,000	4,000	2,000
Wisconsin	4.6	6.75	4	8,610	129,150	700	1,400	400
D.C.	5.0	9.5	3	10,000	30,000	1,370	2,740	1,370

The state where you pay income tax depends on where you're domiciled, usually determined by where you have your permanent home and voting residence. Some states' domicile laws are based solely on intent and you can maintain your domicile simply by signing a declaration stating that you intend to live there permanently. In some states, e.g. Texas, you aren't required to spend a minimum period there or even to own a home there. If you earn income from a state other than the one in which you're domiciled, you may also be liable for income tax in that state, although the state in which you're domiciled usually gives you a credit for taxes paid in another state.

Some local governments also levy income taxes, although these are usually at a lower rate than the state tax. State and local income tax forms are less complicated than federal tax forms and state tax inspectors aren't as strict as IRS inspectors, although they have reciprocal agreements with the IRS, so you must ensure that both sets of figures agree in case a cross-check is made. There's often confusion over filing and payment dates for state and local taxes, and you may receive conflicting information.

Take full advantage of your federal deductions for state and local taxes. If you itemise on your federal tax return (see page 388), you can write off state and local taxes on income and property. However, don't forget items such as taxes for a prior year paid late as a result of an audit or filing an amended or late return. Also, ask your local tax authority or tax adviser what local charges are tax deductible, such as water and sewage fees. If you fail to claim a tax allowance, your state tax collector may spot it and give it to you, but don't count on it. Around ten states allow a couple to calculate their tax separately, even if they file a joint federal tax return, and social security benefits are exempt from tax in some 25 states. Pension income is partly exempt in some states and pension income for certain employees, such as teachers, government employees and military personnel, is exempt in around 15 states.

Most states have faced budget deficits in recent years, which have resulted in cuts in services and increases in state and local taxes. When comparing a state's total tax burden, take into account **all** state taxes, including income, property, sales, death, gas and cigarette taxes, plus 'user fees' (a euphemism for taxes on such items as birth certificates, driving licences and telephone calls). Tuition fees at state public colleges and universities are another item that should be taken into account when calculating state taxes. State and local taxes are rising faster than federal income taxes as a percentage of a family's income (some states have also accelerated tax collection by changing tax-due dates).

PROPERTY TAX

Property tax is levied annually on property owners in all states to help pay for local services such as primary and secondary education (which usually account for around two-thirds of property taxes), police and fire services, libraries, public transport subsidies, waste disposal, highways and road safety, maintaining trading standards, and personal social services.

Tax rates are fixed by communities and are expressed as an amount per $100 or per $1,000 (the 'millage' rate) of the assessed market value of a property. For example, if your home is valued at $100,000 and your local tax rate is $15 per $1,000 value, your annual property tax bill is $1,500. The rating method is complicated and highly variable according to the state, county and municipality. Annual property taxes on a house of average value vary considerably from zero (in some areas houses valued below a certain amount, e.g. $75,000, are exempt) or around $500 in low rated states, e.g. West Virginia, to almost $6,000 in 'high value' communities such as New Hampshire.

Middle-income families have been particularly hard hit by increases in property taxes in recent years. In some states, a portion of property tax is reimbursed for senior citizens and blind and disabled people with low incomes, and there are tax breaks for residents in some states where there are a large number of holiday homes (e.g. Florida).

One way of reducing your property tax is to appeal against your property assessment, which may cut your bill by as much as 10 per cent. Check your property record card at your local assessor's office. If you find that your assessment is based on incorrect or incomplete information, ask the assessor for a review. In many communities, properties are assessed at less than their supposed 'true' value, according to an 'assessment ratio'. For example, if the assessment ratio in your community is 70 per cent, divide your property's assessed value by 70 per cent to arrive at its assumed true value (e.g. a property assessed at $200,000 would be valued at $285,714.28). Call your assessor's office to find out the assessment ratio. If you appeal against your property's assessed value, be prepared to back it up with some convincing evidence, e.g. lower assessments on many similar properties and incorrect details, particularly wrong property and land dimensions. If necessary, hire a professional appraiser; however the assessor and tax board are permitted a margin of error, e.g. 15 per cent. Tax appeal deadlines vary according to the state, county and community. Taxes are usually assessed on 1st January and bills despatched on 1st November, with payment due by 1st April the following year. There may be discounts for **early** payment.

There are many books designed to help you reduce your property taxes, including *Challenge Your Taxes: A Homeowner's Guide to Reducing Property Taxes* by James E.A. Lumley (Wiley), *Appeal Your Property Taxes and Win* by Ed Salzman (Panoply) and *How to Fight Property Taxes* published by the National Taxpayers Union (☎ 703-683-5700, 💻 www.ntu.org).

CAPITAL GAINS TAX

Capital gains tax (CGT) is applicable whenever you sell, or otherwise dispose of (e.g. lease, exchange or lose), an asset. Broadly speaking, assets are everything you own and use for personal purposes, pleasure, or investment, including stocks and bonds held in personal accounts, household furnishings, a car used for pleasure or commuting, coin or stamp collections, gems, jewellery, gold, silver and any other collectibles.

Since 1997, a portion of a gain made on the sale of your principal home has been excluded from CGT, so homeowners can avoid tax on a gain of up to $250,000 for a single person and up to $500,000 for a married couple filing jointly. To qualify you must have owned and occupied the property for at least two of the five years before the sale or exchange. You don't need to buy a replacement home to qualify for the exclusion and can take advantage of it every two years, provided you meet the two-year ownership and residence rule. If your gain exceeds the exclusion amount, it's subject to CGT as a long-term capital gain, even if you intend to buy a new residence at a price exceeding the sale price of the old residence.

The Bush tax cuts reduced the CGT rate for sales of assets on or after 6th May 2003, to no more than 15 per cent. For those in the 10 per cent or 15 per cent income tax bracket, the CGT rate is only 5 per cent, and this is scheduled to drop to 0 in 2008, but only for the one year, unless extended by Congress. There's a 25 per cent maximum rate on gains from property that has been subject to depreciation and a 28 per cent maximum for gains from selling collectibles (your prize collection of Victorian tea pots, for example) or certain small business shares. These rates are due to expire after the 2008 tax year and go back to their pre-2003 levels, but it's likely they will be extended or made permanent before then.

In most cases, when you buy and sell capital assets, each transaction is taxed as it's concluded. Losses on property rentals can be carried forward and offset against a capital gain when a property is sold. When you sell a holiday home or investment property, improvements, selling costs and depreciation are calculated to arrive at the net gain. In some states, an amount equal to 10 per cent of the gross sale price of a property must be withheld by the buyer from the seller's funds at closing. This is used to pay any tax due, the excess being refunded.

You can protect yourself and your survivors from CGT, if you bequeath appreciated property in your will rather than give it away while you're alive. This is because the tax basis of the property when you owned it, i.e. the purchase price, is increased to the fair market value on your death. For example, if you purchased a property for $100,000 that's worth $300,000 when you die, the recipient is able to compute capital gains as if he had bought it at $300,000. However, such bequests may lead to a higher estate tax liability (see below), which must be taken into account. If you have a net capital **loss** in any year, you're limited to a deduction of $3,000 ($1,500 if married and filing separately), but any capital loss above $3,000 can be carried forward to future years to offset capital gains.

ESTATE & GIFT TAX

In the US, federal estate tax (called inheritance tax or death duty in some countries) is applied to the transfer of property when a person dies. However, if you can manage to postpone your death until after the 31st December 2009, you won't have to be bothered, as this tax is in the process of being phased out. Until then, if the deceased was a citizen or resident of the US at the time of his death, the value of his entire estate is subject to estate tax, irrespective of where it's located. A non-resident pays estate tax only on the value of property located in the US at the time of his death. Lifetime transfers and transfers made at the time of death are combined for estate tax purposes.

Transfers between spouses are tax exempt, provided the spouse receiving the transfer is a US citizen. For all other transfers, a *United States Estate Tax Return* (form 706) must be filed if the gross US estate of a non-resident is over $60,000 or if the gross estate of a US citizen or resident exceeds a certain value (known as the 'exclusion amount') at the time of death. The exclusion amount is set to be increased until 2009, as shown in the table below. The 'unified credit' is the amount available to offset estate taxes.

Year of Death	Exclusion Amount	Unified Credit
2004 or 2005	$1,500,000	$555,800
2006, 2007 or 2008	$2,000,000	$780,800
2009	$3,500,000	$1,455,800

Estate tax rates are progressive and are calculated according to a 'unified rate schedule,' from 18 to 48 per cent in 2004, with the maximum rate being reduced 1 per cent each year until 2007, when the 45 per cent maximum rate stays in effect until 2009. An estate tax return should be filed within nine months after death, unless an extension has been granted. But overall, only around 2 per cent of all estates are subject to federal estate tax.

A federal gift tax is imposed on the gratuitous transfer of property (whether tangible or intangible) above a certain value, and the person making the gift must usually pay the tax. There is a separate 'unified credit' of $345,800 available to apply against gifts made until the end of 2009, equivalent to an exclusion of the first

$1,000,000 of gifts made. You can give away $11,000 to any individual during any calendar year without incurring gift tax, and a couple can agree to treat gifts to individuals as joint gifts and, therefore, exclude up to $22,000 per year. Gifts made in amounts greater than this require the filing of a gift tax form, but usually don't require the payment of taxes until the 'unified credit' has been used up. There's also an unlimited exclusion from gift tax for medical expenses and school tuition fees. A person who isn't a citizen or resident is subject to gift tax only on gifts of property situated in the US. US citizens and residents who make taxable gifts during the calendar year are required to file a *United States Gift Tax Return* (form 709) by 15th April of the following year.

In addition to federal estate taxes, inheritance taxes may be imposed by the state and many of these state inheritance taxes **won't** be going away after 2009. State inheritance taxes vary wildly according to the state (some have none, e.g. Florida), the size of the bequest, and the relationship between the deceased and the beneficiary. Many states are in the process of revamping their inheritance tax laws to compensate for the phase-out of the federal estate tax. (Just because the federal government can live without the revenue from estate taxes doesn't mean the state governments are ready to give it up!)

WILLS

It's an unfortunate fact of life, but you're unable to take your worldly goods with you when you take your final bow (even if you plan to come back in a later life). Therefore, it's preferable to bequeath them to someone you love, rather than to let the IRS have them or leave a mess that everyone will fight over (unless that's your intention!). A surprising number of people in the US die intestate, i.e. without making a will, with the result that their estates are distributed according to local state law rather than as they may have wished. The biggest problem of leaving no will is often the delay in the winding up of an estate (while perhaps searching for a will), which can cause considerable hardship and distress at an already stressful time. When someone dies, an estate's assets cannot be touched until estate tax (see above) has been paid and probate (the official proving of a will or other distribution plan) has been granted.

There are two main types of inheritance law employed by US states: common law (42 states) and community property law (Arizona, California, Idaho, Louisiana, Nevada, New Mexico, Texas and Washington). In common law states, the estate is divided among all surviving relatives, including the spouse, children, parents and others. In community property states, all assets acquired by a couple during their marriage are usually deemed to be owned jointly, with the exception of property acquired through inheritance, gifts or compensation. Some states have requirements for valid wills, e.g. you may have to leave a certain part of your estate to your spouse or children; otherwise you risk an irate family member being able to 'break' the will.

All adults should make a will, irrespective of how large or small their assets. If your circumstances change dramatically, e.g. you get married, you must make a new will, as marriage automatically revokes any existing wills. Husbands and wives should each make separate wills. Similarly, if you separate or are divorced, you should consider making a new will, but make sure you have one valid will only. You should check your will every few years to make sure it still fits your wishes and circumstances. A change of state may necessitate changing your will to comply with (or take advantage of) local law.

If you're a foreign national and don't want your estate to be subject to US law, you may be eligible to have your will interpreted under the law of another country. To avoid being subject to US estate and gift tax laws, you must usually establish your domicile in another country. If you don't specify in your will that the law of another country applies to your estate, then US law applies and your estate is subject to US estate and gift laws (see above). Many Americans make tax-free bequests to charities in their wills, which is why charities are so keen that you make a will (leaving it all to them).

Once you've accepted that you're mortal (the only statistic you can rely on is that 100 per cent of all human beings eventually die), you will find that making a will isn't a complicated or lengthy process. You can draw up your own will (which is better than none), but you should obtain legal advice from an experienced estate planning and probate lawyer. If you have total assets of over $1,500,000 (2004), you should have your will drawn up by an attorney who specialises in estates, as you will be liable for estate tax (see above). If you aren't domiciled in the US and want your will to be interpreted under the law of another country, you should choose a lawyer who's conversant with the law of that country.

Many states provide 'fill-in-the-blanks' form wills costing a few dollars and designed for parents or married couples with modest estates. These usually help you leave your estate to your children or spouse, let you give money to one other person or to charity, and usually allow you to name a guardian and an executor. You must usually have two witnesses (to your signature, not the contents of the will) who cannot be a beneficiary or your spouse, although some states allow 'self-proved' hand-written wills. If you wish to go it alone, you should consult one of the many books published on this subject, such as the legal guides from Nolo Press (🖳 www.nolo.com). The Nolo website also includes many articles on legal topics, including wills and estate planning. There are also a variety of software programs available for do-it-yourself wills (e.g. *Quicken WillMaker*). The US obsession with television has led to the practice of recording wills on video, where the deceased makes a speech to his relatives and prospective beneficiaries. This is shown after he has departed this life and has no legal validity, as a will must still be drawn up in the usual way.

You also need someone to act as the executor of your estate. Your bank or lawyer usually acts as executor, but you should shop around a few banks and lawyers and compare fees. These may vary considerably according to the size of your estate. Probate can cost up to 10 per cent of the value of an estate and may also result in months or years of delay before final settlement. **It's best to make one or more of your beneficiaries the executors and then they can instruct a solicitor after your death if they need legal assistance.** An alternative to writing a will is to create a 'living trust', thus eliminating the lengthy and costly probate process. There are a number of books about living trusts, including *Understanding Living Trusts* by Vickie and Jim Schumacher (Schumacher Publishing) and *The Complete Living Trusts Program* by Martin Schenkman (Wiley).

Keep a copy of your will in a safe place at home and another copy with your lawyer or the executor of your estate. Don't keep your will in a safety deposit box (lockbox) at your bank, as that's sealed upon notification of your death and isn't accessible to those who need it. You should keep information regarding bank accounts and insurance policies with your will(s), but don't forget to tell someone where they are!

COST OF LIVING

No doubt you would like to know how far your US dollars will stretch and how many (if any) you will have left after paying your bills and taxes. Americans enjoy one of the highest standards of living in the world, although for the average American family it remained static throughout most of the '70s and '80s and the average family's buying power decreased during this period. More than 32 million Americans also live below the official poverty line (estimated to be an annual income of around $19,000 for a family of four), including around a third of African Americans and 25 per cent of Hispanics. There's a huge (and widening) gap between rich and poor, the richest 1 per cent of households owning around 40 per cent of the nation's wealth and the poorest 20 per cent less than 6 per cent.

The cost of living in the US varies considerably according to where and how you live. There is an interesting internet site, 🖥 www.homefair.com which provides a salary calculator giving you a means of comparing the cost of living between two different towns within the US. Not surprisingly, New York is reckoned to be the most expensive US city followed by Boston, San Francisco, Washington, Chicago and Los Angeles.

Of course, your cost of living depends on your particular circumstances (e.g. family size, distance from work and schools) and lifestyle. Food costs around half as much as in most European countries and $250 should be sufficient to feed two adults for a month in most areas (excluding alcohol, fillet steak and caviar). Apart from the cost of accommodation, goods and services, you should also take into account the level of local taxes (income, property, sales and death taxes), which range from an average of around $2,000 per year in Alaska to some $9,000 per year in New York City. The cost of public college or university education also varies from state to state.

The most expensive item for most people is rent or mortgage payments, which can be astronomical in some cities (although if you need to pay your own health insurance, it could be more expensive than your rent or mortgage). For example, in New York City's Manhattan district, the rent for a small studio apartment may be $2,000 or more per month, while in most rural areas you can rent or buy a 3-bedroom house for less than $1,000 per month. You must earn around $50,000 per year to sustain life in a small studio apartment in Manhattan, but an annual salary of $25,000 is sufficient to live quite comfortably in most rural areas and small towns. Even in the most expensive areas, the cost of living needn't be astronomical (apart from rents). If you shop wisely, compare prices and services before buying, and don't live too extravagantly, you may be pleasantly surprised at how little you can live on.

15.

LEISURE

Like most things in the US, leisure is big business (the share of the average American family budget spent on leisure has increased by over 35 per cent in the past 15 years). The US entertainment industry has a bigger income than many countries and boasts the largest, fastest, highest, most expensive and extravagant tourist attractions in the world. Some 50 million tourists visit the US each year, spending around $75 billion. However, despite numerous man-made attractions, the nation's foremost and most enduring appeal is its immense natural beauty, which owes nothing to man's intervention (except on the debit side). No other country boasts such a diversity of natural wonders, such as the vast barren areas of Alaska (the last great American wilderness), the majesty of the Grand Canyon, the wonders of Yellowstone and Yosemite National Parks, the tropical beauty of Hawaii, and numerous other unique landscapes.

Getting away from it all isn't difficult in the US. There are numerous lakes, hundreds of miles of excellent beaches, and areas of wilderness bigger than many countries. In keeping with the size and grandeur of its natural attractions, it's almost inevitable that the US should have the biggest, brashest and grandest man-made attractions, where pride of place goes to the vast Disney World and Disneyland theme parks, which are among the world's top leisure attractions.

Although New Orleans and San Francisco rate highly on almost everyone's list of favourite American cities, New York (the 'Big Apple') is the entertainment capital and its most vital city (the city that never sleeps). Despite its crumbling infrastructure and well-publicised problems, New York is the place everyone loves to hate but cannot keep away from. Whatever kind of diversion you're seeking, you will find it there in abundance, including some of the best theatre, music, museums, clubs, galleries, nightlife, parties, bars and restaurants in the US. New York dominates American arts and is the main centre for the visual and performing arts (traditional and modern), including art, photography, ballet, contemporary dance, opera, and classical and popular music.

Americans believe in working and playing hard and make the most of their free time (due in part to their long working hours and short holidays), aided by the most developed leisure opportunities and facilities in the world. Although admission to major attractions can be expensive, free entertainment is provided in many cities during the summer months, including theatre, classical music, military bands, opera, pop and other music, dance, puppet shows, mime, jugglers and comedians. The US is populated by people from a multitude of cultures, backgrounds and heritages, and this is strongly reflected in the diversity of the arts.

Although popular mass culture such as movies, television (TV), popular music and pop art reap the bulk of receipts, so called high culture such as classical music, ballet, opera, museums and art also flourish. Many Americans are deeply committed to the arts and more people attend arts than sports events. The number of visitors to museums and galleries exceeds attendance at pop concerts. Most Americans live within reasonable distance of one of the 30 American cities classified as regional arts centres, and many provincial cities have a modern arts centre where theatre, concerts, cinema and dance can be enjoyed under one roof.

Tickets for virtually any event of importance anywhere in the country (theatre, music, sport, etc.) can be purchased through national chains of ticket agencies such as Ticketmaster and Ticketron. Reduced price tickets are often available for local events on the day of performances. Look in local newspapers in the 'Arts and

Leisure' section and in local arts and entertainment newspapers and magazines (often free) for information about current and forthcoming shows, ticket prices and availability. In tourist areas, free books of cut-price coupons for attractions, restaurants, etc., are widely available.

Information about local events and entertainment is also available from tourist offices, libraries and town halls. Guides for the disabled are published by many communities, and in many cities there are gay and lesbian entertainment guides. Entertainment newspapers and magazines are published in all major cities and include: *New York*, and *Village Voice* (New York); *Chicago* magazine and *Chicago Reader*; *LA Weekly*, *LA Reader*, *LA Downtown News* and *Virtually Los Angeles*; *San Francisco Bay Guardian* and *Virtually San Francisco*; and the *Washingtonian*. Other entertainment magazines for other cities can be found at local book shops and news stands. All major newspapers provide entertainment news and many have weekly guides on Fridays, e.g. the *New York Times* and *Washington Post* 'Weekend' sections.

The main purpose of this chapter (and indeed the whole book) is to provide information that **isn't** usually found in other books. General tourist information is available in literally hundreds of US travel books, which cover the whole country or concentrate on a city or region. Among the best general travel guides are *Let's Go* and *Fodor's USA* (see **Appendix B** for others). For information about holiday accommodation and sports facilities see **Chapters 5** and **16**, respectively.

TOURIST INFORMATION

The United States Travel and Tourist Administration (USTTA) was abolished in 1996 because of budget cutbacks; however, a wealth of information exists online via the internet. Most tourist promotion is carried out at state level, and each state has its own tourist department, referred to variously as the Division of Tourism, Travel Information Center or Office of Tourism. Most states do a superb job of promoting their attractions through a number of state tourist offices and some also have overseas offices. All states publish excellent guide books, calendars of events, maps and accommodation guides, plus travel and visitors' guides detailing local leisure and sports facilities. If you know which states you will be visiting, you should contact their travel offices (or city tourist offices) for information.

Many towns and counties also have their own convention and visitors' or tourist bureaux, and there are numerous visitor, information and welcome centres throughout the US (often marked on tourist maps and signposted on main highways). Offices stock an amazing variety of leaflets and information on a wealth of subjects, so mention any special interests (such as sports) when making enquiries. Most regions, states, cities and resort towns publish visitors' guides. Tourist offices don't usually make written replies to individual enquiries, but will post information anywhere within the US and even overseas.

CAMPING & CARAVANNING

The US has more than 20,000 licensed caravan (trailer) and chalet parks and campsites (campgrounds – in the US a campsite is an individual camping area within a campground), public and private, serving more than 60 million campers each year. Camping in the US encompasses everything from backpackers sleeping rough or with a folding tent to those touring in a luxury mobile home or recreational vehicle (RV). Facilities at privately-owned campsites range from primitive (with or without water) to luxury (including cabins and cottages). All states with a shoreline provide seafront campsites, ranging from bare stretches of beach to vast developments with all modern conveniences.

A pitch (campsite) usually has a fireplace, picnic table and parking space, and toilets and running water are available nearby. Many campsites provide pitches with hook-ups (see below), tables, flush or dry toilets, hot showers, a children's area, recreation halls, restaurants and snack bars, free ice, laundry facilities and camp shops. Many also provide facilities for tennis, shuffleboard, volleyball, swimming, fishing, canoeing and boating. Many national and state parks have sporting campsites for hunters and fishermen, with lodgings consisting of cabins (or a central lodge with sleeping cabins); meals may be included. A sea-plane (float-plane) is necessary to reach some areas and a guide service is usually available.

For many Americans, camping means using the ubiquitous RV or motor home (numbering some 9 million in the US) or a camper or caravan rather than a tent. RVs equipped for a family of four can be rented throughout the US for between $500 and $1,000 per week. You're usually prohibited from parking a motor home or caravan overnight on a public highway. Tent campers are advised to avoid RV-oriented campgrounds, which although they offer superior facilities are plagued by noise and vehicle fumes. To RV 'campers', getting back to nature means taking all the modern conveniences of home with you, and few stray further than 100 yards from their vehicles. Many national parks provide 'wilderness' camping in designated areas and have facilities for RVs. Those interested in 'RVing' might like to join the Good Sam Club – see page 296. For those wanting to avoid RVs, in some states there are campsites exclusively for hikers and bikers. In addition to camping facilities, many parks maintain a number of cabins and lodges, which can be rented year-round and reserved six months to one year in advance. All campgrounds have minimum age limits and many won't issue permits to anyone under 18.

Most national and state parks permit camping, and sites at certain parks can be booked (essential in summer) up to eight weeks in advance for a single pitch, and 12 weeks for groups, although many sites don't accept bookings. For parks managed by the National Parks Service, contact ReserveAmerica (☎ 1-800-365-2267 for bookings or 301-722-1257 from outside the US, 💻 http://reservations.nps.gov), whose website has a search and booking facility. Where bookings are possible, a percentage of campsites (e.g. 25 per cent) is usually reserved for visitors on a first-come, first-served basis. Try to arrive by 5pm or earlier, as camps fill up quickly in summer (at the most popular parks queuing all night for a space isn't unheard of). Some sites display a 'No Vacancy' sign all summer, so always ask about vacancies. The peak season lasts from mid-May to the end of October at the most popular parks, and many parks have a one or two-week limit on stays during the summer.

Campsites vary considerably, as do their fees, usually ranging from $7 to $100 or more per night (averaging $10 to $20), according to the popularity, season, facilities, location, type of site, tent size and the number sharing (group rates are usually available). Many sites have caravan and RV hook-ups (electricity, water, and cable

TV), usually costing $10 to $20 per day. To protect land and water resources, some parks restrict the use of certain areas, when a wilderness or 'back country' permit (usually issued free) must be obtained from a park ranger's office. State parks and national forests in most states also provide campsites for $7 to $10 per night for cars or caravans, while many states have cheaper rates for hikers and cyclists (from as little as $2). State park campsites are often primitive and without electricity, water, and flush toilets, although some provide comprehensive facilities and cabins at lower rates than private sites. It's possible to reserve a pitch at many state parks, although it's unnecessary except during federal holidays and summer weekends.

A number of excellent camping guides are available in the US, including Woodall's *Campground Directory* (Woodall Publications), which has national, eastern and western editions, and 17 regional directories plus a website (💻 www.woodalls.com). Woodall also publish a *Tenting Directory*, *RV Trips*, *Favourite Recipes from America's Campgrounds* and other campsite cookbooks. Most states publish free camping guides containing a list of caravan parks and campsites, and the services and facilities provided. Senior citizens (over 62) can obtain a free Golden Age passport (see **Parks, Gardens & Zoos** on page 408) and receive a 50 per cent discount at national park and forest campsites.

Kampgrounds of America (*KOA*), a franchising network of campgrounds, publishes a guide to the KOA nationwide network of more than 700 private campsites. These are almost exclusively intended for RVs and, although more expensive (average around $15 to $30 per day) than national and state park campsites, they generally provide the best facilities, including showers, electricity, flush toilets and telephones, and often have swimming pools and shops. A KOA directory ($4) is available from KOA, PO Box 30558, Billings, MT 59114 (☎ 406-248-7444, 💻 www.koakampgrounds.com). Less well-heeled campers may be interested in *Simple Tent Camping* by Zora and David Aiken (International Marine/Ragged Mountain Press).

AMUSEMENT PARKS

The US is a wonderful country for the young (and young at heart) and a great number of leisure facilities are geared to children. If you ask children in most western countries where they want to visit in the US, the answer is likely to be Disney World (Florida) or Disneyland (California). If you want to be 'taken for a ride', the US is certainly the place to be. Amusement parks, including theme, roller-coaster and water parks, are a multi-billion dollar industry and entertain more than 130 million visitors each year.

Disney World is the largest and most popular tourist attraction in the world, and includes the Magic Kingdom, EPCOT Center, Typhoon Lagoon Waterpark, MGM Studios and the Pleasure Island nightclub extravaganza. Disney World is so vast that it takes around five days to see and do everything, so you should read up on it beforehand and identify the things you're most interested in. The website is useful for planning your trip (💻 www.disneyworld.com) and there are numerous guides, including *The Everything Family Guide to the Walt Disney World Resort, Universal Studios and Greater Orlando* by Jason Rich (Adams Media Corp.), Birnbaum's *Walt*

Disney World and *The Luxury Guide to Walt Disney World* by Cara Goldsbury (Bowman Books). There are also a variety of specialised guides, including those for adults, vegetarians and gay tourists, not to mention the 'unofficial' guides.

Among the most popular amusement parks are the roller coaster parks, which have a cult following among many Americans. Parks compete furiously for the title of the scariest, fastest, loopiest and biggest roller coaster in the US (or the world, which is usually the same thing). The best roller coaster parks are mostly in the Midwest. Ardent thrill-seekers may wish to obtain a copy of *The Roller Coaster Lover's Companion* by Steven J. Urbanowicz (Citadel) or *The Amusement Park Guide* by Tim O'Brien (Globe Pequot).

At most amusement parks, daily tickets cost from $10 to $55 per day (with small reductions for children) and allow unlimited rides. Many parks sell multi-day or season passes which reduce the cost substantially. The most expensive is the Disney World Magic Kingdom where a one-day, one-park pass costs $55 for adults and $44 for children aged three to nine (only theme parks classify ten-year-olds as adults!). Multi-day and multi-park passes are also available, as well as an annual pass for fanatics costing between $380 and $500 ($322 to $424 for 'children') depending on the number of parks included. Cut-price tickets are available from authorised ticket agents throughout Florida and save time queuing to buy tickets. Tickets can all be purchased via the internet through ticket brokers, e.g. 💻 www.seligo.com, travel agents, or on the Disney World website (see above).

The entrance fee allows you to enjoy all the attractions, the only limitation being the time spent standing in queues, which can be an hour or more at the most popular rides, although you're usually informed of the waiting time at each ride. It's best to avoid peak periods such as weekends and federal holidays, when crowds of 75,000 a day jam Disneyland and Disney World. Queues (lines) are shorter early and late in the day, including queues for food, so eat early or late to save queuing time.

Water parks, where all rides and activities are water-based, are growing in popularity, and there are now around 150 throughout the country, although the majority are located in Florida and other 'Sunbelt' states. The main attractions include giant tidal wave pools, rapids for tubing, slides that shoot down from seven stories, jet slides, wind and rain tunnels, whirlpools and wave pools, helical rides on water mats, and surf lagoons with four-foot waves. A typical water park is Typhoon Lagoon in Disney World, Florida, where a one day pass costs around $32 for adults and $26 for children under ten. Discount coupons for many amusement parks are contained in local tourist guides and brochures, and discounted tickets are available from ticket agents in local hotels and restaurants.

The US's latest theme park, Celebration City, opened in Branson, Missouri in May 2003, but the ultimate is Florida's Discovery Cove, which opened in July 2000 and where you can swim among giant rays and bottlenose dolphins for a day – that's if you have $190 to splash!

MUSEUMS & ART GALLERIES

US cities contain an abundance of museums and art galleries, including some of the most important collections in the world. The Americans have been buying up everything in sight at international auctions for many years, and some American museums and foundations such as the Getty Center in Los Angeles (California is a cultural backwater full of old masters), have a bigger budget than some countries. What Americans may lack in culture and refinement, they more than make up for in buying power, and they're largely responsible for the huge escalation of international art prices in the last few decades.

Most American museums and galleries are privately funded rather than national institutions. Although many receive some federal and municipal funds, most rely on sponsorship, patronage and donations from corporations and individuals. The patronage of rich philanthropist-collectors has served the US well and many of the nation's most famous collections were endowed or donated by a benevolent benefactor (patronage of the arts is one of the quickest ways to prominence in US society).

Many American museums are refreshingly modern and stimulating (although they also have a plethora of kitsch, of which the Liberace Museum in Las Vegas is a prime example), particularly those offering hands-on exhibits. These bear little resemblance to the traditional image of rows of glass cases full of stuffed animals and dusty static exhibits. Most museums are well designed and, often, the buildings housing museums and galleries are as artistically or historically important as the collections themselves. In cities (and shopping centres) there are also many commercial galleries. If you enjoy contemporary art, they're well worth a visit, even if you have no intention of buying. Many rural museums are operated by local historical societies and private interests, and they often preserve local history or long-departed local industries (e.g. Alcatraz, the former infamous prison island in San Francisco Bay, which has become a Museum of Penal Servitude).

New York City is home to some of the most acclaimed museums and art collections in the US and is the art capital of the world. It's particularly noted for its contemporary art. There are more museums per square mile in Manhattan than in any other city in the world, and the Metropolitan Museum of Art is the world's largest museum (only a quarter of its more than 3 million works of art can be displayed at any time). Washington DC houses the National Gallery of Art, the National Air and Space Museum (the most popular museum in the world – don't miss the films), and the Smithsonian Institute, comprising the world's largest museum complex (14 plus the National Zoo). One of the best modern art galleries is the San Francisco Museum of Modern Art, which opened in 1995. Many museums and galleries have excellent restaurants.

The opening hours of museums and galleries vary considerably. Many close on Mondays and open in the early evening one day a week, e.g. until around 9pm, when admission may be free or fees reduced. Because of their large endowments, many major galleries and museums are unable to charge admission fees, as this would conflict with their charitable status. However, they get round this by suggesting a 'donation', e.g. $5 for adults and $2.50 for students. This is accepted by most Americans as a **minimum** entrance fee and most people wouldn't dare give less. There may be an extra 'charge' for special exhibitions. Most museums offer memberships for an annual fee (usually around $50), that includes free admission and preference booking for special exhibitions and openings. However, special exhibitions often cause regular exhibits to be closed; half (or more) of the exhibits may be closed, e.g. for refurbishment, so you should check in advance. Entrance to many smaller, specialist galleries and museums is often free. Some museums offer free entry to students on certain days or evenings and most provide student and senior citizen discounts. On certain festive occasions, entry to many museums is free in some cities (e.g. New York in mid-June). Many museums and galleries provide reductions for the disabled and some have special access or provide wheelchairs.

PARKS, GARDENS & ZOOS

The US is home to a multitude of internationally acclaimed parks, gardens, aquariums and zoos. The crowning glory is its vast government-protected national park system, which includes some 375 parks and sites comprising 2 per cent of the country's land area (more than 80 million acres or around 35 million hectares). National parks include some of the most awe-inspiring scenery found anywhere on earth, much of it unique. National parks include everything from spectacular seascapes to deep canyons, dramatic volcanoes, crystal lakes and craggy mountains. Among the most renowned parks are Acadia (Maine), Everglades (Florida), Glacier (Montana), Grand Canyon (Arizona), Great Smoky Mountains (Tennessee), Olympic (Washington), Yosemite (California) and Yellowstone (Wyoming), which was the world's first national park (1872). Nobody is permitted to live within the borders of US national parks.

Besides national parks, there are also national forests, national wildlife refuges, fish and wildlife areas, conservation areas, marinas, state and county parks, and other government-protected reserves, many bordering national parks and providing similar landscapes. The chief attraction of state and county parks is that they're usually much less crowded than national parks; although smaller and less grand, they nevertheless offer magnificent scenery. National and state parks contain campsites, caravan parks, cabins for hire, hotels, motels, lodges, restaurants, snack bars and shops. Most also have extensive walking (hiking) trails, cycle and bridle paths, and picnic areas. All parks provide various sports opportunities and facilities, including hiking, cycling, fishing, hunting, horse riding, swimming, cross-country skiing, snowmobiling, mountain climbing and boating (see also **Chapter 16**).

All national parks have an entrance fee, e.g. $2 to $5 per person or $4 to $10 per car load (irrespective of the number of passengers). A number of passes allow holders and anyone accompanying them (e.g. passengers in a private vehicle) free access to national parks. Annual passes for individual parks are also available for $10 or $15. Golden Age (for people over 62) and Golden Access (for blind and disabled people) passports provide free lifetime entrance to all national parks and also provide a 50 per cent discount on federal use fees (e.g. camping, parking and cave tours). **When parking at national or state parks, lock your vehicle and put any valuables out of sight in the boot.**

Generally, national parks are open all year round, closing on Christmas Day and New Year's Day only, although inclement weather restricts activities in some parks. Visiting hours and seasonal opening and closing times vary, so check in advance (some national and state parks are closed from mid-October to mid-April). The high season is July and August, when parking queues are interminable. The most popular parks are overcrowded from May to October, during which period bookings for campsites and other accommodation are essential. It's best to avoid the most popular parks in summer and to visit them in spring or autumn (fall), when many are at their most beautiful.

Many parks provide educational talks, guided tours and walks (hikes), and other organised activities. Park superintendents and staff can tell you anything you wish to know about a park, including its history, ecology and geology. Most parks have a visitor centre providing free literature and often exhibits, films and slide shows. Many guide books are available covering the whole park system or individual parks. Among the best general books is *Frommer's National Park Guide* by Michael Frome (Frommer).

Unfortunately the US's national parks are victims of their own success (visitors increased from 170 million in 1973 to 285 million in 2000, down slightly to 'only' 266 million in 2003) and many are severely threatened by pollution, erosion and conservation problems, a lack of water and too many visitors. Many parks have plans to increase entrance fees (to pay for the backlog of maintenance and repairs), and limit parking and visitor numbers.

The National Park Service (🖥 www.nps.gov) publishes free brochures and information about national park campsites, including a *National Park System Guide and Map* available from the Superintendent of Documents, U.S. Government Printing Office, Stop SSOP, Washington, DC 20402-0001 (☎ 202-512-1800). Regional public information offices are also provided. A wealth of national park handbooks, including *The National Parks: Lesser-Known Areas*, are available from the Superintendent of Documents. For information about national forests contact the USDA Forest Service, 1400 Independence Avenue, SW, Washington, DC 20250-0003 (☎ 202-205-8333, 🖥 www.fs.fed.us). For information about state parks, write to state tourist departments.

Most cities also have extensive park areas that are welcome retreats from the surrounding noise and chaos, the most famous of which is Central Park (843 acres/350ha) in New York City's Manhattan district. Most major cities have botanical gardens, where entrance is often free. Almost every large US city has a zoo, stocked with up to 2,000 animals. Many include a separate children's zoo, where children can mingle freely with man-eating goats, sheep and chickens. Many zoos have taken the animals out of cages and put them into 'natural' (albeit man-made) habitats, where they have more freedom, and some, such as the Metrozoo in Miami, cage the visitors and let the animals roam free. Among the largest and most famous US zoos are: San Diego (the US's and one of the world's best); Chicago's Brookfield and Lincoln Park Zoos; St. Louis and Kansas City in the Midwest; Audubon Park and Zoological Gardens in New Orleans; the Bronx Zoo in New York City; the National Zoo in Washington DC (one of the most beautiful); and Busch Gardens in Tampa, Florida. Some zoos keep animals in appalling conditions and 'performing' animals are often treated abominably.

Entrance fees and opening times vary according to the time of year, so check in advance. Often zoos have amusement parks attached, where you can take your children when they become bored with the animals. Aquariums are also extremely popular, although the largest and best-known bear more resemblance to circuses (with performing whales, dolphins, sea lions and seals) than traditional aquariums.

Among the most famous are the Miami Seaquarium, the Sea World of Texas (San Antonio), and Sea World in Orlando (Florida) and San Diego (California). Like theme parks, entrance fees are high, e.g. Sea World, Orlando costs $48 for adults and $39 for children under ten. Traditional aquariums (i.e. without the circus performances) include the New England Aquarium in Boston and the Monterey Bay Aquarium in Monterey, California.

Circuses are unfortunately (or fortunately depending on your viewpoint) disappearing in many countries, the US included. However, the Ringling Brothers and Barnum & Bailey Circus (the original three-ring circus) still thrives in New York City, as well as on tour around the country, as does the Big Apple Circus.

CINEMAS

Although cinemas (known as 'movie theaters' in the US) face increasing competition from TV and videos, the US film (movie) industry is thriving, particularly in the major cities. Hollywood remains the centre of the world's film industry and US films dominate the cinemas of most countries. In the US itself, 1.63 billion cinema tickets were sold in 2002, a record number. However, most cinemas (virtually all outside the major cities) show the latest box office blockbusters and it's becoming harder to find cinemas showing serious (i.e. anything without gratuitous violence, car chases or aliens), classic, 'art', experimental or foreign-language films. However, foreign-language (sub-titled) films are popular in New York and in other large cities with significant ethnic populations.

There are large multi-screen, e.g. 12 to 18-screen, cinemas in most cities. The main venues for film buffs are Westwood in Los Angeles and Third Avenue in New York (where the New York Radio City Music Hall is the largest cinema in the world). American audiences can be noisy, and audience participation is common, particularly with cult films. Special film series and experimental films are regularly screened by museums and galleries, particularly in New York and Washington.

Cinemas usually fall into three categories: first-run, second-run and re-run. First-run are found in major cities, such as Los Angeles and New York, and are often used to test audience reaction. Films were first made in New York and its audiences still have a huge influence on the success or failure of a film opening there. Second-run cinemas show films on general release throughout the US, and re-run cinemas (often called 'revival' or 'art houses') specialise in showing 'old' classics. First-run cinemas charge $6 to $10 (or more in major cities), second-run $3 to $5 and re-run from $1 to a maximum of around $3 (except for all-night shows). Matinees (afternoon performances) are usually cheaper (e.g. $4 to $5) with shorter queues. In US cinemas, the 'orchestra' refers to the front seats or stalls, while the upper stalls or dress circle are called the mezzanine, and the upper circle or gallery may be called the family circle. In addition to town centre (downtown) cinemas, there are cheaper cinemas on the outskirts of most cities.

Bookings are normally accepted at the cinema itself or online. Advance booking is occasionally necessary for first-run cinemas, which often take millions of dollars in the first few weeks of a popular film. You should plan to arrive at the cinema up to an hour early to obtain a ticket, or even earlier if the film's a major hit, as queues are often interminable. Many larger theatres have their own websites for booking tickets, and there are now some websites where you can order cinema tickets nationwide up to a month or more in advance (e.g. 💻 www.movietickets.com). Most cinemas show one film only (have a single bill) and, surprisingly, there may be no on-screen advertisements (except for forthcoming films). Smoking is prohibited in cinemas and air-conditioning can be freezing, so it pays to take a sweater in summer. Large multi-screen cinemas in shopping centres usually have a vast assortment of food and drink stands offering everything from the traditional popcorn and sweets (candy) to gourmet sandwiches and blended fruit drinks, plus an assortment of electronic games to keep you well fed and amused while waiting for the film to start.

Drive-in films were invented in Camden, New Jersey in 1932 and quickly spread throughout small towns. At a drive-in film, you pay at the entrance and drive to a parking space, where you clip a small loudspeaker to your car window or attach a cord to your radio aerial, tune in your AM dial, and watch the film on a gigantic screen. Obviously, drive-in 'cinemas' operate only when it's dark and often in the summer only (they aren't popular when it's raining, except with couples who don't plan to watch the film). They seldom show new releases or the best movies, but what are known as 'exploitation' films, and in the last few decades they've been badly hit by the spread of videos. Nevertheless, there are still around 500 drive-in cinemas in the US (which are the only ones where you're allowed to smoke!).

All films on general release in the US are given a rating under the motion picture code of self-regulation, as follows:

Classification	Restrictions
G	General audience; all ages admitted.
PG	Parental guidance suggested; some material may be inappropriate for children.
PG-13	Parents strongly cautioned; some material may be inappropriate for children under 13.
R	Restricted; children under 17 must have a ticket purchased by someone over 17 (but don't need to be accompanied by someone over 17).
NC-17	No children under 17 admitted.

Children (or adults) who look younger than their years may be asked for proof of their age, e.g. a school or student card, social security card or driving licence, for admission to age-restricted performances.

THEATRES

The US has the best and most vibrant theatre (spelt theater in the US) entertainment in the world, with New York as its hub. New York's world-famous Broadway theatre district contains the world's greatest concentration of theatres. In the US theatre world, you're considered to have 'arrived' only when you've played Broadway (the

'Great White Way'). Theatre outside New York is generally referred to as regional theatre. New York theatre is classified as Broadway, Off-Broadway or Off-Off-Broadway, signifying a descending order of commercial backing, theatre comfort and ticket prices. Off-Broadway shows include social and political drama, satire, ethnic plays and repertory, while Off-Off Broadway embraces experimental theatre, cabaret acts, student 'showcases' and performance art. More than 10 million theatre-lovers a year attend major shows on Broadway (excluding performances at 20 Off-Broadway and more than 250 Off-Off-Broadway theatres). Broadway is the venue for the annual 'Tony' awards, the theatre's equivalent of the Oscars.

Ticket prices in the major cities are exorbitantly high, even prohibitively so. You need to take out a loan to buy a pair of tickets to a hit Broadway musical and even then the theatres are barely breaking even (Broadway is increasingly losing out to Off-Broadway venues). Tickets for Broadway shows usually range from around $25 to $50 for drama and comedy, and up to $75 or more for musicals or hundreds of dollars if you need to buy from touts (scalpers). Tickets for Off-Broadway shows average around $30, while tickets for Off-Off-Broadway shows start at around $7.50.

Tickets can be purchased via the internet e.g. 🖥 www.telecharge.com and 🖥 www.ticketmaster.com, or direct from box offices, by telephone (credit card sales) or in person. Most people book tickets by telephone and pay by credit card through 24-hour telephone/charge card agencies, which usually add $3 to $10 per ticket for their services. In US theatres (as in cinemas) the 'orchestra' refers to the front seats or stalls, while the upper stalls or dress circle are called the mezzanine. Tickets ordered by credit card can be picked up from the theatre box office on production of your card.

Tickets can also be purchased by writing directly to theatres, when you should apply well in advance and give a number of alternative dates (at least two or three). Enclose credit card details, a cheque or a money order and a self-addressed and stamped envelope with your request. Many theatres have websites where you can order tickets directly. Often certain dates are reserved for charity or other special evenings. In many cities there are theatre clubs, often offering tickets in advance at reduced prices. Discounted tickets are also available through various clubs and organisations. Check performance times with the box office or in a newspaper or entertainment magazine. If you're late for a live performance, you may need to wait until the interval before being permitted to take your seat, although it may be possible to watch the show on a TV monitor. There are usually daily evening performances from Monday to Saturday and matinee performances (2pm or 3pm) on Wednesdays, Saturdays and Sundays. Matinee (and preview) tickets are usually slightly cheaper than evening tickets.

US theatre includes around 400 professional, non-profit theatre companies in cities around the country, many of which perform in city arts centres subsidised by local governments. Modern, experimental and new shows are usually performed only in major cities. In regional theatres, particularly in summer holiday resorts, well-proven classics, comedies and musicals are the most popular shows. Regional theatre is often provided by touring companies, performing shows originating on Broadway, and used as a testing ground for new plays (any new play or show which fails to make an impact on the provincial circuit is virtually condemned). Many universities also have excellent repertory companies.

Experimental theatre usually takes place in so-called 'Equity waiver' theatres with 99 seats or less, often no more than a room or hall with chairs. They're so called because they aren't required to use professional actors and pay Equity (union) rates of pay. This enables them to survive on low budgets, as nothing stirs on the US stage without Equity's approval (even theatre mice must be fully paid-up members!). Many Equity waiver theatres operate on a wing and a prayer, and they often solicit contributions before, during and after performances. Equity waiver theatres include many Off-Off Broadway (fringe) theatres in New York, where ethnic shows are often performed.

Community theatre is strong in many towns and is usually of a high standard. In fact, many US amateur theatre companies, whether drama, comedy or musical, would put professional repertory companies to shame in some countries. However, if you're a budding Brando or Hepburn, don't let the high standards deter you. Community theatre companies are always on the lookout for new talent and people to assist in other areas such as costumes, lighting or stage scenery. Shakespeare festivals are extremely popular and are performed in cities and towns throughout the US (there's a free annual Shakespeare festival in New York's Central Park). Outdoor drama is a popular summer entertainment, and native American epics are performed in woodland amphitheatres across the country.

Most theatres have a number of spaces for wheelchairs, induction loops for the hard of hearing and toilets for wheelchair users (mention when booking). Some theatres produce Braille programmes and brochures, and most allow entry to guide (seeing-eye) dogs for the blind. Most theatres, New York and regional, have restaurants and bars, and some have their own car parks. Many of the points noted above relating to theatre facilities and tickets also apply to concert halls and tickets (see below).

POPULAR MUSIC

Popular music (used here to encompass everything except classical music and opera) flourishes in the US, which has the most dynamic and varied music scene in the world. The US is the birthplace of many forms of music, including jazz, blues, bluegrass, country (the country's most popular music), rock and roll, soul, rhythm and blues, folk, gospel and rap, plus numerous hybrids such as new country and jazz-rock. Whatever your taste in music, you will find something to enjoy (and possibly much to dislike) in the US. Surprisingly, the US is often slow to embrace new pop trends and is usually fairly conservative in its music tastes. Much of the punk, new wave and other fads which originated in the UK in the '70s and '80s hardly made an impact in the US, and the rock music scene can be disappointing for those seeking originality.

American popular music is dominated by what is termed Adult Oriented Rock (AOR), encompassing such diverse performers as Michael Jackson, Prince, Sting, Paul Simon, Bruce Springsteen, Billy Joel, Dire Straits, Pink Floyd, the Rolling Stones and Elton John, to name but a few. Major rock concerts are often held in huge sports stadia and vast outdoor concerts and music festivals are popular in summer. Los Angeles is the rock capital of the US and the most popular venue for top rock acts (amazingly, around a third of the world's pop and rock music is recorded in LA). There are usually a number of top international solo stars and groups touring the US at any time of the year, where a major tour by a top act may take in as many as 60 cities. The US market is vast and profitable, and many old and largely forgotten American and British rock bands do a thriving business recycling their old hits to a new generation of teeny-boppers many years after everyone else has forgotten their names.

The club and bar music scene thrives in US cities and encompasses just about every kind of popular music. Most clubs have an admission (cover) charge, although few are restricted to members only. Shows often start later than advertised, particularly those at venues serving drinks (e.g. clubs), where the general idea is to keep customers waiting so they drink more (club acts often start as late as 1am). All university and college towns have a wealth of musical entertainment at bargain prices or even free and some of the best musical entertainment is provided free by street musicians (buskers). Street music encompasses all popular music tastes, including jazz, rock, folk, blues, country and classical. New York alone provides more free music than there are formal concerts in some countries.

Tickets for rock concerts are often available from agencies such as Ticketron (🖳 www.ticketron.com) and Ticketmaster (🖳 www.ticketmaster.com) and from local record shops, many of which have ticket machines (which may accept cash only). The best source of information about forthcoming concerts are music newspapers and magazines such as *Billboard* (🖳 www.billboard.com) and *Rolling Stone* (🖳 www.rollingstone.com). Local newspapers also list forthcoming concerts and music festivals, and free music newspapers and magazines are available in some areas. Information about local concerts is also available from tourist offices and local radio stations.

CLASSICAL MUSIC, OPERA & BALLET

Americans probably enjoy greater access to classical music and dance than most Europeans and, although ticket prices are high, they're probably lower than in Europe when the generally higher spending power of Americans is taken into account. Classical music concerts and opera and ballet performances are major social events in the US and are regularly staged by the cream of American and international musicians. Fortunately for music lovers, there's considerable competition among US cities and prominent citizens to endow nationally (and internationally) acclaimed orchestras and artistic venues. Any city with any claim to artistic prominence needs at least one symphony orchestra, plus an opera or ballet company if they want to be taken seriously. Concerts generally have a strong following in most cities and performances are of a high (often international) standard.

New York City lays claim to the title of 'Music Capital of the World' (although London might dispute it) and boasts the largest number of resident professional musicians in the world. It excels in all 'traditional' music fields and also in ethnic music such as Chinese opera, Jewish choirs, balalaika orchestras, choral groups and diverse community musicians. Although New York boasts one top ranking orchestra only, the New York Philharmonic, it more than compensates by the number and quality of American and international orchestras, ensembles and soloists it attracts.

The Mecca for the performing arts (for artists and art lovers) is New York's Lincoln Center, housing the Met (the Metropolitan Opera House and home of the American Ballet Theater), the New York Philharmonic Orchestra, the New York City Ballet, the New York State Theater and the Julliard School of Music. Among the many fine American orchestras are the big five of Boston, Chicago, Cleveland, New York and Philadelphia. Many smaller towns and cities also have symphony orchestras, totalling more than 1,200 throughout the country. The leading opera companies include Boston, Chicago, New York (the Metropolitan and City Operas), San Francisco, Santa Fe and Seattle.

New York City is also the world's undisputed centre of dance (classical and contemporary) and is home to five major ballet companies, dozens of modern troupes and hundreds of soloists. The New York City Ballet is one of the most celebrated in the world and the darling of New York society, whose members flock to sponsor it. Among the other leading American ballet companies are the San Francisco Ballet and Opera Company (the oldest in the US), the Joffrey Ballet (which divides its time between New York and San Francisco), the national ballet in Washington, and the Pittsburgh and Philadelphia ballet companies. Major international ballet companies perform regularly in the US, including the Bolshoi and Kirov companies (Moscow), the Royal Ballet (London) and the Paris Opera Ballet.

Tickets to concerts are often subsidised by local money and patronage, which usually keeps ticket prices between $10 and $35, although for major concerts and superstars they can be over $100 (top international performers charge up to $50,000 per concert!). Standing tickets are also sold at some venues (e.g. $10 for the Met). Opera and ballet tickets are also expensive (e.g. $40 to $100) and difficult to obtain, with people queuing all night for popular performances. If you're looking for bargains, it's often best to avoid major concert halls and attend performances at lesser venues where, although programmes vary considerably in quality, seats are usually half the price (you're also more likely to hear contemporary or avant-garde works in smaller auditoria). The best bargains of all are the free concerts, for example those given in New York City's Central Park in summer by the New York Philharmonic, where audiences number up to 250,000. Outdoor classical concerts are also held from July to September at the Hollywood Bowl, Los Angeles.

Most major American orchestras hold a winter season at their local concert hall and, when not touring, a summer season, usually staged in a park or pavilion. All orchestras (and ballet and opera companies) offer season or series tickets, which for many music lovers are the only way to obtain tickets. Enquire early about tickets for the coming season. Renewals for the winter season are usually offered to previous subscribers in June, after which tickets go on general sale. Because of the high price of tickets, two or more people often club together to buy a season ticket. In major cities, there are ticket brokers, permitted to sell tickets for a small surcharge, who handle some 5 per cent of all tickets in New York and other major cities. Brokers are common in top class hotels in major cities.

Many of the points relating to theatre facilities and tickets listed under **Theatres** (see page 411) also apply to most concert halls and tickets. Forthcoming concerts are listed in music and entertainment magazines, and local newspapers contain performance details and reviews. Information can also be obtained from tourist offices.

SOCIAL CLUBS

There are numerous social clubs and organisations in the US (as used here, the term 'social club' embraces any group of people who get together to share a common interest) and all cities and towns have a wide range of clubs. Joining a club is an excellent way to meet new people, make social and business contacts, and be accepted into the local community. In many rural towns, social life revolves around the local church and social clubs, and if you aren't a member your social life can be rather dull.

Common clubs and organisations include the American Legion, Audubon Society, boy and girl scouts, bridge, business, chess, choral groups, church, Democrat, Elks, ethnic and expatriate, gardening, Home and School Association, Jaycees, junior women, Kiwani, Knights of Columbus, League of Women Voters, leisure, Lion and Lioness, Masons, men's, Mensa, Moose Lodges, municipal bands, newcomers, professional (e.g. doctors, lawyers, engineers and journalists), PTA, Republican, rifle, Rotary, Round Table, senior citizens, Shriners, social, sports, Toastmasters, university (alumni), veterans' organisations, women's, YWCA/ YMCA, to name but a few.

Country clubs are popular among power brokers and social climbers, who usually belong to at least one. There's often tremendous prestige in belonging to the right country club, which are usually places to play tennis or golf and enjoy a meal. City clubs are generally a business institution and they're often male dominated places where executives hold 'power' breakfasts, entertain business clients or go simply to get away from their wives (or mistresses). Often clubs are a substitute for college fraternity houses or other 'boys' clubs, where men can get together for a drink and a few laughs and gain relief from the pressures of the office. Most country clubs have facilities for golf, swimming, tennis, squash (or racquetball) and a gymnasium. They may also cater for badminton, basketball, sailing and other sports (use of sports facilities may be included in annual fees). Other facilities generally include a sauna, restaurant, bar and dance floor, and possibly hotel accommodation.

Joining a fashionable country club may be a long-winded and bureaucratic affair, depending on the status (pomposity) and exclusivity of the club. Your application must usually be proposed by a member and sponsored by several (in some cases five or ten) other members before it's put before the membership committee. If you pass this test, you're required to attend an interview and, if accepted, you may still need to wait some time (even years) before becoming a member. Company membership of many clubs is possible, although most don't allow membership to be transferred to successors or colleagues. One of the big advantages of club membership for business people is that expenses for business entertaining (or whatever you can pass off as such) are tax deductible. Family membership of most clubs is also possible.

Membership of many country clubs is expensive and may be associated with home purchase (e.g. you may need to live in the local county). Ask in advance about initiation fees, monthly or annual dues, bonds and shares, capital assessment fees, family fees, plus any extra fees, e.g. for golf, tennis, swimming or other sports. Many clubs have a minimum expenditure at the clubhouse per quarter or month and most exact a non-returnable entrance or initiation fee, typically $1,000 to $2,500 for a couple, plus similar annual fees. New members may also be required to invest in the club by purchasing a non-transferable bond or shares. If you're resident in the US for a short period, make sure that any investment you make in a bond or shares is returned with interest when you leave the country.

In addition to private membership clubs, there are also public non-member clubs in many communities and all major cities, including many sports clubs and gyms. (See **Chapter 17 Sports**). Check with your local library or chamber of commerce for the names of clubs in your area.

NIGHTLIFE

The best nightlife in the US is, not surprisingly, found in the big cities. It embraces everything from the ritziest and most expensive floor shows featuring international stars to the sleaziest back street topless bars and strip joints. The most popular forms of nightlife include music bars, discotheques (discos) and dance clubs, piano bars, musical cabaret, supper clubs (with a dance band), comedy clubs, drag (female impersonators) and satirical cabaret. Discos come and go with amazing speed in the major cities, particularly in New York, where even the hottest discos rarely last more than a year. The most popular discos, with the most amazing sound and light systems, have high entrance fees (e.g. $20) and serve expensive drinks costing around $5.50 to $10 (mixers around $12). Some up market discos and dance clubs admit couples only.

Piano bars provide sophisticated musical entertainment and are popular in most cities. They usually have a minimum order of two drinks, but no entrance fees. Comedy clubs (entrance fee $5 to $25) are popular in most cities (particularly Los Angeles and New York) and feature up-and-coming, young stand-up comics (or old comedians on their way down). Foreigners often have trouble with the accents and humour (which often only Americans find funny). There are gay and lesbian bars and nightclubs in all major cities, particularly Atlanta, New York and San Francisco, often listed in mainstream guides and in free gay guides.

The hottest nightlife is found in New York, where anything goes and the party never stops (some people never see daylight!). New York clubs often don't warm up until midnight or 1am and the revelry continues until 4am or later (after which, if you've any energy left, you can go on to an 'after hours' joint). **Take care when leaving a club or anywhere after midnight, particularly if it's in an unlit street or a run-down area.** Most clubs don't have a strict membership policy and you can usually become an instant member (if the doorman likes your face). Entrance fees are from $5 to $20, depending on the day of the week (Fridays and Saturdays are the most expensive) and who's performing. Often free tickets can be obtained from convention and visitors' bureaux for mid-week access, and discount 'invitation' tickets are common. Many music bars have no entrance fee during the week and $5 on Fridays and Saturdays. **If you're refused entry to a club, never argue with a doorman, as they can be aggressive.** Don't forget to take identification with you, as you won't be allowed into a club serving alcohol without it or if you're under 21 (see **Bars** on page 420). In some clubs those under 18 are allowed entry, but aren't permitted to drink alcohol.

Dress codes vary considerably according to the venue. If you're unsure, smart casual is best (black is safest). This usually **excludes** jeans, leather, T-shirts and trainers, although in some establishments this may be the perfect gear (fashion dictates). If you don't look the part, you may be excluded (or at least feel uncomfortable), so it's best to check in advance. An up-to-date guide giving a run down on local hot-spots is a must if you want to be seen in the best places and avoid the dives. Always check who's playing, show times and entrance fees, as they often change at short notice. Obtain local newspapers and entertainment guides for the latest information.

GAMBLING

Despite the stereotype film and TV images of Americans as hard-drinking gamblers, many are puritanical when it comes to official gambling (casino owners prefer to call it 'gaming'), and many states don't officially allow casinos (although illicit casinos are widespread). Nevertheless, the US has an obsession with gambling and wagers over $400 billion a year ($300 billion in casinos), much of it in the world-famous gambling cities of Las Vegas (Nevada) and Atlantic City (New Jersey), where gambling, alcohol and sex are available on demand 24-hours a day. In Nevada, you can bet on practically anything, and even laundrettes, supermarkets and toilets have slot machines (slots) and most bars have gaming tables. Direct annual state gaming taxes total over $500 million or over 40 per cent of the state budget.

For most people, a visit to Las Vegas (Sodom and Gomorrah/Babylon) or Atlantic City is a memorable and sometimes shocking experience. The sheer scale, architecture, extravagance and opulence of the casinos is guaranteed to take your breath away. Vegas (the US's fastest-growing city) is compelling and repelling at the same time. It's so vulgar and monstrous that it's almost beautiful (and must be seen at night). On the other hand, some visitors are repulsed by these monuments to bad taste and see them as a stark portrayal of the worst of decadent modern America (it's said that there's more culture in a pot of yoghurt than in Las Vegas). Vegas is famous for its floor show extravaganzas, which attract the biggest American and international super-stars and, like everything in Vegas, are larger than life (Vegas has around 15 of the 20 largest hotels in the world).

Somewhat surprisingly to foreigners familiar with European casinos, American casinos have no dress code, and punters in jeans and T-shirts generally outnumber those in more formal attire (the only entrance requirement is money!). Most novice gamblers play the slot machines (100,000 in Vegas alone), which accept anything from a penny (1 cent) to a $500 token, with jackpots running into millions of dollars. It doesn't usually all pour out of the machine (despite the cartoon at the start of this chapter), although there must be worse ways to go than being buried alive in silver dollars (in Las Vegas in 2003, a person won $39.7 million from a slot machine - the largest payoff ever!). The most popular games with high rollers are roulette, poker and craps (played with dice).

If you take advantage of the plethora of special deals and resist the temptation to gamble away too much of your hard-earned cash, a few days in a gambling city can be an enjoyable experience. In contrast to the gambling, almost everything else is inexpensive, including accommodation, meals, drinks and shows. To entice people to make donations to their coffers, casinos offer inexpensive or free accommodation and meals to gamblers. Shop around and compare deals and freebies such as meals, shows and gambling coupons, and don't pay booking agents for accommodation. Meals in Vegas typically cost $5 to $15 for breakfast, lunch or dinner, although you shouldn't expect *cordon bleu* fare. Food is usually served buffet style from non-stop cafeterias to deter customers from wandering off in search of food.

Casinos are temples to man's desire to make a fast, easy buck and their *raison d'être* is to separate as many fools as possible from their loot in the shortest possible time. Many casinos provide free gaming lessons, but don't expect to receive any insider tips. However much you think you have a fool-proof scheme to break the bank, the odds favour the casino and over a period of time they **always** win (otherwise they wouldn't be in business). Don't gamble more than you're prepared to 'happily' lose and don't get robbed of your winnings on the way back to your hotel (winners often want their money in cash, even if it's $100,000).

Gamblers are plied with free cocktails (provided you look as if you're gambling; otherwise they cost around $2) in an effort to dull their senses and speed up the process of parting them from their loot. Casinos are even devoid of windows and clocks, so that customers won't be encouraged to leave at 'bed-time' (or any time while they still have money in their pockets!). If you wish to leave with your shirt, a book such as the *New Complete Guide to Gambling* by John Scarne (Fireside) might help.

Apart from Nevada and New Jersey, most states have little legal gambling. However, Indian (Native American) reservations are exempt from state gambling laws and reservation casinos have spread rapidly with the realisation that they're a licence to print money. American Indian tribes have set up hundreds of casinos in more than 26 states, on their own reservations or land, or through riverboat gambling (which is popular on the Mississippi and Ohio rivers, although stakes are generally low), and the combined revenue is worth billions of dollars a year. Ironically it was the white man's avarice that decimated the native Americans and it's their greed that has saved them from extinction (the Indians still scalp the white man, who now loses his shirt rather than his hair). However, not all Indians are in favour of gambling and many claim that it's destroying their cultural values.

Some 37 states run state lotteries with profits totalling over $32 billion (states pay out only half the receipts). Profits go towards schools, social services, parks, highways and other state programmes. State lotteries pay enormous prizes, multi-state lotteries sometimes paying a top prize of over $100 million, although major prizes are usually shared. Betting pools based on sports are popular at work, in schools and at home (Americans bet on any kind of sport). Only two states (Oregon and Nevada) allow sports gambling. Other forms of legal gambling include horse racing (all forms), greyhound racing and jai-alai. Off-track betting (OTB) is illegal in all states except Connecticut, Nevada and New York, where there are OTB offices. Some towns such as New Haven, Connecticut (home of Yale university), make up for their lack of racetracks with a Teletrack racing theatre, with a 24 x 32 foot screen, 1,800 seats and 40 betting windows.

All horse race betting is based on the totalizer (tote) system, where the total amount bet on a race is divided among the winners (after the organisers and the IRS have taken their cuts). Bets are placed at booths accepting stakes of $1 to $1,000. The different kinds of bets are explained in the official programme, as is the form of the horses and riders. Generally bets are the same as in other countries, although the terminology may be different. Bets can be made for a win ('on the nose'), a place (to come second) and to show (to come third). An 'each way' bet is a bet on a horse to win or be placed second or third.

Illicit gambling is widespread throughout the US and includes the infamous 'numbers' racket, illegal casinos, and informal and undercover gambling on sports results (gambling on the NFL alone is estimated to run into billions of dollars each week during the season). The numbers racket is akin to a raffle and is particularly popular in northern industrial areas, where blue-collar workers are the prime targets of numbers operators. There are different versions, the most common of which involves simply picking a number from 1 to 999 and staking $1. The winning number is usually the last three digits of a publicly quoted index, such as the closing Dow Jones index or the price of rubber futures. As the winner usually collects around $500 only, it's easy to see why this form of gambling is so popular with America's underworld. Another game to avoid is three-card monte, which is a pavement con game where the dupe tries to spot the odd colour among three quickly shuffled cards (similar to trying to find the pea under three shells). Internet gambling is also popular, although the US government has tried to ban the use of US issued credit cards for online gambling.

For most people, gambling is a bit of harmless fun, although it's no pleasure for the estimated 8 million compulsive gamblers in the US, including around 1 million teenagers. If you need help to stop gambling, contact Gamblers Anonymous, Box 17173, Los Angeles, CA 90017-0173 (☎ 213-386-8789, 💻 www.gamblers anonymous.org).

BARS

Social drinking in the US is usually done in bars, including hard-drinking, cocktail, singles, music, piano, hotel lounge, artistic, literary, business, ethnic, gay, neighbourhood, cigar and endless other varieties of bar. At the bottom end of the scale are dingy, mainly men's bars, with a noisy, beer-drinking, working class clientele, while at the other extreme are expensive cocktail bars inhabited by executives and professionals having a quiet drink after a day at the office. The cheaper bars are usually pretty awful places and most are nothing like the inviting pubs and cafés of Europe, where it's a pleasure to get drunk (or be thrown out). There's no US equivalent of the continental pavement café, where you can get anything from a cup of coffee to a cognac at any time of day and enjoy a tasty, inexpensive meal or snack at the same time.

Many bars are dives with a predominantly male clientele (women were originally banned from many bars, until thirsty feminists stormed the barricades), where single women may be unwelcome. However, although most women wouldn't wish to be seen dead in them, they're an excellent place to meet 'real' Americans. In some cities there are chains of bars, e.g. Blarney Stone and McAnn's in New York, serving imported beers and good value food. There are also British-style pubs, some of which are genuine, having been imported piece by piece. They sell a range of imported British beers, although they invariably lack the ambience of a real (British) pub. Many bars serve excellent lunches and snacks, and most serve some kind of food (whether it's edible or not is another matter!).

Those who want a quiet chat over a drink, perhaps at lunch time or after work, are likely to go to a cocktail lounge. Similar to European wine bars in decor and clientele, they're the main venue for middle class social drinkers, particularly in large cities. You're waited on at your table and pay after each round or 'run a tab', which you 'pick up' when you leave. When in groups, Americans tend to buy their own drinks, rather than rounds. Singles bars are cocktail bars where customers pay high prices (e.g. $4 to $5 for a beer and $8 for a mixer) for the privilege of chatting up the opposite (or same) sex in a 'favourable' atmosphere. At their best they can be good fun, although many are simply cattle markets where casual pick-ups are common.

Many bars are noisy places (often with live music) where people go for an expensive night out to drink, listen to music or dance. Karaoke (singing to recorded music) is popular in many bars, where frustrated pop stars can perform their favourite songs. Bars with live music usually have an entrance fee (cover charge) of $5 to $20, or the price of drinks is increased. Some places allow women free entry in order to attract free-spending men, although these are often the worst kind of cattle markets. Other bars cater for homosexuals and lesbians, so check in advance if this isn't your scene (some 'straight' bars also have gay evenings on certain days of the week). The main gay cities are Atlanta, New York and San Francisco. There are topless bars in some areas (these **aren't** bars without roofs).

Most cocktail bars have a 'happy hour'. This is usually a period of at least two hours during which drinks are sold cheaper than usual, e.g. half price or two drinks for the price of one. Happy hours are usually held in the late afternoon and early evening, e.g. 5pm to 7pm, although some may last all evening ('happy hour forever'). They may also be held on certain days only. If you wish, you can order a number of drinks during happy hour to last all evening, as long as you pay as you go. Usually happy hours are accompanied by free hot and cold food such as various hors d'oeuvres, dips, and cheese and biscuits. Generally, the more up-market the bar, the better the range of free food (if you plan to fill up on the free food, make sure you look respectable or you won't be admitted).

One thing that may influence your choice of watering hole is the cost, as a drink costing $1 in a seedy back street bar may cost as much as $7 or more in a trendy cocktail bar with a view. It's also usual to leave a tip in most cocktail bars, particularly if you want another round and wish to be served on your return. The practice of tipping varies according to the city and bar. For example, in most bars in New York people don't tip when they're drinking beer and may tip only after drinking a few cocktails or after occupying a stool at the bar. Where tipping is customary, it's usual to tip 15 to 20 per cent of the bill or 50 cents if you have a single drink (usually placed in the saucer provided). See also **Tipping** on page 532.

Bourbon (known as whisky) is the US's most popular spirit and got its name from Bourbon County, Kentucky, where it originated. It's distilled from varying mixtures of corn, maize and rye, and can be malted or unmalted. Jim Beam, Jack Daniels (from the oldest distillery in the US, although technically it isn't bourbon, as it isn't made in Kentucky) and Old Grandad are the most popular brands.

Canadian rye whiskies (known as rye) such as Canadian Club and Seagrams 7 are also popular, and are often mixed with Seven-Up (a kind of lemonade). Imported scotch whisky (scotch) is also popular, but is usually twice as expensive as bourbon. When ordering spirits, you're likely to receive an inexpensive 'house' brand if you don't name your poison. Other spirits are also popular, although they're rarely drunk straight (neat) but served in cocktails. The term 'highball' is used to describe such drinks as gin and tonic, whisky and soda, and rum and coke. If you don't want ice, ask for your drink 'straight up'. Drinks served with ice are said to be served 'on the rocks'.

Drinking habits tend to vary according to the establishment. In inexpensive bars, the clientele usually drink beer or bourbon, while in cocktail bars people are more likely to drink cocktails (surprise, surprise) or highballs. Cocktails are highly popular in bars and in restaurants, as an aperitif before dinner. Cocktail fashions change frequently, as customers and bartenders (barkeepers) compete to invent new ones. American bartenders are unique in their ability to mix cocktails. Among the most enduring are Black Russian, Bloody Mary, Daiquiri. Manhattan, Margarita, Martini, Mint Julep, Old-fashioned, Pina Colada, Rusty Nail, Tequila Sunrise, Tom (or John) Collins and Whisky Sour. Cocktails are usually served with cherries and other fruit and little umbrella cocktail sticks, plus the obligatory bucket of ice. The average cocktail price is around $5, although they can be double this in an expensive bar or club. A single shot (measure) of neat spirit costs at least $3 in most cocktail bars and is equivalent to a double in most countries, depending on the generosity of the bartenders (no measures are used). In addition to the large measures, American spirits are usually a lot stronger than in most other countries.

In stark contrast to their spirits, American beer is weak, and most foreigners find it's like drinking flavoured water (you risk drowning before you get drunk). After tasting American beer, you may wonder whether prohibition wasn't a good thing or, indeed, whether it's still in force. Most beer sold in the US is pasteurised draught lager, brewed from maize or even rice, rather than from barley. It's usually served ice-cold and much colder than most foreigners (except Australians) are used to. In addition to lager-type beer, most bars also sell dark beer. The best-known American beers are Budweiser (nothing like the real thing, which is brewed in the Czech Republic), Michelob and Schlitz, although the tastiest beers usually come from small local breweries and 'brewpubs' (where beer is brewed on the premises).

Americans don't usually add lime or lemonade to their beer to make, for example, a shandy, although you can order a beer with a shot of tomato juice, e.g. a 'Bud and blood' (tastes better than it sounds). A uniquely American beer is malt liquor (e.g. Colt 45 and Schlitz), brewed without hops and rather sweet and tasteless. In most states, you will also find low-alcohol, 'three-two' beer (3.2 per cent alcohol), which is even weaker than standard beers and is intended to reduce alcohol consumption. In some states there are three-two 'clubs', where those under 21 are permitted to drink three-two beer only. Low-alcohol (lite) beers such as Bud Light, clear malts (e.g. Zima) and ice beer have become increasingly popular in recent years and constitute a large part of the $45 billion annual beer market.

Draught beer (or beer 'on tap') is sold by the glass in bars and restaurants for $1.50 to $2 per glass. A glass usually contains 12 fl oz (the same as most bottles and cans). Many bars also sell beer by the pitcher, which is a jug containing a quart or half-gallon (32 to 64 fl oz). This is much cheaper than buying beer by the glass and costs around $5.50 per half-gallon. In the US, you usually order a beer or a pitcher, as there are no small and large glass sizes. As in many other countries, there's a considerable difference between bar and shop prices, and a six-pack (six 12 fl oz cans or bottles) costs as little as $3.75 from a shop.

Licensing

One of the biggest problems for social drinkers is knowing the local licensing and drinking laws. In some places you aren't permitted to stand to drink, cannot buy a drink on a Sunday or cannot get a drink at any time. Like most laws in the US, drinking and licensing regulations are set by individual states and are often modified by counties or local communities. Most bars open between 9am and noon (some as early as 6am) and close between midnight and 4am (or when the last customer falls off his bar stool). Some are open later on Saturday nights/Sunday mornings, while others close an hour earlier, e.g. 3am in New York. Where Sunday opening is permitted, licensing hours are usually shorter, e.g. noon to 1am. Generally, licensing laws are tougher than in many other countries and in some states (e.g. Utah) spirits can be bought only in state shops and not in bars. In some states, many counties are dry (e.g. Mississippi and Texas). Nevada has the most liberal licensing laws.

The minimum age for drinking in bars is 21 (since 1984) in all states, although in some areas you can drink beer or low alcohol three-two beer (see above) at the age of 18 or 19. Age limits are strictly enforced in most states, although some are lax. You may be asked to show some identification (ID), even if you're fairly obviously over 21 (some bartenders or doormen ask everyone for identification, even pensioners). If you're a foreigner, always carry your passport or other identification. Needless to say, there's a thriving business in false identification cards sold at print shops where you can have a false name, address, age, social security number or whatever. However, anyone who uses false identification to obtain a drink is guilty of fraud, in addition to drinking under age. In some states (e.g. Louisiana) there's no liability for bar owners and they may therefore be less concerned about under-age drinkers, while in others, e.g. Colorado, a bartender must be insured against being sued for serving someone who later has a car accident. It's even illegal in some states to give anyone under 21 a drink in a **private** house, e.g. at a party or with a meal.

There are strict laws regarding the sale of alcohol in most states (see **Alcohol** on page 481) and there are 'dry' counties and towns in many areas, although there's usually a nearby town where you can get a drink. In some states, such as Kansas and Oklahoma, you may need to join a private club through a hotel or motel, although 'membership' is often included in the price of your first drink. At many state borders, there are 'last chance' bars for those entering a dry state or county (interestingly, newspaper reports in dry counties often involve cases of public drunkenness). In many southern states, it's illegal to advertise alcohol, but not to sell it ('cold beverages of all kinds' usually means beer is sold). Other drinking legislation includes the so-called 'container' laws, which prohibit drinking in public places almost everywhere. This law is largely ignored and has given rise to the custom known as 'brown-bagging', where alcohol is concealed in brown paper bags, used by alcoholics and picnickers to hide their favourite tipple. Alcohol purchased for consumption on licensed premises cannot usually be consumed elsewhere.

There's a much stricter attitude towards drunkenness in the US than in many other countries, and if you look as if you've had one too many you're likely to be refused service and may even be ejected. Business drinking is modest and disciplined, and drunken behaviour is socially unacceptable and regarded with contempt (and can also get you arrested or mugged if you aren't careful). Drinking and driving (see page 285) is a serious offence throughout the US and the federal government has even threatened to cut highway funds to states allowing those under 21 to drink.

Information

There are bar guide books in most large cities, and most guide books contain recommendations. Local newspapers in all cities and towns carry advertisements for local bars, particularly those with live music and other entertainment (e.g. Karaoke). Habitual drunks may like to obtain a copy of *Barhop USA* by 'Awesome Wells' (Permanent Press).

EATING OUT

The US isn't noted for its cuisine, and most gastronomes consider it a benighted country in culinary terms (*haute cuisine* in the US is almost inevitably foreign cuisine). Out in the countryside, however, some of the regional cuisines are surprisingly good: a New England clambake, Cajun cooking in New Orleans, or many of the hearty soups, chowders and gumbos that rely on local ingredients. However, Americans are **BIG** eaters (nearly two-thirds of American adults are overweight) and most cities and towns contain a wealth of restaurants and other eating places, ranging from gourmet restaurants to 'greasy spoon' cafes. Many Americans dine out three or four times a week, with some 40 to 50 per cent of the average person's food budget spent on eating away from home.

In most cities, there's a multitude of eating places, including more than 25,000 in New York, a restaurant for every 200 inhabitants in San Francisco, and more restaurants per capita in New Orleans than any city in the world except Paris. New York is one of the world's top five culinary cities (ranking alongside Hong Kong, London, Paris and Tokyo) and has the most diverse and best value restaurants in the world (the NY foodies' bible is the *Zagat Restaurant Guide*, listing all the city's best restaurants). The secret to eating well in the US is to steer well clear of the plastic highway eateries and fast-food restaurants. However, American menus are written by the best fiction writers in the US and the food may bear little or no resemblance to the mouth-watering delights described on the menu. Americans generally go in for quantity rather than quality, and portions are usually enormous everywhere (American life is fattening!).

It's difficult to generalise about American restaurants, as the quality, price, cuisine and range of establishments varies so greatly. Often restaurants employ gimmicks to attract customers and excess is generally the order of the day, e.g. in the decor, food description or staff appearance. Waiters and waitresses may dress as clowns, lobsters or penguins – anything to appear different and attract custom. Many Americans don't know the difference between quality and kitsch, and menu prices are often determined by the decor, labour costs and hype, rather than the quality of the food.

American restaurants come in every type and class, from lavish expense-account *haute* and *nouvelle cuisine* French restaurants through a veritable maze of American and ethnic restaurants (listed in the yellow pages by speciality or national cuisine and often also by area). Other eating places include family restaurants, cafeterias, fast food joints, diners, truck-stops, cafes, delicatessens (delis), snack bars, lunch counters, take-aways (take-outs or carry-outs), coffee shops and street vendors.

The ethnic potpourri that is the US is most evident in the range and variety of its eating establishments, unrivalled in any other country. The most common types are Chinese (most regional styles), Italian (including innumerable pizza parlours), Japanese (e.g. sushi bars), Jewish, Korean, Mexican (or Tex-Mex), Thai and Vietnamese. Also common in many cities are German, Greek, Lebanese, Polish, Russian, Turkish and Yugoslavian restaurants. Some ethnic restaurants are found only in certain areas, where they reflect the ancestry of the local population, e.g. the Basque restaurants in many west coast farming regions. The US's ethnic restaurants are one of the joys of eating out and they do more to promote international goodwill and cross-cultural exchange in a day than the United Nations does in a year.

The most expensive (and intimidating) restaurants are usually French, where staff often outnumber the diners and the menu is indecipherable, followed by up-market Italian restaurants and the hybrid continental. The majority of exclusive and trendy restaurants, particularly in cities such as Los Angeles and New York, are grossly over-priced (particularly the wine), pretentious and gastronomically unimpressive. Many of the most fashionable establishments are places to see and be seen ('To hell with the food, isn't that Robert Redford over there?'). These places are best visited when someone else is paying. Foreign cuisine is almost always at its best in small family-run restaurants, where generally the less pretentious the decor, the better the food. Sometimes foreign dishes in restaurant chains or family restaurants are Americanised to such an extent that they're unrecognisable.

In most restaurants, you won't need a starter, as single portions are usually enough to feed two (or a whole family for a week in most third world countries) and some restaurants even allow customers to order one meal for two people. In many restaurants, salad (from self-service salad bars) is included in the price of the entree (main course) and is eaten as a starter (appetizer). There's usually a choice of Italian, French, Russian, thousand island and blue cheese dressing. Vegetables other than potatoes (e.g. fries or baked) often aren't included in the price of a meal and must be ordered separately. Potatoes are often cooked with their skins or you can even order potato skins on their own. If you're unable to finish your meal, it's quite usual to be asked if you want a 'doggie bag' to take the remains of your meal home for tomorrow's lunch (although it isn't done in smart restaurants).

Whatever your preference or price range, you will find it somewhere in most cities. Local restaurant guides can be purchased in most large cities and most travel guides provide recommendations at all price levels. Local newspapers in all cities and towns are packed with advertisements for local eating places and bars, many providing coupons and other discounts. Your American friends, colleagues, neighbours and acquaintances are usually also glad to recommend their favourite places (and tell you what to avoid).

Diners

Although diners and roadhouses are at the bottom of the gastronomic league table, they often serve excellent food (it can also be terrible). A diner was originally a roadside caravan (or an old railway carriage) used mainly by truckers, but nowadays it may mean any café or truck-stop with low prices and long menus; many are open 24 hours. They usually have a counter with stools, plus tables and chairs, where you're often waited on by the proprietor and his wife. In many towns, diners and roadhouses (which were an institution) have become extinct, thanks to the ubiquitous franchise fast food outlets.

The *pièce de résistance* of diners remains their hearty breakfasts, costing as little as 99 cents. Most diners have lunch 'specials', which may not offer the best of home-cooking but are usually tasty, filling and inexpensive. Often there are signs saying 'no substitutions'. This means that the special menu is fixed and you cannot, for example, replace the fries with boiled potatoes. Diners are also the place to go for a slice of genuine American pie (apple, blueberry, pecan, pumpkin and banana cream, to name but a few). Some diners are open 24 hours a day. Most don't serve alcohol. Apart from tea and coffee, the only drinks you're likely to find in diners are soft drinks (soda or juice), served in large (small), huge (regular) and gigantic (large) paper cups, with the obligatory bucket of ice. You can also order low-calorie or no calorie ('no cal' or diet) soft drinks, such as ginger ale or cola (or if you prefer, a reactionary brand called 'Jolt', boasting 'all the sugar and twice the caffeine').

Fast Food

Americans invented fast food (the market is worth around $100 billion a year) and have successfully exported it around the world, even invading Eastern Europe and China in recent years. Among the most familiar names are McDonald's, Kentucky Fried Chicken, Burger King, Pizza Hut, Taco Bell, Wendy's, Howard Johnson, and the International House of Pancakes (IHOP). Many Americans rank Wendy's and Burger King above McDonald's, and local chains of independent hamburger joints are often rated highest of all, e.g. Fuddruckers on the east coast. Some fast food joints specialise in home deliveries (which you can even order by computer), particularly pizza parlours serving pizzas as big as a Texan's hat. American fast food is the most diverse in the world and includes hot dogs, hamburgers, fried or grilled chicken, stuffed potatoes, vegetarian snacks, samosas, calamari, dim sum, sushi, gyros, falafel, couscous, tabouleh, Italian beef sandwiches, doner or shish kebab, pitta bread, bagels, pretzels, tortilla, taco and pizzas, to name but a small selection.

In the US, fast food isn't synonymous with junk food and it can be fresh, nutritious, and excellent value for money. (American hamburgers are usually made from pure beef, although it's sometimes mixed with soya beans.) There are even gourmet fast food outlets, which are so good that hosts are proud to tell you where your dinner came from. At many fast food restaurant chains, you're asked whether your order is 'to eat here or to go'. Take-away food doesn't incur sales tax in some states. Drive-in (drive-thru) fast food outlets are popular, where you may order and collect your food from a window, or order via an intercom. Your food is delivered on a tray (possibly by a roller-skating waitress), which you hang from your car window. (Wendy's recently won the 'fastest drive-thru service' accolade with an average service time of 2 minutes and 22 seconds). Fast food outlets on wheels (mobile canteens or 'roach coaches') are also common throughout the US. There's no tipping in fast food restaurants, and you're usually expected to clean up after yourself and deposit your rubbish in the bins provided.

Delicatessens

An American delicatessen (deli) isn't usually an exotic (and expensive) imported food shop, but a gourmet sandwich and salad bar (eat in or 'to go') and the ultimate in fast food establishments. Some delis are celebrated world-famous restaurants (e.g. in New York City) with prices to match and have little in common with humble street-corner delis. Sandwiches are made from a variety of bread with numerous (often unfamiliar) appetising fillings. Classic fare includes chicken, tuna and egg, pastrami (smoked beef) or corned beef served on rye bread with mustard, and bagels with cream cheese or smoked salmon (lox). You can usually choose from black rye bread (rye), brown rye bread (light rye), brown bread (wheat) and white bread, e.g. French and referred to as a hero, sub or submarine, torpedo, hoagy or grinder. Club sandwiches consist of three slices of toast in layers filled with chicken/turkey, lettuce, tomato, bacon and sometimes cheese. Many delis also serve hot meals and toasted sandwiches. In delis, and generally anywhere at lunchtime, in major cities, you're expected to know what you want and to order fast. You can telephone or fax your order to many delis and diners, who deliver to your home or office and also provide home or office buffets and party catering.

Family Restaurants

Roadside diners are slowly being replaced (particularly on or close to main highways) by 'family restaurants', which are chain restaurants somewhere between fast food joints and more up-market restaurants. Typical fare is steaks (American steaks are among the best and biggest in the world), roast beef and lobster. They usually serve beer and wine but not spirits. The largest chains include Cracker Barrel, Denny's, Hungry Tiger, Marie Callender's, Sizzlers and Velvet Turtle (Americans have a way with words). Many family restaurants, such as Cracker Barrel, provide unbeatable value, and most have an all-you-can-eat salad or soup bar and a sweet (dessert) bar. If you're allergic to children, give family restaurants a wide berth (children are usually specially catered for in American restaurants and much more welcome than in some European countries).

Breakfast

For many people, breakfast, costing as little as $3 for a 'breakfast special' is a treat not to be missed (for others, especially those on a diet, it's to be avoided at all costs). It usually consists of any or all of the following: eggs, bacon, sausages, hash browns, grits, toast, cereal, waffles, pancakes, honey, maple syrup (usually all served on the same plate), plus orange juice and an endless supply of coffee. Most Americans eat everything together (often mixing sweet and savoury foods). Eggs can be ordered every imaginable way and in any quantity (one or two is normal). If you order fried eggs, you're asked how you want them cooked; 'sunny side up' is unturned, 'over' is turned and cooked on both sides, 'over easy' is turned but with a runny yolk, and 'over hard' is turned with a hard yolk. For your toast you may be offered a choice of white, rye, whole-wheat, pumpernickel bread or an 'English' muffin.

Brunch

Brunch is a combination of breakfast and lunch (hence the name), usually eaten between 11am and 3pm, particularly on Sundays (Sunday brunch). Favourite brunch food includes smoked salmon (lox) and cream cheese on a bagel, steak and eggs, eggs Benedict, and crepes and waffles (often accompanied by 'free' drinks, e.g. Bloody Marys, Mimosas and Champagne). Many restaurants and hotels serve a buffet-style all-you-can-eat brunch for a fixed price, e.g. $15 or $20. Some hotels and cafes, particularly in major cities such as New York, serve afternoon tea (usually from 3pm to 6pm), which is becoming increasingly fashionable with business people.

Desserts

If you're still hungry (or thirsty) after your Big Mac or Kentucky Fried Chicken, you may like to visit a soda fountain or an ice-cream parlour (although if you're on a diet and have no willpower, give them a wide berth). For a dollar or two you can choose from a 'million' varieties (new flavours are invented daily) of ice-cream, milk shake or malted milk (a milk shake with malt flavouring added). All are made with natural ingredients (milk or cream) and are worlds away from the plastic fare served up by some fast food joints. Ice-cream is the US's national dish and among the best in the world. (Although a recent medical study called American ice cream 'a heart attack in a cup' for all the fat, sugar and cholesterol content in the best brands.) National chains include Baskin-Robbins, Ben & Jerry's, Dairy Queen and Haagen Dazs. A float is a drink combining soda (usually cola or root beer) and ice cream. Frozen (often fat-free) yoghurt is also popular and is sold in chains such as TCBY and 'I Can't Believe It's Yoghurt' (it certainly doesn't taste like it). Cookie shops are also common in many cities.

Drinks

If you want a glass of wine or beer with your meal, you must find a licensed restaurant or bring your own (where allowed); coffee bars, fast food joints and most diners don't serve alcohol (liquor). In some states, you must belong to a private club to get a drink with your meal (see **Licensing** on page 423), while in others you must bring your own wine, beer or spirits (the restaurant provides glasses, ice and mixer drinks, called 'set-ups'). This practice is also common in unlicensed restaurants in states where it's difficult to obtain an alcohol licence. Some restaurants are licensed to sell wine and beer but not spirits. Cocktails are often drunk before lunch and dinner, particularly when entertaining business associates. Most Americans don't drink wine with meals, except in California, and many Americans don't drink alcohol at all, for religious or health reasons. Many Americans drink coffee or tea with (as well as after) their food, possibly served in a mug rather than a cup. Most Americans are unable to eat anything without a copious supply of (iced) water. Usually when you sit down in a restaurant you receive a glass (or pitcher) of iced water, which is constantly refilled.

Wine can be expensive in restaurants, where there's usually at least a 200 per cent mark-up, particularly if you order imported vintage wine. House wine often consists of Italian 'plonk', a half carafe of which can cost around $15. Californian wines are popular and are usually cheaper and better than many inexpensive imported French wines, although even they can cost $25 per bottle or $5 to $6 per glass. (You should always check the cost of a glass of wine, which can be as much as $10!). Often, wines listed on wine lists as 'chablis' or 'claret' are Californian (white and red respectively) and not imported French wines. American wines include good cabernets, rieslings and rosé ('blush' or white Zinfandel). Californian sparkling wine such as Chandon is also popular and rivals some of the best imports. (If only someone could teach Americans not to chill red wine!)

Coffee & Tea

Coffee is the US's national drink, although it's generally weak and often stale or burnt from sitting around on a hot plate all day. If you come from continental Europe where each cup is made fresh and tastes and smells of fresh coffee, you will often be hugely disappointed. However, freshly-brewed espresso, cappuccino, mocha and milk (latte) coffee is available in bars and coffee shops (such as Starbucks), which have spread throughout the US in recent years.

However, buying a coffee can be like being in a quiz show. Coffee usually comes in two varieties, 'regular' or 'decaf' (decaffeinated), sometimes referred to as 'Sanka', a brand name often used as a generic term. As with all their food, Americans like to mess with their coffee, which is also drunk with vanilla, almond and chocolate flavourings, and fruit syrups. Coffee is served 'with' or 'without' cream or milk and you may get a blank look if you ask for a white coffee. A regular coffee is usually black, although in some places 'regular' means white, sometimes with one or two teaspoons of sugar. You generally receive your own jug of 'cream', usually half cream and half milk (called half and half). If you order coffee 'to go', you may be asked if you want cream or milk, and if milk, whether you want 1 per cent or 2 per cent (both low fat).

In most establishments you can drink as many cups of 'house' coffee as you like for the price of one cup (from 75 cents). Take-away coffee, like all American drinks, comes in large, huge and enormous sizes. A 'small' coffee is equal to two normal size cups.

If you think American coffee is terrible, wait until you try their tea! You're usually served with a cup or pot of hot (if you're lucky) water, with a tea bag (it will come as no surprise to discover that the US invented the tea bag) and a cup and saucer. In the US, tea isn't usually made with boiling water and cold milk (as in the UK). You're generally offered lemon with your tea, and you may have to ask for milk, if you prefer it that way. In some places (e.g. the southern states) you may be served iced tea (a strong tea drink served with lemon, sugar and lots of ice) unless you specify the hot variety. Many Americans prefer non-caffeine herbal teas (served 'straight' or with lemon) to the normal 'black' tea variety. Green tea is now popular, as it is believed to be healthier than black tea. Popular flavours include apple and cinnamon, blackcurrant, camomile, emperors (a spicy herb) and ginseng, peppermint, and rose hip. Iced coffee is also a popular American drink in certain regions, particularly in the Northeast. Tea costs around the same as coffee (from 75 cents), although you receive one cup only.

Meal Times

American meal times may differ from what you're used to, although in large cities you can eat around the clock, particularly breakfast. This is often served 24 hours a day in diners, cafes and coffee shops. Working or 'power' breakfasts (invented in Los Angeles) are popular in the main cities and are often offered at hotels. Breakfast is usually served from as early as 6am (in places not open 24 hours) until 10am or 11am, lunchtime is usually from 11am to 2.30pm and dinner (often called supper) between 5.30pm and 9pm. As a general rule, supper is a light meal eaten earlier than dinner, for example between 5.30pm and 6.30pm. Dinner is the main meal of the day for most people. In small towns or anywhere outside the main cities, dinner (or supper) may be served until 7pm or 8pm only, although there's usually a local fast food joint or truck-stop open until much later. Top restaurants often open at 11.30am for lunch and some remain open until late evening. In some areas, restaurants close on one day a week, e.g. Mondays.

Bookings

Many popular restaurants don't take bookings (reservations) and operate on a first-come, first-served basis. Queues, however, usually move quickly, and it's often possible to wait in the bar. Most restaurants have a non-smoking section (often required by law) and in some cities and states smoking is banned by law in all restaurants. When it's possible to make bookings, they should be made at least 24 hours in advance and preferably earlier for parties or at busy times. It's necessary to book weeks in advance for some fashionable restaurants. In most major cities, restaurants open and close with such frequency that you should book just to check that they're still in business. When making a booking, you should specify smoking or non-smoking and any special requirements, such as a private booth. You may be asked for a credit card number when booking. Be warned that if you don't turn up, your account may be debited for an amount equal to the average cost of a meal for each member of your party. If you're going to be late, warn the restaurant or you could lose your table (15 minutes may be too late in a popular restaurant).

Dress

Many restaurants have dress codes ranging from no jeans, shorts or T-shirts to compulsory tie or jacket for men and dresses (or 'dressy' slacks) for women. Dress rules depend on the popularity and standards (or pretensions) of establishments and to a certain extent on the location. If you're planning to eat in a fancy (expensive) restaurant for the first time, check the dress code in advance, particularly if you plan to dress casually. If you arrive 'undressed', a restaurant may lend you a tie or jacket but is unlikely to have a selection of dresses. Serviettes (napkins) are often worn by men like bibs, tucked into shirt fronts or attached to buttons.

Formalities

At most restaurants or anything other than a diner or fast food joint, you should wait to be seated, which is the 11th commandment in the US (unless there's a sign saying 'Please seat yourself'). Often there's a 'Please wait to be seated' sign, when a 'captain' or 'hostess' shows you to your table. Sharing tables is almost never done in the US in any establishment. In a fashionable restaurant, if you aren't a regular customer or aren't rich and famous (or proffer a **very** large tip), you will probably be seated in 'Siberia', the trade term for tables hidden behind pillars or in alcoves where you cannot see or be seen. In some restaurants you may be totally ignored, which can be bad news if you're trying to impress a business client. In expensive restaurants, a woman accompanied by a man may be given a menu without prices (a date menu); great if she is paying!

Americans often go way over the top in their cheerful, effusive, over-attentive service. Your waiter's patter is likely to go something like: 'Hi, I'm Rick and I'll be your waiter this evening. I'd like to tell you about today's specials. We've got . . . enjoy your meal', accompanied by a smile a mile wide. He may also enquire after your health or ask about your day (there's no need to tell him). It can become rather wearing after a time, particularly if you're cynical and see it merely as a stock ritual to encourage a large tip. On the other hand, restaurant staff are usually attentive and often genuinely keen to see you enjoy your meal. Americans often summon their waiter by name ('Hey Rick!'), which, in case you forget it, is usually worn on a name tag. In fancy restaurants, you may be inundated with staff (*maître d'hôtel*, captain, hostesses, waiters, cocktail waiters, wine waiters, busboys, etc.), all of whom have a different task.

Cost

An inexpensive meal in a restaurant in a major city can cost as little as $5 per head, excluding drinks. Expect to pay at least $50 a head in top restaurants. In smaller towns, prices are often as little as half those charged in large cities for the same quality food. Some restaurants have a minimum charge. Prices quoted in guide books generally don't include drinks (see page 429), sales tax (see page 474) or tips (see below and page 532), which may double the cost. However, if you have a tight budget you can usually eat well for around $15 and get a filling meal for less than $10. One of the best American food bargains is the Great American Breakfast (see above), costing a few dollars only. Taking advantage of lunch 'specials' and looking for places serving low-priced 'sunset' or 'early-bird' suppers (usually before 6pm or 6.30pm) also saves money. The lunch menu, even in expensive restaurants, is usually much cheaper than dinner, even though the food may be the same (and as an added advantage, the portions are generally smaller!). As in most countries, city centre restaurants are usually more expensive than those in the suburbs. Hotel restaurants, grills and coffee shops are generally the most expensive of all and are to be avoided by all but the extravagant. Try to avoid restaurants catering mainly to tourists, as the transitory nature of the clientele is often reflected in poor quality food.

Paying the Bill

In fast food joints and cafeterias, you pay when you receive your food. In other establishments you receive a computerised print-out or a hand-written bill ('the check'), which includes local tax but not usually service. You should have your bill itemised and verify that it's correct, as in some places it's likely to be wrong. In quality restaurants you pay your waiter at the table, while in diners and other places you usually pay at a cash desk on your way out. Payment can usually be made in cash, by travellers' cheques or credit card. In some establishments, it's acceptable to leave the amount owed on the table (with the tip). Some restaurants may add a percentage to your bill as a 'suggested' service charge, or when your party includes more than six or eight people. In general, a service charge isn't included in the bill, and you're expected to tip the waiter or waitress around 12 to 20 per cent of the total before tax. The total on credit card slips is usually left blank to encourage you to leave a tip. Don't forget to fill in the total before signing it or your waiter may be tempted to write in his own tip. Americans usually tip even when buying a cup of coffee (usually 10 cents) or a snack (e.g. 25 cents), when the tip may be left under the plate. Don't worry if you've been served by a variety of staff, as tips are usually pooled, although in high class establishments it's common to tip the wine waiter and perhaps the *maître d'* (pronounced 'mayter dee'). You may **need** to tip the *maître d'* to get a seat in a fancy restaurant (see also **Tipping** on page 532). If you don't tip in a restaurant, you would generally be unwise to return (without a disguise).

LIBRARIES

The US has an excellent public library service and there are libraries in all cities and most towns, although membership is surprisingly low at below 5 per cent of the population. In addition to municipally funded public libraries (including mobile libraries), there are also a vast number of private reference libraries (many are part of museums) in US cities, containing important collections on a wide range of subjects. In some states, all state residents are entitled to use state college and university libraries. Many private libraries are more like museums, where valuable books and manuscripts are displayed. Even large public libraries (such as New York City's) house valuable collections of rare books. Admission to private libraries is usually free, although some charge an entrance fee of around $5 to non-members and some are for members only (membership fees vary considerably). Where applicable, members can usually borrow (take out) books, while non-members can use libraries for reference only. Some libraries are reserved for bona fide research.

New York City public library has the third largest collection of books (more than 9 million in 3,000 languages and dialects) in the world after the American Library of Congress and the British Library. Public libraries in major cities have business sections and sometimes have separate business libraries. These are an excellent source of up-to-date business information. However, in some major libraries you don't have direct access to books and must locate the titles required via a file index (often computerised), complete a slip and wait (sometimes a long time) for them to be delivered. Many public libraries are organised on a county-wide or state-wide system (interlibrary loan), where you have access to any book at any library within the county or state. Books can usually be borrowed from (and returned to) any library in the system.

In addition to lending libraries, local libraries also have reference sections where you will find encyclopaedias, dictionaries, trade directories, federal publications, atlases and maps, educational books, telephone books, and any number of other reference works and catalogues. All main or central libraries also have copies of local and national newspapers and magazines, usually found in the reading room. Central libraries in major cities have international telephone directories for many foreign cities and may also provide information in a number of languages. Many libraries have a large selection of foreign-language books, particularly in Spanish.

In order to borrow books from a public library, you need to show proof of residence. Anyone who lives, works or studies in the US can join their local public library free of charge on production of the appropriate identification (e.g. a driving licence) and their current address. Children under 15 or 16 must be 'sponsored' by a parent or guardian. You're given a membership card, allowing you to borrow as many as 10 books at a time or even an unlimited number. Some libraries have restrictions, e.g. a shorter loan period, for the latest bestsellers, and non-residents may need to pay for library membership (there are also usually limits on the number of 'recent fiction' books you can borrow). Books are usually loaned for three or four weeks and there are fines for late returns, e.g. 10 cents per day for books and $1 for CDs (compact discs) and videos. Some libraries have a book return container outside, so you can return books when the library is closed.

Library opening times vary considerably. Main libraries may open from 9am to 9pm from Mondays to Thursdays, and 9am to 5pm on Fridays and Saturdays (hours may be restricted on summer Saturdays, e.g. 9am to 1pm). Many libraries are also open on Sundays, e.g. from 1pm to 5pm. In some areas, branch libraries are closed on one weekday and all libraries are closed on federal holidays. When a library has a separate children's section, opening times may differ from those of the main library. In recent years, many libraries have had to reduce their opening hours in the face of budget cuts and are struggling to maintain their services. Many solicit contributions from the public through 'friends of the library' schemes.

Most libraries carry stocks of books in large print for those with poor eyesight and many also provide 'talking books' (on cassette) for blind and partially-sighted members. Many also have a Kurzweil Reading Machine which can 'read' printed material and convert it into speech. All libraries have collections of books for adults with reading or spelling problems, e.g. dyslexia. Other items for loan may include magazines, audio cassettes, CDs, computer software, video films, DVDs, games, toys, jigsaw puzzles and art (e.g. paintings and posters). There's a rental charge on most of these items and usually a limit on the number of items that can be rented at one time. Many towns have separate toy lending libraries.

In addition to their lending and reference services, most libraries provide a free information service on any subject. Local libraries are one of the best sources of information about local community services and information (e.g. housing, consumer rights, money problems, voluntary work and job search skills), public transport, clubs and organisations. Other services usually include job information, computers and internet access, collections, social services and a range of children's services. Many libraries have children's centres and activities such as story-telling, films, workshops and exhibitions, and many publish a monthly schedule of events for children. Libraries in some cities operate literacy centres, where illiterates are taught to read and write, and help is given to immigrants learning English as a second language.

Most reference libraries provide coin-operated photocopiers (usually 10 cents or 20 cents per copy) for public use (they may accept all coins and give change). Some central libraries have colour laser copiers and many provide telephones and fax facilities.

16.

SPORTS

Sport is a huge industry in the US, where people take their sport extremely seriously, as participants and spectators (sport is **the** national language). Few countries are more sports conscious than the US, where the competitive urge is paramount. Many Americans' idea of relaxation is some form of energetic exercise, such as a vigorous game of tennis or racquetball. However, despite the popular image of a nation of joggers, most Americans get their daily sporting fix via television (TV) or as spectators, rather than by working up a sweat (to many Americans, keeping in shape means drinking a small beer or eating half a slice of pie). Sports facilities throughout the US are generally second to none, although they can be prohibitively expensive in some cities.

It's estimated that some 95 per cent of Americans take part in sports at least once a month, as participants or spectators. The most popular participant sports are walking, with some 70 million regular participants, swimming (65 million), cycling (60 million), fishing (55 million), jogging or running (50 million), hiking (45 million) and callisthenics. The top spectator sports (including nationwide TV audiences) are baseball, American football and basketball, all of which originated in the US and have little mass appeal in other countries (or nothing like the fervour generated in the US). Other popular sports include aerial sports, boxing, golf, handball, (ice) hockey, hunting, motor racing, racquetball, skiing and other winter sports, softball, tennis, tenpin bowling, athletics (track), watersports and wrestling. Many sports that are primarily amateur sports or played purely for fun in other countries are played professionally in the US, often for big money prizes (e.g. tenpin bowling and volleyball).

Exercise and amateur sport is often undertaken as part of the latest fashion craze, rather than for enjoyment or health. Americans pursue the latest fitness fads with a passion and are convinced that staying fit requires more than regular exercise and a balanced diet. Many Americans **agonise** over whether they're getting enough exercise (including those who do no regular exercise at all). Jogging is extremely popular throughout the country and with the exception of swimming (which is usually done for pleasure rather than purely for exercise) is the number one fitness pursuit (or the most popular way of committing suicide for the grossly unfit!). Most cities and towns have official jogging circuits in parks and along beaches. The latest craze to sweep the US in recent years is to have your own personal trainer, i.e. someone to coach and train you in your daily fitness regime. Many wealthy Americans have home gyms, and executives often have the use of a gym at their office. Whatever sport you practise, it's important to look the part and have the latest and best equipment, plus the most fashionable attire (particularly if you belong to a country club).

The cost of using private sports facilities is high in major cities such as Los Angeles and New York, but generally inexpensive in smaller towns. Most communities have recreational parks with tennis and basketball courts, a 'ball park' and a swimming pool, which can usually be used free by residents. Many communities also have an inexpensive YMCA sports centre with a swimming pool, gymnasium, training centre, tennis and racquetball courts, basketball and volleyball. Courses and coaching are provided in a wide range of sports.

Many community schools and municipal recreation departments organise a variety of sports classes, and most large corporations, hospitals and churches have indoor gymnasiums and informal sports teams. For those who can afford the high membership fees, there are exclusive country clubs and health and fitness centres in all areas, catering mainly for basketball, golf, handball, racquetball, squash, swimming, tennis and volleyball, and usually with gymnasiums. Most clubs provide professional coaching and training programmes.

American insularity is most evident in the field of sports, where the US is truly an island unto itself. Most international sporting events outside the US hardly warrant a mention in the American media (except perhaps when an American wins), compared to the lavish coverage devoted to American sports. With a few exceptions, such as athletics, Americans rarely enjoy seeing their country's teams and sports stars compete against other countries, so opportunities for jingoism are limited. However, the fact that Americans compete mostly among themselves doesn't prevent them crowning themselves World Champions (football), or competing for the World Series (baseball) or the World Championship (basketball). Whatever the sport, Americans love statistics, and fans can recite their team's batting, running, passing and scoring averages for the past three seasons (when watching sport on TV you're inundated with statistics and trivial information). American sports fans are nothing if not devoted, and they even turn up in their thousands to demonstrate support for their beloved teams in 'pep rallies' before big matches. Many foreigners find the Americans' passion for spectator sports excessive and even obsessive, although the hooliganism associated with spectator sports in many other countries is largely absent in the US.

Professional sport is a large and profitable branch of show business. Professional teams are owned and run purely as businesses and are occasionally sold or even moved to another location when business is bad (the most famous example is the Brooklyn Dodgers baseball team, which moved from New York to Los Angeles in 1957). Almost all teams and sports events are sponsored, often for astronomical amounts, and star players are also heavily sponsored and often earn more from sponsorship deals, endorsements and appearance fees than they do from wages and prize money. Professional athletes are paid huge amounts, particularly in top sports such as baseball, basketball and American football, where the average player earns over $1 million a year and star players earn astronomical salaries. Michael Jordan (basketball) is reputedly the highest-paid athlete in the world, earning over $30 million per year. In the last few years, confrontation over pay between team owners (many of whom are losing money and want salary caps) and players has resulted in lockouts and strikes in baseball (the 1994 World Series was cancelled) and hockey. The US's obsession with money means that everything must have a price or value, reflected in the Most Valuable Player (MVP) titles awarded to the leading players in professional team sports.

The major TV networks compete vigorously for the TV rights to top sporting events. The National Football League (NFL) and its member teams generate over $5 billion each year in revenue, and major league baseball has a TV contract worth tens of millions of dollars a year to each club. Professional sport is dominated by TV, which often determines the venue and timing of events and even influences the rules of some sports; many sports have what are termed 'official time-outs' (in addition to normal time-outs), which are simply breaks to allow TV advertisements to be screened. The frequency of commercial breaks (or 'messages') makes watching most

TV sport a painful experience for many foreigners. The lack of natural breaks in some sports (e.g. football, known as 'soccer' in the US) is no obstacle to advertisers, as advertisements are simply screened while play is in progress. The major US TV networks each broadcast an average of around 500 hours of sports programmes a year, and cable stations such as the Entertainment Sports Programming Network (ESPN) broadcast 24 hours a day. However, with the over-saturation of sports on TV and a drop in advertising revenue, networks are finding it increasingly difficult to make a profit on sports events and the future doesn't look so rosy for the teams or the networks, who are increasingly turning to pay-per-view TV to recoup broadcast rights to major sports events.

One of the unique show business aspects of American sport is the use of 'cheerleaders'. These are usually scantily-dressed, athletic, young women (but also men) who dance and perform acrobatic feats to incite the crowd to support their team (although it's difficult to imagine American fans needing any encouragement, as most scream, shriek and whoop at the drop of a hat). Other stimuli are marching bands (before and during matches) and electronic organs played during baseball games (to keep the fans awake). American sports fans, many of whom paint their faces and dress up as 'clowns', are notably better behaved and less violent than their counterparts in many other countries. Fans are, however, getting rowdier and more unruly, although you can still safely take your family to most ball games. US sports stadia are all-seat, comfortable, and among the finest in the world. The Houston Astrodome was the world's first air-conditioned domed stadium for baseball and football, with seating for 66,000. However, even this is dwarfed by the New Orleans Superdome, the world's largest domed stadium with 27 stories seating 76,000. Information about sports facilities is available from state tourist offices.

School and college sport is extremely important, as it's the training ground for the nation's professionals. In most sports, playing for a college team is a prelude to becoming a professional player and without the inter-collegiate sports system many professional sports would cease to exist. College sports are organised by the National College Athletic Association (NCAA). Rivalry between colleges and universities for top athletes is intense, and most offer scholarships to promising athletes irrespective of their academic abilities (a football player's IQ is usually measured in pounds and inches). High schools and colleges employ professional coaches (who earn huge salaries) and usually have teams for athletics (track), baseball, basketball, football, gymnastics, tennis and wrestling. Many also have fencing, hockey, golf, soccer, swimming, volleyball and various other teams. The Division One college football programme alone has a budget of over $1 billion. In some cases the most important element of a college or university is its football or basketball team, from which (provided it's successful) it gains huge prestige and a vast income. Sport is one of the few areas of American life where black Americans have equal opportunity; they comprise over half the nation's college and professional football and basketball players and the vast majority of track athletes.

Tickets for top events in many cities can be purchased through ticket agencies such as Ticketron and Ticketmaster (check telephone books for local numbers), both of which have internet sites (🖳 www.ticketron.com and www.ticketmaster.com) and from other online ticket agencies. Tickets for major sports such as baseball, football, basketball and hockey are difficult to obtain, as most seats go to season ticket holders, and tickets can also be expensive. In major cities there are usually 24-hour recorded information numbers where you can obtain sports results or a schedule of local sports events.

In addition to sports with an obvious element of danger such as most aerial sports and mountaineering, certain other sports (e.g. most winter sports, power boat racing, waterski jumping and show-jumping) may not be covered by your health, accident or life insurance policies (see **Chapter 13**). Some US companies prohibit employees from participating in 'hazardous activities and pursuits' such as motor sport and mountaineering. **Check in advance and take out insurance when necessary.** Some sports organisers and clubs require participants to sign a 'release', whereby they agree not to sue the organisers in the event of an accident (suing is one of the US's most popular and lucrative sports).

AERIAL SPORTS

Most aerial sports have a strong following, in particular gliding, hang-gliding, paragliding, para-sailing, hot-air ballooning, microlighting and kite-flying (popular among politicians). Hang-gliding has become increasingly popular in recent years and there are numerous hang-gliding schools in the US. Paragliding (also called para-sailing) and parascending are the cheapest and easiest ways to fly. Paragliding entails 'simply' jumping off a steep slope attached to a parachute. Parascending is being towed by a vehicle or a boat (popular at beach resorts); when you've gained enough height, you release the tow and float off on your own (or come crashing back to earth).

Hot-air ballooning is a popular sport. The relatively low cost and profusion of areas with good ballooning weather has resulted in the largest concentration of balloons in the world. There are balloon meetings throughout the year, the largest being held in Albuquerque, New Mexico, the unofficial centre of world ballooning. Balloon flights are available throughout the US and many operators offer sunrise or sunset, breakfast, picnic and champagne flights. Operating seasons vary considerably, so check in advance. A one-hour flight in a balloon costs around $175 to $200 (lawyers, politicians and Texans get a reduction for supplying their own hot air) and usually includes a ritual champagne breakfast. A flight in a balloon is a marvellous experience, although there's no guarantee of distance or duration, and flights (not to mention a safe landing) are dependent on wind conditions and the skill of the 'pilot'.

The US has the highest number of private aircraft per head of any country and private jets, propeller aircraft and helicopters are common. Aircraft and gliders (sailplanes) can be rented with an instructor or without (provided you have a pilot's licence) from numerous small airfields. There are many gliding (soaring) clubs and parachuting and free-fall parachuting (sky-diving) flights can be made from private airfields. Air, seaplane and helicopter rides are available from small airfields and lakes. The latest American craze is microlight (ultralight) flying, a low-flying 'go-cart' consisting of a hang-glider attached to a motorised tricycle. It's one of the cheapest ways of experiencing powered flight, a two-seater microlight costing less than $10,000. There are two main types of machine, with rigid and flex wings, the cost depending mainly on engine size. Microlight fliers require a private pilot's licence.

Some aerial sports or private aviation may be specifically excluded from insurance policies, including, for example, health, accident and life insurance policies. **Before taking up any aerial sport (apart from kite-flying), you should ensure you have adequate health, accident and life insurance, and that your affairs are in order.** Why not take up fishing instead? A nice, sensible, **safe** sport (unless, of course, you're a fish).

AMERICAN FOOTBALL

American football, which in the US is called simply football (or, popularly, 'gridiron'), is an almost exclusively American sport (Canadian football is similar), but is fast gaining popularity in Europe, where TV and the inaugural World League of American Football (WLAF) brought the game to a wider international audience. Professional football is played by teams in the National Football League (NFL), divided into the National Football Conference (NFC) and the American Football Conference (AFC), each of which comprises an Eastern, a Central and a Western division. Each division contains five or six teams, a total of 31.

Foreigners brought up on a diet of soccer or rugby may initially find American football complicated, slow and boring (there are few sports where so much activity can result in so little action). Nevertheless, once you learn the rules and strategy (like a chess game, with feints to throw your opponents off guard), you may join the millions of Americans who find it fascinating and exciting. However, it can be puzzling for greenhorns and what follows is designed to shed some light (although it may well add to the confusion!).

A football field is 100 yards (91.4m) long and 40 yards (36.6m) wide, plus a 10-yard (9.14m) end-zone at each end, painted with the home team's name. The field has parallel lines painted across it at 5-yard (4.57m) intervals and shorter lines every yard; 10-yard (9.14m) intervals are indicated by huge numbers. Like rugby, American football is played with an oval ball and the basic aims are the same, although that's where the similarity ends. A team can have 11 players on the field at any one time. Professional teams have entirely separate offensive and defensive teams, depending on whether they're in possession of the ball (and attacking) or without the ball (and defending). Because of the highly specialised nature of the game, a defender such as a right tackle may play for ten years and never touch the ball in play, except by accident. Players are huge, averaging around six feet six inches (1.98m) and weighing around 240 pounds (109kg), and look even bigger in battle dress, which includes copious amounts of padding and protective gear.

A game lasts for one hour of **playing time**. This is divided into four quarters of 15 minutes each, with a 12 minute break at half-time. If the score is tied at the end of the fourth quarter, the game goes into overtime, the winner being the first team to score ('sudden death'). However, because the clock runs only when play is in progress, a game can last up to three hours including the half-time break.

When you watch football on TV, you're faced with a barrage of statistics from commentators who continually discuss the play. Rather than clarify what's happening, this may hopelessly confuse you. A match has a total of six officials (wearing black and white 'pyjamas'), who, like the players, wear numbers on their backs, with the match referee making final decisions. If an official spots an infringement during play he throws his flag onto the field to attract the referee's attention, hence the term 'a flag has been thrown'. Instant-replay screens are no longer used by the match referee to make decisions, which are announced to the crowd via a microphone. The team coaches also wear headphones, used to communicate with a battery of specialist advisers housed in coaching booths.

The professional football season runs from August to December and culminates in the Super Bowl in January on 'Super Bowl Sunday', the championship play-off between the champions of the National and American Conferences. This game is watched by over 40 per cent of US households and throughout the world and to Americans is the 'most important sporting event in the universe'. Professional games are played on Sundays and Monday evenings. Tickets cost around $50 and are difficult to obtain because of the number of season ticket holders and the few games played (16 per team a season). Many games are sold out well in advance and most teams have a long waiting list for season tickets (e.g. 20 years for the New York Giants). However, all matches are televised and are a popular event in bars, where they're often shown on king-size screens. All American professional sports competitions are a combination of league and knockout games, where the top-placed league teams compete against each other in a series of knockout matches (playoffs) to decide the champions.

College football is followed almost as avidly as professional football, with crowds regularly numbering over 50,000. The season starts in September and ends with invitation bowl games played over Christmas and on New Year's Day. The major college bowls include the Sugar Bowl, Cotton Bowl, Orange Bowl and the Fiesta Bowl, all of which feature teams from different leagues (conferences). The oldest and most famous college championship is the Pasadena Rose Bowl, contested on New Year's Day between the winners of the Midwest Big 10 universities and the Pacific 10 College Conference. Tickets to college games cost $5 to $10 and are available from college athletic departments. Some 10,000 amateur teams play milder versions of American football called flag or touch football, in which tackling is prohibited, thus removing the need for expensive protective clothing and even more expensive surgery.

If you've never seen a game of American football, your best bet is to watch a few games on TV with an American friend who can explain what's going on. Once you know the difference between a tight end and a safety, and between a guard and a tackle, you can consider yourself no longer a 'rookie' foreigner (all professional sportsmen in their first year are called rookies) and well on your way to integration into the American Way of Life.

BASEBALL

Baseball (known as 'the beautiful game') is the US's national sport and was first played in its modern form in 1839 at Cooperstown, New York. There are two major baseball leagues with a total of 30 teams: the American League (AL), established in

1900, and the National League (NL), which was established in 1876. Both are divided into East (five teams), Central (five or six teams) and West (four or five teams) divisions. The season runs from April to early October, with games (a total of 162 per team in each league) being played almost every day during this period, many at night under floodlights. In October, the top two teams in the American and National leagues compete against each other in the 'playoffs' to decide who will contest the World Series (established in 1903), played over seven games.

In addition to the major league clubs, there are also numerous minor league clubs in small towns known as 'farm' teams, so called because they supply the top clubs with players. College, high school and little league baseball (played by children from the age of seven to their teens) are also hugely popular, but expensive (it can cost over $200 to outfit a child).

Games usually last two to three hours and are normally played in the evening. Ticket prices have risen in recent years, although the average ticket price is still relatively low ($15 to $30) and some tickets are available on the day of the match (the 'bleacher' seats in the sun and furthest from the field are the cheapest). When you buy a ticket for a baseball game that's postponed (called), for example because of a 'rainout', you're entitled to a free ticket for another game (the origin of the term 'rain cheque').

Baseball is a peculiarly American sport, although it has been successfully exported to a few countries including Canada, Japan and Taiwan. It usually takes foreigners some time to understand it (around ten years). However, watching a baseball game is an interesting day out and a real 'slice of American pie', even if you haven't got a clue what's going on. Crowds are vastly entertaining and fans are usually friendly and sociable.

A baseball field ('field of dreams') is laid out in the shape of a 90-foot square diamond, with four bases set at the corners. The bottom corner base is called 'home plate' and the others are, from right to left, first, second and third base. There are nine players in a team and a game consists of nine innings. The home team takes to the field first, the two most important players being the pitcher and catcher (called the battery). The other seven players take up defensive positions at the bases and in the field. Substitute players can enter the game at any time, but once a player (e.g. a pitcher) is removed, he cannot return. Fielders wear gloves and the first baseman and catcher wear a glove on the hand in which they catch the hard ball. The ball has a cork and rubber centre wound with woollen yarn and is covered in horsehide. Balls are expendable and when they're hit into the crowd they aren't returned. The batter carries a hard wooden bat, a maximum of 2.75in (7cm) in diameter and 42in (1.07m) in length.

The basic idea of the game is for the batting team to score runs by hitting the ball with the bat and running around the bases to the home plate without being called out. The team with the most runs after all nine innings have been played is the winner. A game cannot be tied and if there's a tie after nine innings, extra innings are played until one team wins. Each player bats in turn, with each team having three 'outs' per inning. Players normally bat three to five times in a match (players on base aren't out, so you can have more than three batters per inning). A 'play' commences when the pitcher, who stands on a raised 'mound' in the centre of the diamond, throws the ball at up to 100mph towards the batter. The idea is to bend and curve the ball, making it as difficult as possible for the batter to hit it.

Baseball has a language all its own and many baseball terms have found their way into everyday speech, the most common of which is to 'strike out', i.e. to fail. Other terms include walk, bull pen, pinch hitter, slider, double or triple play, switch hitter, curve ball, bottom-of-the-ninth, line drive, steal or stolen base, double steal, pop-up, (sacrifice) bunt, shut-out, no-hitter, perfect game, chopper, fly (out), pop fly, foul out, RBI, ball four and many more. Only when you've mastered these will you become a **real** American (and qualify for a US passport). For those looking for more information, there are literally hundreds of baseball books available in libraries and book shops.

BASKETBALL

Basketball was invented in the US in 1891 and was exported during World War I by American servicemen. The National Basketball Association (NBA, 🖳 www.nba.com) was formed in 1949 and has two leagues: the Eastern Conference with 15 teams (divided between the Atlantic and Central divisions) and the Western Conference with 15 teams (divided between the Midwest and Pacific divisions). Teams play over 80 games during the main season, running from September or October to April. The top teams are involved in the playoffs in late May and June, to determine the NBA playoff teams and world champions.

The skills demonstrated by professional basketball players (often black and seven feet tall) are worlds apart from the amateur game played in many countries. Games last for 48 minutes, which is a long time considering the speed of the game and the ground covered by the players, although as with other sports, there are frequent 'time-outs'. Although they don't play in the NBA, one of the most famous teams is the Harlem Globetrotters (🖳 http://harlemglobetrotters.com), who have been delighting crowds around the world for many years with their entertaining exhibition games, a combination of superb technical skills and clowning.

College basketball teams rival professional teams in popularity and skills, and it's a major spectator sport in its own right, with tickets for the National Collegiate Athletic Association (NCAA) basketball tournament sold out a year in advance. Around 270 colleges (divided into 30 divisions) participate in the NCAA basketball conference. At the end of the season the top two teams in each division (a total of 64) earn a ticket to the NCAA Basketball (knockout) Tournament, played throughout March, when 'March Madness' grips the nation and games are televised live for hours on end. The final four teams, representing the east, west, Midwest and south-east, compete in the final four tournament for the title of NCAA National Champions.

Tickets for professional games can cost from $60 to $1,500 (for a courtside seat, with season tickets costing up to $7,500!) and $15 to $20 for college games. As with all professional sports, high school and college teams are the training grounds for would-be pros, although the rules of professional and collegiate basketball differ slightly. In some midwestern states (e.g. Ohio, Indiana, Illinois), the high school basketball tournaments, which also take place during the month of March, are even more important and carefully followed than the NCAA championships. There's also a strong women's collegiate league (the women are only six-and-a-half feet tall). Unlike football and baseball, in addition to being a major professional sport, basketball is played for fun by many Americans, particularly in poor inner-city neighbourhoods.

CLIMBING & CAVING

Those who find hiking a bit tame might like to try abseiling, rock-climbing, mountaineering, or caving (spelunking). Although experienced mountaineers may not find North America's mountains sufficiently demanding, they offer plenty of challenges for less experienced climbers (they're also an excellent training ground for social climbers and yuppies, willing to risk life and limb to reach the top). If you're an inexperienced climber, you're advised to attend a course at a mountaineering school before heading for the hills. There are mountaineering schools in all the main climbing areas, providing basic to advanced ice, snow and rock climbing courses lasting from one day to several weeks. Most clubs have indoor training apparatus (e.g. a climbing wall) for aspiring mountaineers. Many mountaineering schools organise international expeditions for intermediate and advanced climbers.

Many climbers and cavers are killed each year in the US, where Mount McKinley in Alaska (the US's highest mountain) claims the most victims. Most victims are inexperienced and reckless and many more climbers owe their survival to rescuers, who risk their own lives to save them. **It's extremely foolish, not to mention highly dangerous, to venture off into the hills (or caves) without an experienced guide, proper preparation, excellent physical condition, sufficient training and the appropriate equipment.** Mountain or hill-walking shouldn't be confused with 'ordinary' hiking (see above), as it's generally done at much higher altitudes and in more difficult terrain, and should be attempted only with an experienced leader. It can be dangerous for the untrained or inexperienced and should be approached with much the same caution and preparation as mountain climbing. **The note regarding insurance on page 441 particularly applies to the above sports.**

CYCLING

Cycling has enjoyed a surge in popularity in recent years because of the American obsession with exercise, its low cost, and the establishment of cycle paths and routes in many towns and cities. Unlike many countries, cycling in the US isn't usually necessary as a means of getting from A to B, and is usually done for enjoyment, exercise or as a competitive sport. Competitive cycling includes road and track racing, cycle speedway, time-trialling, cross-country racing, touring, bicycle polo and bicycle motocross. Tandems are becoming increasingly popular among couples.

Before buying a bicycle (bike), compare the advertisements in *Bicycling* (🖳 www. bicycling.com) and other cycling magazines to find the lowest prices. Buying by mail-order is common and inexpensive, and you can usually get a bike (or anything else) delivered within a few days. Buying a bike or accessories from your local bicycle shop is usually more expensive, although you have the advantage of being able to obtain local assistance and advice. Many different types of bike are available, including children's and motocross bikes, one-speed domestic runabouts, three-speed bikes with calliper brakes, touring or racing bikes, usually with drop handlebars and 5 to 15 gears, lightweight competition bikes, and mountain bikes (invented in California). American bikes are rarely fitted with mudguards, as most Americans are strictly fair-weather cyclists. Brakes are sometimes the reverse of what's found in other countries, e.g. the right-hand brake operates on the rear wheel and the left-hand brake on the front wheel (strange lot, Americans!). Some brakes operate on the rear wheel by pedalling backwards (coaster brakes).

When buying a bike, carefully consider your needs, now and in the future, obtain expert advice (e.g. from a specialist cycle shop), and make sure you purchase a bike with the correct frame size. Ten-speed touring (road) bikes are the most common and cost from around $250 new or $150 for a second-hand bike in good condition. More expensive European and Japanese bikes are also widely available. Mountain bikes are popular, not just for off-road use, but for negotiating the potholes in many of the US's roads; expect to pay at least $400 (and up to $2,000 for all-singing, all-dancing models). There's a good trade in used bikes, particularly in college towns where they're popular with students.

Bikes can be rented from bicycle shops (and some hotels) in most cities and towns by the hour, day or week. Rates vary considerably according to the city or area and the type of bike, e.g. a touring bike costs from around $12 per day ($50 per week) in a small town to $7 per hour ($30 per day) in New York City, and for a mountain bike you can pay up to $11 per hour or $50 per day. Older bikes are often available at lower rates. You must provide identification and pay a deposit of $10 or $20. In New York and other major cities, a passport or credit card may be required as security. If you want a bike for a few months, it may be cheaper to buy a bike and sell it when you no longer need it. Some bicycle shops will sell you a bike and agree to buy it back later.

In some cities, such as Los Angeles or New York, you must be crazy or suicidal to cycle in the jam-packed streets on weekdays (weekends are quieter). However, most cities have parks and off-road areas where you can enjoy cycling without risking your life, and many states have a network of marked, off-road bikeways (ask state tourist offices for information). National and state parks have car-free carriage paths and trails exclusively for cyclists. For those with plenty of stamina there's the 4,250 mile TransAmerican Trail, running between Oregon and Virginia through national parks, prairies, deserts, farmlands and country towns. Maps of the route are available from Adventure Cycling (see below).

The premier American cycling organisation is the League of American Bicyclists (LAB, formerly the League of American Wheelmen), 1612 K Street, NW, Suite 800, Washington DC 20006-2850 (☎ 202-822-1333, 🖳 www.bikeleague.org). Membership costs from $30 per year for individuals and $45 for families. The LAB issues a wide range of publications, including *League of American Bicyclists* (their members' magazine) and *Bike League News* (a free email newsletter). The League has some 500 affiliated cycling clubs across the country and organises an annual rally called BikeFest in August. Long-distance cyclists may be interested in joining Adventure Cycling (formerly Bikecentennial), a national non-profit recreational cycling organisation that runs tours for members. Adventure Cycling offers members insurance, guidebooks, maps, books, equipment, route information and tours, and publishes the *Cyclist's Yellow Pages* (free to members, $10 non-members) as well as a member magazine, *Adventure Cyclist*. For further information write to Adventure Cycling, 150 East Pine Street, PO Box 8308, Missoula, MT 59802 (☎ 1-800-755-2453 or 406-721-1776, ☐ www.adventurecycling.org).

Racing cyclists may wish to join the United States Cycling Federation (USCF), 1 Olympic Plaza, Colorado Springs, CO 80909 (☎ 719-578-4581, ☐ www.usa cycling.org), the national body for amateur competitive cycling. If you're a member of a cycling club affiliated to the USCF, you're automatically a USCF member, or you can become a licensed member by completing a racing licence application (cost $45). The USCF is one of several cycling organisations under the umbrella of USA Cycling; others are the USA Cycling Development Foundation, the National Off-Road Bicycle Association (NORBA), which organises mountain biking events, the USCF (for road and track cycling) and the NBL (for BMX racing). All of these can be contacted at the same address as the USCF.

There are a multitude of books for cyclists, including *Greg Lemond's Complete Book of Cycling* by Greg Lemond (Perigee), *Bicycling the Pacific Coast* by Tom Kirkendall and Vicky Spring (Mountaineers), and *Effective Cycling* by John Forester (MIT Press). State cycling and touring guides are published by many state tourist offices and regional tour guides can be found in local book shops.

FISHING

Fishing (or angling) opportunities in the US are boundless and it's one of the nation's biggest participant sports. The US's inland waterways are an angler's paradise, particularly the Great Lakes, and its coastal waters provide some of the best deep-sea fishing in the world. Almost every species of freshwater fish (native and introduced) can be found in the US's lakes, rivers and streams, including trout, bass, coho and chinook salmon, pike, muskie, walleye, catfish and sunfish. Many waters (including the Great Lakes) are restocked each year. As many as 600 species of saltwater fish inhabit the US's coastal waters including striped bass or stripers' (sadly depleted in some areas), cod, mackerel, flounder, crappie, largemouth bass, fluke, weakfish, bonito, red snapper, sailfish, jewfish and jack.

In general, the fishing season extends from the thaw (ice-out) in mid-April until October, although some states (e.g. Nebraska) allow fishing all year round on rivers, streams and man-made lakes. All regulations are precisely formulated and there are strictly enforced seasons and limits for all freshwater and some saltwater fish (although fishing for some saltwater species is permitted all year-round). Some states are vigilant in preventing out of season fishing or fishing in non-designated areas. In most states, a freshwater fishing licence is required by all residents and non-residents over 16 (although in some states, only non-residents require a licence). Licences can be obtained from fishing tackle, sporting goods and general shops, marinas, fish camps, and town and city clerks. Senior citizens, the blind and the disabled can fish (and hunt) free or for a reduced licence fee in many states. Non-resident freshwater fishing licences for lakes and rivers are issued by state authorities, and typically cost $5 to $10 for three days, $15 to $20 for seven days, and $30 to $50 for a year. Licences for residents cost as little as $10 or $15 per year. There's sometimes an additional fee to fish for certain species, e.g. trout, and a licence may be required to fish for species such as Atlantic salmon or for ice fishing. Licence fees may vary by class, purpose and residence, and combined fishing and hunting licences are available in some states. You can be fined up to $500 for fishing without a licence in some states. Information about fishing seasons and permitted catches is available from state Fish and Wildlife departments. Many states publish fishing guides and booklets detailing the species available and the public areas open to sportsmen, and a comprehensive range of lake maps is available in some states, e.g. Minnesota. It's possible to join an organised fly fishing trip for between $75 and $150 per day, depending on the number of people.

A licence isn't usually required for saltwater fishing, although there may be some bag limits and equipment restrictions. Exceptions include Florida and Texas. In Florida, licence fees are similar to those for freshwater fishing (see above), although a licence isn't necessary when fishing from a vessel with its own saltwater licence. Surfcasting can be done from public beaches and town piers (popular fishing spots). In some areas, you need a licence to take certain species of saltwater fish, e.g. smelt, shellfish and salmon.

Deep-sea fishing (or sport fishing) for big-game fish, e.g. marlin, tuna, barracuda, bass, rockfish, tarpon, wahoo and sharks, is an exhilarating, if expensive, sport. Among the most popular deep-sea fishing areas are the Caribbean off Florida, around Cape Cod (Massachusetts), along the Outer Banks off North Carolina, and off the coast of northern California. Operators of charter, party and 'head' boats (so named because they charge per person or head) are plentiful in coastal resorts and charge an average of $30 to $45 per person for day trips (tackle may be included). Luxurious deep-sea charter boats or yachts for up to six people can be rented for $300 to $750 per day or can be chartered for a number of hours only. Lists of fishing-boat captains can usually be obtained from tourist offices.

If you want to get off the beaten track, you might like to try 'fly-in fishing', entailing chartering a seaplane to reach remote inland waterways which are inaccessible by road. If you're adventurous and don't mind freezing to death, you may like to try winter ice fishing in the Midwest or New England, which entails fishing through a hole in the ice from inside a 'fish-house' (a wooden hut located on the ice). In Alaska, which has the best fishing in the US, you can pay more than $3,000 for a week's salmon fishing, inclusive of lodge accommodation and a private plane to the fishing area.

Information about local fishing spots is provided in newspapers and obtainable from local fish and game authorities, marinas, and bait and tackle shops. Sometimes, it pays to hire a professional guide to show you the best spots. Many states have an outdoor guides' association, members of which have met local state licensing requirements. Guides are available year-round and many specialise in fishing, charter fishing, ice fishing, boat and canoe trips, plus numerous other outdoor pursuits. In some areas, there are fishing schools for those who wish to learn fly-fishing or bait and spin-casting techniques. Local and national fishing festivals and contests, e.g. for trout or bass, are held in many towns throughout the season. Joining a local fishing club may give you access to private rivers or lakes.

GOLF

Golf is one of the US's most popular sports (if American men had to choose between golf and sex, most would choose golf) and with many thousands of courses (over 800 in Texas alone!), there's certainly sufficient to satisfy demand in most areas. Although golf is an expensive sport, you don't need to be a millionaire to play in the US (unless you plan to spend all day in the '19th hole'). In addition to the many expensive private golf courses and complexes (usually restricted to members or residents only), there are numerous public courses, ranging from three to nine-hole courses to full championship courses. In addition to being a popular participant sport, golf is also a leading spectator sport in the US, where many major professional championships are held including the Masters (April), the US Open (June) and the PGA Championship (August). The foremost international team competition, the Ryder Cup, is contested between teams from the US and Europe every two years (although, as it must compete for prime TV air time with 'slightly more popular' sports events such as baseball and American football, many Americans are unaware of its existence). American and European female golfers compete biennially in the Solheim Cup, in which the Americans routinely thrash the Europeans.

Membership isn't required to play on a public golf course, although you should book in advance (sometimes it's essential). In some cities, you need a city golf permit to play at a public course. In some areas, there are few public courses, and private clubs may allow you to play only if you're a member of a club and have a handicap certificate. However, many private clubs are open to non-members or 'green fee' golfers, although access may exclude weekends and federal holidays. The US also has numerous resort complexes with as many as three championship courses.

Green fees at public courses are usually between $15 and $25 (but can be much higher) for a round of 18 holes, or around half this for nine holes. Under 16s and senior citizens can usually play for a reduced fee, e.g. holders of a Golden Age Passport (see page 405) can play for half price on weekdays (except on federal holidays) at public courses in national parks. Public course fees are around $5 higher at weekends, when booking is usually necessary (there may also be a booking fee). Club rental usually costs around $15 per round and electric carts can also be rented at most clubs (because of the proliferation of golf buggies, most American golfers expend little energy and would get more exercise walking around the block). Green fees at private courses vary considerably according to the club, the region and the time of year. Clubs that permit non-members usually charge from $35 to over $100 (possibly including use of a golf cart) for a round of 18 holes.

Professional lessons are available at most clubs from around $20 for a half-hour lesson. Many clubs also have driving ranges, practice putting greens and bunkers (sand traps) and a golf shop. In most cities, there are golf studios and schools offering instruction for busy executives and anyone else with the time and money to work on their handicap. Most are equipped with AstroTurf putting greens and teaching nets, and offer a video analysis (demolition) of your swing. Golf clinics (intensive two or five-day coaching sessions) are popular and are held at schools and clubs throughout the country. Golf holidays are popular throughout the US and often include accommodation and green fees. Information is available from state tourist offices.

For further information about golf contact the US Golf Association (PO Box 708, Far Hills, NJ 07931, ☎ 908-234-2300, 💻 www.usga.org).

GYMNASIUMS & HEALTH CLUBS

There are gymnasiums (gyms) and health and fitness clubs in most towns in the US, where the employees are sadists and where masochists go to torture themselves (Americans who aren't bent on killing themselves with drugs or alcohol are obsessive about exercise and physical culture). Health clubs are often combined with sports or racket clubs (e.g. tennis, racquetball and squash). In addition to fitness centres and fully-equipped gymnasiums, health clubs usually also offer swimming (or lap) pools, jogging tracks, and aerobics and keep-fit classes.

Most health clubs are mixed (coed) and many have a variety of membership levels according to the facilities you wish to use, e.g. gym and exercise rooms only or gym plus squash or tennis. New members are often offered discounts or a free trial period. Some health and sports clubs run a number of centres, e.g. citywide or in a number of cities, and members can usually use the facilities at any centre. The cost of membership at a private club varies considerably according to the area, the facilities provided, and the local competition. Some clubs offer reduced rates for husband and wife or family membership. Many health clubs have a joining or initiation fee, e.g. $100 to $250, and all have monthly fees, e.g. $30 to $60. Most clubs are for members only, although there are gyms and health clubs in most major cities allowing guests to pay on a per day or per class basis. Individual classes are usually quite expensive, e.g. $10 to $15 per exercise class, or around $20 per day for the use of gym and exercise facilities, although there's often a reduction for ten or more classes or sessions.

Clubs are usually open seven days a week from around 6am until 9pm or 10pm Monday to Friday, usually with shorter hours on Saturdays and Sundays (when some clubs are closed). Most health and fitness clubs have facilities such as saunas, solariums, Jacuzzis, steam baths, whirlpools and massage, and many have a child care service. Many top class hotels have health clubs and swimming pools, which are usually open to the general public (although usage may be restricted to residents at certain times). Fitness classes are also organised by local community schools. Some municipal swimming pools have gymnasiums and exercise facilities that can be used free of charge by local residents.

Gyms have tons of expensive bone-jarring, muscle-wrenching apparatus, designed to get you into shape or kill you in the attempt. Middle-aged 'fatties' shouldn't attempt to get fit in five minutes (after all, it took years of dedicated sloth and gluttony to put on all that weight), as over-exertion can result in serious injuries and heart attacks. Most gymnasiums and health clubs will ensure this doesn't happen and carry out an initial physical assessment including a blood pressure test, fat distribution measurements and heart rate checks, produce personal training programmes for members and follow up with regular fitness testing. In your headlong rush to become one of the bodies beautiful, it pays to take the long route and give the intensive care unit (or mortuary) a wide berth!

HIKING

Hiking (a grand word for walking) is popular in the US (despite the fact that most Americans never get out of their cars) not least because it has some of the most dramatic and unspoiled hiking country in the world. This includes more than 80 million acres of national parks and numerous state parks, all with marked hiking routes. Almost every state boasts vast areas (many running into millions of acres) of outstanding natural beauty. Among the most popular hiking regions are Alaska, the Appalachians, the Cascade range, the Colorado Plateau, the Columbia Plateau, the Great Desert, the Northwest Coast ranges, the Ozarks, the Rockies, the Sierra and the wooded areas of northern Michigan, Minnesota and Wisconsin. National forests are popular with those seeking wilderness hiking areas.

The US has a number of long-distance hiking routes, including the Pacific Crest Trail, extending 2,400mi (3,862km) from the California/Mexico border north through Oregon all the way to Canada. The famous Appalachian Trail runs for 2,135mi (3,436km) from Maine to Georgia traversing wilderness areas of great beauty along the crests and ridges of high mountains. An estimated 4 million hikers enjoy it annually, experienced hikers travelling its entire length. For detailed maps, guidebooks, information about shelters, hiking conditions, highlights, and food and other supplies along the Appalachian Trail, contact the Appalachian Trail Conference (ATC), PO Box 807, Harpers Ferry, WV 25425-0807 (☎ 304-535-6331, 🖳 www.appalachiantrail.org). Membership of the ATC costs from $30 per year (or $600 for lifetime membership). Information about the Pacific Crest Trail is available from the Sierra Club (see address below).

If you're hiking in national parks and camping or sleeping rough, you may require a wilderness permit and should obtain information about weather conditions and general information regarding your intended route. In some parks and forests, there's a system of hosted 'huts' for hikers, usually located around a day's hiking distance apart. Inexpensive accommodation is also available in many hiking areas in lodges and camps. There are numerous hiking and mountain clubs in all areas, many of which maintain their own mountain lodges, publish guidebooks, and produce books about local wilderness and nature topics.

Among the many hiking organisations are the Appalachian Trail Conference (mentioned above) and the Sierra Club (85 Second Street, 2nd Floor, San Francisco, CA 94105, ☎ 415-977-5500, 🖳 www.sierraclub.org), North America's premier hiking and environmental organisation. Membership costs $39 for individuals and $49 for couples, although there are cheaper introductory offers. Hikers can also join the American Hiking Society (1422 Fenwick Lane, Silver Spring, MD 20910, ☎ 301-565-6704, 🖳 www.americanhiking.org) and support its work in protecting hiking routes (membership starts at $25 per year for individuals and $35 for families, but you can pay up to $1,000 for life membership for a couple). The National Audubon Society (700 Broadway, New York, NY 10003, ☎ 212-979-3000, 🖳 www.audubon.org), which is concerned with preserving natural ecosystems, manages a system of 75 nature centres and sanctuaries, with marked trails and footpaths open to the public. Annual membership costs $20.

Orienteering, a combination of hiking and a treasure hunt (or competitive navigation on foot), is also popular. It's unnecessary to be super fit and the whole family can enjoy it. The only equipment that's required (in addition to suitable walking attire) is a detailed map and a compass.

If you're an inexperienced hiker, you may wish to attend a course in backpacking and learn how to survive in the wilderness. Courses are run by a number of organisations, including Outward Bound USA, 100 Mystery Point Road, Garrison, NY 10524 (☎ 845-424-4000, 💻 www.outwardbound.org) and the National Outdoor Leadership School (NOLS), 284 Lincoln Street, Lander, WY 82520-2848 (☎ 1-800-710-NOLS, 💻 www.nols.edu).

There are literally hundreds of books available about hiking, ranging from general national guides containing a wide selection of walks, to simple booklets (many free) produced by local hiking and rambling clubs. Among the best hiking books are *The Hiker's Bible* by Robert Elman and Claire Rees (Doubleday), *The Complete Walker IV* by Colin Fletcher (Knopf) and the *Backpackers' Sourcebook* by Penny Hargrove and Noelle Liebrenz (Wilderness Press). If you're interested in the US's unique wildlife or flora and fauna, obtain a copy of the *Audubon Society Beginners Guide* to birds, reptiles, amphibians and wildflowers (see address above). The National Wildlife Federation, 11100 Wildlife Center Drive, Reston, VA 20190 (☎ 800-822-9919, 💻 www.nwf.org), organises field trips and classes for nature lovers (membership involves a 'donation' of at least $20), and the Appalachian Trail Conference (see address above) publishes official guides to the Appalachian Trail (and numerous other hiking publications although their 'Ultimate Trail Store'). The Sierra Club (see address above) publishes a multitude of information for hikers including *The Best About Backpacking* and a free *Annual Outing Catalog*.

Topographical maps of the US are available from the US Geological Survey, Information Services, PO Box 25286, Denver, CO 80225 (💻 www.usgs.gov). If you're hiking in national parks, *US Geological Survey Maps of National Parks* published by the Department of the Interior will prove invaluable. They contain detailed information on topography, roads, trails and other features of national parks. *National Forest Maps* published by the Department of Agriculture provide the same information about national forests. The *Atlas and Gazetteer* series of maps published by the Delorme Mapping Co. are among the best privately published topographical maps in the US.

For more information about visiting national parks, see **Parks, Gardens & Zoos** on page 408.

HUNTING

Hunting is extremely popular in the US, where, unlike many countries, it isn't the preserve of the wealthy or upper classes. Hunters enjoy almost unrestricted access to literally millions of acres of land (often owned by state governments or paper, timber and mining companies), much of which is teeming with wildlife (or was before the hunters arrived on the scene). The National Rifle Association (NRA) is the premier organisation for hunters; it has more than 3 million members and is one of the most powerful and influential organisations in the US (many Americans are frustrated gunslingers and, when not shooting their neighbours, relieve their frustrations on the US's hapless wildlife).

The type of game available varies considerably from state to state and includes bear, caribou, moose, elk, deer, antelope, wild hog, bighorn sheep, rabbits, racoon, opossum, coyote, nutria, skunk, beaver, squirrel and game (e.g. partridge, pheasant, grouse, wild turkey, waterfowl, quail, geese and duck). Moose and elk hunting is limited by lottery in most states and all non-resident hunters must obtain permission via a draw (Alaska is the favourite venue for big game). It's strictly illegal to kill buffalo (or bison) in protected reserves such as Yellowstone Park; however, if they stray outside reserves, they can be shot. The huge herds of buffalo roaming the North American plains were wiped out in the 19th century, when some 60 million were slaughtered, and conservationists wage a constant battle to protect the remaining few thousand from hunters.

Hunting is closely regulated in all states and illegal hunting is severely penalised. Some states are aggressive in preventing out of season hunting or hunting in non-designated areas, and there are precisely stated and strictly enforced seasons and bag limits for most game and fur bearing animals. Hunting on certain Indian territories is controlled by the tribes and permission must be obtained.

Licences issued by state authorities are required by all hunters on public land. Fees usually vary by class, purpose and residence. Hunters must generally be 16 or over to hunt big game (often younger for small game) and must have completed a hunter's safety course. To discourage out-of-state hunters, licences for non-residents in some states are much more expensive than those for residents. The cost of non-resident permits depends on the type of game and varies from a few dollars to hunt waterfowl up to hundreds of dollars to hunt bear or moose.

In many states, licences are required to hunt with a bow and arrow or muzzle loaders, and bow hunters may be required to complete a training course. In many states, you must also be licensed to trap game. Most states generally recognise licences and training certificates issued by other states. In some states (e.g. Texas) there's a hunting lease system, where private landowners sell leases to hunters for a day or longer. Senior citizens, the blind and disabled can hunt (and fish) free or for a reduced licence fee in many states (but steer well clear of blind hunters!).

Hunting licences can be obtained from fishing tackle and bait shops, sporting goods and general shops, town and county clerk offices or courthouses, and by post from the relevant state department. Information about season dates, bag and possession limits, licences, permitted weapons, and public areas and private reserves is available from state Fish and Wildlife departments (the department name varies from state to state; e.g. in New York, it's the Department of Environmental Conservation). Many states publish hunting guides listing local regulations, the species available and the public areas open to sportsmen. The duration of licences may vary from state to state (e.g. in Texas, licences are valid from 1st September to 31st August). Combined hunting and fishing licences are available in some states.

Often it's wise to hire a professional guide when hunting (ask at local hunting shops for information). Many states have an outdoor guides' association, members of which have met local state licensing requirements.

ICE HOCKEY

Ice hockey (called simply hockey in North America, where hockey played on grass is called field hockey and isn't a major sport) was invented in Canada in around 1879 and is a major sport in the US. Canada produces most ice hockey players (around 65 per cent), with most of the rest coming from Europe (plus a few token Americans making up the numbers). The National Hockey League/NHL (💻 www.nhl.com)

was formed in 1917 and is divided into two conferences, Eastern and Western, each with three divisions. Each division has five teams, most of those in the Northwest and Northeast divisions being Canadian. The NHL competition runs from October to May, during which period teams play around 80 games, culminating in the playoffs for the Stanley Cup (played over a seven game series). Inaugurated in 1892, the Stanley Cup was originally contested between Canada and the US, but is now competed for by all 30 league teams.

Hockey is a violent sport and striking opponents often appears to be more popular then hitting the puck (hence the joke 'I went to a fight and a hockey game broke out'). It's the only sport where violence is an integral and accepted part of the game, for which there are usually no penalties, other than a few minutes in the 'sin bin'. Tickets for hockey games are expensive (e.g. $40 to $50) and hard to come by. In northern states, high schools and universities host hockey teams and offer a somewhat less-violent version of the sport (at more reasonable ticket prices). It's possible to find amateur hockey teams, sponsored by employer groups or local ice skating rinks, if you want to try the sport for yourself.

JOGGING & RUNNING

Competitive running has a strong following in the US and jogging is extremely popular (joggers are runners who compete against themselves). At times it may seem as if every man (and his dog) is a jogger, and what's more they're all jogging in your neighbourhood. In towns and cities, there are usually marked jogging trails (many with exercise stations en route), although you may have to compete for space with roller-skaters and skateboarders. You shouldn't jog on your own in deserted areas, particularly in major cities, where you run the risk of being mugged or raped. Women can expect stares and cat calls when running along streets.

Races are organised throughout the year in all areas, from fun runs of a few miles up to half and full marathons. The New York City marathon (organised by the New York Road Runners Club, the world's largest running club) takes place on the third or fourth Sunday in October, and attracts around 16,000 competitors and 2 million spectators. The Boston marathon, held on the third Monday in April, is the oldest marathon in the US and was first run in 1897. There are running clubs in all major cities, most organising extensive race programmes, clinics and running classes.

MOTOR SPORTS

Motor racing has a huge following in the US and somewhat surprisingly attracts more spectators than any other sport. The US has the most varied motor sport in the world, which embraces everything from single-seat formula racing to stock car and drag racing. Most major events are held from spring to autumn on literally hundreds of vast, purpose-built tracks and on (closed) public roads. The Indianapolis 500, held on the Memorial Day weekend (the last weekend in May), is the US's premier event for racing cars and the biggest single spectator event in the world (some 500,000 spectators pay over $10 million). The race is run over 500mi (805km) and lasts for three hours at speeds averaging over 170mph/275kph (many believe it's now **too** fast). The Indy 500 is one of the CART IndyCar World Series of races for single-seat cars, the US equivalent of the international Formula One Grand Prix series, and in recent years, the Formula One circuit has included an American Grand Prix event at the Indianapolis Motor Speedway (although it has to be completely reconfigured for the event). Around half the Indy series of races are held on purpose-built oval tracks, with the rest on street circuits.

However, the most popular form of car racing is stock car racing, which is highly professional and attracts many of the US's best drivers. Unlike those of most other countries, American stock cars aren't old wrecks, but highly modified, 200mph/322kph, production line models, with races held at specially built tracks such as Daytona (Ohio). Stock car racing is run under the auspices of North American Stock Car Auto Racing (NASCAR) in the Winston Cup series, with races including the Daytona 500, Winston 500, Coca-Cola 600 and Heinz Southern 500.

Other popular motor sports include demolition derbies (where the aim is literally to demolish and outlast the other cars) and drag racing, where cars reach 100mph/161kph in seconds and go on to 300mph/483kph. Drag meetings are organised by the National Hot Road Association (NHRA), with a wide range of classes including gas, supercharged, funny and top fuel. Other forms of motor sport include off-road and desert driving, for which you can buy special (expensive) off-road vehicles. The dates and venues of all US motor sport events and racing calendars are published in *Motor Sport* magazine (🖳 www.motorsport.com).

RACKET SPORTS

There are excellent facilities in the US for most racket sports, particularly tennis, racquetball and squash, although badminton isn't popular and facilities are scarce. Tennis is easily the most popular racket sport and is played outdoors all year round in many southern states. Most outdoor tennis courts are clay or hard (i.e. asphalt or cement) courts, while indoor courts may be synthetic (e.g. AstroTurf) or hard. There are many public tennis courts in parks in US cities, and many communities have municipal tennis courts that can be used free (or for a small fee) by local residents. However, courts are often available on a first-come, first-served basis and it may be impossible to book. Annual or season permits (e.g. badges) are required in some towns and are inexpensive, e.g. $30 to $65 per year for adults, with reductions of up to 50 per cent for senior citizens and nominal fees (or none at all) for children under 17. Non-permit holders can play on some public courts at an hourly or daily rate, e.g. $2 to $4 per hour. Many towns have floodlit courts for evening games, and some courts can be used all night. YMCAs often have tennis courts and organise coaching at all levels.

There are numerous private tennis clubs in cities and rural areas, and some top-class hotels also have tennis courts that can be rented by non-residents. The cost of renting a court at a private club is high and varies from $25 to $40 per hour at member-only clubs to $40 to $100 per hour at non-member clubs in major cities (e.g. New York). Most member-only clubs have a guest fee, e.g. $20. Annual membership costs anything between $500 and $1,500 (plus an entry fee in some cases). In cities, particularly in northern states, most clubs have indoor courts for use in winter. Some private tennis clubs also incorporate health and fitness clubs, where tennis membership entitles members to use all the club's facilities. Most private clubs have resident pros who charge from $50 to $75 per hour for lessons (usually with reductions for ten or more lessons) and some tennis centres and clubs specialise in tennis packages and coaching by top pros.

Tennis camps, clinics, schools and resorts are popular throughout the country and are an excellent way to quickly improve your game. Tennis camps usually offer five to eight hours' tuition daily and are held at colleges, private schools or children's summer camps (out of season). Cost for room and board (which may be fairly basic) plus instruction is normally around $100 per day. Tennis clinics are a more expensive affair and are usually held at hotels, resorts or tennis schools, where coaching may be provided by a resident tennis pro or visiting coaches. Clinics usually last from a few days to a week and the daily cost may be double that of attending a tennis camp, e.g. $200 per day.

Most tennis camps and clinics are intended for reasonably fit serious beginners or improvers, and aren't for those who play just a few social games of doubles each year. Inexpensive tennis coaching for children and adults is organised in many communities through the Community Tennis Foundation. Whatever course of lessons you sign up for, make sure that they're designed to match your ability and fitness (this applies to all sports instruction).

Professional tennis was introduced to the US in 1926, but only gained international acceptance in 1968 when Wimbledon opened its doors to pros. The US is one of the world's leading tennis nations and hosts a comprehensive calendar of men's and women's professional tournaments throughout the year. The highlight is the US Open held at the United States Tennis Association's national tennis centre at Flushing Meadow in New York City in October.

Hardball is the American form of squash, played on a longer, narrower court (indoor and outdoor) than squash and with a harder ball. Squash (softball) is gaining in popularity and there are now many world-class tournaments throughout the US, notably the Tournament of Champions, which takes place inside Grand Central Station, New York. Racquetball can be played on a hardball or squash court, but uses a bigger, bouncier ball and shorter rackets. It's a less skillful game than hardball or squash and isn't popular outside the US. Many YMCAs have racquetball courts and organise clinics and lessons at all levels. Hardball, squash and racquetball courts usually cost around $20 for half an hour, depending on the time of day. Some private clubs allow guests to play, although there's usually a guest fee, e.g. $10. There are few dedicated hardball/squash or racquetball clubs in the US, and most are combined with health clubs and are for members only. Hardball/squash is played mostly at universities (colleges) and there are few professional players. Further details can be obtained from the US Squash Racquets Association, PO Box 1216, 23 Cynwyd Road, Bala-Cynwyd, PA 19004 (☎ 610-667-4006, 🖳 www.us-squash.org).

Court costs for all racket sports are usually lower before 5pm on weekdays and after 5pm at weekends, although lunch periods may be charged at peak rates. You must usually cancel a booked court 24 or 48 hours in advance or pay for it if it isn't re-booked. Rackets, shoes and towels can usually be rented (or purchased) from public and private clubs. Most clubs organise internal leagues and knockout competitions, and also participate in local and national league and cup competitions. To find racket clubs in your area, look in the yellow pages or enquire at your local library or tourist office.

SKIING

Skiing is one of the biggest participant sports in the US, which has the most reliable skiing conditions in the world and more than 1,200 skiing areas. When the weather is uncooperative, extensive snowmaking systems (covering up to 95 per cent of runs in some resorts) ensure uninterrupted skiing in all but the smallest of resorts. In recent years, snowboarding has become a fashionable sport, particularly among the young trendy set (nicknamed the 'teenage death dwarfs' by one commentator because of their danger to skiers). Snowboarding was previously banned in many resorts, although it's now permitted in some 90 per cent of resorts and is an official event in the Winter Olympics.

The North American ski season lasts from October or mid-November until May or even June in some areas. Most resorts are extremely crowded over Christmas, New Year, Presidents' Day holiday (the third Monday in February) and Easter. During these periods, it's usually necessary to reserve well in advance (or better still, avoid them altogether). Ski queues (lines), although practically unknown in many resorts, are orderly, and staff everywhere are usually friendly and helpful (a pleasant change from many European resorts). As in most countries, skiing is an expensive sport and few skiers can expect to spend less than $100 per day. However, accommodation and amenities in the major resorts are superb, and comfort, service and attention to detail are second to none. Most resorts have a huge range of accommodation including hotels and inns, self-catering 'aparthotels', studios, apartments and condominiums.

If you're taking your family skiing, you may find it best to choose a resort with a centralised lift system on one mountain, making it easier to get together for lunch or at the end of the day. Most resorts have excellent facilities for children, including a wide range of non-skiing entertainment. All major resorts have ski schools, many of which teach the Graduated Length Method (GLM), the US equivalent of the French *ski évolutif* (which starts beginners on short skis around three feet long). Most nursery and children's ski schools provide all day supervision, although some require parents to pick up their children for lunch. Many resorts provide a nursery for children aged from two months to three years, costing from $35 to $50 per day ($25 to $35 per half-day). Children's ski school (usually ages 3 to 12) costs from $25 to $100 per day, depending on the resort, and usually includes equipment hire (it may also include lunch and lunchtime supervision). Babysitters are available in most resorts for around $15 per hour.

If you're an advanced skier, it's best to choose a multi-centre area of two or three resorts, as even the biggest US ski areas are small compared to the large inter-linked areas in Europe. Even many intermediate skiers find that they can ski most of the trails in the majority of US resorts within around five days. Most resorts have a variety of graded runs for all standards from beginners to experts. Black runs may be graded as single (steep) or double diamond (help!), which are for expert skiers only. Many resorts also have night skiing on illuminated runs. In most resorts, there's a lack of decent mountain restaurants, although there's usually no shortage of self-service cafeterias (however, local licensing laws may make obtaining an alcoholic drink difficult).

Although *après ski* entertainment isn't always up to European standards, facilities in the best resorts are excellent, and most have a wide choice of restaurants and bars. Most resorts provide a variety of sports and leisure facilities, including cross-country skiing, sno-cat skiing, bob-sledding, snowmobiling, ice-skating, swimming (heated indoor and outdoor pools), aerobics, racket sports, horse-riding, rock and ice climbing, and hot-air ballooning. Other diversions may include sleigh rides, dog-sledding, snowshoe tours, natural hot springs and snowmobile tours. Most resort hotels and inns have saunas, Jacuzzis, steam baths and hot tubs, and many have their own health clubs, fitness rooms, gymnasiums, aerobics and games rooms, all of which are usually free to residents.

Skiing ranges from immaculately groomed pistes ('freeway' trails) to challenging off-piste (back-country) skiing. Signs indicate the trails that have been groomed in the past 24 hours and are therefore likely to be in the best condition. Off-piste skiing is strictly controlled and areas are usually clearly marked. If you're an experienced off-piste skier (and rich), you can go heli-skiing in some areas, which entails renting a helicopter to reach virgin skiing areas (you can also take a balloon to the top of a mountain in some resorts). Off-piste skiing can be dangerous because of avalanches (particularly in the west), and all off-piste skiers should attend seminars and wear avalanche beacons.

Skiing in US resorts is generally much more regulated than in Europe and to avoid overcrowding some resorts restrict the number of passes sold. Stewards armed with walkie-talkies are commonly posted everywhere and, like traffic police, signal frantically to skiers to slow down in crowded areas where pistes converge (some resorts such as Vail even boast a network of skiers' traffic lights). If you ski recklessly you're given a warning, and repeat offenders lose their ski lift passes (this also applies to anyone who skis out of bounds, which is illegal). Not surprisingly in this litigation-crazy country, resort owners are keen to avoid accidents. **All skiers should have personal liability insurance (in addition to accident and health insurance).**

Lift passes (lift tickets) in the US are the most expensive in the world and cost from $30 to $70 per day, or $150 to $400 for six days (children $10 to $40 per day, $50 to $200 for six days – passes for those under five are usually free), depending on the size of the skiing area and the number of ski lifts. (Children over 11 normally count as adults.) Rates are usually lower on weekdays than at weekends and with multi-day passes. Package deals, including transport, lodging and lift passes for several days or weeks, can reduce costs considerably. Skis, boots and poles can be rented from $20 to $35 per day by adults, around $15 to $25 by children. In many resorts, there are special deals to attract skiers at the beginning and end of the season, possibly including free skiing for women. Most resorts offer discounted passes (up to two-thirds reduction) for senior citizens (usually those aged 65 to 69) and free passes for those aged 70 or over. Most lifts are chair-lifts (double, triple and quadruple), gondolas and cable cars. T-bars and drag (poma) lifts are thankfully rare and are usually used only for teaching (as are rope tows). Somewhat surprisingly, many resorts operate chair-lifts without safety bars (strictly illegal in European resorts). Adult ski school costs around $50 to $75 per 'day' (which may be around four hours' instruction); private tuition costs up to $400 per day. The best skiing areas are as follows:

East

Maine (Sugarloaf, Sunday River), New Hampshire (Loon Mountain, Waterville Valley), New York (Hunter Mountain and Lake Placid, site of the winter Olympic Games in 1932 and 1980) and Vermont (Killington, Mount Snow, Smugglers' Notch, Stowe, Stratton).

West

California (Lake Tahoe, including Heavenly and Squaw Valley, and Mammoth Mountain), Colorado (Aspen, the most fashionable US resort, Beaver Creek, Breckenridge, Crested Butte, Keystone, Park City, Snowmass, Steamboat, Summit County, Telluride and Vail, the US's largest skiing area), Idaho (Sun Valley, the world's first purpose-built ski resort), Montana (Big Mountain, the new 'in' place to ski), New Mexico (Taos), Utah (Alta, Park City and Snowbird) and Wyoming (Jackson Hole, one of the best resorts for scenery).

There's also good skiing in hundreds of smaller resorts and superb skiing over the border in Canada (e.g. Whistler in British Columbia, reckoned by many to have the best skiing in North America).

California and the Pacific north-west generally have the best snowfalls, but it's often heavy and slushy because of the high moisture content. The east has the longest queues and most skiing is done at relatively low altitudes. This can result in a lot of freezing and thawing, creating icy trails (also true of the Midwest). The best skiing is usually to be found in the Rockies (particularly Colorado), where huge snowfalls combined with the area's dryness can create the kind of powder snow most skiers dream about (powder hounds will think they've died and gone to heaven). All ski resorts and ski regions provide telephone snow reports (usually 24-hour).

There are many books about skiing in North America, among the best of which are *The White Book of Ski Areas, U.S. & Canada, The Greatest Ski Resorts in North America* by Robert E. Weber (Guidebook Publishing Co.) and *Skiing America* by Charles Leocha (World Leisure). A number of skiing magazines are published, including *Ski* (🖳 www.skimag.com/skimag) and *Skiing* (🖳 www.skiingmag.com/skiingmag). *Ski* magazine has a monthly section, 'Where to Ski in Your Region', containing information about lift fees, children's programmes, lift queues and other important information. Local ski guides are published in many states.

Cross-Country Skiing

Cross-country skiing is popular throughout the US and is an inexpensive alternative to downhill skiing. The best cross-country skiing is to be found in the New England states and in California, Colorado, Minnesota, Montana, Wisconsin and Wyoming. Although you can enjoy cross-country skiing anywhere there's sufficient snow, cross-country skiing centres are becoming increasingly popular and offer lessons, ski rental and machine-made trails (a lot easier, although less adventurous, than making your own). Trail maps are provided and are a necessity when you're faced with miles of trails. You must pay around $15 to $20 per day for a trail pass in the US, unlike European resorts, where cross-country skiing is usually free. Skis can be rented in most resorts for $15 to $20 per day. For information about cross-country routes across the US contact National Parks Service, Department of the Interior, Washington, DC 20240 (for details of national parks with cross-country trails). A good reference book is *Cross Country Skiing for Everyone* by Jules Older (Stackpole Books).

An alternative to cross-country skiing and the latest craze in winter sport is 'snowshoeing', which is essentially walking on snow (using special shoes) and can be enjoyed by anyone wherever there's snow.

SOCCER

Soccer was at its most popular in the US after its introduction as a professional sport in the '70s, when (ageing) overseas stars such as Pele, George Best and Franz Beckenbauer were imported by American professional teams (e.g. New York Cosmos). It fell into a slump in the '80s, with falling attendances and huge losses. Soccer has, however, experienced a revival in the last few years and is the fastest growing amateur sport in the US with more than 16 million players (only basketball is played by more American children) and average league game attendances of around 15,000. Soccer is played by thousands of children and college students of both sexes (women can even get college soccer scholarships!) throughout the US, although it has rather an intellectual middle class image, unlike in most other countries where it's traditionally a working class sport. Two big advantages soccer has over (American) football are that equipment and clothing are inexpensive, and it can be played on any area of grass or concrete.

Its progress as a professional sport is hampered by the absence of a college structure (many promising players are enticed into other sports when they enter college) and the lack of natural breaks for TV advertising. The American Professional Soccer League (💻 www.mlsnet.com) has a Major League Soccer (MLS) competition with ten teams, divided between a Western and an Eastern division, which started in 1996. Two new teams are being added in 2005. Outdoor soccer is usually played on artificial grass fields or on baseball fields.

Professional soccer is also played indoors during the winter months (on AstroTurf laid on ice hockey rinks) in the Major Indoor Soccer League (MISL), which merged with the World Indoor Soccer League in 2002, and is now up to nine teams. Indoor soccer teams have a pool of 16 players, 13 of whom must be Americans. Six players may be on the field at any one time. Some fouls are penalised by sending players to the 'sin-bin' for a specified period, as in ice hockey. As with most imported sports, the Americans like to mess around with the rules in order to attract sponsors and TV advertisers and 'make it more entertaining'. Indoor soccer employs huge instant replay screens to help referees make offside and other decisions.

The popularity of soccer in the US was heightened by their hosting the 1994 World Cup, the first time it had been held in a country where it isn't a major professional sport (although the American women's team had previously won the Women's World Championship). The competition was watched by record numbers of spectators and made record profits, although some two-thirds of Americans didn't even know it was being staged. The American national team has made huge progress in recent years and reached the quarter finals in the World Cup in 2002.

SWIMMING

Swimming is the most popular sport (or pastime) in America, where some 75 million people regularly take a dip. Private pools are common, particularly in the Sunbelt states, where they're often a standard feature of family homes and condo complexes. There are public, heated indoor and outdoor swimming pools in most towns, and numerous sandy beaches (the best are in Florida) along the US's thousands of miles of ocean and lake shores. Other popular swimming spots are gravel pits, disused quarries and ponds. Lakes and rivers are generally colder than sea waters and can have dangerous rapids and whirlpools. Springs are a popular place for a natural Jacuzzi, although if you use a sulphur spring you won't be too popular with your friends until after you've had a shower. Huge water theme parks covering many acres are common throughout the US and are extremely popular with children (see **Amusement Parks** on page 405).

Considering the US's thousands of miles of coastline, it's surprisingly difficult to get to the sea in many places. In many coastal areas there are numerous private beaches and there's no general view that beaches should be open to everyone (90 per cent of the US coastline is privately owned). Most public beaches are spotlessly clean, although in some areas (such as New York City) the sea and beaches are severely polluted and some have even been closed. Many public beaches are overcrowded (particularly those close to major cities) and highly commercialised with numerous concessions (everything from umbrellas and chairs to catamarans). Facilities may include toilets, picnic areas, barbecue pits, showers, rangers, first-aid, cabanas, volleyball courts, and parking. Pets, alcohol and fires are prohibited on most public beaches. Americans don't change on the beach and in some resorts it's illegal (they're also prudish about going topless, and nude bathing is illegal in some states, even for small children, although it flourishes in many places).

Resort beaches are more organised than in most countries, with strictly controlled opening and closing times and lifeguard patrols during daylight hours. You're advised to check ocean conditions and hazards with lifeguards. Before swimming at beaches without lifeguards, check the local sea conditions, as many waters (particularly on the west coast) are unsafe because of strong currents (rip tides) and undertows. Some areas of the US's coastline are inhabited by sharks and jellyfish (which are common in some areas off Florida and Hawaii). The Pacific is, surprisingly, usually colder than the Atlantic, because of the Humbolt current, the cold counterpart of the Gulf Stream (which warms the Atlantic).

In addition to being an enjoyable pastime, swimming is a serious sport and children usually take lessons at local municipal pools. Although usually more crowded and smaller than privately owned swimming pools, municipal pools are much cheaper. Admission is usually through annual membership and may be free for residents (or there may be a nominal fee only). Residents may receive a badge and be required to sign in on each visit. In northern states, municipal outdoor pools are open from May to September. Many YMCAs have indoor pools open to non-members and provide excellent teaching programmes for children and adults. Most colleges and universities have Olympic size pools which are often open to the public for a small fee. The majority of hotels and motels have pools that are much less crowded than municipal pools, although they're supposed to be for hotel residents only! Most health clubs have indoor swimming pools, but they're generally for members only. Many pools, public and private, also provide gymnasiums and other facilities such as diving boards, paddling pools for toddlers, sunbeds, saunas, solariums and Jacuzzis. Most pools provide swimming lessons and classes for all ages, including children from six months (with their parents) as well as life-saving courses.

WATERSPORTS

Watersports are hugely popular in the US and include sailing, windsurfing, waterskiing, rowing, power boating, canoeing and kayaking, surfing, yachting and sub-aqua. This is hardly surprising when you consider the thousands of inland waterways and the seemingly endless coastline. The whole of the US is a Mecca for watersports, many of which originated there, including surfing, waterskiing and windsurfing. New watersports are continually being devised and you may come across some you haven't encountered before, such as 'tubing' (see below). Boats and equipment can be rented at coastal resorts, lakes and rivers, and instruction is available for most watersports in towns and vacation areas. Sailing boats (sailboats) and power boats, canoes, and rowing (row) boats are generally available for hire in coastal towns and at inland waterways. Jet and surf skis can also be rented at many resorts.

Boat launch sites are provided on most lakes and rivers, many of which can be used free of charge. Pleasure boating is forbidden in 'fishing access areas', which may be used by licensed fishermen only. Wetsuits aren't usually required for surfing, windsurfing, waterskiing and sub-aqua sports in summer, although they're essential in northern states during the winter months. In many states (e.g. New York), a life jacket or buoyancy aid (known as a personal flotation device or PFD) is mandatory for each passenger. Some states have a law specifically prohibiting 'boating while intoxicated (BWI)', so don't drink and 'drive'. Most states publish a free 'boater's guide' detailing local laws and regulations, and local US Coast Guard auxiliaries offer boating safety courses for small boats in most areas. **Wherever you practise watersports, be sure to observe all warning signs.** Each year hundreds of people die and thousands more are injured in watersport accidents in the US.

Canoeing & Kayaking

Canoeing and kayaking are popular on inland waterways. Canoes for several paddlers are popular as a way of exploring the calmer lakes and waterways (previous experience isn't necessary). However, if you want to use a kayak (a one-man enclosed boat) on a river, you need some previous experience or training. Canoes, rowing boats, kayaks and 'duckies' (inflatable kayaks) can be rented for between $10 and $30 per hour, depending on the area (usually a deposit and identification is necessary). Rentals are cheaper by the day or week, e.g. a day's rental usually costs the same as two or three hours. Most rental companies offer instruction for a half or full day (costing $60 to $75) and also organise trips from a few hours up to a week in duration (when camping equipment and food is usually included). On some waterways you need a launch permit for all boats, which, although usually free, are restricted in number (they can be booked in advance). In some states (e.g. Minnesota) rivers are classified for canoeists according to their degree of difficulty and danger, ranging from class I (easy, small waves, few obstructions) to class VI ('You must be kidding!').

Diving & Snorkelling

Scuba diving and snorkelling are also popular, particularly in California, Florida and Hawaii. Florida Keys is reportedly the best venue, closely followed by Southern California. To buy or rent scuba gear, you must be able to show proof of having passed a special certification ('C' card) course. The main scuba diving certification organisation is PADI (30151 Tomas Street, Rancho Santa Margarita, CA 92688-2125, ☎ 1-800-729-7234, 🖳 www.padi.com), which can provide you with a list of affiliated dive centres and resorts. Many schools provide equipment rental and certification training, involving 25 to 50 hours' tuition spread over a number of evenings or weekends. The US is one of the safest places in the world to learn scuba diving, and in resort areas you can obtain your certification in three or four days, while on holiday.

Motorboating & Waterskiing

In many states, power boats (and sailing boats) above a certain size (e.g. 12 feet) must be registered before they can be used in inland waters (fees depend on size). All mechanically propelled vessels must carry a valid registration number. Many states subscribe to an out-of-state reciprocity system, under which full recognition is granted to valid registration certificates issued in other states. There may be a maximum permitted period of operation for out-of-state boats, e.g. 90 days. In most states, children (e.g. those aged 10 to 16) must be qualified (have a certificate) to operate a motorboat without adult supervision and some states have also introduced a mandatory licensing system for adults. On many waterways you're prohibited from using motor-propelled craft, or their horsepower is restricted and there are speed limits in most areas (check state and local regulations). Offshore power boating is the formula one of watersports and is popular in the US among the well-heeled and heavily-sponsored. The speed of the fastest boats is over 100mph (160kph), which is exceeded only by the speed at which they eat up dollars. Waterskiing was invented in the US in 1922 (on a Minnesota lake) and is popular on lakes and in calm coastal areas. In many areas you can rent a ski-boat (tow-boat) and skis for a reasonable fee (e.g. $90 per hour).

Rafting

White water rafting (or river running) is hugely popular throughout the US, particularly on the fast rivers of New England and the Rockies, e.g. the Colorado River, and is an unforgettable experience (better than the hairiest of roller coasters). The best (or worst, if you're terrified) time to go is in April or May, when waters are at their most turbulent because of melting snow. Experience is usually unnecessary, as the inflatable, rubberised, pontoon-type boats are virtually unsinkable (although you won't be if you fall out). However, not all trips are suitable for families or novices. If you're inexperienced you should be accompanied by a professionally trained guide, who will (you hope) reduce the danger, but not the thrills. Trips cost from $20 to $30 for half a day, $40 to $100 for a day or up to hundreds of dollars for a week-long excursion with meals. On rivers designated 'national wild' and 'scenic', it's necessary, when rafting independently, to apply for a permit many months in advance (e.g. the previous year), as access is strictly limited. Dozens of companies organise white water rafting expeditions throughout the US, and there are a number of books for white water fans, including the *Whitewater Handbook for Canoe and Kayak* published by the Appalachian Mountain Club (AMC Books, 5 Joy Street, Boston, MA 02108, 🖳 www.outdoors.org) and *Whitewater Rafting in Eastern North The US* by Lloyd D. Armstead (The Globe Pequot Press).

Sailing

From the early days of the Union, when the 'American rebels' were busy evading the British naval blockade, to the latter-day trouncing of (most) opponents in the America's Cup, there has been huge interest in sailing. Sailing clubs and schools are numerous throughout the US, and boats of all shapes and sizes, from ocean-going racing yachts to modest sailing dinghies, can be rented or chartered in resorts (dinghies cost around $40 to $50 per hour). The most famous east coast sailing centres are Long Island South (New York and Connecticut), Cape Cod (Massachusetts), Newport (Rhode Island), Chesapeake Bay (Maryland and Virginia) and Fort Lauderdale (Florida). On the west coast, the most renowned sailing centres are San Diego (California) and Seattle (Washington). Always check with the Coast Guard before setting sail, as sudden storms are common in some areas. Navigation charts for all coastal and inland waterways are published by the National Oceanic and Atmospheric Administration and sold by a network of sales agents, including the Federal Aviation Administration (FAA Distribution Division, AVN 530, National Aeronautical Charting Office, Greenbelt, MD 20770-1479 ☎ 301-436-9301, 🖳 www.noaa.gov).

Surfing

Surfing was invented in California, which shares with Hawaii the distinction of having the world's best surfing beaches. The best Californian surfing is to be found at Malibu on Point Duma and Surfrider, Santa Monica State Beach (north of the pier), and at La Jolla on Windandsea and Boomer. Hawaii is the ultimate venue for surf groupies, where the north shore of Oahu Island is reckoned to have the best (i.e.

biggest) surf in the world. Surfing varieties include traditional board surfing, body surfing and bogey-boarding (body surfing with a short foam board). Surfboards, bodyboards and wetsuits can be rented at most locations.

Tubing

One of the latest crazes is 'tubing', which entails floating down a river on an inflatable 'rubber ring' (originally a tyre inner tube, hence the name) – a rather more leisurely and less dangerous method of river travel than rafting. It's one of the most popular summer sports in Arizona, where thousands of enthusiasts strap beer-filled ice chests and their bottoms to old inner tubes. Tubes can be rented for $5 to $10 per day (or for a few dollars more with a seat) or can be purchased at petrol stations for around $15. Life jackets can also be rented in some places. Organised 'floats' start at around $15 for a couple of hours.

Windsurfing

Windsurfing (also called sailboarding) was created in California around 1969 and is popular on coastal waters and inland lakes, where instruction and equipment rental is usually available. The ultimate windsurfing experience is to be had in Hawaii, where boards can be rented for around $20 and instruction had for around $60 (for 90 minutes).

MISCELLANEOUS SPORTS

Outlined below is a selection of other popular sports:

Athletics

Most towns and villages have athletics (track) clubs and organise local competitions and sports days. The US had genuine professional athletes long before the rules of amateur athletics were changed to allow athletes to earn a living from their sports. The US is one of the most successful nations in world and Olympic athletics competitions.

Bowling

Ten-pin bowling is an inexpensive family game and is one of the US's favourite participation sports, with more than 80 million people taking part at least once a year. There are also many professional competitions. The US has more than 7,000 bowling centres, some with over 100 lanes. A game usually costs around $5 and shoe rental around $1.50. Most bowling centres are open from 10am until 2am or later. Some centres are closed to the public when league games are being played. There are bowling leagues and clubs in all areas and many companies have teams.

Boxing

Boxing is popular throughout the US, particularly with spectators (many people enjoy watching a good fight, so long as they're out of arm's reach). Most towns have a boxing club, and boxing gymnasiums for budding professionals are common in major cities. The US is the most successful boxing nation in the world, at amateur and professional levels.

Bungee Jumping

If your idea of fun is jumping off a bridge with an elastic rope attached to your body or limbs to prevent you merging with the landscape, then bungee jumping may be just what you're looking for. American bungee jumpers make around a million jumps a year. Most bungee venues use purpose-built platforms and cranes, rather than natural locations (you can even jump from a hot-air balloon). However, due to a number of deaths, bungee jumping has been banned in some states.

Handball

Handball is played indoors on a court similar to a five-a-side soccer court and involves passing the ball around by hand and attempting to throw it into a small goal. It's an extremely popular game in the US, where there are thousands of courts (there are 2,000 in New York state alone). It's particularly popular among soccer players with two left feet.

Horse Riding

Horse riding and equestrian sports have a large following throughout the US, in urban and rural areas. Most city parks have riding trails, and horses can be rented in most areas for around $20 to $30 per hour, with lessons costing $35 to $45 per hour (most stables give discounts for children and groups). Most national and state parks have a network of bridle paths and riding trails, and horses can be rented in many parks, where horse riding is an excellent way to get off the beaten track. Organised riding holidays are arranged on ranches throughout the US.

Ice Skating

Ice skating is a fashionable indoor and outdoor sport, particularly among the under 25s, and major cities have numerous skating rinks, most of which are open all year round. All rinks offer skate hire, a skate sharpening service, and lessons for individuals and groups. Some indoor centres hold disco ice-skating evenings, e.g. on Fridays and Saturdays. Indoor rinks charge around $5 for adults (children $3) in smaller cities and rinks, up to $10 for adults ($7 under 12s) at top rinks in major cities, e.g. New York. Use of an outdoor rink is usually free. Skate rental costs from $2 to

$4. American skaters achieve considerable success in international competition, and speed skating is also a popular sport.

Jai Alai

Jai alai (pronounced 'high lie') is a local version of the Basque (Spanish) sport of pelota, a combination of handball, tennis and lacrosse, requiring great nerve, endurance and experience. It's played on a three-walled court and the object is to catch the ball and hurl it against the wall with a reed-basket called a cesta. It's played mostly in Florida (by Cubans), where you can catch the action nightly at the Miami Jai-Alai Fronton, the largest in the US. Gambling is legal at jai alai matches, which explains the huge crowds.

Martial Arts

For a country brought up on a diet of cops and robbers armed to the teeth with everything from pistols to automatic assault rifles, unarmed combat such as Aikido, Judo, Karate, Kung Fu, Kushido, Taekwondo and T'ai Chi Ch'uan is surprisingly popular. There are also clubs in all areas.

Pool

Pool is played widely throughout the US and there are pool rooms in all large cities and towns. Snooker and billiards (with pockets) are also popular with an estimated 40 million participants. Snooker tables are available in most clubs, where competitions are held for amateurs and professionals (who play for huge prizes).

Softball

Similar to baseball, softball is played with a larger, slightly softer ball and teams have ten players per side instead of nine. It's played by children and adults and is the most popular recreational team sport in the US (more than 30 million participants). A form of beach softball called over-the-line (OTL) is played by three-person teams in many states.

Volleyball

Volleyball is a hugely popular game in the US and is played indoors or on beaches, where there are usually public courts. The two games have different rules and indoor volleyball has six players to a team compared with just two for beach volleyball. It costs nothing to play on a beach, but if you're challenged to a game you must accept and win to keep the court. Volleyball is played competitively at schools and colleges and there's also a thriving professional beach volleyball season, where top players earn up to $300,000 per year. It's also an Olympic sport for men and women and has world championships.

Wrestling

The 'real' sport of wrestling (as practised in the Olympics) and cabaret wrestling are popular in the US. Amateur wrestling has a large following, particularly the NCAA wrestling championships. However, when it comes to mass popularity, showbiz wrestling (as staged by the World Wrestling Federation) is streets ahead and has spawned a huge industry of magazines, books, videos, computer games, toys, etc.

Other Sports

Other popular sports in the US include archery, chess, fencing, field hockey, gymnastics, lacrosse (the US are world champions), lawn bowls, table tennis and weightlifting. Almost unique American 'sports' include duckpin and candlepin bowling, Frisbee (also exported), horseshoe pitching, paddleball and shuffleboard. Many imported sports and pastimes have a group of expatriate fanatics, including bocc (bocci ball), cricket (which is catching on with Americans), Gaelic sports (e.g. hurling, Gaelic football), polo and rugby. If they class as sports, skateboarding, roller-skating and rollerblading, and BMX biking are also popular, particularly among the young.

17.

SHOPPING

The US is the ultimate consumer society, with annual consumer spending totalling over $4 trillion ($4,000,000,000,000)! Towns and cities are jam-packed with bustling shopping centres (malls), vast department stores, colourful markets, discount warehouses, chic boutiques and numerous specialist shops (stores). In American cities, you can buy anything and everything at almost any time of day or night, and enjoy the most competitive prices anywhere in the world. Americans believe in abundant choice and everything is available in every size, colour and flavour imaginable. New York is the US's premier shopping city, where a walk down Fifth Avenue is one of the quickest ways of emptying your wallet known to man.

Not surprisingly, the US is a major importer of famous and exclusive international labels and branded goods, which can often be purchased for less than in their country of origin. Designer products (designed to look as if they aren't mass-produced and double the price) are much in vogue and include coffee, beer, ice cream, health food, clothes, perfume and numerous other items. Most consumer goods are inexpensive (never ask for something 'cheap', which is synonymous with poor quality) compared with other countries, including electronic goods, cameras, computer hardware and software, stereo systems, compact discs (CDs) and DVDs, video cameras, sports equipment, and clothes (particularly jeans and casual clothes), all of which are excellent value.

What matters most to Americans are low prices and hardly anyone pays 'full' price for anything (many shops meet any advertised price). If you're an avid bargain hunter it's important to 'comparison shop 'til you drop', as recommended retail prices are almost extinct in the US. However, you should avoid stores that don't display their prices; if you need to ask the price, it usually means you cannot afford it! Most people save their spending sprees or major purchases for the sales or shop at discount and factory outlets where huge savings can be made (see **Sales, Discounts & Factory Outlets** on page 490).

Most Americans live life in the fast lane and long working hours and commuting times make one-stop shopping popular. Most people shop in department stores, supermarkets and suburban shopping centres, rather than in small specialised shops in city and town centres (downtown). In most cities, there are even professional shoppers, who charge $40 to $50 per hour and shop for you or accompany you while you shop. Their knowledge of what's on offer can save you more than their fee, particularly if you're shopping for designer clothes. Many department stores provide customers with a free 'personal shopper', who gathers a selection of goods from which customers can choose.

Shop assistants (store clerks) usually fall into two main categories. On the one hand they may be friendly, helpful and polite, and treat you as a long lost friend, asking after your health (like waiters) and sending you on your way with a cheery 'Have a nice day'. Conversely, in some shops (particularly in New York City) staff are astonishingly rude, and their 'sales patter' may include 'Don' waste my time if yer ain't buyin'!', 'Do you wanna buy it or doncha?' and 'Quit the please and thanks lady, waddyawan?'. American shoppers are often equally blunt and usually dispense with the niceties; 'I'll take' or 'Gimme' suffices for most things (no please and thank-you). With the exception of the occasional exclusive boutique with foreign clientele, shop assistants rarely speak foreign languages (apart from their native tongues). In major cities such as New York, many shops employ doormen to keep street people at bay and shops everywhere don't allow food or drink, smoking, bare feet or men without shirts.

Most shops accept all major credit cards, although you may be required to make a minimum purchase. Many accept a personal cheque only if your bank is located in the same city and you show at least two forms of identification (ID). In some shops, you may need to go to a special desk and have a cheque approved before going to the checkout, and some shops accept personal cheques only from customers to whom they've previously issued an identification card. Almost all retailers accept $US travellers' cheques and most give change. You will be pleased to hear that most shops also accept cash (some even insist on it). If you run out of the folding stuff, many shops, supermarkets and malls have automated teller machines (ATMs) accepting most cash and credit cards.

Most retailers (particularly supermarkets) regularly offer discount coupons, found in most local newspapers and magazines, particularly at weekends. Shopping with coupons is a way of life in the US and it's a rare shopper who never uses them. If you don't use coupons, you will simply pay too much, as prices are set with the expectation that customers will use them. In order not to lose business to their rivals, many shops and businesses also accept coupons issued by their competitors. The ultimate coupon book is *Entertainment* published annually for all regions and cities by Entertainment Publications Inc., 1414 East Maple Road, Troy, MI 48083 (☎ 1-888-231-SAVE, 🖥 www.entertainment.com). It costs $25 to $45 (depending on the area) and contains literally hundreds of coupons issued by local businesses such as restaurants, fast food outlets, cinemas, hotels, car hire companies, dry cleaners and numerous shops.

In the US, the customer is always, but **always** right! Most retailers, particularly department and chain stores, exchange goods or give refunds without question. Americans enjoy a high degree of consumer protection and almost any complaint is dealt with promptly and favourably (particularly if you threaten to sue!). If you have any questions about your rights as a consumer, contact your local consumer protection agency or better business bureau (see also **Consumers' Organisations** on page 499).

Many shops, particularly department and chain stores, provide free catalogues at various times throughout the year (catalogues are delivered to homes with other junk mail) and free shopping guides are published in all areas. If you're looking for a particular item or anything unusual, you will find that the yellow pages saves you a lot of time and trouble (and shoe leather). For those who aren't accustomed to buying goods with American measures and sizes, comparative weights and measures are listed in **Appendix C**.

In the US, shopping is all things to all men and women and is variously a sport, pastime, entertainment, game, business, amusement, love, all consuming passion and the Meaning of Life (some 50 per cent of American women prefer shopping to sex). However, for those with an uncontrollable urge to spend, spend, spend, life can be hell, and compulsive shopping is a serious addiction that bankrupts thousands of families every year. An estimated 6 per cent of adult Americans (around three million people) are shopaholics, buying things they don't need, don't want and often cannot afford. However, don't despair, American researchers have come up with a cure using an antidepressant drug (fluvoxamine) to suppress the urge to shop. (You'd better believe it!) In stark contrast to the frenzied consumption of most Americans, the latest fad among a dedicated minority is penny pinching (the cult of thrift). Thrifties even have their own newsletters, one of which, *The Tightwad Gazette*, by Amy Dacyczyn (Villard) has been published as a book! And, of course, there are websites devoted to pinching pennies, e.g. Tightwad Central (⌨ www.tightwad.com).

When you're shopping in crowded towns and cities, keep a firm grip on your belongings, as pickpockets and bag snatchers are an integral part of the American free enterprise system.

SALES TAX

Prices of goods and services are always shown and quoted exclusive of state sales tax, which is the most complicated tax you must deal with. Sales tax varies from zero (no tax) in five states (Alaska, Delaware, Montana, New Hampshire and Oregon) to 7 per cent or more (see table below). Sales taxes are the largest source of revenue for most state and local governments, raising around $150 billion nationwide. Not all items are taxable, however, and taxable items vary from state to state (and often appear to have been selected at random). The table below shows in which states (most types of) food and medicines are exempt from sales tax. (In Idaho, Kansas, South Dakota, Vermont and Wyoming, low-income families are given an income tax credit to offset state sales tax on food.) Newspapers and magazines are exempt in most states and professional services are exempt in some states. In most states, sales tax is applicable to all items over 20 cents and meals over $1. Clothing costing up to $175 is exempt in Massachusetts and all clothing is exempt in New Jersey. Even the definitions of goods such as 'snack food' and 'sportswear' vary from state to state. (There are bizarre examples: In New York there's sales tax on ordinary shampoo, but not on anti-dandruff shampoo, in Indiana you can avoid sales tax on doughnuts if you buy at least six, and in New Jersey you won't pay tax on your running shoes if you don't use them to run!)

State	Tax Rate (%)			
	General	Food	Prescription Medicines	Other Medicines
Alabama	4	4	0	4
Arizona	5.6	0	0	5.6
Arkansas	5.125	5.125	0	5.125
Califorinia	7.25	0	0	7.25
Colorado	2.9	0	0	2.9
Connecticut	6	0	0	0
Florida	6	0	0	0
Georgia	4	0	0	4
Hawaii	4	4	0	4

Idaho	6	6	0	6
Illinois	6.25	1	1	1
Indiana	6	0	0	6
Iowa	5	0	0	5
Kansas	5.3	5.3	0	5.3
Kentucky	6	0	0	6
Louisiana	4	0	0	4
Maine	5	0	0	4
Maryland	5	0	0	0
Massachusetts	5	0	0	5
Michigan	6	0	0	6
Minnesota	6.5	0	0	0
Mississippi	7	7	0	7
Missouri	4.225	1.225	0	4.225
Nebraska	5.5	0	0	5.5
Nevada	6.5	0	0	6.5
New Jersey	6	0	0	0
New Mexico	5	5	0	5
New York	4.25	0	0	0
N. Carolina	4.5	0	0	4.5
N. Dakota	5	0	0	5
Ohio	6	0	0	6
Oklahoma	4.5	4.5	0	4.5
Pennsylvania	6	0	0	0
Rhode Island	7	0	0	0
S. Carolina	5	5	0	5
S. Dakota	4	4	0	4
Tennessee	7	6	0	7
Texas	6.25	0	0	0
Utah	4.75	4.75	0	4.75
Vermont	6	0	0	0
Virginia	5	4	0	0
Washington	6.5	0	0	6.5
West Virginia	6	6	0	6
Wisconsin	5	0	0	5
Wyoming	4	4	0	4
D. C.	5.75	0	0	0

Many people cross state borders (lines) to buy alcohol and cigarettes, as there are often wide variations in prices due to different tax levels. When you're planning to make an expensive purchase, it may pay you to shop by mail-order, as sales tax often isn't applied to mail-order purchases and shipping costs are low within the continental US (see **Mail-order & Internet Shopping** on page 492). With internet sales reaching $50 billion in 2004, the question of sales tax on mail-order purchases is becoming a national issue and could pave the way for rationalisation of the state sales tax system. (The government is currently considering a 'Streamlined Sales Tax Project'.)

Sales tax applies not only to new goods and goods sold by businesses, but also to private sales of certain used products, e.g. cars, motor homes, boats and aircraft. Sales tax is calculated on the amount paid for a used item (usually less any trade-in) and is paid by the buyer. Certain types of consumer (e.g. schools, churches and non-profit organisations) are exempt from paying sales tax in some states. In 2004, some thirteen states held 'sales tax holidays' where certain categories of goods could be purchased sales tax free for some period of time, from a single day in Massachusetts, to week-long tax holidays in Connecticut and the District of Columbia! Sales tax holidays tend to fall during the back-to-school season in the month of August, and are often limited to clothing and school supplies.

Sales tax, not only varies from state to state, but is increased in many areas by local taxes (e.g. city and county taxes). There are more than 6,500 state and local taxing jurisdictions in the US. Taxes are regularly reviewed (there are around 600 changes per year throughout the US), and many states have increased their sales tax in recent years. If you're running a business and you're getting a headache trying to keep up with local and state sales tax rates, two companies (Vertex in Pennsylvania and Taxware in Massachusetts) sell software that automatically applies the latest tax rates. (You may or may not have to pay sales tax on the software, depending on where and how you buy it!)

SHOPPING HOURS

One of the most surprising and pleasant discoveries for foreigners in the US is the long shopping hours. Many supermarkets, drugstores and petrol stations remain open 24 hours a day, seven days a week in most areas (some people actually shop at 3am). When not open 24 hours, supermarkets and drugstores generally open from 8am or 9am to 9pm. At least one drugstore or chemist (pharmacy) is open until midnight or 24 hours in major cities (see page 309). In smaller towns, shops have more 'normal' shopping hours and usually open between 9am and 10am, and close between 5pm and 7pm, Mondays to Saturdays. In central shopping areas, major stores may be open from 9.30am to 10pm Mondays to Fridays, and from 9.30am to 7pm on Saturdays and Sundays. Most shopping centres open at around 10am and close at 9.30pm or 10pm. It's best to avoid shopping at lunchtimes and on Saturdays, when shops are packed.

Sunday opening is subject to state and/or local county 'blue' laws (see **Alcohol** on page 481) and in some counties, Sunday trading is prohibited (in which case shops in neighbouring counties do a roaring trade). The most lively shopping areas on Sundays, in some cities (e.g. New York) are Jewish neighbourhoods, where shops are closed on Saturdays (the Jewish Sabbath) and open on Sundays. Shops in some ethnic neighbourhoods, such as the New York City and San Francisco Chinatowns, are open every day of the week. Some department stores in New York City (e.g. Bloomingdales and Macy's) and other large cities (e.g. Boston, Chicago, San Francisco) are open from noon until 6pm on Sundays. Officially, shops close on two days a year only: Thanksgiving and Christmas Day (sales are often held on other federal holidays).

MALLS & MARKETS

All US cities and suburban areas have huge indoor shopping centres, usually called malls (pronounced 'mawls'), often housing 50 to 100 shops. Malls vary from basic everyday shopping centres to plush 'plazas' catering exclusively for big spenders. Some malls are housed in beautiful historic landmarks or extravagant modern buildings and many occupy the lower floors of office blocks. Among the major attractions of shopping malls is that they're usually enclosed (some are underground), air-conditioned, provide free or inexpensive parking (many are accessible by car only) and offer competitive prices. Discount or outlet malls (see page 490) are also common throughout America. Discount malls may offer entertainment as well as unbeatable prices and are often located alongside amusement parks.

Malls typically contain at least one supermarket, a number of department stores, chain stores, banks, launderettes (laundromats), hairdressers, optometrists, restaurants, fast food outlets (the food court), and a wide selection of boutiques and specialist shops. In some malls, there are car hire offices, airline booking desks and even medical clinics, and many house, leisure and entertainment facilities such as a skating rink, tenpin bowling, cinemas, amusement arcades and art galleries (you can even get married in a mall!). Malls are usually open from around 10am to 9.30pm or 10pm. One of the world's largest malls is the appropriately named Mall of America in Minneapolis, dubbed the megamall. It covers an area of 4.2 million square feet (390,180m^2) and contains more than 400 shops, 45 restaurants, 14 cinemas, 9 nightclubs, a seven-acre amusement park, a miniature golf course and a marriage chapel. The Mall of America attracts 40 million customers a year and is the second most popular 'attraction' in the US after Disney World.

In most cities, there are daily food markets (including 'farmers' and 'green' markets), although street markets are generally poor compared with those in Europe. Flea (junk) markets are common in major cities and specialise in clothing, jewellery, antiques, and miscellaneous bric-a-brac. In states with severe winters, markets may be held between spring and autumn only. There are often small impromptu markets in many cities, although it's illegal to sell goods in the street without a licence. Some towns organise regular street markets for local artisans and craftspeople. Ask at your local tourist office, library or town hall for information about local markets.

DEPARTMENT & CHAIN STORES

There are many excellent department and chain stores in the US. For those unfamiliar with department stores, they're usually large shops with several floors and may sell everything from clothes to perfume, electrical items to furniture. Each floor may be dedicated to a type of goods, such as ladies' or men's fashions, or furniture and furnishings, and stores usually have restaurants, cafeterias, telephones and toilets (restrooms). A chain store is a store with two or more branches, often located in different towns. There are dozens of chain stores in the US, selling everything from electrical items to food, books and clothes. Many department and chain stores specialise in fashions.

The US has some of the world's best and most famous department stores, including Bloomingdales (popularly known as Bloomies), Macy's and Saks Fifth Avenue (fashion), which, although renowned for their New York City stores, also have branches in many other cities. Macy's New York City store is the world's largest, with over 2 million square feet (185,800m²) of floor space. Here you can shop (or get lost) for days and still not see everything (seven restaurants and cafés will sustain you).

Few American department stores are nationwide chains, with stores in all areas, but there are many with branches in more than one city. These include Sears Roebuck, J.C. Penney, Lord & Taylor, Neiman Marcus, Marshall Field's, Nordstroms, Sangar-Harris and May & Co. Nordstroms fashion department stores (based in Seattle) set the standards for other stores and are famous for their attractive design and layout, well trained, polite and knowledgeable staff, and a pianist who regales shoppers during peak hours. There are also excellent independent department stores in major cities. Most department stores operate a home delivery service and many deliver goods anywhere in the world.

In a department store the floor at street level is designated the first floor (not the ground floor), the floor below the ground floor is usually called the basement and the floor above may be called the mezzanine. The basement or lower basement is usually occupied by a bargain department where reduced price or inexpensive goods are sold. Some stores, such as Filene's (Basement), Marshalls, Syms and T.J. Maxx operate basement stores famous for their cut-price branded clothes and unbeatable prices on other items.

In the last decade, department and chain stores (and supermarkets) have faced increasing competition from discount and outlet stores and warehouse clubs, and many have failed in the past decade. The largest nationwide discount department stores, sometimes called mass merchandisers, include Kmart, Target and Wal-Mart (nearly 3,000 stores). Warehouse clubs, the fastest-growing retail sector in the US with a $25 billion turnover, include Costco and Sam's Club (owned by Wal-Mart). Warehouse clubs charge an annual membership fee of $25 to $35 (which can be recouped in one visit) and offer discounts on branded goods (particularly food, where prices for bulk quantities are typically 20 per cent below supermarket prices). The hackneyed slogan 'the more you spend, the more you save' is literally true, although discerning shoppers profit most.

Most department and chain stores accept all major credit cards, although some issue their own credit cards and don't accept others. If you have a store credit card, you will be inundated with pre-sale mail, special offers and seasonal catalogues. Some store credit cards allow customers to write personal cheques without providing further identification, and a number of stores issue their own identification cards to enable regular customers to pay by cheque.

SUPERMARKETS & FOOD SHOPS

As in most western countries, the majority of people buy their food in supermarkets, many of which are open 24 hours a day, seven days a week (especially in cities and metropolitan areas). The US supermarket business, which is worth over $200 billion a year, is dominated by three chains, Albertson's, Kroger and Safeway, although there are numerous smaller chains. The cost of food depends on the area and the origin of the produce; for example fruit and vegetables are usually cheapest in California, where most are grown, and beef is cheapest in the Midwest where the big cattle ranches are located. Food is cheapest overall in Texas and most expensive in Alaska (except for salmon), where most foods must be imported. In general, $1 buys you a pound of bread or chicken or a dozen large eggs. Like department stores, supermarkets are losing business to warehouse clubs (see above), where a family of four can save around $75 per month on their food bill. However, clubs cannot compete with supermarkets for variety and typically stock some 4,000 products (lines) only, many of them non-food, compared with a supermarket's 20,000.

The quality, variety and (often regulation) size of produce (fruit and vegetables) in American supermarkets is excellent and often overwhelming to the newcomer. Shops are huge and packed year-round with the most exotic produce, mountains of meat and dairy products, and convenience foods by the truckload. US supermarkets invariably carry larger stocks and offer a much wider variety of merchandise than their counterparts abroad. The choice is mind-boggling (e.g. literally hundreds of breakfast cereals) and everything seems to come in giant cartons or gallon bottles (which can be a problem when you're shopping for one person). Most supermarkets provide giant shopping trolleys, called caddies or carts.

A common criticism of American produce is that it's grown almost exclusively for its colour and appearance, with little thought given to taste or nutrition. Everything is aimed at marketing and convenience, and American farmers would happily produce square fruit and vegetables for easier packing if they could (they're probably working on it!). Produce is usually graded, for example from A to C, grade A being the best quality (i.e. best looking), and grade C, broken or sliced pieces suitable for cooking. Many fruit and vegetables are sprayed with a variety of chemicals and herbicides to kill pests, speed growth or promote longevity, none of which do much for the taste, or in some cases, your health (some fruit even has a wax coating). However, organically grown produce is also available in many shops and many food shops in areas with a large Jewish population have a Kosher section. Produce departments are self-service and fruit and vegetables aren't pre-packed, so you can buy as little or as much as you like (although you save nothing by buying in bulk). Many large supermarkets are equipped with a microwave oven, where you can heat your 'TV dinner' free of charge (although it may then attract a sales tax levied on warm take-away food in some states) and often sport delicatessen sections, salad bars and on-site bakeries.

American meat usually tastes excellent, particularly beef, although animals are usually stuffed with hormones (e.g. anabolic steroids) and antibiotics. Most cattle are scientifically bred using production-line methods in order to produce better and larger animals in the shortest possible time (although meat from naturally reared livestock is also available). Remember that when buying frozen foods, they defrost or melt much quicker in the hot weather experienced in some states if they aren't stored in freezer bags (available along with ice from most supermarkets). Supermarkets are often the cheapest place to buy cigarettes (sold in cartons of ten packs) and alcohol.

Most American supermarkets sell their own brand (private-label) foods and also have a 'generic' section, where tins and packets bear the name of the product only, statutory information (e.g. weight, contents) and a bar code. These may sell for as much as 70 per cent (average 25 per cent) less than their branded counterparts. One survey estimated that a family of four could save over $1,500 per year by buying private-label or generic items. In some cases, the product is virtually the same as the branded item and may even be produced in the same factory. When comparing different brands, ensure that the grade and quantity is the same.

All supermarkets have bargain offers on certain items to attract customers, when goods are often sold at below cost price ('loss leaders') and displayed at the ends of aisles. Coupons are issued by manufacturers (they can be used in any shop) and also by chain stores and individual shops. Shops often advertise that they honour coupons issued by other shops in order to prevent competitors luring away their regular customers. If a shop has sold out of an offer item, it may offer you the same deal on another brand or a 'rain cheque', where you're given a voucher entitling you to buy at the offer price when new stocks arrive. You can save around 10 to 20 per cent on your weekly shopping bill ($10 to $15 per week for most families) by becoming an avid coupon clipper. Many people keep their coupons in coupon holders, given away as promotional items. (Most coupons have an expiry date.) Most supermarkets also now have customer loyalty cards which entitle you to discounts on featured items if you present the card when paying. You also get in-store coupons when using your customer loyalty card.

Most American supermarkets use scanners to scan bar codes at cash desks (checkout counters). Purchases and prices are usually displayed on computer screens. Check your bill, as the people who enter prices into computers sometimes make mistakes. It's usually unnecessary to take a shopping bag, as most shops provide free strong brown paper bags or plastic sacks at the checkout (and you may be asked whether you prefer 'paper or plastic'), where an assistant not only packs your bags for you, but may even carry them to your car. Many supermarkets are introducing 'self-checkouts' or 'self-scan stations', where you can scan and bag your own purchases. Payment can be by cash, cheque or credit/debit card, even at 'self-checkout' stands. You may need to go to a 'courtesy' desk in some shops to have your cheque approved. Some shops accept cheques only if you have an identification card issued by the shop. Several of the supermarket chains also offer home delivery services, which you can access over the internet.

In some suburban areas, separate produce shops (e.g. butchers' and bakers) are rare, so you may have little choice but to shop at a supermarket. (American bread is often bland and sweet-tasting.). It's possible to buy inexpensive naturally grown fruit and vegetables from local farmers or co-operatives in all rural areas (including 'pick your own' farms). Many have roadside stalls or signs advertising their produce. In many cities, there are 'farmers' or 'green' markets, where local farmers sell fresh and reasonably priced produce most days of the week (see **Malls & Markets** on page

477). Local fishermen usually set up stalls in fishing towns. As in most countries, markets are usually the best place to shop for fresh food and are a good place to buy an assortment of bread and a wider variety of cheeses than you find in most supermarkets. However, unlike the markets in the rest of the world, local regulations may prevent you tasting the goods before you buy.

Many foreign foods and ingredients are available in supermarkets and there are also ethnic food shops and supermarkets in many neighbourhoods. In neighbourhoods without local supermarkets, corner produce shops may be open up to 20 hours a day (often run by Asians, e.g. Koreans in New York City). There are also numerous specialist or 'gourmet' food shops in all major cities, selling every luxury food imaginable, although they **aren't** the place to shop for basic foodstuffs. Larger food shops provide catering services for anything from a small dinner party or picnic to a 100-head banquet or wedding reception, complete with crockery, furniture, flowers and staff.

ALCOHOL

The sale of alcohol (liquor) in the US is strictly controlled in most states and liquor laws are also set by counties, municipalities and towns (see **Licensing** on page 423). In some places, you can buy alcohol at practically any time of the day or night, although in most states the sale of spirits is more restricted than that of beer and wine. Not all supermarkets sell alcohol, and in many states, spirits (and sometimes beer and wine) can be purchased from official state off-licenses (liquor stores) only, e.g. Alcohol Board of Control or ABC shops, generally called package liquor stores (packies). In states with liberal licensing laws, e.g. New Jersey, off-licenses may open from 9am to 9pm or 10pm Mondays to Saturdays and from 10am to 5pm on Sundays. On the other hand, in almost a third of the counties in Texas and the whole of (Mormon-dominated) Utah, the sale of alcohol is prohibited. In some states, drinks can be sold to members in private clubs only, although it's easy to become a temporary member. There are 'dry' towns or counties in most areas, although you can usually buy alcohol in a nearby town. It's illegal to take alcohol into some states, e.g. Arkansas and Michigan, and other states permit only a limited amount to be imported, e.g. a quart or a gallon.

In many Midwestern states, there are 'blue laws' (nothing to do with pornography) restricting Sunday trading, particularly the sale of alcohol. Blue laws are usually set by counties and may prohibit the sale of any alcohol, including beer and wine, on Sundays or holidays (or on election voting days until after the polls close). In some states, only low-alcohol beer can be bought from package shops on Sundays, where alcohol is packaged in plain brown paper bags (hence the term 'brown bagging', i.e. drinking from a bottle concealed in a brown bag). An 'open container' law forbids the consumption of any alcoholic beverage in public and in many states, it's illegal to have an open container of alcohol in your vehicle, even in the boot. It's illegal to sell alcohol on Sundays in Connecticut, Louisiana (unless decided otherwise locally), Mississippi (except in resort areas) and South Carolina (excluding non-profit clubs).

The minimum age for purchasing alcohol is usually 21 (except for low-alcohol beer in some states). Twenty-one is also the minimum drinking age in bars and restaurants in most states. A retailer is supposed to ask your age and may ask for identification. In practice, however, this rarely happens if you look old enough, particularly in supermarkets. Acceptable identification usually consists of a driving licence or a 'liquor purchase identification card' issued by the Registry of Motor Vehicles in many states. Technically, a supermarket checkout assistant isn't permitted to sell alcohol if he is under 21, and he may ask an older clerk or even the customer to ring up a sale. In some states, supermarkets, drugstores and grocery shops may sell only beer or beer and wine only (this may be decided on a county basis), and bars may be permitted only to sell beer or spirits 'to-go' (i.e. for consumption elsewhere).

The standard size of bottles for most forms of alcohol (i.e. other than wine) is 757 ml (25.6 ounces), known colloquially as a fifth (of a US gallon). Wine is likely to be sold in standard 750 ml bottles, as it is elsewhere in the world. The cheapest wine (sold in screw top bottles) costs around $3 to $5 per bottle, while quality American wines are considerably more expensive, although generally excellent. Usually, you receive a discount when you buy wine by the case (12 bottles). 'Jug' wines are inexpensive, blended, Californian red wines, often sold in half-gallon jugs (usually excellent value). Beer is sold in 12fl oz and 16fl oz sizes, bottles or cans being sold individually or in packs of six (a 'six-pack') from $3 to $4; imported beer is more expensive (but worth the extra). The price of a bottle (a fifth) of bourbon or other spirits (hard liquor) is around $15. Prices vary little (if at all) in state liquor stores, although in some states, e.g. New Hampshire, prices are low and people travel from other states to stock up. Duty on alcohol varies from state to state.

Most wine sold in supermarkets and off-licences is from California or New York state, although European, Australian and other foreign wines are widely available. Californian wines are recognised as among the best in the world and include many first-class chardonnays, cabernet sauvignons, sauvignon blancs, pinot noirs and zinfandels. The US doesn't adhere to international naming conventions or labelling standards (e.g. as are common in most European countries) and names such as burgundy, claret, chablis, port, and sherry, to name but a few, are used with impunity and may have little, or nothing, in common with the genuine article. Quality California wines are labelled according to grape type, and must contain at least 51 per cent of the variety of grape indicated on the label, e.g. cabernet sauvignon.

A few states have 'bottle laws' to discourage litter and encourage recycling. This involves paying a deposit of 5 cents or 10 cents on all beer or soft drink bottles (but not usually wine, spirit or fruit-juice bottles), that's added to the price at the checkout. Deposits are refunded when empties are returned to shops or redemption centres.

For further information on alcohol and drinking, see **Drinks** on page 429 and **Bars** on page 420.

CLOTHES

Clothes are generally of excellent quality in the US, particularly those from famous manufacturers producing classic styles and traditional clothes made to last (and outlive ever-changing fashions). With the exception of pop stars, prostitutes (hookers) and members of certain ethnic groups, most Americans are surprisingly conservative in their dress. Not all Americans wear loud checked trousers or garish Bermuda shorts, although some American clothes are so loud they should carry a health warning. The east coast is more conservative than the west, where people are more likely to dress casually, due mainly to the warmer climate.

The US's most enduring contribution to fashion is the humble blue jeans, excellent value at around $30 for top brands such as Levi's, Lee and Wrangler (although you can pay a fortune for designer jeans such as Calvin Klein and Ralph Lauren). T-shirts (said to have originated in the US), often with original, outrageous or distasteful designs and slogans, are fashionable and sold everywhere.

Shops selling designs from the world's top fashion houses flourish in the largest (and richest) cities and include Yves Saint Laurent, Gucci, Polo, Chanel, Boss, Jaeger, Giorgio Armani, Hermès, Givenchy and Burberry. Even more exclusive are clothes designed by Calvin Klein, Ralph Lauren (the arbiter of urban American taste), Donna Karan, Norma Kamali and Liz Claiborne. Some establishments (dubbed 'designer showrooms') cater exclusively to the famous and seriously rich (men's perfume at $3,000 a bottle!) and shopping is by appointment only (the stars don't wish to rub shoulders with the hoi polloi when buying their underwear). Trendy boutiques, where the emphasis is on designer clothes and chic accessories, are found everywhere.

Among the most popular mainstream clothes shops are Banana Republic, Benetton and Gap (also GapKids shops). Gap (who also own Banana Republic) was the US's biggest retail success story of the '80s and is renowned for its reasonably priced, brightly coloured, basic clothing, including T-shirts, trousers (pants) and sweaters. The best value specialist clothing chains include Talbots, Eddie Bauer and Timberland. Among the most famous men's shops are Brooks Brothers, who have a reputation for selling high quality, classic men's clothing (they also sell women's clothes). Many mainstream fashion shops are unisex. One of the most surprising things about shopping for quality clothes in the US, is the number of shops selling quality branded clothes at much lower prices than in other countries. However, in smaller towns, the reverse may be true. Some successful clothing companies such as L.L. Bean and Land's End sell almost entirely by mail-order.

There's a large market in used (often called 'antique' or 'vintage') clothes in major cities, sold by consignment shops which sell second-hand clothes on commission. Charity shops are also a good place to pick up inexpensive and fashionable new and second-hand clothing, donated by shops and individuals. Many thrift shops also sell inexpensive second-hand clothing. Designer clothes can even be purchased from handcarts in some cities, although these are usually shop-soiled or seconds (or even counterfeit!). In the garment districts of major cities such as Los Angeles and New York, there are factory outlets, clothing clearance centres and clothes discount shops, where designer clothes can be bought at discounts of 25 to 75 per cent (see **Sales, Discounts & Factory Outlets** on page 490). One of the best outlets for bargain-priced designer clothes are the 'off-price' chains such as Burlington Coat Factory, Filene's Basement, Syms, Marshalls and T.J. Maxx, who buy factory overruns and clothes that department stores cannot sell (although there may be no refunds or exchanges).

In American and British English, different names are often used for the same items of clothing, or both use the same name but with different meanings. Among the many items occasionally causing confusion (or hilarity) are stockings (hose or socks to an American), nightdress (nightgown), dungarees (overalls), trousers (pants), tights (panty hose), bathrobe or dressing gown (robe or housecoat), underpants or short trousers (shorts), pants (underpants or panties), braces (suspenders), vest (undershirt), and a women's coat or other outer garment (wrap). In the US, a jumper is equal to a British pinafore, which is a dress worn over a blouse, and not a sweater. An American vest is a men's waistcoat or sleeveless pullover.

Shoes

Although many clothes shops sell shoes, there's also a wide variety of specialist shoe shops. Among the best American brands of shoes are Alden, Bass, Dockside, Florsheim, Hush Puppies, Mephisto, Rockport, Sebago, Selby, Sioux, Sperry and Timberland (famous for their boots). Good children's shoes are produced by Bass, Capezio and StrideRite. Famous imported brands are also widely available, e.g. Bally and Clarks. American-made shoes are generally good quality, particularly cowboy boots, which are made in a multitude of styles, leather and skins. Although they're generally expensive, if treated with care they will last for many years. Shoe repair shops can be found in all towns and in department stores, where repairs may be done while you wait.

There are sports shoe shops in most cities and towns, selling specialist sports shoes, leisure shoes and 'sneakers' (includes everything from tennis shoes to trainers and running shoes). Sports shoes are excellent value for money and almost all Americans own at least one pair. A bizarre and common sight in cities, is women wearing trainers with their formal office clothes or even with a fur coat, although they usually change their footwear when they get to the office.

Sizes

Clothes sizes often vary wildly according to the manufacturer (as we all know only too well!). Often small, medium and large are meaningful only in the mind of the manufacturer, where one man's (or woman's) small can be another's extra large. The average size American (male and female) is usually larger than the average person in most other countries and therefore American clothes are often cut larger. Men's shirts sometimes come in different sleeve lengths (and collar sizes), which is fine as long as you know the size you need. If possible, try on all clothes before buying and don't be afraid to return them if they don't fit or are a different colour from what you imagined. Most American shops exchange clothes or give a refund (if you're unsure, ask when buying) unless they were purchased during a sale, although the exchange period can vary considerably. Some clothes shops offer a 30-day money-back guarantee on unworn garments (shops usually advertise their refund policy or it's printed on receipts). See **Appendix C** for comparison tables for American, British and continental European clothes' sizes and **Receipts & Warranties** on page 498.

LAUNDRY & DRY CLEANING

There are self-service launderettes (laundromats) in most towns (the Americans like to wash their dirty linen in public), open from around 7am until 9pm or 10pm, seven days a week. A wash usually costs from around $1.50 (top load) to $3 (front load) and a drier around 50 cents for 5 to 10 minutes. In some areas, launderettes have pool tables and a bar and many offer free coffee, special offers and coupons to attract customers. In some establishments, it's common for machines to be out of order. For an extra dollar or two per load, launderette staff usually wash and dry your clothes for you. Soap powder is sold in vending machines, but it's expensive (e.g. $1 per load) and it's better to bring your own. There are also Chinese laundries in most cities (around 2,000 in New York alone) taking around four days. The cost usually depends on the location and whether you require any special services.

Towns usually have at least one dry cleaner, which also does minor repairs, invisible mending, alterations and dyeing. Some dry cleaners offer a one-hour service, same day alterations, and will remove stains within a day or two. Many provide a free local delivery and collection service (e.g. within a ten block radius). Americans consider dry cleaning to be expensive, although most outlets issue coupons and accept coupons issued by competitors. Some launderettes have self-service dry-cleaning machines. Most hotels provide an expensive laundry and dry cleaning service, and some have coin-operated machines in the basement for residents' use.

NEWSPAPERS, MAGAZINES & BOOKS

The US has more daily newspapers than any other country, a total of around 1,500 morning and evening newspapers and more than 850 Sunday newspapers, or more than 9,000 when weekly and free newspapers are included. More than 60 million newspapers are printed daily, including Sundays, many in full colour. However, the number of newspapers published has been falling for some years and only four cities (Chicago, Los Angeles, New York and Washington DC) have competing daily newspapers, i.e. newspapers owned by different publishers. Foreign-language newspapers are published in all major cities. In addition to newspapers, more than 11,000 different periodicals are published in weekly, monthly, bi-monthly, quarterly or bi-annual editions. As in many other countries, most states don't tax newspapers or magazines, although most tax books.

The US has no genuine national press or national newspapers, such as are common in many European countries, and most newspapers are regional (city or state) or local (e.g. county). The nearest to a national newspaper is the tabloid *USA Today*, although the *Wall Street Journal* and *Christian Science Monitor* are also distributed nationally. *USA Today* (nicknamed 'McPaper', as it's the journalistic equivalent of fast food) is transmitted by satellite throughout the country and also internationally (there's an international edition), and sells more than 5 million copies daily. It provides readers with the minimum amount of news and the maximum sports coverage, mostly printed in glorious colour with lots of pictures. The *Wall*

Street Journal is printed in several American cities and has four regional editions: eastern, midwestern, western and south-western, selling a total of 2 million copies daily (it's **the** paper for business people, brokers and bankers).

Among the most influential and respected regional newspapers are the *New York Times* and the *Washington Post*, both available throughout the country. These newspapers syndicate staff-written articles and features to regional newspapers throughout the US. Other quality regional newspapers (almost all broadsheets) include the *Boston Globe* (owned by the *New York Times*), *Chicago Tribune, Denver Post, Los Angeles Times, Miami Herald* and the *San Francisco Chronicle*. Tabloid newspapers are also published in most cities and include the *Herald* (Boston), *Sun Times* (Chicago) and the *Daily News* (New York). There are also afternoon or evening newspapers in most major cities, and thriving and respected local newspapers everywhere. Free newspapers (some of which are surprisingly good) containing local community news are published in all regions and are delivered to homes.

Most daily newspapers also publish Sunday editions, which are usually huge and contain ten or more sections. The Sunday edition of the *New York Times*, which consists largely of advertisements, can weigh over ten pounds (4.5kg). Sections may include national/world news, local news, sport, entertainment, money or finance, home or lifestyle, TV and radio programmes, and car and property-buying information. Sunday newspapers are often on sale from mid-afternoon on Saturdays (without the news section) and usually cost two to five times as much as daily editions.

As in many western countries, the serious newspapers are usually broadsheets, while the tabloids are more interested in scandal, sex and sport (not necessarily in that order). Most Americans read newspapers for the comics, sports, fashions, crime reports (e.g. local murder count and gory details) and local news, and rely on TV for 'serious' news. While all major American newspapers contain comprehensive sports and entertainment sections, few include much international news or foreign sports coverage. Most newspapers rely heavily on stories from news services such as the Associated Press (AP), which collect national and international news stories and sell them to subscribing newspapers. Some newspapers are published in 'zoned' editions for different regions and many have magazine-format 'lifestyle' and 'home living' sections in order to compete with magazines.

Weekly news magazines such as *Newsweek, Time* and *US News and World Report* are hugely popular, nationally and internationally, and are a good way to catch up on the most important American and international news. The *New Yorker* and *Fortune* are also highly rated magazines with an international readership. However, among the most popular American magazines are those featuring stories about war, serial killers and female icons, all of which hold a fascination for many Americans. Local entertainment magazines and newspapers are published in all major cities. At the bottom of the journalistic heap are weekly gossip tabloids such as the *National Enquirer*, the *National Examiner* and the *Star*. These specialise in celebrity sex, fad diets and arresting headlines such as 'JFK is Alive!' and 'I Married a UFO Alien'.

Around one in three Americans have newspapers delivered to their homes or rather thrown onto their front garden or drive (they're inserted in a plastic cover to protect them from inclement weather). Newspapers aren't delivered by newsagents, but by the newspaper companies themselves. Newspapers are sold in towns from 'honour' vending machines located on street corners, in shopping centres, and at railway and bus stations. You insert the exact price (usually 25 cents to 50 cents) in a slot and pull down a handle to open the door (you're trusted to take one copy only, hence the term 'honour'). In major cities, newspapers and magazines are sold from news stands.

Foreign Publications

Some foreign newspapers and periodicals are available from specialist news stands in major cities, although they're expensive and newspapers are usually a few days old. A few foreign newspapers, such as the London *Financial Times*, publish an edition printed in the US and available daily in major cities. Many British and foreign newspapers produce weekly editions, including the *International Express*, the *Guardian Weekly*, and the *Weekly Telegraph*. Some public and university libraries keep a selection of foreign daily newspapers in their reading rooms, although they're usually old copies. Most foreign (and American) newspapers and magazines can be purchased on subscription at huge savings over news stand prices (most foreign publications aren't available in the US at any price) and many American magazines offer gifts to new subscribers. Most popular foreign (and American) magazines maintain websites where you can order a subscription, and often subscribers have privileged access to the magazine websites, such as being able to search archives of articles and features. Magazines are often sold in book shops, where they may be discounted, e.g. a 10 per cent reduction.

Newsletters

The US invented the newsletter, probably the most widespread form of printed publication in the US. A newsletter is a subscription publication offering specialised information and written in suitable language for a targeted readership. The information may be 'insider' news, stock market tips, industry gossip, government statistics, club calendars, alumni updates, personal predictions, travel news or shopping bargains. Whatever your special interest, there's probably a newsletter published somewhere that covers it. One of the most popular is the fortnightly *Bottom Line Personal*, which prides itself on 'insider' tips on 'How To Do Everything Right', from managing your money to relaxing with music. *Bottom Line Personal* is available from the Subscription Service Center, PO Box 58446, Boulder, CO 80323-8426 (⌨ www.bottomlinesecrets.com). Many newsletters are now available online or in email form.

Books

The US is the cheapest country in the world in which to buy books, particularly paperbacks. There are cut-price and remainder book shops in major cities, and most general book shops have a bargain basement or rack where discount books are sold. Some book shops discount all books, e.g. Barnes and Noble, where there's typically 10 per cent off paperbacks, 15 per cent off hardbacks, and 30 per cent off hardback books on the *New York Times* best-seller lists (although best-sellers are generally cheapest at warehouse clubs). The biggest nationwide chains include Doubleday, B. Dalton (owned by Barnes & Noble) and Walden Books.

In major cities, there are second-hand (pre-owned) and exchange book shops for collectors and bargain hunters. Specialist book shops are common, including some selling foreign titles only. Most large book shops also keep a selection of foreign-language books. Credit card orders are accepted by telephone and fax, and orders are shipped overnight, e.g. via UPS. In major cities, many book shops are open until late evening (some until midnight) and on Sundays. Many book shops now offer coffee bars, complete with internet access (via Wi-Fi connections) to entice you to spend time (and money) on a regular basis. In city book shops (e.g. in New York), you're usually required to check your bags when entering and collect them when you leave (alternatively some shops and libraries may examine the contents of your bag when you leave).

There are also mail-order book clubs, most offering introductory offers at hugely discounted prices. Some book clubs offer a wide range of general books, while others specialise in a particular subject, e.g. photography or computers (clubs advertise in newspapers and magazines). Many organisations and clubs run their own libraries or book exchanges, and public libraries in all towns have an excellent selection of books (see **Libraries** on page 432). The US also has a number of internet book shops, including Amazon (🖥 www.amazon.com), which is the biggest in the world.

FURNITURE

Furniture is usually good value in the US and top quality furniture is often cheaper than in many other countries. There's a huge choice of traditional and contemporary designs in every price range, although as with most things the quality is usually reflected in the price. Exclusive modern designs, American and imported, are available, usually with matching exclusive prices. The best value-for-money imports include quality leather suites and a wide range of cane furniture from the Far East. Most furniture shops have personal designers and decorators, whose services may be provided free to high-spending customers. There are also shops specialising in beds, leather, reproduction and antique furniture, and companies that manufacture and install fitted bedrooms and kitchens. Many shops offer 'rooms-to-go', where you can buy a complete roomful of furnishings in one go.

A number of manufacturers sell directly to the public, although you shouldn't assume that this results in large savings and should compare prices **and** quality before buying (the least expensive furniture may be poor value for money if you want something that will last). If you want reasonably priced, good quality, modern furniture, there are a number of companies selling furniture for home assembly, which helps keep down prices, e.g. the Bombay Company and Ikea. All large furniture retailers publish catalogues, generally distributed free of charge.

Furniture and home furnishings is a competitive business. You can often knock the price down by some judicious haggling, particularly when you're spending a large amount. Another way to save money is to wait for the sales, when prices may be marked down by as much as 75 per cent. If you cannot wait and don't want or cannot afford to pay cash, look for an interest-free credit deal. Check the advertisements in local newspapers (particularly 'home' or 'habitat' magazine sections) and national home and design magazines. Most American furniture is produced in the Carolinas and manufacturers often sell their wares from the back of trucks, strategically positioned on street corners in northern states (usually on Sundays). Second-hand furniture can be purchased from charity shops, through advertisements in local newspapers, and yard, garage (see page 491) and estate sales.

If you're buying a new home, most developers offer furnishing packages which include everything from a fitted kitchen to a corkscrew, although deals may not offer savings over selective buying of individual items and are mainly intended for owners wishing to let their properties. Check other homes that companies have furnished and comparison shop before committing yourself. Furniture rental for home and office is common, although it isn't cost-effective in the long term.

HOUSEHOLD GOODS

The electricity supply in the US is 110/120 volts AC with a frequency of 60 Hertz (cycles), so imported electrical equipment made for a 220/240V 50 Hertz (Hz) cycle supply won't function unless it has a 'dual voltage' switch or is used with a transformer (see page 139). Similarly, when buying electrical items that you intend to export to a country with a 240V 50Hz electricity supply, ensure that they have a voltage and frequency selector (or that they operate on 50/60Hz). Don't bring a TV or video equipment made for a different market (e.g. Europe), as it won't work (see page 183). In general, it isn't worthwhile bringing electrical equipment to the US, as a wide range of American-made and imported items are available at reasonable prices. Most new homes come complete with major appliances such as a cooker and dishwasher and may also include a microwave, refrigerator and washing machine (washer).

Large household appliances such as cookers (stoves or ranges) and refrigerators are usually provided in rented accommodation. Dishwashers (the mechanical type, not the wife/husband) are common, although they aren't usually found in rented accommodation. Practically nobody brings large household appliances to the US, as the standard width isn't the same as in other countries. American refrigerators are huge and usually have the capacity to store a year's supply of dairy products for a family of 14 (plus the dog). Small appliances such as vacuum cleaners, grills, toasters and electric irons are inexpensive. Shop around when buying large appliances and be prepared to haggle over prices, even when goods are at sale prices. Look for interest-free credit deals, but also make sure that the price is competitive. Some inexpensive deals don't include delivery and installation (or sales tax), so always compare **inclusive** prices.

If you want kitchen measuring equipment and cannot cope with American measures, you must provide your own measuring scales, thermometers, jugs, cups (American and British recipe 'cups' **aren't** the same size). American beds, pillows and quilts (comforters) aren't the same size or shape as in most other countries, so your sheets, pillowcases and duvet covers may not fit. For a list of comparative measurements, see **Appendix C**.

SALES, DISCOUNTS & FACTORY OUTLETS

Although haggling (bargaining or bartering) isn't a way of life in the US, you should never be shy about asking for a discount, particularly when buying an expensive item or a large quantity of goods. Most American retailers are wheelers and dealers and are open to offers, even when goods are already discounted. Although prices are fixed in supermarkets, department and chain stores, many shops will match any genuinely advertised price. In the tough trading times experienced in the early '90s, retailers discovered that the only thing which attracted shoppers was discounts and low prices.

Most shops hold sales at various times of the year, the largest of which are held in January and July or August when bargains are plentiful, particularly in major cities. Top department stores usually have pre-season fashion sales, e.g. autumn/winter clothes are reduced (on sale) for a limited period in August or September. Sales are also common on federal and local holidays such as Presidents' Day and Veterans' Day weekends. Traditionally, sales start after Thanksgiving in November. Most Americans have an eye for a bargain and many only shop for luxury or expensive items when they're in a sale. It pays to stock up on non-perishable everyday items during sales, as this can save you hundreds of dollars a year.

If you're planning to buy an expensive item, for example a TV, computer or camera (the US is a paradise for hi-tech freaks), compare prices in advertisements in local newspapers (particularly Sunday editions) and consumer magazines, or call several local shops before buying. **However, when comparing prices, make sure that you're comparing the same or similar goods and services, as anyone can 'save' money by purchasing inferior products.** Ask your friends, neighbours and colleagues for their advice, but do your own research as well. Be wary of bargains that seem too good to be true, as they probably are!

The best bargains can be found at warehouse clubs, factory outlets (see page 490), discount centres (shopping malls comprised entirely of discount and factory-outlet shops). Many discount shops operate on the 'pile 'em high and sell 'em cheap' principle, with no fancy displays or customer areas, usually no demonstrations and little customer or after-sales service – just rock-bottom prices. You should know exactly what you want when shopping at discount shops, as staff don't waste time discussing products and are likely to employ the hard sell if you're undecided. When shopping with a money-off voucher, it isn't wise to tell the assistant until you've checked that the goods are in stock. If he knows you have a discount voucher, you may find the shop is suddenly out of stock, as your discount comes out of his commission.

Competition between the 'big two' discount chains, Kmart and Wal-Mart (the world's largest retailer), ensures that their prices are low enough. Factory outlets usually have rules stating that tenants **must** discount merchandise a minimum of 10 per cent compared with any local discount shop or offer at least one third off regular retail prices. Factory outlets, owned and operated by manufacturers, are common in the US. Although they may sell obsolete or overstocked items, most factory outlets don't sell poor quality goods or 'seconds' (flawed or damaged goods), **but sell quality products at bargain prices**. Ask your friends and neighbours if there are any factory outlets in your area and look out for them on your travels. Designer clothes can also be purchased from factory outlets in cities. Factory outlets may accept cash only. In most cities, there are also huge warehouse shops, specialising in selling remainders, leftover stock, overruns and cancelled orders at reduced prices, typically 25 to 75 per cent below normal retail prices.

If you're a keen bargain hunter, obtain a copy of *The Outlet Shopper's Guide: A Field Guide to Outlet Shopping* (Lazer Media) or *Guide to the Nation's Best Outlets* by Randy Marks (Outlet Bound). There are many national and regional guides to factory outlets, available free or sold in local book shops, including *Fabulous Finds* by Iris Ellis (Writer's Digest Books). Several are published by The Globe Pequot Press (PO Box 480, Guilford, CT 06437, ☎ 1-888-249-7586, 💻 www.globepequot.com).

SECOND-HAND BARGAINS

There's a lively second-hand market in the US for everything from cars to computers and photographic equipment. You name it and somebody will be selling it second-hand (used, prepossessed or previously owned). There are junk shops and second-hand 'thrift' shops in cities and large towns, some run by charities such as Goodwill or the Salvation Army. With such a large second-hand market, there are often excellent bargains to be found, particularly if you're quick off the mark. There's also a huge interest in collecting antiques, although you're unlikely to pick up many bargains, as prices are high and competition fierce.

If you're looking for an item such as a camera, boat or motorcycle, you may be better off looking through the small advertisements in specialist magazines, rather than in general newspapers or magazines. The classified advertisements in local newspapers, e.g. 'sales and bargains' columns, are also a good source, particularly for furniture and household appliances. Shopping centre bulletin boards and company notice boards may also prove fruitful. Expatriate club newsletters are a good source of furniture and household items, often sold cheaply by families returning home. Newspapers and magazines exclusively advertising second-hand goods are published in most areas (some with separate editions for automotive and general merchandise and many available free).

One of the most common places to obtain second-hand bargains in the US, is at private 'yard' and 'tag' (i.e. garage) sales, another American invention. Families moving house or just periodically emptying their attics, store rooms and wardrobes often sell unwanted clothes, furniture, records, books and assorted oddments, from their garage or drive or on their front lawn. Sometimes people moving abroad or across the US sell practically the entire contents of their homes. Most garage sales are confined to spring or summer Saturdays and are advertised in local newspapers and via posters, leaflets, supermarket bulletin boards, home-made street signs and word of mouth. They can also be found simply by driving around neighbourhoods on a Saturday. They're often a good place to find interesting Americana, considered junk by Americans, but collectibles by foreigners. Prices are negotiable and items are sold at knockdown prices; Americans don't ask or expect to receive much for second-hand goods. At the end of the day, anything left is practically given away. It's possible to furnish an entire apartment with items purchased at garage sales. The best bargains and quality goods are found in high and middle class areas (where some people sell their designer clothes after wearing them once or twice only). The biggest yard sale in the world is held in Tennessee along highway 127 on the third weekend in August (it's so big, it overflows into neighbouring states!)

Another place to pick up a bargain is at an auction, although it's usually necessary to have specialist knowledge concerning whatever you're planning to buy, as you will probably be competing with experts. Auctions are held throughout the year for everything from antiques to paintings, cars to property. Craft fairs and flea markets are also good hunting grounds. These are typically organised as fund raisers and held in local schools, churches, women's clubs, town squares and on college campuses. Local auctions and fairs are widely advertised in local newspapers and through leaflets. For information about local markets, ask at your local tourist office, chamber of commerce or library.

MAIL-ORDER & INTERNET SHOPPING

Mail-order has a long tradition in the US and since the late 19th century, those living in remote areas have purchased the latest fashions and consumer goods by post. Today mail-order business generates some $200 billion in annual sales and around 13 billion mail-order catalogues are circulated (you will regularly receive unsolicited catalogues in your post). Over 50 per cent of Americans shop by post and almost anything (even guns) can be bought from the comfort of your home and delivered overnight (although you pay extra for this service). One of the advantages of mail-order purchases is that they're often exempt from sales tax (see page 474).

Before committing yourself to buying anything by post, make sure you know what you're signing and don't send cash through the post or pay for anything in advance unless absolutely necessary. It's foolish to send advance payment by post in response to an advertisement (or to anyone) unless you're sure that the company is reputable and provides a money-back guarantee.

Catalogues

Many American manufacturers sell their products by mail-order only, to corporate and private customers. Specialist companies such as J.C. Penney, Orvis, Spiegel, and Lane Bryant produce extensive and elaborate catalogues. The top American mail-order companies by sales are J.C. Penney, Fingerhut, Spiegel, Land's End and L.L. Bean, while the best companies for mail-order clothing include L.L. Bean, Patagonia, Land's End, REI and Cabela's. Orders can usually be placed by telephone (toll-free) and delivery can be made to your home or office. Catalogues are free or cost around $5 and often come with free gifts and/or discount coupons.

A number of companies operate mail-order clubs for books, CDs or cassettes, computer software and videos and DVDs. New members are offered a number of items at a nominal introductory price (e.g. CDs for 1 cent and videos for 39 cents each!), in return for an agreement to purchase a further number of items at full price during the following one or two years. There's no catch, although the choice may be restricted and if you want to resign before you've fulfilled your side of the bargain, you may be required to repay the savings made on the introductory offer. Many American shops publish catalogues and send goods anywhere in the world. (Although be sure to ask about international shipment, as the charges can be expensive.)

There's generally little risk when buying goods by mail-order, as federal consumer-protection laws regarding mail-order sales are strict. If you have any doubts about a company's reputation, you can check with the US Postal Service, your state or local consumer protection agency, or a Better Business Bureau before ordering. Keep a copy of the advertisement or offer and a record of your order, including the company's name, address and telephone number, the price of items ordered, any handling or other charges, the date you posted or telephoned your order, and your method of payment. Also keep copies of all cancelled cheques and statements.

The mail-order merchandise rule adopted by the Federal Trade Commission (October 1975) states that when you order goods by post you must receive the goods when the seller says you will. If you aren't promised delivery within a certain period, the seller must ship the goods not later than 30 days after receiving your order. If you don't receive the goods within a few days after the 30-day period has expired, you may cancel your order and receive a full refund (if you paid in advance). The seller must notify you if the promised delivery date or time (or the 30-day limit) cannot be met and give you a new shipping date. You then have the option of cancelling the order and receiving a full refund or agreeing to the new shipping date. The seller must provide you with a free method of giving your answer, e.g. a toll-free telephone number or a postage-paid postcard. If you don't answer, it means that you agree to the shipping delay. If the delay is going to be longer than 30 days and you don't agree to it, the seller must return your money (if applicable) by the end of the first 30 days of the delay. If you cancel a pre-paid order, the seller must post your refund within seven business days or, in the case of a credit sale, adjust your account within one billing cycle.

Exceptions to the mail-order merchandise rule are photograph developing, magazine subscriptions and other serial deliveries (except for the initial shipment), seeds and plants, and cash on delivery (COD) orders, where the buyer's account isn't debited in advance of shipment. Postal regulations allow you to write a personal cheque payable to the sender (not the delivery company) for COD orders. If after examining the goods you feel there has been a fraud or misrepresentation, you can stop payment on the cheque and file a complaint with the US Postal Inspector's Office. If you pay by credit or charge card, you can have a charge removed from your bill if you don't receive the goods or services, or if the order was obtained through fraud or misrepresentation. You must notify the card company in writing less than 60 days after the charge first appears on your bill.

Mail-order catalogues in the US don't usually offer credit (instalment) plans, as in some other countries.

Telephone

Shopping by telephone has increased dramatically in recent years, particularly with the proliferation of charge, credit and debit cards. One of the most popular methods of telephone shopping is via TV through companies such as the Home Shopping Channel, QVC and Prodigy. Cable TV shopping shows offer goods at seemingly bargain prices, some even providing a 24-hour service for insomniac shoppers.

Orders are placed by telephone and goods are posted to you. Payment can be made by credit card, personal cheque or money order. However, before placing an order, check that an item isn't available cheaper in local discount shops and set a spending limit before switching on the box! In-flight shopping is also possible via SkyMall catalogues found on most US airlines. Orders are placed on toll-free numbers via Airfones and charged to credit cards.

Be extremely wary of unsolicited telemarketing sales, which have increased greatly in recent years. A caller will try to sell direct or arrange an appointment to visit you and may offer a variety of gifts and inducements to tempt you. If you aren't interested, just say 'no thank you' and put the telephone down. If you're tempted, ask for written information by post and check out the company or organisation, e.g. with a Better Business Bureau. **Never give a credit card number or bank account details over the telephone to someone who has called you.** As a general rule, it's wise to ignore all unsolicited telephone calls, as you never know whether the caller is a crook. Although many reputable companies sell their products or services by telephone, they rarely resort to unsolicited telephone calls to obtain business. (See also **Unsolicited Mail & Mail Fraud** on page 156.) If you want to stop unsolicited telemarketing calls, you can sign up for the national Do Not Call list, maintained by the Federal Trade Commission (☎ 1-888-382-1222, ⌨ www.donotcall.gov). For more information about the Do Not Call list see **Using the Telephone** on page 163.

Internet

Despite predictions to the contrary (and widespread internet access), internet shopping hasn't taken off in the US, where online sales amount to a mere 1 per cent of total retail spending. Nevertheless, with internet shopping, the world is literally your oyster, and savings can be made on a wide range of goods, including CDs, clothes, sports equipment, electronic equipment, jewellery, books, wine, computer software, and services such as insurance, pensions and mortgages. Huge savings are also possible on holidays and travel, and most rail and airline tickets can be booked online, with postal delivery of tickets, collection from a local travel agency or electronic ticketing. Small, high-price, high-tech items (e.g. cameras, watches and portable or hand-held computers) can usually be purchased cheaper than in shops, with delivery by courier within a few days. Nearly all the major catalogue stores (see above) have websites where you can place orders and contact customer service representatives.

Shopping via the internet is, in most cases, safer than shopping by phone or mail-order. However, internet fraud is big business in the US, where it's estimated to cost consumers at least $5 million per year. To avoid being defrauded you should:

- Make absolutely sure you're on the seller's actual website (i.e. by typing in the website URL yourself or using your own bookmark rather than a click through link from an unsolicited email or unknown website). Thieves have set up realistic looking websites in order to lure unsuspecting shoppers into giving up credit card numbers and other identifying information that can be used for identity theft (see **Credit Rating** on page 364). This practice is known as 'phishing';

- Look for the seller's postal address and telephone number posted on the website and evidence that he belongs to a scheme that fosters good business practice;

- Pay by credit card rather than money order;

- Ask your credit card issuer if you can have 'substitute' or 'single-use' numbers, so that you don't have to give your real credit card number;

- When you submit payment information, check that the 'http' at the beginning of the address bar changes to 'https' or 'shttp', indicating a secure server, and check what is done to safeguard your information during transmission;

- Obtain full details of the purchase before committing yourself, e.g. description of items, total price including shipping, delivery time, warranty information and return policy.

Further information about internet shopping can be obtained from the National Consumers League (see page 499). Information about 'phishing' and other forms of online fraud is available from the Federal Trade Commission (💻 www.ftc.gov) and the Anti-Phishing Working Group (💻 www.antiphishing.org).

Duty

If you buy goods from outside the US, **you shouldn't be charged customs duty, which cannot be paid in advance**. The US Postal Service collects any duty owed on delivery of the goods (unless the goods are worth more than $2,000, in which case you must collect them from your nearest Customs International Mail Branch or appoint a customs broker to do so on your behalf). Approximately 65 per cent of items are zero rated for duty, the highest rates of duty generally applying to textiles. The various rates of duty for goods are listed in the *Harmonized Tariff Schedule* (*HTS*), which is a dictionary-size book containing thousands of entries! If you need to know the amount of duty you will be charged, your local library should have a copy or you can go to the US International Trade Commission internet site (💻 www.usitc.gov) and follow the link to the 'Official Harmonized Tariff Schedule' on the left, although it might be simpler to ring your local port and ask to speak to an import specialist. A customs processing fee of $5 is also payable on all dutiable shipments. For further information about international mail imports obtain a copy of *International Mail Imports* (publication # 0000-0514) from the US Customs and Border Protection Service, 1300 Pennsylvania Avenue, Washington, DC 20229 (☎ 202-927-1000). This publication can also be downloaded from the CBP website, publications section (💻 www.cbp.gov).

DUTY-FREE ALLOWANCES

Most 'personal shipments' worth up to $200 and gifts worth up to $100 can be received in the US free of duty, provided you don't receive more than those values in shipments in one day. Gifts must not include alcoholic beverages, tobacco products or perfume containing alcohol, and packages must be marked 'personal purchases', 'personal goods returned' or 'unsolicited gift – value less than $100', as appropriate.

Your duty-free allowance when entering the US depends on how long you've been out of the country and whether you've imported any duty-free goods in the previous 30 days. Your allowance is also based on whether you're a resident or a non-resident. Generally speaking, if you leave the US to travel, work or study abroad and return to resume residence in the US, you're classified as a resident by customs. US residents living abroad temporarily are classified as non-residents and receive more liberal customs exemptions on short visits to the US, provided they export any goods acquired abroad when they leave the country. US citizens who are residents of American Samoa, Guam or the US Virgin Islands are considered to be US residents. The respective allowances are as follows:

Residents

US residents who are returning from a stay abroad of at least 48 hours (excluding Mexico and the Virgin Islands) are permitted to import goods duty and tax-free to the total value of $800 (or $600 if they're returning from one of the 24 Caribbean Basin countries, or $1,200 if they're returning from American Samoa, Guam or the US Virgin Islands). As part of these exemptions, you may bring in duty-free:

- Up to 200 cigarettes or 100 cigars or 3lb of smoking tobacco (up to 1,000 cigarettes if returning from American Samoa, Guam or the US Virgin Islands) **and**

- Up to one litre (33.8 fl oz) of alcoholic drinks, provided that you're over 21, it's for your own use or a gift, and alcoholic drinks are permitted in the state you're arriving in. (The limit is two litres if you're returning from a Caribbean Basin country and five litres if you're returning from American Samoa, Guam or the US Virgin Islands, provided that at least one litre was produced in that country.)

If you exceed these allowances, you must make a written declaration (see below). You must not have used any part of your allowances during the preceding 30-day period. If you don't qualify for the normal exemption because of the 48-hour or 30-day limits, you have a $200 exemption only, including any of the following: 50 cigarettes, 10 cigars and 150ml (5 fl oz) of alcoholic beverages or 150ml (5 fl oz) of alcoholic perfume.

Articles imported in excess of your customs exemption are subject to duty unless entitled to free entry. The items with the highest rate of duty are allowed under your exemption and duty is assessed upon the lower rated items. After deducting your exemptions and the value of any duty-free articles, a flat duty rate of 2 per cent (1.5 per cent if the articles were purchased in American Samoa, Guam or the US Virgin Islands) is applied to the next $1,000 (fair retail) value of goods. Duty on any article(s) valued above $1,000 is payable at the current rate(s) applicable.

You may import household effects (e.g. furniture, carpets, paintings, tableware, stereos, linen) that were purchased abroad duty-free provided that you've used them for at least a year and that you don't sell them after your return to the US. Clothing, jewellery, photographic equipment, portable stereos and vehicles are regarded as personal effects and are subject to duty.

Further details are listed in a booklet, *Know Before You Go*, available free from US customs offices or from the US Customs and Border Patrol (CBP) or on 💻 www. cbp.gov. (See also **Returning Residents** on page 110.)

Non-residents

A non-resident is allowed to import gifts not exceeding a total value of $100 duty-free. The exemption is valid only if the gifts accompany you, you stay 72 hours or more and you haven't claimed this exemption within the previous six months. Non-residents can also bring in 200 cigarettes or 100 cigars or three pounds of smoking tobacco (or proportionate amounts of each), and one litre of alcoholic beverages free of duty. Children of US citizens who were born abroad and have never resided in the US are entitled to the customs exemptions granted to non-residents, and with the exception of alcoholic beverages, are entitled to the same exemptions as adults.

Declarations

You may declare verbally to the customs officer any articles acquired abroad if they're accompanying you and you haven't exceeded your duty-free exemption (see above). However, you're required to provide a written declaration, using *Customs Declaration* form (6059B), when:

● You have more than your allowance of goods, alcoholic drinks or tobacco products (see above);

● You're importing items that aren't intended for your personal or household use, such as commercial samples, items for sale or use in your business, or articles you're bringing in for another person;

● Articles acquired in American Samoa, Guam or the US Virgin Islands are being sent to the US;

● Customs duty or internal revenue tax is payable on any article in your possession;

● You've used your exemption (or part of it) in the last 30 days;

● A customs officer requests a written list.

The value of all imported goods is based on the fair retail value of each item in the country where it was acquired, not necessarily the price paid. **If you underestimate the value of an article or misrepresent an article in your declaration, you may need to pay a penalty in addition to duty.** If you're in doubt about the value of an article, declare it at the actual price paid. If you fail to declare an article acquired abroad, you're liable to a personal penalty in an amount equal to the value of the article in the US. **In addition, the article is subject to seizure and forfeiture and you may be liable to criminal prosecution.** If in doubt about whether an article should be declared, always declare it and let the customs official decide. Articles exempt from duty must have been acquired for your personal or household use, must be brought with you when you enter the US, and must be properly declared to customs.

The head of a family may make a joint declaration for all members residing in the same household and entering the US together. Family members may combine their personal exemptions, even if the articles acquired by one family member exceed his personal exemption. (See also **Customs** on page 108.)

RECEIPTS & WARRANTIES

When shopping in the US, you should insist on a receipt as proof of payment (this is useful when an automatic alarm is activated as you're leaving a shop!). It may also be impossible to return or exchange goods without a receipt, and you may need it to return an item for repair or replacement under a warranty. You should check receipts immediately on paying (particularly in supermarkets); if you're overcharged, you cannot usually obtain redress later. Although it isn't required by law, most shops will give you a cash refund or credit on a charge account or credit card within a certain period, e.g. one to two weeks (although you may be offered only a shop credit or exchange on discounted goods). Some discount and outlet shops don't allow any returns. The latest trend is 'unshopping', i.e. returning unused goods bought in previous shopping binges (around 10 per cent of all goods are returned for a refund). As a consequence, many retailers have tightened their refund policies in recent years to prevent abuses. Shops usually advertise their refund policy or it's stated on your receipt.

All goods sold in the US carry an implied guarantee of 'merchantability', meaning that goods must perform the function for which they were designed. If they don't, you can return them to the dealer from whom you bought them and demand a replacement or your money back. In addition to the implied warranty, some goods carry written warranties, although these are voluntary. When provided, warranties must by law be written in clear everyday language and the precise terms and duration must be specified at the top of the warranty document. Warranties for items costing over $15 must be included with the product and a copy must be available in the shop for you to read before making a purchase.

The period of a warranty varies considerably, e.g. from one to five years, and may be an important consideration when making a purchase. Warranties can also be full or limited, a full warranty providing you with maximum protection, although usually for a limited period. Warranties may be transferable when goods are sold or given away during the warranty period. You're often asked to complete and post a warranty card confirming the date of purchase, although under a full warranty this isn't necessary. Most warranties are with the manufacturer or importer, to whom goods must usually be returned for repair.

A local or state consumer protection agency or association or a Better Business Bureau can usually advise you of your rights in a given situation (see also **Legal System** on page 516). If you have a complaint against a retailer and cannot obtain satisfaction, you can report it to the Federal Trade Commission (FTC), Sixth Street and Pennsylvania Avenue, Washington, DC 20580, or an FTC regional office.

CONSUMERS' ORGANISATIONS

There are many consumers' organisations and publications in the US, including the following:

Consumers Union

The Consumers Union (CU), 101 Truman Avenue, Yonkers, NY 10703-1057 (☎ 914-378-2000, 💻 www.consumersunion.org), is a non-profit organisation aiming to provide consumers with information and advice on consumer goods and services, and to initiate and co-operate with efforts to maintain acceptable living standards. The CU publishes a monthly *Consumer Reports* magazine containing test reports, product ratings, and buying guidance, available on subscription from Consumer Reports, Subscription Department, PO Box 53000, Boulder, CO 80322-3000.

National Consumers League

The National Consumers League (NCL) is a consumer organisation, founded in 1899, concerned primarily with health and safety protection, and aiming to promote fairness in the market and workplace. Membership costs $20 per year and members receive *NCL Bulletin*, a bi-monthly newsletter, plus discounts on a range of NCL publications. For further information contact the National Consumers League, 1701 K Street, NW, Suite 1200, Washington, DC 20006 (☎ 202-835-3323, 💻 www.nclnet.org).

Consumer Federation of America

The Consumer Federation of America (CFA) is primarily an advocacy organisation promoting consumer rights to Congress, regulatory agencies and the courts. It's also an educational organisation, distributing information on consumer issues to the public and the media, and a membership organisation providing support to national, state and local organisations. Individuals cannot join the CFA, but can subscribe to *CFA News* for $25 per year. You can contact the CFA at 1424 16th Street, NW, Suite 604, Washington, DC 20036 (☎ 202-387-6121, 💻 www.consumerfed.org).

Better Business Bureaux

Better Business Bureaux (BBBs) are non-profit organisations sponsored by local businesses, offering a variety of consumer services, including providing consumer education material, answering consumer questions, mediating and arbitrating complaints, and providing general information on companies' consumer complaint records. For the address of your local BBB, consult your telephone book or contact the Council of Better Business Bureaux, 4200 Wilson Boulevard, Suite 800, Arlington, VA 22203 (☎ 703-276-0100, 💻 www.bbb.org).

Around 200 free or low-cost consumer information booklets covering a wide range of subjects are published by the federal government. For a free *Consumer Information Catalog* contact the Consumer Information Center, PO Box 100, Pueblo, CO 81002 (☎ 719-948-4000, 💻 www.pueblo.gsa.gov). The Consumer Information Center also distributes an excellent free *Consumer's Resource Handbook* published by the US Office of Consumer Affairs. Most Consumer Information Center publications can be downloaded from the website for free. One of the US's best consumer magazines is *Consumers Digest*, published bi-monthly and available from news kiosks or by subscription from Consumers Digest, 8001 Lincoln Avenue, 6th Floor, Skokie, IL 60077 (☎ 847-763-9200, 💻 www.consumersdigest.com).

18.

ODDS & ENDS

This chapter contains miscellaneous information. Although not all topics included are of vital importance, most are of general interest to anyone living or working in the US, including everything you ever wanted to know (but were afraid to ask) about religion and restrooms.

AMERICAN CITIZENSHIP

With few exceptions, anyone born in the US has an automatic claim to US citizenship (even children born of illegal immigrants). Under a law which came into force in March 1995, children of US citizens born abroad can also claim US citizenship without living in the US. To qualify, one parent must be a US citizen and the child must be under 18 years of age and in the legal custody of the American parent. Adopted children must have been adopted before age 16. If the American parent hasn't lived in the US for five years before the child's birth (at least two years after the parent was 14 years of age), one of the child's American grandparents must have lived in the US for this period.

The easiest and most popular way of becoming a US citizen is to marry a US national, although it's prohibited to do so purely to obtain US citizenship (or residence in the US) – a situation light-heartedly explored in the film Green Card. A green card (see **Chapter 3**) is no longer issued for life (it must be renewed after ten years), and many immigrants prefer to become US citizens, which costs less in the long run.

An immigrant aged 18 or older can become a US citizen under a process called naturalisation, which has been speeded up in recent years and should take six to nine months. Naturalisation involves living in the US for a minimum of five years (three years when married to a US citizen) and passing a naturalisation examination. To pass the examination, you must be able to read, write and speak simple English and correctly answer around 20 questions about the US government and American history, such as 'Who drafted the Declaration of Independence?' and 'What is the 4th of July?' Currently the examinations are given informally (usually orally), but by 2006 officials hope to have new uniform testing standards in place that will most likely include group testing of the English and history and government sections. Except in extremely rare cases, it's impossible to become a naturalised US citizen without first obtaining a green card. Citizenship is conferred by a judge in a 'naturalisation ceremony' when an 'oath of citizenship' is taken. US law permits dual nationality for naturalised citizens, who have virtually the same rights as native-born Americans (but cannot become President or Vice President!). There's no compulsion for immigrants to become US citizens and they're free to live in the US for as long as they wish, provided they abide by the laws of the land. In fact, fewer immigrants become naturalised (under 10 per cent) than a generation ago, when as many as 80 per cent became citizens.

Naturalisation forms can be obtained by calling ☎ 1-800-870-3676 or downloaded from the USCIS website (🖳 www.uscis.gov). The questions you may be asked in the naturalisation examination and other information about naturalisation are listed in a free booklet, *Guide to Naturalization*, available from USCIS offices or the

Superintendent of Documents, US Government Printing Office, Washington, DC 20402-9325 and on the USCIS website.

CLIMATE

Because of its vast size and varied topography, ranging from sub-tropical forests to permanent glaciers, from deserts to swamps, the US's climate varies enormously. The range of weather in the contiguous states is similar to what is experienced in Europe (from northern Finland to the south of Spain), with a few cyclones, hurricanes and tornadoes (twisters) thrown in for good measure. Temperatures in the Midwest prairies vary from 104°F (40°C) in summer to -40°F (-40°C) in winter. A high of 134°F (57°C) has been recorded in California's Death Valley, while in Montana and Alaska the temperature has dropped to -70°F (-56.5°C) and -80°F (-62°C) respectively. Fortunately, not too many people live in these inhospitable areas. Not surprisingly, the northern states are referred to as the Frostbelt, while the warm southern states are known as the Sunbelt. The cities in the Pacific coastal region have the smallest annual temperature swings (between the highest and lowest), while the largest variations are experienced in the Midwest away from the Great Lakes.

In winter, it's cold or freezing everywhere except in the Sunbelt. However, even in Florida (which has the highest annual average temperatures) and California the temperature occasionally drops below freezing between December and February, although southern cold spells never last long and can be followed by a heat wave. In all northern states, winters are severe with heavy snow, ice storms and blizzards (most of the world's snowfall records are held by North America). Temperatures are often reduced considerably by the wind, known as the 'wind chill factor' where a temperature of 10°F (-12°C) combined with a wind of 25mph (40kph) results in a wind chill factor of -29°F (-34°C). The wind chill factor can cause temperatures to drop as low as -60°F (-51°C), when people (not surprisingly) are warned to stay at home. The coldest areas include the plains, Midwest and Northeast, where temperatures may remain well below freezing (32°F/0°C) for weeks on end. If you're a keen skier you will welcome some snow, but you won't perhaps be so enthusiastic when snowdrifts make roads impassable, engulf your home and cut you off from the outside world for days on end. In some areas, summer snowfalls are also fairly common. Torrential rain and violent thunderstorms are frequent in many regions, often creating floods and mudslides.

A long, hot summer is normal throughout the US, with the exception of northern New England, Oregon and Washington state. The most temperate regions in summer are the Pacific north-west, Maine and the upper Great Lakes region of Minnesota, Wisconsin and Michigan. Everywhere else it's hot to sweltering (heat waves are common and occasionally cause many deaths), particularly in the south-west, with its many desert areas. The east coast, south and the Midwest are often extremely humid, making it feel even hotter. Smog is a problem in many cities, e.g. Los Angeles, where it's at its worst in August and September. Insects can also be a problem in many states during the summer, and many homes have screens to keep them out.

Spring and autumn (fall) are usually fairly mild and are generally the most pleasant seasons, although temperatures can vary considerably from week to week. Spring and autumn are warm and sunny in most regions and the humidity is low, although it can be very wet in some areas (particularly in the Pacific north-west). Hurricanes are fairly common in summer until late autumn along southern parts of the east coast and around the Gulf of Mexico. Spring (April to June) is the tornado season in the Midwest, between the Appalachians and the Rockies, when winds can reach 300mph/483kph.

Forest fires and earthquakes (along the San Andreas fault line) are a constant threat in California and there have been a number of earthquakes in recent years (although they're still nervously awaiting 'the BIG one', which could be the US's worst natural disaster). Severe flooding was experienced in California and Texas in 1992 (after record rainfall caused the worst floods since 1938) and in 1993 the Mississippi and Missouri rivers broke their banks and flooded some 23 million acres. The '90s were a bad time for natural disasters in many regions, where it's said (only half-jokingly) that they have four seasons: fire, flood, drought and hurricanes. The good news is that your chances of experiencing a cyclone, hurricane, tornado, flood, earthquake or forest fire are rare in most areas.

American meteorologists are constantly on the alert for severe weather patterns indicating hurricanes, tornadoes and thunderstorms. Warnings are issued if a hurricane, tornado or storm is expected, and storm alerts are broadcast on television (TV) and radio. Some radios have a national weather service band. 'Travellers advisories' are broadcast when road conditions are expected to be bad because of ice, snow, high winds or fog. Hailstones in the US can be the size of baseballs and can severely damage your car, while sleet often refers to small hailstones rather than frozen rain.

Americans usually overreact to extremes of climate with freezing air-conditioning in summer and sweltering heating in winter. Because most buildings are too hot or too cold, it's often a problem knowing what to wear and many people dress in layers that they take off or put on, depending on the indoor or outdoor temperature. Most people use humidifiers to counteract the dry air caused by powerful air-conditioning.

The American fascination with statistics is highlighted in weather forecasts. These may include pollution or air quality indexes, pollen counts, ultraviolet (UV) forecasts (to help people avoid potentially dangerous exposure to the sun's rays), record high and low temperatures, and heating (winter) and cooling (summer) 'degree days' (the number of degrees by which the average temperature deviates from 65°F/18°C). The likelihood of rain may be expressed as 'a 40 per cent chance of precipitation' (the term precipitation or 'precip' is often used to refer to rain and snow).

Frequent weather forecasts are given on TV, radio and in daily newspapers, and there's even a 24-hour cable TV Weather channel! Radios can be purchased that are programmed to automatically tune to the nearest weather station. A number of newspapers and other sources provide telephone weather forecasts for some 650 US cities and online weather forecasts are popular.

The average daytime temperature range (in Fahrenheit) for selected major cities is shown below:

City	Jan–Mar	Apr–Jun	Jul–Sept	Oct–Dec
Chicago	32 – 45	59 – 81	76 – 84	35 – 65
Los Angeles	67 – 69	71 – 77	83 – 84	68 – 78
Miami	76 – 89	83 – 88	88 – 90	77 – 85
New Orleans	62 – 70	78 – 90	77 – 85	64 – 80
New York	39 – 48	61 – 81	77 – 85	41 – 67
San Francisco	59 – 60	61 – 65	64 – 69	57 – 68

A quick way to make a rough conversion from Fahrenheit to Centigrade is to subtract 30 and divide by two (see also **Appendix C**).

CRIME

The purpose of this section isn't to scare you, but to warn you about the high level of crime and violence in the US, which in the major cities is much higher than in many other countries, especially western Europe. **The 'ground rules'** (see **Crime Prevention &Safety** below) **aren't the same in the US, as in many other countries.** If you follow the rules, your chances of being a victim are as low as in most European cities – but **break the rules and they rise dramatically.**

The US has always had an extremely high crime rate, due in no small measure to the vast number of guns (over 200 million) in circulation. However, the trend over the last decade has been improving, from 49.9 violent crimes per 1,000 people in 1993 to a 'mere' 22.6 per 1,000 in 2003. Every day on average, 25 people are killed by guns and a further 600 or more are robbed or raped at gunpoint. In the past 20 years, over 700,000 Americans have been shot dead – more than the population of Washington state. Most Americans support gun registration, although few favour a complete ban on the sale and possession of guns (Americans cannot understand why foreigners fail to grasp their obsession with guns). However, owning a gun is little deterrent against crime, as you must be ready and able to use it. Most people could never react quickly enough to a threatening incident, and statistics show that a gun is over 20 times more likely to kill a family member, friend or acquaintance than to kill an intruder. Many children accidentally kill themselves or their playmates with guns that are left lying around homes (half the guns in US households aren't kept under lock and key). Despite the statistics, the National Rifle Association (NRA) insists that any connection between gun ownership and crime is purely coincidental!

Black-on-black crime is the biggest problem in the US and the middle-class US has largely ignored the urban warfare raging in inner-city areas. Most whites live in rural areas and communities hermetically sealed from the trigger-happy chaos of the US's black urban life (some 8 million Americans live in 'gated communities' with high fences, security floodlights and bullet-proof guard boxes). However, there are increasing signs that the horror of the US's romance with the gun is spreading to small town, white America. One of the most worrying aspects is the increase in violent crime committed by children: in recent years there have been a number of high-profile 'massacres' perpetrated by children aged as young as eight. Schools routinely check children for weapons (using metal detectors), and many inner-city schools have armed security guards and a prison-like regime in order to reduce crime.

The crime rate varies considerably according to the region (the west has the most crime, the Northeast the least) and city, although the recent application of a 'zero tolerance' policing policy (i.e. imprisoning an increasing number of offenders – the prison population has swollen to almost 2 million, compared with 300,000 in 1970) in many major cities has resulted in a dramatic reduction in crime rates, which are currently at their lowest for 25 years. In recent years, the right wing view has held sway, the majority believing that crime will go away if only they get tough, build more prisons, lock offenders away longer and execute more murderers.

Despite the statistics, the vast majority of Americans manage to get through the day without being molested, mugged, knifed or shot (or even witnessing such events), and most live to a ripe old age and die natural deaths (if over-consumption can ever be called natural!). Although crime and violence are among the most disturbing aspects of life in the US, it's important to maintain a sense of perspective, as heightened anxiety or paranoia about crime can be just as bad or worse than being a victim (and is a complete waste of time and effort). Nevertheless, anyone coming to live in the US would be wise to choose a low-crime, middle class suburb and avoid 'high-crime' areas (e.g. most inner cities) at all times, as well as following the guidelines below.

Crime Prevention & Safety

Staying safe is largely a matter of common sense and you should observe the following guidelines:

- At night, stick to brightly lit main streets and avoid secluded areas (best of all, take a taxi). Avoid parks and keep to a park's main paths or where there are other people during the day. If you find yourself in a deserted area late at night, remain calm and look as though you know where you're going by walking briskly. If you must wait for a train or bus at night, do so in the main waiting room, a well lit area, or where there's a guard or policeman. If possible, avoid using subways in the late evening or after midnight.

- Walk in the opposite direction to the traffic so no-one can kerb-crawl (drive alongside you), and walk on the outside of the pavement, so you're less likely to be mugged from a doorway.

- When you're in an unfamiliar city ask a policeman, taxi driver or local person if there are any unsafe neighbourhoods (all major cities have 'no-go' areas at night and some have areas that are to be avoided at any time) – and avoid them! Women should take care and should never hitchhike or accept lifts with strangers (rape statistics are extremely high and most go unreported).

- Carry the bare minimum of cash with you, say $20 to $50, often referred to as 'mugger's money', because in the event that you're mugged, it's usually sufficient to satisfy a mugger and prevent him from becoming violent (or searching further). In some cities, parents give their children mugger's money as a matter of course whenever they leave home. **Never resist a mugger. It's far better to lose your wallet and jewellery than your life. Many muggers are desperate and irrational people (officially known as emotionally disturbed persons or EDPs) under the influence of drugs, and can turn violent if resisted.**

Some experts advise you to keep your cash in at least two separate places and to split cash and credit cards. Don't keep your passport, green card, driving licence and other important documents in your wallet or purse where they can be stolen. Anaesthetic sprays or ordinary hair or insect sprays are carried by some people to deter assailants (as are pepper sprays and mace). These are, however, of little use against an armed assailant and may increase the likelihood of violence. Many cities and states require registration or licensing for those carrying mace or pepper sprays and local police forces sometimes offer training classes in their use.

- Warn your children of the dangers of American 'street life', particularly if you've been living in a country where it's taken for granted that you can safely go almost anywhere at any time of day or night. It may be necessary to totally re-educate your family regarding all aspects of public life. Wherever you live and whatever the age of your children, you should warn them against taking unnecessary risks and discourage them from frequenting remote or high risk areas, talking to strangers, or attracting unwanted attention.

- Don't leave cash, cheques, credit cards, passports, jewellery and other valuables lying around or even hidden in your home (the crooks know all the hiding places). Store anything of value in a home safe or a bank safety deposit box and ensure that you have adequate insurance (see page 349). Good quality door and window locks and an alarm helps, but may not deter a determined thief (see page 136). In many cities, triple door locks, metal bars and steel gratings on windows are standard fittings. Most city dwellers always lock their doors and windows, even when going out for a few minutes.

  Apartments are often fitted with a security system, so you can speak to visitors before allowing them access to your building. Luxury apartment buildings have armed guards in the lobby with closed-circuit TV and voice identification systems. In addition, most apartments have a peephole and security chain, so you can check a caller's identity before opening the door. Be careful who you allow into your home and always check the identity of anyone claiming to be an official inspector or an employee of a utility company. Ask for identification (ID) and confirm it with their office **before** opening the door.

- If you live in a city, you should be wary of anyone hanging around outside your home or apartment block. Have your keys ready and enter your home as quickly as possible.

- Never make it obvious that no-one is at home by leaving tell-tale signs such as a pile of newspapers or letters. Many people leave lights, a radio or a TV on (activated by random timers) when they aren't at home. Ask your neighbours to keep an eye on your home when you're on holiday. Many towns have 'crime watch' areas, where residents keep an eye open for suspicious characters and report them to the local police.

- If you're driving, keep to the main highways and avoid high-risk areas. Never drive in cities with your windows or doors open or valuables (such as handbags or wallets) on the seats. Take extra care at night in car parks and when returning to your car, and **never** sleep in your car. If you have an accident in a dangerous or hostile area (any inner-city area), police advise you not to stop, but to drive to the nearest police station to report it. In remote areas, accidents are sometimes staged to rob unsuspecting drivers (called highway hold-ups) and cars are deliberately bumped to get drivers to stop (again, seek out the nearest police station). If you stop at an accident in a remote area or are flagged down, keep the engine running and in gear and your doors locked (ready to make a quick getaway), and only open your window a fraction to speak to someone. In some states, hire car drivers are targeted by muggers (after a spate of attacks on tourists in Florida, rented cars are now indistinguishable from private vehicles) and you should be wary of collecting a hire car from an airport at night.

Police forces, the federal government, local communities and security companies all publish information and advice regarding crime prevention, and your local police department will usually carry out a free home security check. See also **Keys & Security** on page 136, **Underground & Urban Railways** on page 235, **Car Theft** on page 289, **Legal System** on page 516 and **Police** on page 524.

GEOGRAPHY

The US covers an area of 3,615,000 square miles (9.36 million km²), including Alaska and Hawaii, and is the fourth largest country in the world after Russia, Canada (most of which is uninhabited) and China. America is a federal republic comprising 50 states and the District of Columbia, the nation's capital.

Forty-eight states (the 'contiguous' states) make up the mainland US, stretching some 2,500mi (4,023km) from east to west from the Atlantic to the Pacific. The country measures around 1,200mi (1,931km) north to south, from the Canadian border to the Gulf of Mexico. The remaining two states are Alaska and Hawaii. Alaska joined the union as the 49th (and largest) state in 1959, having been purchased from Russia a century earlier for around 5 cents per acre. Alaska is situated north-west of Canada and separated from Russia by the Bering Strait. Hawaii joined the union in 1960 as the 50th state and comprises a group of islands in the mid-Pacific Ocean some 2,500 miles (4,023km) to the south-west of the continental US. The US also administers more than 2,000 islands, islets and atolls in the Pacific and Caribbean, including American Samoa, Guam, Puerto Rico and the US Virgin Islands. Geographically, the contiguous states consist roughly of the highland region of Appalachia in the east, the Rocky Mountains in the west and the Great Plains in the centre. The highest point in the US is Mount McKinley (20,320ft/6,193m) in Alaska and the lowest Death Valley in California (282ft/86m below sea level).

The US is divided into a number of geographical regions, although regional terms are often vague and can be confusing. If you ask an American where he's from, the answer is usually a city or a town first, a state second and a region last, if at all. The states can be **roughly** divided into the following four regions:

- **East** – Connecticut, Delaware, District of Columbia, Maine, Maryland, Massachusetts, New Hampshire, New Jersey, New York, Pennsylvania, Rhode Island, Vermont and West Virginia;
- **South** – Alabama, Arkansas, Florida, Georgia, Kentucky, Louisiana, Mississippi, North Carolina, Oklahoma, South Carolina, Tennessee, Texas and Virginia;
- **Midwest** – Illinois, Indiana, Iowa, Kansas, Michigan, Minnesota, Missouri, Nebraska, North Dakota, Ohio, South Dakota and Wisconsin;
- **West** – Alaska, Arizona, California, Colorado, Hawaii, Idaho, Montana, Nevada, New Mexico, Oregon, Utah, Washington and Wyoming.

The following sub-regions are also widely referred to:

- **New England** – Connecticut, New Hampshire, Maine, Massachusetts, Rhode Island and Vermont;
- **Northeast** – New England states (see above) plus Delaware, Maryland, New Jersey, New York, Washington DC and eastern Pennsylvania (for those in the west, the Northeast may also include the Midwestern states listed below);
- **Deep South** – Alabama, Georgia, Mississippi, perhaps including Louisiana, South Carolina and northern Florida;
- **Plains** – Kansas, Nebraska, North and South Dakota, and maybe Colorado, Montana, Oklahoma and Wyoming;
- **Rockies or Mountain West** – Colorado, Idaho, Montana, Wyoming and usually Utah;
- **Southwest** – Arizona, New Mexico and possibly southern California, Nevada, Texas and Utah;
- **Northwest** – Oregon, Washington and maybe northern California and Idaho;
- **West Coast or Far West** – California, Oregon, Washington.

Alabama, Illinois, Indiana, Kentucky, Michigan, Mississippi, Tennessee and Wisconsin are considered by some to be part of the Midwest, while others contend they're eastern states. Many westerners consider that the east begins at the Mississippi river, although to some easterners these states represent the beginning of the Midwest. Others reckon that the Dakotas, Kansas, Montana, Nebraska, Oklahoma and Wyoming are in the west and that the term Midwest applies to Arkansas, Illinois, Indiana, Iowa, Michigan, Minnesota, Mississippi, Missouri and Wisconsin. The only thing you can be sure of when discussing geographical regions is that most Americans disagree.

The nation's capital, Washington in the District of Columbia, is usually referred to as Washington, DC (see below), to distinguish it from Washington state, which **isn't** usually referred to simply as Washington for the same reason. Similarly, the city of New York (known affectionately as the 'Big Apple') is often referred to as New York City to distinguish it from the state of New York, referred to as New York state or upstate New York.

GOVERNMENT

The US is a federal republic consisting of 50 states and the federal District of Columbia (known locally as 'the district'). Although it's geographically situated in Maryland, DC is a separate autonomous area, chosen to be the nation's capital and seat of government.

The US system of government is based on the Constitution of 1787, a concise document comprising just a few thousand words but containing a number of checks and balances to ensure that power isn't concentrated in a few hands. The Constitution lays down the division of power between the executive, the legislature (see below) and the judiciary (see **Legal System** on page 516). A unique feature of the US political system is that the executive and the legislature are elected, housed and function separately. Power is also split between federal, state and local governments. Each state has its own semi-autonomous government headed by a governor, who's elected for four years.

Executive

The executive branch of government is responsible for administering the laws passed by Congress (the legislature – see below). It's presided over by the President, who's the head of state and chief executive of the government, and whose official residence is the White House in Washington, DC. He (there have been no female presidents) is elected for a term of four years and can be re-elected for a further term, making a total of eight years. He and his Vice President (veep) are the only members of the government elected by a nationwide vote. The Vice President has just two official constitutional duties (regularly making a fool of himself is an extra-constitutional duty): presiding over the Senate and taking over the presidency if the President dies, is unable to perform his duties or is removed from office. However, everyone knows the veep's **real** job is to make the president look good and to act as a deterrent against assassination, which is why most presidents pick a 'jerk' as their veep! The President's main job is to veto bills originated by Congress (and to avoid being caught with his trousers down).

There are usually just two candidates for the presidency, one from each of the two major parties, the Democrats and the Republicans, the latter also being called the Grand Old Party (GOP). Together they provide the President, every seat in Congress, and most state governors and posts at state and local level. There are few major differences between the parties, although the Democrats are to the left of the Republicans and considered liberals (a dirty word to many Americans). Democrats are usually in favour of increased public spending and taxation, to expand the economy and increase welfare. In contrast, Republicans are more conservative, strongly in favour of big business and private enterprise, and opposed to the welfare state. The Democrats traditionally garner most of their support from blue-collar workers and ethnic and religious minority groups, while the Republicans are supported by the large middle class, big business and farming interests.

The US presidential election process is long, complicated and expensive, costing millions of dollars. Campaigning, in earnest, begins almost two years before the election. The spring and summer of a presidential election year are dominated by the battle for party nominations, beginning with primary elections (or primaries) in February, in which voters choose their party's presidential candidate. The list of candidates put forward by a party, e.g. for president and vice-president, is called the 'ticket'. Final nominations are supposed to be decided at the parties' national conventions in July or August, although increasingly the nomination has already been decided months earlier based on the results of a few early primaries. After his first term of office, a president is almost never challenged for his party's nomination and rarely fails to be elected for a second term (unless he has made an almighty mess of things and is unpopular, and sometimes even that doesn't stop his re-election!).

There's no system of proportional representation and elections are based on the 'winner takes all' system. This system guarantees that minor 'third' parties are excluded from the political system, as most people are reluctant to 'waste' their vote on someone who cannot win (Americans hate losers). Presidential elections are based on an electoral 'college' system of voting, where voters cast their votes for electors (not for the presidential candidate) who are pledged to one party and its candidate on the ballot. Each state has as many electors as it has senators and representatives, a total of 538 (100 senators, 435 representatives, plus three electoral votes for the District of Columbia). The electoral votes assigned to each state go to the party polling the most votes, and the party's candidate who receives the majority of the 538 votes becomes the president elect. Thanks to the close outcome of the last two elections, there has been talk of changing or doing away with the electoral college system, although this would need a Constitutional amendment, something which is difficult to do and which would take several years to complete.

When voters select their President, they're in effect choosing an entire administration or government. On taking office, the President makes more than 2,000 appointments, from his Cabinet down to key officials in the myriad government departments and agencies. The Cabinet is comprised of the heads (or secretaries) of the 15 executive departments: agriculture, commerce, defence (defense), education, energy, health and human services, homeland security, housing and urban development, interior, justice, labour, state, transport, the treasury, and veterans' affairs. Apart from key political appointments, government departments are manned by permanent civil servants.

Although the office of President has enormous prestige and symbolic significance, the President's authority is limited by Congress, particularly when the presidency and the majority in Congress are held by different parties. The President has no authority to make laws himself, although as head of the executive he is expected to ensure that laws are faithfully executed. He can veto legislation passed by Congress, although a two-thirds majority in both houses overrides a presidential veto. However, although Congress can throw out or amend legislation, it's often the President who provides the initiative. A bill must be passed by both houses of Congress and signed by the President before it becomes law.

Legislature

Congress is the legislative branch of government responsible for making laws. It consists of two houses, the Senate and the House of Representatives (referred to as 'the House'), both with their seat in the Capitol building in Washington, DC. The Senate is the senior house and consists of 100 senators, two from each state. The House has a total of 435 members or congressmen (only a few of them are women, thus proving conclusively that women are more intelligent than men), who represent electoral 'districts'. The number of congressmen per state is based on each state's population, e.g. California has 52 representatives while 16 other western states have a total of 50 between them. Senators are elected for six years, so around a third of the seats are up for election every two years. Congressmen are elected for a two-year period and voting is held for the entire House of Representatives at the same time as the Senate elections (elections held between presidential elections are called 'mid-term' elections).

Each house has specific duties. For example, the Senate's duties include confirming or rejecting presidential appointments (including those of supreme court judges) and the ratification of foreign treaties, while laws concerning the raising of revenue originate in the House of Representatives. The real power of Congress lies in the numerous standing, select and special committees, the most important of which are 'rules' committees, whose job is to decide which bills will be considered. Both houses initiate legislation that begins as a bill and is sent to the appropriate committee.

One of the most unusual features of the political system is the thousands of lobbyists and pressure groups. These have considerable influence in Washington, particularly those representing commercial and business interests. Powerful corporations, associations, organisations and myriad special-interest groups employ professional lobbyists (often with huge staffs), whose job is to co-ordinate financial support and disburse funds to suitable members of Congress (as lampooned in the film *The Distinguished Gentleman* with Eddie Murphy). In some countries, this is called bribery, although in the US 'buying' votes is an accepted and traditional part of politics. Consequently, it's practically impossible to get Congress to enact legislation going against the interests of any powerful lobby group (unless a more powerful group outbids them).

One of the failings of the US political system is that members of Congress spend most of their time arguing for local interests (with a wary eye on the next election), while neglecting more important issues. Self-preservation and self-interest are at the root of all US politics, and when it comes to the crunch hardly any American politicians have the courage to cast unpopular votes. Every vote on Capitol Hill comes down to the same question: 'Will my vote lose me votes in my own backyard?' (the amount of federal money politicians get for their district is called pork-barrel spending). A vote on any issue possibly adversely affecting local issues is immediately recorded and used as ammunition by opponents. Congressmen and senators spend most of their time in office fund-raising, much of which is spent on TV advertisements savaging the records of their political opponents. The US has the most entertaining and expensive political campaigns in the world and American politicians **never** stop campaigning. No tricks are too dirty or cheap for American politicians on the campaign trail.

The federal government is responsible for foreign trade and commerce between states, borrowing and minting money, foreign relations, the post office, federal highways, defence, internal security, immigration and naturalisation, and customs and excise.

State Governments

The states have a large degree of autonomy to control their own affairs, including setting their own taxes (in addition to federal taxes) and drafting state laws with regard to trade and commerce, education, state highways and driving, marriage, divorce, licensing, weapons, social services (e.g. health and welfare), wages, and criminal justice. Like the federal government, each state government consists of three branches: the executive, legislature and the judiciary. Each state also has its own great seal, flag, song, motto, flower, bird and tree.

States are subdivided into counties, municipalities, towns, school districts and special districts, each with its own 'government'. Municipalities include cities, boroughs, towns and villages. In most large cities, local government consists of a mayor and a city council, although some have administrative managers and a board of 'selectmen' or a commission. Mayors aren't ceremonial figures, but chief executives with broad powers. Counties may be governed by a council-commission, council-administrator or a council-elected executive, the powers of which vary widely.

Local Government

There are some 500,000 elected officials in the US, mostly at the local level where local governments establish policy and set local laws in their communities. Their responsibilities include primary and secondary education (school district governments), police, fire and ambulance services, libraries, health and welfare, public transport subsidies, parks and recreation, waste disposal, highways and road safety, and trading standards. Local laws, e.g. licensing and trading laws, are often decided at county level, rather than by individual towns.

Voting

Only US citizens and naturalised citizens are permitted to vote, which is a major source of contention among the millions of immigrants who are permanent residents of the US and who vainly clamour for 'no taxation without representation'. It's also illegal for foreigners without permanent resident status to make financial contributions to political parties (although why any of them would want to beggars belief!).

Even among those eligible to vote, many aren't registered, and participation in local, state and federal elections is less than in most other democratic countries (around 30 per cent of the population, some 65 million people, don't bother to vote or register). The voter turnout for presidential elections is usually around 50 per cent and even lower for state and local elections (only a quarter of Americans under 35 vote in presidential elections). The 2004 presidential election drew record numbers of voters, estimated to be nearly 120 million, or some 60 per cent of eligible voters, largely thanks to press reports about how close the race was expected to be. (Although the actual results were close, they weren't nearly as close as the polling organisations had predicted.) Midwestern and western cities have the highest voter turnout, the south the lowest. Not surprisingly, voter apathy is at its highest in poor areas, where experience has taught people that whoever is in power their prospects are the same – i.e. dim.

Like all wise people, most Americans distrust politicians (whom they consider to be corrupt) and have a negative view of politics, although paradoxically most are proud of their political system. Political scandals are common and are widely publicised. Americans make a point of washing their dirty linen in public and many Americans are more interested in a politician's sex life than his policies (some politicians are evidently well aware of this!). Corruption is rife and local politics are inherently criminal (Americans have a saying that a person is 'so crooked he could run for public office'). Not surprisingly, many politicians are also lawyers! However much Americans criticise or complain about their politics and politicians, they aren't keen for ignorant foreigners to join in!

LEGAL SYSTEM

The US legal system is based on federal law, augmented by laws enacted by state legislatures and local laws passed by counties and cities. Most rights and freedoms enjoyed by Americans are enshrined in the first ten amendments of the US Constitution (written in 1787) and popularly known as the 'Bill of Rights'. American law and the US Constitution apply to everyone in the US, irrespective of citizenship or immigration status, and even illegal immigrants have most of the same basic legal rights as US citizens. Under the US constitution, each state has the power to establish its own system of criminal and civil laws, resulting in 50 different state legal systems, each supported by its own laws, prisons, police forces, and county and city courts. There's a wide variation in state and local laws, making life difficult for people moving between states. **Never assume that the law is the same in different states** (Conflict of State Laws is a popular course in American law schools).

The US judiciary is independent of the government and consists of the Supreme Court, the US Court of Appeals and the US District Courts. The Supreme Court, the highest court in the land, consists of nine judges who are appointed for life by the President. Its decisions are final and legally binding on all parties. In deciding cases, the Supreme Court reviews the activities of state and federal governments and decides whether laws are constitutional. The Supreme Court has nullified laws passed by Congress and even declared the actions of US presidents unconstitutional. Momentous judgements in recent years have involved the Watergate scandal, racial segregation, abortion and capital punishment. However, when appointing a Supreme Court judge, the President's selection is based on a candidate's political and other views, which must usually correspond with his own. The Supreme Court was for many years made up of members with a liberal or reformist outlook, although this trend has been reversed in recent years with the appointment of conservative judges by successive Republican presidents.

A separate system of federal courts operates alongside state courts and deals with cases arising under the US Constitution or any law or treaty. Federal courts also hear disputes involving state governments or between citizens resident in different states. Cases falling within federal jurisdiction are heard before a federal district judge. Appeals can be made to the Circuit Court of Appeals and in certain cases to the US Supreme Court.

There's a clear separation and distinction between civil courts, which settle disputes between people (such as property division after a divorce), and criminal courts that prosecute those who break the law. Crimes are categorised as minor offences ('misdemeanours') or serious violations of the law ('felonies'). Misdemeanours include offences such as dropping litter, illegal parking or jay-walking, and are usually dealt with by a fine without a court appearance. Felonies, which include robbery and drug dealing, are tried in a court of law and those found guilty are generally sentenced to prison (jail). In many counties and cities, there are often eccentric local laws (usually relating to misdemeanours rather than felonies).

People who commit misdemeanours may be issued a summons (unsuspecting foreigners who violate local by-laws may be let off with a warning), while anyone committing a felony is arrested. An arrest almost always involves being 'frisked' for concealed weapons, handcuffed and read your rights. You must be advised of your constitutional (Miranda) rights when arrested. These include the right to remain silent, the right to have a lawyer present during questioning, and the right to have a free court-appointed lawyer if you cannot afford one. You will be asked if you wish to waive your rights. This isn't recommended, as any statement you make can then be used against you in a court of law. It's better to retain your rights and say nothing until you've spoken with a lawyer. At the police department, you're charged and have the right to make one telephone call. This should be to your embassy or consulate, a lawyer or the local legal aid office, or (if necessary) to someone who will stand bail for you. You're then put into a cell until your case comes before a judge, usually the same or next day, who releases you (if there's no case to answer) or sets bail. Bail may be a cash sum or the equivalent property value. For minor offences, you may be released on your 'personal recognisance'. In serious cases, a judge may oppose bail.

In many areas, lawyer (or attorney) referral services are maintained by local (e.g. county) bar associations, whose members provide legal representation for a 'reasonable' fee. Before retaining a lawyer, ask **exactly** what legal representation costs, including fees for additional services such as medical experts, transcripts and court fees. Most importantly, hire a lawyer who's a specialist and experienced in handling your type of case. If you cannot afford a lawyer and your case goes to court, a court-appointed lawyer represents you.

An unusual feature of the US legal system is plea bargaining, which involves the prosecution and the defence making a deal where the defendant agrees to plead guilty to a lesser charge, thus saving the court time and leading to a reduced sentence. This has made the US legal system something of a lottery, often with victims' lives at stake, and in high profile cases (such as the O.J. Simpson case) a media circus. In the US, you're normally considered guilty until proven innocent, at least in the eyes of the general public, and you may be tried and convicted by the media (there are virtually no reporting restrictions in the US), long before your trial comes to court (as happened in the case of Louise Woodward in 1997–98). Penalties are often harsh, particularly for less serious crimes, while professional and white-collar criminals who can afford the best defence often get off with a light sentence or a fine. Many American judges are elected, rather than appointed from qualified members of the legal profession, which often results in bad legal decisions and a lack of consistency in sentencing (at the lower court levels, corrupt judges aren't unknown). In 1994, a new 'three-strikes-you're-out-law' was introduced in response to the clamour for longer sentences, whereby anyone convicted three times of violent federal crimes automatically receives a life sentence.

Litigation is an American tradition and national sport, and every American has a right to his day in court (as well as to his 15 minutes of fame). There are 15 to 20 million civil suits a year, which leads to a huge backlog of cases in all states and even the Supreme Court. One of the most unusual aspects of US law is that lawyers are permitted to work on a contingency fee basis, whereby they accept cases on a 'no-win, no-fee' basis. If they win, their fee is as high as 50 per cent of any damages. If you must hire a lawyer on a non-contingency basis, the cost is usually prohibitive. Many people believe this system helps pervert the cause of justice, as a lawyer's only concern is winning a case, often irrespective of any ethical standards or the facts of the matter. The contingency-fee system is responsible for the proliferation of litigation cases, which lawyers are happy to pursue because of the absurdly high awards made by US courts.

The litigation system is primarily designed to make lawyers rich, while ensuring that almost everyone else ends up a loser. Not only must individuals have liability insurance to protect against being sued, but everyone from doctors to plumbers must have expensive malpractice insurance to protect themselves against litigious patients or customers. The whole US economy and legal system is underpinned by litigation (in which it seems half the population are directly employed and the other half are plaintiffs or defendants!). Everyone (except lawyers) agrees that litigation is out of control and is seriously undermining the US's competitiveness. Nobody, however, seems to know what to do about it. Meanwhile, lawyers spend their time dreaming up new and lucrative areas of litigation. (They even follow ambulances in an attempt to be first in line to represent accident victims, hence the term 'ambulance chasers'!)

In many states, there are hair-raising product liability, personal liability and consequential loss laws. Some of these have limited liability, while others don't, meaning that multiple warnings are printed on the most unlikely articles. In fact, most companies attempt to anticipate the most ridiculous and implausible events in order to protect themselves against litigation. Taken to ridiculous extremes a bottle of beer would have warnings about drinking and driving, choking on the stopper, breaking the glass and cutting yourself or someone else, swallowing broken glass, taking alcohol where it's prohibited, drinking under age or giving a drink to someone under age, alcoholism, carrying alcohol in your car or over certain state borders, being mugged or falling over while drunk, etc, etc. – and this is hardly an exaggeration!

In fact, alcohol **does** carry a number of health warnings regarding cancer risk and other health problems, birth defects, driving and operating machinery. In Colorado, a barman must insure himself against being sued for serving someone who's later involved in a car accident. In the US, you can sue a tobacco company for causing your cancer, a car manufacturer for causing an accident, a ski firm for contributing to your ski accident, or a computer software company for fouling up your tax return. In fact anything that can (however remotely) be blamed on someone else, will be! If you're the victim of an accident, you must never discuss your injuries with anyone connected with the other party and must never sign any documents they present to you without legal advice. Put the matter in the hands of an experienced litigation lawyer and let him handle everything. And in case you might forget, there are television adverts advising you of your rights to sue in accident situations, by attorneys claiming special competence at winning huge settlements.

Most companies and professionals are so frightened of the courts that many cases don't go to trial, e.g. personal injury and medical malpractice cases, which, apart from the cost of losing, are bad for business. This adds to the proliferation of law suits, as it's expensive to fight a legal battle even if you win, and litigants know that most companies are happy to settle out of court. If you're in business and not being sued by at least 100 people, it's usually a sign that you're broke and therefore not worth suing. If someone sues you for your last dime, don't take it personally – it's simply business.

Not surprisingly there are **a lot** of lawyers in the US (more than 500,000, i.e. one for every 600 Americans (compared with one for every 10,000 people in Japan). The chief role of lawyers is to make themselves (very) rich and to make business as difficult as possible for everyone else. Never forget that lawyers are in business for themselves and nobody else and, although they may be representing you, their brief never strays far from the bottom line (i.e. how much they will be paid). If you have a dispute with a person, company or government agency involving a sum of from $100 to $5,000 (depending on the state), you can use the small claims court, which doesn't require a lawyer (hurrah!).

Many social service agencies provide free legal assistance to immigrants (legal and illegal), although some may serve the nationals of a particular country or religion only. There are help lines and agencies offering free legal advice in most towns and cities, many with legal aid societies (offering free advice and referral on legal matters), Better Business Bureaux (dealing with consumer-related complaints, shopping services, etc.) and departments of consumer affairs (who also handle consumer complaints). See also **Crime** on page 507, **Liability Insurance** on page 352 and **Police** on page 524.

MARRIAGE & DIVORCE

In order to get married in the US, the bride and groom must usually be at least 18 or 16 if they have parental consent (also applies to foreigners), although ages vary according to the state. The minimum age for marriage with parental consent ranges from 14 for a girl in Alabama, Kansas, Massachusetts, Texas and Utah (though generally it requires the consent of a judge in addition to that of the parents), to 18 for a male in several states. Without parental consent it may be as high as 21 for men and women (Arkansas). In most states, marriage licences are issued by local city or county clerks and an application must usually be made in the municipality where either the bride or the groom lives. A witness, aged 18 or older, may need to accompany the couple at the time of the application.

In around 30 states, marriage partners must undertake a compulsory 'Wassermann (blood) test' to show that they're free from venereal and other communicable diseases before a marriage licence is granted. In some states, e.g. California, if a couple are over 18 and living together, a blood test isn't required. Results of a blood test must be submitted with the application and there's usually a waiting period of two to seven working days before a marriage licence is issued. Licence fees vary considerably from less than $10 to over $50 in some states. After the marriage license is issued, the couple must have a marriage ceremony, which can be performed by a religious clergyman or by a judge or 'justice of the peace'. The completed license (signed by the person conducting the ceremony and witnesses) is then returned to the town hall to be registered. Common law marriages don't require a blood test, licence or ceremony and are legal in 11 states (Alabama, Colorado, Iowa, Kansas, Montana, Oklahoma, Pennsylvania, Rhode Island, South Carolina, Texas and Utah) and in the District of Columbia. They essentially consist of a man and woman living together as man and wife sharing a common name.

You can get married practically anywhere and in any surroundings, e.g. in a shopping precinct, in a car, on roller-skates, under water, in the air (e.g. in a hot-air balloon or while parachuting or skydiving), on a roller coaster, in a theme park, in a hot tub on the back of a limousine (in Las Vegas of course) . . . even in the nude! Gay marriages are commonplace (there's even an *Essential Guide to Lesbian and Gay Weddings*) although they aren't recognised legally except in the state of Vermont, where you can register a 'domestic partnership' granting many of the same rights as a marriage certificate. The issue of gay marriage has become quite heated recently, with several states passing laws against the practice and there's now a move to amend the US Constitution to define marriage as 'a relationship between a man and a woman'. Nonetheless, many churches perform ceremonies for gay and lesbian couples on request and some employers allow unmarried household partners coverage in benefits plans.

Nevada (with no blood test or waiting period) is the most popular state for quickie marriages, which are the second biggest industry after gambling. Las Vegas has 280 churches and 120 wedding chapels (some 30 of which are open 24 hours a day). Around 80,000 marriages are performed in Las Vegas annually (more than 11,000 on Valentine's Day weekend alone). Weddings in Las Vegas stretch credulity and vulgarity to breaking point and why anyone would want to get married there at all is a complete mystery, as it's one of the least romantic places on earth. The only people they won't marry are drunks and people of the same gender. (Be careful, as some countries don't accept Las Vegas weddings as valid if you try to register your marriage at your home country consulate!)

Despite the apparent enthusiasm for marriage, more people are remaining single and becoming divorced than ever before. In 1931, Nevada made divorce legal and for many years Reno and Las Vegas were the divorce capitals of the US. This led to more liberal divorce laws in many other states. Today, the US has the highest divorce rate in the world (over 50 per cent of American marriages fail, although the statistics are misleading, as many people have a number of failed marriages). The number of divorced people has more than quadrupled since 1970 to almost 20 million (over 10 per cent of the adult population). Americans divorce and re-marry so often that in some states you can renew a marriage licence if you remarry again within a certain period. Two-thirds of states have a 'no-fault' divorce law, making it unnecessary to prove that a marriage partner has committed an act giving grounds for divorce (thus depriving private detectives of much lucrative work). This allows either partner to seek a divorce simply because he or she no longer wishes the marriage to continue. More than a million children experience parental divorce each year; almost one in three American children are born out of wedlock and more than one in four families are single parent families.

If you're contemplating divorce, the most important consideration is to hire a good divorce lawyer (i.e. a divorce specialist), particularly if the divorce will be contested and there's significant property and the legal custody of children at stake. Because of the high probability of divorce in the US, many (rich) marriage partners insist on a (decidedly unromantic) marriage contract or prenuptial agreement, limiting a spouse's claims in the event of a divorce. All states have an alimony law (Texas, previously the only state without an alimony law, introduced one in 1991 for marriages lasting at least ten years).

Foreigners living in the US who are married, divorced or widowed should have a valid marriage licence, divorce papers or death certificate. These are necessary to confirm your marital status with the authorities, e.g. to receive certain legal or social security benefits. Foreigners married abroad come under the marriage laws of the country where they were married, although they may be subject to property and child welfare laws in the state where they're resident when it comes to getting a divorce.

MILITARY SERVICE

There's no conscription (draft) in the US (it was last used during the Vietnam war) and all members of the armed forces are volunteers. Nevertheless, all male permanent residents and US citizens aged 18 to 25 must register for military service with their local board of the Selective Service System (SSS, see notices at US post offices) or online at 🖳 www.sss.gov. Resident, 18-year-old men must register within 30 days of their birthday. All qualifying immigrant men are required to register within six months of entering the US, but may be exempted if they've served at least one year in the armed forces of another country. SSS registration is a requirement of eligibility for state-funded higher education, state jobs and job training, and citizenship. Failure to register can result in a fine of up to $25,000 and/or a five-year prison sentence.

There have been constant rumours in recent years concerning the resurrection of the draft, particularly since the beginning of the various campaigns in the War on Terror. The Bush Administration has repeatedly denied all such rumours, and in October 2004, a potential law to resurrect the draft was resoundingly defeated in the House of Representatives. The armed forces in the US consist of the Army, Navy, Air Force, Marines, Coast Guard, Merchant Marines and the National Guard. Until the start of the War on Terror, the National Guard were considered 'weekend warriors' who kept their civilian jobs while training one weekend a month and for a few weeks during the summer. Active duty for the National Guard normally consisted of domestic service, after a natural disaster or major accident, but increasingly, the

National Guard units are being called into active combat roles in the Middle East and elsewhere for periods of up to a year or more.

Homosexuals are officially prohibited from serving in the armed services and acknowledged homosexuals are discharged. There are around 200,000 women in the military (some 10 per cent of the total) and women are permitted to serve in combat roles, although they aren't required to register for military service. Despite the number of servicewomen, sexual harassment and prejudice against women is rife throughout the military. A veteran is an ex-serviceman of either sex and any age. Veterans are entitled to a number of benefits, including tuition grants and assistance for attending university (a common motivation for enlisting in the armed forces).

Although the federal government was reducing defence spending and manpower in recent years, expenditures have increased with the War on Terror, launched shortly after the September 11th attacks, in 2001. The government currently spends over $400 billion a year on defence, which accounts for some 25 per cent of the federal budget and around 5 per cent of GDP.

PETS

The import of all animals and birds into the US is subject to health, quarantine, agriculture, wildlife and customs regulations. Pets, particularly dogs, cats and turtles, must be examined at the first port of entry for possible evidence of disease that can be transmitted to humans. Pets excluded from entry must be re-exported or destroyed. Dogs, cats and turtles may be imported free of duty, although duty may be payable on other pets, the value of which can be included in your customs exemption if they accompany you and aren't for resale.

Dogs must be vaccinated against rabies at least 30 days before their entry into the US. Exceptions are puppies less than three months old and dogs originating or located for six months or longer in areas designated by the Public Health Service as being rabies-free. All domestic cats must be free of evidence of diseases communicable to man when examined at the port of entry and vaccination against rabies isn't required (though it is highly recommended). Birds must be quarantined upon arrival for at least 30 days in a facility operated by the US Department of Agriculture (USDA) at the owner's expense. For regulations concerning the import of other animals, contact your local US embassy or consulate or write to the US Public Health Service, Center for Disease Control, Foreign Quarantine Program, Atlanta, GA 30333 (☎ 404-639-3311, 💻 www.os.dhhs.gov/phs). A leaflet, *Pets, Wildlife: US Customs*, is available from the US Customs and Border Protection Service, Office of Public Information, PO Box 7407, NW, Washington, DC 20229 (☎ 202-927-1770, 💻 www.cbp.gov, then follow the links for 'Travel' and 'Pets'). The publication number is 0000-0509 and it can be downloaded from the Travel section of the CBP website.

If you're travelling with pets within the continental US, they must have a valid Interstate Health Certificate and be fully vaccinated (documentation is required). All but four states require dogs to be inoculated against rabies (costing $30 per year) and some also require it for cats. To take a dog, cat or bird to Alaska or Hawaii, you need a valid Interstate Health Certificate, signed by an accredited veterinarian and issued no more than ten days before shipping. Hawaii has strict anti-rabies laws and all dogs and cats (including those from the continental US) must be quarantined for 120 days, with the exception of those coming from a rabies-free area (e.g. Australia, the UK and New Zealand). Alaska requires a written statement from a veterinarian certifying that your pet is free of rabies. Further information about interstate pet transportation can be obtained from the USDA's information hotline (☎ 202-720-2791) or in the Travel section of the USDA website (🖳 www.usda.gov).

Mexico and the US enforce stringent regulations regarding pets, and visitors to Mexico usually find it more convenient to leave their pets at veterinary boarding facilities in the US. When pets are taken into Mexico and returned to the US, owners must present a rabies vaccination certificate dated not less than one month or more than 12 months previously. A booklet, *Traveling With Your Pet*, is available from the ASPCA (see address below) and contains inoculation requirements by territory and country.

You can take your dog or cat to a veterinary surgeon for a course of vaccinations, some of which (e.g. rabies) are mandatory. Some municipalities provide free rabies shots for cats and dogs. After vaccination, your pet must wear a rabies tag attached to its collar. (In most areas, all dogs are required to wear collars and those without are considered to be strays.) If you live in a rabies area, don't let your pets run free and don't allow your children to play with or approach strange or wild animals. If you're bitten by an unknown animal, you may require a series of anti-rabies injections. You can also take your dog or cat to a vet for neutering (recommended by the ASPCA), the cost of which varies according to the region and the vet. Shop around and compare veterinarian fees. It's possible to take out health insurance for your pets in order to reduce veterinary bills. The American Animal Hospital Association (☎ 800-883-6301, 🖳 www.healthypet.com) provides help in finding vets near your home. Tattooing of dogs and cats for identification purposes isn't commonly done (except for valuable show animals), although the ASPCA encourages the use of a small tattoo at the site of the incision to identify neutered animals. Chipping (the insertion of a small electronic chip under the skin) is also not commonly used, except for pedigree pets or those likely to travel overseas to countries where chipping is more commonly used.

Many Americans aren't content with just keeping a cat or a dog like 'normal' people, but keep exotic pets such as leopards, cougars or boa constrictors. Although most states have strict regulations regarding the keeping of wild animals as pets, many Americans keep them illegally, particularly in Florida, one of the main gateways for the import of illegal animals. Note also the following:

● Many municipalities and cities require cats and dogs to have a licence, usually costing around $10 per year (possibly less if an animal has been neutered). Licensing may depend on a pet's age. Proof of rabies vaccination may be required to obtain a licence and the license is normally in the form of a small tag that must be worn on the animal's collar whenever they're outside. Check with your local town hall or city clerk.

● It's illegal not to clear up after your dog (you can be fined). Take a 'poop-scoop' and a plastic bag with you when walking your dog. Dog excrement is called 'doodie' or 'doo-doo' in polite circles.

- Cities and large towns have professional dog walkers who walk your dog for around $10 per hour.

- With the exception of guide (Seeing Eye) dogs, which may travel on trains and buses free of charge, dogs aren't allowed on public transport or in most restaurants and shopping centres.

- Many cities have strict leash laws and pets may not be permitted on beaches (or must be kept on a leash).

- Many apartments and rented accommodation have regulations forbidding the keeping of dogs and other animals (cats are usually accepted). The number of cats and dogs per residence may also be limited (by number or by combined weight), and large animals such as horses may be prohibited (particularly in condos). The internet site of the Humane Society of the US (🖳 www.rent withpets.org) includes information on moving with pets and a list of rental accommodation which allows pets.

- Most major cities and towns have animal hospitals and clinics, and individuals and organisations in many areas operate sanctuaries for injured or orphaned wild animals and abandoned pets. However, using an animal hospital may be much more expensive than going to a local vet. Many cities and towns have animal shelters where you can obtain a stray dog free of charge. Animal shelters usually require that you have the dog neutered.

- Your vet will arrange to collect and cremate the body of a dead pet (for a fee), although you may bury a dead pet in your garden in some areas. There are many commercial pet cemeteries, where the pets of the rich and famous are given a send-off befitting their privileged position in life.

Animal lovers can join the American Society for the Prevention of Cruelty to Animals (ASPCA), 424 East 92nd Street, New York, NY 10128-6804 (☎ 212-876-7700, 🖳 www. aspca.org) for $25 per year (members receive the quarterly *Animal Watch*). The ASPCA campaigns vigorously against the killing of wildlife and the destruction of their habitats and publishes a wealth of free information for pet owners.

POLICE

There's no national police force in the US, where policing is organised on a state and local basis. The country has around 500,000 police officers and a total of 40,000 separate police forces, over half of which are simply one or two-man sheriffs' offices in small towns (sheriffs are normally locally elected officials with no formal training). Police forces include city police (possibly with separate departments to deal with schools, traffic and even refuse), county police, transport police, sheriffs' departments, state police (state troopers) and highway forces such as the California Highway Patrol. An ordinary policeman is usually called a patrolman. In addition to regular full-time police officers, many towns have auxiliary, part-time police officers, special duty and volunteer sheriff's posses (which assist sheriffs' offices in some areas). The American response to increasing crime is usually to put more cops on the beat.

The division between federal and state law can be confusing; for example murder is classified as a state crime, while less serious crimes such as taking a woman across state lines for immoral purposes is a federal crime (although it may be dealt with by a local police force). City police are concerned with local crime, and offences outside their jurisdiction are usually dealt with by state police or federal investigators (the FBI). With the increased emphasis on fighting and preventing terrorism, more and more responsibility has fallen on the local police forces, and many jurisdictions are being stretched to the limit, with promised federal funds for fighting terrorism proving inadequate for the measures proposed.

All police are armed and popular weapons include .38 specials and shotguns. Police officers also carry truncheons (night-sticks), and some forces are issued with an electronic tazer gun administering a charge of 50,000 volts for around eight seconds (originally a cattle prod), used to knock out aggressive drug addicts. In many areas, police wear bullet-proof vests, although even these are no defence against the Teflon-coated bullets (known as cop-killers) used by some criminals. Police officers also carry mace, a riot gas similar to CS gas. Police officers are among the most frightening looking Americans you're likely to meet, with their carefully developed tough-men looks, truncheons and guns. In some states, police can legally shoot suspected criminals trying to evade arrest, so don't even think about it!

As in most countries, the efficiency, honesty and politeness of police officers vary from city to city and state to state. Police corruption is reportedly widespread, particularly in the major cities such as New York, where many officers are involved in criminal activities such as selling drugs seized from pushers. Although some people claim to present their driving licence to a traffic cop along with a $20 bill, **you should never attempt to bribe a police officer, even if he gives you an open invitation**. As in many countries, most complaints against the police are dismissed out of hand by police review boards, and most people consider it a waste of time reporting cases of bad cops.

If you're stopped by a policeman, either in a car or when walking, don't make any sudden moves and keep your hands where they can be seen. Some policemen are extremely jumpy (often justifiably so) and may interpret any movement as an attempt to reach a concealed weapon. Always be courteous and helpful. It may not do any harm to emphasise that you're a foreigner (depending on your nationality) or to tell the officer you're a visitor or newcomer. If you've broken the law, you should apologise and stress that it was innocently and inadvertently done (although they may not be convinced if you've just held up a bank with an AK-47).

In addition to federal and state police forces, there are around 75 federal law enforcement agencies such as the Federal Bureau of Investigation (FBI), who deal with interstate crime. The FBI has some 20,000 plain clothes agents who normally concern themselves with major offences such as murder, kidnapping and robbery. It publishes a list of the 'ten most wanted fugitives' and provides state and local police forces with information. In the last few years, however, the FBI has had its role expanded to include 'homeland security' and there's talk of merging or at least co-ordinating the activities of the FBI with those of the Central Intelligence Agency (CIA). Each state also has a reserve national guard under the command of the state governor that can be called on to deal with civil unrest such as riots, as well as dealing with natural catastrophes, e.g. earthquakes, fires, floods and hurricanes. The

National Guard has had its role vastly increased in recent years. (See **Military Service** on page 521.) Many companies and individuals also employ private armed guards. (See also **Crime** on page 507 and **Legal System** on page 516.)

POPULATION

The US is the third most populous nation in the world after China (1.2 billion) and India (1 billion). The population is expanding at the rate of around 1 per cent per year and it's estimated that it will reach 400 million by the year 2050. According to the last national census (conducted every ten years), the population of the US on 1st April 2000 was 281,421,906, an increase of almost 33 million since the last census in 1990 due mainly to a continued influx of migrants from Central and South America. (By 1st July 2003, the US population was estimated to have grown to over 290 million.) Hispanics are the fastest growing population group and are expected to outnumber African-Americans by 2010. They currently account for almost 10 per cent of the population, 80 per cent of which is Caucasian, 12 per cent African-American, 3 per cent Asian, 1 per cent native American (no longer referred to as 'red Indians'), and 4 per cent other races, including those who claim two or more different races in their background. The largest Spanish-speaking communities are Mexicans in the south-west (Arizona, California, New Mexico, Texas), Cubans in the south-east (Florida) and Puerto Ricans in New York City. A total of over 28 million Americans were foreign-born, the highest proportion since the '30s. There are 6 million more women in America than men.

The population density of the US is around 70 people per square mile (27 per km), which contrasts with around 600 per square mile in the UK. However, some 75 per cent of Americans (around 190 million people) live in urban areas and are concentrated in just 2.5 per cent of the country's land area. There are some 40 metropolitan areas with a population of over 1 million, comprising a total of 130 million inhabitants or around 50 per cent of the total population. The US has some of the world's largest urban areas, such as greater Los Angeles, which stretches almost 100mi (160km) along the west coast and around 50mi (80km) inland. The east coast from Boston to Washington, DC (taking in New York City and Philadelphia) is virtually a continuous 250mi (400km) long urban sprawl. New York is the largest city, with 7.5 million inhabitants (1.5 million in Manhattan alone), followed by Los Angeles (3.5 million) and Chicago (2.8 million). Washington, DC, the nation's capital, has a population of around 600,000.

Despite its huge metropolitan areas, 97.5 per cent of the US is classified as rural, where the population density may be just a few people per square mile. Between the major population centres in the east and west are the huge almost unpopulated areas of the wheat belt and Great Plains in the Midwest, the Rocky Mountains, and the desert lands of Colorado, Nevada, New Mexico and Utah. However, only Alaska can be defined as true frontier land, where most of the state has a population density of less than two people per square mile.

Although the most densely populated region remains the Northeast, population growth there is slowing as people move to the west and the Sunbelt, lured by 'sunrise', high-tech industries and newly booming centres such as Atlanta and Las

Vegas. In the decade 1990–2000, the population of the Northeast rose by just 2.8 million compared with increases of 10.4 million in the west and 14.8 million in the south, with the result that Texas has overtaken New York as the US's second most populous state after California, whose population (almost 34 million) is larger than that of the 21 least populous states (plus the District of Columbia) combined. (Wyoming has the smallest population, with fewer than half a million inhabitants; even Alaska has more.) The states with the largest population increases in percentage terms were Nevada (66 per cent) and Arizona (40 per cent), but in absolute terms California, Texas and Florida have grown the most (by more than 3 million people each) in the last decade.

Like other western countries, the US is faced with the problem of an ageing population due to a declining birth rate (the average number of children per family is 2.1) and an increasing life expectancy (72 for men and 78 for women). In 1960, over 35 per cent of the population was under 18; this figure had fallen to 26 per cent by 2000. During the same period, the number of people over 65 doubled to around 35 million. The number of people over 50 rose from 33 million in 1950 to 77 million in 2000 and is expected to increase to 100 million by 2020 as the 'baby boomers' (people born in the decade after the Second World War) reach retirement age.

RELIGION

The US has a tradition of religious tolerance and every resident has total freedom of religion without hindrance from the state or community. The establishment and free exercise of religion is enshrined in the First Amendment of the US constitution. For this reason, prayer isn't permitted in schools or at the start of sports games and was ruled unconstitutional by the US Supreme Court (although you may privately pray for your team to prevail). Although the influence of religion declined in most western societies in the latter part of the 20th century, the US has remained solidly religious (it's one of the world's most deeply religious nations). The national motto 'In God We Trust' is inscribed upon US coins, and the pledge of allegiance to the American flag still refers to the US as 'one nation under God' despite sporadic legal attempts to have the words removed. Religion is conspicuous in the US, where it's a part of everyday life (only sport is taken more seriously). More than 90 per cent of Americans claim to believe in God (and Mammon), two-thirds are members of a local church or temple and around 45 per cent attend religious services at least once a week. Some 60 per cent of Americans are Protestant, 25 per cent Roman Catholic, 2 per cent Jewish, 1 per cent Orthodox and 4 per cent belong to other religions such as Buddhist, Hindu or Moslem (the remaining 8 per cent claim no religion). Not surprisingly, more Americans believe in heaven (around 80 per cent) than hell (65 per cent), and 70 per cent believe in life after death (they hope they can take their pile with them or at least come back and enjoy it in their next life). As a consequence of the diverse religions, Americans refer to 'first' or 'given' names, rather than 'Christian' names.

Astonishingly, around a third of Americans claim to be 'Born Again Christians', so called because they believe life starts anew when you commit yourself to Jesus Christ (being born again doesn't, however, guarantee you a longer life!). They, and other fundamentalists, contend that every word in the bible is literally true and that Darwin's theory of evolution is false. The southern and south-west regions are known as the 'bible belt' because of the prominence of fundamentalist Protestants. In many parts of the US, there's a relentless determination by religious zealots to impose their views on non-believers, often through so-called street preachers. The most famous (or infamous) evangelists conduct their business via radio and TV (the 'electronic' church). A staggering 1,300 radio and TV stations (television ministries) are devoted full-time to religion. Although TV religious broadcasts may look like game shows, they're a deadly serious, multi-million dollar business (God is BIG business in the US). The chief aim of TV ministries is to encourage viewers to donate pots of money to pay for their salvation (or the preacher's high life). Enterprising readers should note that one of the fastest ways to get seriously rich in the US is to start a religious organisation, which enjoy tax-exempt status.

Many religious groups have considerable influence in US society and politics, locally and nationally. (The backing of religious organisations was credited in part with President Bush's victory in the 2004 elections and many expect the 'religious right' to influence the administration's decisions during Bush's second term in office.) Religion pervades political life and prominent politicians (and sportsmen) often praise or call on God in public or share their religious beliefs with millions of TV viewers (atheism is bad for business). Often sportsmen state that they won 'with God's help', although losers don't usually blame divine indifference.

The US, particularly California, is also the birthplace of many of the world's most bizarre religious organisations, including Hare Krishna, the Moonies, the Rajneeshies, Scientology and Transcendental Meditation (TM). Many 'cults' seek the total commitment and involvement of their members, which means giving up their worldly possessions or donating a large percentage of their salaries to the cult. Some cults have a fundamentalist outlook, while others are based on oriental religions or philosophies. Many Americans consider cults to be dangerous, as they appear to indulge in brain-washing techniques (which is why some have been banned in a number of countries).

Churches and religious meeting places representing a multitude of faiths can be found in every town (often outnumbering bars), and Sunday traffic jams are common, as people commute to church (some even have drive-in services). Recent years have seen the advent of mega-churches (known as 'God's shopping malls') with seating for up to 6,000 worshippers or more than 30,000 a week. They generally offer a computerised, pulsating, video-age service packaged as big-time entertainment and dished up with a variety of added attractions. In some towns, practically everyone attends church or Sunday school, when people dress in their Sunday best. The bible remains the nation's best-selling book and most book shops have a section for religious books. In smaller towns and communities, churches are often the main centres of social and community life. Most churches organise a wide range of social activities, including sports events, dances, coffee hours, dinners and suppers, discussion groups and outings. Many also operate nursery schools and after-school and youth programmes for older children. Most colleges and universities have 'campus ministries' affiliated with churches. Many of the US's largest charities are administered by religious groups, which run hospitals, homeless shelters, canteens, workshops for the disabled, refugee centres, youth centres, special schools, and many other establishments and projects. In many cases, these charities have now become eligible for federal government funding under programmes developed to encourage 'faith-based' initiatives to replace social services previously cut back due to budgetary constraints.

For information about local religious centres and service times, contact your local library or telephone religious centres for information (listed in the yellow pages under 'Religious Organisations' or 'Churches'). Many religious centres hold services in a number of languages. In some areas, a church directory is published and local religious services are usually listed in tourist guides and published in local weekend newspapers, where a whole page may be devoted to religious news.

SOCIAL CUSTOMS

All countries have their social customs and peculiarities, and the US is no exception. Good manners, politeness and consideration for others are considered important by most people. Americans are generally informal in their relationships and won't be too upset if you break the social rules, provided your behaviour isn't outrageous. As a foreigner you may be forgiven if you accidentally insult your host (although you may not be invited again). On the other hand, **you** may consider normal American behaviour occasionally shocking. Here are a few American customs you may like to familiarise yourself with:

- Americans often greet total strangers, particularly in small towns and communities. This may vary from a formal 'good morning' to a more casual 'Hi!'; it's considered polite to respond likewise. On parting, it's customary to say 'Have a nice day' (don't, however, say it to the bereaved at a funeral), although this habit is reportedly dying out as Americans become weary of ritual insincerity. Americans often reply 'You're Welcome' or something similar when somebody thanks them, and they may think you're impolite if you don't do likewise. If someone asks 'How are you?', it's usual to reply 'Fine thanks' (even if you feel dreadful).

- When introduced to someone, it's common to follow the cue of the person performing the introduction, e.g. if someone is introduced as George, you can usually call him George (although it might not be such a good idea if his last name is Bush and he happens to be the President, when Mr. President would be more appropriate). Americans generally dislike formality or any sort of social deference due to age or position, and most quickly say 'Please call me Rick (or Rita)'. To Americans, informality shows no lack of respect. Because of the rise of women's liberation in America, women may be introduced with the title 'Ms' (pronounced 'mizz') and some women object to being addressed as 'Miss' or 'Mrs'. In some social circles, women are introduced after their husbands, e.g. Mrs Chuck Whizzkid, in which case you shouldn't address her as Chuck! Some American women retain their maiden (family) names after marriage. Many American first names can be confusing and it's often difficult to know whether a name refers to a man or a woman.

- After you've been introduced to someone, you usually say something like, 'Pleased to meet you' or 'My pleasure' and shake hands with a firm grip (although more common among men). When saying goodbye, it **isn't** customary to shake hands again, although some people do. Among friends, it's common for men to kiss ladies on one or both cheeks. Men don't usually kiss or embrace each other, although this depends on their nationality or ethnic origin (or sexual proclivity).

- Americans don't have status or inherited titles (e.g. Sir or Lord) but do defer to people with a professional title which has been earned. These include foreign diplomats (e.g. Sir), members of the Senate (Senator) or Congress (Congressman/Congresswoman), judges, medical doctors and others with a doctorate, military officers (e.g. General, Colonel), professors, priests and other religious ministers (e.g. Father, Rabbi, Reverend).

- If you're invited to dinner, it's customary to take along a small present, e.g. flowers, a plant, chocolates or a bottle of wine (but nothing extravagant or ostentatious). Flowers can be tricky, as to some people carnations mean bad luck, chrysanthemums are for cemeteries and roses signify love. Maybe you should stick to plastic, silk or dried flowers (or a nice bunch of weeds). Wine can also be a problem, particularly if you bring a bottle of Italian plonk and your hosts are wine connoisseurs or members of a religious group that considers alcohol consumption a sin. If you stay with someone as a guest for a few days, it's customary to give your host or hostess a small gift when you leave.

- A wedding or baby 'shower' isn't a communal bath or an invitation to watch baby have its first wash, but a party organised by female friends to shower presents on a prospective bride or new mother. Presents may be of a particular kind, as in a china or linen shower or you may be directed to the gift registry the guest of honour has established at a local department store.

- Although many foreigners have the impression that Americans are relaxed and casual in their dress, they often have strict dress codes. In the puritanical New England states, people usually dress conservatively and more formally than in most other regions. This is particularly true of office workers, who are usually expected to wear a suit and tie (and have short hair). In the east, casual wear (jeans or casual trousers, open-necked shirt) is acceptable for the beach or the garden but is unacceptable in many restaurants. In the south and west, casual dress is more acceptable, in the office and socially, and only the most expensive restaurants insist on ties and formal dress. Many offices have introduced a 'dress-down' day on one day a week (usually Friday), when employees may wear casual attire (although jeans may still be off limits).

  When going anywhere that could be remotely formal (or informal), it's wise to ask in advance what you're expected to wear. Usually when dress is formal, such as evening dress or dinner jacket, this is stated in the invitation (e.g. 'black tie'), and you won't be admitted if you turn up in the wrong attire. On the other hand, at some informal gatherings you may feel out of place if you aren't wearing jeans and a T-shirt. If you're invited to a wedding, enquire about dress (unless you want to stick out like a sore thumb). Black or dark dress is almost always worn at funerals.

- Guests are normally expected to be punctual, with the exception of certain society parties, when late arrival is *de rigueur* (provided you don't arrive after the celebrity guest). It's usual to arrive half an hour to an hour after the official start of a dance. Invitations to cocktail parties or receptions may state 5pm to 7pm, in which case you may arrive at any time between these hours. Dinner invitations are often phrased as 8pm for 8.30pm. This means you should arrive at 8pm for drinks and dinner will be served (usually promptly) at 8.30pm. Anyone who arrives late for dinner or, horror of horrors, doesn't turn up at all, should expect to be excluded from future guest lists, unless he has a good excuse (e.g. he has been murdered or kidnapped). On the other hand, you must **never** arrive early (unless you plan to help with the cooking). You should never be late for funerals, weddings (unless you're the bride, who's always late) or business appointments.

- Some families say grace before meals, so follow your host's example before tucking in. If you're confused by a multitude of knives, forks and spoons, don't panic but just copy what your neighbour is doing (the rule is to start at the outside and work in). If he's another ignorant foreigner, you will at least have some company in the social wilderness to which you will both be consigned.

- You will notice that most Americans don't eat with a knife and fork like 'normal' people. When not eating with their hands they usually eat everything with a fork held in the right hand (unless left-handed). If anything cannot be broken up into bite-size pieces with a fork (e.g. steak), you're permitted to use a knife, but must dispense with it afterwards (knives are generally reserved for killing people!). Even desserts are eaten with a fork, and a spoon is usually for your coffee.

- Don't overstay your welcome. This becomes obvious when your host starts looking at his watch, talking about his early start the next day, yawning, or in desperation, falling asleep.

TIME DIFFERENCE

The 48 continental states of America are divided into four time zones: Eastern Standard Time (EST), Central Standard Time (CST), Mountain Standard Time (MST), and Pacific Standard Time (PST), which are often marked on maps and shown in telephone directories. The difference between local time and Greenwich Mean Time (GMT) is:

Zone	Difference from GMT
EST	Minus 5 hours (includes Atlanta, Boston, Cleveland, Miami, New York, and Washington, DC)
CST	Minus 6 hours (includes Chicago and New Orleans)
MST	Minus 7 hours (includes Denver, Houston and Phoenix)
PST	Minus 8 hours (includes Los Angeles, San Francisco and Seattle)

When it's noon in New York (Eastern), it's 11am in Chicago (Central), 10am in Denver (Mountain) and 9am in Los Angeles (Pacific). Time zone boundaries don't always coincide with state boundaries and ten states have two time zones: North and South Dakota, Kansas, Kentucky, Idaho, Indiana, Nebraska, Oregon, Tennessee and Texas. Alaska has four time zones: Pacific Standard Time (Juneau and Ketchikan), Alaska Standard Time (Anchorage and Fairbanks), Bering time and Yukon time. Hawaii is GMT minus ten hours. When driving from one time zone to another, local time is sometimes indicated by a sign at the roadside. When telephoning someone in a different time zone, bear in mind the time difference, as you may not be terribly popular if you wake someone at 3am.

Daylight Saving Time (DST) is observed in all states except Arizona, Hawaii and parts of Indiana (which can make life confusing for residents). Clocks are put one hour ahead in spring, usually on the last Sunday in March or the first Sunday in April, and one hour back in autumn (fall), usually on the last Sunday in October (remember: spring forward, fall back), the change officially taking effect at 2am local time.

When stating the time, Americans say 'twenty of three' for 'twenty minutes **to** three' or 2.40. Similarly 'twenty after three' is 'twenty minutes **past** three' or 3.20. Times are commonly written with a colon, e.g. 2:40 or 3:20. Americans don't usually use the 24-hour clock and on transport timetables (bus, rail, air) am and pm times are often shown as 'A' or 'P', or pm times may simply be indicated in bold print.

TIPPING

There's a long tradition of tipping in the US, where greasing palms is both an integral part of the American way of life and a social disease (tippititus), and has nothing whatsoever to do with the quality of service. Without tipping the whole economy would grind to a halt, although there's often a thin line between tips and payoffs, a fact of everyday business life in most cities (where everyone has their price). Americans are prodigious and prolific tippers, which **isn't** normally regarded as discretionary. Non-tippers are considered cheap (the ultimate insult to an American) and are treated with contempt, particularly by taxi drivers. Most Americans are shocked by anyone who doesn't tip or who tips too little, and some go to extremes and tip everybody in sight, including air hostesses and theatre attendants. Tipping has become so ingrained that it's generally impossible to get a decent seat at a cabaret or floor show (e.g. in Las Vegas) without bribing the attendant $5 or $10. Even if all other seats are empty, you will end up behind a pillar if you don't cross the attendant's palm with silver. Although it's customary to show your pleasure or displeasure by the size of your tip, most Americans would have to receive atrocious service not to tip at all (most wouldn't dare refuse to tip a taxi driver, irrespective of how tortuous or roundabout their journey).

Many restaurant owners and other employers exploit the practice of tipping by paying starvation wages (the person who delivers your take-away pizza or Chinese meal may get no wages at all), in the knowledge that employees supplement their wages with tips. If you don't tip a waiter, he may not starve (unless the restaurant's food is bad), but he'll certainly struggle to survive on his meagre salary. In general, a service charge isn't included in the bill in restaurants and you're expected to tip the waiter, waitress and bartenders 15 to 20 per cent, depending on the class of establishment. In top class restaurants the 'captain' may also receive 5 per cent of the total bill and the wine waiter (*sommelier*) around $2 for each bottle of wine served. Most people also tip the *maître d'hôtel* (at least $5) if he finds them a seat or arranges a party (often the only way to **get** a seat in a fashionable restaurant is to tip the *maître d'* $10 or $20).

The situation with regard to tipping is anything but clear, however, and it can often be embarrassing (it's surprising that some enterprising American hasn't established a 'tipping counselling service' for foreigners). In restaurants, for example, many bills have 'service not included' printed on them to make sure you leave a tip. However, even when service **is** included in the bill, this doesn't mean that the percentage added for service goes to the staff (if you don't leave a tip and the waiter tips the soup in your lap the next time you go there, you will know why). Don't be bashful about asking whether a tip is expected. Restaurant tips can be included in credit card payments or given as cash. The total on credit card slips is often left blank (even when service is included in the price) to encourage you to leave a tip. Some bills even include separate boxes for gratuities for waiters and captains, but don't forget to fill in the total before signing it. Most restaurant staff prefer you to leave a cash tip, as tips included in credit card payments often aren't passed on to them.

In a bar, you may be presented with the bill after each round of drinks and if you don't tip that could be the last you see of the waiter for the rest of the evening. In some bars (or where you're well known), you can 'run a tab' and pay (pick up the tab) when you leave. Some people place a $5 or $10 bill on the table or bar at the start of a drinking session to ensure they receive good service. As in restaurants, bar staff usually expect 15 to 20 per cent, although tips depend on the class of establishment. Bar staff in a five-star hotel are used to receiving large tips, whereas in a seedy back street bar they aren't.

When using taxis, a tip of 10 to 15 per cent is normal and the fare is usually rounded up to the nearest dollar. Tipping in hotels depends on whether you're staying at The Plaza (where you're expected to tip everyone in sight) or some back street hovel (where no services are provided). Petrol station attendants (who clean your windscreen) and cinema and theatre ushers aren't usually tipped. Fifty cents is generally the lowest tip for anything and $1 is normal for small services. Other typical tips include porters (50 cents to $1 per bag), doormen/bouncers (50 cents to $10, e.g. at a nightclub), chambermaids ($1 to $1.50 per day), hotel room service (20 per cent), toilet attendants (50 cents to $1), sleeping car attendants ($2 to $5, depending on the service), cloakroom attendants (25 cents to $1), valet parking attendants ($1 to $5, depending on the establishment), delivery people ($1 to $5 or $10, depending on the value and size of what was delivered), hairdressers (15 to 20 per cent or $1 or $2 for the washer, cutter and the colourer), and tour guides ($1 or $2).

Most people give the doorman or superintendent of their apartment block a tip (or 'sweetener') for extra services, ranging from 50 cents to $5. It's usually essential to tip your apartment block's handyman (if you want to see him again). Postmen aren't tipped (it would be expensive to tip them every day) but Americans traditionally give them $5 or $10 at Christmas (despite the fact that US postal employees are prohibited from accepting gifts). Christmas is generally a time of giving tips to all and sundry and can be expensive. It's customary to tip all tradespeople who serve you regularly, e.g. your doorman, newspaper boy, parking attendant, hairdresser, laundryman, handyman, etc. The size of a tip depends on how often someone has served you, the quality and friendliness of service, and how rich you are. Generally, tips range from a few dollars up to $20 or more for the superintendent of your apartment block (it pays to be nice to him), which is usually placed inside a Christmas card. If you're unsure who or how much to tip, ask your neighbours, friends or colleagues (who will all tell you something different!).

TOILETS

For some reason Americans find the word 'toilet' distasteful and they use a myriad of 'genteel' terms such as restroom, powder room, washroom, bathroom, ladies' or men's room, and even 'comfort station' to refer to their toilets. When enquiring after a toilet, most people ask for the restroom, bathroom or the men's or ladies' room. Take care when using public toilets, as it isn't always easy to tell from the sign on the door whether it's the ladies' or men's.

One of the biggest problems you may initially encounter is finding a public toilet, as there are few in most cities (e.g. around three in Manhattan, although New York has introduced new pay toilets in recent years). Public toilets can, however, be found in airports, hotels, hospitals, colleges and universities, restaurants, bars, department stores, office buildings (usually in the foyer), and public buildings such as libraries and museums. Most petrol stations have clean toilets and they can also be found at bus and railway stations (although they're often dirty). Toilets in undergrounds are rare and often dangerous and therefore to be avoided.

It isn't always easy to stroll in off the street and use a toilet in a private building, such as an office block, although it helps if you look the part. Bars and restaurants usually try to deter non-customers with intimidating signs such as 'Restrooms for Patrons Only', although you can usually get away with using the toilets in a busy bar and many people use the facilities in large hotels. Some toilets in large hotels and restaurants have an attendant, when it's customary to tip 25 cents to 50 cents, but by law most toilets must be available free of charge.

Some American 'comfort stations' are anything but comfortable. Cubicles in low-life bars and roadside toilets may even be missing doors (usually because derelicts have stolen them for firewood), which can be a bit unsettling when you're desperate to relieve yourself. You cannot always expect to find towels, toilet paper or cleanliness in public toilets. Women are warned not to put their handbags on the floor in a public toilet, as they run the risk of having them stolen (most toilet cubicles have an opening at the bottom of the doors and walls). Toilets in hotel rooms usually have a paper seal showing they've been 'sanitised for your protection', which is simply the American way of saying the toilet bowl has been cleaned (Americans are paranoid about toilet hygiene and cleanliness, which probably explains the lack of public toilets). Many toilets provide nappy (diaper) changing facilities or facilities for nursing mothers (breastfeeding isn't usually performed in public). Many shopping centres have toilets for the disabled, as do airports and major railway stations, although most public toilets for motorists aren't accessible to disabled drivers.

19.

THE AMERICANS

Everybody knows Americans are an eccentric lot, but who are they and what are they really like? Let's take a tongue in cheek, candid and totally prejudiced look at the American people, and hope they forgive my flippancy or that they don't read this chapter (which is why it's hidden away at the back of the book).

The typical American is brash, friendly, competitive, industrious, rude, forthright, impatient, spontaneous, loud, optimistic, conscientious, litigious, patriotic, naive, wealthy, serious, demonstrative, ignorant, unworldly, fun-loving, racist, corrupt, altruistic, a shopaholic, effusive, parochial, dynamic, outrageous, efficient, excessive, virile, garrulous, intense, a religious zealot, ambivalent, helpful, crude, boastful, demanding, an exhibitionist, individualistic, selfish, ebullient, gluttonous, aggressive, a hustler, ambitious, proud, extrovert, flashy, compulsive, humorous, insecure, enthusiastic, greedy, uninhibited, decisive, arrogant, insincere, fickle, innovative, extravagant, pragmatic, vulgar, puritanical, artificial, overweight, unsophisticated, kind, shallow, materialistic, laid-back, entrepreneurial, tasteless, thrusting, insular, energetic, honest, hard-living, unethical, accessible, bigoted, warm, sporting, determined, abrasive, stressed, paranoid, ruthless, polite (except for New Yorkers), conservative, generous, egotistical, vain, ostentatious, promiscuous, neurotic, narcissistic, approachable, prudish, exuberant, compassionate, violent, intransigent, blunt, dramatic, hyperbolic, brusque, superficial, predatory and a baseball fan.

You may have noticed that the above list contains 'a few' contradictions (as does life in the US), which is hardly surprising, as there's no such thing as a typical American and few people conform to the popular stereotype (whatever that is). The US is the most cosmopolitan country in the world and a nation of foreigners (except for a few native Americans) who have as much in common with one other as Eskimos have with Africans or Mongolians with Europeans. However, despite its diverse racial mix, the US **isn't** always the popularly depicted melting pot, but a potpourri of ethnic splinter groups often living entirely separate lives with their own neighbourhoods, shops, clubs, newspapers, and television (TV) and radio stations.

Americans pride themselves on their lack of class-consciousness and don't have the same caste distinctions and pretensions common in the old world. There's no sense of class as portrayed by the eternal struggle between the bosses and workers in some European countries. In the US, workers don't want to do away with the wealthy – on the contrary, they adore the rich and famous and simply want to get a piece of the action (they care more about opportunity than equality). Americans have almost unlimited social mobility, and class isn't your birthright, but something you acquire (in the US you are whatever you decide to be).

However, the US is far from being a classless society and status is as important there as it is anywhere else, if not more so. Class is usually based on your profession and position (not to mention your salary), which has led to the executive, management and professional business classes. One of the most common manifestations of class distinction is the division between white and blue-collar workers. Many things are classified as white or blue-collar, including neighbourhoods, jobs, clubs, sports, pastimes, restaurants, bars and shopping centres. A wife automatically acquires the same status as her husband (unless she has a better job, and more money) and is accorded the same deference (women are generally far more class and status conscious than men).

If there's an American class system, it consists of old (usually pre-World War I) and new money (mostly post World War II). The American establishment is predominantly Anglo-American and made up of long-settled families with pots of old money, who take it for granted that everybody else is rich. While it's possible to convert new money into old, it's rare. However, although a few pretentious clubs and societies are barred to the *nouveaux riches*, new money (if you have enough of it) opens almost any door in the US. The fastest way for aspiring social climbers to gain entry to American society is to donate a small fortune to fashionable charities or to establish a foundation in their own name.

Americans are usually sociable and, when not bent on mugging or killing you, are **intensely** friendly and agreeable, although some foreigners are suspicious of the American propensity for instant friendship, which they interpret as insincere and shallow. Newcomers are invariably warmly welcomed with a firm, dry handshake (wet and feeble handshakes are for wimps and foreigners) and Americans ask and remember your name and use it often, which can be embarrassing when you haven't got a clue who they are! Americans yearn to be loved by everyone and popularity is a sign of success and hugely important. However, in the major cities, Americans can be as unfriendly and aloof as anyone, and it's common for city folks only to be on nodding terms with their neighbours.

Americans don't stand on ceremony and usually insist that you call them by their first name on first meetings. Titles are seldom used except when addressing public officials and politicians (although what they're called behind their backs is something else!). Most Americans are extremely polite and police officers are generally addressed as 'sir' or 'officer', especially when they're holding a gun or truncheon! Americans are forthright in their opinions and can be insensitive in their interrogation of strangers, which can be unsettling. They're uncomfortable with shyness and diffidence and expect foreigners to be equally candid (although criticisms of the US aren't well tolerated when coming from foreigners). Some Americans are likely to ask you straight out what you earn, why you aren't married or don't have any children, and whether you're gay. Nobody **ever** accused Americans of being bashful.

If there's one single motivation uniting all Americans, it's their desire to be rich and famous (I want it **all** NOW!). It's the American Dream to be rich (Americans live on dreams, particularly rags-to-riches dreams) and money is openly admired and everyone's favourite topic. Many Americans will do (almost) anything for money, which is the country's national language (along with sport). To be considered seriously rich in the US, you must be fabulously wealthy with a fleet of gold-plated Cadillacs, luxury yacht, private jet and a mansion 'on the hill' with scores of servants.

Americans are the greatest consumers in the history of the world and their primary occupation is spending money – when not spending money they're thinking about spending it. In the US, everything and everyone is a commodity to be bought and sold for dollars (Americans believe every man has his price). Displaying the correct 'labels' is vital, as your status is determined by what you wear, drive, inhabit or own. Status is everything to Americans, who buy more status symbols than any other nation and believe there's no point in buying anything expensive if it isn't instantly recognisable and desirable. Ostentatious consumption is the order of the day (if you've got it, flaunt it!) and modesty is un-American and to be condemned. Most Americans can never have enough money (they firmly believe that anyone who thinks money cannot buy happiness has simply been shopping in the wrong places!).

Size is everything and bigger is **always** better; big cars, big buildings, big breasts, big homes, big butts, big jobs, big pay cheques, big cities, big football players, big Macs, big guns, big stores – everything is big (most things in the US come in three sizes: big, huge and gigantic!). The US is a land of GIANTS, where everyone is twice as BIG and three times as LOUD as 'normal' people (and not just Texans). To Americans, size and quality are inextricably linked and your success in life is illustrated by the size of your office and the number of zeros on the end of your salary (Americans are impressed by numbers). Likewise new, which **always** equates to improved, is infinitely better than old in the American throwaway society. Americans are continually 'trashing' or trading in last year's model, whether it's their car, home or spouse.

When an American buys a new toy or car, friends and acquaintances are summoned from miles around to admire it and hear what it cost (provided, of course, that it was expensive). Money is the measure of your success and wealth announces that you're one of life's winners (as Americans are fond of saying "If you're so smart, how come you ain't rich?"), although inherited wealth is less praiseworthy than a fortune amassed by a self-made person (stealing is acceptable, provided you aren't caught). Americans not only believe that you **can** have everything, but that you owe it to yourself to have it all; beauty, education, fame, health, intelligence, love, money, etc. – if they cannot have it all, most Americans will settle for money. The best of everything is every American's birthright, and they will borrow themselves into bankruptcy if they have to, to provide the best of everything for themselves and their families.

Unlike many foreigners, Americans have no ambition to retire as soon as they have enough money (they **never** have enough) – they cannot bear the thought of someone else getting a bigger slice of the pie while they're idle. Americans love winners (losers are instantly consigned to the trash can of history) and being on the winning team isn't just everything – it's the **only** thing (in the US, you aren't allowed to admit defeat until you're dead – not that rich Americans believe in dying.

Americans are raised with a 'can do' mentality and to believe that they can achieve anything, from world champion horseshoe pitcher to President of the United States of America. They think that if they dedicate enough energy they can have a bigger house, more intelligent children, and an option on immortality (preferably in California or Florida). Most Americans have a rose-tinted view of the world, where provided you rise early, work hard and fight fairly, everything will turn out fine. America peddles dreams, hopes and lifestyles, where life's a giant candy bar and all you've got to do is take a BIG bite!

The American attitude towards sex is indicative of their philosophy that everything must be available on demand. Sex is open, available and free for the taking (just do it!). Like their obsession with all good things in life, the Americans' sexual appetite is insatiable (they even live in condoms) and many just cannot get enough of it. Most Americans (apart from the few oddballs who would rather watch TV, play golf or shop) wish they could spend more time making love, although not necessarily with their wives or girlfriends. Americans analyse their sexual performance to death and every stroke is examined, reviewed and evaluated (aided by a torrent of books, articles and TV programmes advising people how to enjoy better sex). Americans have few inhibitions about discussing sex and do so incessantly.

Somewhat surprising is the sharp contradiction between the official puritanical attitude towards sex and the facts of life. The taboo concerning topless and nude sunbathing and showing too much bare flesh in public (and on TV, where Americans make love with their clothes on) contrasts starkly with many Americans' casual attitude towards sex, which has led to epidemics of illegitimacy, AIDS and divorce (and politicians getting caught with their trousers down!). Americans are much more at home with violence than they are with nudity. However, contrary to the popular image of sex-mad Americans, according to some surveys the US is a hotbed of marital bliss and most husbands profess that they would refuse an offer of $1million from someone who wanted to sleep with their wife (if you believe that . . .).

Life in the US is lived in the fast lane and if you aren't on the fast track you had better move over and let someone else make the running. It's no coincidence that the US invented fast food, as life is far too important to waste time eating (time is money and money is everything!). Life in cities is lived at a frenetic pace, where stress and pressure are unremitting and yuppies (young urban professionals devoted to their careers and status) compete vigorously to fashion their first million dollars (or coronary). Fast is one of the US's favourite buzz words; fast cars, fast living, fast women/men and fast bucks are all extremely popular. The only way for a newcomer to cope with the US is to sit back, relax and let it flow over him.

Although the American Dream isn't always what it's cracked up to be, the US remains the supreme land of opportunity. Nowhere else on earth is it possible to become seriously rich in such a short time. However, although you can rise rapidly, the route from the penthouse to the poorhouse can be equally swift. When you're down (or on the way down) you're a schmuck and on your own. 'Friends' will stop calling and may even cross the road to avoid you – nobody wants to be tainted with failure, which many fear is contagious. Failure is even more shameful than poverty, as it's assumed to be your own fault and nothing to do with luck (the buck stops with you!).

Patriotism (or nationalism) is like a religion in the US, both of which are branches of show business. Most Americans are deeply patriotic and demonstrate their love of their country through their reverence and allegiance to the Stars and Stripes (Old Glory!). The flag is the nation's symbol and flies over all government offices, including post offices, and many businesses use it to demonstrate that they're more patriotic than their competitors. Theoretically, the bigger the flag, the more patriotic you are, which is why the White House and used car dealers (both of whose integrity can use any help it can get) fly the biggest flags of all! The US flag is held in high regard and must never be ridiculed. Flag desecration is a capital offence and it mustn't be left in the dark or be allowed to become soiled, wet or fall on the ground. (Although the sorry state of the many US flags flying on SUV aerials since '9/11' doesn't count as desecration apparently.) After a spate of flag-burning in the '70s, the US Supreme Court surprisingly declared that a citizen has the right to burn the flag, although most Americans believe it's tantamount to treason (it certainly isn't wise in public unless you have a death wish!).

The flag is paraded before every sports event, no matter how small or unimportant, and the national anthem (Star-Spangled Banner) is played and sung by the crowd. At major events, such as football's Super Bowl, a famous personality is employed to sing the anthem and Americans stand to attention, remove their hats and put their right hands on their hearts, while tears fill their eyes. American schoolchildren pledge an oath of allegiance to the flag every day: "I pledge allegiance to the flag of the United States of America and to the Republic for which it stands – one nation, under God, indivisible, with liberty and justice for all" (Amen). Americans wrap themselves in the flag like no other nation and during a recent presidential election the House of Representatives even voted to salute the flag every morning (American politicians will do **anything** to get re-elected!). However, despite their nationalism, Americans aren't xenophobic, which would be highly hypocritical considering they're mostly foreigners themselves.

Some cynical foreigners believe that the US's patriotism is a substitute for history and tradition. After all, when your nationhood goes back only 'a few years' you need something to provide a sense of identity and to remind immigrants that they're no longer Irish, Italians, Polish or whatever. Americans are bombarded with patriotic messages, and any politician who wants to be elected must take the sacred icons of God (who's naturally an American), the flag and motherhood seriously. Americans fervently believe that the US is the promised land, the most favoured nation (not a mere country) and unquestionably the greatest place in the world – and what's more it was planned that way by God (if they did away with all the lawyers and politicians and threw away all the guns, many foreigners might even be inclined to agree with them). Americans are continually reminded of their great and wonderful nation (low self-esteem isn't an American trait) by advertisers, politicians and anyone trying to sell something.

Like many democratic countries, the US is a victim of its political system and politicians. In the US, election to public office depends on how much TV time you can afford, whether you make the most persuasive TV advertisements, and your camera appeal. At election times, you're subjected to the most offensive of all advertisements, the negative political advertisement, where politicians dish the dirt on their opponents (nobody fights dirtier than American politicians). There's no limit to the amount of air-time candidates can buy and some spend millions of dollars to get elected. However, if the American political system produces the best politicians money can buy, it proves that contrary to popular American philosophy money **cannot** buy everything. It will come as no surprise to learn that the vast majority of Americans distrust their politicians and hold them in low esteem.

Americans think they're (or should be) the role model for the rest of the world and the collapse of communism and the 'winning of the cold war' was seen as a tribute to the US and American values. They feel aggrieved when ungrateful foreigners don't share their good opinion of themselves (the US's warm and admiring sense of itself doesn't export). Many Americans would be surprised to learn that, on the contrary, many foreigners see the US as the prime example of the sort of mess you can get into if you aren't careful! Most Americans know nothing about the wider world (many couldn't even place **their own** country on the globe) and care even less about what happens beyond their shores (to most Americans the world ends at the US border). War has been something fought 'over there' since before the beginning of the last century, even those wars the US has started. Home-grown conflicts threaten the long-term wellbeing of the US, not least the rapid growth of a permanent under-class (the African-American and Hispanic, uneducated, under-skilled inhabitants of inner-city ghettos). There has long been a breakdown of moral and spiritual values and an erosion of the family unit, and many Americans are no longer prepared to work to save a marriage or even take responsibility for their children or ageing parents.

Crime (although falling) remains the fastest growing sector of the economy, despite the ever-increasing number of police officers and bulging prisons. Law enforcement and crime prevention are a bottomless pit and second only to the Pentagon in devouring the nation's resources. Crime and terrorism are the most serious threats to Americans' rights and freedoms and the biggest problem facing the nation. The high crime rate has hardened attitudes towards criminals, who many believe get a better deal than their victims. The vast majority of Americans believe in capital punishment and a third of them would gladly pull the switch to fry a convicted murderer. Americans are becoming increasingly intolerant of anyone and anything they disapprove of, including smoking, gays, gambling, sex, lawyers, politicians, feminists, immigrants, street people, abortion and alcohol. Oddly enough, most Americans approve of increasingly intrusive measures taken to improve 'security' from detaining potential terrorists without charges or access to an attorney to ever more intimate pat-downs and searches at US airports.

Although racial minorities theoretically enjoy a high degree of protection against discrimination, many find it difficult to get well-paid jobs, or indeed any job at all (despite 'affirmative action'). Unemployment rates are twice as high for African-Americans as for whites, and Hispanics fare only slightly better. African-American and Hispanic job opportunities have been further eroded by the flow of immigrants from Asia in recent years, which has seen the fiercely ambitious and hard-working Asians scrambling up the ladder over the heads of other ethnic groups. Although African-Americans have made tremendous strides towards equality since the '60s, they still have a long (long) way to go to compete on equal terms with whites.

In no other western country is there such a stark contrast between rich and poor (the fabulously wealthy and those living in grinding poverty) as in the US, where 1 per cent of households own over 40 per cent of the wealth (most of which is inherited). That the wealthiest nation the world has ever known, as well as the most liberal and democratic, should harbour so much poverty, hunger and homelessness is a national disgrace. Like the ruling classes in many developing countries, many Americans turn a blind eye to poverty in their own backyard and firmly believe that giving the poor handouts prevents them from earning an honest living. Rich Americans have little sympathy with poverty, which they see as un-American (the poor get what they deserve!). However, without a dramatic improvement in education standards and job opportunities for the poor and underprivileged, their ability to lift **themselves** (without handouts) out of the poverty trap is receding year by year.

To be fair (who the hell's trying to be fair?), Americans do have a 'few' good points; they're kinder, more generous and more hospitable than almost any other people. Their benevolence is legendary and American philanthropists are the world's most generous. The US produces the majority of the world's leading sportsmen and women (admittedly many in sports nobody else plays) and also leads the world in most artistic fields. Despite the occasional rumours of the US's imminent economic collapse, it remains the fount of invention and innovation and is the most technologically advanced and productive nation in the world. It also produces the world's best hamburgers and ice cream and has one of the world's highest standards of living, while at the same time enjoying the lowest cost of living in the western world (you don't **need** to earn a fortune to live well in the US).

Despite the doom-laden predictions from some quarters, most Americans have extraordinary faith in themselves and eternal optimism for the future, firmly believing there's always a bright dawn ahead. To an American, **nothing** is impossible. In the US, the competitive spirit is paramount and when their backs are to the wall they invariably come up trumps. Although immigrants may criticise some aspects of American life, few ever consider leaving and most are proud to call themselves Americans. In fact, most immigrants appreciate the fruits of the American way of life even more than many 'early' Americans, who don't realise how fortunate they are to inhabit such a beautiful, bounteous and wonderful country. No other nation provides such endless opportunities and has such an irrepressible and exciting lifestyle. For sheer vitality and love of life, the US has no equals and is, above all, the ultimate land in which to turn your dreams into reality.

Finally, one last tip for success. Newcomers must take care **never** to criticise the US or Americans; taking cheap shots at honest, hard-working lawyers and politicians is in particularly bad taste (but fun).

God bless America!

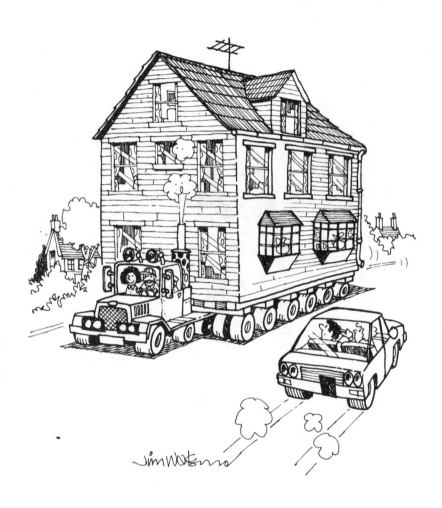

20.

MOVING HOUSE OR
LEAVING AMERICA

When moving house or leaving the US, there are many things to be considered and a 'million' people to be informed. The checklists below will make the task easier and with luck help prevent an ulcer or nervous breakdown (only divorce or a bereavement cause more stress than moving house), provided of course you don't leave everything to the last minute. (See also **Moving House** on page 134 and **Relocation Services** on page 126)

MOVING HOUSE

When moving house **within** the US, particularly when changing states, the following items should be considered:

- Give notice to your employer, if applicable.

- If you live in rented accommodation, you must give your landlord the necessary notice, as specified in your lease. If you don't give your landlord sufficient notice, you're required to pay the rent until the end of your lease or for the full notice period.

- If you aren't moving into permanent accommodation, book temporary accommodation and have it confirmed in writing.

- Inform the following:

  - Your employer (if not giving notice);

  - Your utility companies, e.g. electricity, gas and water companies. Make sure that any security deposits are returned if you're moving to a new area.

  - Your telephone company, preferably at least 14 days in advance. If you're moving home and remaining within the same local code area you may be able to retain your existing number. If not, you can often have your calls automatically forwarded to your new number, or have an announcement put on your old line giving callers your new number. Don't forget to have your telephone line disconnected when moving; otherwise the new owners or tenants will be able to make calls at your expense.

  - Your insurance companies (for example health, car, homeowner's, life, etc.); banks, savings and loans, stockbroker and other financial institutions; credit card, charge card and loan companies; lawyer and accountant; and local businesses where you have accounts. Make sure you have valid insurance if you're moving to another state.

  - Your doctor, dentist and other health practitioners. Health records should be transferred to your new doctor and dentist, if applicable. Contact your vet for information and health records for your pets, and any transportation requirements.

  - Your family's schools. If applicable, arrange for schooling in your new community. Try to give a term's notice and obtain a copy of any relevant school reports or records from your children's current schools.

- Give or send all regular correspondents your new address and telephone number. These may include subscriptions, social and sports clubs, church and other organisations, professional and trade journals, and friends and relatives.

- Arrange to have your post redirected by the post office (see **Change of Address** on page 155).

- If you're moving to another state and have a US driving licence or a US registered car, inform your new state's Motor Vehicle Department as soon as possible after moving (see page 255). Inform your motoring organisation (see page 295) of your new address.

- Return any library books and other borrowed or rented items.

- Book a moving company (see page 134) well in advance to transport your furniture and personal effects to your new home. If you have only a few items of furniture to move, you may prefer to do your own move, in which case you may need to rent a vehicle or trailer (e.g. 'U-Haul'). Keep a record of all moving expenses for tax purposes.

- Arrange for a cleaning and/or painting (decorating) company for rented accommodation, if necessary (see page 130).

- If renting, contact your landlord or the letting agency to have your security deposit returned (with interest, if applicable).

- Cancel newspaper and other regular home deliveries.

- If necessary, arrange for someone to look after your children and pets during the move.

- **Ask yourself (again): 'Is it really worth all this trouble?'**

The United States Postal Service produces a useful *Mover's Guide*, regularly updated and including a mail forwarding form (the USPS forwards mail to your new address free for up to 12 months), change of address cards, an information booklet and some junk mail. The *Mover's Guide* is available online on the USPS website (🖳 http://moversguide.usps.com). The USPS even sends you a Welcome Kit 'with valuable information about your new community' – you've guessed it, more junk mail!

LEAVING AMERICA

Before leaving the US permanently or for an indefinite period, the following items should be considered **in addition** to those listed above under **Moving House**:

- Check that your family's passports are valid and aren't out of date.

- Check whether any requirements (e.g. visas, permits or inoculations) are necessary for entry into your country of destination by contacting the local embassy or consulate in the US. An exit permit or visa isn't required to leave the US, but if you have a green card (Alien Registration Receipt Card), you may need to surrender it if you're leaving the US permanently (see page 77).

- If you're shipping household and personal effects, find out the exact procedure from the local embassy of your destination country. Forms may need to be completed before arrival. If you've been living in the US for less than a year, you're required to re-export all imported personal effects, including furniture and vehicles (if you sell them you should pay duty). Contact an international shipping company (see page 134) well in advance and arrange shipment of your furniture and personal effects.

- Notify any utility companies well in advance if you need to have security deposits returned.

- You must pay your federal taxes and obtain a sailing or departure permit from the IRS to confirm this before leaving the US (see page 383). If you're leaving permanently and are a member of a company pension plan (or have a personal pension plan), you should receive a lump sum payment in lieu of a pension (see page 336). Contact your company personnel office, local IRS office or pension company for information.

- Arrange to sell anything you aren't taking with you (car, furniture, etc.). If you have a US registered car which you're exporting, check the procedure and cost (e.g. shipping, tax and import duty) of exporting it and make arrangements for its shipment.

- Sell your house, apartment or other property, or arrange to rent it through a friend or an agent (see **Chapter 5**).

- Depending on your destination, your pets may require inoculations or may be required to go into quarantine for a period (see page 522). Make arrangements well in advance. If you're travelling by air, you must make arrangements for their shipment.

- Arrange health, travel and other insurance as necessary (see **Chapter 13**).

- Depending on your destination, arrange health and dental check-ups for your family before leaving the US. Obtain a copy of your family's health and dental records, and a statement from your health insurance company stating your present level of cover.

- Settle any loan, lease or instalment contracts and pay all outstanding bills (allow plenty of time, as some companies may be slow to respond).

- Check whether you're entitled to a rebate on your car registration and car and other insurance. Obtain a letter from your car insurance company stating your number of years' no-claims bonus (good-driver discount).

- Check whether you require an international driver's permit or a translation of your driving licence for your country of destination or any countries you pass through.

- Give friends and business associates a temporary address and telephone number where you can be contacted abroad.

- If you're travelling by air, allow yourself plenty of time to get to the airport, check your luggage in, and clear security and immigration (see page 105).

● Buy a copy of *Living and Working in ********* published by Survival Books (see page 587) before leaving America. If we haven't published it yet, drop us a line and we'll get started on it right away!

Have a safe journey!

APPENDICES

APPENDIX A: USEFUL ADDRESSES

Embassies & Consulates

A selection of foreign embassy addresses is shown below. In addition to their embassies in Washington DC, many countries have consulates in a number of other US cities (see local telephone directories). Links to most embassy Internet sites can be found at 🖳 www.firstgov.gov. (Enter 'foreign embassies & consulates' in the search function.)

Algeria: Kalorama Road, NW, Washington, DC 20008 (☎ 202-265-2800).

Antigua & Barbuda: 3216 New Mexico Avenue, NW, Washington, DC 20016 (☎ 202-362-5122).

Argentina: 1600 New Hampshire Avenue, NW, Washington, DC 20009 (☎ 202-939-6400).

Australia: 1601 Massachusetts Avenue, NW, Washington, DC 20036 (☎ 202-797-3000).

Austria: International Court, NW, Washington, DC 20008-3027 (☎ 202-895-6700).

Bahamas: Massachusetts Avenue, NW, Washington, DC 20008 (☎ 202-319-2660).

Barbados: 2144 Wyoming Avenue, NW, Washington, DC 20008 (☎ 202-939-9200).

Belgium: Garfield Street, NW, Washington, DC 20008 (☎ 202-333-6900).

Brazil: 3006 Massachusetts Avenue, NW, Washington, DC 20008 (☎ 202-238-2700).

Bulgaria: 1621 22nd Street, NW, Washington, DC 20008 (☎ 202-387-0174/0365).

Canada: Pennsylvania Avenue, NW, Washington, DC 20001 (☎ 202-682-1740).

Chile: 1732 Massachusetts Avenue, NW, Washington, DC 20036 (☎ 202-785-1746).

China: 2300 Connecticut Avenue, NW, Washington, DC 20008 (☎ 202-328-2500/2501).

Costa Rica: 2114 S Street, NW, Washington, DC 20008 (☎ 202-234-2945/2946).

Cyprus: 2211 R Street, NW, Washington, DC 20008 (☎ 202-462-5772/0873).

Congo (Democratic Republic) (formerly Zaire): 1800 New Hampshire Avenue, NW, Washington, DC 20009 (☎ 202-234-7690).

Czech Republic: 3900 Spring of Freedom Street, NW, Washington, DC 20008 (☎ 202-274-9100).

Cuba: 2630 16th Street, NW, Washington, DC 20009 (☎ 202-797-8518).

Denmark: 3200 Whitehaven Street, NW, Washington, DC 20008 (☎ 202-234-4300).

Ecuador: 2535 15th Street, NW, Washington, DC 20009 (☎ 202-234-7200).

Egypt: 3521 International Court, NW, Washington, DC 20008 (☎ 202-895-5400).

Finland: 3301 Massachusetts Avenue, NW, Washington, DC 20008 (☎ 202-298-5800).

France: 4101 Reservoir Road, NW, Washington, DC 20007 (☎ 202-944-6000).

Germany: 4645 Reservoir Road, NW, Washington, DC 20007 (☎ 202-298-8140).

Greece: 2221 Massachusetts Avenue, NW, Washington, DC 20008 (☎ 202-939-1300).

Hungary: 3910 Shoemaker Street, NW, Washington, DC 20008 (☎ 202-364-8218).

Iceland: 15th Street, NW, Suite 1200, Washington, DC 20005 (☎ 202-265-6653–6655).

India: 2107 Massachusetts Avenue, NW, Washington, DC 20008 (☎ 202-939-7000).

Iran: Wisconsin Avenue, NW, Washington, DC 20007 (☎ 202-965-4990).

Ireland: 2234 Massachusetts Avenue, NW, Washington, DC 20008 ((202-462-3939).

Israel: International Drive, NW, Washington, DC 20008 (☎ 202-364-5500).

Italy: 3000 Whitehaven Street, NW, Washington, DC 20008 (☎ 202-612-4400).

Jamaica: 1520 New Hampshire Avenue,, Washington, DC 20036 (☎ 202-452-0660).

Japan: 2520 Massachusetts Avenue, NW, Washington, DC 20008 (☎ 202-238-6700).

Jordan: 3504 International Drive, NW, Washington, DC 20008 (☎ 202-966-2664).

Kenya: 2249 R Street, NW, Washington, DC 20008 (☎ 202-387-6101).

Korea: 2450 Massachusetts Avenue, NW, Washington, DC 20008 (☎ 202-939-5600).

Luxembourg: 2200 Massachusetts Avenue, NW, Washington, DC 20008 (☎ 202-265-4171).

Malaysia: International Court. NW, Washington, DC 20008 (☎ 202-572-9700).

Malta: 2017 Connecticut Avenue, NW, Washington, DC 20008 (☎ 202-462-3611/3612).

Mexico: 1911 Pennsylvania Avenue, NW, Washington, DC 20006 (☎ 202-728-1600).

Morocco: 1601 21st Street, NW, Washington, DC 20009 (☎ 202-462-7979).

Netherlands: 4200 Linnean Avenue, NW, Washington, DC 20008 (☎ 202-244-5300).

New Zealand: 37 Observatory Circle, NW, Washington, DC 20008 (☎ 202-328-4800).

Nigeria: International Court, NW, Washington, DC 20036 (☎ 202-986-8400).

Norway: 2720 34th Street, NW, Washington, DC 20008 (☎ 202-333-6000).

Pakistan: 2315 Massachusetts Avenue, NW, Washington, DC 20008 (☎ 202-243-6500).

Peru: 1700 Massachusetts Avenue, NW, Washington, DC 20036 (☎ 202-833-9860).

Philippines: 1600 Massachusetts Avenue, NW, Washington, DC 20036 (☎ 202-467-9300/9363).

Poland: 2640 16th Street, NW, Washington, DC 20009 (☎ 202-234-3800).

Portugal: 2125 Kalorama Road, NW, Washington, DC 20008 (☎ 202-328-8610).

Romania: 23rd Street, NW, Washington, DC 20008 (☎ 202-232-3694).

Russia: 2650 Wisconsin Avenue, NW, Washington, DC 20007 (☎ 202-298-5700).

St. Kitts and Nevis: 3216 New Mexico Avenue, NW, Washington, DC 20016 (☎ 202-686-2636).

St. Lucia: 3216 New Mexico Avenue, NW, Washington, DC 20017 (☎ 202-364-6792).

St. Vincent and the Grenadines: 3216 New Mexico Avenue, NW, Washington, DC 20016 (☎202-364-6730).

Saudi Arabia: New Hampshire Avenue, NW, Washington, DC 20037 (☎ 202-342-3800).

Singapore: 3501 International Place, NW, Washington, DC 20008 (☎ 202-537-3100).

South Africa: Massachusetts Avenue, NW, Washington, DC 20008 (☎ 202-232-4400).

Spain: Pennsylvania Avenue, NW, Washington, DC 20037 (☎ 202-452-0100).

Sweden: 1501 M Street, NW, Washington, DC 20005 (☎ 202-467-2600).

Switzerland: Cathedral Avenue, NW, Washington, DC 20008 (☎ 202-745-7900).

Thailand: 1024 Wisconsin Avenue NW, Suite 401, Washington, DC 20007 (☎ 202-944-3600).

Trinidad and Tobago: 1708 Massachusetts Avenue, NW, Washington, DC 20036 (☎ 202-467-6490).

Tunisia: 1515 Massachusetts Avenue, NW, Washington, DC 20005 (☎ 202-862-1850).

Turkey: 2525 Massachusetts Avenue, NW, Washington, DC 20008 (☎ 202-612-6700).

United Arab Emirates: 3522 International Court. NW, Washington, DC 20008 (☎ 202-243-2400).

United Kingdom: 3100 Massachusetts Avenue, NW, Washington, DC 20008 (☎ 202-588-6500).

Uruguay: 1913 I Street, NW, Washington, DC 20006 (☎ 202-331-1313).

Venezuela: 30th Street, NW, Washington, DC 20007 (☎ 202-342-2214).

Vietnam: 1233 20th Street, NW, Suite 400, Washington, DC 20036 (☎ 202-861-0737).

Yugoslavia: 2134 Kalorama Road, Washington, DC 20008 (☎ 202-332-0333).

Zimbabwe: 1608 New Hampshire Avenue, NW, Washington, DC 20009 (☎ 202-332-7100).

Government Departments

Information about the federal government is available from the Federal Information Center via state and regional toll-free telephone numbers (see your local telephone book or ask information) or by contacting the Federal Information Center, PO Box 600, Cumberland, MD 21502 (☎ 1-800-FED-INFO, 🖥 www.FirstGov.gov), whose Internet site has links to most government department sites.

Department of Agriculture: 1400 Independence Avenue SW, Washington, DC 20250 (🖥 www.usda.gov).

Department of Commerce: 1401 Constitution Avenue NW, Washington, DC 20230 (☎ 202-482-4883, 🖥 www.commerce.gov).

Department of Defense: (☎ 703-697-5737, 🖳 www.defenselink.mil).

Department of Education: 400 Maryland Avenue, SW, Washington, DC 20202 (☎ 202-872-5327, 🖳 www.ed.gov).

Department of Energy: 1000 Independence Avenue, SW, Washington, DC 20585 (☎ 1-800-dial-DOE, 🖳 www.energy.gov).

Department of Health and Human Services: 200 Independence Avenue, SW, Washington, DC 20201 (☎ 1-877-696-6775, 🖳 www.hhs.gov).

Department of Homeland Security: Washington, DC 20528 (☎ 202-282-8000, 🖳 www.dhs.gov).

Department of Housing and Urban Development: 451 7th Street, SW, Washington, DC 20410 (☎ 202-708-1112, 🖳 www.hud.gov).

Department of the Interior: 1849 C Street, NW, Washington, DC 20240 (☎ 202-208-3100, 🖳 www.doi.gov).

Department of Justice: 950 Pennsylvania Avenue NW, Washington, DC 20530 (☎ 202-514-2000, 🖳 www.usdoj.gov).

Department of Labor: 200 Constitution Avenue, NW, Washington, DC 20210 (☎ 1-866-4-USA-DOL, 🖳 www.dol.gov).

Department of State: 2201 C Street, NW, Washington, DC 20520 (☎ 202-647-4000, 🖳 www.state.gov).

Department of Transportation: 400 7th Street, SW, Washington, DC 20590 (☎ 202-366-4000, 🖳 www.dot.gov).

Department of the Treasury: 1500 Pennsylvania Avenue NW, Washington, DC 20220 (☎202-622-2000, 🖳 www.ustreas.gov).

Department of Veterans' Affairs: 810 Vermont Avenue NW, Washington, DC 20420 (☎ 202-273-5400, 🖳 www.va.gov).

Internal Revenue Service: 500 N. Capitol St. NW, Washington, DC 20221 (☎ 800-829-1040, 🖳 www.irs.gov).

Social Security Administration: 6401 Security Blvd., Baltimore, Maryland 21235-0001 (☎ 800-772-1213, 🖳 www.ssa.gov).

Publications

American Holiday & Life: PO Box 604, Hemel Hempstead, Herts, HP1 3SR, UK.

Essentially America Magazine: 120–126 Lavender Avenue, Mitcham, Surrey, UK (☎ 020-8646 5389).

Going USA: Outbound Newspapers, 1 Commercial Road, Eastbourne, East Sussex, BN21 3XQ, UK (☎ 01323-412001).

International Property Magazine: 2a Station Road, Gidea Park, Romford, Essex, RM2 6DA, UK (☎ 01708-450784).

International Property Tribune: Welbeck House, High Street, Guildford, Surrey, GU1 3JF, UK (☎ 01483-455110).

Overseas Property News: E.W. Publicity, 15 King Street West, Stockport, Cheshire, SK3 0DT, UK.

Private Villas (Rentals): 52 High Street, Henley-in-Arden, Solihull, West Midlands, B95 5BR, UK (☎ 01564-794011).

Resident Abroad: Subscriptions Department, PO Box 461, Bromley, BR2 9WP, UK (☎ 020-8402-8485).

World of Property: Overseas Property Match, 532 Kingston Road, Raynes Park, London, SW20 8DT, UK (☎ 020-8542 9088).

APPENDIX B: FURTHER READING

There are many useful reference books for anyone seeking general information about the US, including the *World Almanac & Book of Facts* (Primedia Reference) and *The Time Almanac* (Time), which can be accessed online (💻 www.infoplease.com). The ultimate reference guides to US government experts and information are *Information USA* by Mathew Leasko (Viking/Penguin Books) and the *Arco Blue Pages USA*, containing 25,000 government and public service telephone numbers nationwide. The US government publishes a wealth of books, posters, pamphlets and maps available from government book shops in major cities or the US Government Printing Office, Mail Stop: SDE, 732 N. Capitol St. NW, Washington, DC 20401 (☎ 202-512-1530 or 888-293-6498 toll free). See also **Consumers' Organisations** on page 499.

In the lists on the following pages, the publication title is followed by the name of the author(s) and the publisher's name (in brackets). Books prefixed with an asterisk (*) are recommended by the author.

Tourist Guides

Berlitz Country Guide USA (John Wiley & Sons)

*Birnbaum's United States (Houghton Mifflin)

*The Rough Guide to California (Rough Guides Ltd.)

Crossing America (National Geographic Society)

*Fodor's USA (Fodor's Travel Publications)

*Let's Go USA (Let's Go Publications)

The Moneywise Guide to North America (BUNAC)

*New York: The Rough Guide (Rough Guides Ltd)

*The Time Out's New York Guide to Eating and Drinking (Time Out Publishing)

*The Rough Guide to the USA (Rough Guides Ltd)

Visitor's Guide USA (Moorland Publishing Co.)

Travel Literature

*Alistair Cooke's America (Weidenfield Nicolson Illustrated)

*Blue Highways, William Least Heat Moon (Pimlico)

Going to Miami: Exiles, Tourists and Refugees in the New America, David Rieff (University Press of Florida)

*The Great Divide, Studs Terkel (Hamish Hamilton)

*Hunting Mr. Heartbreak, Jonathan Raban (Picador)

In God's Country, Douglas Kennedy (Harper Collins)

*L.A. Lore, Stephen Brook (Sinclair-Stevenson)

Los Angeles: Capital of the Third World, David Rieff (Pocket Books)

*The Lost Continent, Bill Bryson (Black Swan)

*New York Days, New York Nights, Stephen Brook (Picador)

*Notes from a Big Country, US Title: I'm a Stranger Here Myself, Bill Bryson (Black Swan)

*The State of America, Trevor Fishlock (Faber & Faber)

Storm Country, Pete Davis (Heinemann)

*A Walk up Fifth Avenue, Bernard Levin (Jonathan Cape)

*Whicker's New World, Alan Whicker (Weidenfeld & Nicolson)

Yankee Doodles, Michael Leapman (Viking)

*A Walk in the Woods, Bill Bryson (Black Swan)

Living & Working in the US

Applying for a United States Visa, Richard Fleischer (International Venture Handbooks)

Buying a Home in Florida, David Hampshire (Survival Books)

*The Complete Guide to Life in Florida, Barbara Brumm LaFreniere & Edward N. LaFreniere (Pineapple Press)

Finding a Job in the United States, Joan Friedenberg & Curtis Bradley (NTC Contemporary Publishing Co.)

How to Get a Job in America, Roger Jones (How To Books)

Immigrating to the USA, Dan Danilov (Self Counsel Press)

*New Rating Guide to Life in America's Small Cities, G. Scott Thomas (Prometheus Books)

*US Immigration Made Easy, Laurence Canter & Martha Siegel (Nolo Press)

Welcome to New York, Roberta Seret (American Welcome Services Press)

Miscellaneous

America, Americans, Edmund Fawcett & Tony Thomas (Collins)

Americans, Desmond Wilcox (Hutchinson)

*America: What Went Wrong? Donald Bartlett & James Steele (Andrews & McMeel)

American Ways, Gary Althen (Intercultural Press)

*Brit-Think Ameri-Think: A Transatlantic Survival Guide, Jane Walmsley (Penguin)

The Day America Told the Truth, James Patterson & Peter Kim (Prentice Hall Press)

*The Economist Guide: United States (Economist Books)

*Made in America, Bill Bryson (Black Swan)

*Xenophobe's Guide to the Americans, Stephanie Faul (Oval Books)

Appendix C: USEFUL WEBSITES

There are dozens of expatriate websites and as the Internet increases in popularity the number grows by the day. Most information is useful, and websites generally offer free access, although some require a subscription or payment for services. Relocation and other companies specialising in expatriate services often have websites, although these may only provide information that a company is prepared to offer free of charge, which may be rather biased. However, there are plenty of volunteer sites run by expatriates providing practical information and tips. A particularly useful section found on most expatriate websites is the 'message board' or 'forum', where expatriates answer questions based on their experience and knowledge and offer an insight into what living and working in the US (or in a particular state or town) is **really** like.

Below is a list of websites not otherwise mentioned in the text. Websites are listed under headings in alphabetical order and the list is by no means definitive.

General Websites

British Expatriates (🖳 www.britishexpat.com). A site designed to keep British expatriates in touch with events in and information about the UK.

British in America (🖳 www.british-expats.com). Another site designed for the British in the US.

Direct Moving (🖳 www.directmoving.com). Information, tips and advice about moving within the US and internationally, and numerous links. This site is part of the ExpatBoards site mentioned below.

ExpatAccess (🖳 www.expataccess.com). Aimed at those planning to move abroad, with free moving guides.

ExpatBoards (🖳 www.expatboards.com). A comprehensive site for expatriates, with popular discussion boards and areas for the British and Americans.

ExpatExchange (🖳 www.expatexchange.com). Reportedly the largest online 'community' for English-speaking expatriates, including articles on relocation and a question and answer facility.

ExpatFocus (🖳 www.expatfocus.com). News, community and advice for expatriates.

ExpatNetwork (🖳 www.expatnetwork.com). The UK's leading expatriate website, which is essentially an employment network for expatriates, although it also includes numerous support services and a monthly online magazine, *Nexus*.

ExpatWorld (⌨ www.expatworld.net). Information for American and British expatriates, including a subscription newsletter.

ExpatExpert (⌨ www.expatexpert.com). Run by expatriate expert Robin Pascoe, providing advice and support.

Global People (⌨ www.peoplegoingglobal.com). Includes country-specific information with emphasis on social and political issues.

Living Abroad (⌨ www.livingabroad.com). Includes an extensive list of country profiles, which are available only on payment. The site is designed for human resources (HR) staff of international companies and requires a membership to use.

Outpost Information Centre (⌨ www.outpostexpat.nl). Contains extensive country-specific information and links. Operated by the Shell Petroleum Company for its expatriate workers, but available to everyone. Information on the US focuses on Houston, TX and New Orleans, but includes general information.

Real Post Reports (⌨ www.realpostreports.com). Includes relocation services, recommended reading lists and 'real-life' stories written by expatriates in cities throughout the world.

SaveWealth Travel (⌨ www.savewealth.com/travel/warnings). Travel information and warnings.

Trade Partners (⌨ www.tradepartners.gov.uk). A UK government-sponsored site providing trade and investment (and general) information about most countries, including the US.

The Travel Doctor (⌨ www.tmvc.com.au). Includes travel health advisories and a country by country vaccination guide.

World Health Organization (⌨ www.who.int). Health information.

World Travel Guide (⌨ www.wtgonline.com). A general website for world travellers and expatriates.

American Websites

AARP (formerly the American Association of Retired Persons) (⌨ www.aarp.org). Information of interest to retirees.

Administration on Aging (⌨ www.aoa.gov). Information about retirement and related issues.

American Universities (⌨ www.usuniversities.com and ⌨ www.petersons.com). Two sites offering searchable listings of US universities, plus general information about selecting a school and information for foreign students.

American School Directory (⌨ www.asd.com). Facts about local schools. Requires a subscription to access information, but offers annual and monthly subscriptions.

Federal Government FirstGov (⌨ www.firstgov.gov). The US Government's Official Web Portal with all 47 million federal web pages, indexed and organised by subject.

Gov Spot (⌨ www.govspot.com). Offers information and links to State and Federal government sites, publications and more.

Housing and Urban Development (⌨ www.hud.gov). Information on home ownership, renting and more. Information can be accessed online or ordered in pamphlet form.

The Humane Society of the US (⌨ www.rentwithpets.org). Includes information on moving with pets and a list of rental accommodation which allows pets.

Life in the USA (⌨ www.lifeintheusa.com). General information for immigrants.

Monster (⌨ http://globalgateway.monster.com). General information about working in the US. Part of the job hunting website, Monster.com.

National Center for Health Statistics (⌨ www.cdc.gov/nchs). Official health statistics.

See America (⌨ www.seeamerica.org). General travel information.

Third Culture Kids (⌨ www.tckworld.com). Designed for expatriate children.

USA Services (⌨ www.info.gov). Official US government site with links to documents and consumer information.

US Census Bureau (⌨ www.census.gov). Information and statistics derived from the census conducted on 1st April 2000.

US Department of State (⌨ http://travel.state.gov). Groups together all the various information on the State Department site related to travel, to and from the US. Includes travel warnings, warnings about drugs and a list of useful travel publications for foreigners coming to the US and Americans travelling abroad.

US Postal Service (USPS) (⌨ www.usps.com/moversnet). A guide to moving house.

Visit USA (⌨ www.visitusa.org.uk). General travel information.

Women Connect (⌨ www.uswc.org). Women Connect is an online networking group, with information about women's organisations and issues around the world.

Worldwise Directory (🖳 www.suzylamplugh.org/worldwise). Run by the Suzy Lamplugh charity for personal safety, the site provides practical information about a number of countries with emphasis on safety, particularly for women.

Appendix D: WEIGHTS & MEASURES

Unlike the rest of the industrialised world, America remains stubbornly wedded to inches, miles, gallons, pounds and Fahrenheit. Although America decimalised its currency before most European countries, it continues to use measures derived from the British Imperial system and has abandoned plans to convert to the metric system (*Système International* or SI) for international trade and scientific purposes.

Nationals of countries who are more familiar with the metric system of measurement will find the tables on the following pages useful. Some comparisons shown are only approximate, but are close enough for most everyday uses. The clothes sizes shown include the equivalent European (continental) and British sizes, both of which are different from American sizes (see also page 482).

Women's Clothes

Continental	34	36	38	40	42	44	46	48	50	52
UK	8	10	12	14	16	18	20	22	24	26
US	6	8	10	12	14	16	18	20	22	24

Pullovers

	Women's						Men's					
Continental	40	42	44	46	48	50	44	46	48	50	52	54
UK	34	36	38	40	42	44	34	36	38	40	42	44
US	34	36	38	40	42	44	sm	med		lar	xl	

Men's Shirts

Continental	36	37	38	39	40	41	42	43	44	46
UK/US	14	14	15	15	16	16	17	17	18	-

Men's Underwear

Continental	5	6	7	8	9	10
UK	34	36	38	40	42	44
US	sm	med		lar		xl

Note: sm = small, med = medium, lar = large, xl = extra large

Children's Clothes

Continental	92	104	116	128	140	152
UK	16/18	20/22	24/26	28/30	32/34	36/38
US	2	4	6	8	10	12

Children's Shoes

Continental	18	19	20	21	22	23	24	25	26	27	28	29	30	31	32
UK/US	2	3	4	4	5	6	7	7	8	9	10	11	11	12	13

Continental	33	34	35	36	37	38
UK/US	1	2	2	3	4	5

Shoes (Women's and Men's)

Continental	35	36	37	37	38	39	40	41	42	42	43	44
UK	2	3	3	4	4	5	6	7	7	8	9	9
US	4	5	5	6	6	7	8	9	9	10	10	11

Weight

Imperial	Metric	Metric	Imperial
1oz	28.35g	1g	0.035oz
1lb*	454g	100g	3.5oz
1cwt	50.8kg	250g	9oz
1 ton	1,016kg	500g	18oz
2,205lb	1 tonne	1kg	2.2lb

Length

Imperial	Metric	Metric	Imperial
1in	2.54cm	1cm	0.39in
1ft	30.48cm	1m	3ft 3.25in
1yd	91.44cm	1km	0.62mi
1mi	1.6km	8km	5mi

Capacity

Imperial	Metric	Metric	Imperial
1 UK pint	0.57 litre	1 litre	1.75 UK pints
1 US pint	0.47 litre	1 litre	2.13 US pints
1 UK gallon	4.54 litres	1 litre	0.22 UK gallon
1 US gallon	3.78 litres	1 litre	0.26 US gallon

Note: An American 'cup' = around 250ml or 0.25 litre.

Area

Imperial	Metric	Metric	Imperial
1 sq. in	0.45 sq. cm	1 sq. cm	0.15 sq. in
1 sq. ft	0.09 sq. m	1 sq. m	10.76 sq. ft
1 sq. yd	0.84 sq. m	1 sq. m	1.2 sq. yds
1 acre	0.4 hectares	1 hectare	2.47 acres
1 sq. mile	2.56 sq. km	1 sq. km	0.39 sq. mile

Temperature

°Celsius	°Fahrenheit	
0	32	(freezing point of water)
5	41	
10	50	
15	59	
20	68	
25	77	
30	86	
35	95	
40	104	
50	122	

Notes: The boiling point of water is 100°C / 212°F.

Normal body temperature (if you're alive and well) is 37°C / 98.6°F.

Temperature Conversion

Celsius to Fahrenheit: multiply by 9, divide by 5 and add 32. (For a quick and approximate conversion, double the Celsius temperature and add 30.)

Fahrenheit to Celsius: subtract 32, multiply by 5 and divide by 9. (For a quick and approximate conversion, subtract 30 from the Fahrenheit temperature and divide by 2.)

Oven Temperatures

Gas	Electric	
	°F	°C
-	225–250	110–120
1	275	140
2	300	150
3	325	160
4	350	180
5	375	190
6	400	200
7	425	220
8	450	230
9	475	240

Air Pressure

PSI	Bar
10	0.5
20	1.4
30	2
40	2.8

Power

Kilowatts	Horsepower	Horsepower	Kilowatts
1	1.34	1	0.75

APPENDIX E: MAP

The map opposite shows the 50 states which constitute the United States of America, listed in alphabetical order below (official abbreviations are shown in brackets). The District of Columbia (DC), the nation's capital and seat of government, is geographically situated in Maryland (MD).

Alabama (AL)	Montana (MT)
Alaska (AK)	Nebraska (NE)
Arizona (AZ)	Nevada (NV)
Arkansas (AR)	New Hampshire (NH)
California (CA)	New Jersey (NJ)
Colorado (CO)	New Mexico (NM)
Connecticut (CT)	New York (NY)
Delaware (DE)	North Carolina (NC)
Florida (FL)	North Dakota (ND)
Georgia (GA)	Ohio (OH)
Hawaiian Islands (HI)	Oklahoma (OK)
Idaho (ID)	Oregon (OR)
Illinois (IL)	Pennsylvania (PA)
Indiana (IN)	Rhode Island (RI)
Iowa (IA)	South Carolina (SC)
Kansas (KS)	South Dakota (SD)
Kentucky (KY)	Tennessee (TN)
Louisiana (LA)	Texas (TX)
Maine (ME)	Utah (UT)
Maryland (MD)	Vermont (VT)
Massachusetts (MA)	Virginia (VA)
Michigan (MI)	Washington (WA)
Minnesota (MN)	West Virginia (WV)
Mississippi (MS)	Wisconsin (WI)
Missouri (MO)	Wyoming (WY)

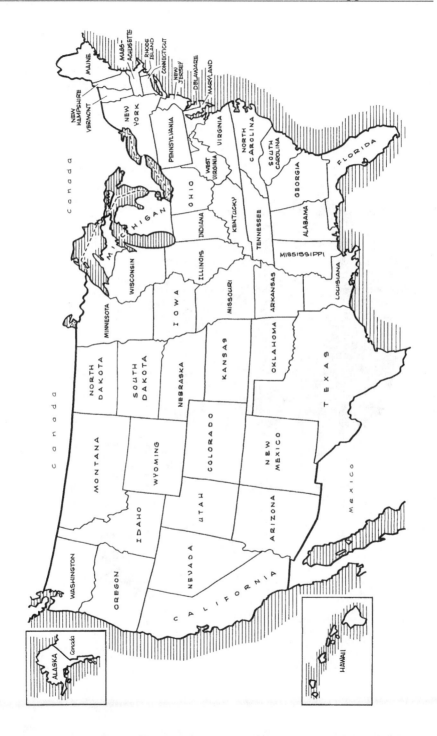

INDEX

M

N

T

LIVING AND WORKING SERIES

Living and Working books are essential reading for anyone planning to spend time abroad, including holiday-home owners, retirees, visitors, business people, migrants, students and even extra-terrestrials! They're packed with important and useful information designed to help you **avoid costly mistakes and save both time and money.** Topics covered include how to:

- Find a job with a good salary & conditions
- Obtain a residence permit
- Avoid and overcome problems
- Find your dream home
- Get the best education for your family
- Make the best use of public transport
- Endure local motoring habits
- Obtain the best health treatment
- Stretch your money further
- Make the most of your leisure time
- Enjoy the local sporting life
- Find the best shopping bargains
- Insure yourself against most eventualities
- Use post office and telephone services
- Do numerous other things not listed above

Living and Working books are the most comprehensive and up-to-date source of practical information available about everyday life abroad. They aren't, however, boring text books, but interesting and entertaining guides written in a highly readable style.

Discover what it's *really* like to live and work abroad!

Order your copies today by phone, fax, post or email from: Survival Books, PO Box 146, Wetherby, West Yorks. LS23 6XZ, United Kingdom (☎/▤ +44 (0)1937-843523, ✉ orders@ survivalbooks.net, ▯ www.survivalbooks.net).

BUYING A HOME SERIES

Buying a Home books, including **Buying, Selling & Letting Property**, are essential reading for anyone planning to purchase property abroad. They're packed with vital information to guide you through the property purchase jungle and help you **avoid the sort of disasters that can turn your dream home into a nightmare!** Topics covered include:

- Avoiding problems
- Choosing the region
- Finding the right home and location
- Estate agents
- Finance, mortgages and taxes
- Home security
- Utilities, heating and air-conditioning
- Moving house and settling in
- Renting and letting
- Permits and visas
- Travelling and communications
- Health and insurance
- Renting a car and driving
- Retirement and starting a business
- And much, much more!

Buying a Home books are the most comprehensive and up-to-date source of information available about buying property abroad. Whether you want a detached house, townhouse or apartment, a holiday or a permanent home, these books will help make your dreams come true.

Save yourself time, trouble and money!

Order your copies today by phone, fax, post or email from: Survival Books, PO Box 146, Wetherby, West Yorks. LS23 6XZ, United Kingdom (☎/▤ +44 (0)1937-843523, ✉ orders@ survivalbooks.net, 🖥 www.survivalbooks.net).

OTHER SURVIVAL BOOKS

The Alien's Guides: *The Alien's Guides to Britain and France* provide an 'alternative' look at life in these popular countries and will help you to appreciate the peculiarities (in both senses) of the British and French.

The Best Places to Buy a Home in France/Spain: The most comprehensive homebuying guides to France or Spain, containing detailed profiles of the most popular regions, with guides to property prices, amenities and services, employment and planned developments.

Buying, Selling and Letting Property: The most comprehensive and up-to-date source of information available for those intending to buy, sell or let a property in the UK.

Foreigners in France/Spain: Triumphs & Disasters: Real-life experiences of people who have emigrated to France and Spain, recounted in their own words – warts and all!

Lifelines: Essential guides to specific regions of France and Spain, containing everything you need to know about local life. Titles in the series currently include the Costa Blanca, Costa del Sol, Dordogne/Lot, Normandy and Poitou-Charentes; Brittany Lifeline is to be published in summer 2005.

Renovating & Maintaining Your French Home: The ultimate guide to renovating and maintaining your dream home in France: what to do and what not to do, how to do it and, most importantly, how much it will cost.

Retiring Abroad: The most comprehensive and up-to-date source of practical information available about retiring to a foreign country, containing profiles of the 20 most popular retirement destinations.

Broaden your horizons with Survival Books!

Order your copies today by phone, fax, post or email from: Survival Books, PO Box 146, Wetherby, West Yorks. LS23 6XZ, United Kingdom (☎/▤ +44 (0)1937-843523, ✉ orders@ survivalbooks.net, 🖳 www.survivalbooks.net).

ORDER FORM

Qty.	Title	Price (incl. p&p)			Total
		UK	Europe	World	
	The Alien's Guide to Britain	£6.95	£8.95	£12.45	
	The Alien's Guide to France	£6.95	£8.95	£12.45	
	The Best Places to Buy a Home in France	£13.95	£15.95	£19.45	
	The Best Places to Buy a Home in Spain	£13.95	£15.95	£19.45	
	Buying a Home Abroad	£13.95	£15.95	£19.45	
	Buying a Home in Florida	£13.95	£15.95	£19.45	
	Buying a Home in France	£13.95	£15.95	£19.45	
	Buying a Home in Greece & Cyprus	£13.95	£15.95	£19.45	
	Buying a Home in Ireland	£11.95	£13.95	£17.45	
	Buying a Home in Italy	£13.95	£15.95	£19.45	
	Buying a Home in Portugal	£13.95	£15.95	£19.45	
	Buying a Home in South Africa	£13.95	£15.95	£19.45	
	Buying a Home in Spain	£13.95	£15.95	£19.45	
	Buying, Letting & Selling Property	£11.95	£13.95	£17.45	
	Foreigners in France: Triumphs & Disasters	£11.95	£13.95	£17.45	
	Foreigners in Spain: Triumphs & Disasters	£11.95	£13.95	£17.45	
	Costa Blanca Lifeline	£11.95	£13.95	£17.45	
	Costa del Sol Lifeline	£11.95	£13.95	£17.45	
	Dordogne/Lot Lifeline	£11.95	£13.95	£17.45	
	Poitou-Charentes Lifeline	£11.95	£13.95	£17.45	
	Living & Working Abroad	£14.95	£16.95	£20.45	
	Living & Working in America	£14.95	£16.95	£20.45	
	Living & Working in Australia	£14.95	£16.95	£20.45	
	Living & Working in Britain	£14.95	£16.95	£20.45	
	Living & Working in Canada	£16.95	£18.95	£22.45	
	Living & Working in the European Union	£16.95	£18.95	£22.45	
	Living & Working in the Far East	£16.95	£18.95	£22.45	
	Living & Working in France	£14.95	£16.95	£20.45	
	Living & Working in Germany	£16.95	£18.95	£22.45	
	Total carried forward (see over)				

ORDER FORM

Qty.	Title	Price (incl. p&p)			Total
		Total brought forward			
		UK	Europe	World	
	L&W in the Gulf States & Saudi Arabia	£16.95	£18.95	£22.45	
	L&W in Holland, Belgium & Luxembourg	£14.95	£16.95	£20.45	
	Living & Working in Ireland	£14.95	£16.95	£20.45	
	Living & Working in Italy	£16.95	£18.95	£22.45	
	Living & Working in London	£13.95	£15.95	£19.45	
	Living & Working in New Zealand	£14.95	£16.95	£20.45	
	Living & Working in Spain	£14.95	£16.95	£20.45	
	Living & Working in Switzerland	£16.95	£18.95	£22.45	
	Normandy Lifeline	£11.95	£13.95	£17.45	
	Renovating & Maintaining Your French Home	£16.95	£18.95	£22.45	
	Retiring Abroad	£14.95	£16.95	£20.45	
				Grand Total	

)rder your copies today by phone, fax, post or email from: Survival Books, PO Box 146, /etherby, West Yorks. LS23 6XZ, UK (☎/▤ +44 (0)1937-843523, ✉ orders@ urvivalbooks.net, 💻 www.survivalbooks.net). If you aren't entirely satisfied, simply turn them to us within 14 days for a full and unconditional refund.

enclose a cheque for the grand total/Please charge my Amex/Delta/Maestro vitch)/MasterCard/Visa card as follows. (delete as applicable)

d No. _ _ _   _ _ _ _   _ _ _ _   _ _ _ _   Security Code* _ _ _

ry date _____   Issue number (Maestro/Switch only) _____

ature _____   Tel. No. _____

= _____

ESS _____

_____

_____

urity code is the last three digits on the signature strip.